Magical Images:
A Handbook of Stereo Photography
with B&W Photographs

By G. R. OGRAM BSc PhD
Second Edition - 2016

Magical Images:
A Handbook of Stereo Photography
with B&W Photographs

By G. R. OGRAM BSc PhD
Second Edition - 2016

Copyright © 2001, 2016 by G. R. Ogram

ISBN - 9781626130746

Published by ATBOSH Media ltd.
Cleveland, Ohio, USA

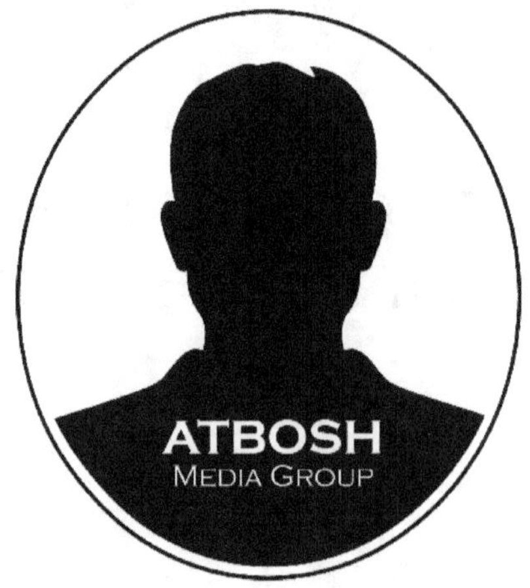

www.atbosh.com

At a fairly early stage in my childhood, I can recall being fascinated with the "magic pictures" of animals presented in anaglyph form in a book that had been given to me. From that moment I was converted to stereoscopy, even though I had never heard of the word. I can also remember attending a show of some kind in which the audience wore the familiar red and cyan spectacles and watched 3D shadows on a white sheet lit from behind; the "shadows" illusion is described in this book.

During my undergraduate days in the 1950's I purchased a copy of the STEREO REALIST MANUAL, mainly to enjoy the stereo illustrations, dreaming that one day I would be able to afford a real stereo camera. That finally happened in 1965 when I purchased a Wray Stereo Graphic together with a viewer. As a 3D practitioner, then, I can claim over thirty years' experience, but I have to say that for most of that time I knew only very basic practice and principles and understood very little of the subtleties of the subject. At that time, books on stereo photography were either compilations of 3D pictures for viewing, or, if more technical in nature, fairly basic. As an applied science student, I suppose that I should have been more interested in the nuts and bolts of the subject, but as my life changed from being a student to developing a career, many other activities took over. Effectively, I remained a beginner.

On retirement in 1995, after thirty years of teaching metallurgy, I decided that it was time to learn something about stereo, and thought about writing a book on the subject. By now I was taking stereoscopy more seriously, with a greater regard for good practice. I sold the Wray and bought a FED and later replaced that with a Stereo Realist (which I regard highly). More recently I purchased an RBT "Siamesed" XRP3, so that I now have a choice of 5P and full frame formats. A FED projector and an older Hawk (both modified to use QI lamps) complete the line-up of my stereo hardware. During this period I also dabbled with a Nimslo camera and a Pentax Stereo adapter.

Most stereo books published over the years treated the subject in a rather haphazard way, until Ferwerda produced his "The World of 3D", and examined stereoscopy more rigorously, although I found that some of his explanations and analyses were rather condensed and difficult to comprehend.

I felt that there might be a market for a book that would develop some of the principles more fully and extensively, to provide a logical basis for the practical side of stereo photography. Added to that was the need to update the subject so that some of the more recent technology could be included.

I set out, therefore, in 1995 to produce an all-purpose book, which would provide not only practical information and advice for the beginner but also a comprehensive and logical treatment of the theoretical principles involved, so that the more experienced worker could study the subject in more detail. At the same time I wanted the book to be a kind of reference text that one could "dip into" to find advice on a specific topic or the answer to a particular problem. Various publishers in the UK saw some of the early drafts and commented favourably, but declined to take up the project commercially because they felt it was "too specialist". Eventually I decided to self-publish.

A book on stereo photography that has no 3D photographs in it would be somewhat of a disappointment, so I have included a selection of stereo pairs purely for "entertainment".

Although stereo photography is essentially very simple, there are many factors that need to be considered if consistently good results are to be produced. I hope that this book will help the enthusiast to follow good practice and to understand better how it all works.

Geoff Ogram - 2001

PREFACE to the 2nd Edition

The principal change in this second edition is in the expansion of Chapter 14 on digital photography to take account of the tremendous increase in that technology as it affects photography in general and stereoscopic photography in particular. The rapid advance that began at the beginning of the twenty-first century has seen a significant diminution in the use of film, though there are many photographers who have resisted the change. The theoretical aspects of stereoscopy theory as explained in this book are not altered by the use of digital technology and so remain in their original form.

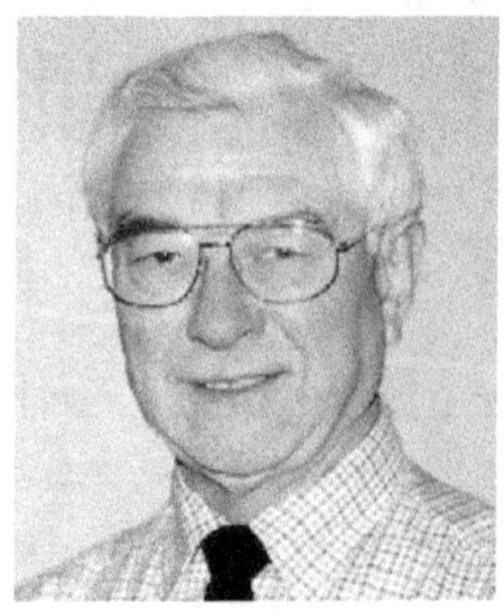

Geoff Ogram - 2016

ACKNOWLEDGMENTS

A book of any kind, especially one of this magnitude, cannot be prepared without assistance and I have been fortunate in being able to benefit from the generosity of others.

First and foremost, I am indebted to my brother Laurence, who worked long and hard during the early years of preparation of the manuscript, deciphering my scruffy longhand with its many afterthoughts to produce a readable draft. His advice on style and presentation was also helpful and I hope that it shows in the final text.

Many members of the Stereoscopic Society in the UK have been most unselfish in providing ideas and information at a time when I was, as a new member, unknown to them. Past President Donald Wratten kindly read and commented on some of the early chapters and offered sound advice and encouragement.

Colin Clay not only encouraged me but also offered to proof-read the "final" manuscript, which he did meticulously, making many useful suggestions and additions that have led to the current version.

I would also like to thank the following:

Fred Everett, and his brother, the late Harry Everett, for sending me many cuttings and articles from their archives; Bernard Makinson, current President of the Stereoscopic Society, for information on the View Magic System; Past President David Burder, for the picture of the "Siamesed" digital camera; Brian Temple, for a wealth of photographs and information relating to the View-Master system; Marcus Warrington, for information on the NuView video attachment.

Ray McMillan expertly scanned the stereo slides I sent him so that I could include a selection of stereograms "purely for entertainment" in the form of the Plates at the end of the book. His advice on presentation was also helpful and I am most grateful for his contribution. I only hope that the images I chose will be judged favourably in terms of their entertainment value!

David Rainbow of Advanced Illustration kindly provided the example of a three-point perspective grid.

I thank Jared Bendis for his enthusiasm for this book (in its original edition), so much so that he offered to publish it in this new format. For that I am extremely grateful.

Last, but not least, I thank my wife Peggy for her tolerance while I was spending so many hours at my desk and, later, my computer; unfortunately she did not live to see this new development. I tried not to let the desire to complete this book quickly take over my life completely. It would be gratifying to know that I made sufficient effort to play my part in more important matters, the home and family.

This book is designed to provide practical guidance to the stereo photographer and a logical analysis of the basic principles of stereoscopic photography. It can also be used as a reference text.

Part 1 (Chapters 1 to 15) is essentially practical in nature, and is particularly appropriate for beginners because it describes the equipment and basic techniques required to produce satisfying 3D pictures. At the same time, the fundamental principles that lie behind good practice are explained, mainly in a qualitative manner. However, some simple mathematical evaluation is included where this is felt to be helpful in the discussion or explanation of a particular topic. At various points in the text, the reader is referred to one or other of the Supplements in Part 3 for further information on, or further development of, a specific topic.

Part 2 (Chapters 16 to 21) is devoted to the underlying theory and principles of stereo photography. It includes subjects such as vision and optics, to provide a background for the discussions of topics specific to stereoscopy. The approach is to develop the theory logically and to treat it quantitatively where relevant.

A mathematical approach is valuable because it can help to identify important variables and show how changes in technique or practice will affect results. Also, a mathematical approach can show the limitations, approximations or boundary conditions of a technique or a particular item of equipment. The level of mathematics in this book is not too advanced; it is based mainly upon GCSE geometry, trigonometry and algebra. The various derivations and formulae are used in numerical examples wherever possible, in order to show the practical relevance of the theory. Readers who feel that their mathematical skills are somewhat rusty can, however, avoid the derivations and equations if they wish, and concentrate on the text. The essential ideas can still be grasped.

Part 3 (Supplements) contains more detailed discussion and explanation of topics that appear within the main text. Some of the Supplements deal with theoretical principles while others provide additional information. A few are concerned with the construction of stereo apparatus.

The book is structured to provide a logical development of the subject starting at Chapter 1 and reading through to Chapter 21, but this path is not obligatory. The newcomer may benefit by working through Chapters 1 to 15 in order to gain an overall view. Those with experience can pick topics at random, to find out more details of a technique, perhaps, or to solve a problem.

B&W Edition

Please note that this is the B&W Edition of this book. It was published as a cost saving alternative to the Color Edition (which is also available). A PDF supplement containing all stereoscopic images (both photographs and drawings) contained in the book is available on the ATBOSH Media website (www.ATBOSH.com).

CONTENTS

Part 1 - Basic Principles and Practice

CHAPTER 1: INTRODUCTION - THE NATURE OF 3D

1.1 Space

We, and the real world in which we live, are three-dimensional. That is a straightforward, uncomplicated statement that trips easily off the tongue and is one that is understood by the majority of people. We were born into this three-dimensional space, we grew up in it, we handle it with ease, without conscious effort, as part of our daily lives. We do not need to contemplate its characteristics in great detail or to philosophize on its significance; we take it for granted.

Nevertheless, if we are to understand the principles and practice of stereoscopic photography in particular, or stereoscopy in general, it is beneficial to examine three-dimensional space in some detail and to find out "how it works".

The word "space" itself is not easy to define in meaningful ways, despite the fact that we understand what it means and use it freely in common parlance. My dictionary gives the following: "noun: that in which material bodies have extension: a portion of extension: room: intervening distance: an interval: an open or empty place". There are other definitions, too, that apply to specific usages of the word that are not relevant in this context, so let us be content with no more than those quoted. Perhaps a more helpful interpretation of "space" can be achieved by turning to mathematics.

One of the many functions of mathematics is to describe our physical world in a succinct and accurate way, in this instance through the applications of algebra, trigonometry and geometry. Our dictionary definition covers two- and three-dimensional space but we shall concentrate on the second of these, with but passing reference to the first as required.

Applications of mathematical techniques enable us to "map out" our space, to locate key points and to show the relationships between the various points within that space, be it the distance between two points, the angle between two lines or whatever. All mapping has to be done with reference to some fixed point, or scale, or both. This principle will be familiar to anyone conversant with map reading. Britain, for example, can be mapped accurately, despite the curvature of the earth and the topography of the landscape, onto flat sheets of paper. Here we have two-dimensional space, and our reference lines are the **N-S** and **E-W** axes upon which the Ordnance Survey references are based. This enables the map-reader to locate places and, from the scale of the map, to measure distances in a two-dimensional world. Only two reference axes are required to allow all such information to be recorded or measured unambiguously and with precision. Flat objects can be mapped in terms of height and width axes, chosen to lie at right angles to each other so that they are independent. In mathematics, these are normally denoted as the **y** and **x** axes respectively. Although the **y** axis is usually taken as the height axis in two-dimensional mathematics, with three dimensions height information is allocated to the additional (**z**) axis. This is merely a matter of convention.

The space in which we live and move cannot be fully represented on a two-dimensional frame. A third reference axis is required, mutually at right angles to the other two (height and width) to give us a scale that is concerned with dimensions and distances "towards us and away from us" as observers, in addition to those distances and dimensions measured in a vertical sense and horizontal (left and right) sense. We now have a depth axis (**Fig 1-1a**). In the field of mathematics, the three axes are referred to as **x**, **y**, and **z** axes as shown in **Fig 1-1b**. Any point in this three-dimensional space can be identified uniquely by reference to the **x**, **y** and **z** axes, as can two- and three-dimensional shapes, their orientation in that space and so on.

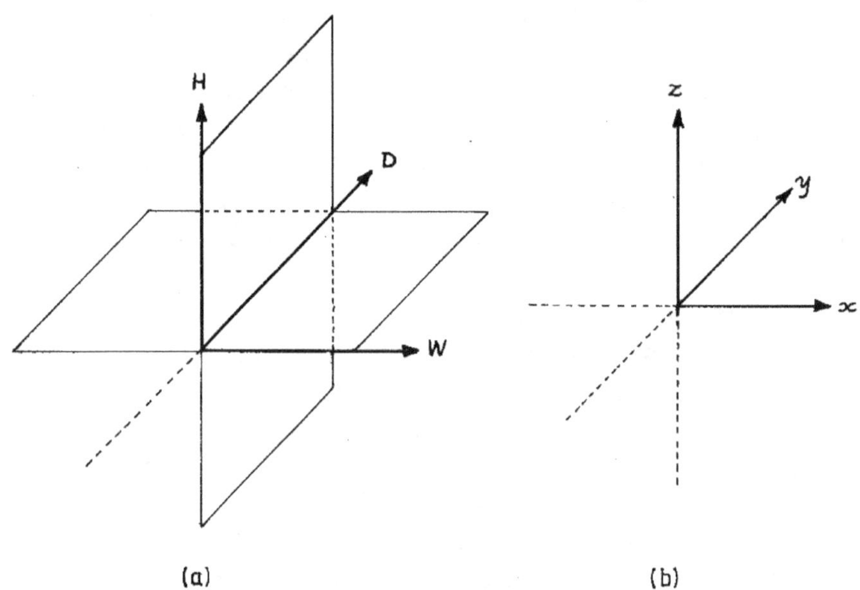

Fig 1-1
a. *Three axes mutually at 90° relating to height (**H**), width (**W**) and depth (**D**)*
b. *Conventional labelling of axes **x**, **y** and **z** in mathematics.*

1.2 The Perception of Depth

The word stereoscopy, from the Greek, simply means "seeing solid"; it is concerned with the ability to perceive the "depth" element in space, as well as the "height and width" information. A more formal definition, given by K.B.Chibisov[1], is "the science of the visual perception of the three-dimensional space surrounding us".

N.A.Valyus[2] states that the word is "usually used to convey appreciation of relief, plasticity, roundness or spatial qualities of the visual images of the objects viewed."

Our ability to appreciate these qualities derives principally from our having two eyes; we have "binocular vision". Those people who, for whatever reason, have to rely on the vision of a single eye, will be unable to receive the kind of visual information that enables the two-eyed person to understand fully the spatial relationship of objects or images before him. Nevertheless, information about depth exists even in the image received by one eye, although it is interpreted on the basis of experience, albeit subconsciously, as distinct from information obtained specifically from the use of two eyes simultaneously. These monocular "clues" are important, too, in binocular vision.

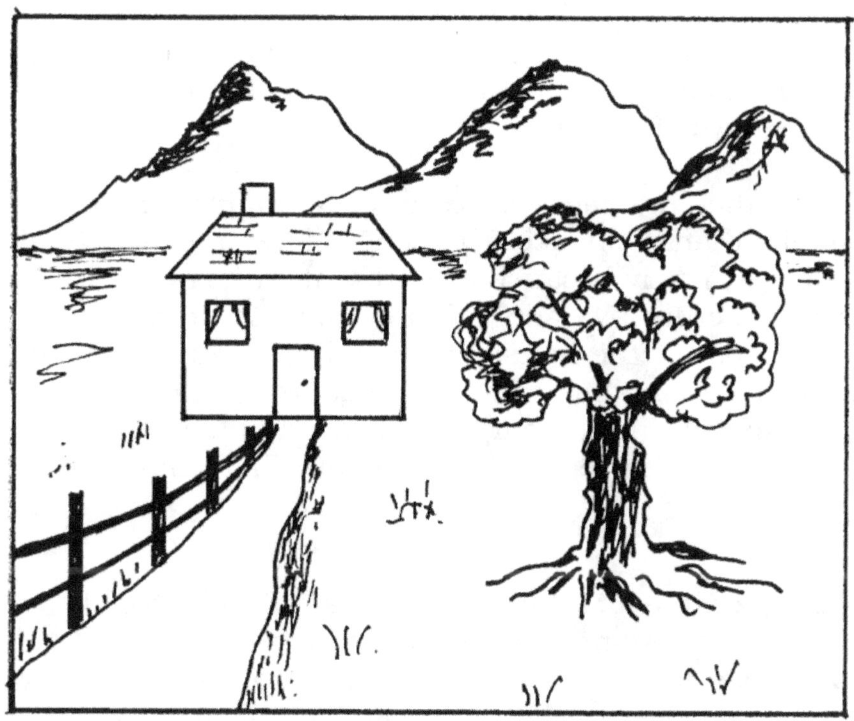

Fig 1-2
Stylised two-dimensional scene for the analysis of depth clues.

Consider the simple scene shown in **Fig 1-2,** which could represent a drawing, painting, or a photograph of a landscape. In this monocular view, there is no direct information about the spatial distribution of the various features. The images of the mountains, house and tree are all in the same plane (the plane of the diagram itself) and hence equidistant from the viewer. However, from our visual experiences and memories we can deduce that the tree is nearest to us, the house further away and the mountains still further in the distance. This is based upon the following observations:

1. the mountains are partly obscured by the house - therefore the house (from our experience) is the nearer.
2. the path appears to get narrower as it reaches the house. We are accustomed to paths of constant width (approximately) and we know that parallel lines appear to converge as they recede. We sense, therefore, that the path extends from the bottom of the picture away from us to a more distant point where the house is located.
3. the tree appears to be nearer than the house mainly because of the position of the base of the trunk, where it meets the ground, in relation to our viewpoint and eye level. If one tries to imagine that the tree is further away than the house, the brain would be forced to accept that the house was now very small, like a doll's house, floating in mid-air.
4. the fence posts diminish in size as they "approach" the house. We expect fence posts to be the same size as each other in reality, but we know (again from experience) that an object appears smaller if it is further away from us.

Without other evidence, we cannot determine whether the tree is bigger or smaller than the house. The image of the tree in the diagram itself is certainly bigger, partly because it represents a nearer object. If we were to place in our picture two adult figures, one standing by the tree and another by the door of the house, we could estimate the relative sizes of house and tree by using the height of the figures (which would be roughly equal) as a yardstick. In summary, from the simple image of **Fig 1-2**, we can identify the following visual clues to depth that will also exist in a real scene:

1. **masking of objects**: nearer objects will completely or partially obscure more distant ones, but not vice versa.
2. **perspective**: for example, parallel lines appearing to converge away from the observer (**Fig 1-3**). (See also Supplement S1).
3. **relative size**: objects of the same size placed at different distances from the observer appear smaller as the distance increases.

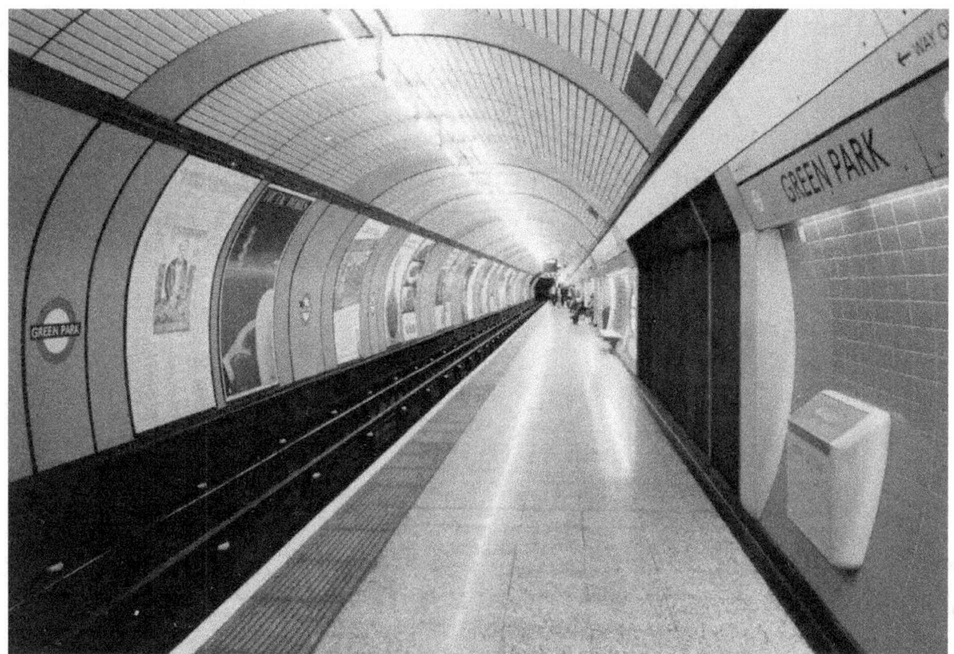

Fig 1-3
The effect of perspective in causing parallel lines to appear to converge into the distance. (Photograph by Laurence Ogram).

However, these are not the only clues to depth in a monocular image. When we consider actual scenes or photographs, we benefit from other information, depending upon the circumstances. Not all the clues are necessarily present in every image, but they certainly exist in various combinations. These clues are:

4. **lighting and shadows**: suppose the sun is behind us and slightly to one side and we view a scene comprising a house with a telegraph pole in front of it and nearer to us. The pole casts a shadow along the ground and onto the front wall of the house. We know from experience that this can only occur if the pole is nearer to us than the house. There will be many other examples of this kind of effect in which our brains process information subconsciously and lead us to deduce relative positions of the objects displayed before us. Shadows also confirm the shape and solidity of an object, its roundness for example. We can thus distinguish between an object that is in the shape of a flat circular disc and one of identical diameter and colour that is a solid sphere. The direction of the lighting and whether it is harsh or diffused helps (or hinders) our interpretation of the depth of the object itself. In some flat, diffused lighting conditions even real, solid objects can appear to be flat and two-dimensional so that the scene appears to be a collection of cardboard cut-outs.

5. **aerial perspective**: the presence of haze in a landscape has the effect of making distant objects less distinct, both in colouring and detail. Again, our previous experience in encountering this effect helps us to interpret new images displaying the same effect. Aerial perspective is captured by the camera and can be imitated by the artist, so we can gain these clues not only from reality but also from photographs and paintings (**Fig 1-4**).

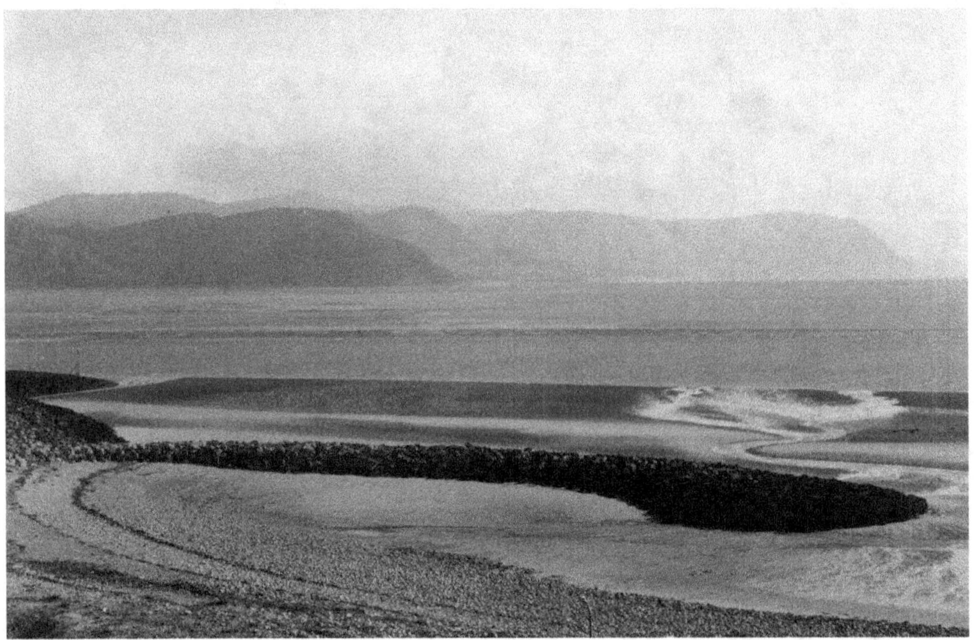

Fig 1-4
Aerial perspective. Distant parts of the scene can be affected by haze, causing loss of detail and colour

6. **colour**: we have already noted that aerial perspective is responsible for muting colours, but it is also a fact that bright, bold colours seem to stand out from paler, more pastel shades and tints (and also darker tones). In particular, reds seem to jump out at the observer, whereas blues tend to recede. A startling effect, arising from this phenomenon, can sometimes be experienced on the cinema screen or on television. For example, bold lettering in a title (especially in white, yellow or red) against a plain blue background can often appear to float on the surface of the screen and the blue background appears to recede into the TV set. The effect is rather like looking through a rectangular hole into an empty box with the words of the title painted onto a transparent window. Because bright, bold colours tend to be prominent against weaker, subdued hues, brightly coloured objects may dominate even if they are further away than less "colourful" nearer objects; this can lead to some visual confusion about the relative positions in space of the objects concerned.

Momentarily, at least, the perceived positions of the objects may be interpreted as the opposite of their actual locations (the further object appearing to be the nearer). With the specific depth information received from a two-eyed view of a real scene or stereo pair, this is unlikely to cause any problems, however.

7. **observer movement**: if the observer moves his head slightly sideways the relative positions of objects appear to change in a lateral sense within the image. Vertical movements of the head will likewise cause apparent movement of objects in a vertical direction. This apparent movement is greater for objects close to the observer and diminishes progressively with distance for objects further away. The detail of the effect is that as the observer moves his head to the left, for example, near objects appear to move to the right relative to infinity or other objects further away, and vice versa. An object at a great distance, such as a mountain, will effectively define a reference plane against which the relative "movements" of nearer objects can be judged. These apparent shifts in relative positions are registered and processed by the brain and, again by virtue of experience, the observer concludes which objects are closer. The technical term for this apparent movement is **parallax.** This effect is particularly noticeable when the countryside is viewed from inside a moving train. Distant objects appear almost stationary, nearer ones passing more rapidly the closer they are to the observer. Reproducing this effect on cine film or video gives the viewer an enhanced sense of depth and reality in the two-dimensional image.

It is worth repeating that all the above visual clues are important in judging spatial distribution of the various components in a flat image, such as a photograph, painting or an image reproduced on a TV or cinema screen. They are the only factors that contribute to the observer's relating the image he sees to the real spatial world he lives in, and this ability will have been developed subconsciously from childhood days. The visual image alone is insufficient; it has to be assessed in conjunction with other stimuli. The classic scenario of the infant reaching out to grasp the moon is a valid one. Over the first few years of life, the child, by touching and feeling objects and by moving around the real world, will gain the experience required to relate the visual data to that real space; furthermore, he will learn later to interpret flat images representing that space.

It will be clear from the above that the child is, in fact, learning these spatial skills with two eyes (in most cases) and it follows that the visual depth clues analysed in this section are as relevant to three-dimensional images as they are to two-dimensional ones. With binocular vision we have the ability to gain additional information that is denied us if we restrict our observations of real space by employing only one eye. Stereoscopy enables us to reproduce the visual experiences of the real world with a kind of uncanny accuracy, if we follow certain rules; on the other hand, we might introduce distortions to a greater or lesser extent that may or may not spoil the illusion. In this, the eye and brain combination can be tolerant, and these distortions may not be noticed in many situations.

1.3 Binocular Vision - the true perception of depth
1.3.1 The two image principle

The apparent movement of objects relative to each other that occurs when the observer moves his head slightly when viewing a scene (see Section 1.2 (7) above) gives the clue to true stereoscopic or binocular vision. Because our two eyes are separated by a short distance (around 65mm (2.5 inches)), each eye sees the one scene slightly differently.

When we view a scene with the right eye closed, the left eye simply sees a flat image. If we move the head about 65mm to the right, so that the left eye now lies at the point previously occupied by the right eye, it will see a different flat image. The two images are seen in succession in this case. However, when looking at the scene with both eyes, these two flat images are perceived simultaneously. The brain combines them to provide us with the true sense of depth that is lacking in a monocular image. The capacity to perceive depth in stereo vision is known as **stereopsis**.

In normal vision, we are not aware of the two separate images; instead, we appear to be looking out as if from a single eye positioned at the bridge of the nose. This is the so-called **cyclopean image** named after the mythological Greek giant Cyclops who was blessed with but a single eye, though in his case a little higher up, in the centre of his forehead.

A simple experiment will easily reveal the different views seen by our two eyes:

1. close the right eye and hold out upright at arm's length, a pencil, aligning it with some more distant object in the scene, such as the edge of a window frame (**Fig 1-5a**).
2. without moving either the head or the pencil, close the left eye and open the right. The pencil will no longer line up with the edge of the window frame but will appear to have jumped to its left (**Fig 1-5b**).

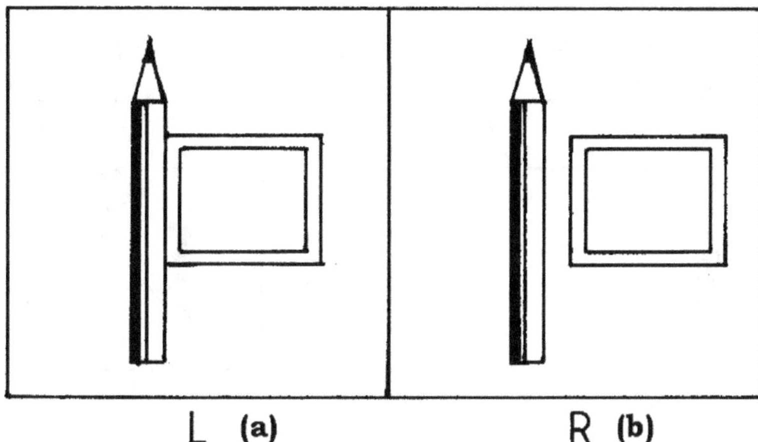

Fig 1-5
The 'pencil and window' experiment illustrating the difference between the left and right eye images of two objects at different distances from the observer. In the right eye view, the nearer object (pencil) appears to be displaced towards the left, or the further object (window) to the right.

Two such images are termed a **stereoscopic pair.** In the experiment, these images are formed within the eyes and interpreted by the brain. However, we can recreate these visual images as drawings or photographs made from the two viewpoints occupied by the eyes. If these drawings or photographs are viewed in such a way that the left image is seen by the left eye only and the right image by the right eye only, the brain will combine them to reproduce the scene in depth as a three-dimensional sketch or, with colour photographs, an uncanny replica of the original objects. There are several ways of achieving correct viewing conditions for a stereoscopic pair and these are discussed in Chapter 5.

1.3.2 Lateral displacements in stereo pairs

The pencil experiment described above shows in a simple arrangement of two principal objects how the nearer one (the pencil) appears to be laterally displaced relative to the background, when the left and right images are compared. Because the pencil is closer to the left border of the right image than it is in the left image, it means that when the image pairs are placed side by side, as in **Figs 1-5a** and **b**, the separation of the pencil images is less than the separation of the window images.

The nearer an object is to the observer the greater will be the relative lateral displacement of its image in the left and right views; a consequence of this is that the separation of these images in a stereoscopic pair mounted side by side will be smaller than the separation of more distant objects. All such separations must be measured between corresponding points in the two images, known as **homologous points** or **homologues.**

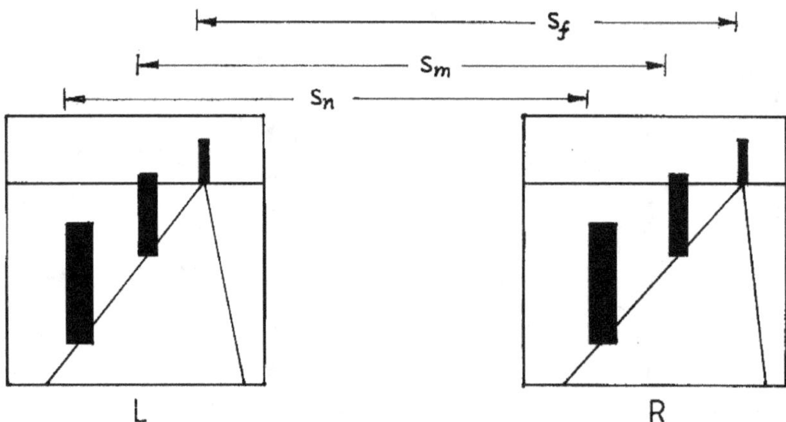

Fig 1-6
The image separations for three objects at different distances have different magnitudes. In this diagram **s$_f$** *has the greatest value and* **s$_n$** *the smallest.*

Fig 1-6 shows a stereo pair with three objects, one far away, one at a mid-distance and the third close up. In this diagram $s_f > s_m > s_n$.. (This picture can be viewed as a genuine stereo pair allowing the observer to verify that the objects are at the relative distances described).

These differences in the two images of a stereo pair also enable us to identify which of them represents the left view of the scene and which the right, although this is often difficult with small-sized pictures or with scenes which have no close up objects, because the displacements will be very small. In the pencil and window experiment, the relative displacement is large, rather too large for comfortable viewing of the images stereoscopically (see also Supplement S7). If the same experiment is repeated with a distant tree (acting as the pencil, as it were) against a mountain background, the lateral displacement will be much smaller. If the objects are very far away, the lateral movement can be so small as to be undetectable to the observer, even though the two objects are actually separated by a great distance. Since it is precisely these differences that provide the information about depth, the inference is that we should be able to perceive depth differences more easily with close objects than with distant ones. This is indeed the case. The stereoscopic effect diminishes with distance from the observer. In practical terms, there is a distance beyond which no differences in depth can be detected and all objects appear to lie in the same plane. The very distant trees and mountain appear as flat as if they were painted on a backcloth in a stage set. This far limit of stereoscopic perception is, at best, of the order of 1350 metres (about 0.8 miles)[3] but it varies from person to person and with the conditions, such as the light or the presence of haze (see also Chapter 16, Section: 16.2.2).

However, in converting the retinal images into a sense of depth, the brain does not act in any way like an automatic direct-reading rangefinder. It does not, for example, tell us that the tree is exactly 10.5 metres from us or that the house is 348 metres away. We possess only a crude sense of distance and those who can estimate distances with a fair degree of accuracy do so only from practice and experience.

1.3.3 Perspective differences in stereo pairs

If we imagine a scene that consists of no more than a number of flat cardboard cut-out shapes situated at various distances from the observer, then all that has been discussed in Section **1.3.2** will apply, and the left and right views of the scene will show the expected lateral displacements. In reality, the majority of objects themselves have depth and this gives rise to other differences in the images that are related to differences in perspective. The left eye sees slightly more of the left side of a solid object than does the right eye and vice versa, as illustrated in **Fig 1-7a**. Here, the object is placed close to the eyes to exaggerate the effect. As the object moves further away, the region **BC** (seen by both eyes) increases and the regions **AB** and **CD** (seen only by the left and right eye respectively) diminish (**Fig I.7b**).

Fig 1-8 shows the left and right images of a solid cube. To illustrate the effect just discussed let us examine the left hand face of the cube (**HKLM**). The difference in the appearance of this face is, of course, due to the different viewpoints (see also Supplement S1). It is also consistent, following the explanations given in Section 1.3.2, with the difference in separation of the rear vertical edges, s_r, compared with the separation of the near vertical edges s_n. As in the case of **Fig 1-6b**, the separation of a near object is less than that of a more distant one, so in **Fig 1-8**, $s_r > s_n$. When viewing such an image in 3D we can locate the rear edge and near edge positions and see the left face of the cube as a receding plane, giving depth to the cube itself.

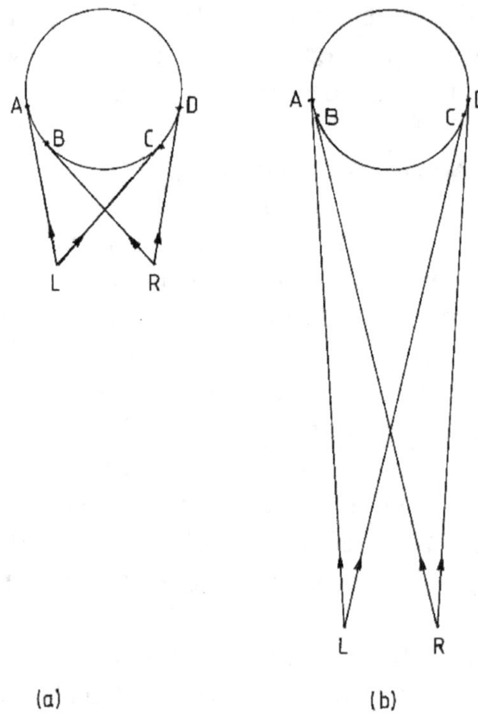

(a)　　　　　　(b)

Fig 1-7

Perspective differences in stereo pairs
a *The left eye sees the portion* **AC** *of the object*
whereas the right eye sees **BD**.
b *From a greater distance the regions* **AB** *and* **CD**
(for left and right eye respectively) become smaller.

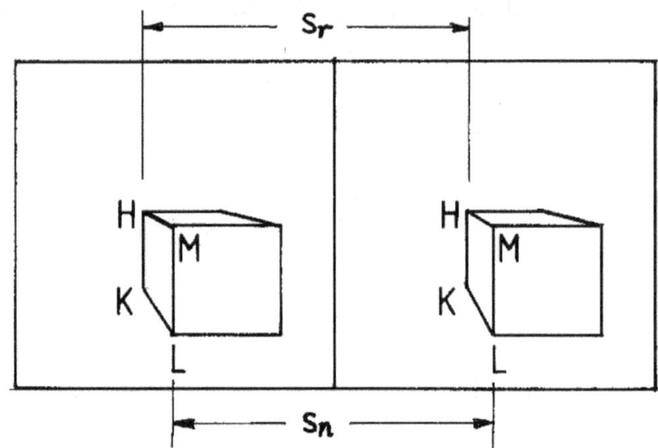

Fig 1-8

Left and right images of a cube. The left face **HKLM** *appears different in each diagram because of the oblique view. Since the vertical edge* **HK** *is further away than the edge* **ML**, *the separation* s_r *will be greater than* s_n.

CHAPTER 2: STEREOSCOPIC PHOTOGRAPHY WITH AN ORDINARY (MONOCULAR) FILM CAMERA

2.1 Principles

Until the large-scale use of digital cameras, smartphones and tablets in the early part of the twenty-first century, film has been the main medium for capturing images since photography began some one-hundred-and-fifty years before, so this chapter and the next are devoted to the use of film cameras for stereoscopic work.

It will be welcome news for the beginner in stereo photography that he can, without purchasing any special equipment, make a few experiments in the art simply by using his standard, single-lens camera, whether this be an advanced technology single lens reflex, a medium format, or a compact camera. To produce stereo pairs photographically it is necessary to take two photographs from two viewpoints, usually spaced about 65mm apart, using the principle discussed in Chapter 1, Section 1.3.1. By doing so, two images will be produced that correspond to the views seen by the two eyes from the same position. The camera is simply positioned for the first exposure, and, after winding on the film, moved 65mm or so to the right (or left) for the second exposure. Indeed, this is one of the traditional methods used by many 3D photographers and it can work very well, but only when the subject matter consists entirely of static objects. Anything in the scene that moves during the time interval between the first and second exposures will produce differences in the left and right images that are nothing to do with purely stereoscopic differences, and it will be difficult, if not impossible, to view the resultant photographic pair as a true stereoscopic image.

2.2 Traditional (or Classic) Stereo Photography

For the purpose of this book, traditional stereo photography is defined as: "the use of a camera (either monocular or stereo) to take two pictures spaced horizontally about 65mm apart (the average eye separation) to form a stereo pair when suitably processed and mounted."

This basic technique can be applied to the majority of photographic subjects, provided that the objects within a scene are located between about 2 metres (about 7 feet) and infinity. It is most effective when the subject matter lies between 2 metres and a few hundred metres. For subjects closer than 2 metres, or very distant scenes where there is little or no foreground of significance, variations on this standard technique need to be adopted in order to achieve satisfactory stereoscopic effects. Principally, this means taking the pair of pictures with a reduced or increased lens separation, from a few millimetres to perhaps hundreds of metres. The inter-lens spacing, or **stereo base**, differs significantly from the norm of around 65mm. Use of a stereo base smaller than the norm is referred to as **hyposteroscopy**; for a base greater than the norm, the term is **hypersteroscopy**.

In addition to these variations from traditional stereoscopy, there are special cameras available that are designed to take 3 or 4 pictures simultaneously. The resulting images are processed to produce a single print (on special photographic paper) that can be viewed directly as a 3D image, without any additional optical aid. This belongs to another branch of stereoscopy known as **autostereoscopy**. Hypersteroscopy, hyposteroscopy and autostereoscopy are discussed in Chapters 7 and 9 in this book.

2.3 Guidelines for Successful Stereo Photography

As indicated in section **2.1**, the method involves no more than taking two separate pictures approximately 65mm apart horizontally. The camera may be used in landscape format, in which the camera is held with the film running left to right (or vice versa, depending upon the direction of film transport in the camera), which means that the longer edges of the picture frame are horizontal. Alternatively, one may use portrait format, where the camera is rotated by 90° so that the longer edges of the picture are vertical. It almost goes without saying, of course, that the two separate pictures should be in the same format! It is probably fair to say that most stereo workers favour the landscape format, although, as its name suggests, the portrait format is satisfactory for portraits and certain other subjects with an essentially vertical shape.

Despite the apparent simplicity of the method, there are a number of techniques, including the use of simple items of equipment, which can assist the photographer in producing a satisfactory stereo pair. In addition, there are a few simple guidelines that should be followed for optimum results. There are good reasons for these, but they are not all explained in this section. For the moment, the reader is merely recommended to adhere to them. They are as follows:

1. the subject must be static: any moving object, even foliage, blowing in the wind, can cause oddities in the stereo image as it shifts its position in the time interval between the two shots.
2. the nearest object should be no closer than about 2 metres
3. the whole image should be sharp: the aperture should be set and the lens focused to ensure that the whole scene is rendered sharp from the nearest to the furthest object (see Chapter 10, Section 10.5).
4. the camera should not be tilted: whether in landscape or vertical format; the camera must be held level, so that the image frame edges are vertical and horizontal (**Fig 2.1**). It is permissible, however, to tilt the camera forward or backward about a horizontal axis running left to right through the camera body, as for example tilting the camera

back to include the top of a tall building. This technique is best used sparingly (**Fig 2.2**).

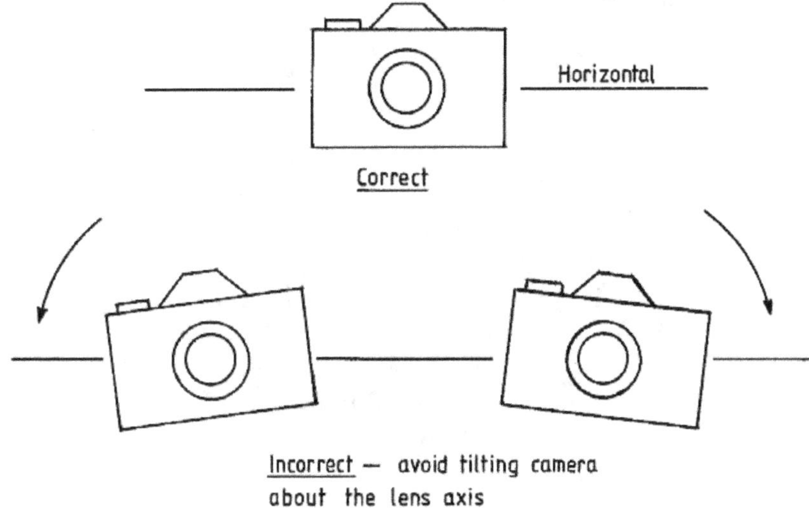

Fig 2.1

With sequential exposures, the camera should be held horizontally for each shot.

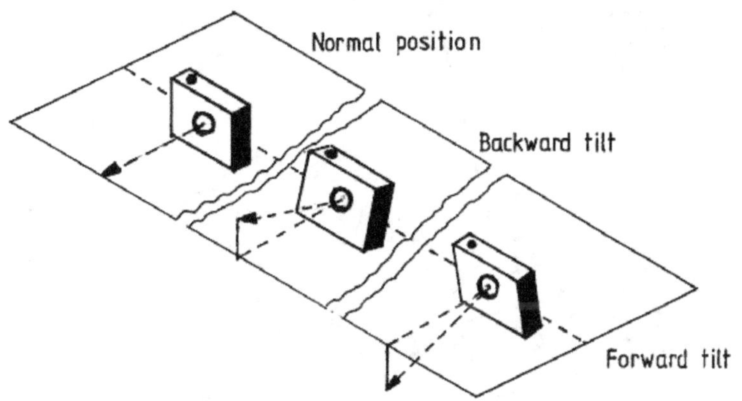

Fig 2.2

The camera can be tilted backwards or forwards for certain shots, for example to include the top of a building. With sequential shots, the amount of tilt should be the same for both exposures.

5.   the camera should not be twisted: "twisting" here refers to any rotation about a vertical axis passing through the centre of the camera body. In shifting the camera from the first to second shooting positions, there should be no "toeing-in". The camera should be moved parallel to itself when it is repositioned (**Fig 2.3**).

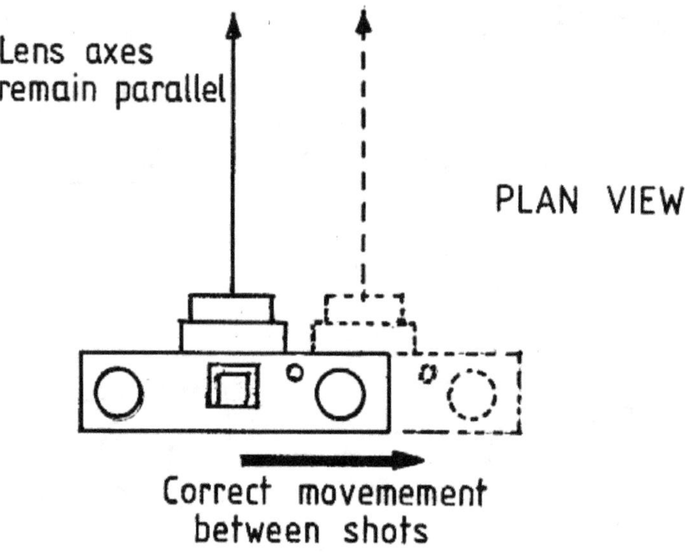

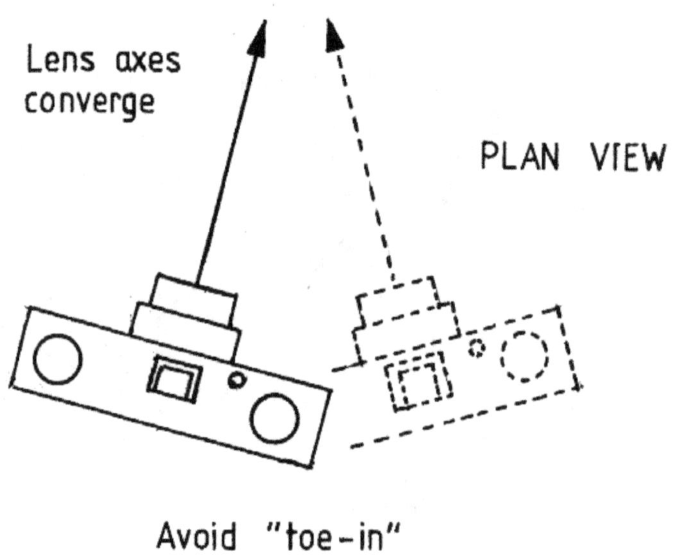

Fig 2.3
With sequential exposures, the camera should be moved parallel to itself. "Toe-in" (lower diagram) should be avoided or at least kept to a minimum.

6. the camera should move horizontally between shots: there should be no upward or downward shift in camera position between the two shooting positions. In taking the first picture, the configuration of objects, in particular those near the bottom edge of the frame, should be carefully noted so that when the camera is relocated for the

second shot, the configuration of these objects is essentially the same. Of course there will be some differences caused by the horizontal movement itself; objects on the left or right may be nearer or further from the vertical frame edges. For example, the edge of a low wall in the foreground should appear at the same distance from the bottom edge of the frame in both shots (**Fig 2.4**).

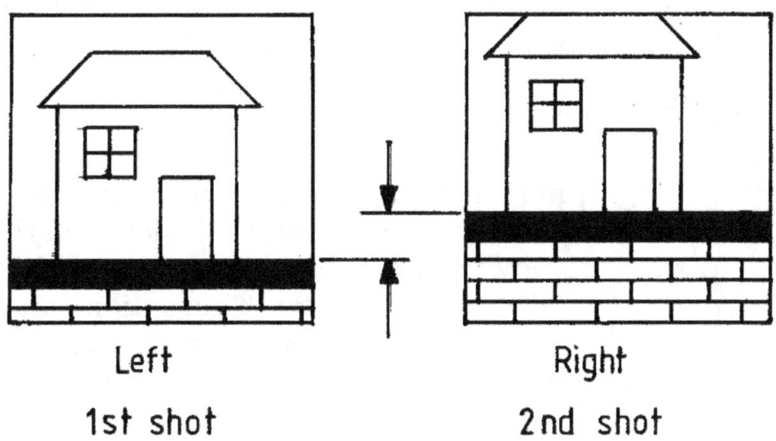

Fig 2.4
Unsatisfactory stereo pair showing a height error caused by a vertical shift of the camera between sequential exposures.

7. the lighting conditions should be the same for both shots: generally, this will not be a problem if the two shots are taken with only a short time interval between them. However, weather conditions can change rapidly and if, for example, the first shot is taken in sunshine but the sun is obscured by a cloud for the second shot, the resulting photographs will be unsatisfactory as a stereo pair. If using a flashgun, it must be in the same position for both shots; it should not, therefore, be attached to the camera.

8. the exposure settings should be the same for both shots: do not, for example, use 1/125 sec at f/11 for one shot and 1/1000 sec at f/4 for the other. Although these are equivalent exposures, the two pictures will differ in their depth of field because of the different apertures used (see Supplement S13). Parts of the image, sharp in the f/11 shot, are likely to be blurry in the f/4 shot. If the camera is used in an auto-exposure programme mode, there might be slight changes in the shutter speed/aperture settings if the lighting conditions change marginally (but see rule 7); this is outside the photographer's control. However, the differences should not be critical.

***(N.B**. Numbers 1 to 4, 7 and 8 are also relevant when using a stereo camera.)*

Finally, a general tip: it is recommended that the two shots are always taken in the same order, (e.g. left first, right second). This makes it easier to identify the left and right shots after processing, when they are being mounted.

Now let us examine the various photographic techniques that can be used for stereo photography.

2.4 Freestanding Methods
2.4.1 Using the eyes

Here, the photographer stands absolutely still and takes the first picture with the camera viewfinder placed against the left eye. Having taken the first shot, and without moving the head, the camera is shifted so that the viewfinder is relocated against the right eye. This action can be repeated on any other occasion with a high degree of reproducibility and consistency. There will be little difference in the stereo base for each stereo pair of photographs.

2.4.2 Using the feet

Much less consistent or reproducible is to stand with feet slightly apart, lean slightly to the left to put all the weight on the left foot for the first photograph, then to shift the weight to the right foot for the second shot. The stereo base cannot be controlled as accurately with this method, but minor variations in stereo base from one shot to the next will go unnoticed.

Both of the above methods can be used in good lighting conditions, but if slow shutter speeds are necessary (as in night shots) then there is a danger of camera shake.

2.5 Mechanical Aids

Various simple devices can be used to assist in positioning the camera correctly and accurately for the two exposures. Some are available commercially, but it is not difficult for even the most ham-fisted DIY worker to produce home-made versions!

2.5.1 Ruler and flat surface

Although this hardly comes into the category of mechanical aids and may seem blindingly obvious as a method, nevertheless there will be occasions when a suitable horizontal surface, such as a fence rail, can be used as a camera support. A ruler (or even guesswork!) can be used to locate two suitable positions for the exposures. If the surface used is rather large compared with the camera, care should be taken that part of this surface is not inadvertently included in the images. The camera needs to be at the front edge, and in some instances what appears to be an ideal surface may turn out to be unusable because of restricted access to the camera's viewfinder.

2.5.2 Tripod

A tripod provides the photographer with a portable support that can be adjusted in height. However, unless it is used on a flat surface it can be awkward to move it by 65mm between exposures with any degree of accuracy and the second exposure can suffer from being tilted with respect to the first or having its horizon line higher or lower.

A small table tripod could prove more useful in conjunction with available flat surfaces. The extra height provided by the tripod can overcome the problem of including part of the surface itself in the picture and may allow one to use a surface that otherwise would be impracticable.

Other devices, obtainable from camera shops, such as clamps or bean bags might find a use in certain circumstances but generally all such supports, including tripods, do not provide any great advantage over the hand-held freestanding techniques explained earlier, apart from allowing the use of long exposures with less risk of camera shake. Even so, it is advisable to attach a cable release to the camera when using such devices, because they are not necessarily as rigid as they might appear.

2.5.3 Stereo Slide Bar

The slide bar can take on several forms with various levels of sophistication. Whatever the actual design, it is fixed to a tripod for support and allows the camera to be moved accurately to two predetermined positions without moving the tripod itself.

Fig 2.5 shows one of the simplest designs of slide bar; it can be constructed very easily from wood. It consists of a tray with built up edges to form a recess into which the camera is placed. The width of the recess is made equal to the width of the camera, **W**, plus 65mm. Thus, when the camera is placed to the left of the recess, butting it up to the left and rear edges of the tray, it can be slid to the right, using the rear edge as a guide, and it will move a distance of exactly 65mm.

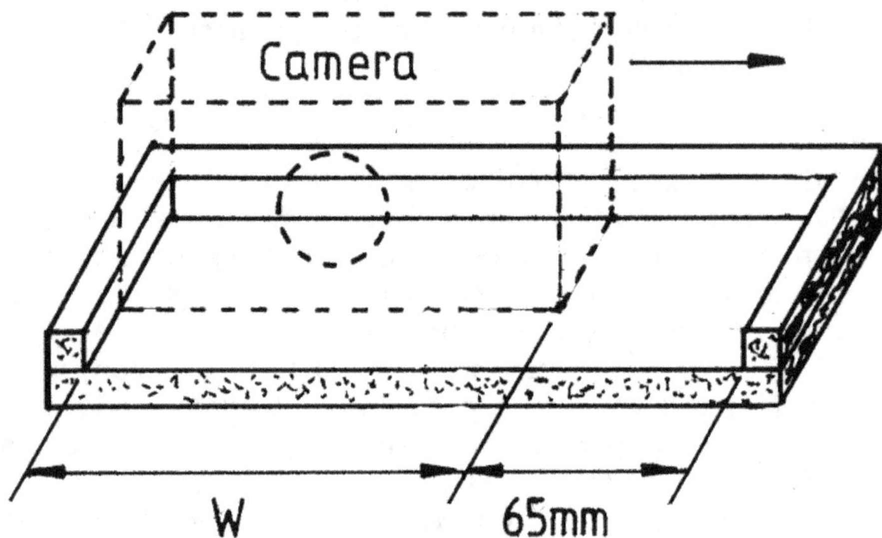

Fig 2.5
A simple slide bar in the form of a recessed tray. Here it is designed to give a shift of 65mm quickly and accurately.

As described, the tray is suitable only for cameras whose width is the same as that for which it is designed. However, the tray can be made wide enough to allow different cameras to be used in conjunction with appropriately sized blocks to retain the 65mm movement, as illustrated in **Fig 2.6**. The same principle can be used to reduce the stereo base to less than 65mm, which is a technique that has to be used for objects in close-up, nearer than 2 metres (see Chapter 7).

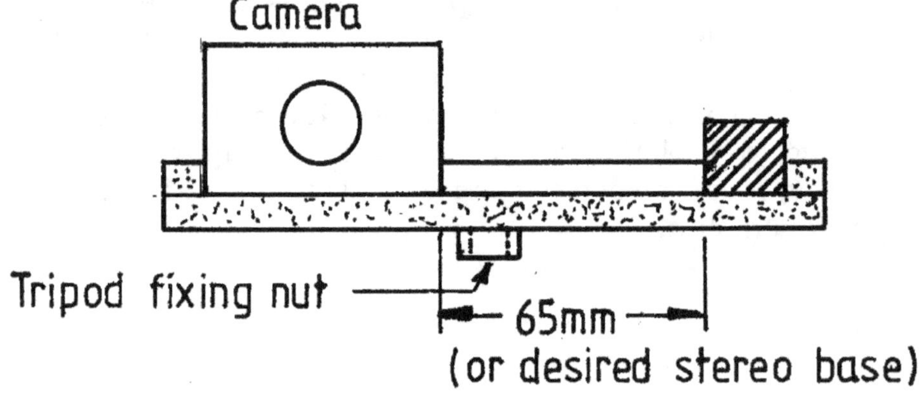

Fig 2.6
*Front view of a slide bar with a temporary block in position (on the right) so that it can be used with a camera of width less than **W** (see **Fig 2.5**. Blocks of greater width can be used to reduce the stereo base in close-ups.*

Even more simply, the slide can be constructed from two pieces of wood as shown in Fig 2.7. With a reference line on the camera back and a graduated scale on the back ledge, any camera and stereo base can be employed.

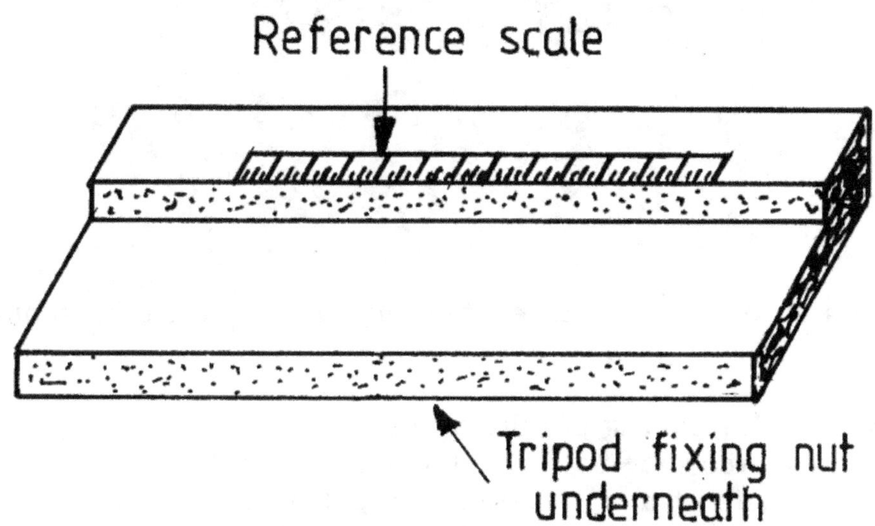

Fig 2.7
Another simple slide bar incorporating a reference scale.

One might be tempted to think of increasing the slide width to allow for larger stereo base values in addition to short stereo bases. However, there would be little point in doing this, because the 65mm base is adequate for most stereography (apart from close-ups). When a larger base is necessary, it is more likely to be measured in metres than in millimetres to have any real advantage.

Now that the principle has been explained, the reader can doubtless think of more sophisticated designs in wood or metal, with precision engineering in mind. Such slides are available from specialist photographic dealers, but they can be expensive. Further information and designs can be found in books by Ferwerda[4] and Waack[5]

Even those who use a true stereo camera might find the stereo slide bar a useful device when they wish to take close-up shots with a reduced base and adopting the separate exposure technique (See Chapter 7).

The author's own stereo slide bar is constructed from a discarded bathroom shower fitting, the vertical metal tube along which the shower head can be raised and lowered. A short piece of this tube, together with the end stops and the shower head carrier (which locks via a button at any position along the tube) were used as the basis for the slide bar. Part of a plastic ruler provides a reference scale against which the camera movement can be measured (**Fig 2.8**).

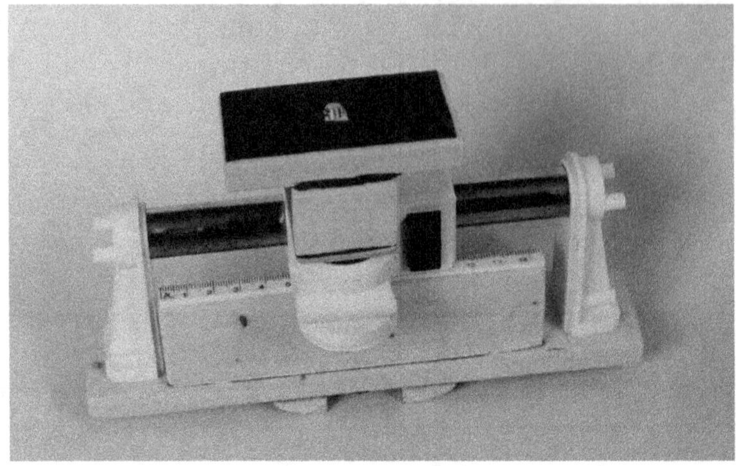

Fig 2.8
The author's slide bar constructed from wood and part of a shower head slide.

2.5.4 Pantograph (moving parallelogram)

Like the stereo slide bar, this device is relatively simple and quick to operate. It consists of a flat platform (**Fig 2.9**) to which the camera is attached. Four linkage bars (two each side), which are pivoted at the points of attachment, connect the platform to a flat base. A suitably threaded hole in the centre of the base allows it to be fixed to a tripod. The linkage bars allow the platform to be swung in an arc into two resting positions on a central block; the dimensions are calculated to give a lateral movement of 65mm, or whatever stereo base the pantograph is designed for. **Fig 2.10** shows the operation of the pantograph. The platform carrying the camera remains horizontal and is at the same height in the two extreme positions.

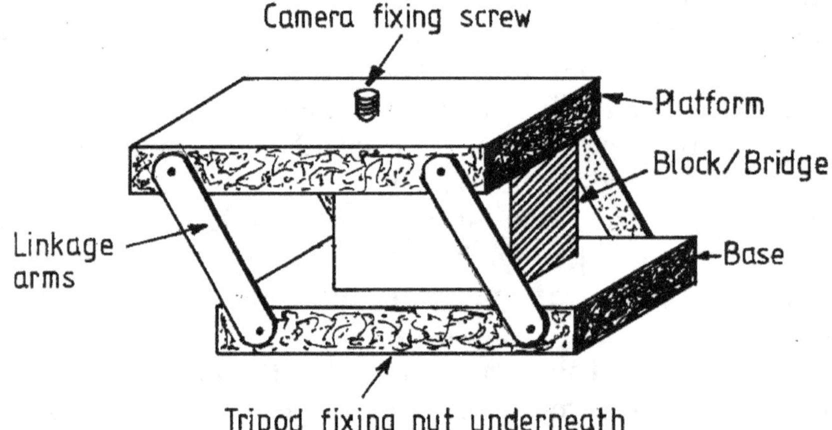

Fig 2.9
Basic pantograph or moving parallelogram.

Although demanding a little more skill in construction than that required for the stereo slide bar, the reasonably competent DIY worker should not find the work too difficult. Once the principle of operation is understood, refinements in the design and basic engineering construction can easily be incorporated.

Some suggested dimensions for a pantograph are given in **Fig 2.11**, as a starting point. These dimensions can be modified to suit the individual camera. The method of fixing the camera to the platform is not shown in this diagram.

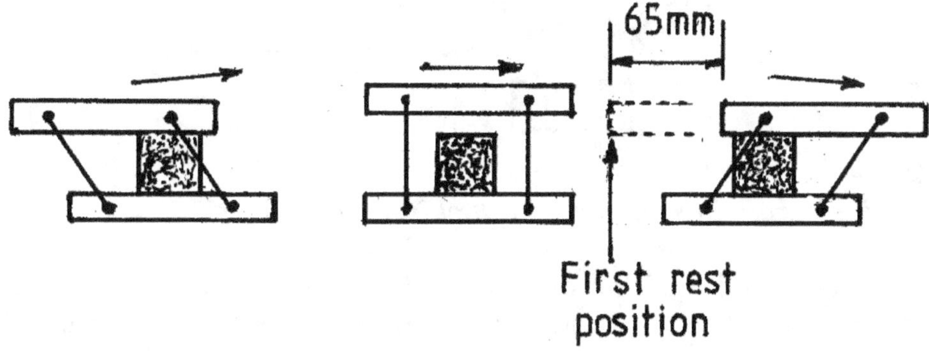

Fig 2.10
Operation of a pantograph showing the "up and down" movement to give a predetermined shift of the .camera Varying the bridge height will change the stereo base.

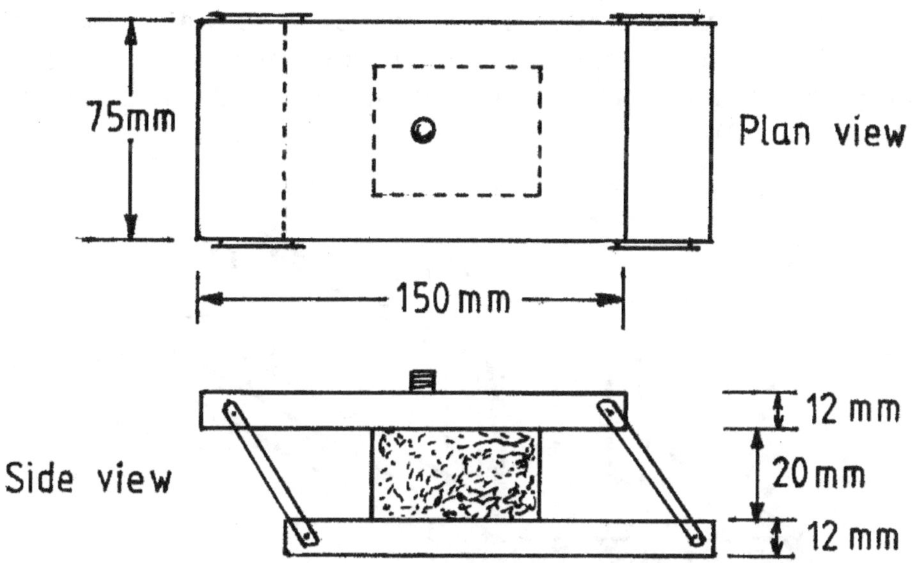

Fig 2.11
Suggested dimensions for a pantograph.

The fixing device can take the form of a central screw located in a threaded hole and protruding above the surface; this screw fits into the tripod socket on the camera. A locking nut on the underside will be required to ensure that the camera can be orientated correctly and fastened securely in place (**Fig 2.12**). In this case the platform can be shorter than the camera.

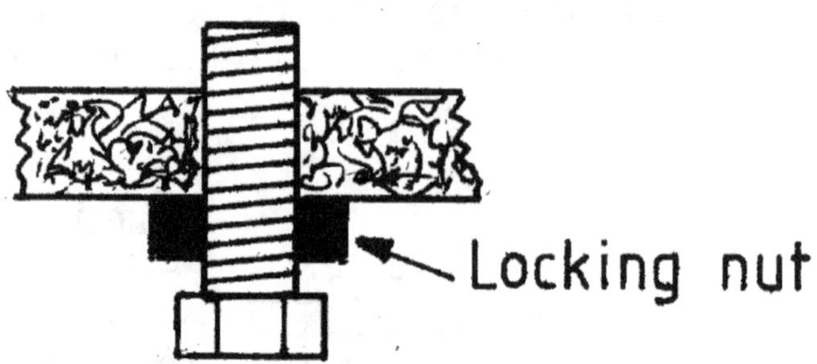

Fig 2.12
Camera fixing screw incorporating a locking nut.

The overall dimensions of 150 x 75mm (6 x 3in approximately) are large enough to allow for the addition of raised edges to form a recessed tray into which the camera can fit snugly, as an alternative to the screw-fixing device. The easiest material to use is wood and the 12mm thickness (about ½in) gives rigidity and a reasonably large dimension within which holes can be drilled in order to fix the linkage pivots. The more skilled craftsman will be able to construct a rigid but more elegant model in metal, but even the most basic design will function correctly.

The central block or "bridge" must be placed so that it does not make contact with the camera fixing screw on the platform. One way to achieve this is to replace the solid bridge with two thinner bridges spaced apart, or four pillars (**Fig 2.13**).

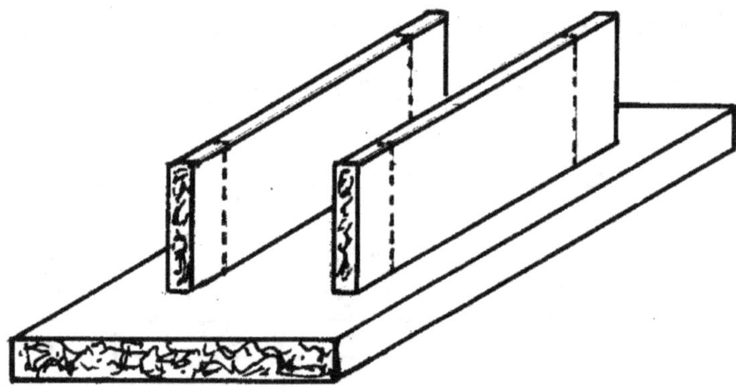

Fig 2.13
Alternative to a central block using two thinner bridges or four pillars (dotted lines) thus reducing bulk and weight.

This also has the advantage of reducing the weight of the pantograph. The bridge would normally be fixed to the base, but it could be designed to be easily removable, so that bridges of different heights can be interchanged. This will allow the lateral movement of the platform (and hence the camera) to be varied. In other words, the apparatus can be adapted for stereo photography with a stereo base less than 65mm. Supplement S2 gives more details of this modification.

The bridge is not an essential component of the pantograph and can be omitted. If we assume that the platform and base are of moderate thickness (say 12mm) then, without a bridge, the platform will swing over from one rest position to the other in an almost complete semi-circle, **Fig 2.14a**. We can make the "up and over" movement trace a flatter path by increasing the thickness of both platform and base, **Fig 2.14b**, but this adds weight. The use of a bridge acts as a compromise, **Fig 2.14c**. If the bridge is too high, the device becomes rather more top-heavy. Anyone constructing a pantograph will have to decide which design features suit him best.

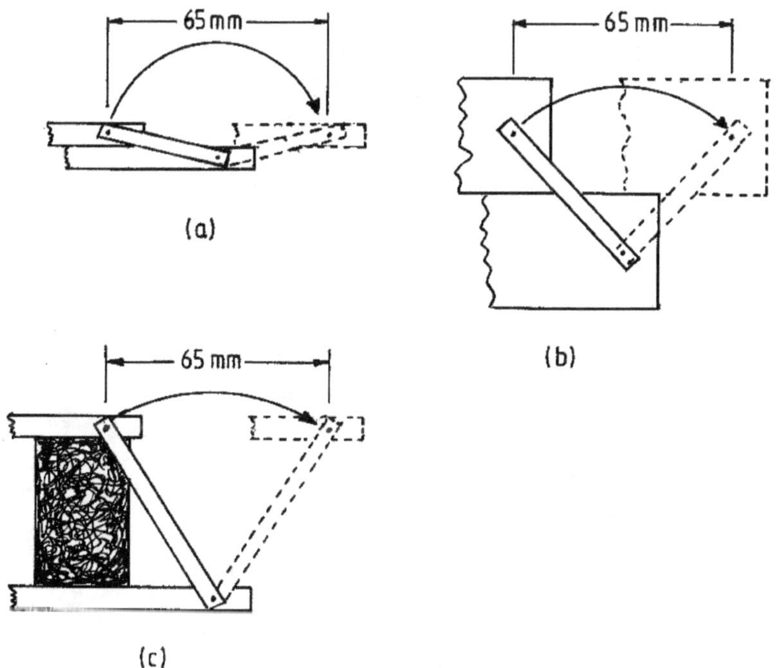

Fig 2.14
Trajectory of platform for a given horizontal shift.
a *Near semi-circular movement using thin material for platform and base.*
b *Flatter trajectory achieved by using thicker material.*
c *Flatter trajectory achieved with a bridge together with thinner material for platform and base.*

The pantograph can easily be adapted for close-up photography using a stereo base less than 65mm. By adding extra layers of wood, say, the height of the bridge can be increased; this reduces the lateral movement of the platform. Trial and error can be used to determine what extra height is needed to produce a specific (reduced) stereo base. Conversely, removal of the bridge will produce a stereo base greater than 65mm but, as has been explained in connection with the stereo slide bar (Section 2.5.3), there is little advantage unless the enlarged stereo base is several metres or more, which would be outside the scope of the device. The relationship between the bridge height and the stereo base for any given pantograph can be calculated by following the principles explained in Supplement S2.

CHAPTER 3: STEREOSCOPIC PHOTOGRAPHY WITH A STEREOSCOPIC FILM CAMERA

3.1 Introduction

Since the early days of stereo photography, special twin lens cameras have been constructed to enable the two images to be captured on film simultaneously; this use of specialist stereoscopic cameras is by far the most convenient way of working. In the twenty-first century, the use of digital cameras became available, as discussed in Chapter 14.

The basic design of a stereoscopic camera is illustrated schematically in **Fig 3.1**. In essence, it consists of a camera body rather wider than a conventional camera so that it can accommodate two identical lenses separated by about 65mm. The actual separation varies in different models for reasons that will become clear when the various types of camera are discussed individually, later in this chapter. Usually the lenses are coupled together so that the act of focusing one lens automatically focuses the other at the same time. Similarly, the aperture settings for the two lenses are linked, as are the shutter speed controls.

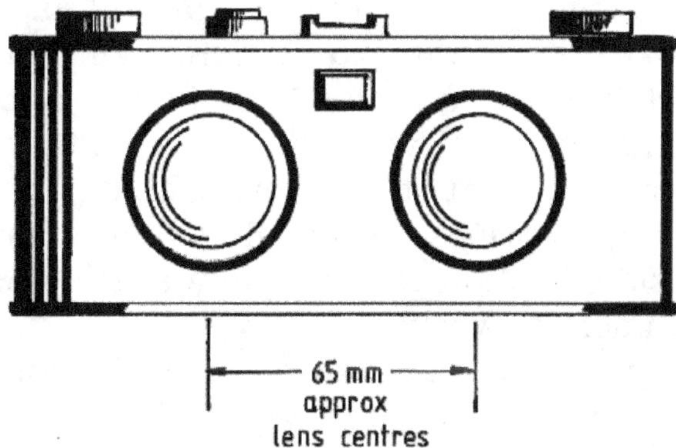

Fig 3.1
Schematic stereo camera.

With these facilities, the stereo photographer has a much greater scope for capturing images in a wide range of situations. He is no longer restricted by the limitations of the sequential exposure technique outlined in Chapter 2, Section 2.3. Nevertheless, many of the guidelines described in that section are still relevant when using a stereo camera.

3.2 Availability of Equipment

Within the broad scope of photography, stereo photography still represents only a minority interest; it is a specialist hobby. Consequently, there are relatively few new specialist cameras on the market and many enthusiasts still seek out good second-hand equipment. It is perhaps quite surprising to discover just how many different models have been manufactured over the years, ranging from the simple to the highly sophisticated. However, a note of caution must be introduced here. The general photographer is accustomed nowadays to handling very well specified equipment with all the latest electronic gadgetry; even the more modest compact camera is better equipped with facilities than its counterpart in the past. The stereo photographer is not so fortunate. Having to rely on yesterday's technology or to buy new stereo equipment that is less well specified than mono cameras, he has to accept that his stereo camera will not be quite as versatile as his latest single lens reflex. He must, therefore, get to know the limitations of his equipment and not expect it to perform adequately in all situations.

Apart from certain photographic retailers who handle second-hand or even new stereo cameras and equipment, there are in existence various stereoscopic societies that further the art of stereo photography and play an important part in keeping equipment in circulation.

3.3 Stereoscopic Formats

The history of photography shows clearly how the development of better emulsions for film stock, improvements in lens design and technological advances made in camera design and exposure control have led to a considerable degree of miniaturisation. From the early use of glass plates (giving rise to the terms 'full plate', 'half plate' and 'quarter plate' for the older negative image sizes), we, nowadays, find a preponderance of 35mm format cameras. We must not forget that larger image sizes on negatives lead to superior prints (especially when enlarged several times) and today's professional photographer tends to use medium format cameras in most commercial work.

Early stereo cameras were, of course, based upon the negative sizes of the time. However, in this chapter we shall concentrate mainly upon stereoscopic cameras that use 35mm film; there are several good reasons for this:

1. the 35mm format is the most popular and widely available format today
2. 35mm film is much cheaper in terms of the number of pictures produced at a given cost
3. most of the stereoscopic cameras manufactured in the last fifty years or so have been in the 35mm format
4. 35mm cameras are generally cheaper than medium format cameras
5. 35mm cameras are lighter, easier to handle and very versatile
6. 35mm projectors are readily available for those interested in viewing stereo slides on a screen. Even stereo projectors (with twin lenses),

can be obtained, though in restricted numbers and mostly second-hand

7.   35mm stereo slide mounts in various shapes and sizes are currently manufactured and available commercially. This is very helpful to the stereo worker as making one's own mounts is very exacting.

Before we review various cameras, it is instructive to examine the different image sizes that exist, and the ways in which the images are arranged along the length of the film. It is also helpful to our general understanding of stereo photography to begin by examining a larger format, as exemplified by the 120 or 620 roll film and using (or imagining!) a stereo camera designed for this size film, known today as **medium format**.

3.3.1 Medium Format Images
Fig 3.2 shows the image sizes that are currently produced by various monocular medium format cameras. Medium format cameras are used mainly to produce prints rather than transparencies and the size of the image in each of the three formats lends itself conveniently to the production of contact prints which, with a couple of reservations explained below, are ideal for stereo work

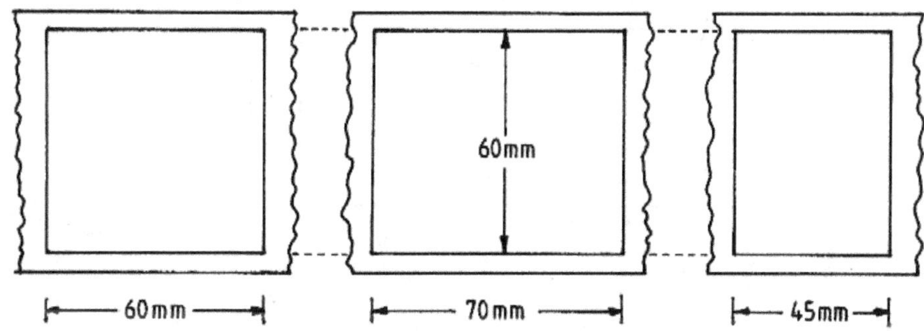

Fig 3.2
Standard medium format image sizes on 120/620 roll film.

The 60x60mm size, which gives 12 exposures per roll of film (6 stereo pairs), is probably the best in this respect, since a stereo pair of contact prints can be mounted side by side (with 65mm between the centres of the prints) to give comfortable viewing conditions. Some older stereo cameras produced two side-by-side images within a 60 x 130mm area, which gives similar sized individual images.

The 60 x 70mm format (8 exposures per roll, or 4 stereo pairs) will produce "landscape format" prints, which cannot be mounted closer than 70 mm separation. This is a little too far apart for comfort, unless a more specialised viewing technique is used (See Chapter 5, Sections 5.3.5 to 5.3.7). The prints can, of course, be trimmed to about 65mm in width, but this rather defeats the object of using this format, and the photographer would have to allow for any such loss in the image when composing the picture in the camera.

There is no such problem with the 60 x 45mm format, except that the upright portrait format is generally less favoured. One advantage of the 60 x 45mm size is that it is the most economical, with 16 frames (8 stereo pairs) per roll of film.

Any stereo camera based upon these formats could be designed with the left and right images (in both the 60 x 60mm and 60 x 70mm sizes) side-by-side. The lens separations would be around 65mm and 70mm respectively (**Fig 3.3**). The film winding mechanism would need to advance the film by two frames between exposures to produce the sequence shown in **Fig 3.4**. The film can be cut conveniently between the 'pairs' of images, which is useful for storage. Because the images are inverted (as shown in **Fig 3.4**) a direct contact print of the pair has to be cut and the left and right images transposed for viewing. This is explained more fully in Chapter 5. Transposition of the left and right images is necessary in stereo shots produced by most stereo cameras.

The sequence of images produced in medium format is quite straightforward. With 35mm film the story is a little more complex.

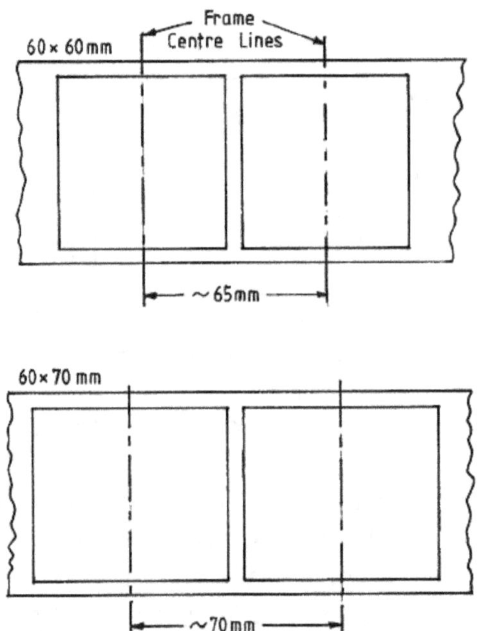

Fig 3.3
Possible configurations for "side-by-side" stereo pairs in the 60 x 60 and 60 x 70mm formats. The image widths dictate the lens separation required (stereo base) on any camera designed to produce these formats.

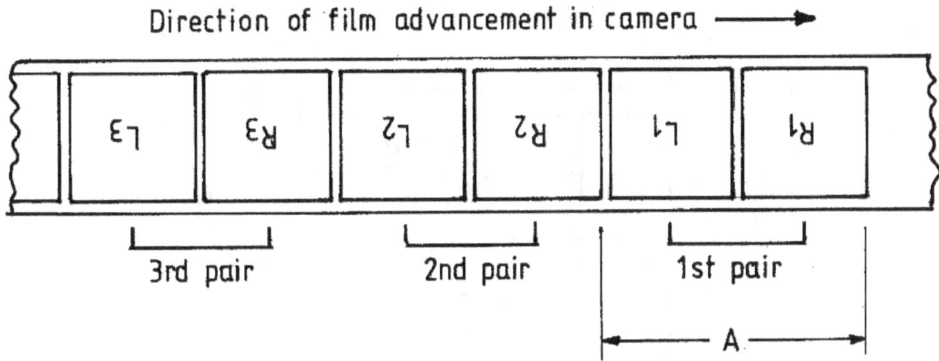

Fig 3.4

Sequence of stereo image pairs for a medium format stereo camera (60 x 60mm frames). Dimension A (essentially two frame widths) is the distance by which the film must be advanced between exposures. Although the left and right images of a given pair are adjacent, they are inverted, so transposition is necessary for correct viewing.

3.3.2 The Standard 35mm Format

This is the image produced in monocular cameras and the individual frame measures 24 x 36mm (**Fig 3.5a**) and would be the image size produced by the sequential exposures method described in Chapter 2. As will be seen, this is a slightly wider image than that produced on 35mm film in true stereo cameras, and whilst the transparencies can be mounted in commercially available stereo mounts, some image loss at the edges is inevitable (see Chapter 6, Section 6.3.2).

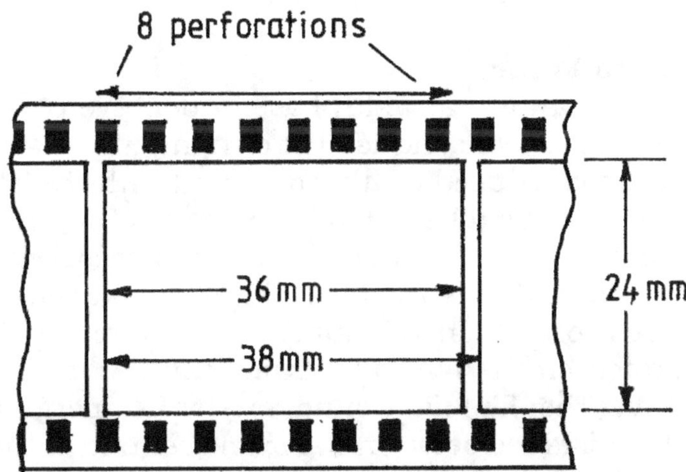

Fig 3.5a

Standard 24 x 36mm frame on 35mm film. The frame width is 8 perforations and the frame separation 38mm.

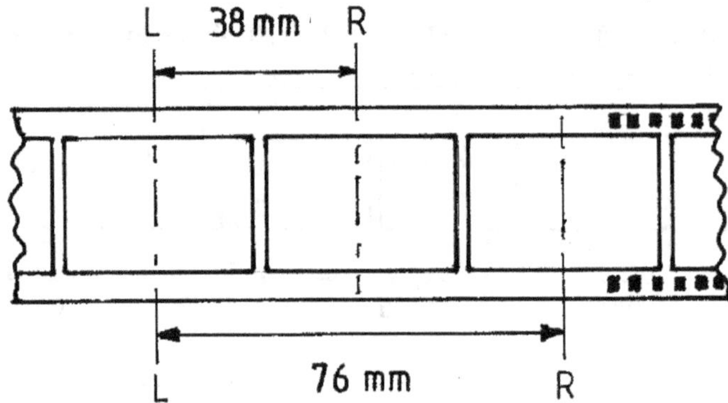

Fig 3.5b
Possible values of stereo base **b** *for cameras using 35mm film and standard 24 x 36mm frames.*

The image width corresponds to 8 perforations on the film, and the winding mechanism in ordinary 35mm cameras advances the film by this amount.

If we were to design a stereo camera around this format we could either base the lens separation on adjacent frames (38mm apart, which is too small in general as a stereo base) or on alternate frames with a stereo base of 76mm, which would be more acceptable (**Fig 3.5b**). However, by reducing the individual image width to less than 36mm we can keep the camera to a more manageable size, and gain more exposures per roll of film. This is the principle employed in nearly all the stereoscopic cameras designed for the 35mm format. There are two principal image formats and these are discussed in the following sections.

3.3.3 The 5P Stereo Format

This format has an image width based upon five perforations (hence "5P") rather than eight. The individual (left or right) image size is 24 x 23mm approximately, and the reduced width (compared with the 'standard' frame) allows 28 stereo pairs to be taken on a "36 exposure" film.

Fig 3.6 shows that the distance between successive perforations on the film is 4.75mm and this is the critical dimension that determines the stereo base for this format. In 5P cameras, the individual left and right images are separated on the film by 2 frame widths, to give the sequence shown in **Fig 3.7**. The film is wound on by 10 perforations between exposures, and the distance between the frame centres of the two images of a given stereo pair is 15 perforations. This separation will therefore be 15 x 4.75 = 71.25mm

Clearly, the camera lenses must be separated by the same distance. Although greater than the 65mm 'norm', this is an acceptable value. In actuality, the lenses in most stereo cameras are set slightly closer together than the corresponding frame separation to give a built-in **stereo window**.

This is explained fully in Chapter 18, Section 18.2 The most common stereo base is 70mm.

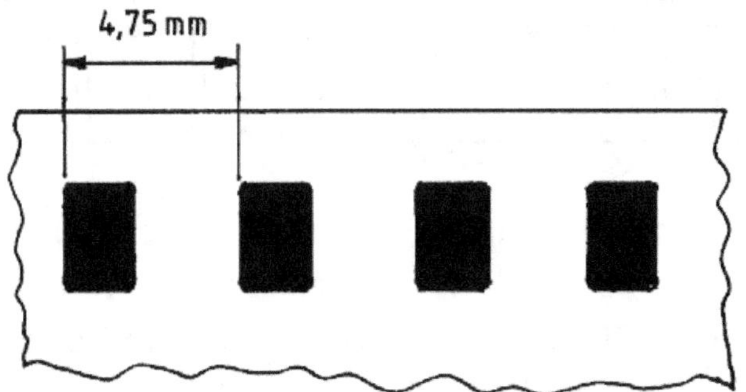

Fig 3.6
Spacing between perforations in 35mm film. Multiples of this value are usually used to establish a suitable stereo base in 35mm stereo cameras.

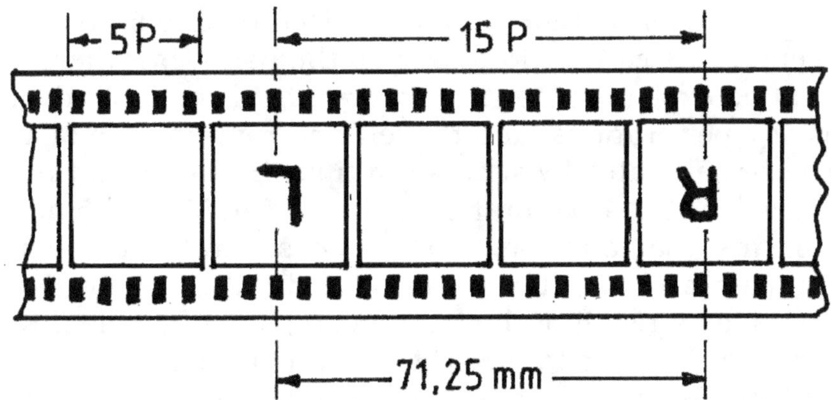

Fig 3.7
Basic geometry of the 5P format. The left and right images of a stereo pair are separated by two frames, fifteen perforations, to give a stereo base of 71.25mm. In practice, the camera lenses are often set slightly closer, at 70mm.

The two-frame advance gives rise to two blank frames on the film when all 28 shots have been completed, one near each end. The sequence of frames is shown in **Fig 3.8**. This method of film advance is known as the **Colardeau** progression after its inventor.

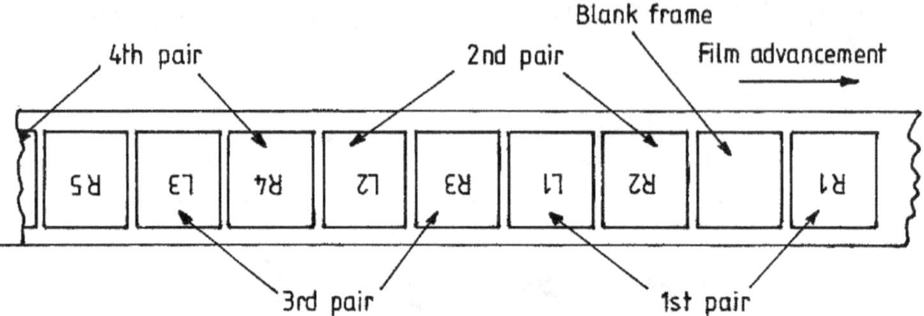

Fig 3.8

Sequence of images in 5P format, as seen from the back of the camera. The film is advanced by two frames after each exposure (the Colardeau progression), which results in a blank frame near to each end of the film.

3.3.4 The 7P European Format

This is an alternative major format that gives slightly wider images (nominally 24x30mm) than those obtained with 5P format cameras. Some workers prefer the slightly wider coverage given by this system.

In essence, it uses 7 perforations as the basis, but there is a rider to this statement as explained later. In theory, then, the film advancement is in multiples of 7 perforations, and the left and right images of a stereo pair would have to be separated by such a multiple. In this case, the stereo base would be equivalent to 14 perforations, viz: 14 x 4.75 = 66.5mm.

This means that only one full frame separates the left and right images of a pair and not two frames as in the 5P format. The film advancement is, as a result of this, more complex. After the first exposure, the film is advanced by one frame. The second exposure can now be taken, and at this point the configuration of images will be as shown in **Fig 3.9**.

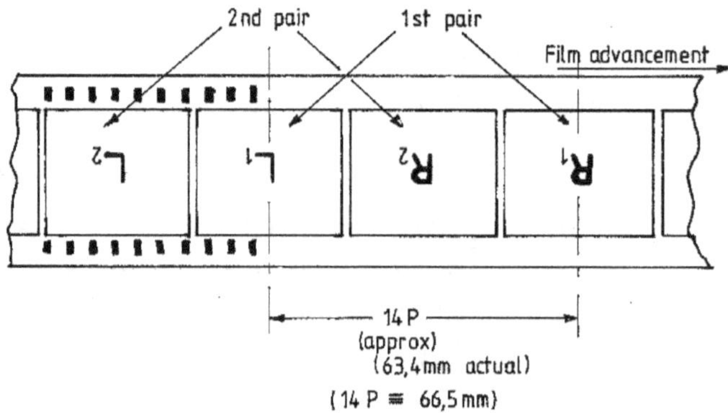

Fig 3.9

The 7P format. The frame width is approximately seven perforations (nearer 6¾ in practice), and the film advances by one and three frames alternatively. The stereo base is approximately fourteen perforations, at 63.4mm.

If the next advance of the film were to be only one frame, one of the exposed frames would be re-exposed and this would occur repeatedly throughout the rest of the film. So, after the second exposure (**Fig 3.9**) the four exposed frames must be by-passed, and this requires a three-frame advance. The whole cycle is repeated, which means that the film is advanced in the sequence: 1,3,1,3,1... etc. Usually, the shutter button is automatically locked until the correct number of frames is advanced after any given exposure. **Fig 3.10** shows how the images are located as a result of this sequence. One minor advantage of this system is that the film can be cut into lengths of four images (two interlaced stereo pairs). In the 5P format, no matter where the film is cut between adjacent frames, one stereo pair is always separated onto different pieces of film.

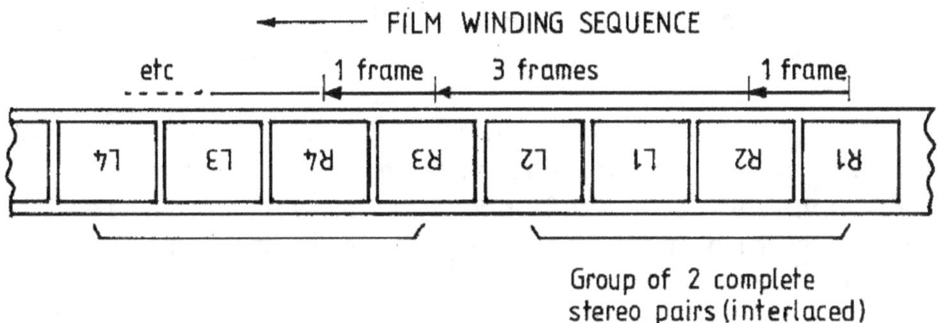

Fig 3.10
Sequence of images on film in the 7P format. With the 1,3,1,3,1... winding sequence, the images are in groups of four, each group comprising two interlaced stereo pairs.

As implied earlier, the seven-perforation measure is a notional one and only approximate. In 7P cameras the actual frame separation of the left and right images is 64mm (this figure is measured from an exposed film) rather than 66.5mm as calculated earlier. This corresponds to about 6¾ perforations as the unit of frame width and the winding mechanism is designed to produce this amount of film advance. For convenience, however, the format is referred to as 7P.

Again, the actual lens separation is often made slightly smaller than this to create the built-in stereo window; the resulting stereo base is 63.4mm.

The 70mm stereo base of the 5P format will give a very slightly superior 3D effect (in theory) than the 63.4mm stereo base of the 7P format, but the difference is marginal and unlikely to be noticed in practice. Values of eye separation of the human race vary from about 55mm to 75mm in adults, though the majority of people (90%) have inter-pupillary distances of between 60 and 70mm. These figures are based on Hofstetter's findings[6] for adult, white male inhabitants of the USA. From these figures, one can see clearly why 65mm is taken as a convenient yardstick for theoretical stereoscopic analysis, and this value has been used for various calculations in this book.

3.3.5 Other 35mm Formats

There are one or two special formats in use for specific viewing systems. These will be discussed in the next section in conjunction with particular camera details.

3.4 Review of 35mm Stereo Cameras

The cameras reviewed in this section have been chosen as being representative of the various formats and levels of sophistication available. They are not necessarily the best of their kind; some indeed are quite basic but, within their own limitations, capable of producing satisfactory stereo images. Most of these cameras can still be found on the second-hand circuit, though not in large numbers. A few are available as new models in specialist camera retailers.

An attempt has been made in the individual reviews to make some kind of value judgement on performance and handling; these are the author's opinions, but it is to be hoped that they will help the reader to form his own assessment of the worth of any particular camera.

3.4.1 Wray Stereo Graphic

This camera was manufactured by Wray (Optical Works) Ltd. of Bromley, Kent under licence from Graflex Inc. of the USA. It first appeared in Britain in the 1950's at a time when there was a surge of interest in 3D, prompted perhaps by the production and screening of a number of 3D movies. Whilst having a modest set of specifications the camera is capable of producing excellent results. An example is shown in **Fig 3.11**.

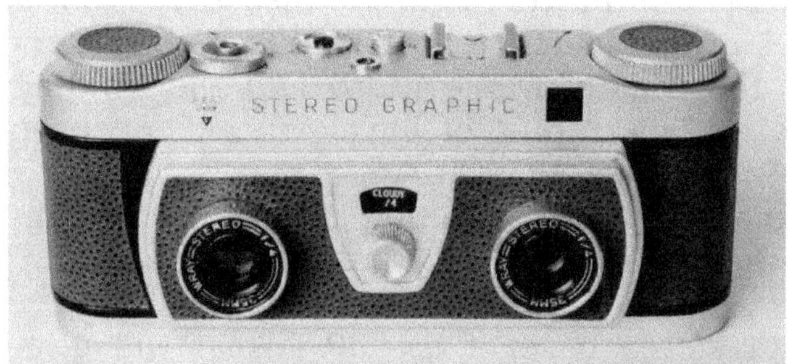

Fig 3.11
Wray Stereo Graphic camera – 5P format.

The camera is designed around the 5P format yielding 28 stereo pairs on a standard 36 exposure 35mm film, individual frames measuring a nominal 24 x 23mm.

Brief Specification:

Lenses:	Two matched 35mm f/4 Wray, fixed focus. Horizontal angle of view 36°22' (see Supplement S3)
Stereo Base:	(lens separation) 70mm
Frame Separation:	71.25mm between the frame centres of the left and right images of a stereo pair.
Shutter Speeds:	1/50 sec (I setting) and bulb setting
Apertures:	f/4 to f/16 (Waterhouse stops)
Other Features:	Flash socket and shoe, frame counter, double exposure prevention, cable release thread.

Comments:

The manufacturers point out that: "*the Stereo Graphic is different from other stereo cameras. The exclusive 'DEPTHMASTER' lens system eliminates the need for focusing mechanisms and gives greater depth of field than ever before. Compare the slides from a Stereo Graphic with those taken with any other stereo camera and you will see the difference. Stereo Graphic slides are always in focus from foreground to deepest background.*"

In the handbook it is claimed that the camera will give sharp focus as close as 1.2 m (4ft). This large depth of field (see Supplement S13) is actually achieved by the particular method of lens mounting in the camera. There is an extra shim in the mount of one lens, so that it is pre-focused on a nearer distance than is the other lens. No detailed information is given but it is probable that the one lens is pre-focused to about 2m (7ft) while the other is pre-focused to about 5m (16ft).

A ring around the shutter release button can be set to two positions, **I** (instantaneous) giving 1/50 sec and **B** (bulb) where the shutter remains open until the button is released, for time exposures. In the **I** setting, since there is only one shutter speed, exposure is controlled by varying the aperture. This is achieved by rotating the small knob situated between the two lenses on the front of the camera. Metal plates behind the lenses are turned by this action to bring various diameter holes (Waterhouse stops) into position. A window above the aperture knob displays the f/number and words such as Hazy, Cloudy, Bright etc. These descriptions were designed to suit the original Kodak slide film popular at the time when the camera was first produced, but rather slow by today's standards. Now, with faster films and very bright conditions, the shutter speed of 1/50 sec can be somewhat too slow in some situations, but there are some excellent 50 ISO speed films available that minimise this minor disadvantage. There is a bonus in that they produce a very fine-grained image, which is always desirable in stereo photography.

Because double exposure prevention is built into the design, the camera does not lend itself easily to close-up work, using a supplementary lens, two separate exposures and a reduced stereo base (see Chapter 7).

Overall, the camera works well, within its limited design features, and produces excellent results. Some care is necessary when advancing the film not to force the winding knob too far or the film can move slightly more than 15 perforations, resulting in overlapping images. Two notches, one in each of the upper and lower frame edges in the camera allow the right image to be identified clearly on the film (**Fig 3.12**). Similar notches, located variously, are included in most stereo cameras to identify the (usually) right image as an aid during mounting.

Fig 3.12 *Back view of the Wray Stereo Graphic camera (with back removed) showing the location of notches to identify the image produced by the right lens.*

3.4.2 Stereo Realist

This camera was developed in the USA by the David White Co., Milwaukee, and was first on sale in 1947 (**Fig 3.13**). It uses the 5P format and was most probably the inspiration for a number of 3D cameras that also used the "Stereo Realist format" as it has come to be known. In fact, two models were produced, the **ST-41** and the **ST-42**, differing mainly in the lenses provided. The later **ST-42** is better specified in this respect.

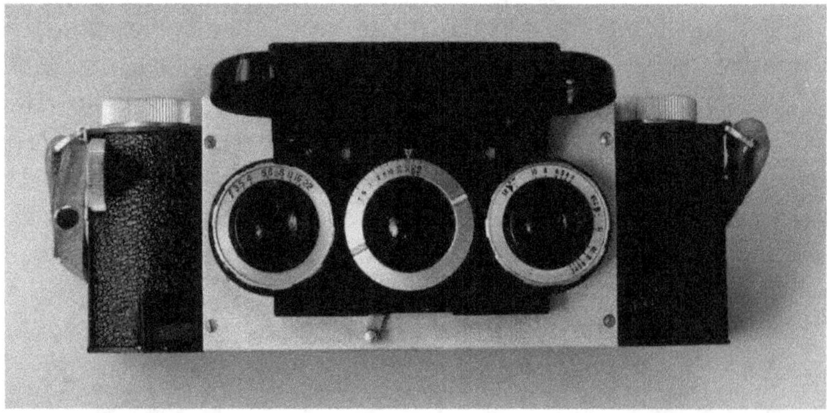

Fig 3.13 *Stereo Realist camera – 5P format.*

Brief Specification:

Lenses:	Two matched f/3.5 3-element colour-corrected, coated anastigmat lenses of focal length 35mm (Model **ST- 41**); Two matched f/2.8 4-element colour-corrected, coated anastigmat lenses (Model **ST- 42**) Horizontal angle of view quoted as 35°
Stereo Base:	70mm
Frame Separation:	71.25mm (15P)
Shutter Speeds:	**ST- 41**: 1 sec to 1/150 sec plus Time (T) and Bulb (B) **ST- 42**: 1 sec to 1/200 sec plus T and B. (In the T setting, the shutter button is pressed and released; the shutter remains open until the shutter release is pressed again. In the B setting, the shutter stays open for as long as the button is depressed.)
Apertures:	f/2.8 (or f/3.5) to f/22
Other Features:	Coupled rangefinder focusing down to about 760mm (2ft), flash shoe, double exposure prevention (can be over-ridden), automatic exposure counter, cable release socket.

Comments:

This well-specified (for the time) camera proved to be extremely popular in the USA from the late 1940's into the 1950's, and it was also available in the UK. With full manual control of exposure and focusing, it is a versatile camera that can be used in most situations. Unusually, the lenses do not rotate when focusing; instead, the focusing knob controls the position of the film plane. The viewfinder window is located between the lenses and on the same level. This is an ideal position because it avoids parallax problems when composing the picture. In any viewfinder camera, what the photographer sees is not exactly what the camera lens "sees" because the viewfinder window and camera lens are in different positions. Parts of the viewed image may be cut off in the photographic image, particularly with close subjects. Only in single lens reflex (SLR) cameras does the photographer see exactly what will appear on film, since he is looking through the actual camera lens.

The built-in rangefinder with a base of 120mm (4¾ in) provides a fairly accurate means of focusing, and together with a depth of field scale enables the photographer to ensure that the whole scene being photographed is in focus from front to rear, by suitable choice of aperture.

Since the rangefinder is coupled to the camera focusing mechanism, the operation is very straightforward.

In 1954, the "Stereo Realist Manual"[7] was published. This book is a comprehensive guide to the camera and its associated equipment (viewers, projectors) produced by the company and covers operation of the camera, techniques including slide mounting, close-ups, photomicrography and many others. It is liberally illustrated with many stereo photographs and is an extremely useful handbook for any stereo photographer, even if he does not own a Stereo Realist.

More recently (1999), another book ("How to use and maintain your STEREO REALIST")[49] has appeared. This gives much new information about the camera and its production history, the numerous accessories that were (and still are in some cases) available and is a valuable guide to its use. Particularly helpful are the sections on maintenance and modifications. The book is highly recommended to all Realist users[49].

The Stereo Realist is still available from time to time on the second-hand circuit and is a favourite with many stereo photographers.

3.4.3 FED Stereo

This camera (**Fig 3.14**) is one of the few that are currently available new and originates from the FED factory, Kharkov, in the Ukraine.

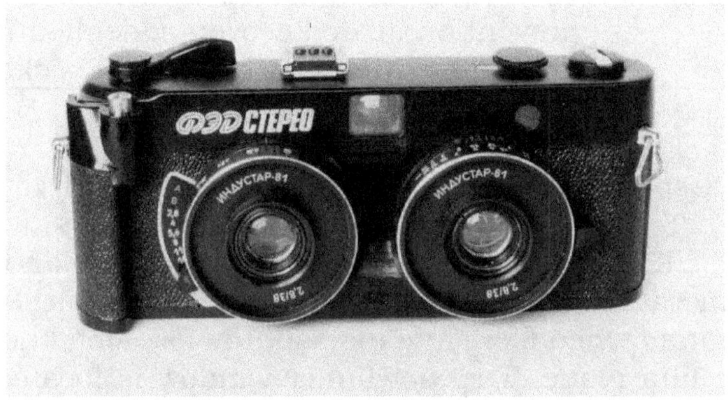

Fig 3.14
FED stereo camera – 7P (European) format.

The specification is somewhat curious; the build is reasonably rugged but with some lack of refinement, yet the camera is capable of producing very good results. It is designed around the 7P, European format, giving an individual frame size of 24 x 30mm and 21 stereo pairs on a standard 36 exposure 35mm film. Three models, the FED Stereo, the FED Stereo M and the FED B.O.Y are available. The B.O.Y. version is a modified form of the earlier models.

Brief Specification:

Lenses:	Two matched f/2.8 lndustar-81 lenses, focal length 38mm. Horizontal angle of view 43°05'
Stereo Base:	63.4mm
Frame Separation:	64mm between frame centres of the two images of a stereo pair.
Shutter Speeds:	1/30 to 1/650 sec (automatic); 1/30th sec manual; 'B'
Apertures:	f/2.8 to f/16 (down to f/11 only on B.O.Y.)
Exposure Modes:	Programmed automatic mode: from 1/30 sec at f/2.8 to 1/650 sec at f/14. Manual mode: 1/30 sec from f/2.8 to f/16. 'B' setting: aperture fixed at f/2.8 (FED Stereo) aperture fixed at f/5.6 (FED Stereo M)
Other Features:	Flash hot shoe, film speed settings from 20 to 800 GOST/ISO, manual focusing from 1 metre (3.3ft) to infinity, automatic frame counter, cable release socket. Uses button cell for automatic operation.

Comments:

The two models FED Stereo and FED Stereo M differ in that they use different battery types to power the automatic exposure mode and operate at different apertures in the B setting.

A lever set around the "right hand image lens" can be adjusted to position A (automatic exposure mode), B (which selects f/2.8 or f/5.6 according to the model) and apertures f/2.8 to f/16, which represent the manual settings using a fixed shutter speed of 1/30 sec. The choice of 11/30 sec is rather odd as it only just allows hand holding without too much risk of camera shake. The fact that the aperture is fixed at f/2.8 for time exposures on the FED Stereo model does not give the photographer a lot of scope for obtaining a large depth of field.

No information is provided about the programme exposure mode other than the boundary limits quoted in the specification. Presumably, it is biased towards small apertures.

The viewfinder is centrally placed but on a higher level than the lenses (unlike the Stereo Realist camera) so some parallax problems might occur at closer distances. There is a so-called "bright" frame outline in the viewfinder, although it is not in fact very bright and the markings defining the close-up frame are rather confusing.

The back is removed completely for film loading and unloading, and some care is needed to ensure that it is clipped properly into place. Some models have suffered from light leakage.

Despite these shortcomings, results have proved to be satisfactory and the automatic exposure mode seems to work well, though some reports note that the camera tends to underexpose by about one stop.

The 1-3-1-3... frame advance is interlocked with the shutter release mechanism so that there is no possibility of accidental double exposure; the shutter cannot be fired, for example, at any intermediate stage in the 3 frame advance part of the sequence.

By pressing in the rewind release button in the base of the camera, the shutter can be primed by operating the film advance lever, without actually advancing the film. This, in theory, will allow two separate exposures to be made, as might be used in close-ups with a reduced stereo base. However, the film take-up after such a procedure may be rather hit and miss in terms of accurate framing, so the method is not recommended.

A minor disadvantage is that there is no way of switching off the camera to conserve power, which means that there is a continuous drain on the battery from the built-in exposure meter, even during manual operation. A suggestion that appeared in a French Stereo Magazine[8] is to construct a simple cap from black PVC to cover the exposure meter window (**Fig 3.15**). This cover is attached to the camera with double-sided tape so no permanent 'damage' is caused. The front piece of plastic can be rotated by 90° to uncover the exposure meter window when required.

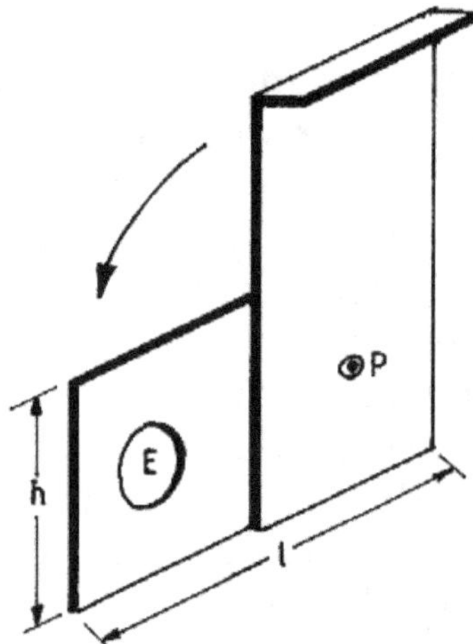

Fig 3.15
Cover for FED Stereo camera's exposure meter window, made from black plastic. The cover can be rotated as shown. Approximate dimensions: hole diameter (E) 8mm; **h** *= 18mm; 1 = 25mm.*

3.4.4 Nimslo 3D

Launched in 1980 by Jerry Nims and Allen Lo, this camera was intended to re-awaken an interest in 3D, the gimmick being that no special glasses would be required to view the results. Strictly speaking, this camera is out of place in this section (which is concerned with "traditional" stereo photography) because it is designed to produce special prints with a ribbed plastic surface (lenticular coating); these can be viewed directly as 3D images without the need for a special viewer. This principle is covered in Chapter 9, Autosteroscopy.

It differs from traditional stereo cameras in that it has four lenses (**Fig 3.16**). For all the jargon-loaded blurb that accompanied the introduction of the camera in the UK, a kind of "blinding with pseudo-science", the basic principle involved was to take the four recorded images and, by virtue of a computer-controlled printer, convert them into narrow strips onto the special photographic paper with its lenticular coating to produce the final picture.

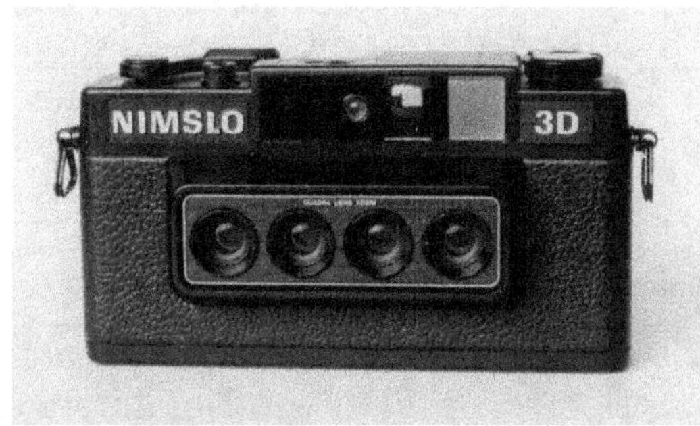

Fig 3.16
Nimslo 3D camera, designed for the production of stereo prints for direct viewing. It uses a half-frame (4P) format, taking four images simultaneously.

The camera did not prove to be very popular, doubtless because it was relatively expensive and the extra costs involved in the special processing did not convert many photographers to stereo. Nevertheless, many stereo enthusiasts realised that it could be used effectively for traditional stereo photography, by selecting just two of the images and ignoring the others. This is probably the most common use for this camera at the present time. Even though it did not become the runaway success envisaged by its inventors, and is no longer available new, the Nimslo 3D camera has inspired the production of a range of similar cameras, with 3 or 4 lenses, made by other companies, and there is a minor revival of interest in autosteroscopic prints.

Brief Specification:

Lenses:	Four matched f/5.6 air spaced triplets with coated, high index optical glass elements. Focal length 30mm, pre-focused for a depth of field from about 2m (7ft) to infinity. Horizontal angle of view 33°24'
Stereo Base:	18mm (approx) inter-lens spacing. The two outer lenses are about 55mm apart.
Frame Format:	Four half-frame (22 x 18mm vertical format) images occupying 2 standard 35mm film frames of width 36mm (4P format).
Shutter:	Automatic, electronically programmed from 1/30 sec to 1/500 sec
Apertures:	Maximum f/5.6, minimum not stated. Selected automatically in conjunction with shutter speed by the program.
Film Speed:	100 ISO and 400 ISO only.
Other Features:	Dedicated hot-shoe contact for Nimslo Electronic Flash (other flash units can also be used), double exposure prevention, green and red LED warning lights (red is low light warning), cable release facility.

Comments:

The programmed exposure and fixed focus lenses virtually guarantee successful stereo photographs in the majority of situations and this relatively sophisticated exposure control is accurate enough when using slide film in place of colour print film. Most traditional stereo photographers use the Nimslo with slide film (which cannot be used for producing autostereoscopic prints, of course) and employ only the outer pair of images to produce their stereograms. Traditional mounts in cardboard or plastic designed for other formats, such as the Stereo Realist, can be adapted for Nimslo images, but specially designed mounts can now be purchased (see Chapter 6, Section 6.8). The stereo base, using the outer images, is about 55mm, somewhat less than the norm, but perfectly acceptable. Results are generally very satisfactory.

A neat way of taking close-up photographs is to use any adjacent pair of lenses with a supplementary lens in front (of sufficient diameter to cover both), giving a stereo base of 18mm. By combining the images of alternate lenses instead of adjacent ones, a stereo base of 36mm is available.

Even if the photographer is not interested in producing autostereoscopic prints, he can produce traditional ones by using colour print film and mounting the images produced by the outer lenses. Since two full frames of the 35mm film are used for each exposure, only eighteen stereo photographs will be created on a 36 exposure film. This is marginally more expensive than using the Stereo Realist or European formats.

The image is basically portrait format, and the height of the image is slightly less than the standard 24mm. Being only 18mm wide, the images might be thought to be rather narrow compared with the 5P and 7P formats, but the lenses of 30mm focal length lenses, give a horizontal angle of view of just over 33°. Although this does not quite match up to the 36° and 43° of the 5P and 7P formats, it is quite acceptable.

Operation of the film advance lever automatically winds the film by two full frames, to give separate blocks of four images along the film.

A valuable publication is "The Nimslo 3D Book"[9] published in 1986, which covers standard and special techniques, tips and modifications that will enhance the usefulness of the camera.

3.4.5 Loreo 35mm Compact Camera

This is a simple-to-use compact camera of unusual design aimed at the popular market or beginners in 3D (**Fig 3.17**), designed to be used with colour print film. It is currently available new. A companion stereo viewer is also available and the two items can be bought singly or as a kit.

In essence it consists of a conventional 35mm compact camera with the addition of a specially designed lens assembly consisting of two closely spaced lenses behind a mirror type "beam splitter" integral with the camera body. It produces two side-by-side images on a single frame, in much the same way as a separate beam splitter accessory used on a conventional SLR camera (see Chapter 4 Section 4.2.2). Unlike a conventional stereo camera, the left and right images are automatically transposed on the film so that the resulting 152xl02mm (6x4in) print (long edge horizontal) has two adjacent images, each 102x76mm (4x3in), in the correct position for viewing.

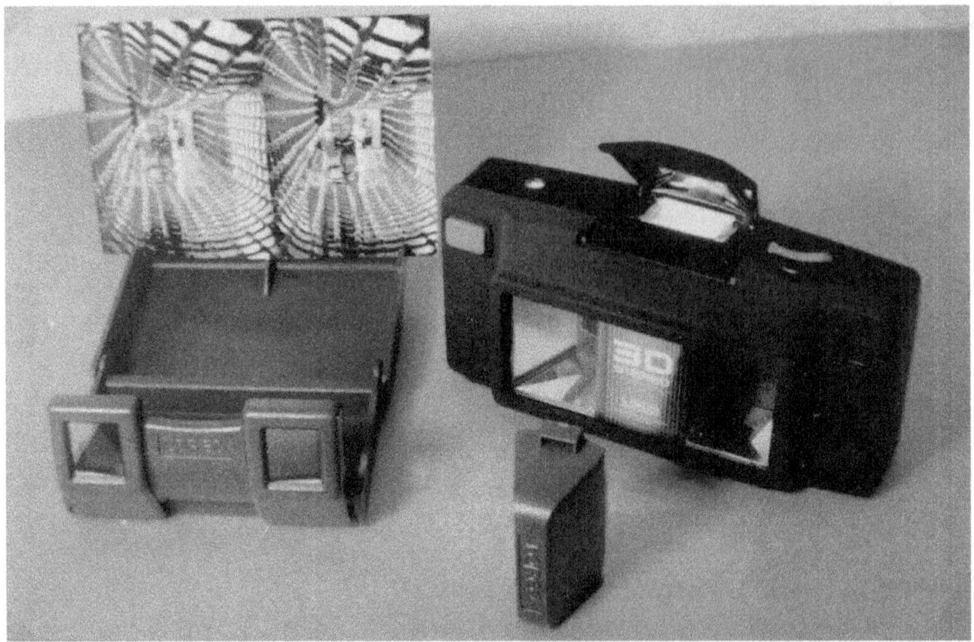

Fig 3.17
Loreo stereo camera (with lens shade) and stereo viewer (Picture taken from an advertising brochure).

Brief Specification:

Lenses:	2 stereo wide-angle type, focal length 28mm, used in conjunction with a mirror optical system. Horizontal angle of view 35°38' (estimated). Fixed focus.
Shutter Speed:	1/90 sec
Aperture:	f/11
Focusing:	Lenses are pre-focused to the hyperfocal distance of the 28mm lenses (about 2.4m (8ft)) giving a depth of field from about 3ft to infinity.
Film Speed:	200 and 400 ISO, possibly 100 ISO
Other Features:	Built in flash fitted with reflector to give wide coverage. Flash range is approximately 1.5 – 3.7m (5 – 12ft) with 200 ISO film and 1.5 – 4.9m (5 – 16ft) with 400 ISO film. A lens shade can be purchased separately to provide extra shielding against cross-reflection.

Comments:

For the general snapshotter, or even the more advanced photographer who wishes to experiment, this camera is a useful introduction to stereo photography because, apart from the camera and viewer, no special mounts are required. Once exposed, the film can be processed along with "mono" films by any photographic processor. The stereo pairs are self-contained and ready to insert in the simple viewer.

Results are extremely effective, though with such a simple camera relying on 200 or 400 ISO film one cannot expect the image quality to match that of a transparency taken in a more conventional stereo camera.

The "patented optical system", as it is described in the promotion literature, is a kind of hybrid between a conventional beam splitter and a stereo base enlarger (see Chapter 4, Sections 4.2.2 and 4.2.5). The two lenses, presumably set at about 18mm apart, provide the essential stereo effect; the mirror components simply extend the stereo base to around 65mm, whilst directing the left and right images to the opposite sides of the frame so that they are in the correct configuration for viewing, without the need for transposition.

With a fixed shutter speed and aperture, good results rather rely on the wide exposure latitude of currently available colour print film films. The use of higher speed films is necessary because of the small aperture (f/11), and to allow for half to one stop of light loss through the mirror sections.

It is unlikely that reliable results would be obtained with slide film in this camera, because slide film does not have the same exposure latitude as print film. A different viewing system would be needed for transparencies, in any case. The type of viewer used with beam splitter attachments (Chapter 5, Section 5.3.9) would be suitable for viewing any slides taken in the Loreo camera.

3.4.6 Verascope F40

This camera, made by Jules Richard of Paris, was introduced in 1946 and was one of the first to popularise the 7P European format (**Fig 3.18**), although the original Verascope camera dates back to 1893.

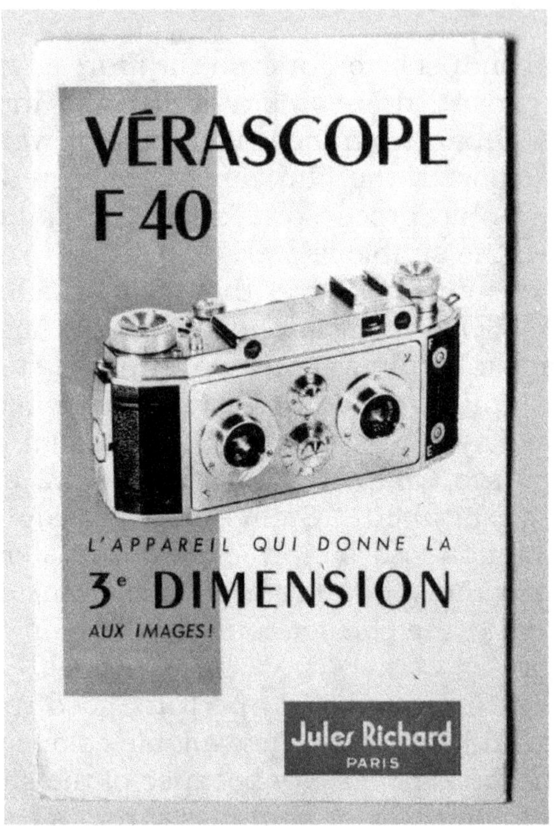

Fig 3.18
The Jules Richard Verascope F40 (European 7P format).

Brief Specification:

Lenses:	Two matched f/3.5 Berthiot Flor patent treated, focal length 40mm. Horizontal angle of view 41°07'
Stereo Base:	Not quoted in instruction booklet but around 62.1mm
Frame separation:	63.3mm
Shutter Speed:	1/250 to 1 second, B and T
Focusing:	From 0.6m to infinity
Aperture:	f/3.5 to f/16
Other Features:	Accessory shoe, flash synchronised for flash bulbs and electronic flash, built-in rangefinder, conversion button to allow use as a mono camera, double exposure facility. In addition, the Jules Richard company supplied various accessories: flashgun, projector, stereoscope with focusing and interocular adjustment, and for close-up work a set of supplementary lenses, a parallax corrector for positioning over the viewfinder and a stereoscopic bench (a form of slide bar) to allow shorter stereo bases to be controlled with a rotational facility to converge the sight-lines (toe-in).

Comments:

Fifty or more years after its first appearance, the Verascope is regarded as one of the classic 3D cameras and is still sought after by enthusiasts. Just as the Stereo Realist has given its name to the "Realist format", the Verascope lives on because the European format is often referred to as the "Verascope format".

3.4.7 View-Master Cameras

The US company Sawyer's Inc., based in Portland, Oregon, introduced to the general public the View-Master viewers and specially designed reels covering a range of subjects, both educational and entertaining. Each reel consisted of seven stereo pairs using a small frame size (11x12 mm). The system was invented in 1938 and was very popular during the 1940's and 1950's. Nowadays, the relatively few reels produced are mainly for children and depict popular cartoon characters, stills from Disney films and the like. Older reels are still sought after by the enthusiast. Despite the small image size, the picture quality is high.

In about 1952, the Stereocraft Engineering Company started to manufacture for Sawyer's the View-Master Personal Stereo Camera (**Fig 3.19**), which allowed amateurs to produce their own View-Master stereograms. In this camera the film is transported across twice. During the first transport, 36 pairs are taken on the lower half of the film. Operating a lever then shifts the lenses and diaphragms upward to allow a further 36 exposures to be taken as the film is wound back into the cassette, so giving a very economical 72 stereo pairs on a standard 35mm film.

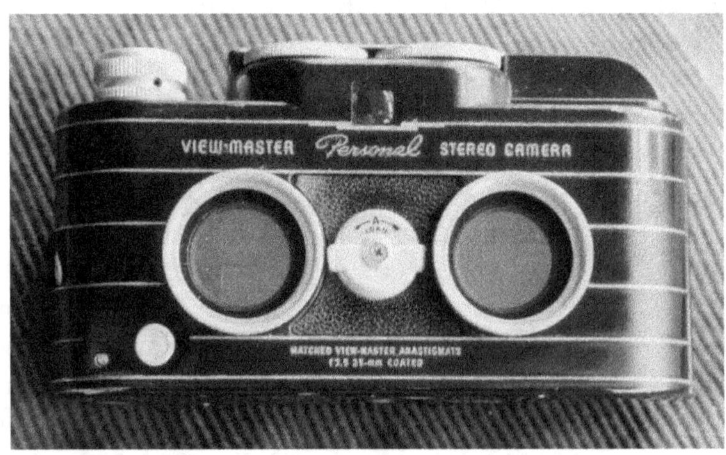

Fig 3.19
One type of View-Master camera, the PERSONAL.
(Photograph by Brian Temple).

Around 1962, two German companies began to produce another type of View-Master format camera in which the film advance was reduced from the standard 8 perforations (as used in the Personal Camera above) to 3.5 perforations, with the film running diagonally to give a unique arrangement of interlaced pairs, the film being transported only once past the lenses. The diaphragms were fixed. This camera was known as the View-Master Color Camera. The frame configurations for both the Color camera and the Personal camera are shown in **Fig 3.20**.

Special film cutters were also made to suit both types of camera so that the tiny film chips could be cut accurately from the film. Blank reels were available so that the pairs could be mounted and a stereo projector was produced, to complete the system.

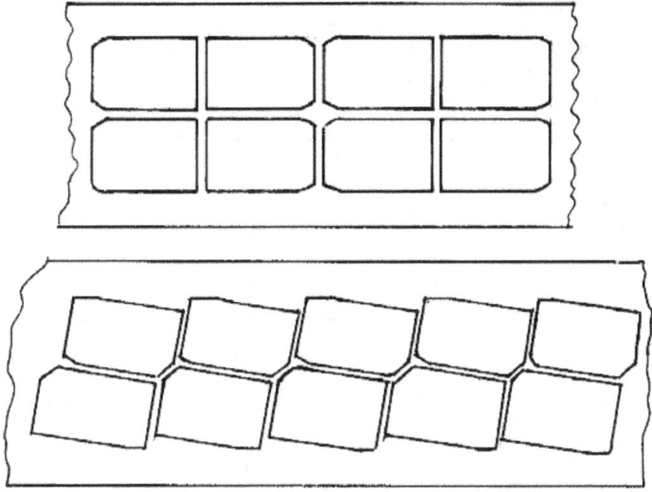

Fig 3.20
Configuration of images on film for the two designs of View- Master camera.

Brief Specifications:

Personal stereo camera

Lenses:	View-Master Anastigmat f/3.5, focal length 25mm, fixed focus. Horizontal angle of view 27°
Stereo Base:	61.5mm
Frame separation:	62.7mm
Shutter Speed:	1/100 to 1/10 sec, continuously adjustable, B
Focusing:	Fixed
Aperture:	f/3.5 to f/16, continuously adjustable
Other Features:	Flash synchronisation (special connection necessary), cable release socket, mechanical exposure guide, Newton type viewfinder (reduced size image), tripod socket, double exposure prevention incorporated.

Stereo Color camera

Lenses:	Rodenstock Trinar f/2.8, focal length 20mm, fixed focus. Horizontal angle of view 33°24'
Stereo Base:	65mm
Frame separation:	65.5mm
Shutter Speed:	1/30, 1/45, 1/60 sec, I (instant), B. For exposure values 8, 8½ and 9 the camera operates at f/2.8 and speeds 1/30, 1/45 and 1/60. For higher exposure values it operates with 1/60 and the respective apertures
Focusing:	Fixed
Aperture:	f/2.8 to f/22, continuously adjustable (in effect, exposure values between 8 and 15 are set)
Other Features:	X and M flash synchronisation, PC outlet, Newton type viewfinder with bright-line frame, tripod socket, double exposure prevention incorporated, accessory shoe, cable release socket

Comments:

These cameras are ideal for general stereo photography and can produce excellent results, even with its small image size. The View-Master system has its own group of devotees who will have their own opinions about the merits of both types of camera. Second-hand cameras, and especially film cutters and projectors, are not widely available and tend to become collectors' items.

CHAPTER 4: STEREO ATTACHMENTS AND TWO-CAMERA SYSTEMS

4.1 Introduction

Besides using a single mono camera or a stereo camera, a number of other devices, techniques or adaptations either exist or can be constructed, all of which have the merit of producing a pair of images simultaneously

The apparatus and techniques covered in this chapter are as follows:
1. stereo attachments, such as beam splitters, for mono cameras
2. using two mono cameras simultaneously
3. custom-built stereo cameras, constructed from a pair of identical mono cameras

All of the above have their advantages and disadvantages compared with the traditional stereo camera, but they are popular with many stereo photographers. Provided that one can use sufficiently fast shutter speeds, pictures that include moving objects can be taken successfully.

4.2 Stereoscopic Attachments

These are usually in the form of a self-contained unit, which can be attached by means of a screw thread to the standard lens of a camera. The apparatus consists of either mirrors or prisms, or a combination of both, designed to provide two separate optical paths corresponding to the left and right images of the resultant stereo pair. By using the device, the two images are produced side-by-side (usually) within a single frame. Because of this, the use of such attachments is best suited to wider formats so that the individual images of the stereo pair do not end up too narrow in proportion to their height.

Relatively few stereo attachments are available commercially. Most of them have been designed to fit a range of 35mm cameras using a 50mm lens; a few have been made by camera manufacturers for specific models in their production range. Many keen DIY photographers have built their own versions of these, or have produced new designs.

Devices that use prisms to divert the light rays are usually superior to those that rely on mirrors. However, mirror attachments are more widely available. In order to maintain good image quality the mirrors are front-surface silvered, to prevent any possibility of double images that frequently occur with traditional back-surface silvering. The front glass (non-silvered) surface of ordinary mirrors can produce a secondary image, the strength of which can vary according to the lighting conditions but which is always present to some degree (**Fig 4.1**).

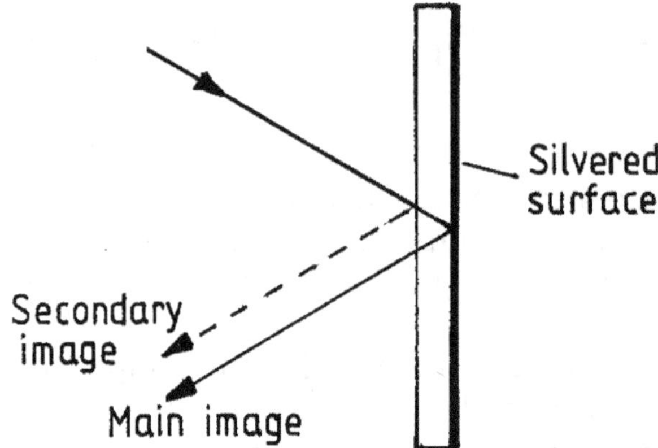

Fig 4.1
*Double image produced by a conventional back surface silvered mirror.
Reflection from the front glass surface can produce a secondary image.*

The "ghost" image will be displaced laterally, vertically or in any other
direction according to the geometry of the reflecting surface in relation to
the location of the subject. Front-surface silvering avoids this problem but,
since the mirror now lacks the protective paint covering normally applied to
the silvered surface of an ordinary mirror, the reflecting surface is
vulnerable to scratches and must be handled with care; the same, of course,
applies to the mirror in a 35mm SLR camera.

Basically, there are two types of attachment. The first, often referred
to as a **beam splitter**, is designed to cause the two bundles of light rays
(that produce the two images) to cross over as they pass through the single
lens of the camera. The second type, referred to as a **beam spreader** or
stereo base extender, keeps the two optical paths separate and directs
them to the individual lenses of a stereo camera, usually one which has a
smaller than normal stereo base. As its name suggests, this type simply
acts to increase the stereo base rather than to generate two separate images
in its own right. The details of the workings of both types are discussed in
the sections that follow.

4.2.1 Double mirror

This is a simple unit, at least in its principle of operation, but to the
author's knowledge it has never been available as a manufactured item. It
is attributed to F.A.P Barnard and was used by him from 1853 for making
Daguerreotypes. To construct one would appear to be relatively
straightforward, but as with all optical instruments, however basic, a
certain degree of precision is required, which usually involves careful
assembly and some means of finely adjusting the positions of the mirrors.

The device consists simply of two mirrors placed in front of the
camera lens and set at a slight angle to each other (**Fig 4.2**).

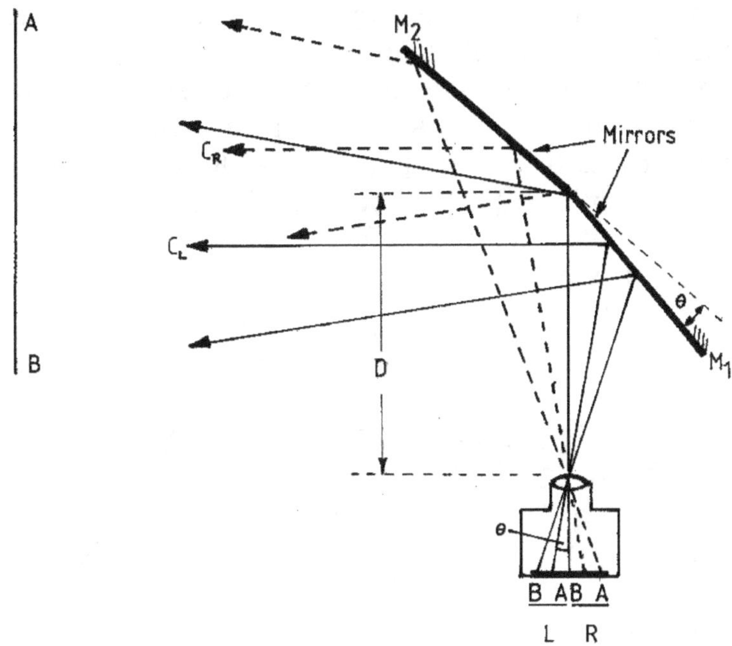

Fig 4.2
Two-mirror device. Mirrors **M₁** *and* **M₂** *are set at a small angle* **θ** *to one another and placed at a nominal 45° to the lens axis. The left and right images must be transposed for correct viewing.*

The mirror pair is set at an overall angle of 45° to the lens axis; thus one mirror is angled slightly less than 45° and the other slightly greater than 45° to the camera lens axis.

It should be apparent from this diagram that there are at least two disadvantages inherent in the device. Firstly, the camera does not point directly at the object, which can be mildly disorientating for the photographer; secondly, and more seriously, is the fact that the images will be laterally reversed owing to the single reflection in the mirror experienced by the light rays. These images are, indeed, "mirror images". Whilst this problem can be overcome by viewing the resultant transparencies from the emulsion side of the film, or by printing negatives the opposite way round, such solutions are not entirely satisfactory. An alternative approach is to add a third, single mirror placed parallel to the mirror pair; this will provide an additional reversal of the images laterally and also means that the camera can be pointed directly towards the object, though slightly offset. Although the arrangement (as shown in **Fig 4.2**) means that the left and right images of the stereo pair are in the correct configuration for viewing without the normal transposition (if the film is turned over and viewed from the emulsion side), these images are too close to each other to be used directly in a normal stereoscope without first being separated. So, using a third mirror to remove the lateral reversal reintroduces the need for transposition of the two images.

The stereo base is determined by the angle between the two mirrors and the distance of the assembly from the camera lens. Increasing either of these will increase the stereo base. Symons[10] suggests that the easiest way to obtain the correct adjustment is to set up two pins 65mm apart located a distance **f** from the double mirror (**f** = focal length of camera lens), and alter the angle between the two mirrors until the images of the two pins coincide when viewed from a suitable distance (**Fig 4.3**), but this technique will give only an approximate setting.

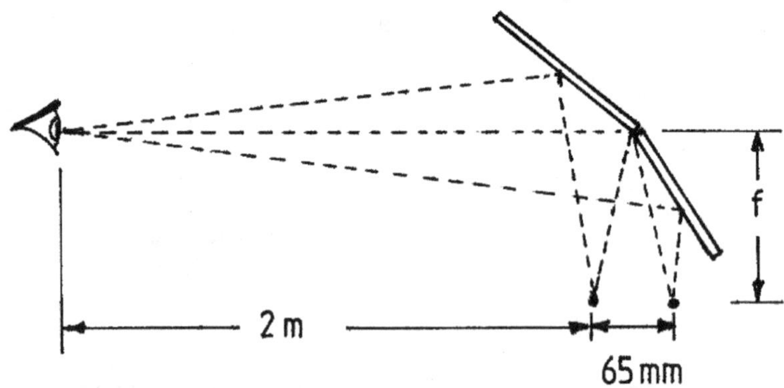

Fig 4.3
Method for setting up the two-mirror beam splitter according to Symons[10] (See text for explanation).

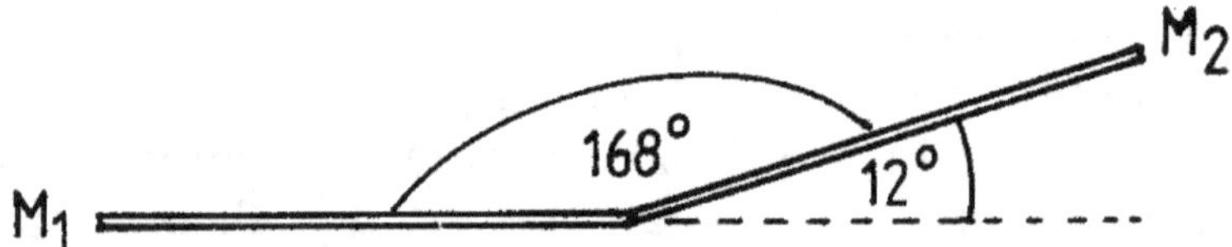

Fig 4.4
Typical mirror setting according to Symons[10] with an obtuse angle of about 168°. In calculations it is more convenient to use the acute angle (12° in the diagram).

An angle of about 168° between the mirrors is a typical value for such devices (**Fig 4.4**), according to Symons, but the value actually depends upon the film format in use. The acute angle (marked 12° in **Fig 4.4**) is more useful in calculations and the angle between the mirrors will be so defined in this chapter.

The correct setting is achieved by placing the two mirrors at the correct angle for the film format being used and at a suitable distance from the camera lens, to minimise convergence distortion and to create the desired stereo base. Convergence distortion has the form shown in **Fig 4.5**.

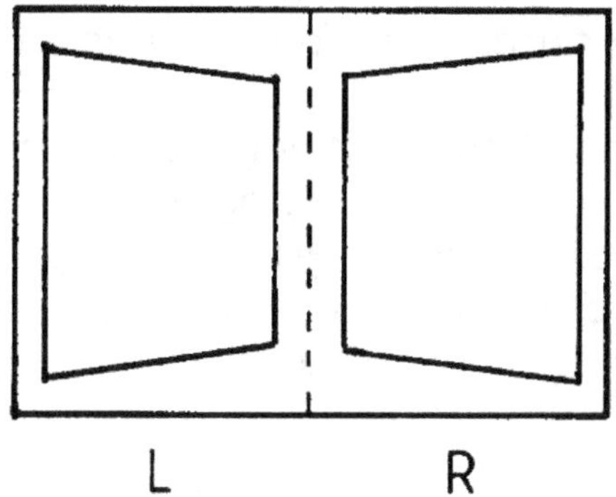

Fig 4.5
Typical convergence distortion, exaggerated for clarity that occurs in the images produced by a beam splitter on a mono camera. Rectangular shapes are distorted as shown, a form of "keystoning".

To control the convergence distortion, it is necessary to make the mirror angle equal to the half angle of view for one image (see **Fig 4.2**). For a 35mm format in which the left and right images (side-by-side) occupy a standard frame, this angle is about 10°, approximately a quarter of the horizontal angle of view of the lens. This angle ensures that the left and right sight lines, marked C_L and C_R in **Fig 4.2,** which lead to the centre of each image on the film, are parallel. It remains only to fix the distance **D** (measured from the mirror junction to the lens) to achieve the desired stereo base. Now the stereo base depends upon the angle θ and the distance **D.** Increasing **D** or θ individually, or together, will increase the stereo base. As shown in Supplement 4, the magnitude of the stereo base, **b**, is given by the following expression:

$$b = 2D\sin\theta \quad \textit{(In Supplement 4, the critical angle } \theta_c \textit{ is used)}$$

There is an infinite number of combinations of θ and **D** that will give a particular stereo base, but we must restrict our calculations to the appropriate θ value for the film format, to minimise convergence distortion, as discussed above.

For a 35mm format, where $\theta = 10°$ and for a normal stereo base **b** = 65mm the value of **D** will be:

$$D = b/2\sin\theta = 65/(2 \times 0.174) = 187\text{mm approx.}$$

This would require mirrors of about 150mm width to include the whole width of the image, so the device is not particularly compact. Using the same angle (10°), other values of **D** can be calculated for smaller stereo bases, as used in close-up work. In these situations the mirror assembly will be closer to the camera, and the mirrors can be made smaller.

As long as the **θ** value is known for a particular image format, similar calculations can be performed to determine the correct settings (see Supplement S4).

Although this device has effectively been superseded by four-mirror or prism beam splitters, the stereo photographer might well consider it for the purposes of experimentation. In terms of design, it is likely to be rather too large to be conveniently attached to a camera lens and it must be regarded as a separate piece of equipment for use in a static situation rather than out in the field.

4.2.2 Four-mirror beam splitter

This device is a variant of the two-mirror adapter, but, because of its optical design, is a more compact affair and it can be attached directly to the camera lens by means of a screw thread. This makes it readily portable. As it is an adapter, it can be used at any time so that mono and stereo shots can be mixed on the same film. Commercially available for a number of years, they have a certain following, especially amongst those who are perhaps interested in stereo photography but not committed to buying a stereo camera.

According to Symons[11] the first four-mirror beam splitter was designed by Theodore Brown and first appeared in 1894 under the name "Stereophoto Duplicon".

Currently available models include the Pentax stereo adapter, which can be bought as a kit with its own special viewer (see **Figs 4.6** and **4.7**) and the Stereo World adapter and viewer, which are considerably cheaper than the Pentax versions. The Pentax adapter is made to fit either a 49mm or 52mm diameter screw thread, to suit these camera lens diameters, but adapter rings can be purchased which allow the device to fit virtually any 35mm SLR camera. There is also a model known as the Stitz adapter, which has adjustable mirrors and apertures and can be set for any focal length in the range 50 to 300mm. Other adapters are usually restricted to a single focal length of 50mm or thereabouts.

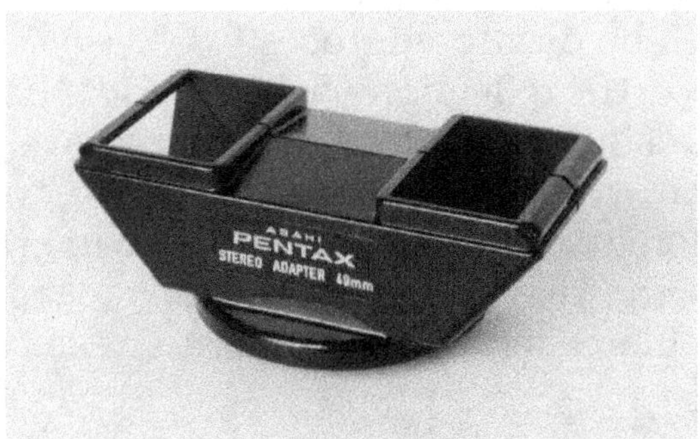

Fig 4.6
Pentax Stereo Adapter. When attached to the camera lens by the circular fitting (at the bottom of the picture), the two rectangular apertures face the subject being photographed.

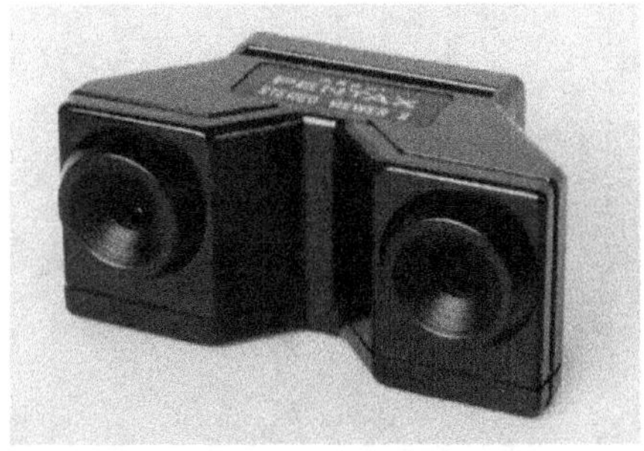

Fig 4.7
Pentax viewer used to view the transparencies taken with the stereo adapter shown in **Fig 4.6.**

Although designed for use with slide film, whereby the individual frames containing both images side-by-side can be viewed directly in the special viewer, this type of adapter can equally well be used with colour print film. The stereo pair will appear side-by-side within a normal print format and can be processed along with any mono prints on the film by any commercial laboratory. If the print size is 152 x 102mm (6 x 4in) the resulting stereo pair can be viewed in single viewers, for example those supplied with the Loreo stereo camera (Chapter 3, Section 3.4.5), which are available commercially.

Using the adapter
The aperture setting on the camera normally has to be f/5.6 or f/8 for satisfactory results, using a 50mm focal length lens. The transition region between the two images of the stereo pair is a few millimetres wide and indistinct; there is no clear-cut boundary. It arises from the mirror junction of the two mirrors closest to the lens. This central "discontinuity" in the apparatus causes some inconvenience in that it is usually impossible

to use viewfinder focusing aids, such as a microprism or split image. Autofocusing may well be disrupted, too.

Because of the extra reflections and the fact that less light is picked up as a result of the restricted angle of view imposed by the front apertures of the attachment, an exposure increase of up to two stops is required. Naturally, this is automatically corrected if the camera has a built-in light meter, but it implies the use of slower shutter speeds when the ambient light is poor, with an increased risk of camera shake.

Optical geometry

The arrangement of the four mirrors is shown in **Fig 4.8**. They are held within a plastic enclosure and form two pairs set at approximately 45°, in opposite senses, to divert the light paths as indicated.

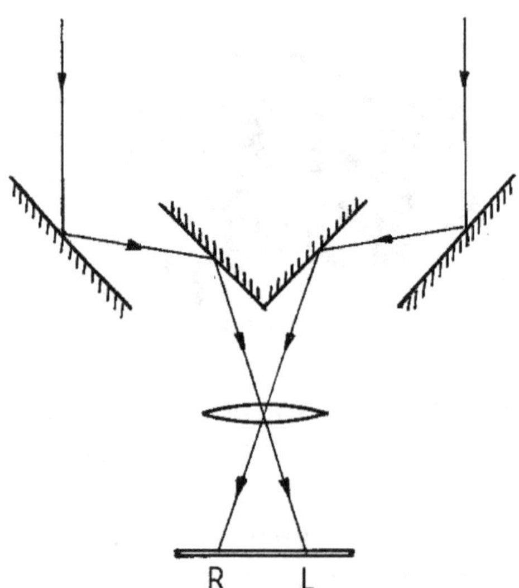

Fig 4.8

Basic optical path through a four-mirror attachment such as the Pentax, showing how the images are located for correct viewing in the transparency or print without the need for transposition.

The two mirrors at the extreme left and right of the attachment act as the two viewpoints, which are set 70mm apart in the Pentax version; this forms the stereo base. The left and right sets of light rays are reflected to the two inner mirrors and then cross over through the lens. The images on the film as seen from the back of the camera are upside down and correctly located for direct viewing, without the need for transposition. The single frame is merely turned the right way up for viewing in the special stereoscopic viewer that forms part of the standard kit. If desired, the left and right images could be separated and mounted for viewing in a more traditional stereoscope.

In the Pentax attachment the outer mirrors are set at about 50° to the long axis of the attachment, whereas the inner mirrors are at 45° (from measurement on an actual model). Thus, the outer mirrors are turned in towards each other by 10° from a nominal 90° reference angle. The image centre rays, which lie at an angle of 10° to the common central ray from the boundary between the two images (**Fig 4.9**), diverge from the lens until they reach the inner mirrors when they emerge parallel as they proceed towards the subject. Rays from the subject trace the same paths but in reverse.

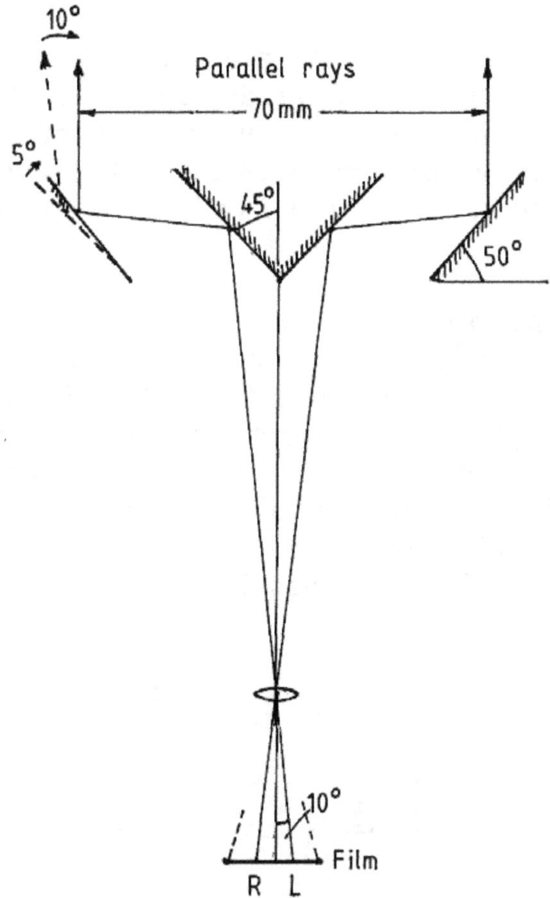

Fig 4.9

Geometry of the Pentax stereo attachment. The inner mirrors are set at 45° but the outer ones at 50°. This produces parallel sight lines for recording the subject.

The outer mirrors are set in a similar way to those in the two-mirror attachment, less 90°. This 90° difference is "recovered" by the reflections at the two inner mirrors, which have the additional effect of causing a second lateral inversion of the images. Thus each image, twice laterally inverted by the optics, ends up the correct way round on the film, but, because of the cross-over of the optical paths, the two are transposed.

The optical geometry is essentially the same as that of the two-mirror device in terms of the relative angle between the mirrors, and the images will be subject to the same convergence distortion. The individual image size, approximately 24 x 18mm, is rather narrow for general use, although it is satisfactory for subjects about 2 to 4 metres from the camera, as in portraits. Subjects should be no nearer than about 1.5 metres.

The advantage of this apparatus over the two-mirror set-up lies in its compactness and portability. For the Pentax adapter, the width is 110mm, height 50mm and depth from the lens to the front surface 45mm (4.5 x 2 x 1.75 in).

The Pentax adapter and viewer are rather expensive items, together costing as much as a well-specified middle of the range 35mm SLR camera. The "Stereo World" adapter kit is about a third of the price; both are available at the time of writing from specialist 3D photographic retailers.

Details of the special viewers used with these attachments are given in Chapter 5.

4.2.3 Prism beam splitter

This is a variant of the four-mirror beam splitter in which two prisms replace the left and right mirror pairs (**Fig 4.10**). The optical geometry is basically the same as that of the mirror version but there is less light loss and the boundary between the left and right images is more clear-cut. The increased exposure is of the order of half a stop (as opposed to 1.5 to 2 stops with the mirror version). It still exhibits convergence distortion. Such a device has been marketed by the Zeiss Company.

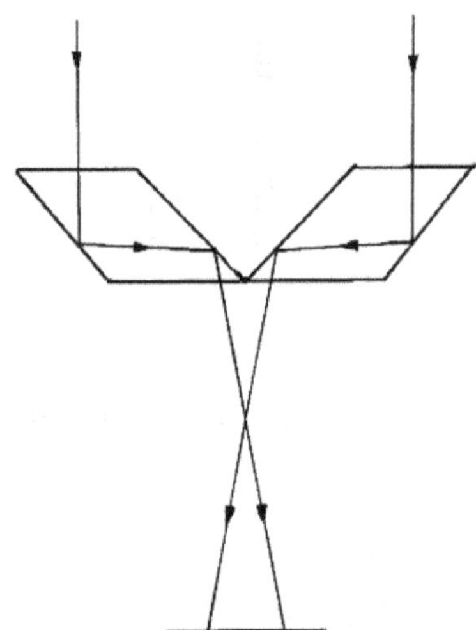

Fig 4.10
Optical paths through a prism stereo attachment. Because of the angles of incidence at the prism faces, total internal reflection occurs so they effectively act as mirrors.

4.2.4 TRI-DELTA stereo attachment

This is a more unusual version of the standard beam splitter design in that it produces pictures in a horizontal format with the top edge of the left image adjacent to the top edge of the right image (**Fig 4.11**). It was manufactured by the American company Tri-Delta Engineering.

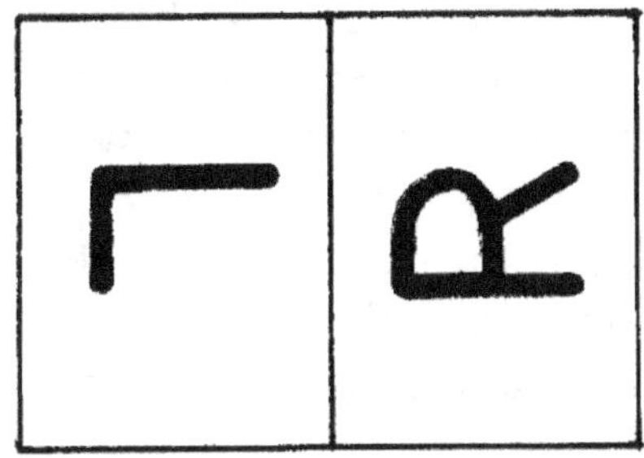

Fig 4.11
Configuration of the two images within a single frame produced by the TRI-DELTA stereo attachment.

The attachment consists of a prism and two mirrors that divert the beams through 90° and give them a twist; this unusual geometry means that the camera has to be pointed vertically upwards (**Fig 4.12**) with the Tri-Delta in place and facing the subject.

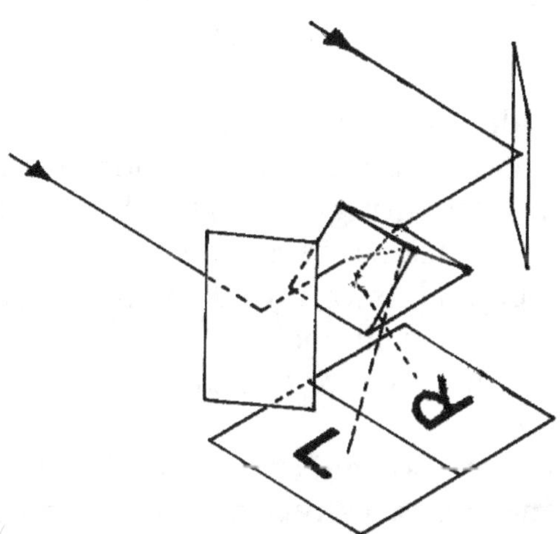

Fig 4.12
Basic optics of the TRI-DELTA stereo attachment. Light rays from the subject are reflected by the mirrors through the prism, which rotates them through 90°. They then pass through the camera lens, the camera itself lying on its back with the lens pointing upwards.

One of the advantages of the design is that it eliminates the normal convergence distortion (**Fig 4.5**). Nevertheless, it does produce a slight convergence of the vertical lines. A viewfinder is mounted on top of the unit, as it is not possible to use the one on the camera when it is lying on its back.

For viewing the stereoscopic image, a specially designed viewer is available. Otherwise the two images have to be separated and mounted in standard stereo mounts.

Eddie Butt[12] from Salisbury in Wiltshire, has experimented with a number of beam splitters, but has never been completely satisfied with the results. Not only has he constructed his own version of the Tri-Delta attachment, but he has attempted, with some considerable success, to counteract the vertical distortion by using the device upside down. By this means the camera points vertically downwards instead of upwards, and the two images have their baselines, instead of their top edges, adjacent (**Fig 4.13**).

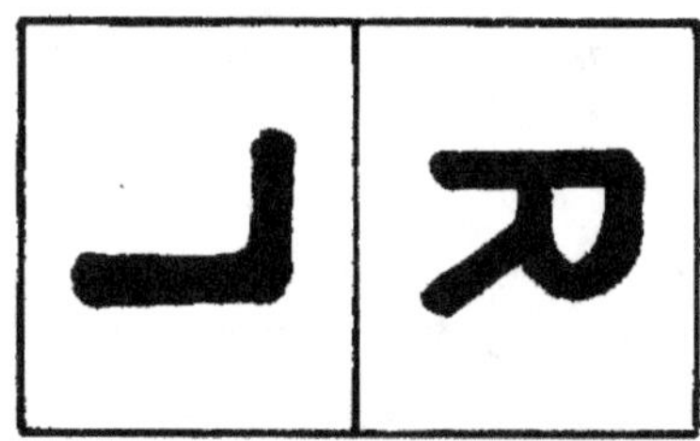

Fig 4.13
Image configuration produced by using the TRI-DELTA stereo attachment upside-down, a technique devised by Butt[12].

Since vertical parallel lines would diverge slightly from bottom to top with this set-up, Butt counteracts this by shooting from a slightly lower viewpoint than normal, and tilting the assembly in an upward direction, which in itself tends to produce convergence of verticals from bottom to top. Thus the two convergence effects will tend to cancel out.

With this reversal of the images (i.e. with their bases adjacent) the resulting pair can no longer be viewed in the special viewer, so they have to be separated.

As Butt points out, the normal use of the Tri-Delta attachment means that in a landscape scene the two sky areas will be adjacent in the centre of the standard 35mm frame; this could lead to underexposure with SLRs having TTL (through-the-lens) metering systems, many of which are centre-weighted. In his adaptation of the device the main subject, rather than the sky, will appear at the centre of the frame.

When using this attachment it is best to avoid cameras with lenses in which the front element is heavily recessed, or vignetting might occur. Unlike normal beam splitters, the aperture is not restricted to f/5.6 or f/8; successful results have been achieved down to f/11.

4.2.5 Beam spreader

Beam spreaders should not be confused with beam splitters, though they are similar in appearance externally. Basically they provide an extended stereo base for cameras with a shorter than normal base, without causing any convergence distortion. The optical paths of the left and right images do not cross over in these devices (**Fig 4.14**). Prisms can be used in place of mirrors, as with beam splitters.

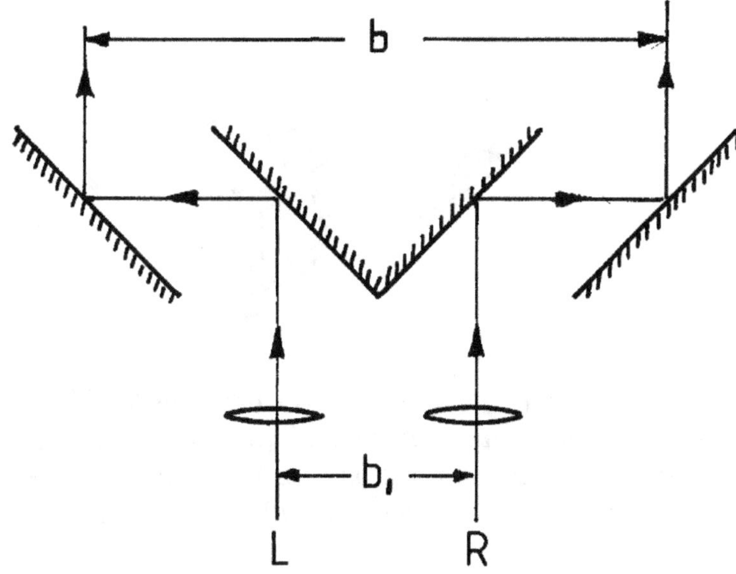

Fig 4.14

*Four-mirror beam spreader. This differs from the beam splitter in **Fig 4.8** because all mirrors are set at 45° and the optical paths do not cross over. It is used with a twin lens camera or twin lens attachment to increase the stereo base from* b_1 *(the lens spacing) to* **b***.*

In the past, various manufacturers have introduced special lens attachments either for their own brand of camera, or for more universal application (**Fig 4.15**). These consist of two smaller lenses separated by perhaps 18 – 20mm (the distance varies with different devices) mounted into a single housing which is attached to the camera in place of the standard lens. This produces two images side by side on a single frame and effectively converts the mono camera into a stereo camera with a reduced stereo base. Whilst this is moderately satisfactory, but not ideal, for normal stereo photography, it does lend itself to close-up work, limited only by the lens separation (see Chapter 7, Section 7.3.2). These devices are also known as **Clemetson attachments**, after their inventor.

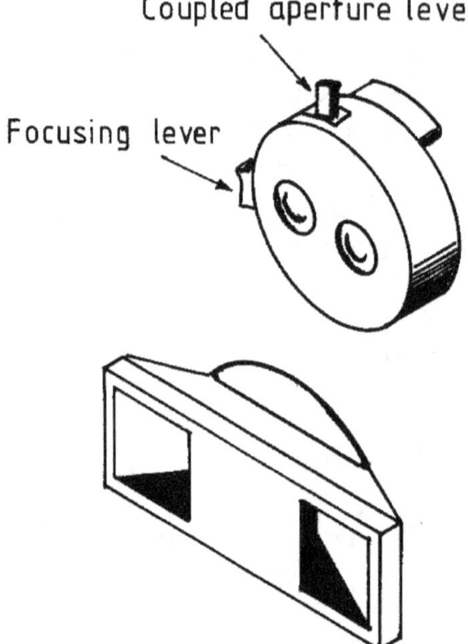

Fig 4.15
Main components of the Leica Stemar stereo attachment. The lens assembly has two 33mm focal length lenses about 19mm (¾in) apart, to replace the normal camera lens. This is used for close-ups from about 1 – 3m (3 – 10ft). The prism attachment is a beam spreader, which can be added to increase the stereo base from 19 to 72mm.

They can be used for normal stereo photography by the addition of a beam spreader, which is designed to increase the stereo base from 18mm to 65 or 70mm. As shown in **Fig 4.14** the left and right sets of light rays are simply turned twice through 90° without the introduction of any convergence distortion.

The availability of many beam spreaders and special twin lens attachments is more or less confined to the second-hand market.

4.3 Use of Two Coupled Mono Cameras

This is a logical development of the use of a mono camera. By using two similar cameras mounted side-by-side, the two exposures can be taken simultaneously instead of sequentially. However, for the best results, the following advice is offered:

1. the two cameras should be identical models; ideally the two lenses should be matched as they are in stereoscopic cameras. Individual lenses of the same type and manufacture will differ marginally in their actual focal lengths, although nominally they are identical. In practice, one may have to rely on chance to get a really good match, but modern technology, manufacturing methods and quality control should be enough to avoid any serious mismatches.

2. the cameras should be lined up accurately so that their lenses are level horizontally. Some kind of jig or mounting frame, or a method of joining the cameras together, is required.
3. a double cable release or electronic device should be employed to ensure that both shutters are released simultaneously.
4. the same make and type of film should be used in each camera, preferably from the same batch; this will minimise colour differences. The films should be processed together to eliminate possible differences in processing. This is less of a problem with transparency film, but colour prints can vary considerably in density or colour balance when processed by different laboratories, or even by the same laboratory at different times.

A typical arrangement is shown in **Fig 4.16**, but there are other configurations that may produce better, or at least more orthodox, stereo. The main difficulty lies in finding appropriate cameras that can be coupled to produce a normal stereo base of 65mm (or 70mm). Most cameras are too wide, and whilst the larger stereo base will give good results, the 3D image will technically suffer from distortions under normal viewing conditions. In most cases, the results will be perfectly acceptable since the human eye-brain combination is remarkably tolerant. The distortion is one of scale only and is described in Chapter 19, Section 19.3.3.

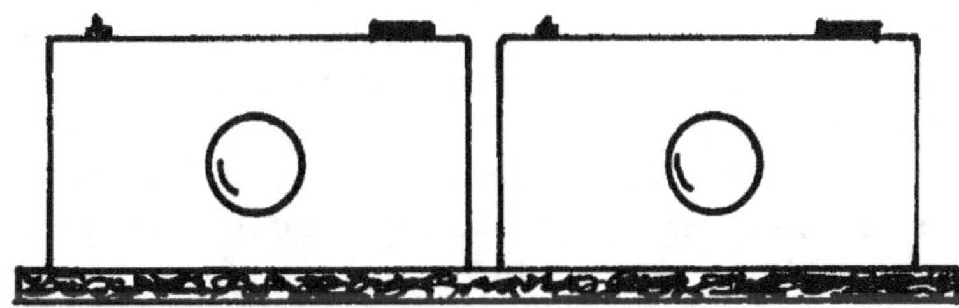

Fig 4.16
Two identical mono cameras mounted side-by-side. The stereo base depends upon camera dimensions but is likely to be greater than 65-70mm.

One possible solution, which can help to reduce the stereo base to something nearer 70mm, is to mount the cameras base-to-base (**Fig 4.17a**). If the lens is not centrally placed within the camera body, then the two cameras will have to be offset; this may make the design of a suitable mounting jig more awkward. The base-to-base arrangement may also be inconvenient with some cameras as access to battery compartments or rewind buttons in the base will be blocked. Also, the tripod sockets would be unavailable as part of the mounting device. The whole unit would have to be dismantled each time access was required. Access can be improved by mounting the two cameras on separate baseboards that are joined at one end by a hinge (**Fig 4.17b**)

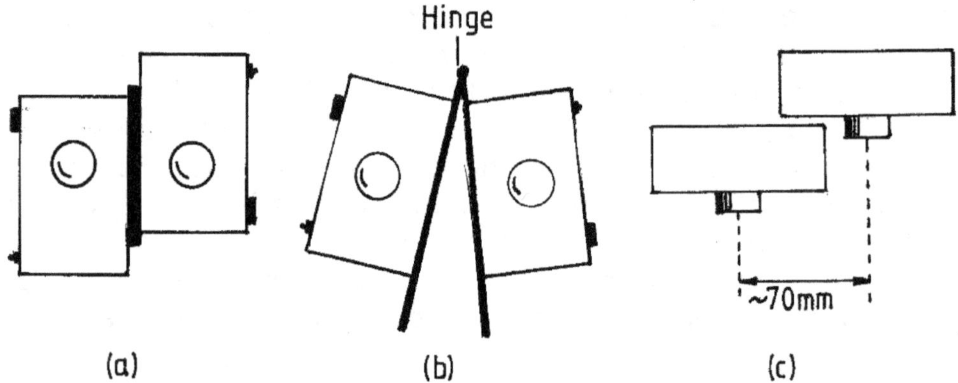

Fig 4.17
Three ways to couple two mono cameras for stereo photography:
a) Base-to-base
b) Base-to base or side-by-side using a hinged baseboard
c) Staggered

Some photographers reduce the stereo base to around 70mm by staggering the cameras, as shown in **Fig 4.17c**. Theoretically, the image in the rearmost camera will be slightly smaller than that in the forward one, but for normal scenes beyond 2 metres the difference will be negligible, and probably no more significant than variations in image size resulting from slight differences in the focal lengths of the two lenses.

Any construction of the kind described is going to be somewhat bulky compared with a traditional stereo camera but that does not detract from its popularity as a practical design. Compact cameras, rather than the larger and heavier SLR's, are the obvious choice for this technique, and there is a wide variety of new models about, amongst them several of small dimensions that may fit together easily to give the desired stereo base.

Many photographers simply press the individual shutter release buttons simultaneously when taking photographs with twin-rigged cameras, but it is safer to use some form of coupling, either mechanical or electrical. Although twin cable releases can be obtained (at a price!), many modern cameras are not provided with the necessary screw thread within the shutter release button. Various adapters are available for just this contingency, and some of these may be suitable. The alternative is to devise one's own solution. Some means of holding the sleeve of the cable release stationary while the plunger operates to push the shutter button has to be devised. Another method, though somewhat crude, is to glue short wooden or plastic rods to the existing shutter release buttons and to glue a longer rod or bar across these two to form a simple mechanical link (**Fig 4.18**). This will not work if the cameras are mounted base-to-base, however. A better method is to connect the shutters electrically as described by Speel[13], who has described two methods of wiring together the shutter contact buttons of two Olympus XA compact cameras. In one method, the contacts are connected directly by fine wires; in the second, an extra camera flash socket is built in to each camera body, wired internally to the shutter release button contacts. The auxiliary flash sockets can be connected externally by a short lead, which can be removed. The extra flash sockets are not, of course, used to operate a flash unit.

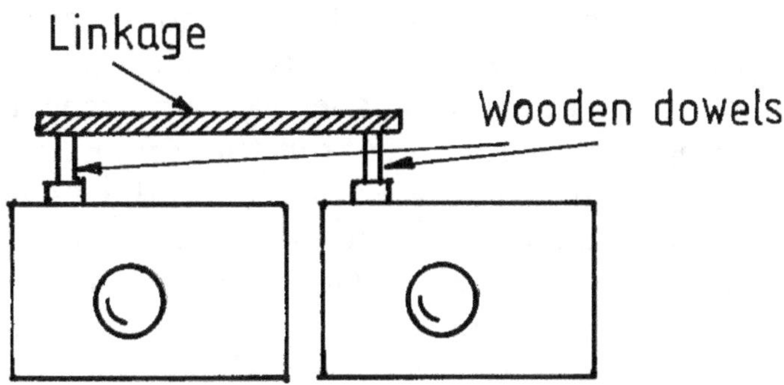

Fig 4.18
Simple mechanical linking of shutter release buttons on two mono cameras

A number of compact cameras include the option of taking "panoramic format" negatives; this facility is widely available in APS (advanced photographic system) cameras, for example. In most cases this option is a gimmick, because the negative image is merely masked top and bottom to produce the "pillar-box slot" shape that is no wider than a standard frame. When processed, it is just given a greater degree of enlargement than the standard negatives. Nevertheless, panoramic prints have caught the public's imagination and two cameras with this facility could be set up to produce panoramic stereo views. These can be viewed most easily with the View Magic viewer (see Chapter 5, Section 5.3.8).

Some photographers use 35mm SLR cameras in a two-camera rig. The advantage lies in having all the latest technological features at one's disposal, especially with the greater versatility of the SLR over the compact camera. The disadvantage lies in the extra weight and rather awkward handling, not to mention the greater potential cost. The chances of being able to keep the stereo base down to the 65–70mm norm are less, but that is likely to upset only the purist.

At the time of writing, it is possible to purchase, from a specialist retailer in 3D equipment, a set of two matched compact cameras (Russian FED 50's) together with a mounting bar and twin cable release. The cameras are arranged side by side and the stereo base is around 110mm, so the kit represents a compromise, because the stereoscopic effect will be exaggerated as described previously.

An easy way to experiment with a two-camera rig is to use a pair of inexpensive "recyclable" (sometimes called "disposable") cameras and simply pressing the shutter buttons simultaneously.

4.4 Custom-built "Siamesed" Stereo Cameras

Strictly, these come under the heading of true stereo cameras, but they are related to the use of two coupled mono cameras. Some stereo enthusiasts, who possess considerable precision engineering skills, have constructed stereo cameras by cutting and assembling components from two identical mono cameras. In principle, the mono cameras are cut into "halves" and the relevant pieces fixed together, although there is clearly a great deal of work involved in linking the film wind mechanism, focusing, shutters and any other functions present in the original cameras.

As this is not a suitable undertaking for the novice or the faint-hearted, ready built "Siamesed" cameras are available from certain specialist companies. For example, the German firm RBT (Raumbildtechnik Gmbh) constructs a range of such cameras based upon the Ricoh XRX at the top of the price range, and the Cosina C1 as the basis of a cheaper range. The company also manufactures stereo projectors and other stereo accessories.

The Ricoh is available in three variants:
1. stereo base 65mm: 24 x 33mm format (20 exposures)
2. stereo base 75mm: 24 x 36mm format (18 exposures)
3. stereo base 65mm: 24 x 36mm format (13 exposures)

The Siamesed version retains all of the features such as spot and centre-weighted metering, multiple exposure functions and flash modes that are available on the original XRX cameras. **Fig 4.19** shows one of the Ricoh models.

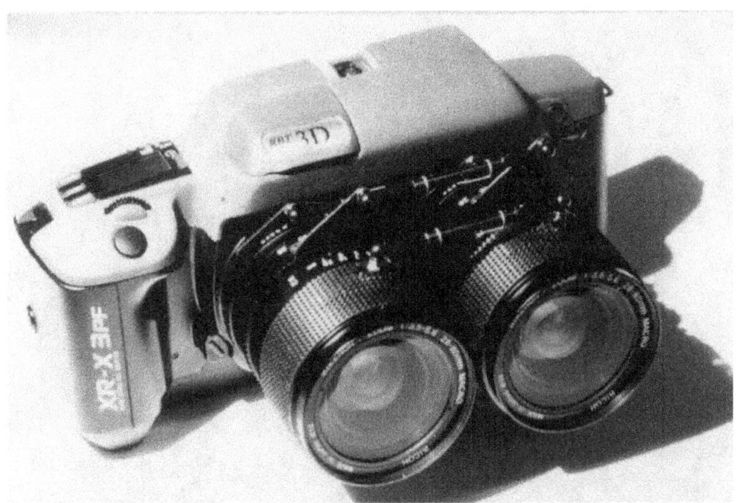

Fig 4.19
RBT "Siamesed" camera, model X3, built from two Ricoh XR-X 3PF mono cameras.

As might be expected, such cameras do not come cheap, but they possess many worthwhile features such as sophisticated metering and exposure control not available on the older stereo cameras.

CHAPTER 5: VIEWING STEREOSCOPIC PAIRS - FREE VIEWING AND THE USE OF STEREOSCOPES

5.1 Introduction

In this chapter, various methods of viewing mounted pairs of images will be discussed, ranging from free viewing techniques and the use of simple aids to the employment of more sophisticated optical viewers, or stereoscopes. However, the viewing of stereo pairs by projection onto a screen will be discussed in Chapter 8, because this method of displaying 3D images brings with it a different set of conditions and problems.

For the moment, it will be assumed that mounting of the stereo pairs has been carried out correctly, that is according to certain pre-conditions and recommendations. Strictly, "correct mounting" is only a relative term. It implies that the images are set in a way that reproduces the original scene exactly with respect to size and location in space. Because eye separation varies from one person to another, each will see a particular stereogram slightly differently. In addition, the lens spacing in stereoscopes and their focal lengths usually differ from those in the camera, introducing additional distortions, even though they may only be slight ones.

The single underlying principle of stereoscopic viewing is to arrange that the left eye sees only the left image and the right eye only the right image. Certainly, the easiest and most comfortable means of achieving this is to use a stereoscope. However, the ability to view a stereo pair as a 3D image without recourse to any apparatus is an extremely useful skill. Developing this ability requires some time, effort, perseverance and practice and not everyone will succeed.

5.2 Free Viewing

The eyes can be trained to fuse the left and right images of a stereo pair without the use of any optical aid. However, in the majority of instances the viewing conditions will not be ideal and the resultant image will be distorted in some way, e.g. compressed, stretched or smaller than intended. This is not a serious problem because the free viewing technique is adopted merely as a quick and convenient way to gain a general impression of a 3D image, to assess its effectiveness, for example; serious viewing is best done with stereoscopes. Currently, many people are acquiring this free viewing skill in order to enjoy the hidden 3D images and shapes in the wide variety of so-called "Magic Eye" posters and pictures. These computer-generated designs, often resembling abstract wallpaper, cunningly conceal a stereo image pair that transforms the picture into recognisable 3D shapes.

Essentially there are two methods for free viewing:
1. viewing with the sight lines parallel (**Fig. 5.1a**)
2. viewing with convergent sight lines (crossing the eyes) (**Fig 5.1b**)

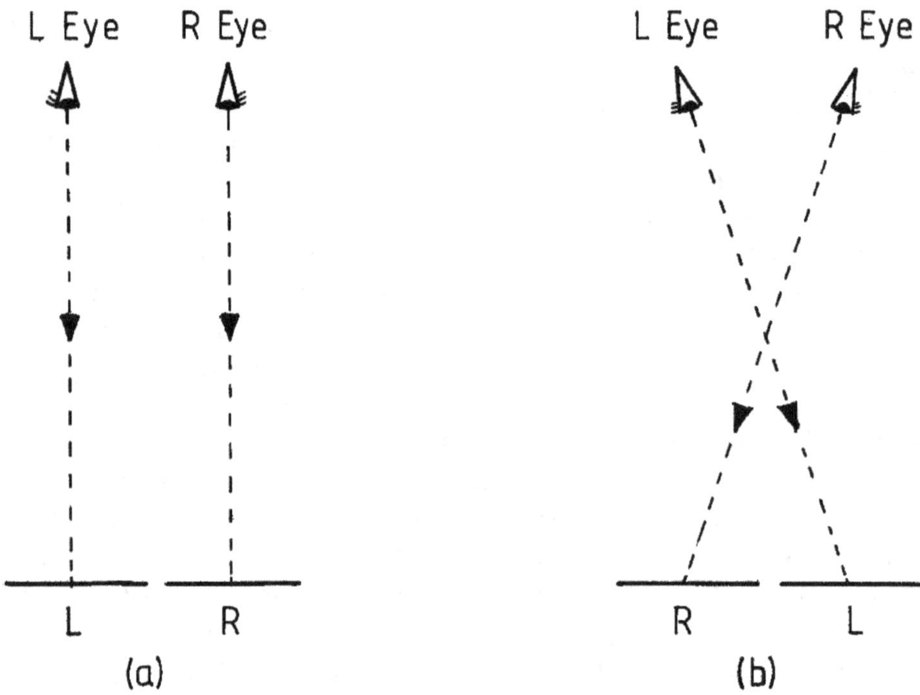

Fig1
Methods of free viewing.
a *Parallel sight lines method*
b *Converging sight lines method (crossing the eyes) With this method the left and right images must be transposed.*

Fig 5.2
Two dots set 65mm apart for free viewing practice.

In the first method the stereo pair is mounted in the normal way (left image on the left, right image on the right) and the 3D image produced will appear correctly. For correct image formation when using the second method, the two pictures have to be interchanged. If they are not, the image will be **pseudoscopic**; all the depth information will be reversed - near objects will appear distant and vice versa. With abstract subjects this may not matter, but for images of people, landscapes and the like, the effect is somewhat surrealistic. However, the crossed-eyes method, probably the easier of the two techniques to master, comes into its own when viewing stereo pairs on a 35mm film, exposed in a traditional stereo camera. Since the image pairs require transposition before they are mounted for conventional viewing, it follows that they lie correctly on the uncut roll of film for crossed-eye free viewing.

In the next section, the two methods are described in greater detail.

5.2.1 Method 1 - parallel sight lines

In this method it is essential that the two images that form the stereo pair are no more than about 65mm apart, as measured between homologous points. If they are further apart, the eyes will need to diverge if the image is to be seen stereoscopically, and this is usually difficult for most people to achieve because it is unnatural. A small amount of divergence can be tolerated without too much discomfort but it is best avoided. Conversely, there is no problem if the sight lines converge slightly, as will occur when the two images are set closer than the eye spacing. When the images have been fused successfully the observer will usually be aware of three images; only the centre image will be in 3D. The other two images are a result of each eye seeing both components of the original pair. Although the left eye, for example, is directly looking at the left image, it is still aware of the right image peripherally, and likewise for the right eye and left image. At first, seeing three images may be confusing but the observer soon learns to ignore the outer two. Indeed, when practising the technique, one may even see four images momentarily, until the eyes are adjusted to fuse the inner pair.

The basic skill that must be acquired is to focus the eyes on the images placed at, say, 380mm (15in) away while at the same time maintaining parallel or near parallel sight lines; this is not something we do in everyday life. As will be explained more fully in Chapter 16, there are two particular adjustments made by the eyes in normal vision: **accommodation**, whereby the lens shape is altered in order to focus the image on the retina and **convergence**, or rotation of the lines of sight towards each other when looking at near objects. These are independent functions but in normal vision they tend to be strongly linked. When we focus on a near object, through habit our eyes converge at the same time so that each eye is directed to a specific point on the object. In free viewing of stereo pairs we have to focus the eyes at the viewing distance (380mm, say) whilst rotating the eyes so that the sight lines converge on the near object.

If from the above description the technique seems rather formidable, it should be pointed out that the brain does not have to carry out a series of "commands to numbers", as it were; the whole thing is more of a knack acquired by following a few simple procedures.

Various ways of assisting the observer to learn the technique have been devised. The reader may wish to try these methods with the aid of the two black spots in **Fig 5.2** which are placed at the top of the page for convenience.

Before attempting the free viewing techniques, the following exercise should be tried; it is designed to make one aware of the eye rotation that has to be avoided in order to succeed in free viewing.

1. Look at a distant object, say a picture on the far wall of the room, and fix the gaze on this.
2. Without removing the gaze from the picture, place the right hand in front of the eyes about 300mm (12 in) away from the face. The hand will be out of focus and appear as a double image.
3. Now direct the gaze away from the picture to the hand. The eyes will re-focus onto the nearer object, but you should also be conscious of movements caused by the eyes rotating in their sockets to converge on the hand. Try this a few times so that you clearly recognise these eye movements.

Once this eye rotation has been recognised, you will understand why earlier attempts to free view failed. It will almost certainly be due to your inability to prevent the rotation.

We can now turn to free viewing proper. To practise the method, the reader should make use of the two black dots in **Fig 5.2**.

Technique 1

1. Focus the eyes on a distant or semi-distant object. This will ensure that the sight lines are parallel (or nearly so). Fix the gaze.
2. Holding the book at arm's length away from you, gradually raise it, keeping the two dots in line horizontally, until it intersects the line of sight. Do not attempt to focus the dot images. If you do, you will find that you are looking directly at one point on the page. If this happens, start again. You have to imagine you are looking through the page into the distance.

3. Having managed to retain your original gaze you should now be aware of aware of three dots on the page. You may see four, especially if the page is not level. The two centre dots are to be fused into one. If necessary, twist the book slightly to keep the dots horizontal. At first the dots may be out of focus, but without making any conscious effort (and trying to avoid the tell- tale eye rotation) concentrate on the dots and you should find that they come into focus. There will be no 3D effect because the two original dots are identical; their purpose is to act as simple images for practising the technique. It is important, if the dots are to come into focus, that the book is not too close. It has to be at normal reading distance.

If the dot exercise is found to be difficult, try it with two dots placed closer together. Draw two dots, as in **Fig 5.2,** but spaced about 40mm apart (just over 1½in). They should be easier to fuse successfully. You can then try the exercise with two dots about 50mm apart (about 2in) and progress to the 65mm separation of the dots in **Fig 5.2**.

If, after several attempts, you cannot achieve a satisfactory result, you may find a variation more helpful, as explained below.

Technique 2
1. As in technique 1, fix the gaze on a distant object.
2. Without changing the gaze, suddenly place the book right up against the face so that the eyes are opposite the two dots. Do not "shift the gaze".
3. Now slowly move the book away from the face, still "looking through the page". You should be aware of three dots that should come into focus as the book continues its movement.

Once the technique has been mastered, it becomes easy to repeat. It can now be applied to a genuine stereo pair, such as the geometric figure in **Fig 5.3**. What looks like two squares, each subdivided into four triangles, is actually a stereo pair of a pyramid seen from above. If the two pictures are viewed by either of the above techniques, the point of intersection of the diagonal lines in the image will appear to be nearer to the observer; the pyramid should stand up from the page. If the observer, in fusing the two images, appears to be looking into a hollow pyramid, from underneath, the convergent sight line technique is being inadvertently used.

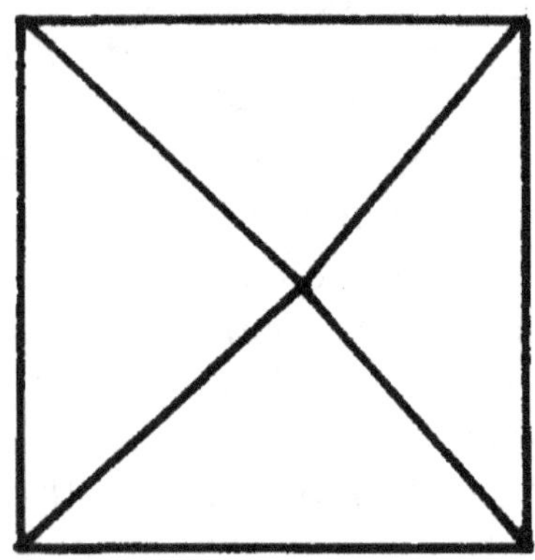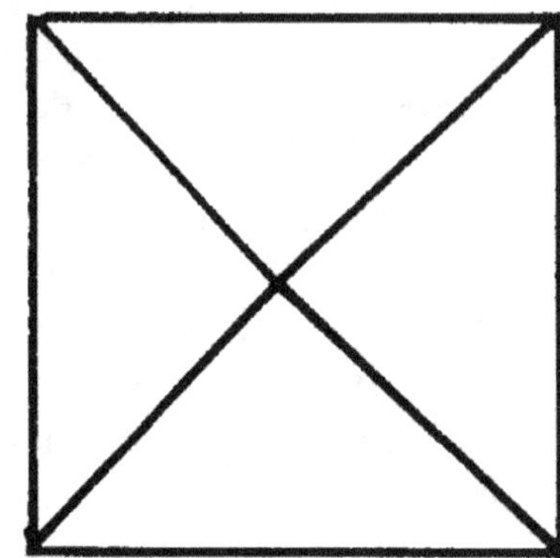

Fig 5.3
Stereo pair for free viewing practice. Using the parallel sight lines method, this will be seen as a pyramid with the apex nearer to the observer. With the "crossed eyes" method it will appear as a hollow pyramid seen from below, with the apex furthest away.

5.2.2 Method 2 - convergent sight lines (crossing the eyes)

Many people find this method easier than Method 1, but as has already been pointed out, a correct rendition of the 3D image can only be obtained if the left and right images of the stereo pair are transposed, to place the left image on the right and vice versa.

The technique is straightforward: with the image pair at a comfortable reading distance away (use **Fig 5.2** or **Fig 5.3**), look at the two images and slowly cross the eyes. Momentarily you will see four images and the centre pair will move towards each other and lock. In the case of **Fig 5.2**, the observer will be looking into a hollow pyramid, with the apex further away than the outer square.

One advantage of this method is that it can be used even if the left and right images are further apart than the 65mm norm, as long as they are not excessively so. A certain amount of eye-strain may be experienced so this method should not be used for too long a time at one viewing. It is perhaps best employed as a quick test to establish, for instance, that two images are correctly placed. If two photographs side by side are viewed by this method and a normal 3D image is seen, then the observer will know that the two images are wrongly located for normal viewing. Conventionally mounted stereo pairs will produce pseudoscopic images when viewed by the crossed-eye method.

5.2.3 Simple aids to assist in free viewing
Vertical divider

A piece of stiff card, of length about 300mm (12in) and width equal to the height of the images to be fused, can be placed between the two images at 90° to act as a separator, so that each eye sees only the correct image (**Fig 5.4**). This should be used only for the "parallel sight lines" method of free viewing, for conventionally mounted stereo pairs.

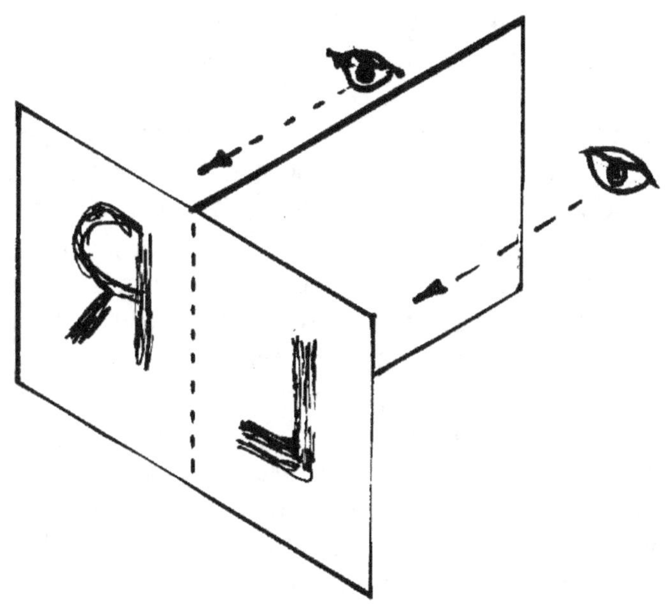

Fig 5.4
Use of a partition or divider as an aid to free viewing

Black card may be the least distracting but the colour is not particularly important. It is best to ensure that the divider does not cast a shadow over either image or it will prove more difficult to fuse the pictures; the observer should arrange for the light to come from above. For complete masking, the divider should be long enough to extend from the stereo pair to the observer's nose, at a comfortable viewing distance. It is possible to use a divider that is shorter than the actual reading distance adopted, but whether it is placed against the images, the nose, or somewhere between, almost certainly each eye will see part of the "wrong" image; this rather defeats the object of using the aid.

The Elliott stereoscope

This is an early form of viewing device, having no lenses or mirrors that can be used only for non-transposed left and right images; it is based upon the "converging sight lines" or "crossed-eyes viewing" method, with the left image located to the right of the right image.

Essentially the stereoscope consists of a closed box with two eyeholes at one end and a central aperture at the other. Strictly speaking, a given model is designed to work with a particular image size, format and separation, individually tailored, as it were, but it will work with other formats provided that they are not drastically different. A basic design, with essential dimensions, is given in **Fig 5.5** (the top is excluded for clarity).

This is designed for use with stereo pairs in which each image measures 60x60mm (maximum) and the image separation between infinity points is 65mm. The comfortable viewing distance is assumed to be 300mm (12in).

In use, the stereoscope is oriented towards the stereo pair so that the far end of the box, containing the central aperture, is 150mm (6in) away from the images; the central aperture will now lie half-way between the eyes and the stereogram (**Fig 5.6**). As should be clear from **Fig 5.6**, each eye sees only its correct image when the stereoscope is set at the correct distance. Moving the stereoscope further away from the stereo pair will cause parts of each image to be lost (the left edge of the left image and the right edge of the right image). This means that only part of the visible image can now be fused, the portions that are common to both. Moving the stereoscope too close to the stereo pair will mask the outer edges of each image, and each eye will now see part of the wrong image, the right edge of the right image being seen by the left eye, for example. In practice, one simply views the images at approximately the correct distance and moves the stereoscope slightly towards and away from the pair to find the exact spot.

The stereoscope can, of course, be made twice as long to incorporate a clip to hold the stereo pair in position at the far end. The aperture will now be correctly placed for all stereograms in the appropriate format (**Fig 5.7**).

In the above design the aperture size is easily determined. Its linear dimensions are simply half the values of the infinity separation points and the picture height of the images. The first value gives the width and the second the height of the aperture. Thus, for an image height of 60mm and an image separation of 65mm the dimensions will be 30mm height and 32.5mm width. The size of this

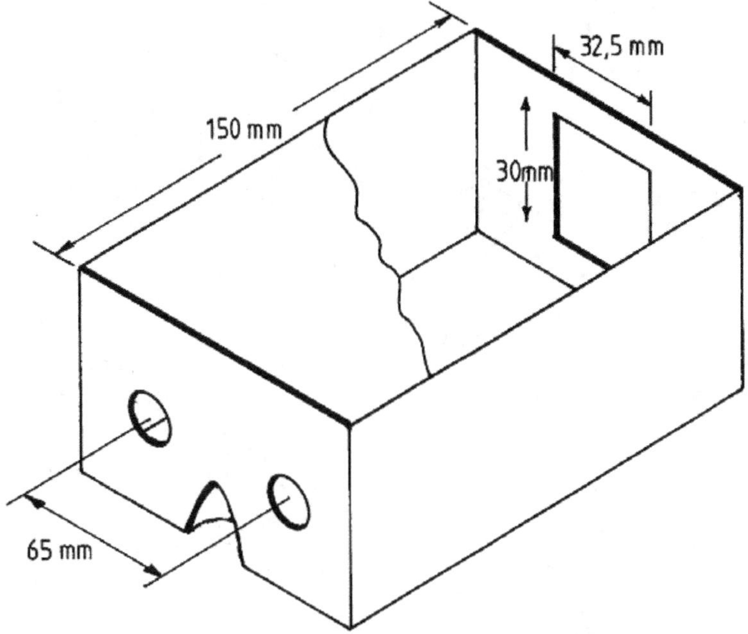

Fig 5.5
The Elliott Stereoscope, in the form of a closed box. It is essentially an aid for crossed eye viewing of transposed left and right pairs.

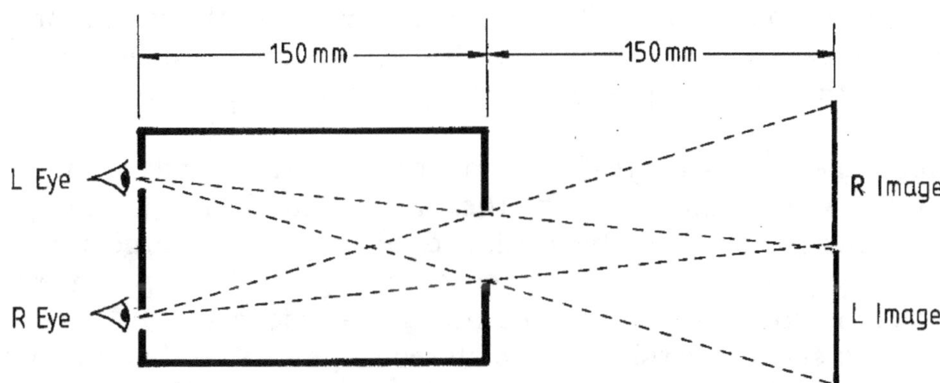

Fig 5.6
Principle of operation of the Elliott Stereoscope. When it is used at the correct distance with transposed images, each eye sees only the image intended for it.

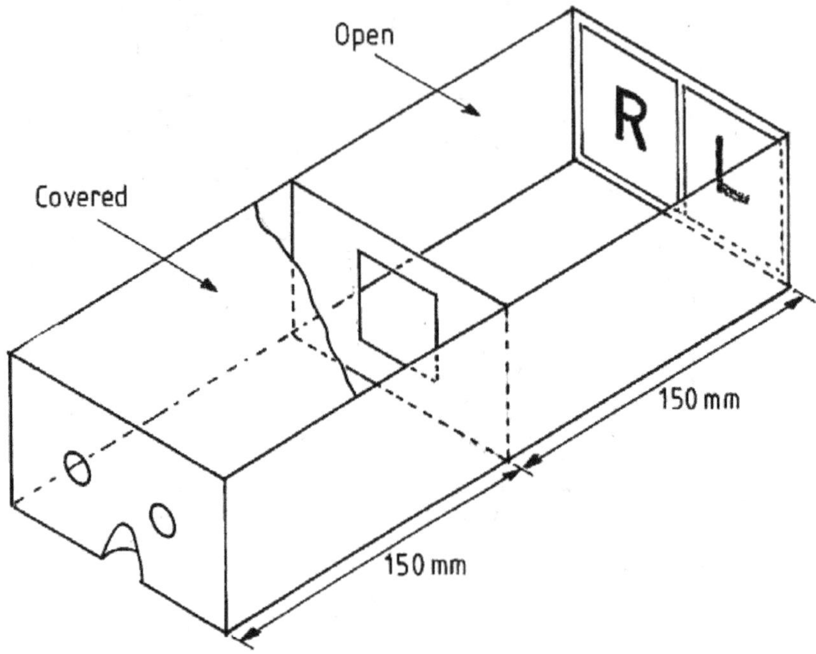

Fig 5.7
Basic design for a self-contained Elliott Stereoscope.

Aperture is independent of viewing distance, so if the basic design of **Fig 5.7** is to be modified for a 380mm (15in) distance, the length of the box is simply increased to 190mm (7½in) and the aperture end positioned 190mm from the stereo pair when viewing. The aperture size is the same as before.

Since the "crossed-eyes" method can be employed when the two images of the stereo pair are set further apart than 65mm (within reason), the Elliott Stereoscope can be designed to work with large images. An analysis of the geometry of this stereoscope is given in Supplement S5 so that correct dimensions can be calculated for any format.

An even simpler version of the stereoscope can be made by ignoring the box design and cutting an aperture of the recommended size in a single sheet of card, which can be held halfway between the observer's eyes and the stereo pair. Exactly the same effect will be produced but it may be slightly more difficult to locate the exact position for it to function correctly.

Mirror viewing

Although an optical device in the form of a mirror is involved, the method is more akin to free viewing techniques than to the use of a true stereoscope incorporating a number of mirrors, prisms or lenses. Mirror viewing has the advantage that large images can be fused; the disadvantage, whatever the image size, is that one of the images has to be reversed laterally.

The mirror is placed between the two images, like the divider in **Fig 5.4** with the reflecting surface to the right. The left eye looks directly at the left image, whereas the right eye is directed to the mirror so that it sees the reflection of the (laterally reversed) right image (**Fig 5.8**). The reflecting surface can, of course, be situated on the left if the left image is the one that is reversed.

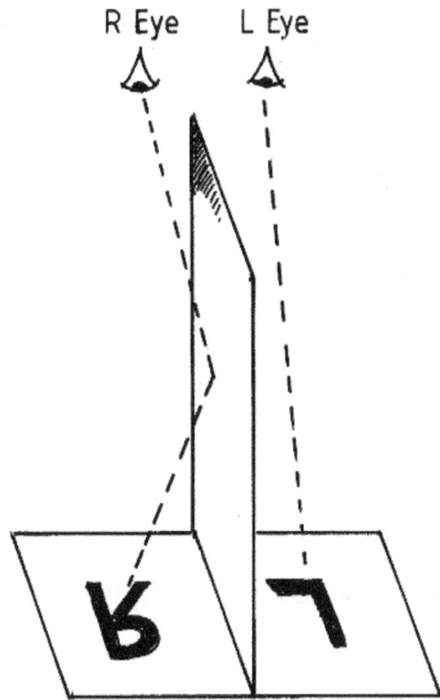

Fig 5.8
Use of a mirror and one laterally reversed image to assist in free viewing.

Tilting the mirror slightly will shift the reflected image into the correct position. There will be some slight distortion of the stereo image, but most people will hardly notice it. Generally, it is better to use a large mirror that can rest in the space between the two images and allow for a comfortable reading distance. Alternatively a smaller mirror can be held close to the right hand side of the nose. Moving the head and adjusting the mirror will quickly lead to successful fusion of the images.

In 1999, the publisher Dorling Kindersley produced a series of children's books of 3D images for viewing with a mirror. The books are designed so that the pages can be turned with the mirror assembly in place.

Tilting the images

The eye-crossing method of free viewing (Method 2) is subject to convergence distortion similar to that shown in **Fig 4.5** (Chapter 4), except that the left and right images will be transposed. Because the sight lines converge, the left eye sees its image at a slight angle rather than head on, as does the right eye and the images will not be perceived as true rectangles, but trapeziums (**Fig 5.9**)

This distortion will be only slight but it is worse for close viewing distances and greater separation of the images. If the mount is folded along the dividing line between the left and right images (**Fig 5.10**), so that the images are tilted, the distortion can be reduced or even eliminated. Only a small amount of tilting will be necessary in most cases, but the result is that fusion of the images is more comfortable to the eyes, especially with larger pictures.

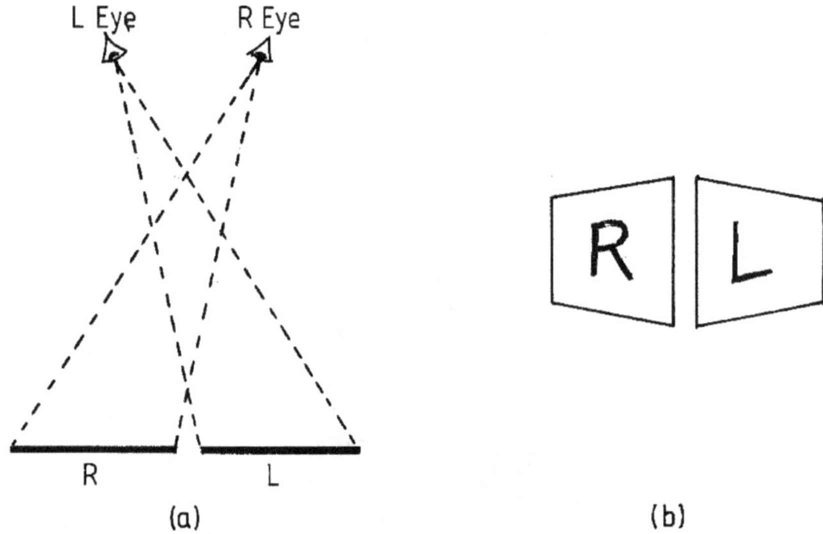

Fig 5.9
*In crossed eyes viewing the sight lines are not at 90° to he images (**a**) and this leads to convergence distortion (**b**).(The effect is exaggerated in the diagram, for clarity).*

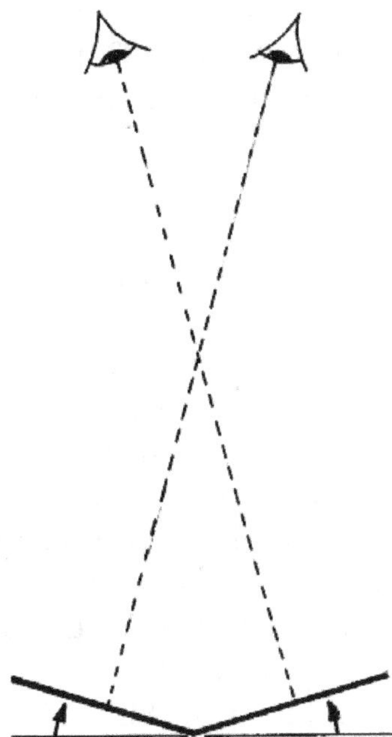

Fig 5.10
Tilting the images as shown can eliminate convergence distortion in crossed eyes viewing.

5.2.4 Free viewing and the stereo image

The shortcoming of most of the free viewing methods is that the stereoscopic image is not re-created under the correct conditions. The basic problem is linked to correct viewing distance and its relation to the image size, as discussed in Supplement S1. The correct viewing conditions for stereo images are explored fully in Chapter 18.

Any photographic image, mono or stereo, should be viewed so as to reproduce the perspective as "seen" by the camera lens when the picture was taken. This means that when viewing a contact print (in which the image size is the same as the original negative) or a transparency, the viewer's eye should be set at a distance equal to the focal length of the lens used for producing that original image. If the original image is enlarged, say four times linearly, then the correct viewing distance will be four times the focal length.

Let us consider two 60 x 60mm images as an example, set about 65mm apart and taken with an 80mm focal length lens on a medium format camera. Such a stereo pair should be viewed at a distance of 80mm for correct realisation of the stereoscopic effect. This distance is too close for free viewing, which is more likely to require a viewing distance of around 300mm, the least distance of distinct vision (LDDV) for most people. The 3D image will appear smaller than the original subject, but elongated in the depth direction.

In summary, free viewing is a useful skill to acquire, but in general it will not provide ideal viewing conditions. Certainly it is advantageous to be able to check the effectiveness of a particular stereo pair (and that the images are correctly located) prior to their being mounted.

5.3 Stereoscopes
5.3.1 General observations on stereoscopes

The use of a proper stereoscope, incorporating such optical aids as lenses, mirrors or prisms (or a combination of these) allows the observer to look at stereograms under controlled viewing conditions (ideally, orthostereoscopic). This means viewing at the correct distance as determined by the camera lens focal length and the degree of enlargement of the final print (Supplement S1). The stereoscope used should, of course, be one designed for the particular image format being viewed

A properly designed stereoscope is particularly valuable when viewing transparencies, because the actual film images are used, without any enlargement, as with a print. The problem of viewing such images at the close distances required for correct perspective is overcome because, if the stereoscope is constructed with two lenses of focal length equal to (or close to) that of the camera lens, then the "impossibility" becomes a reality. Each lens creates a virtual image at a suitable distance for viewing, so that the two images can be fused easily. That is the basic function of any stereoscope, though not all of them will rely on lenses. Some use only mirrors or prisms which produce no magnification; these stereoscopes will tend to be used for larger image formats, where the degree of enlargement and the viewing distance will, ideally, have been chosen for correct viewing perspective. For the best quality images, all mirrors should be silvered on the front surface.

Optical stereoscopes can be categorised broadly into three groups, based upon the design and the principles of operation. First, there is the Wheatstone group, which relies on the use of mirrors. Invented by Sir Charles Wheatstone in 1832. This type pre-dated photography and was originally used for viewing geometric drawings. In 1843, Sir David Brewster designed a more compact stereoscope, using prisms, in simple box form, for viewing smaller images than the Wheatstone type could handle. Brewster first demonstrated this stereoscope publicly in 1844, in a lecture given to the Royal Scottish Society of Arts. Later, lenses were used and this design has formed the basis of many modern stereoscopes. In 1861, Dr Oliver Wendell Holmes invented the open form of stereoscope that bears his name.

5.3.2 The Wheatstone Stereoscope

Charles Wheatstone was a pioneer in the art and science of stereoscopy and to him is accredited the first stereoscope. He invented and made prototypes of both reflecting and refracting types of stereoscope from

1832 onwards. In 1838 he demonstrated the simple reflecting type that still has its place today in the world of stereoscopy, mainly in modified forms. His original demonstration used geometrical drawings of his own construction but later the apparatus was used for photographs

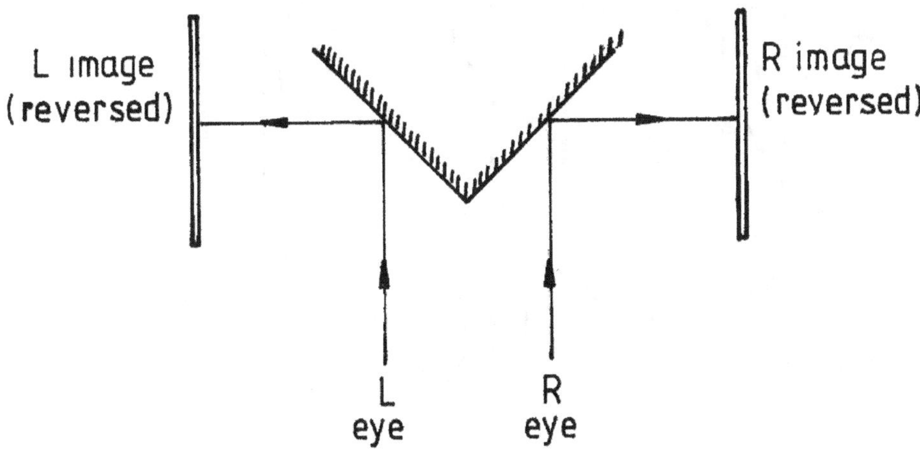

Fig 5.11
The Wheatstone Stereoscope.

The stereoscope consists essentially of two mirrors facing outwards at 45° to the line of sight, one mirror for each eye (**Fig 5.11**). The images are placed parallel to each other, facing inwards. There is one obvious disadvantage. Because the mirrors will reverse the images laterally via the single reflection, the original images have to be laterally reversed if a correct 3D image is to be created. If the images are prints, then they must be printed from the wrong side so that, for example, any lettering will read from right to left as mirror writing. Transparencies can, of course, simply be turned round so that they are effectively viewed from the back. **Fig 5.12** makes this clear.

There is also an advantage in the design. Because the left and right images are parallel and not side-by-side, there is no limit to their size, within reason. This method of viewing is still used for viewing large images such as X-ray film stereo pairs for medical and other scientific purposes.

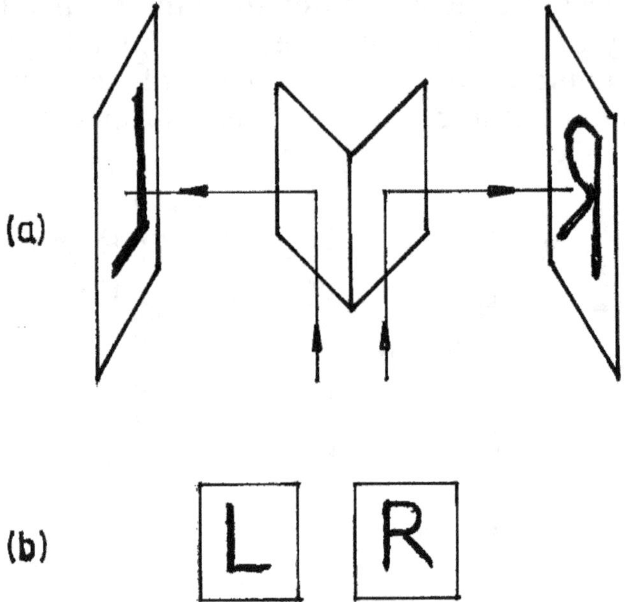

Fig 5.12
a *Laterally reversed images shown in a Wheatstone Stereoscope.*
b *Images as seen after reflection*

The Wheatstone stereoscope can be used for viewing ordinary images (ie ones not laterally reversed) if one is prepared to see the final 3D image as laterally reversed. To achieve this, surprising though it may seem, the right image has to be placed in the left holder and the left image in the right. This apparent paradox can be explained as follows.

Consider a conventionally mounted pair of transparencies. As discussed in Chapter 1, Section 1.3.2, the lateral spacing s_n of the images of the foreground rectangle in **Fig 5.13**, being smaller than s_i, the spacing of the mountain, means that the rectangle will appear to be nearer to the observer when the images are fused. If the whole slide is turned over, each image is laterally reversed. The right image is now on the left, and vice-versa (**Fig 5.14**).

When fusing the images we will see a laterally reversed 3D image but since the separations s_n and s_i have not changed, the post still appears nearer. If we had interchanged the left and right images as well as turning over the slide, the resulting image would have been pseudoscopic.

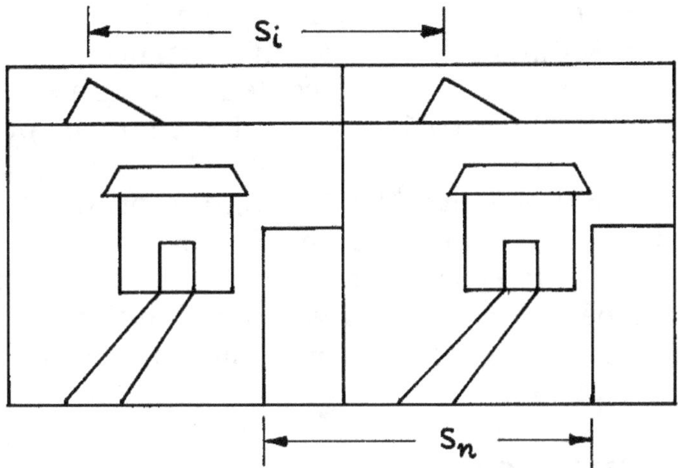

Fig 5.13
Simple stereogram representing a pair of transparencies as viewed from the front.

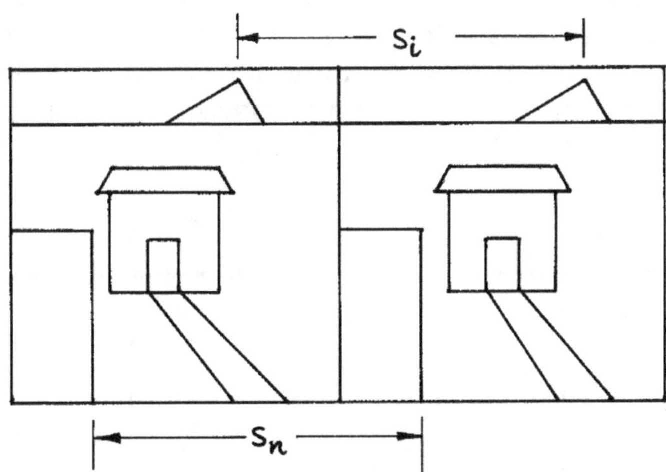

Fig 5.14
The stereogram of Fig 5.13 viewed from the back. Separations s_i and s_n are unchanged ($s_i > s_n$) so all objects, though laterally reversed, are still seen at their proper distances.

The arrangement of **Fig 5.14** is essentially the same as putting normal prints (not laterally reversed) into a Wheatstone stereoscope such that the left eye sees the right image and the right eye the left image. The final 3D image will be laterally reversed, as stated before.

Since the print size is not restricted, the prints should be large enough to satisfy the perspective conditions for correct viewing. If the eye-mirror-print distance is of the order of 300mm (12in), for example, then landscape format pictures printed from 35mm negatives should be of a size as calculated below:

Using	$\mathbf{D_V}$	$= \mathbf{fV}$	(Supplement S1)
we have	$\mathbf{D_V}$	= 300mm	(viewing distance)
and	$\mathbf{f}$	= 50mm	(focal length of camera lens)
Therefore	$\mathbf{V}$	$= \mathbf{D_V/f}$ = 300/50 = 6	(the enlargement factor)

From the original negative (24x36mm), the prints should be 6x24 = 144mm (5½in) high and 6 x 36 = 216mm (8½in) wide.

The Wheatstone stereoscope, as the above calculation leads one to suspect, is going to be a somewhat large piece of equipment, of the order of 600mm (2ft) wide, with the mirrors and image holders attached permanently to a solid base.

5.3.3 The Cazes stereoscope

This stereoscope was designed by L. Cazes in 1895 and represents a development of the Wheatstone stereoscope. In principle it functions in a similar way to a beam-spreader used on a camera with closely spaced lenses (Chapter 4, **Fig 4.14**). By adding two more mirrors to the basic Wheatstone design, pairs of images mounted side-by-side can be viewed. The extra reflecting surfaces result in an additional lateral inversion of each image, which means that normal pictures can be used. The basic design is shown in **Fig 5.15**.

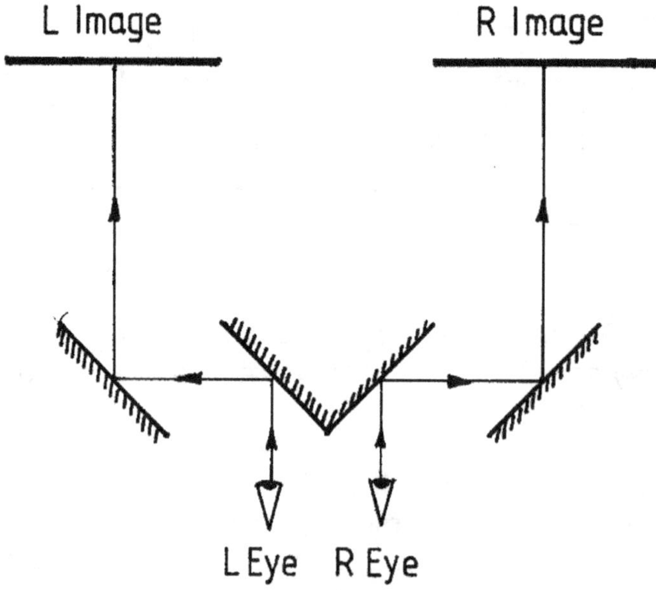

Fig 5.15
Basic design of a Cazes Stereoscope, consisting of four mirrors at 45° to the sight lines. Acting like a beam spreader in reverse, it can be used to view larger images separated by more than the normal 65mm.

Such a stereoscope can be designed for viewing large prints, as the image size is not critical. The distance between the outer and inner mirrors can be made to suit any image spacing, within reason. Indeed, the design can be made with adjustable holders for the outer mirrors, allowing than to be positioned at various distances from the inner pair, while maintaining the 45° set angle.

For viewing large prints, the two outer mirrors will have to be placed further apart and will need to be fairly large if the images are to be seen complete, without cut-off at the edges. For example, to view prints of maximum dimension 216mm (8½in) at an approximate distance of 300mm (12in), as would be the case for 6x enlargements from 35mm negatives, the inner mirrors would have to be just over 50mm (2in) wide, with the outer mirrors around 140mm (5½in) wide.

For convenience and lightness of construction this stereoscope, in its commercial form, is usually designed for vertical viewing, the prints being placed flat on a table. A light framework holds the eyepiece and mirror together as a unit which is supported by four legs angled outwards to leave a sufficiently large central area to contain the photographs (**Fig 5.16**).

Large versions of this stereoscope, usually bench mounted, are used to analyse photographs taken from the air in such activities as cartography, surveying, forestry studies and the like. Often the equipment will incorporate a floating index mark that can be adjusted to coincide with features in the picture so that their heights can be measured with a fair degree of accuracy. Stereo pairs in aerial photography have to be photographed with a very large stereo base, in order to exaggerate the depth of features within the landscape.

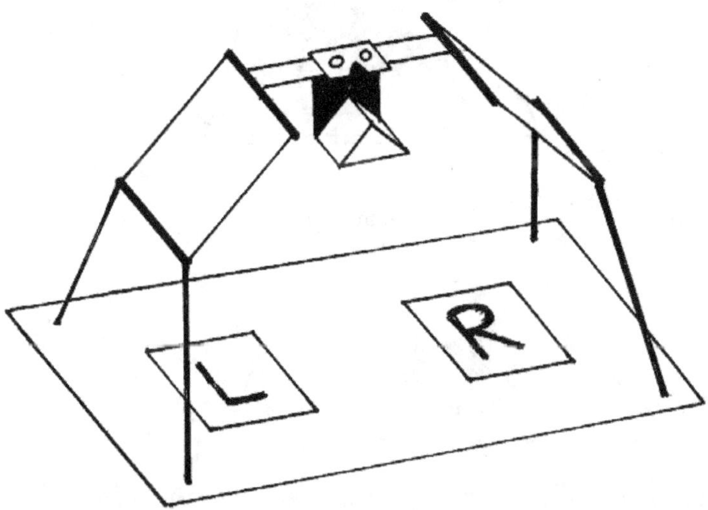

Fig 5.16
An example of a free-standing Cazes Stereoscope.

Cazes stereoscopes in the form described are ideal for large images that have to be viewed from 300mm (12 in) or more, but they can be constructed in smaller sizes, bringing the images nearer to the observer.

This requires lenses to be fitted to the eyepiece to magnify the smaller images and adjust the perspective conditions for correct rendition of the 3D picture.

A marketed version of the Cazes stereoscope (the Mirrorscope) about 8 inches wide incorporated a dial which, when turned, caused the outer mirrors to rotate in opposite directions back and forth to enable viewing of side-by-side stereo pairs of different sizes as prints or on a computer monitor.

In Supplement S6 the design of the Cazes stereoscope is analysed in more detail to assist anyone wishing to construct one.

5.3.4 The Brewster stereoscope

The original stereoscope, which forms the basis of many present-day stereoscopes, consisted of a simple tapered box, the narrower, front end of which contained apertures for the eyes and a cutaway for the nose. Behind the eye apertures two lenses (actually the two halves of a large lens cut into two) were mounted with the thinner edges nearest to the nose aperture. At the far, wider end of the box was a holder to take the stereo pairs (**Fig 5.17**).

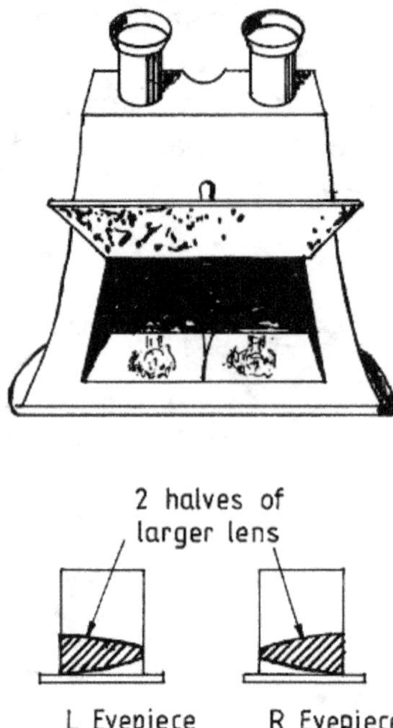

Fig 5.17
Brewster's lenticular or refracting stereoscope showing the wedge-shaped lenses that form the eyepiece.

By using two halves cut from a single lens (original size about 40mm diameter) the difficulty of obtaining two perfectly matched lenses was overcome. Lens manufacture at that time was not of the standard of accuracy or reproducibility that we have today.

Sometimes, quarter lenses were used, or two circular lenses cut from a single larger lens (**Fig 5.18**).

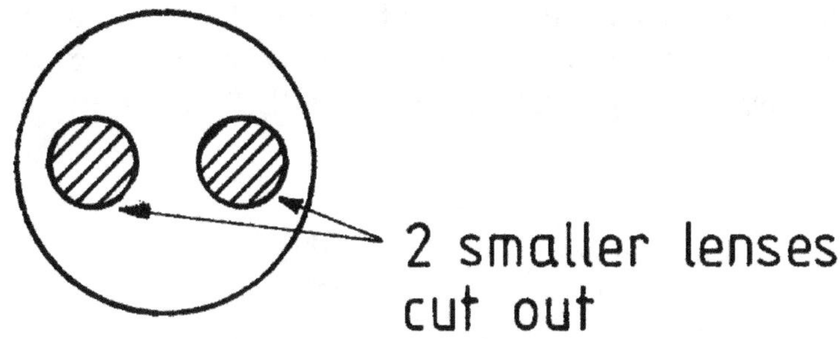

Fig 5.18
Cutting two small wedge-shaped lenses from a single large diameter lens.

The frame containing the lenses was also constructed in two parts so that the interocular separation of the lenses could be adjusted. Later models had the lenses, by now mainly circular, mounted in tubes that could be moved in and out for focusing.

The wedge-shaped lenses of the original model had a basic characteristic that is still used today, even though it is not an essential feature of a Brewster stereoscope. The wedge shape, acting as a prism, causes the originally parallel sight lines from the eyes to diverge. The significance of this is that larger images, separated by a distance greater than the standard 65mm can be viewed comfortably without eye divergence (**Fig 5.19**).

With two normal lenses, as in modern viewers, this divergence will be absent, and the stereo images must be mounted no more than about 65mm apart.

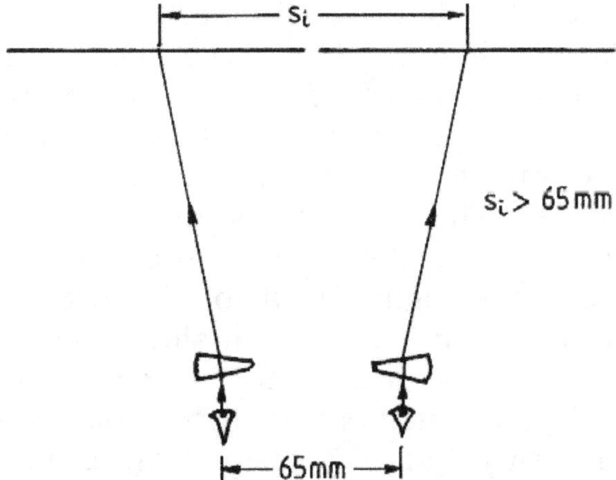

Fig 5.19
Divergence due to wedge-shaped lenses allowing larger images, separated by more than 65mm, to be viewed comfortably.

5.3.5 Stereo Realist viewer and similar stereoscopes

Various models of this stereoscope appeared on the market in the late 1940's and early 1950's. Originating in the USA, they formed part of the range of accessories based upon the Stereo Realist cameras; the range included projectors, screens, flashguns and mounting kits. One such stereoscope is shown in **Fig 5.20**, an early 1950's version.

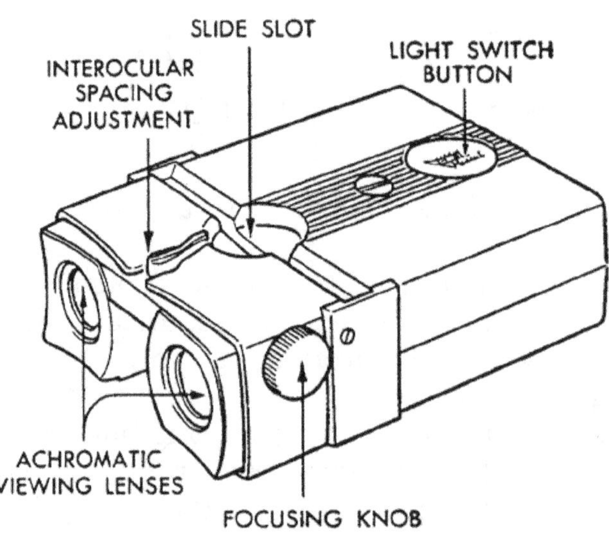

Fig 5.20
Stereo Realist viewer (c, 1950's). (Drawing reproduced from the Stereo Realist Manual[7] page 207).

It has two 44mm focal length lenses, of slightly longer focal length than that of the 35mm camera lenses. This means that the viewing conditions are not orthostereoscopic. There will be a slight exaggeration of the depth effect, namely "stretch" (see Chapters 18 and 19).

The interocular spacing of the lenses can be varied by turning a lever just above the nose cavity, whilst focusing is achieved by rotating the knob at the side, causing the lens mount section to move in or out.

About 40mm from the front is a slot into which the Realist format stereo slides are inserted. The whole of the rear section of the stereoscope contains a bulb and batteries. Pressing down on the button at the rear of the top panel switches on the light. Releasing the button switches it off. The light is reflected from a white surface insider the casing to give even illumination. The whole of the rear section is removable so that the front half of the viewer, complete with its translucent plastic backing piece, can be used as a straightforward stereoscope for use in daylight. With overall dimensions of 140mm length, 135mm width and 50mm depth (5½ x 5¼ x 2in) and a weight of 480g (1lb 1oz) including batteries, it is a compact and convenient piece of equipment. Whilst intended for Stereo Realist format images it will accept European (7P) format mounts, but there is some cut-off of the images at the outer edges.

Of very similar design is the Wray Stereoscope, (**Fig 5.21**), another product of the 1950's. This also accepts slides of the Realist format, and can be split to form a very neat daylight viewer in the same way as the Realist model. Focus adjustment and variable lens spacing is also provided.

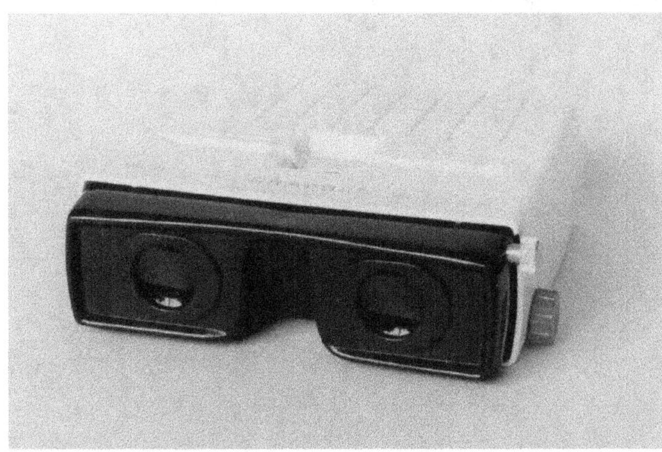

Fig 5.21
Wray Stereo Graphic stereoscope.

A more recent stereoscope, the Star viewer, will take slides of the Realist, European and half-frame formats. Essentially similar to the Wray and Realist viewers, it has built-in illumination, focusing adjustment (but no interocular adjustment) and plastic lenses.

Over the years, many such viewers, ranging from the simple to the more sophisticated, have been produced. Their main characteristics are exemplified by the Wray and Realist models; a detailed survey of other models would serve no further purpose. However, some additional stereoscopes, often produced in conjunction with commercially produced sets of stereograms, are reviewed later. Some are still available (**Figs 5.22 and 5.23**).

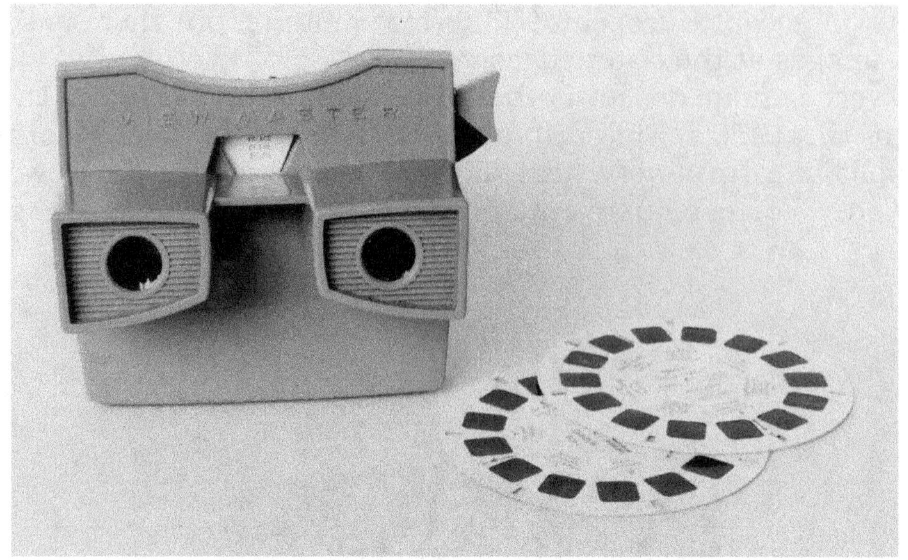

Fig 5.22
View-Master viewer (c.1950's) and reels with seven pairs of images.

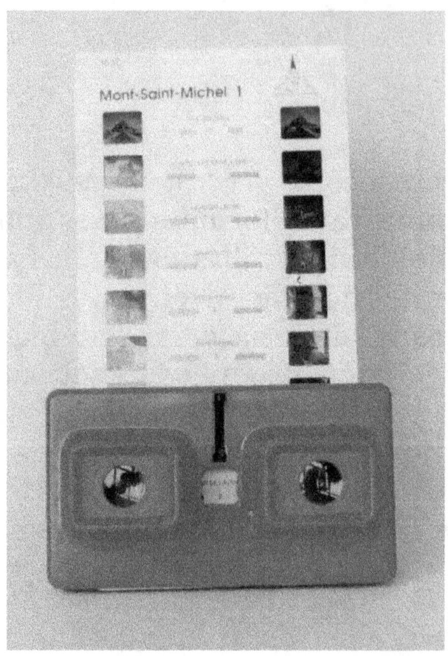

Fig 5.23
Lestrade viewer (France) dating from the mid 1990's and card containing ten pairs of images.

5.3.6 The Holmes stereoscope

Brewster stereoscopes have been around since the 1830's. In the Victorian age they were usually made of wood in the form of closed boxes, both hand-held types and table-top models. Dr Oliver Wendell Holmes was responsible for a characteristically lighter design, which he introduced in 1861, and which has become associated with his name. There was nothing new in its optics that was not already present in the Brewster stereoscope, but Holmes reduced its weight and increased accessibility by transforming the heavy box to a skeletal framework (**Fig 5.24**).

A hood or face mask holds the two wedge-shaped lenses in place. On the far side of this hood, a slide bar protrudes; this carries a simple crossbar and holder for the stereogram, which can be moved along the slide bar to focus the image. A handle is fixed below for support when viewing. The general design has changed little since its first appearance, although it is to J.L. Bates that credit is due for the sliding carrier. The first models had a fixed mount.

The prismatic lenses allow larger pictures to be viewed. The original design was used for pictures up to 3¼in (83mm) square, the infinity homologues being this distance apart in the stereogram.

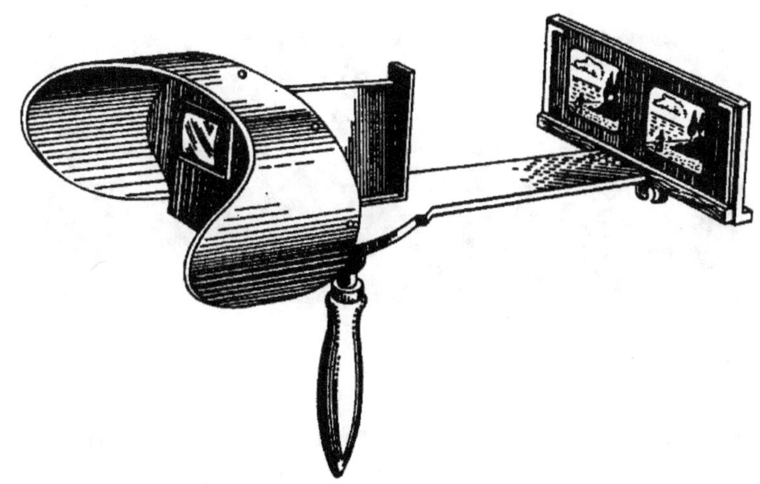

Fig 5.24
Holmes Stereoscope. (Diagram from "Stereoscopy" by Valyus[19])

Later developments have included such features as a detachable mount so that the hood/lens section can be used alone, for viewing stereograms in books, and the incorporation of a translucent background that can be swung into place to allow for the viewing of transparencies.

In recent years, a "Classic Stereoscope" has been advertised in the USA. This is in the form of a reproduction Holmes stereoscope and comes with sets of stereo cards, copies of the originals. Another Holmes style viewer is available in the form of a kit that can be assembled at home, including some modern colour stereograms. This is marketed in the USA as "The American Stereoscope Kit".

Original stereograms from the Victorian period and later are still fairly widely available in a number of formats, some of which are suitable for viewing in a Holmes stereoscope. One can obtain these old black and white or sepia images relatively cheaply through specialist dealers in second-hand equipment and are often on sale at camera fairs together with some of the hardware relating to stereo photography.

5.3.7 Lorgnette

This is one of the simplest means of viewing stereograms, particularly prints for which they are especially designed. As the name implies, the lorgnette consists of two lenses fixed in a frame with a handle attached, and is something that can be made easily. Nowadays they are available commercially as a single unit moulded in clear plastic (**Fig 5.25**). More often than not, the lenses are wedge-shaped, as in the original Brewster and Holmes stereoscopes, so that larger stereograms, with infinity points more widely separated than 65mm, can be viewed easily. Being compact, they can be included in books of stereograms to allow the reader to view them conveniently, as is the case with the Stereo Realist Manual[7].

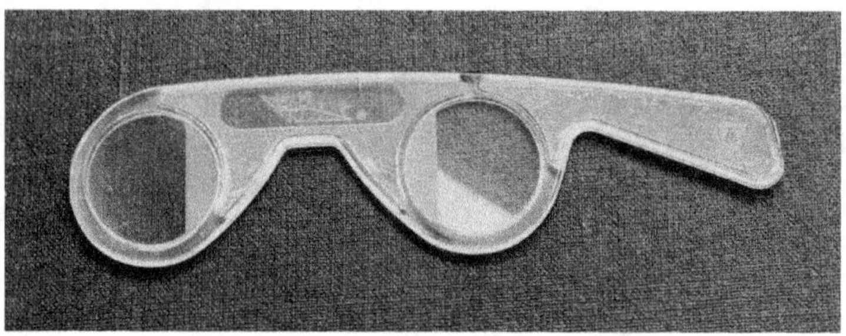

Fig 5.25
Plastic lorgnette.

Indeed, in that book, there is some inconsistency in the mounting of the many stereo pairs included. The maximum separation of infinity homologues is about 71mm; such pairs are somewhat difficult to fuse by free viewing as most people would have to diverge their eyes, but the lorgnette allows more comfortable viewing. In contrast, several other stereo pairs are set closer and can be free-viewed more easily. Even so, the lorgnette can still be used for these.

Lorgnettes are compact and inexpensive and one can easily construct a simple stereoscope from a box with a holder at one end for the stereograms and a slot or clip at the other end so that the lorgnette can be held in place temporarily whilst in use, and removed later.

5.3.8 "Over and under" viewing devices

An alternative method of viewing is currently gaining popularity, although the principle is much older. Instead of mounting the two images of the stereogram side by side, they are mounted one above the other. Conventionally, the right image is placed above the left (**Fig 5.26**). Each eye is made to see its correct image by means of a specially designed optical device. This can be in the form of a lorgnette in which the wedge lenses are set at 90° to their orientation in a normal lorgnette, so that the sight line for the right eye is diverted upwards and that for the left eye downwards (**Fig 5.27**).

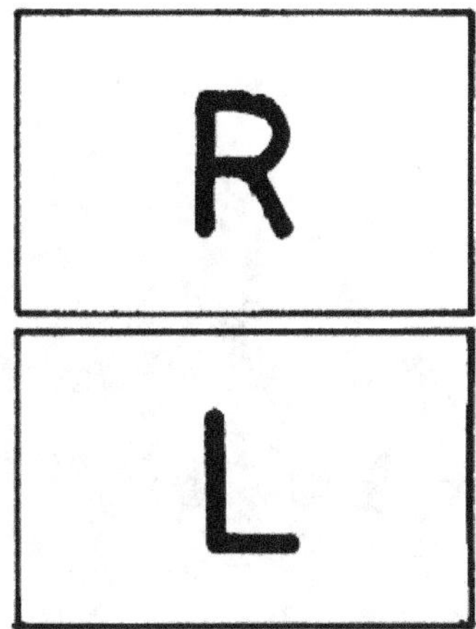

Fig 5.26
Standard image configuration for "over and under" viewing of stereo pairs.

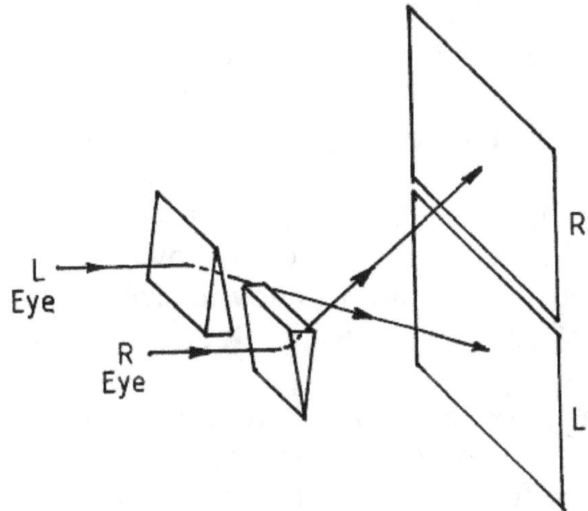

Fig 5.27
Wedge-shaped lenses bend the sight lines for successful "over and under" viewing.

The lenses from a standard lorgnette can easily be cut off and remounted in a simple frame to produce an over/under version.

Other over/under viewers have been based upon mirrors to divert the sight lines. One such device, currently popular with many enthusiasts, is the View Magic system developed in the USA by Dennis Brown (**Fig 5.28**). It consists of a plastic housing within which four mirrors are set, in pairs, to form a kind of double periscope. The left half works as a downward periscope for viewing the lower image while the right half diverts its sight line upwards. Ultimately, the right eye's line of sight ends up 100mm (4in) higher than that of the left eye. The two images are set so that their horizontal centre lines are 100mm apart.

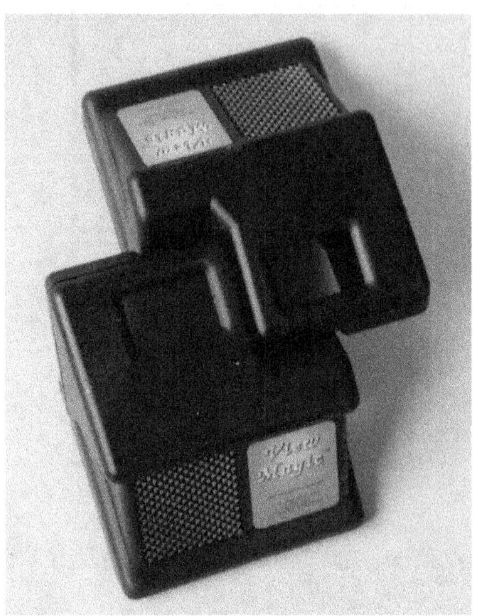

Fig 5.28
View Magic viewing device for over and under viewing of standard prints.

The system is ideal for viewing 152 x 102mm (6 x 4in) standard prints. Because of the over/under mounting there is no restriction on the width of the images (within reason) as the angle of view is relatively wide. In fact, panoramic format prints can be viewed by moving the viewer from one side to the other. The mounting system is advantageous as pairs of prints can be included, correctly spaced vertically, in the pages of traditional photographic albums.

The View Magic viewer does not magnify the images. Because of the two internal reflections the actual viewing distance is about 50mm (2in) more than it appears from the viewer/print distance. It can be used at greater distances than, say, the normal reading distance around 300mm, provided that the images are no more than 100mm apart, measured between the centre-line horizontals. As long as this separation is adhered to, smaller images can be viewed (**Fig 5.29**).

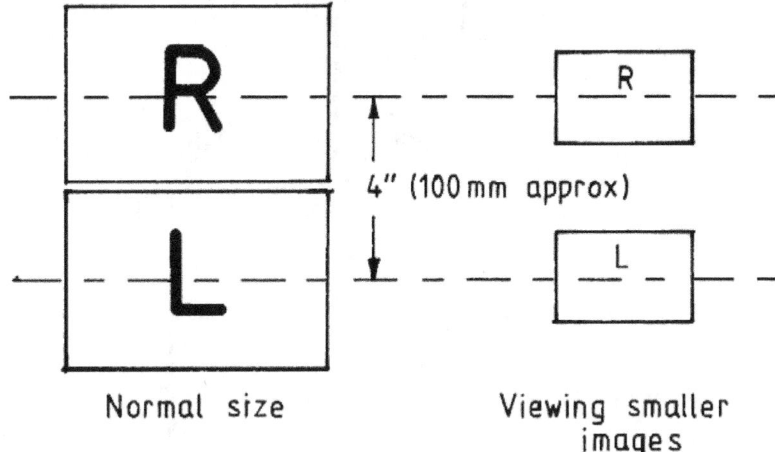

Fig 5.29
Method of mounting prints for the View Magic system. Smaller prints can also be viewed as long as their horizontal centre lines are 4in apart.

Overall, the View Magic system offers a convenient viewing system for standard prints made from 35mm camera pairs, stereo cameras or mono cameras using the sequential exposure technique. Mounting is considerably easier than it is with 35mm film chips.

All the mirrors are front-surface silvered. Although bulkier than a lorgnette, the viewer weighs only 170 grams (6oz) and its dimensions are 170 x 124 x 50mm (6¾ x 5 x 2in) deep; it can be mounted on a stand.

One disadvantage is that the viewing conditions are not orthostereoscopic. A small infinity point separation (as recommended by the handbook) and a longer viewing distance than is correct for the print size combine to produce a small image of limited depth. This is discussed further in Chapter 20, Section 20.5.

5.3.9 The Pentax viewer

This is illustrated in **Figs 4.7** and **5.30.** It is designed to be used in conjunction with the Pentax (or equivalent) stereo attachment (see Chapter 4, Section 4.2.2). In fact it is restricted to this particular format and can be used only for viewing transparencies. Similar models made by other manufacturers work in the same way and often appear as part of a kit along with their own stereo attachment. Usually, pictures taken with one particular brand of stereo attachment can be viewed in any other make of viewer.

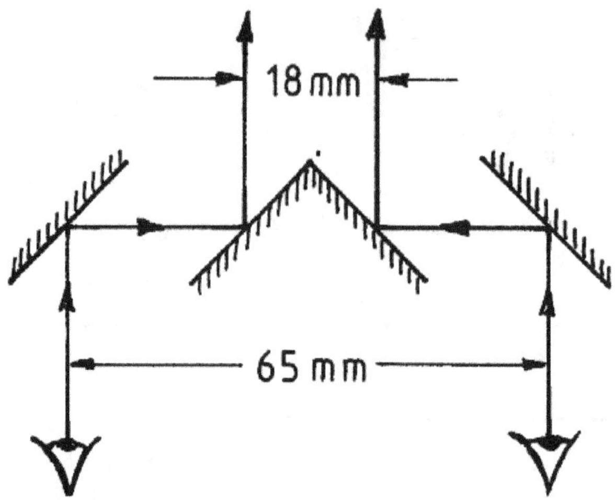

Fig 5.30
*Optics of the Pentax type stereoscope for viewing non-transposed pairs on a
single frame taken with the Pentax stereo attachment on a mono camera
(Chapter 4,* **Figs 4.6** *and* **4.7***).*

As previously discussed in relation to camera attachments, the
standard horizontal format 35mm transparency shows two half-frame
images side by side with the left image on the left, ready for viewing. Normal
viewing is not possible without an aid because the infinity homologues will
be separated by only about 18mm, whereas the true stereo base is 70mm.
While the images could be separated and mounted in suitable counts, the
Pentax viewer allows the combined pair to be viewed directly.

In essence, it is a miniature Cazes stereoscope working in reverse
with the addition of two lenses to form the eyepieces. The distance between
the sight lines is reduced from 65mm to 18mm by reflection at the internal
front-surface silvered mirrors (**Fig 5.30**). In the Pentax viewer, the inter-
lens spacing can be adjusted from about 59 to 65mm. The transparency is
inserted in a slot at the top of the viewer, and there is a translucent screen
at the back but no internal illumination.

5.3.10 Miscellaneous stereoscopes and viewers

To complete this survey of stereoscopes, some unusual or specialist
types of stereoscope, for various formats, will be reviewed.

Folding stereoscopes

Many basic Brewster-type stereoscopes have been made available
from time to time, often in the form of simple viewers given away or sold at
low cost to accompany the purchase commercially produced sets of
stereograms. Often, these stereoscopes were designed to fold flat, and were
constructed from metal, plastic or even cardboard, fitted with a pair of
simple meniscus lenses. Although extremely basic, they served to

popularise stereo photography, at least for short periods. Some of the pictures were given away in the form of cigarette cards. They were really no more than a novelty for the general public, but are now very collectable amongst the stereo fraternity.

Table and cabinet stereoscopes

Even from the early days of stereo photography, large versions of the Brewster type of stereoscope have been made in cabinet form, containing a number of stereograms that could be viewed in succession by operating a lever or turning a handle. Usually the set of pictures could be cycled continuously. Modern counterparts to these taxiphotes (an alternative name), on a smaller scale, are the hand-held viewers made for the View-Master system, with seven views to a reel (**Fig 5.22**) and the Lestrade system with ten views per card. They are hardly cabinet viewers but they serve a similar purpose.

Cabinet viewers are ideal for use at exhibitions and like events. They can be left on display and can be programmed to illustrate a particular theme. The Dutch company Hugo de Wijs manufactures a number of viewers of high quality in materials such as stainless steel, including some table viewers holding up to 21 slides. The illumination system switches off automatically 30 seconds after use to conserve the lamp and to avoid slide deterioration.

Transposing stereoscopes

Although not generally available, various stereoscopes have been designed to view non-transposed pairs of images, having the left image on the right and vice versa. A transposing stereoscope avoids the need to separate and mount the images and could be a useful device for viewing the image pairs on a 35mm film taken with a standard stereo camera, for example. An ideal application would be to view the single 35mm frame containing the side-by-side images produced with stereo attachments of the Leica type (Chapter 4, Section 4.2.5).

A simple four-mirror type of transposing stereoscope is shown in **Fig 5.31**. It is a kind of Cazes stereoscope in reverse, but with the pairs of mirrors at different distances from the eyes and staggered to allow the sight lines to cross. The eye spacing is effectively reduced to around 18mm.

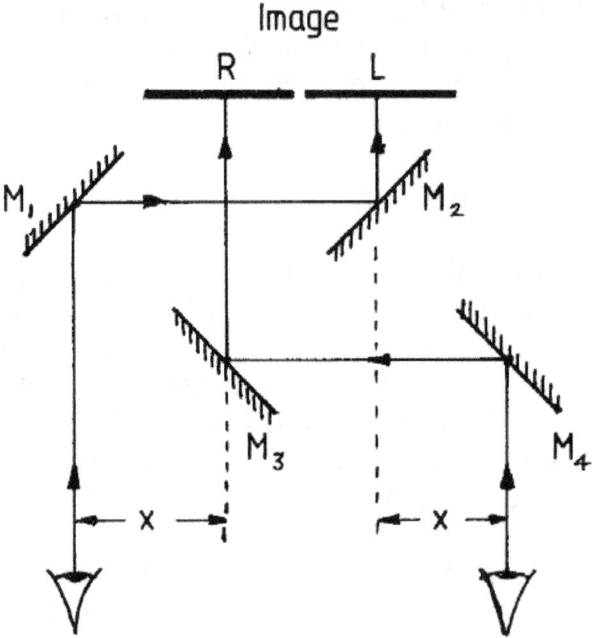

Fig 5.31
Four-mirror transposing stereoscope.

With the design shown in **Fig 5.31**, mirror **M₃** has to be set to the right of mirror **M₁**. With a symmetrical arrangement, mirror **M₂** will be offset from the right eye's sight line by an equal amount. Thus the separation between infinity homologues in any image viewed with this device has to be (65 − 2**x**)mm, that is, less than the norm. While it is true that mirror **M₂** could be moved further to the right to increase the separation of the sight lines, this will increase the optical path length from the left eye, which will see its image as smaller. The two images will be of different sizes. If a Cazes style four-mirror module is set up between this transposing mirror arrangement and the image, then the distance between the parallel sight lines can be increased to 65mm (or even more) to allow wider images to be viewed. However, the whole thing then would become too cumbersome, larger mirrors would be required, and there would be significant light loss by virtue of the many reflections.

Twin monocular viewers

An extremely economical but effective stereoscope for slides can be constructed by joining two monocular viewers side by side (**Fig 5.32**).

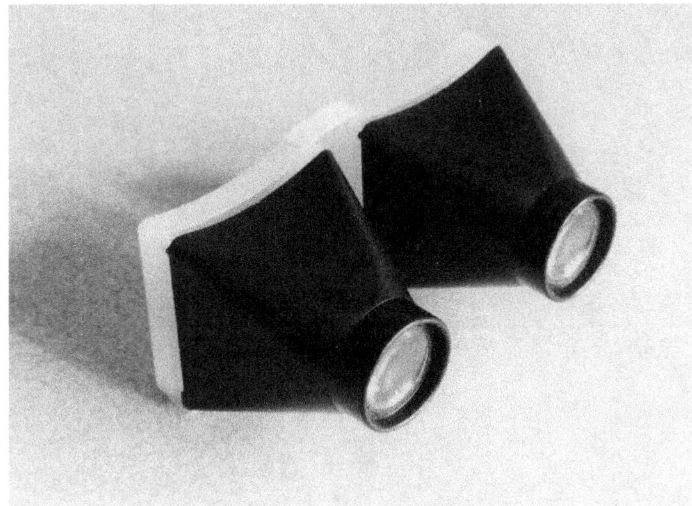

Fig 5.32
Simple stereo viewer for use with two 50 x 50mm slide mounts. It is made from two mono slide viewers fixed together to give an interocular spacing of 65mm.

This type of viewer is ideally suited for viewing separated pairs, taken sequentially or with twin cameras. The viewers should be joined to give a lens separation of about 65mm. It is best to ensure that the slide mounts fit reasonably tightly in their slots to avoid movement of the images.

This viewer can be used for a variety of formats – 5P, 7P, Nimslo and so on, and is ideal for those who wish to try out stereo photography without a lot of initial expense.

One or two versions (e.g. the Pinsharp viewer) have been marketed at moderate prices, but still dearer than can be made by the handyman.

CHAPTER 6: MOUNTING OF STEREO PAIRS

6.1 Introduction

Taking stereoscopic photographs is not a particularly difficult thing to do, even with the simplest of equipment, provided one obeys the basic guidelines outlined in Chapter 2, Section 2.3. Likewise, viewing the results is straightforward, with a variety of stereoscopes and other devices available or easily constructed. Mounting of film or print stereo pairs, however, is a little trickier and rather more time-consuming if proper results are to be obtained. The basic principles discussed in this chapter apply equally well to digital images but the methodology is different in that adjustments are made on a computer (see Chapter 14).

The principal objectives of mounting can be summarised as follows:
1. to enable the observer to view the desired 3D image without difficulty
2. to recreate the image in such a way that it matches as exactly as possible the original subject of the photograph
3. to ensure that the reconstructed 3D image is located realistically in space in relation to the regions forming the frame or border
4. to provide a convenient storage system for stereo pairs, so that they are always available for viewing without the need for any readjustment.

By way of brief explanation:

In (1) the aim is to arrange the images in such a way that the observer, either by free viewing or by using an optical aid such as a stereoscope, will be able to fuse the two images without excessive eye-strain.

Point (2) represents the ideal situation in which the original scene and its recreated 3D image are spatially identical. This implies that, were the observer to stand at the exact point where the camera was located when the picture was taken, the 3D image would superimpose exactly onto the actual scene. In reality, this perfection will hardly ever be achieved because of differences between the geometries of the picture-taking and picture-viewing conditions. Nevertheless, with good mounting techniques, this ideal can be approached closely.

Objective (3) is particularly important. In life the peripheral regions of normal vision are not clear cut. On the other hand, a photograph or slide has distinct borders, so when viewing a stereogram we will observe a sudden transition at the edges from a 3D image to a 2D one of the surrounding frame. Correct mounting is designed to place this border at a position in space such that the 3D scene appears behind it. The effect should be that of looking through a window. The position of this stereo window is controlled by the mounting technique, and when located correctly in front of the scene it adds to the naturalness of the 3D image.

Objective (4) is a matter of common sense in that the images will remain fixed in relation to each other. Assuming that mounting is properly carried out, these positions will be retained for "correct" viewing at any time in the future.

In this chapter, the basic principles of mounting will be reviewed, but only in a general way. To exercise proper control in difficult mounting situations, it is important to understand some of the theoretical background or the process becomes mere guesswork. One needs to know more about the stereo image and how it can be distorted by a number of factors. The more problematic areas of mounting are dealt with in Part 2 of this book, in Chapter 20.

6.2 The Stereo Window

The desired effect when viewing a stereogram is to see the 3D image in the same way as if one were looking at the actual scene through a window set in a wall, preferably from a darkened room so that the area surrounding the scene is neutral and unobtrusive. Usually, the window is located at about 2 metres (7ft) from the observer; this relates to the capacity of the human eye to view the entire depth (to infinity) of a scene without experiencing any visual discomfort. This also ties in with recommendation (2) in Chapter 2, Section 2.3, that the nearest object should be no closer than 2 metres for normal stereo photography.

Generally, one should avoid having objects in front of the window, a situation that can arise in three ways, viz:

1. including objects nearer than 2 metres in the scene
2. incorrectly setting the film chips in the mount. If they are too close together, near objects may appear closer than they should and protrude through the window.
3. using a mount with incorrectly located apertures.

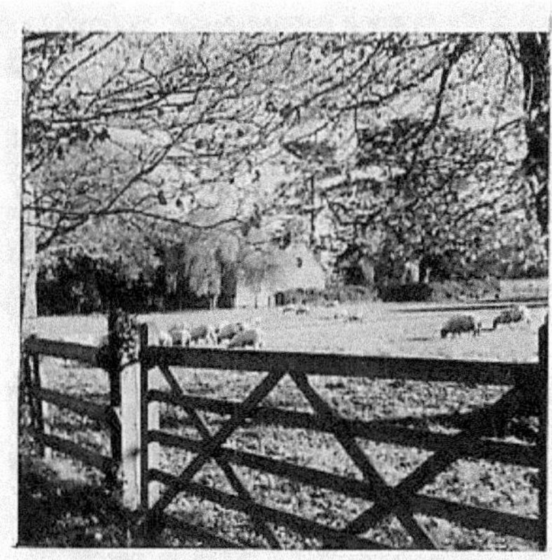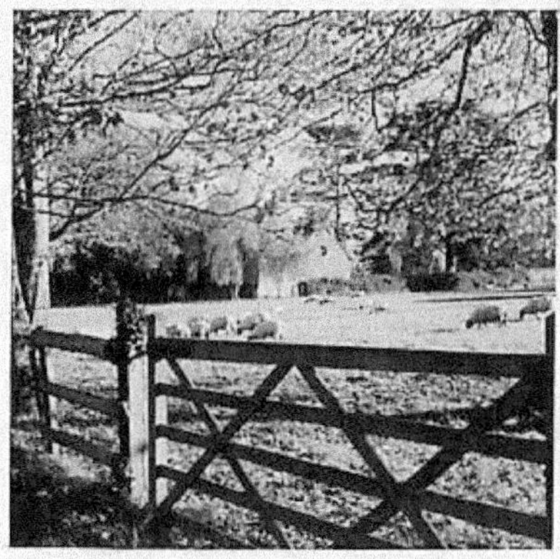

Fig 6.1
Stereo pair with a stereo window set normally so that the whole scene lies behind it.

Mounting to produce a window at 2m will give results typified by **Fig 6.1**. In this diagram, the picture frame itself becomes the window. The various objects in the scene all lie behind the window at different distances. (Because of the scale of reproduction of this, and similar diagrams, the window will not actually be located at 2m in the stereoscopic image when it is viewed. However, the relative positions of window and objects will be preserved, to illustrate the relevant points made in the text.)

The problem caused by "errors" outlined earlier in (1) to (3) can best be appreciated by considering a head and shoulders portrait taken at a distance of 1m. When viewed stereoscopically, the image appears in front of the window. The lower halves of the figures are missing, because the bottom edge of the frame appears to mask them. The anomaly is that the frame is actually further away than the figures, which is an unnatural effect (**Fig 6.2a**), though the brain may refuse to accept the evidence and the observer may "see" the window in front of the subject in that region. Bringing the stereo window forward restores normality (**Fig 6.2b**) and this can usually be done fairly easily, but is not always possible. Artificial "cutting" of part of a scene by one or more of the frame edges of the window is referred to as **window violation**. Either a closer window has to be created or the image moved back. This is discussed in Chapter 20.

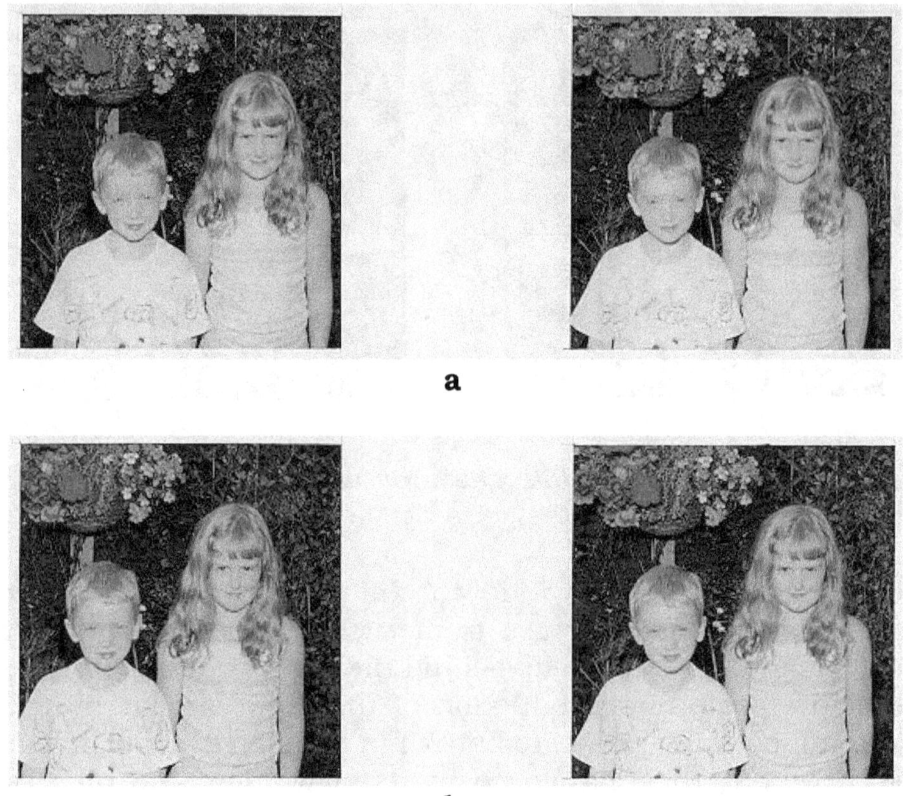

a

b

Fig 6.2
a *Head and shoulders portrait mounted incorrectly because the figures are "cut" by the lower edge of the stereo window.*
b *The same portrait mounted correctly*

For special effect, however, some objects can be allowed to protrude through the window, as long as they are clear of the frame edges (**Fig 6.3**). This kind of presentation can give a stereo picture dramatic impact, but it should be used with discretion.

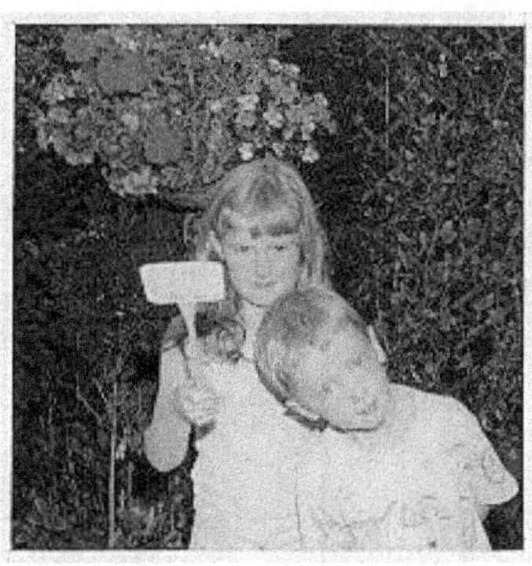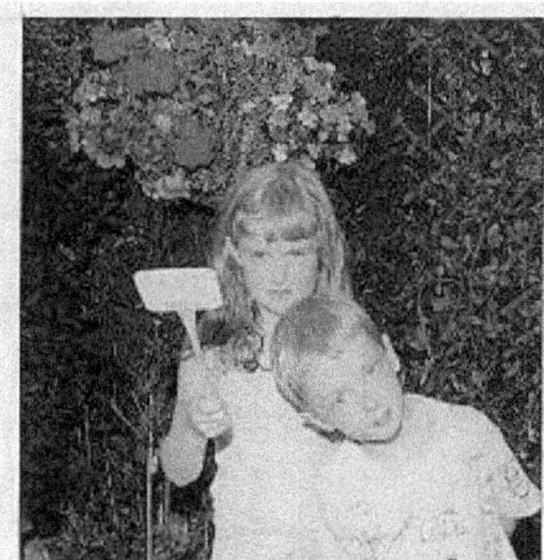

Fig6.3
Stereo pair with part of the subject protruding through the window. This is acceptable because the relevant part of the subject is not intersected by the frame.

6.3 General Approach to Mounting
6.3.1 Ground rules

Whether the images to be mounted are prints or transparencies, large or small, there are certain rules that must be adhered to for successful results. For the present, we shall concentrate on conventional stereograms (images side-by-side with the left image on the left).

Leaving aside for the moment the question of the stereo window location and how it is controlled, there are four important rules. To make the explanations clear we need to consider the significance of **homologous points** (or **homologues**). As mentioned in Chapter 1, Section1.3.2, these are corresponding points in the images, the top front left corner of a cube-shaped object or the top of a distant tree for example, that can be recognised easily in each of the two views forming the stereogram. Particularly important are homologues for very distant objects (infinity homologues) and those for the nearest object.

Rule 1 Homologues must be at the same height. Any given pair should lie on a horizontal line parallel to the top of the frame (**Fig 6.4**).

Rule 2 Infinity homologues should be set at a specified distance apart, of the order of 65mm (but different mounting techniques may require this distance to be varied slightly) (**Fig 6.5**).

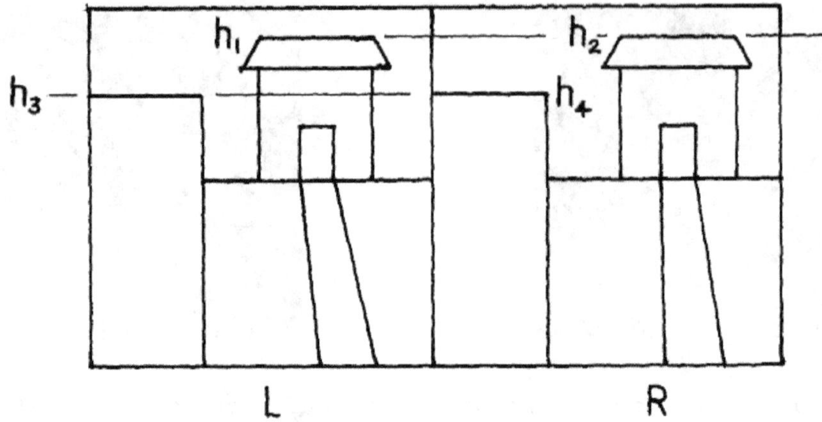

Fig 6.4
A correctly mounted stereo pair will have homologues at the same height, e.g. **h₁,h₂** *and* **h₃,h₄**

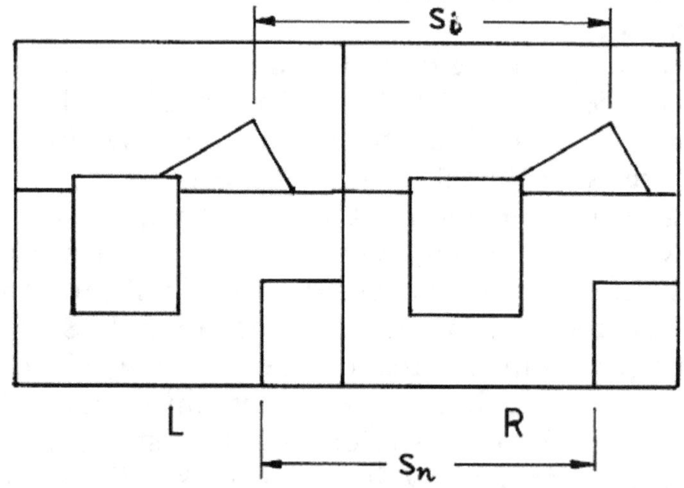

Fig 6.5
For correct mounting, infinity homologues must be set at a specific separation **s$_i$**, *in the region of 63 to 65mm depending upon the format. Alternatively, the separation of near objects can be set to a separation* **s$_n$**, *smaller than* **s$_i$**.

    Rule 3 Near point homologues should not be set closer than a specified distance, which will also depend upon the particular mounting technique.

    Rule 4 There should be no rotational differences between the two images, with reference to an axis perpendicular to the image plane (**Fig 6.6**).

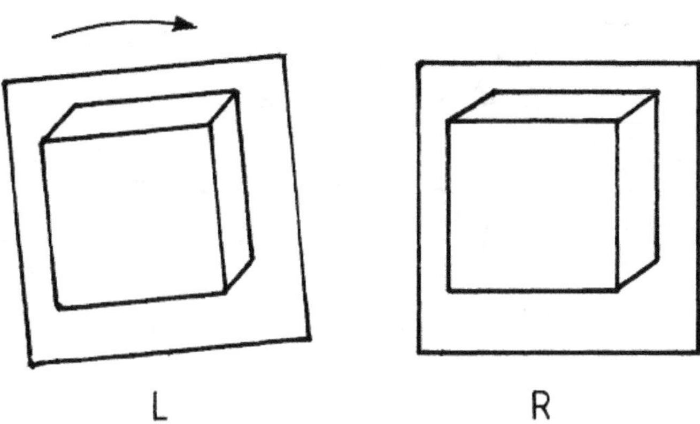

Fig 6.6
Rotational error in a mounted stereo pair. The left image needs to be rotated in the direction shown by the arrow.

If the photographs have been taken correctly, with the camera horizontal then there should be no height errors in the images themselves, or at least they will be very small. This will make mounting easier. Separate shots taken with a mono camera, without the assistance of slide bars, tripods or such aids, are more prone to height errors. However, if the individual photographs are truly horizontal, the error can easily be corrected during mounting. Even so, height errors can be introduced during mounting, which is the reason for Rule 1.

If the stereo camera is tilted about the lens axis when the scene is photographed (**Fig 2.1**) then mounting the film chips with their top and bottom edges parallel to the mount edges will give a proper stereo effect, but the images will also be tilted (**Fig 6.7a**). Rotation of the chips before securing them in the mount may correct the problem (**Fig 6.7b**) but this is a situation to be avoided, because it is more complex than it might at first appear.

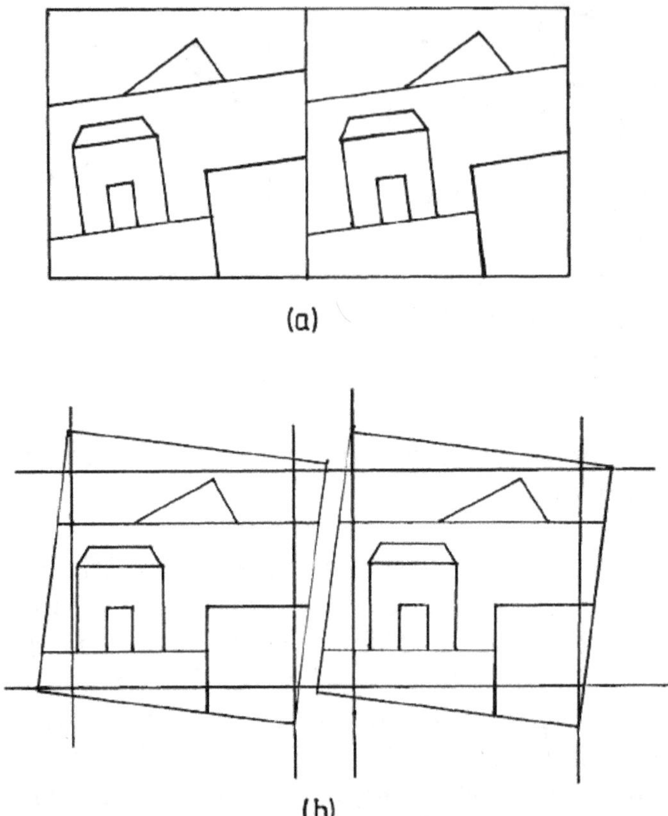

(a)

(b)

Fig 6.7
a *Stereo pair produced when the stereo camera is not horizontal when the picture was taken.*
b *Rotation and trimming may allow the images to be mounted successfully but there will be residual discrepancies in the location of homologues, worse towards the outer areas.*

6.3.2 Basic principles of mounting
Slides

With transparencies taken with a conventional stereo camera, it is necessary to cut the individual images from the film in order to transpose them into the correct configuration for viewing. Locations of the two images on the film vary with the image format (see Chapter 3, **Figs 3.8** and **3.10**, for example).

The individual film chips must be fixed accurately in place in the mount, which generally consists of a card or metal mask with two pre-cut apertures, over which the chips are secured. The mount apertures are slightly smaller than the images so that the positions of the latter can be adjusted without the margins being brought into view.

It is advisable to use a light box to illuminate the slides from the back and to incorporate a couple of lenses above the light box surface so that the images can be seen in greater detail to facilitate fine adjustments. The two lenses allow the image to be seen in 3D during the procedure. The film chips should be handled carefully throughout the mounting operation, to avoid dust, finger marks or scratches. The use of tweezers is recommended.

Ultimately, the images will be viewed from the non-emulsion side of the film (the shinier side) but it is sometimes convenient to mount from the back, placing the right image chip emulsion side up onto the left aperture of the (upside-down) mount and the left image chip over the right aperture (**Fig 6.8**).

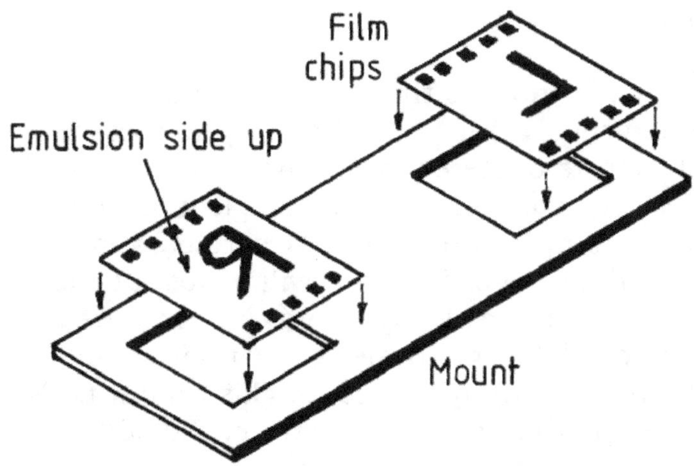

Fig 6.8
Recommended method of mounting from the back of the mount.

The chips, once positioned correctly, are then secured in place by clear adhesive tape strips. To allow for expansion and to avoid "popping" when slides are placed in a projector, it is advisable to affix only one edge of each chip in the mount. When the finished mount is turned over, the images will be seen in their correct configuration. Thin metal foil masks are an alternative form of mount; in these, the chips are usually inserted into cut-out tongues, which hold them securely but at the same time allow for some re-positioning, both horizontally and vertically (**Fig 6.9**).

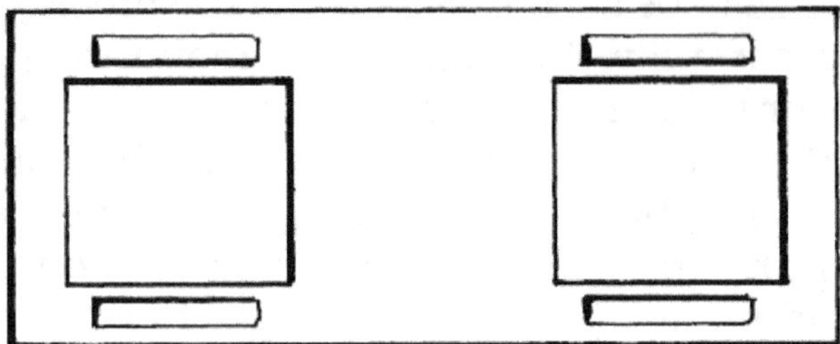

Fig 6.9
Typical aluminium foil mask with twin apertures and pressed-out flanges to hold the film chips.

The actual separation of the two film chips in the finished mount depends upon the format being used. Getting the right separation is one of the most critical aspects of stereo mounting.

When slides are taken either with a single mono camera or twin mono cameras, then the two-aperture mounts described above can still be used, but a substantial amount of each image will be lost at the sides by virtue of the narrower mount aperture. Many photographers like to retain the wider format of the standard 35nm frame and prefer to mount the slides in separate 50 x 50mm (2 x 2in) plastic or glass mounts. Because the two images of the stereo pair are entirely separate, the slides must be mounted in such a way that the images are correctly positioned when they are viewed. With this format, therefore, the plastic mounts are best taped together side-by-side, temporarily, with a 12mm (½in) wide spacer between them, to set the frame centres approximately 64mm apart.

Prints

With prints, the same principles apply. The left and right images have to be correctly aligned and positioned, and secured to a backing sheet. The separation of the prints will depend upon their size and the type of viewer that is to be used.

The photographer who makes his own prints and enlargements can simply print the negatives in sequence to give two images side-by-side on a single sheet of photographic paper, correctly transposed for viewing. However, to obtain a correctly positioned pair of images with correct framing to give a proper stereo window requires rather more care and thought, and a good understanding of the theoretical principles.

6.4 Mounting of 35mm Slides
6.4.1 Introduction

The first stage in mounting slides is to align the two images vertically and horizontally in the mount; the image of a given object must be at the same height in each of the finished frames and there must be no rotational errors, following the rules outlined above. The second stage is to adjust the relative positions of the two chips by sliding them towards or away from each other, until they are at the correct separation. The exact distance depends partly on the dimensions of the mount but should be around 65mm. Although various standards pertaining to the dimensions of stereo mounts have been published, one still finds small differences in the key dimensions of card mounts and masks made by different manufacturers.

By using commercially available mounts one of the problems of mounting is immediately overcome. This relates to the stereo window, which in standard mounts is designed to be located at about 2 metres. All the stereo photographer has to do is to position the film chips so that the whole of the image lies behind this pre-set window; this makes the task so much easier.

Ideally, the film chips have to be located with a degree of accuracy of a fraction of a millimetre, which seems formidable. However, there are ways of achieving this that are relatively painless! With the best will in the world we may still end up with minute discrepancies but these will be well within the margins of error; it is important, however, to aim at this ideal and to produce all stereograms to the same standard.

6.4.2 Depth range of subject matter

The stereo photographer will accumulate a large number of images of a variety of subjects, some of which will prove more difficult to mount accurately than others, because of the range of distances over which the subject extends. The easiest images to mount are those that include a very distant object, far enough away to be regarded as being at infinity, or those in which the nearest object is located exactly at 2 metres. To understand the precise placement of the film chips, assume that a scene of the form shown in **Fig 6.5** is to be mounted. This has been chosen because it contains an object at infinity (the mountain) and another at 2 metres, the closest permissible distance (following the rules outlined in Chapter 2, Section 2.3). Either the mountain or the near object individually would be sufficient to make mounting easy, but having both in the same image is a bonus which helps with the explanation.

When we understand the correct procedures for mounting this type of image, we will be in a better position to deal with stereo images in which objects at neither of these easily identifiable distances are present, For example, a stereo pair might have the furthest object at only 6 metres (20ft) away, or the nearest object no closer than 3 metres (10ft).

6.4.3 Separation of homologous points

Brief mention has already been made of homologues and their separations. Since these are important factors in mounting, their roles need to be explained.

As illustrated in Chapter 1, **Fig 1.6**, the separation of homologous points decreases as the object distance from the observer decreases. In **Fig 6.5**, the value of s_n for the nearest object at 2 metres distance (which we will denote as s_2) will be the smallest, compared with the separations for other objects further away, particularly those at infinity (separation s_i). Of course, s_i and s_2 are not fixed in value because they simply depend upon how far apart the film chips are placed. However, they are fixed in relation to each other; the difference between the two separations is constant (for a given image format). This arises from the geometry of image formation in the camera and the process of transposition of the images prior to mounting.

Any difference such as (s_i - s_2) is known as a parallactic difference or **deviation** (**d**), which will have a maximum value when measured between infinity homologue separation s_i and "nearest permissible object" homologue separation s_2, where s_2 refers to objects at 2 metres.

For 35mm stereo pairs in 5P or 7P format the deviation is given by:

$$\mathbf{d} = s_i - s_2 = 1.2\text{mm}$$

The reasons for this particular value are explained in Supplement S7, but all we need to know is its magnitude in order to understand its significance in mounting.

If the images are set so that s_i = 65mm, s_2 will be equal to 63.8mm; if s_i = 63.4mm, s_2 = 62.2mm and so on, the difference always being constant at 1.2mm. Setting appropriate s_i (and hence s_2) values according to the mount being used enables us to place the 3D image correctly in relation to the stereo window.

6.5 Mounting of 5P Format Images
6.5.1 Positioning the film chips in the mount

Stereo pairs taken with cameras such as the Stereo Realist use a stereo base of about 70mm which means that, strictly speaking, the film chips should be mounted such that s_i = 70mm. However, this would require divergent sight lines for most people if they were to view the resulting stereogram. For this reason the s_i value has been standardised at a lower value, 63.4mm in this format.

Various mounts for the 5P format, some made of card or plastic, others in the form of thin aluminium metal masks that can be incorporated into a card cover, are obtainable from specialist dealers. The important dimensions are those of the size and location of the two identical rectangular apertures. A typical mask (or card mount) is shown in **Fig 6.10**. This represents a normal mount, designed for use with subject matter in the range 2 metres (7ft) to infinity. (Other mounts exist with different window settings but they need not concern us here).

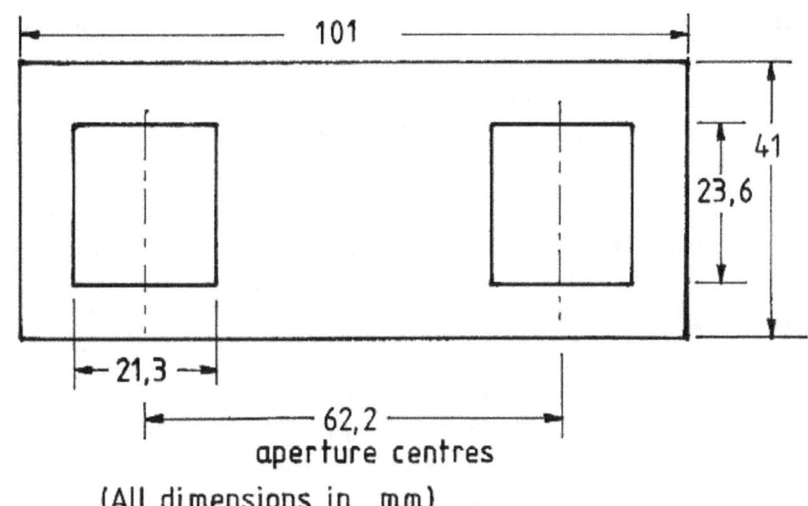

Fig 6.10
Dimensions of card mount for the Stereo Realist (5P) format.

The apertures themselves are slightly smaller than the film images to allow for adjustments when positioning the chips, without exposing the frame edges. Mounts from different suppliers may differ slightly in dimensions, but this is not significant. The key dimension is the distance between the aperture centres, which is set at 62.2mm; this corresponds also to the distance between corresponding edges of the two apertures. This sets the window position in relation to infinity.

Working from the back of the stereogram, if the film chips are now placed over the mount apertures as shown in **Fig 6.8**, and carefully aligned to avoid height and rotational errors, they can be adjusted towards or away from each other until the s_1 separation (measured between the mountain peaks) is equal to 63.4mm. This particular value can be estimated at a pinch with a good ruler because it is not too difficult to estimate the midpoint between two millimetre marks.

At this stage we can allow an error of about ± 0.1mm; 63.4mm can be set reasonably accurately at "just less than 63.5mm". Alternatively, a mounting gauge can be used (see section 6.6), which simplifies the measuring process.

Let us suppose for the moment that we have located the chips accurately, with s_1 = 63.4mm. From Section 6.3.4 above we know that the value of s_2 will be 63.4 − 1.2 = 62.2mm. This is exactly the same value as the mount aperture spacing, which means that the two left vertical edges of the aperture (and, similarly, the two right edges) will be located at exactly the same distance from the observer as the nearest object, at 2 metres. Thus the aperture forms a fixed window, located at 2 metres.

If the film chips had been set slightly further apart, with s_i = 63.5mm, for example, then s_2 would now have the value 62.3mm, marginally greater than the mount aperture separation. This will place the near object a short distance behind the window. Conversely, with the chips closer together, with s_i = 63.3mm, say, then s_2 becomes 62.1mm and the near object will be located in front of the window, nearer to the observer. This, of course, must generally be avoided.

Rather than relying purely on measurements of this kind, when an accuracy of 0.1mm is generally beyond the capability of a plastic ruler (apart from the case above, when estimating 0.5mm), the procedure usually adopted is as follows:

1. set the film chips with s_i = 63.4mm as accurately as possible
2. view the result in a stereoscope
3. readjust the film chips towards or away from each other until the near object is marginally behind the window, as seen in the stereoscope
4. repeat 3 as necessary.

With card mounts, the chips can be held in place temporarily with small strips of adhesive label, the kind that can be removed easily (non-permanent adhesive), until they are correctly located. They can then be fixed with small pieces of adhesive tape, taking care not to allow the tape to intrude into the aperture area.

When metal masks are used, the chips are held under the pre-cut tongues which hold the film securely yet allow some movement for final positioning (**Fig 6.9**).

The key to the fine tuning involved in adjusting the chip positions is to remember that:

1. moving the chips apart shifts the 3D image further away from the observer. All objects will appear more distant.
2. moving the chips closer together brings the 3D image closer to the observer. At some point, near objects will end up wholly or partly in front of the stereo window. This contravenes Rule 3 in Section 6.3.1.

If, in the extreme case, we were to set the film chips with s_i = 62.2mm, then in our hypothetical scene the mountain would appear to be located at the stereo window, just 2 metres away. All other objects in the scene would lie in front of the window. In theory, the whole scene would now resemble a small model with everything scaled down. It would also be distorted in other ways, as discussed in Chapter 19. However, the brain may still interpret the image as being of normal size. It seems to have a facility to ignore the evidence in favour of experience. Although the viewing geometry tells us that we are looking at a model, we can still "see" a life-sized scene. With viewing experience, we learn to recognise these distortions more easily for what they are.

When the chips are separated in order to "push" objects further away the image will become elongated in the depth direction. When the chips are moved closer to each other, the stereo image moves towards the observer and becomes more compressed in this direction. In the extreme case described, the original scene, originally extending from infinity to 2 metres, is now compressed into the range from 2 metres to I metre.

There is an additional clue to correct positioning of the film chips. When looking through a real window, the left eye will see a little more than the right eye of the right hand side of the scene. Similarly, the right eye sees more of the left hand side of the scene. These are monoscopic regions (each seen by only one eye) and they should also rightly appear in the stereogram when the chips are correctly masked by the frame (**Fig 6.11**). The amount of monoscopic image increases with distance behind the stereo window. It is zero at the window itself and is a maximum at infinity. The monoscopic areas will appear at the left edge of the right image and at the right edge of the left image. If the chips are correctly located with reference to the s_i or s_2 values, this should happen automatically.

The danger of moving the film chips too close together, perhaps in an attempt to bring the main subject of a rather distant scene nearer to the observer, is that **floating edges** can be created. For the purposes of explanation, imagine a correctly mounted stereo pair showing, quite properly, a monoscopic area on the left side of the right image and then moving the left chip towards the right. As the left chip is moved, more of the previously hidden part of the left side of the image will come into view, and at some point will match the corresponding part of the right chip. Further movement of the left chip will bring a new monoscopic area on the left of the left image. There will be a new monoscopic area on the right of the right image caused by the disappearance of the original right hand side of the left chip. The result is monoscopic areas on the wrong sides of the two images. When the stereogram is viewed, the edges will not fuse properly. The effect is unnatural and is irritating when present. Floating edges can also occur at the top and bottom of a frame if the film chips are not fixed at the same height in the mount, apart from the other problems that will arise in this circumstance.

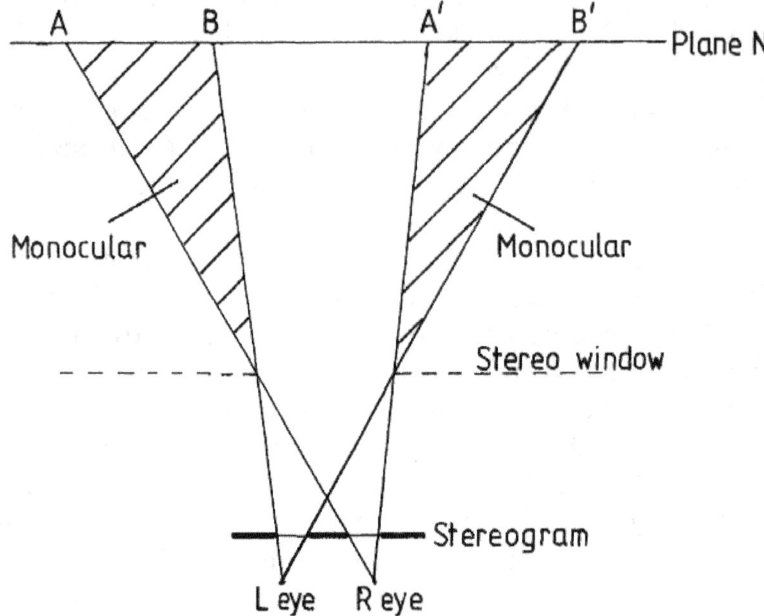

Fig 6.11
*The field of view of the right eye extends from A to A' on the reference plane
N, whereas that for the left eye extends from B to B'. Thus monocular areas
(shaded) appear in normal stereograms as in reality.*

6.5.2 Infinity vs near point referencing

So far, the mounting process has been described in terms of setting
the film chips to an infinity separation determined by s_i = 63.4mm (or the
value recommended for the format being used). If this is done, the near
point separation s_2 takes care of itself. We could equally well have mounted
the chips by setting the near point homologues to a separation s_2 = 62.2mm.
We know that if s_i = 63.4mm, s_2 must equal 63.4 – 1.2 = 62.2mm. By setting
the film chips with reference to s_2, s_i will "take care of itself". In other words
we can mount successfully by using either s_i or s_2 as the reference
homologue separation, depending upon whether the photograph includes
objects at infinity or at 2m. In our "ideal" scene we have the choice of both.

The problem is that many stereo pairs will not include objects either
at infinity or at 2 metres to act as references in this way. If the nearest object
distance is known exactly, it is possible to calculate its s_n value and
separate the relevant homologues accordingly. This is a rather tedious
solution and unlikely to be used much because it relies on remembering the
distance of the nearest object when the picture was taken. Not many
photographers would think about recording this kind of information, except
perhaps when using specialised techniques, as in close-up work for
example. However, for those who may wish to use the method, information
on s_n values is given at the end of Supplement S7.

Nevertheless, in order to mount pictures in which there are no infinity points or 2 metre objects, we can use our knowledge of s_1 and s_2 and make a compromise. One must first look at the stereogram carefully to find the most distant object or the nearest object, preferably one of each.

To position the chips correctly one must ensure that the distant object homologues are closer than s_1 and the near object homologues further apart than s_2. Since s_1 and s_2 represent the separations for infinity and nearest possible (2m) objects respectively, it follows that all objects at distances between will have homologue separations between the values 63.4 and 62.2mm. Either the distant object or the near one can be used as the initial reference, the other being used as a check.

The procedure might follow this sequence:

1. set the distant object homologues at 63.4mm and then move the chips fractionally closer
2. check that the near point homologues are not closer than 62.2mm
3. view the result and adjust the chips if necessary, by separating them slightly to move objects away or moving them slightly closer to bring the scene forward.

The overall result is a matter of judgement and there will be some flexibility in deciding the final location of the image in stereo space. The guideline should be that it "looks right", because there is no way of guaranteeing perfection.

6.5.3 Frame centre and film perforation referencing

Most stereo cameras using the 5P format have a built-in stereo window. As mentioned in Chapter 3, Section 3.3.3, the frame centres are set at 71.25mm apart, based upon 15 perforations. The lenses are each set slightly closer by 0.58mm giving a total of 1.16mm (= 1.2mm rounded up). The lenses are therefore 70.05mm apart. The 1.2mm difference sets the stereo window at 2m approximately and is linked to the value of $s_1 - s_2 =$ 1.2mm discussed earlier.

The significance of this is that another pair of reference points (apart from infinity and closest object homologues) is available for use in mounting. When the images are formed in the camera, the homologues for an object at infinity will be separated by 70.05mm and the frame centres by 71.25mm as shown in **Fig 6.12.**

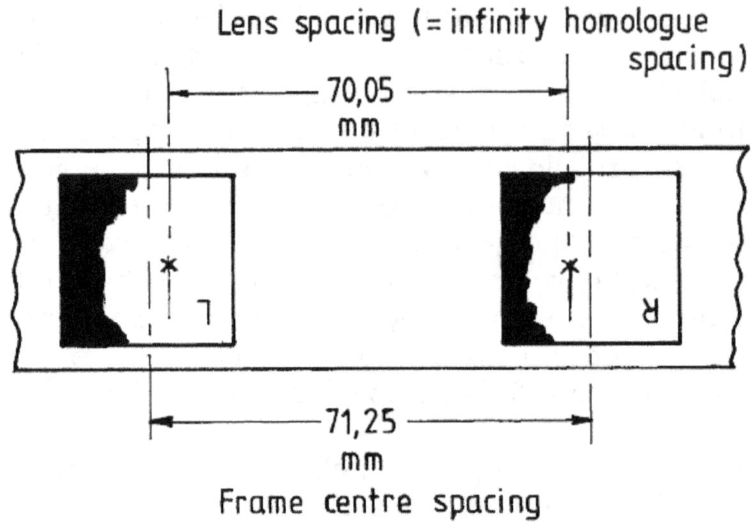

Fig 6.12
*Relationship between the lens spacing and frame separation in 5P format cameras. The difference of 1.2mm gives rise to a "built-in stereo window" at approximately 2m. The **x**'s mark infinity homologues. After transposition and mounting, the frame centres will be 1.2mm closer together than the infinity homologues (see also **Fig 6.13**).*

After the images have been transposed for mounting, the frame centres will be closer together than the infinity homologues (by 1.2mm) as in **Fig 6.13**. The infinity homologues can, therefore, be set correctly at 63.4mm apart if the frame centres are separated by 62.2mm. Now 5P format cameras are designed so that the vertical frame centre line passes through the centre of a film perforation (**Fig 6.13**). Although slack or wear in the winding mechanism of the camera may cause the image positions on the film to fall slightly off-centre, the 62.2mm distance can just as easily be measured between any two corresponding perforations in the two film chips

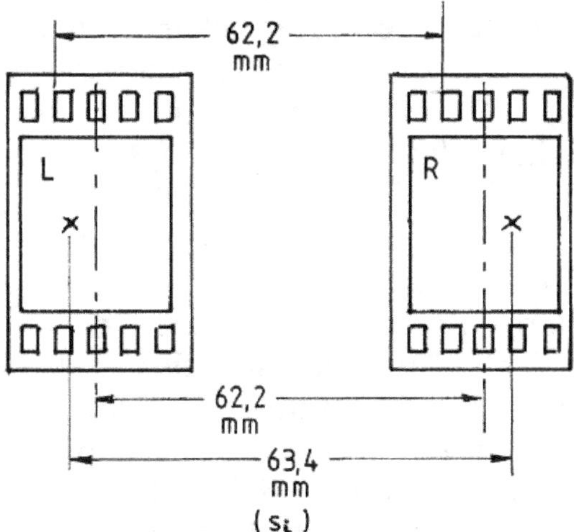

Fig 6.13
Film chips, originally located in the camera as in Fig 6.12, now transposed and separated for mounting. The infinity point separation is now reduced to 63.4mm from 70.05mm. This means that the frame centres will now be 1.2mm closer, at 62.2mm. In the 5P format, the centre perforations are located as shown. Mounting can therefore be based upon a 62.2mm separation between corresponding perforations.

The beauty of this method of spacing the film chips is that all homologues will be set automatically. It does not matter whether the scene covers a depth range from 2m to infinity or merely from 3m to 5m; everything should slot correctly into place. Even so, the resulting stereogram should be checked in a stereoscope and fine adjustments made, if necessary, as previously described. Film is subject to dimensional changes during processing and some shrinkage or stretching may occur and this can affect the positioning slightly.

For cameras that do not have a built-in stereo window, then the infinity homologue spacing will be equal to the frame centre spacing. This means that the film chips should be mounted with the frame centres (or corresponding perforation edges) set at 63.4mm apart (instead of 62.2mm). Again, all parts of the image should correctly fall into place once this is done.

6.6 Mounting Gauges

The need for accuracy in mounting has been emphasised in the preceding sections; references to fractions of a millimetre may well have convinced the reader that mounting is a fearfully difficult task. Certainly it requires patience and it is not something that can be hurried. Working consistently to the key separation values (e.g. s_i = 63.4mm) is important, but one does not have to rely on measuring them with a plastic ruler, a rather rough and ready method at best.

One can simply ignore measurements altogether and proceed by placing the film chips roughly centrally over their apertures, viewing the result in a stereoscope and making adjustments as necessary until the stereogram "looks right". The 3D image should be studied carefully at each stage of adjustment to identify:

1. parts of the image in front of the window. The remedy is to move the chips further apart
2. compression - not much apparent depth from the nearest to furthest objects. This also signifies that the chips are too close
3. stretching - the image extends too far from front to back. This means that the chips are set too far apart. In these circumstances it may be difficult to fuse the images without eyestrain, as the lines of sight may be divergent rather than parallel for objects at infinity.

These distortions are discussed more fully in Chapter 19; at this stage it is helpful just to be aware of them.

Perhaps the ideal solution to simple, accurate mounting is to use some kind of device to assist in precise placing of the film chips. A mounting gauge is an excellent example. Essentially, it consists of a few vertical lines on a transparent sheet, spaced accurately to give reference separations for s_1 and s_2. Examples of such gauges are shown in **Fig 6.14**; these are made by Reel-3D Enterprises in the USA and are available worldwide. Each format has its own gauge. The reference, near and far lines enable the film chips to be placed at the correct distance apart within the mount, while the horizontal lines allow height errors to be corrected.

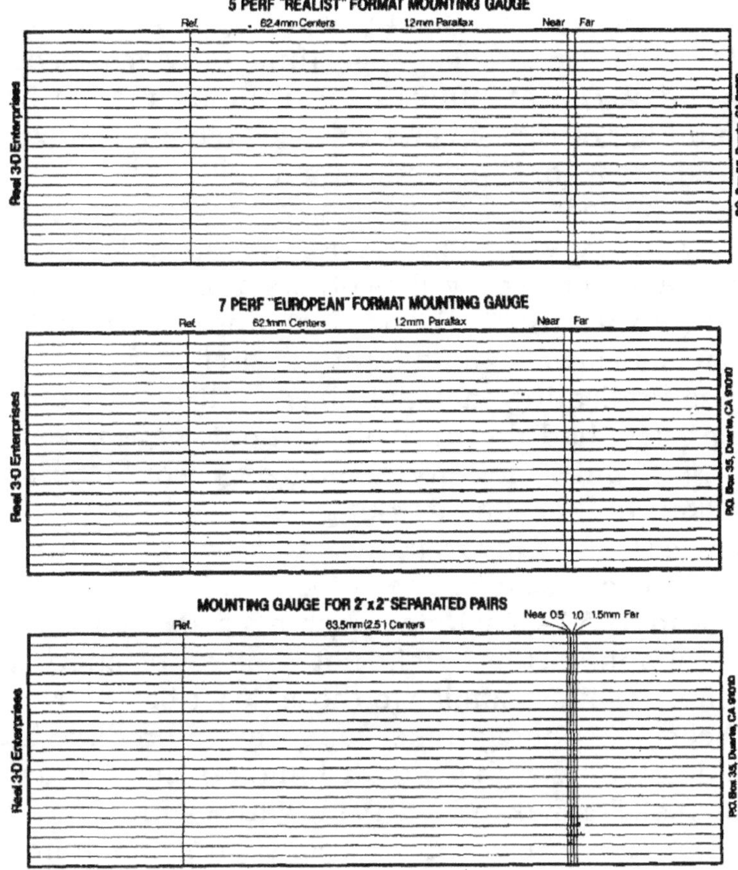

Fig 6.14
Mounting gauges for 5P, 7P and 50x50mm separated pairs. (Copyright: Reel 3D Enterprises. Reproduced with the permission of David Starkman and Susan Pinsky, proprietors.)

There is a minor difference between the dimensions quoted earlier and those marked on the Reel-3D Enterprises Realist (5P) Format gauge. On the latter, the frame centre separation is taken to be 62.4mm (instead of 62.2mm), which means that the infinity homologue separation will be 63.6mm (instead of 63.4mm). The difference $s_1 - s_2 = 1.2$mm, unchanged. Apart from this, the principles are exactly the same.

In use, the gauge can be taped onto a light box (for viewing slides) and preferably aligned against a straight edge or ledge on which the mount can also be placed. After setting the film chips roughly in position, the mount can be temporarily taped over the gauge so that the vertical reference line (marked "Ref") is aligned with a clearly defined near or distant object. The corresponding object point on the right image should fall either exactly on or to the right of the "Near" reference line. One can choose either a near or distant object as the initial reference and use the appropriate "Near" or "Far" reference line as the final marker. For slides with objects within the range 2m to infinity, all homologous points in the right image will fall on or between these two lines, if the corresponding point in the left image is aligned with the "Ref" line. The gauge thus provides clear markers for nearest objects and objects at infinity. During mounting, It will be necessary to move the mount left or right to enable specific homologues to be lined up with the "Ref" and "Near" or "Far" indicators.

Using the gauge will easily reveal any "problem" pictures, those that contain objects over too great a depth range, for example. If a scene includes an object at I metre distance as well as others at infinity, then after aligning infinity homologues with the "Ref" and "Far" lines, it will be found that the near object homologues will extend from the "Ref" line to a point to the left of the "Near" line, indicating that the object will be in front of the stereo window. Alternatively, had the near object homologues been aligned with the "Ref" and "Near" lines, infinity homologues would be spaced further apart than the "Ref" to "Far" line markings.

Other gauges of a similar nature are available through specialist dealers or stereoscopic societies. The Stereo Realist mounting kit, made in the late 1940's and 1950's, included a pronged tool for inserting the film chips into the mounts; this tool, not unlike a short plastic ruler, incorporated reference lines similar to those described above.

For the keen DIY photographer, one way to produce a simple gauge is to score fine lines with a sharp craft knife on the surface of a piece of clear plastic, such as Perspex. A measuring gauge with a Vernier scale could be set accurately to the required distances, such as 63.4mm and 62.2mm. The scribed piece could form the working surface of a mounting jig.

6.7 Mounting of 7P Format Images

Mounts for the 7P (European) format are similar to those for the 5P Realist format, except that the mount apertures are wider to allow for the greater picture width of the individual frames (**Fig 6.15**).

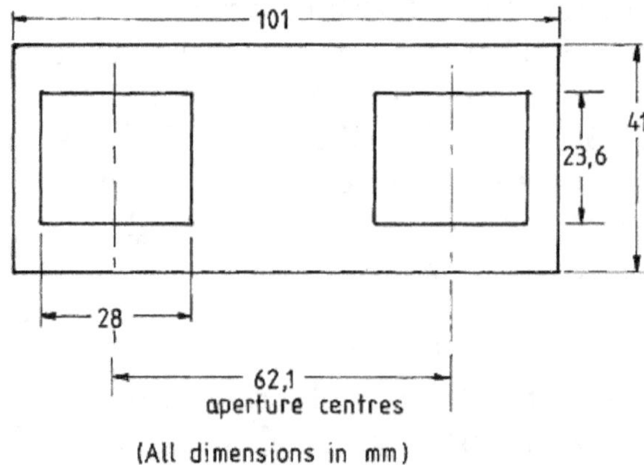

Fig 6.15
Dimensions of mount for the European 7P format for use with 35mm film images.

According to the Reel-3D Enterprises mounting gauge for the 7P format, the key dimensions for mounting (s_1 and s_2) are slightly different from those used in the Realist 5P format. The frame centre separation is quoted as 62.1mm, which together with the 1.2mm parallax displacement gives a value of 63.3mm for s_1.

There is so little difference between these values for the two formats that one could interchange the mounting gauges without serious effect. The key dimensions can vary by this amount in masks and mounts from different manufacturers. For example, the aperture centres on some metal 7P format masks, as measured by the author, are spaced at 62.5mm apart. It is probably best to regard this as the "near" reference dimension and to use 62.5 + 1.2 = 63.7mm as the infinity spacing.

Owing to the winding sequence of 7P format cameras, and the fact that the film advance distance is not a whole multiple of perforations (see Section 3.3.4), the configuration of sprocket holes along the top and bottom of the individual film frames will vary from one image to another. It means that the 7P format images cannot easily be mounted by using frame-centre or perforation edges as references marks. Having said that, stereo mounting of pairs taken with a Belplasca camera (with a 7P format) was at one time carried out in mounts containing pegs over which the perforations were located. This was possible because the winding system in this camera was designed to position the image frames on the film with alternate narrow and wide margins between them to produce some regularity in the location of perforations with respect to the frame margins.

6.8 Mounting of 4P Format Images (Nimslo)

Many stereo photographers use the Nimslo camera for slides, selecting the outer pair of the four half-frame images for the final stereogram. As described in Chapter 3, Section 3.4.4, these outer frames give a pair of images with a stereo base of only 55mm, less than that used in the 5P and 7P formats. Nevertheless, acceptable stereo results can be obtained, except that, with an approximate 15 % increase in the stereo base from taking to viewing (55mm to 63.4mm), there will be some distortion in the image, which, in theory, should appear slightly larger than life. This is a mild form of **giantism** but it is doubtful that the average observer will notice it.

An individual image frame in the Nimslo format measures 22 x 18mm. Mounts akin to those available for the 5P and 7P formats can be obtained for Nimslo 4P images, differing only in the size of the mount apertures, which are 21 x 16mm in size. The frame separation is the same as in the Realist and European formats, i.e. 62.2mm.

Either 5P or 7P mounts can be used for Nimslo slides by masking off 3mm each side of a Realist aperture or 6mm each side of a European format aperture (**Fig 6.16a** and **b**). This has to be done fairly accurately to ensure that both final apertures are of equal width and that the newly formed edges are vertical. Another way to achieve the desired masking is to use two card mounts or metal masks, overlapped as in **Fig 6.16c** and trimmed at the ends.

Although not essential, it is recommended that 3mm is masked from either the top or bottom edges of the 5P or 7P apertures, because the Nimslo images do not use the full width (24mm) of 35mm film for the picture height. There is sufficient margin above the image on the film to cover the gap but the right image is marked with a red dot for identification, and this might be distracting when the stereogram is viewed.

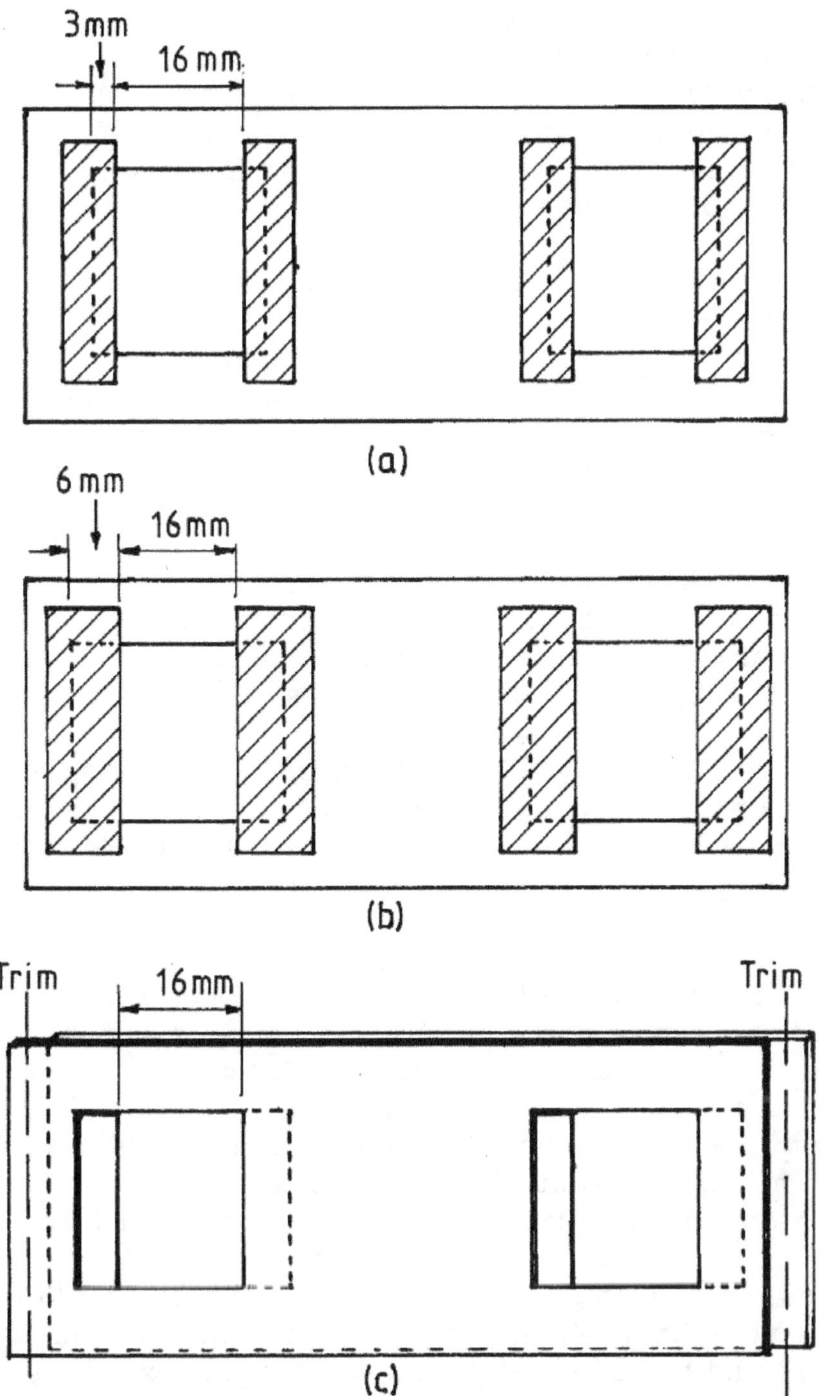

Fig 6.16
Adapting mounts to take Nimslo transparency pairs.
a *5P Realist mount with apertures masked by a total of 6mm using tape.*
b *7P European mount masked by a total of 12mm.*
c *Overlapping two 5P mounts to give apertures of 16mm width. The mount ends must be trimmed as shown.*

6.9 Mounting of 8P Format Images (35mm full frame)
6.9.1 Use of European format mounts

Landscape format 35mm full frame slide pairs can easily be mounted in 7P format mounts, provided that the principal content of the scene will fit within the 28mm width of the mask aperture, because about 8mm of the original frame width will be lost. This means that the left edge, right edge, or parts of both will be masked. The actual film may not need to be physically trimmed unless it protrudes from the end of the mount, which could occur in the extreme.

Using 7P mounts in this way is recommended only in special circumstances rather than as normal procedure. For example, it may be easier to take close-ups with a mono camera by sequential exposures. Employing 7P mounts enables the stereogram to be included in a set of others taken with a stereo camera, thus maintaining a constant image frame width in the series.

With some "Siamesed" full frame cameras, there is no built-in stereo window. This means that there will be additional monoscopic regions in each image that have to be masked off (Chapter 18, Section 18.2). Full frame mounts are not appropriate in this case, so the 7P mount is a useful alternative.

Mounts are now available for full frame 35mm images; these have double apertures, as in the Realist and European mounts already described, but with widths of 33mm. It should be pointed out, however, that if such mounts are used in Realist type stereoscopes, there will be some image cut-off.

6.9.2 Use of two separate 50 x 50mm (2 x 2in) mounts

In order to view or project full frame stereo pairs (or the 33mm width frames that are produced in some "Siamesed" stereo cameras, standard 50 x 50mm (2 x 2in) mounts can be used. Although process-paid transparency films are returned in such mounts, the photographer will not only wish to use something more substantial, but will need to remount the film chips to obtain the proper homologue separation when the two pictures are used as a 3D pair.

The standard adopted is that the frame centres should be set apart at a distance of 63.5mm (2.5in) in the mount. Since the mounts are 2in wide, they should be laid side-by-side with a gap of exactly 0.5in between them. This can be done quite easily with a plastic or card spacer piece, temporarily taped to the two mounts (**Fig 6.17**).

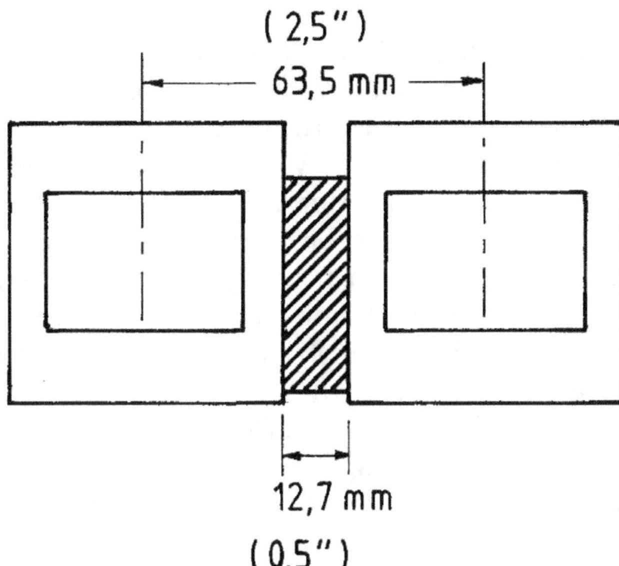

Fig 6.17
Mounting two 50 x 50mm separated pairs. The mounts should be temporarily joined by a spacer to give a 63.5mm (2½in) frame centre separation. The spacer should be ½in wide (the imperial unit is more convenient here).

Because many of these separated pairs are viewed by projection, using two separate slide projectors, it is important to standardise the infinity homologue separation. In projection it is necessary to ensure that infinity homologues are, say, 63.5mm (2.5in) apart on the screen, once the projectors have been set up (see Chapter 8). Because the two beams of light are not parallel, then slides which produce a 63.5mm homologue separation on a typical home screen of just over 1.2m (4ft.) would give a separation of some 190mm if projected onto a 3.6m (12ft.) screen. It is sometimes recommended that the s_i value should be chosen to suit the projecting conditions that are to be used. For the larger sized screens the s_i value will have to be smaller and vice versa. The following values are generally suggested:

	s_i
1.2m (4ft) screen (home viewing)	65mm
1.8m (6ft) screen	64.5mm
3.6m (12ft) screen	64mm

The values quoted above are set during mounting while the two mounts are temporarily joined. The values chosen are all greater than the frame separation itself, which places infinity objects behind the stereo window. However this creates a difficulty because by choosing, say, 64mm for s_i means that the parallax deviation will be 64 − 63.5 = 0.5mm, instead of the usual 1.6mm. This will place the stereo window much further back than the notional 2m location. Reducing the frame separation is no answer because this will simply restore the status quo.

In the long run, it is probably better to ignore these alternative s_i values of 64.5 and 64mm and stick to a 1.5mm difference between frame separation and s_i during mounting. With longer projection distances, the infinity point spacing on screen can be more easily controlled by adjusting the inter-lens spacing on the projector (see Chapter 8, Section 8.3.1).

The Reel-3D Enterprises mounting gauge for separated 50 x 50mm pairs shows three "Far" reference lines for parallax displacements of 1.5 (replacing the more usual 1.6 mm in this instance), 1.0 and 0.5mm. The s_i values quoted above are obtained by adding these displacements to the frame centre spacing (e.g. 63.5 + 1.5 = 65mm).

Whatever the s_i value chosen, the slides can be comfortably viewed in simple viewers such as the Pinsharp, described in Chapter 5, Section 5.3.10.

6.10 Mounting of Prints
6.10.1 Introduction

There is much less standardisation regarding print sizes and mounting practice than with transparencies. Because prints are usually enlarged from the negatives, they can often be viewed with stereoscopes that do not incorporate any magnification of the images. It is probably true to say that print viewing conditions are generally less "correct" than slide viewing conditions, not that the latter are always orthodox. Whereas most slide viewers are designed to give near-orthostereoscopic viewing conditions, in many stereo print systems the viewing perspective is considerably different from that in the camera (see Supplement S1). To the average person, the results may be quite acceptable, but the purist will tend to follow the best practice at all times, and make the necessary changes to achieve it.

6.10.2 Normal configuration (side-by-side)

Compared with the mounting of transparencies, there is a little more freedom in mounting prints because there are many stereoscopes and other viewing aids that enable the prints to be more widely separated than the 65mm norm for infinity points. It is important, therefore, to mount the two images to suit the particular viewer to be used. As with slides, the prints must be correctly aligned horizontally and vertically. This should be done with reference to homologous points and not the print borders. The reason for this is that the print borders will not coincide with those on the negatives owing to the slight cropping that occurs during commercial printing. These will be arbitrary, and the amount of cropping may be slightly different in each image of the stereo pair.

Once the positions of the prints in the stereogram have been established, the edges can be trimmed to produce a proper stereo window. To do this, the prints are trimmed at the sides. In effect, "apertures" have to be created corresponding to the pre-cut ones in slide mounts. The difference is that with transparencies we have to shift the film chips until they lie in the correct location relative to the fixed apertures in the mount. With prints, they are first spaced correctly and then the window has to be created at the right distance by trimming the left or right edges as appropriate. The exact location of the window is not critical as long as the image lies behind it in the finished stereogram, unless special effects are desired.

The procedure is not too difficult, as illustrated in **Fig 6.18** and outlined below:

1. place the prints temporarily as shown to a predetermined s_i value (say 64mm for illustration)
2. locate the nearest object (the gate in **Fig 6.18**) and measure its distance from (in this case) the right hand side in each print
3. trim the right hand edge of either the left or right print so that the distance a_L is greater than a_R. Usually it will be the right hand print that is trimmed, but it depends upon the techniques used in taking the stereo pair. The difference between the two measurements should be no more than a few millimetres, in accordance with the monoscopic areas within the image (see Section 6.5.1)
4. with the prints separated as shown (s_i = 64mm) measure s_n, the separation between near point homologues. Trim the left hand side of each print to make them of equal width s_w, where s_w is slightly less than s_n.
5. fix the pictures permanently in place according to the s_i value selected.

By making s_w smaller than s_n, the subject should lie entirely behind the window. This assumes that the nearest object has been correctly selected as a reference. One may find on viewing that other objects present are actually nearer than that originally used and they will protrude through the window. As long as there is no window violation, nothing more need be done. If there is interaction between objects and the frame edges, then more must be trimmed from each print, from opposite sides (e.g. left side of left print and right side of right print). This will bring the window further forward in relation to the subject.

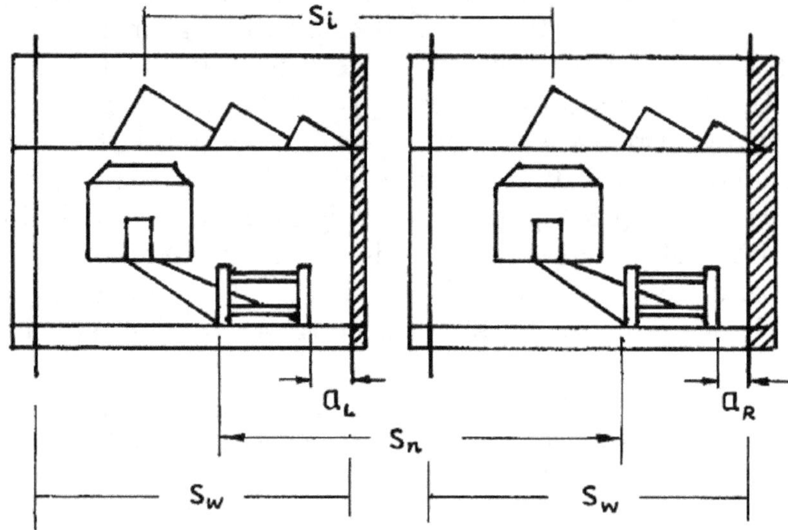

Fig 6.18
Mounting of prints to produce a correct stereo window Using a suitable near object (the gate) as a reference, the prints are trimmed, here on the right hand side, so that **aL** *is slightly larger than* **aR**. *Then both prints are trimmed to the same width* **sw**. *They are then separated to give a specified* **si** *value, around 65mm*

6.10.3 Homologous points in prints

The principles discussed in Section 6.4.3 regarding s_i, s_n and s_2 values can equally be applied to the mounting of prints. We can use these values to set the stereo window at 2m with some precision, assuming that we view the prints with correct perspective.

Since a print is an enlarged version of the negative, all parallax deviations of homologous points (ie $(s_i - s_n)$ values) will be magnified values of what appears on the negatives.

To illustrate this, let us assume that we have 152x102mm (6x4in) prints from 35mm negatives in portrait format. Because the prints are so wide (102mm) we shall have to make s_i about 100mm and view with a suitable stereoscope that can accommodate this setting.

The magnification **V** is given by:

$$V = 100/24 = 4.2$$

This is approximate because of the cut-off in commercial printing. The actual **V** value will be slightly greater, but our calculation will be accurate enough.

On the negative the parallax displacement $(s_1 - s_2) = 1.2$mm for 35mm lenses as used in the 5P format. Therefore on the print this difference will be 4.2 times larger, i.e. 4.2 x 1.2 = 8.4mm.

For a 2m stereo window the print has to be trimmed so that its width s_w is equal to the s_2 separation (or just less than this to play safe).

$$\text{Thus} \qquad s_2 = s_i - d$$
$$= 100 - 8.4$$
$$= 91.6\text{mm}$$

Trimming the prints to a width of 91mm will give the desired stereo window close to 2m under ideal viewing conditions.

The parallax displacement will depend upon the in-camera geometry, so for 50mm lenses the value of 1.2mm should be replaced by 1.6mm (see Supplement S7).

6.10.4 View Magic mounting ("over and under")

The principle of mounting and viewing stereograms in which the right image is placed above the left, instead of side-by-side, was outlined in Chapter 5, Section 5.3.8. Although the basic idea is simple, the mounting procedure needs to be tailored to the particular viewing device used.

The View Magic system is designed to use a viewing distance of around 12in (300mm) and the prints have to be mounted with the horizontal centre lines 4in (102mm) apart (**Fig 5.29**). The basic procedure is as follows:

1. align the prints by eye with the right print above the left
2. fix the lower print in place on the mounting card ensuring that it is horizontal
3. align the right print to an accurate 4in separation by reference to a simple transparent mounting guide which has two horizontal lines spaced by this distance
4. fix the top print in place.

The prints are mounted with their vertical edges in line. Before they can be fixed to the mounting card they have to be trimmed to produce a suitable stereo window. There are two recommendations (**Fig 6.19**):

1. trim the two prints at the right and left edges of both prints to the same foreground detail in order to produce a normal window, with the rest of the scene behind it
2. trim the two prints to the same background points to produce a "distant" window with the subject standing above the print plane. This "pop-out" technique is effective with some subjects provided that there is no window violation.

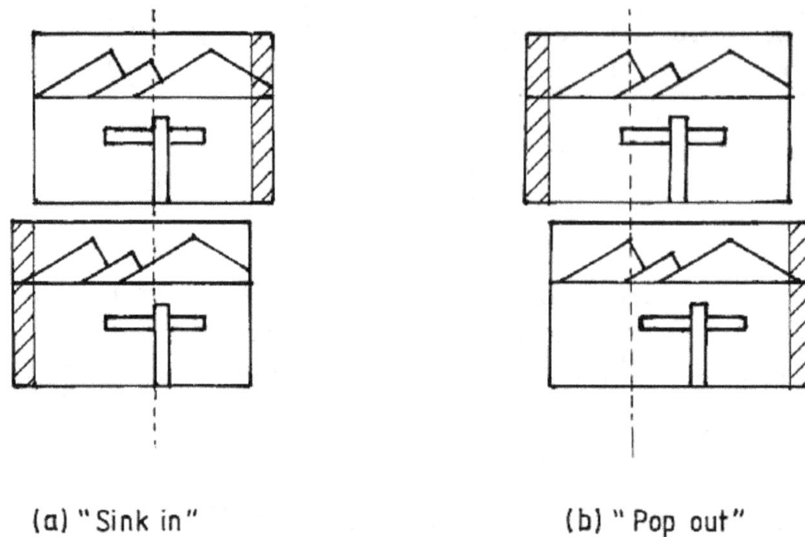

Fig 6.19
Trimming of prints for the View Magic system to give a "sink-in" effect (image below the plane of print) as in **a**, *or a "pop-out" effect (image wholly or partly above plane of print) as in* **b**. *For* **a**, *nearest objects are aligned before trimming the shaded portions. In* **b**, *the most distant objects are aligned before trimming.*

When taking the photographs, it is recommended in the View Magic Manual that the amount of camera shift (i.e. stereo base) with sequential exposures should be adjusted to produce no more than a ¼in (6mm) shift of foreground relative to the background in the print. This is approximately equal to the standard parallax deviation of 1.6mm for a 50mm lens multiplied by 4.2, the enlargement factor for 150 x 100mm prints. It is also another way of expressing the "one in thirty" rule (Chapter 7, Section 7.2.4) and not having too great a subject range (Supplement S9).

The implications of the over and under mounting technique as described above are that infinity homologues in the final stereogram will either be in line vertically (for images that pop out) or separated by about 6mm, for images that sink into the page. The infinity sight lines in both cases will converge when viewing, and the image will appear small, like a model, an example of the **puppet theatre effect** (see Chapter 8, Section 8.11 and Chapter 19, Section 19.3.4). An alternative method of mounting is suggested in Chapter 20, Section 20.5.

CHAPTER 7: HYPERSTEREOSCOPY AND HYPOSTEREOSCOPY
Changing the Stereo Base

7.1 Introduction
7.1.1 The stereo base

In order to reproduce our spatial world as a 3D image, it is logical to use a stereo base equal to the natural one, the average eye-spacing; the mean value (around 65mm) is normally adopted, even though to achieve a perfect reconstruction of the original scene the stereo base should exactly match the eye spacing of the person viewing the stereogram. It is impossible, therefore to use a stereo base that is perfect for everybody, but the differences in the appearance of any one stereogram to various observers will be only marginal.

Most stereo photography does in fact make use of either 70 or 63mm (for the 5P or 7P formats respectively), although slightly larger stereo bases are becoming more common owing to the increasing use of twin mono cameras coupled together. It is often impossible to rig the two cameras side-by-side or base-to-base to give a stereo base as "low" as 65mm. These differences are not detrimental in any way; the slightly larger stereo bases will enhance the depth effect, which is all to the good.

7.1.2 The need for stereo base changes

The reader has been advised not to include any object closer than 2m in a scene, for general stereo photography. If this advice is followed, satisfactory stereo images are virtually guaranteed, as far as the technicalities are concerned. Whether the results are well exposed, sharp and aesthetically satisfying is another matter.

Our perception of depth is more pronounced at close distances and diminishes as the distance between subject and observer increases; this has already been mentioned in Chapter 1, Section 1.3.2. At first, it may seem rather odd to restrict the near distance to about 2 metres. Although subjects closer than this can be photographed in 3D, standard techniques do not give satisfactory results. With very close subjects the normal lens spacing may not allow each lens to capture the entire scene. To overcome this it is necessary to reduce the stereo base; the closer the object, the smaller is the stereo base required. Reduced base (i.e. less than the 65mm "norm") stereoscopy is termed **hypostereoscopy**.

At the other end of the scale, stereo photographs of scenes that include mainly distant objects are often disappointing as 3D images. A sense of space will be experienced, if the stereogram has been correctly mounted, but little depth will be seen in the objects themselves. A distant mountain, for example, will appear to be flat; the impression may be one of viewing a two-dimensional mountain, but at some distance away. The solution is to enhance the depth of the object by increasing the stereo base to several metres or even more; stereoscopy using a larger than normal base is known as **hyperstereoscopy**.

7.1.3 Effect of stereo base on image perception

As the heading implies, there are differences in the way that we see a 3D image that has been produced by using a smaller or larger stereo base but it takes some experience to appreciate them and they will probably go unnoticed by the majority of people.

From a theoretical viewpoint, the changes in the appearance of the image can be understood if one thinks of the two lens positions as eye positions. For simplicity, assume that the sequential exposure method is being used with a mono camera. If two pictures of a distant mountain are taken with the lens positions 65 metres apart, for example, it is as if a giant with an eye spacing of 65 metres is viewing the scene When we view the stereogram with our 65mm eye spacing, the scale is reduced and the scene appears like a model exactly 1000 times smaller.

When a small stereo base is used, the effect is similar, but in reverse. The image will appear larger than life, as if we had become smaller, with an eye spacing of only 13mm, for example.

To summarise, in hypostereoscopy the image appears larger than it does in reality; this effect is known as **giantism**.

With hyperstereoscopy, the converse is true, the image appearing smaller than in reality; this effect is known as **lilliputism** or **dwarfism.**

Whether we become aware of these changes depends on the degree of reduction or enlargement of the stereo base and to a great extent on the individual, as suggested earlier. Our brains can tolerate considerable distortions (which, technically, is what these changes are) without experiencing any sense of "something being wrong"; the image may well be accepted for what we know it to be rather than what it actually is as an optical image. The scene of the mountain will probably be accepted without comment as a true representation. It can in part be attributed to our experience. We see images of familiar objects and we are aware of the fact that mountains are large objects, that the people in the scene are mostly between 5 and 6 feet in height, and so we are led to believe that the scene is natural in size, even though the optical information which is being fed to our brain is that the image corresponds to a model of, perhaps, a few metres in size.

We are partly conditioned in this by our experience of two-dimensional images as mono photographs, television images and so on, most of which are viewed under incorrect conditions of perspective and scale. We accept magnified images of insects, for example, without feeling that they represent giant creatures of horrific appearance. All in all, the changes need not concern us too much, but it is important to know that they exist.

7.2 Hyperstereoscopy
7.2.1 Basic principles

The use of a much larger stereo base presents few problems and successful results can be produced relatively simply. In contrast, short base photography (hypostereoscopy) requires a little more thought and some additional techniques in certain circumstances.

In hyperstereoscopy, one simply takes two shots of a scene from two separate viewpoints in a line, several metres or greater apart, moving the camera parallel to itself (Chapter 2, **Fig 2.3**). Certain procedures, dealt with later, should be followed for the best results. The object of hyperstereoscopy is to increase the observer's depth perception of distant scenes and relatively close objects should not be included. The greater the stereo base, the more pronounced is the effect, bearing in mind that so is the miniaturisation of the image.

To give some indication of the effect of the larger stereo base, we need to consider the potential of the human eye to distinguish small differences in depth. This quality is known as **stereo acuity** or the **stereopsis threshold**, and is discussed in Chapter 16, Section 16.2.2. Stereo acuity can be defined as the angle **p** in **Fig 7.1** such that the objects **A** and **B** can just be distinguished as two separate entities.

Angles p_1 and p_2 represent the parallaxes of points **A** and **B** respectively. Geometrically, $p_1 - p_2 = p$ so if the difference in parallax between two points such as **A** and **B** is just equal to the stereo acuity, we shall just be able to separate them in space. As **Fig 7.2** indicates, the minimum distinguishable depth difference between two objects increases with viewing distance; in fact it increases approximately in proportion to the square of the distance ($\mathbf{D^2}$). Stereo acuity varies from person to person and is also affected by the conditions under which the scene is viewed. The smaller the value of the parallax angle **p** the better one can distinguish small depth differences. If we take **p** as 30 seconds of arc (30") as a representative value[3] (though optimistic for many conditions, perhaps) we can compare stereo depth perception in different situations. For example, with a stereo base of 65mm the distance $\mathbf{\Delta D}$ in **Fig 7.1** (which can be regarded as a depth step based upon angle **p**) varies with the distance $\mathbf{D_N}$ as shown in **Table 7.1**.

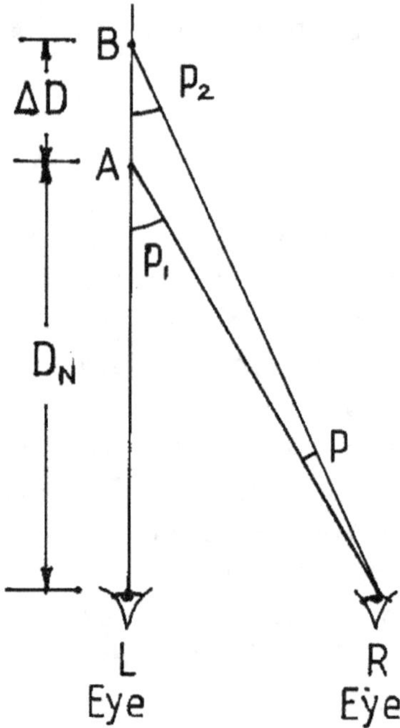

Fig 7.1

Definition of stereo acuity as the angle **p** *subtended by two points* **A** *and* **B** *that are just distinguishable as separate points.* **p** = **p₁** − **p₂**

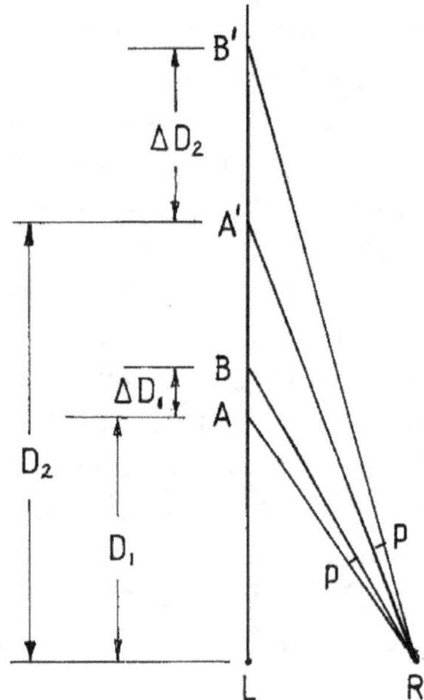

Fig 7.2

Variation of depth step **ΔD** *with distance. For a given stereo acuity* **p**, **ΔD** *(the minimum distinguishable depth step) is larger at greater distances (* **ΔD₂** *is larger than* **ΔD₁**). *Small details of depth are thus more easily discerned at close distances.*

TABLE 7.1

D_N (metres)	ΔD
2	8.65mm (⅓in)
10	228mm (9in)
200	160m (525ft)

(The stereo base b = 65mm)
(See Chapter 16, Section 16.2.3 for fuller details of stereo acuity)

This means that if an object is located at 10m, for example, a second object 228mm behind it can just be distinguished as separate. From **Table 7.1** it can be seen that the size of the depth step that enables the observer to distinguish that two objects are at different distances increases markedly with distance.

The effect of increasing the base can be appreciated from the following. With a near distance D_N = 200m and a stereo base b = 5m the ΔD value is reduced from 160m to 1.2 m approximately (3.75ft). Using the larger base enables the observer to distinguish finer depth detail at this distance.

The above figures are for comparison purposes only and should not be taken as absolute values. Stereo acuity will be poorer in the photographic image than in the original scene; it will also be worse for a projected image compared to one viewed in a stereoscope, so it is not easy to select a truly representative value for p. The examples above at least illustrate the qualitative variation of depth perception with distance and stereo base.

7.2.2 Hyperstereoscopy in practice

The recommendations set out in Chapter 2, Section 2.3 are still valid for photography with a larger than normal stereo base except that the 2metre limit for nearest objects has to be modified as will be explained later.

On most occasions requiring a large stereo base, the sequential exposure technique is the most likely one to be used, with a single mono camera, rather than two simultaneous shots, using two cameras. This means that static scenes will tend to be the norm, although any moving objects are less likely to cause serious false stereo effects if they are far away and moving slowly. Even so, it is best to take the two exposures with as short a time interval between them as possible. Apart from obvious moving objects such as people or vehicles, clouds can be troublesome as they drift. The general rule is to follow their movement as best as possible. If clouds are moving from right to left across the sky, for example, the right exposure should be taken before the left.

Distant objects moving towards or away from the camera will cause less trouble; the apparent change in size will be negligible.

Because of the need to have two cameras widely spaced or having to walk several metres between exposures, it is particularly important to keep the camera parallel to the subject and to avoid height errors, as shown in Chapter 2, **Figs 2.3** and **2.4**. A particular difficulty in some situations is that near objects might intrude and appear in only one of the images.

If the two exposures are made from a relatively high viewpoint, the photographer will be more remote from nearby foreground, and this helps to avoid the inclusion of close objects.

The techniques that can be used for hyperstereoscopy are outlined below:

1. **mono camera** - two separate exposures spaced by an appropriate distance. The two separate exposures could be made in different ways, for example, by walking from viewpoint 1 to viewpoint 2, or by taking separate shots from a moving car, train, boat, or aeroplane and, to some extent, trusting to luck! It is not so much the stereo base that matters as the avoidance of unwanted foreground objects.

2. **"traditional" stereo camera** - if the camera has a double exposure facility, the camera can be used as a mono camera. The left image is taken with the right lens covered, then without winding the film, the right image is taken from the new position with the left lens covered. If the camera will not allow double exposures then a standard (normal base) stereo shot can be taken at each of the two viewpoints forming the extended stereo base. Either image from the first exposure position can be used together with either image taken from the second viewpoint to make a hyperstereogram. The remaining images will make another, almost identical to the first. This method does use more film, of course, but is the only solution when no other facilities are to hand.

3. **two separate mono cameras** - these can be spaced and lined up correctly to avoid foreground and the two views checked in advance. They may even be fired simultaneously. It may be possible to use a remote control firing device, though electronic systems are likely to be expensive. As an alternative, the two shutters can be fired simultaneously by two people. As always, the two cameras should really be identical models with closely matched optics.

7.2.3 Choice of stereo base

For hyperstereoscopy the size of the base is not critical; on the other hand, the choice has to be a sensible one. Ferwerda[16] points out that if we assume that the stereo effect will be good from 2m to 65m, for a stereo base of 65mm, then increasing the stereo base by a factor of 10, to 650mm, means that the stereo effect will be observable at distances ten times as large, that is from 20 to 650m. While it may be argued that the 65m upper limit is rather pessimistic, the general point is valid.

Ferwerda concludes, therefore, that the best stereo effect is achieved in the range 30**b** to 1000**b,** where **b** represents the stereo base. With a standard base of 65mm the range will be 2m to 65m as stated above. The lower value (30**b**) is based upon the "one in thirty" rule, which allows the stereo base to be calculated to suit the prevailing circumstances. This is discussed in the next section.

7.2.4 The "one in thirty" rule

This is a rule of thumb that, in a sense, applies to all stereo situations. It is especially useful in hypostereoscopy as will be discussed later, but its merit in hyperstereoscopy is that it keeps a kind of balance between selecting too small or too large a stereo base.

Fig 7.3 shows the geometry of normal stereoscopy with a base of 65mm and a nearest object distance of 2 metres, a combination that should be by now a familiar one. The "one in thirty" rule is based upon preservation of this geometric configuration when using different stereo base values. By retaining the same geometry we shall avoid having too great a depth range, from nearest to furthest object, within the scene (see Supplement S9).

In **Fig 7.3** the ratio **b**/**D$_N$** = 65/2000 = 0.0325. This approximates to a ratio of 1/30 and the rule is interpreted by making the stereo base equal to one-thirtieth of the distance **D$_N$** of the nearest object that will be included in the scene, ie **b** = **D$_N$**/30.

Application of this rule is not obligatory, but it is worth considering if only to avoid using too large a base in relation to the nearest object. It is better to use a stereo base less than that determined by the rule than one which exceeds it. In making **b** = **D$_N$**/30 one is effectively placing the near object close to the stereo window when the image is mounted in the conventional way. In fact, keeping the stereo base as small as is practicable minimises the miniaturisation of the image (lilliputism).

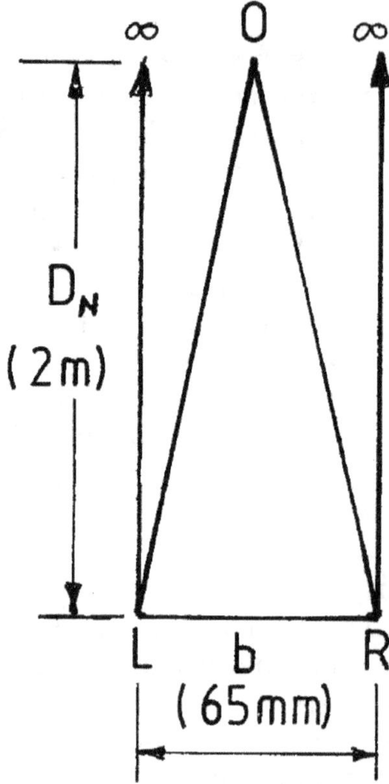

Fig 7.3
*Geometry of nearest permissible object location with reference to the camera lenses (**L** and **R**) leading to the "one in thirty" rule. **b**/**D_N** = 65/200 = 0.0325 = 1/30 approximately.*

Some representative **D_N** and corresponding **b** values are given in **Table 7.2** below:

TABLE 7.2

	Metres				Feet			
Distance of closest object **D_N**	60	100	300	500	200	300	1000	1500
Stereo base **b** (=**D_N**/30)	2	3.3	10	16.7	6.7	10	33.3	50

(Other values can easily be calculated)

Rigid application of the rule is not helpful in situations where near objects are relatively close to the camera. Perhaps this can best be explained with an example. Suppose the nearest object is at 4m. Using **b** = **D_N**/30 we obtain a value for stereo base of 133mm, roughly double the 65mm norm. Whilst one could use this value and obtain satisfactory results, it is an unnecessary complication. After all, a normal 65mm stereo base will produce a good stereo effect up to 65 metres, to use Ferwerda's example, and this range certainly includes near objects at 4 metres. In this case, and by extension of the principle, the 65mm stereo base will be perfectly satisfactory for near objects up to 65 metres, let us say. This 65 metre "minimum" can be taken, therefore, as the starting point for hyperstereoscopy; applying the one in thirty rule gives us a base of around 2 metres as a minimum.

In summary, there is little to be gained by using stereo base values between 65mm (or thereabouts) and about 2m. This was touched upon in Chapter 2 in connection with the use of slide bars or pantographs, neither of which needs to be designed to work with a stereo base greater than, say, 70mm.

Sometimes, as pointed out in Section 7.1.1, a base greater than 70mm (although much less than 2m) is unavoidable; the fact remains is that there is little point in deliberately choosing a stereo base within this range.

7.3 Hypostereoscopy (Close-Up Stereoscopy)
7.3.1 Basic principles

Hypostereoscopy (or reduced stereo base stereoscopy) will apply to all subjects that include objects closer than about 2 metres, through what may be termed normal close-up situations to macro imaging (where the image is near or equal to life size) and stereomicroscopy. There will be some exceptions; for example, the normal base would still be used for a scene that included an object that protruded through the 2m stereo window, towards the observer.

If an object is placed on the centre-axis (midway between the two lens axes) of a traditional stereo camera and moved towards the camera, the two images on the film will move towards the outer frame edges, eventually crossing them and maybe even disappearing. Appropriate supplementary lenses would be needed to enable one to focus properly at the close distances (Section 7.3.5 i) but this does not affect the image positions. Mounting would require the film chips to be separated more than normal, as the images will be too close after transposition. Also, the cut film edges are likely to come into view in the mount apertures. The amount by which film chips can be adjusted laterally in conventional mounts is only 2-3mm.

Unless one possesses a stereo camera with two lenses set closer than the usual 70mm or so, then most hypostereoscopic photography will have to be carried out by using sequential exposures on static subjects. Even a small base stereo camera is limited to a specific near object distance, unless the lens separation is designed to be adjustable. From this discussion, it should be clear that hypostereoscopy, to be successful, is going to require either specialist equipment or more elaborate techniques.

Unlike hyperstereoscopy, which is less rigid in this respect, hypostereoscopy requires very careful choice of stereo base. Usually, it is determined from the one in thirty rule, with some modifications for certain very close conditions. If too large a value is chosen for the stereo base in a particular circumstance, the problem is analogous to that in normal stereo photography when objects closer than 2m are included with extremely distant ones. The distance of the nearest object is not the only criterion; the range of depth, from nearest to most distant object, is also important. The closer the nearest object in the photograph, the smaller is the depth range from front to back that can be tolerated, or viewing may be uncomfortable. This is discussed in Section 7.3.4 below.

Another factor that may cause difficulties is that of depth of field (see Chapter 17, Section 17.5). When focusing any camera on close objects the depth of field is much less than it is for a more distant one. To keep the image sharp from front to back, a small aperture (probably f/11 or smaller) will be required. This may require the use of slow shutter speeds, and a tripod. Even with fast shutter speeds, it will be a lot easier to use some kind of camera support.

In hypostereoscopy, the slide bar and pantograph come into their own. As discussed in Chapter 2, Sections 2.5.3 and 2.5.4, the slide bar can be used for any stereo base below 70mm or so, and the pantograph can be adapted, by changing the bridge height, to cater for reduced stereo bases.

Cameras can only focus as close as the design allows; in many situations this distance may not be close enough to obtain the required result. This means that accessories such as supplementary lenses or extension tubes will be required.

7.3.2 Hypostereoscopy in practice

Leaving aside for the moment the choice of stereo base, we shall consider the various techniques available to the close-up stereo photographer.

Sequential exposures with a mono camera

For close-up work an SLR will generally be more adaptable than a compact camera. An SLR can usually be focused more closely and the image can be monitored in the viewfinder more accurately. For distances closer than can be focused with the normal camera lens, then the use of a supplementary lens is the answer. These lenses are relatively inexpensive and can easily be attached to the camera.

Accuracy in focusing and acceptable sharpness over the total depth range of the subject are paramount. Use of a tripod and slide bar (or a pantograph) is recommended.

The best technique is first to centralise the subject in the viewfinder and then to focus at a distance between the near and far points of the subject in order to achieve the required depth of field in combination with the appropriate aperture. If the stereo base to be used is **b**, the camera should be moved by a distance **b**/2 to the left of the original reference position for the first exposure. The camera should then be moved to a position **b**/2 to the right of the central position for the second exposure (**Fig 7.4**). Whilst this technique is ideal when using a slide bar, it is less convenient with a pantograph because the camera is not at a constant height during its swing from left to right. However, by mounting the pantograph on a tripod, fixing the upper platform temporarily in the central position, the camera can be set up as described earlier. Then, after releasing the platform to its left position, the tripod can be cranked up so that the camera is at the same height as that used for setting up. After the first exposure, the platform can be swung over to the other extreme for the second shot. Suitable bridges will have to be used to give the desired stereo base (see Supplement S2).

If the close-up shots are to be included in a series of 3D slides taken with a stereo camera, say with a 5P or 7P format, then it is sensible to use a 35mm or 40mm lens on the SLR, to match the focal length of the stereo camera, but this is not critical.

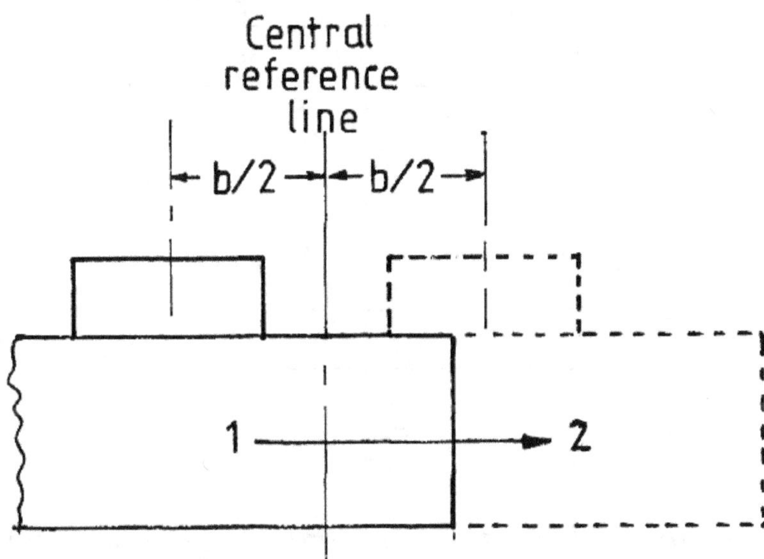

Fig 7.4
*Reduced base stereo with a mono camera, using two exposure positions, **1** and **2**. The desired stereo base is **b**.*

Sequential exposures with a stereo camera

This technique relies on the camera having a double exposure facility, which means that not all stereo cameras will be suitable. However, a modified form of the method can be used in these cases (described later).

The two exposures are taken sequentially, using the left lens for the first and the right lens for the second, the "unused" lens being covered in each case. The shutter is reset after the first exposure without advancing the film, and the camera is moved sideways by a predetermined distance to give the required stereo base. This technique can also be used for hyperstereoscopy, as explained in Section 7.2.2.

Because a different lens is used for each exposure, moving the camera laterally by a distance equal to the desired stereo base **b** is incorrect. This procedure will give a base of (70 + **b**) or (70 − **b**) mm depending upon which way the camera is moved and which lens is used for the first exposure, assuming a camera lens separation of 70mm. The correct way to move the camera is shown in **Fig 7.5**. To explain the method, suppose that the first exposure is made with the left lens. At this point the right lens is, say, 70mm to the right. If the required stereo base is 20mm, the camera has to be shifted to the left (rather than to the right) by (70 − 20) = 50mm. This will place the right lens 20mm to the right of the position initially occupied by the left lens.

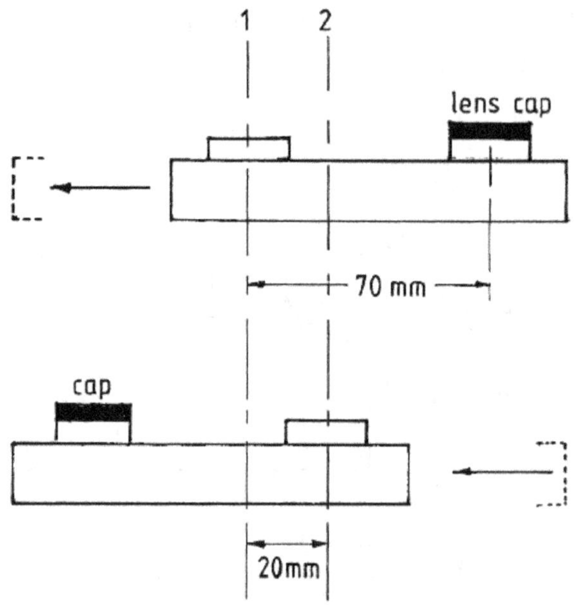

Fig 7.5
Reduced base stereo with a stereo camera that has a double exposure facility. Two separate exposures are made, through each lens in turn, the other being capped. The camera is moved between exposures by a predetermined amount to give the desired stereo base, in this case 20mm.

In general, if $\mathbf{b_L}$ = lens spacing (mm) and $\mathbf{b}$ = desired stereo base (mm) then the procedure can be summarised as follows:

1. align the subject with the axis of the left lens
2. shift the camera by an amount equal to $\mathbf{b}/2$ to the left
3. take the first exposure with the left lens alone (the right lens is covered). Use the double exposure facility to reset the shutter without advancing the film
4. shift the camera by an amount $(\mathbf{b_L} - \mathbf{b})$mm to the left
5. take the second exposure with the right lens (left lens covered)

When the camera viewfinder is located midway between the two lenses, as in the Stereo Realist, one can use the technique recommended in the Stereo Realist Manual[7]. The camera back is marked to indicate the lens centre positions $\mathbf{A}$ and $\mathbf{B}$ and the mid-point $\mathbf{O}$ (**Fig 7.6**).

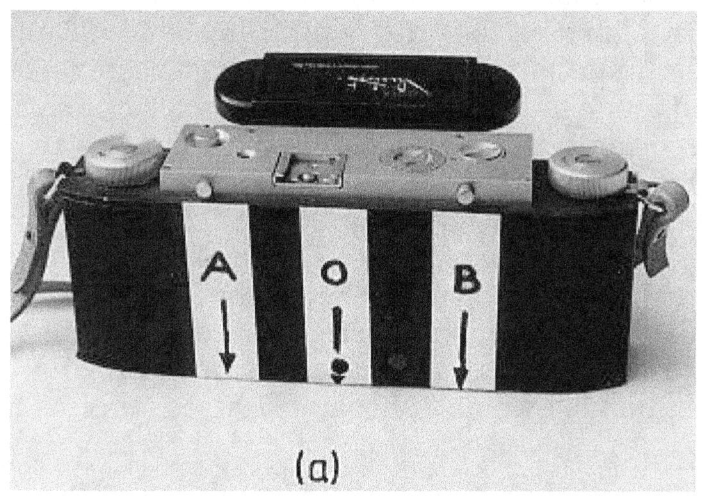

Fig 7.6
a *Back of Stereo Realist camera marked with arrows to indicate the lens positions (**A** and **B**) and the centre (**C**).*
b *Scale for use with the above for hypostereoscopy, marked in millimetres.*

The camera is placed on a slide bar with a scale, preferably marked with a centre zero as shown In the diagram and calibrated in millimetres (plus in one direction, minus in the other). Any normal scale can be used, of course, provided it has a clearly marked reference point at about its centre. The technique is to set the camera with its mid-point $\mathbf{O}$ aligned with the zero (or central reference mark) on the slide bar. The subject is centred in the viewfinder. If the stereo base is to be 30mm, for example, then the camera is moved to the right along the slide bar until pointer **A** is set at -15mm (i.e. 15mm to the left of the scale centre) and the first exposure taken with the left lens (right lens covered). For the second exposure, the camera is slid to the left until pointer **B** is set at +15mm (15mm to the right of the scale centre). A table can be drawn up showing the **A** and **B** pointer positions for any stereo base (**Table 7.3**). This is based upon the one given in the Stereo Realist Manual.

Note that all dimensions in this table are in inches. The second column (total lens separation) gives the stereo base; these values are related to the lens-to-subject values in column 1 by a factor of 1/15. Here, then, a "one in fifteen" rule is being advocated. This could lead to problems because it represents the equivalent of working with near objects at 1 metre in traditional stereo photography. This is likely to give unsatisfactory results if the range of depth extends to infinity. Likewise, in close-up stereo, using a one in fifteen rule means that the depth range will have to be restricted. In **Table 7.4** the information in **Table 7.3** has been re-calculated using metric units and a one in thirty rule, which is safer to use.

If the stereo camera does not have a double exposure facility then, in an emergency it can be used as a mono camera as in (1) above. It is probably best to use just one of the lenses (e.g. the left) for both shots. The film is wound as normal between exposures. The images from the right lens will have to be discarded as they will not be aligned properly with the subject. Unlike the similar technique for hyperstereoscopy we will not end up with two sets of pictures. This method is recommended only for occasional use, when no other option is available, because it uses twice as much film.

TABLE 7.3
Interocular Separation for Close-up Photography
(From the Stereo Realist Manual[7])

Lens to subject distance (inches)	Total lens separation (inches)	Scale position for pointer **A** (inches)	Scale position for Pointer **B** (inches)	Dioptre lens #
30	2.0	-1.0	+1.0	1
27	1.8	-0.9	+0.9	1
24	1.6	-0.8	+0.8	1
21	1.4	-0.7	+0.7	1
18	1.2	-0.6	+0.6	2
15	1.0	-0.5	+0.5	2
12	0.8	-0.4	+0.4	3
9	0.6	-0.3	+0.3	4
6	0.4	-0.2	+0.2	6

#Use +1, +2 or +3 dioptre lenses singly or in combination to get the total power required. The dioptre is an old unit now replaced by "radians per metre". 1 dioptre = 1 rad m^{-1}

TABLE 7.4
Modified Version of "Stereo Realist" Table of Interocular Spacings for Close-up Photography
(Metric version based upon a 1 in 30 rule)

Lens to subject distance (mm)	Total lens separation (mm)	Scale position for Pointer **A** (mm)	Scale position for Pointer **B** (mm)	Dioptre lens#
750	25	-12.5	+12.5	1
650	22	-11.0	+11.0	1
600	20	-10.0	+10.0	1
550	18	-9.0	+9.0	1
500	16	-8.0	+8.0	2
450	15	-7.5	+7.5	2
400	13	-6.5	+6.5	2
350	12	-6.0	+6.0	3
300	10	-5.0	+5.0	3
250	8	-4.0	+4.0	4
200	7	-3.5	+3.5	5
150	5	-2.5	+2.5	6

 # Now rad m^{-1}

Use of specialised stereo cameras

Throughout the history of stereoscopic photography, cameras of all shapes and sizes have appeared; many are no longer around but some have survived. Among the many and varied designs, a number have been produced with lens separations less than 65mm and can therefore be used for close-up stereo. It has to be remembered, however, that if the one in thirty rule is followed, the nearest object can be placed no closer than $30\mathbf{b_L}$ where $\mathbf{b_L}$ is the lens spacing, so even these cameras are somewhat limited in scope.

We shall not review such cameras at length but merely highlight some of the models that have been available in the past, some of which can still be found in use today.

Duplex Super 120

Originating in Italy this camera first appeared in 1965 and uses a lens separation of 30mm to give two 25 x 23.5mm images side-by-side across the width of 120 film. Twenty-four pairs can be obtained on each film. The images have to be transposed in the normal way.

Realist Macro Stereo Camera

This camera was launched in 1971 and has a stereo base of 15mm. It was designed to take pictures at a fixed distance of 100mm as there are no focusing facilities. Two rods protrude forward horizontally, one on either side of the lens pair, to indicate the focusing distance and image width.

The design raises questions since the $\mathbf{b/D_N}$ value is 15/100, or "one In seven", which is well above the "one in thirty" guideline. The implication is that the camera is likely to be successful only with subjects of limited depth, a few millimetres from front to back.

Nimslo 3D. Any adjacent pair of lenses, spaced at 18mm, can be used in close-ups for subjects at 30 x 18 = 540mm distance, or thereabouts. The Nimslo lenses are set for fixed focus, to give a depth of field range from about 2 metres to infinity. Supplementary lenses will be required for close-ups. Alternatively, one large lens can be used if it covers two adjacent Nimslo lenses. The focal length of the supplementary lens should be around 500 to 600mm (about 2 rad m^{-1} in power terms).

Ferwerda[17] suggests that the top and bottom sections of a large supplementary lens could be cut off and the resulting strip fitted into the recess at the front of the camera, to cover the middle two of the four lenses. The advantage of this arrangement is that the camera can be used at will for normal and close-up work. The outer pair of images can be used to produce stereograms for "standard" stereo photography, and the inner pair for close-ups. Of course, only one of these "pairs" at a time will produce a sharp image when used in this way. The other pair of images will have to be discarded.

Using the images from alternate lenses (in conjunction with supplementary lenses if necessary) will produce a stereogram with a stereo base of approximately 36mm, which gives additional flexibility in using the camera. With this lens separation, two separate close-up lenses would almost certainly be necessary. The subject distance would be about 1 metre.

According to the "Nimslo 3D Book"[9] the following supplementary lens/focus distance combinations can be used (**Table 7.5**):

TABLE 7.5

Power of supplementary lens (rad m^{-1}) or (dioptres)	Distance focused	
	inches	mm
1	28	711
1.25	24	610
2	18	457
4	9	229

(See also Section 7.3.5)

Custom-built Stereo Macro Cameras

Several eminent stereo photographers have designed and built their own stereo cameras (usually for 120 film formats) for specialist use in close-up work.

The Dutch photographer, Jacobus Ferwerda, constructed a single lens camera with two diaphragms that form the lens base. As the light rays enter the camera they are deflected by prisms (acting as a beam spreader within the camera) to form two images 40x40mm side by side along the length of 120 film Lens separation can be adjusted to 9, 6 or 4mm.

The English photographer, Mrs Pat Whitehouse produced many excellent photographs using a "Baby Bertha 2" camera, both designed and built by her. This used two 75mm focal length lenses, ground flat on one side each so that they could be placed as close as 12mm, measured at the lens centres. The lens separation was adjustable from 12mm to 30mm, making the camera much more versatile for close-up work.

Further details of these two cameras can be found in Ferwerda's book, "The World of 3D"[18].

The advantage of these cameras, and the reason that some workers are prepared to go to such lengths to create them, is that they can be used for such subjects as wildlife in close-up. Birds, insects and other small creatures can be photographed in natural surroundings (or mock-ups in the studio) to provide interesting and often stunning stereoscopic images, which could not be produced with sequential exposure techniques.

Such cameras are very much the domain of the specialist/enthusiast and equipment of this kind is most unlikely ever to be available commercially.

Use of two coupled mono cameras

A cumbersome set-up, and not without other disadvantages, is to rig two mono cameras together in a special rig to give a reduced (and adjustable) stereo base. The arrangement is shown schematically in **Fig 7.7**.

It uses semi-silvered glass; one camera points at the subject through the glass while the other, set at right angles, relies on the reflection. Since both cameras make use of the semi-silvered surface, the loss of light will be roughly the same for each. The use of grey glass is said to equalise the brightness.

By moving the upper camera, the base **b** can be adjusted accurately from zero to any greater value compatible with the dimensions of the rig.

As is usually the case with stereo attachments, loss of light intensity means that either wider apertures or slower shutter speeds will often be necessary. This might preclude some subjects being photographed successfully.

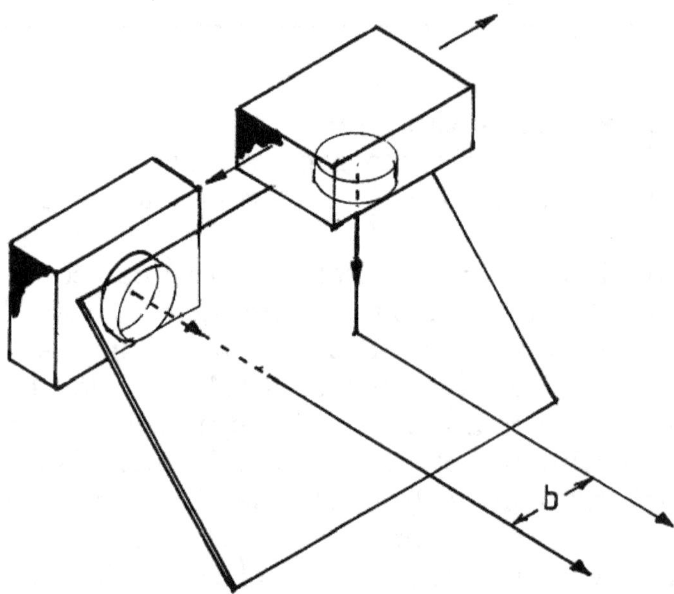

Fig 7.7
*Hypostereoscopy with two mono cameras set at 90° to each other with one behind and the other above a semi-silvered glass plate set at 45°. The cameras can be moved sideways to produce any desired stereo base **b**.*

Use of stereo attachments

The kind of attachment suitable for close-up stereo work has already been described in Chapter 4, Section 4.2.5, and exemplified by the Leica model illustrated in Chapter 4 **(Fig 4.15)**. As far as hypostereoscopy is concerned, the method is to use the twin lens attachment on an SLR camera, in place of its own lens, but without the beam spreader mirror (or prism) addition. The camera is thus neatly converted into a true stereo camera with two lenses separated by 18mm or thereabouts. Two images will be produced side by side within a standard 35mm frame but the left and right images will have to be transposed for viewing, as in any other stereo camera. This differs from the situation found in beam-splitters, where no transposition is required.

As with all fixed base devices or cameras, one is restricted to a working distance no closer than about 30$\mathbf{b_L}$ as discussed earlier.

In summary, for the stereo photographer who occasionally wishes to experiment with close-up work, methods 1 and 2 above will probably be the easiest to adopt. Obtaining specialist stereo macro cameras or designing and building one's own equipment implies a greater devotion to close-up work but one must accept certain limitations with some of the equipment.

7.3.3 Limitations of the "one in thirty" rule

The reason for using the 1 in 30 rule is that the maximum parallactic difference (deviation) must not exceed a certain value, equal to 1.2mm for the 5P and 7P formats, to reduce the likelihood of eyestrain when the stereogram is viewed. This 1.2mm difference is linked to the rotation of the eyes in viewing when the gaze changes from the 2 metre object to one at infinity, or vice versa. It represents a rotation of just less than 2° and allows the observer to see the whole scene from front to back without experiencing diplopia, or double vision of the near objects when looking at the distant ones, or vice versa.

As shown in Supplement S7, the deviation $\mathbf{d}$ is given by:

$$\mathbf{d} = \mathbf{fb}/\mathbf{D_N}$$

where $\mathbf{f}$ = focal length of the lens (strictly it should be the **working focal length**, ie the actual lens/film distance $\mathbf{v}$), $\mathbf{b}$ = stereo base and $\mathbf{D_N}$ = distance of nearest object from the lens.

Rearranging:

$$\mathbf{d}/\mathbf{f} = \mathbf{b}/\mathbf{D_N} = 1/30 \qquad \text{(for the 1 in 30 rule to apply)}$$

Now $\mathbf{d}$ must be no more than 1.2mm and as long as $\mathbf{v}$ is close to $\mathbf{f}$ (35mm) the ratio will be more or less constant. However, as $\mathbf{D_N}$ decreases, the lens/film distance $\mathbf{v}$ starts to increase rapidly and this reduces the $\mathbf{d}/\mathbf{v}$ value to less than 1/30.

For example, with $\mathbf{D_N}$ = 2 metres, $\mathbf{v}$ = 35.6mm and:

$$\mathbf{d}/\mathbf{v} = 1.2/35.6 = 1/29.7.$$

However, if D_N = 200mm then **v** increases to 42.4mm so:

d/**v** = 1.2/42.4 = 1/35

This revised value should be used to calculate the stereo base **b**. Doing so gives **b** = 5.7mm whereas the one in thirty rule would suggest 6.7mm. The difference is even more marked at closer focusing distances.

A fuller explanation of the 1 in 30 rule is given in Supplement S8, which also includes a guide to stereo base values that should be used in extreme close-up situations.

7.3.4 Permissible depth range

If the distance D_N of the nearest object that we wish to include in a 3D image is reduced, so also the distance of the furthermost object that can be safely included must be reduced. In other words, including objects closer than the usual 2 metres necessitates a reduction in the total allowable depth range, from nearest to furthest object. This depth range decreases markedly as D_N is reduced. The permissible depth range is determined by the maximum allowable eye swing of just less than 2° for comfortable viewing of both nearest and furthest objects. If the nearest object is at 2 metres then we can comfortably view a scene that extends from 2m to infinity. When the nearest object is only 1 metre away, however, then the most distant object can be no further away than 2m, a dramatic difference. The table below gives various depth ranges that can be safely used, based upon the nearest object distance. Supplement S9 gives an explanation of the principles involved in calculating these depth ranges.

TABLE 7.6
Permissible Depth Ranges of Subjects

Metric (metres)								
D_N	0.6	0.8	1.0	1.2	1.4	1.6	1.8	2.0
D_F	0.86	1.33	2.0	3.0	4.67	8.0	18.0	∞
ΔD	0.26	0.53	1.0	1.8	3.27	6.4	16.2	∞

Imperial (ft. & in.)								
D_N	2'	2'6"	3'	3'6"	4'	4'6"	5'	6'	7'
D_F	2'10"	3'11"	5'3"	7'	9'4"	12'7"	17'6"	42'	∞
ΔD	10"	1'5"	2'3"	3'6"	5'4"	8'1"	12'5"	36'	∞

***KEY*:**
D_N = *distance of nearest object to be included*
D_F = *distance of furthest permissible object that can be safely included*
ΔD = *permissible depth range* (**D_F – D_N**)
(Additional data are given in Supplement S9)

7.3.5 Techniques for close-up photography

All cameras, whether mono or stereo, compact or SLR, have a minimum focusing distance, which is determined by the design. For a modern SLR camera, with a standard lens, the distance will perhaps be as close as 450mm (1.4ft), whereas it will be no closer than about 1 metre at best for a compact camera. Older stereo cameras will tend to be less versatile, because the typical stereo base of 70mm is too large for close-ups. The Stereo Realist can be used at about 750mm (2.5ft) whereas the Wray Stereographic is limited to just under 2 metres. Therefore, for "extreme" close-ups some external means of focusing more closely distances has to be devised. It is not that the camera lenses themselves are incapable of close focusing, but limitations in the camera design that prevent them from being screwed out far enough.

Various accessories can be used to enable the camera to be used more closely than normal; they are summarised below.

Supplementary lens (or lenses)

In order to focus more closely than normal, a positive supplementary lens is required (bi-convex or plano-convex; see Chapter 17). Commonly used supplementary lenses range in focal length from about 250mm to 2000mm (4rad m^{-1} to 0.5rad m^{-1}, where the reciprocal of the focal length in metres gives the power of the lens in rad m^{-1}; thus if **f** = 250mm = 0.25m then the power is 4rad m^{-1}). The old unit for rad m^{-1} was "dioptre", still used popularly.

Only one supplementary lens will be required if the sequential exposure method is used, either with a mono or stereo camera. If the stereo camera is being used with its normal stereo base of around 70mm then two supplementary lenses will be required for the standard stereo shot using simultaneous exposures. If the stereo camera has a small inter-lens spacing it may be possible to use one supplementary lens if it is large enough in diameter to cover both lenses.

If the camera lens is set to infinity then the focused distance will be equal to the focal length of the supplementary lens being used. This is the easiest setting to use and one can rely on a sharp image at that distance plus whatever depth of field is present. Using this technique, the following subject distances are relevant for various powers of supplementary lens (**Table 7.7**):

TABLE 7.7

Power of supplementary lens (rad m^{-1})	Closest focused distance (mm) #
0.5	2000
1	1000
1.5	670
2	500
3	330
4	250

 # with camera lens set to infinity
(These distances are equal to the focal lengths of the supplementary lenses).

By setting the camera lens to distance values other than infinity, even closer distances than those given in the table above can be focused with the supplementary lens in place. To give some idea of the range, setting the camera lens to 1m on its focusing scale will enable it to focus (with the aid of the supplementary lens, to the following distances (**Table 7.8**):

TABLE 7.8

Power of supplementary lens (rad m^{-1})	Closest focused distance (mm) #
0.5	670
1	500
1.5	400
2	330
3	250
4	200

 # with camera lens set to 1m on focusing scale

One can, of course, set the camera lens to other distances on the focusing scale to give a range of closer focused distances. The relationship between the distance **u** set on the camera and the actual focused distance **D**, with the supplementary lens in place, is given by:

$$\mathbf{D} = \mathbf{us}/(\mathbf{u} + \mathbf{s})$$

where **s** is the focal length of the supplementary lens. The focal length of the camera lens is irrelevant; what matters is the distance to which it is set.

Supplementary lenses can be used in combination and the merit of the "dioptre" (rad m^{-1}) system for the designation of focal length is that rad m^{-1} values are simply added to determine the power (and hence focal length) of the combination. For example, using 3 rad m^{-1} and 2 rad m^{-1} lenses together, the power of the combination is 3 + 2 = 5 rad m^{-1} i.e. the focal length is 1/5 m = 200mm. When such lenses are used together, it is recommended that the one with the greater power should be placed closer to the camera lens. With simple lenses of this type there will be some slight loss of image quality. Nevertheless, results can be very effective.

Extension tubes

These are tubes of differing lengths, usually provided as a set of three that can be used individually, or in combination, with an SLR camera (**Fig 7.8a**). They are threaded (or fitted with the appropriate bayonet fitting) to take the camera lens at one end and to be attached to the camera lens mount at the other, thus providing a range of (fixed) subject distances. Tube lengths range from about 13mm (½in) to 150mm (6in).

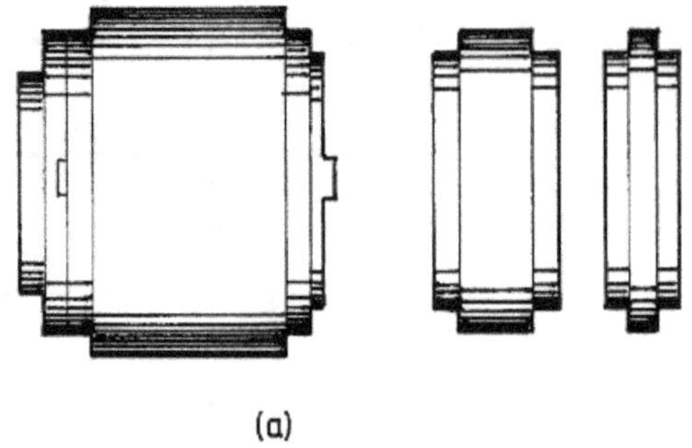

(a)

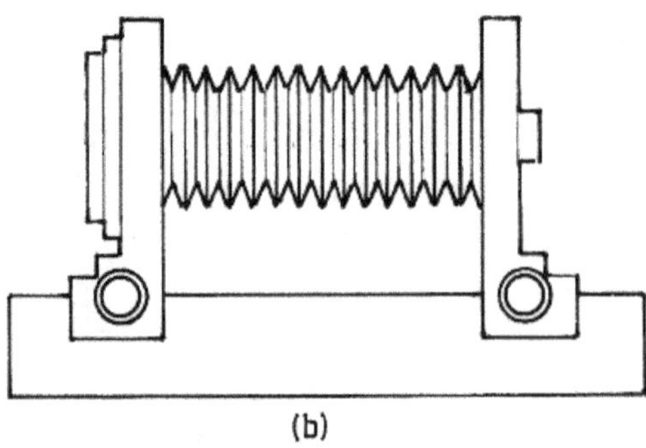

(b)

Fig 7.8
a *Extension tubes.*
b *Extension bellows.*

With straightforward tubes the electronic connections between camera and lens will be lost, so it is worth spending a little extra for auto extension tubes, designed for the specific make of camera, so that all the lens settings can be controlled from the camera body in the normal way.

With the lens much further from the film, extra exposure is necessary, and the effective aperture is reduced (with longer tubes). Exposure compensation can be calculated but with modern cameras, which include TTL (through-the-lens) metering, the exposures are determined automatically.

Extension bellows

These are based upon the same principle as extension tubes, in that the camera lens is held further away from the film plane. In this case, the lens is fixed to the front of a bellows attachment (**Fig 7.8b**) mounted on the camera. Although more expensive than extension tubes, the bellows allow the lens to be set at any position within the range available.

Reversing ring

Again, this is for use only with an SLR camera. It consists of a ring, which is either double threaded or made with the relevant bayonet fitting for the camera being used (**Fig 7.9**). This ring sits between the camera lens mount and the lens itself, which is attached with its front surface towards the film plane. Thus the lens is reversed.

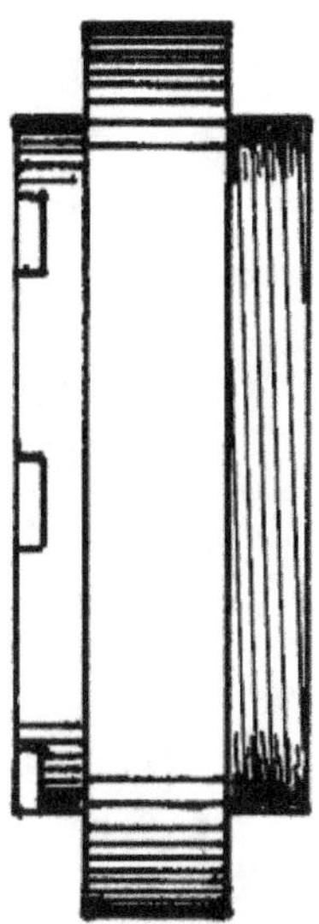

Fig 7.9
Reversing ring for use with an SLR camera.

This arrangement allows close objects to be focused at a specific distance, which is dependent upon the lens focal length. With a 50mm lens, for example, the relevant distance is about 80mm. Greater versatility is gained, however, by using the reversing ring with extension tubes to give a range of focused distances. The advantage is that the lens is designed in normal use to give better results with the image distance shorter than the object distance. Reversing the lens for close-ups makes best use of lens performance by interchanging object and image positions.

One disadvantage, apart from the single usable subject distance, is that all electronic communications between lens and camera will be lost with the lens reversed. It also means that the lens will have defaulted to its widest aperture. To employ a smaller aperture, for greater depth of field (already limited to a few millimetres at such a close distance), it will be necessary to operate the lever by hand. This may not be possible with some modern lenses that are entirely electronically controlled.

The image will be of similar size to the object itself, so one is restricted to small details in objects or small objects of limited depth. Coins and medals are examples of the kind of subject suitable for these extreme close-up conditions.

CHAPTER 8: PROJECTION

8.1 Introduction

In this chapter the emphasis is on the projection of film images (transparencies). Projection of digital images is covered in Chapter 14.

Stereo slides can be seen at their best by viewing accurately mounted stereo pairs in a suitable and properly adjusted stereoscope. In consequence, this method of viewing is to be encouraged as the norm, but it is not ideal when several people are viewing because they are obliged to pass the stereoscope around, re-focus and replace the stereograms, which is both inconvenient and time-consuming. Any linking commentary may have to be repeated and the exercise, as a presentation, becomes somewhat disorganised.

Projection of the images onto a screen, so that all present can enjoy the 3D images simultaneously, is clearly advantageous. The presenter can ensure that the sequence of photographs is logical and designed to fit the commentary.

Viewing by projection, however, introduces its own problems, not that the practice should be discouraged, for it is the only sensible alternative to a single stereoscope. One consequence of projection is that most members of the audience will see a distorted image; this is unavoidable, though it is fair to say that the human brain is capable of accepting such distortions without necessarily causing any distress. The average observer would probably be unaware that the stereo image was flawed in any way.

Many distortions arise from the geometry of the observer's position in relation to the screen. There is only one position from which the observer receives a "correct" image, assuming that the mounting of the stereogram and the projector set-up are carried out properly. Those nearer the screen than this **orthostereoscopic** seat (**OSS**) will experience **compression** of the image in the depth direction, whilst those further away will perceive **stretch**. Observers to the left or right of centre will experience some oblique deformation of the image.

All such differences in the appearance of the 3D image vary in kind and degree according to the observer's position in the auditorium.

We might summarise the advantages and disadvantages of projection as follows:

Disadvantages:
1. The projected image will be slightly degraded compared to that seen in a good stereoscope. The better the optics of the projector, the less degradation will be present.
2. Any slight variations in mounting of the stereograms will be magnified on the screen. This may necessitate constant

readjustment of the image positions on the screen, which can be annoying, and may cause eyestrain. Stereograms for projection should all be mounted with precision and to the same criteria.

3. The projector has to be set up carefully according to the room size and hence projection distance; this takes time.
4. Special twin lens stereo projectors must be used; these are expensive and not available in large numbers. Alternatively, two mono projectors have to be employed to accept two separated left and right mounts. Whether these are used side by side, or, more frequently, one above the other, there will be some convergence distortion (see Section 8.4.2), although this will usually be minimal.
5. Spectators must wear polarising spectacles (matched to polarising filters in the projector) to see the images correctly; this can be mildly irritating to some people, not accustomed to wearing glasses.
6. A special metallic silver screen has to be used for the polarising to be effective.
7. For most spectators, the image is distorted, as explained earlier, although most may be unaware of this.
8. Although a stereo window is produced by projection (at, say, 2 metres) it may or may not coincide with the position of the screen. This depends upon the projection conditions and may cause some minor distraction in the perception of the images.

Advantages:
1. Many people can experience 3D viewing at one time.
2. Proper "presentations" can be made, with commentary and music perhaps, so that the viewing experience is truly entertaining.

Although the disadvantages appear to outweigh the advantages, it should be realised that many of the former are relatively minor. Some can be minimised, even if one accepts that they cannot be eliminated entirely; the main advantage (1) is by far the over-riding factor in all the arguments for and against. A fair assessment might be that projection is a very acceptable alternative to the use of stereoscopes but that the viewing conditions are to some degree inferior. By examining the limitations, however, we can ensure that projection conditions are as good as possible, when it comes to actual practice.

8.2. The Use of Polarised Light for Stereo Projection
In projecting the left and right images onto a screen, it is not just a case of arranging the two images side by side in the normal configuration (left image on the left) and expecting the observer to free-view the result. For a start, most spectators would not have acquired such a skill and, more importantly, the infinity homologues would be so far apart that considerable

divergence of the eyes would be needed to fuse the images, if, indeed, this were possible in the circumstances. In theory, each spectator could be provided with a suitably proportioned Cazes stereoscope (see Section 5.3.3 and Supplement S6) but this is, at the very least, a ludicrous solution.

The first rule of stereo projection is that infinity homologues must be spaced at around 65mm (usually slightly less). It follows that the projected left and right images will overlap for most of their widths.

To ensure that each eye sees only its correct image, polarised light (more strictly, plane-polarised light) is used to provide the means of unscrambling the superimposed images.

All light is a form of electromagnetic energy that essentially travels in straight lines, by wave propagation. The waves vibrate in all directions perpendicular to the direction of travel of the wave itself. Now certain crystals allow electromagnetic waves to pass through them only if the latter are vibrating in a particular plane. Light emerging from such a crystal will be vibrating only in this particular plane (**Fig 8.1**); it is said to be plane-polarised.

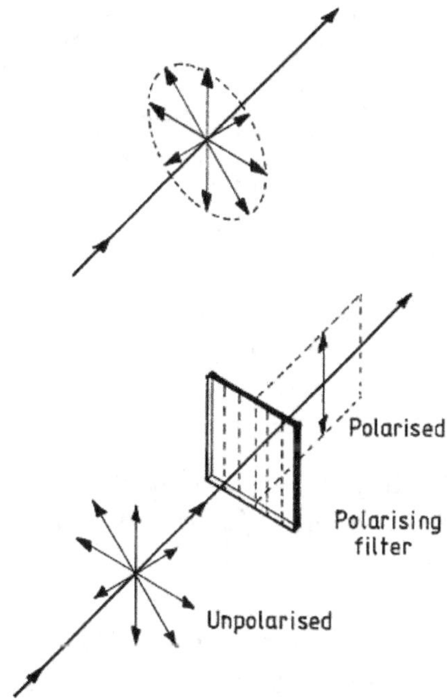

Fig 8.1
Normal light is unpolarised and vibrates in all direction at 90° to the direction of travel (upper diagram). When passed through a polarising filter (lower diagram) the emergent light vibrates in only one plane (plane-polarised).

Certain organic materials can be stretched to orientate the molecules and used to make polarising filters. Commercially produced Polaroid (a trade name) is made from small crystals of quinine iodosulphate aligned in a sheet of nitrocellulose. It is used widely for the "lenses" in sunglasses.

Most surfaces, when they reflect light, will cause some degree of polarisation. A polarising filter (and Polaroid sunglasses) will reduce reflections from smooth, glossy surfaces if the reflections are at angles between about 40° to 70° to the normal. Thus, the photographer can cut out unwanted reflections in a scene by using a polarising filter and rotating it to achieve maximum darkening of the unwanted secondary images. This technique is often used in "mono" photography, but the use of polarising filters in 3D projection represents quite a different application.

Light emerging from a polarising filter and falling onto a second polariser can only pass through if the latter is correctly aligned with the first, with parallel polarising directions. Rotating the second filter about the optical axis will block the light (**Fig 8.2**)

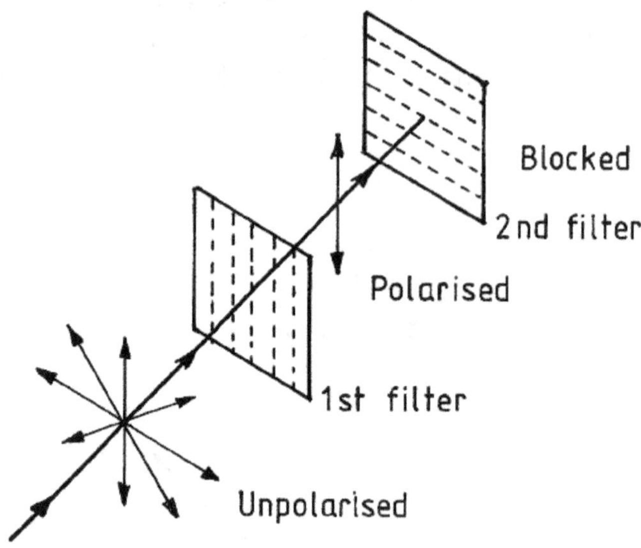

Fig 8.2
Crossed polarisers block the passage of light. Polarised light from the first filter cannot pass through a second if the latter has its polarisation direction at 90° to that of the first filter.

As the rotation of the second filter is increased, the amount of light transmitted gradually decreases to a minimum. This occurs when the two polarisers are "crossed", that is, when the polarising directions of each filter are at 90° to each other. No polarising filter is perfect in this respect and some light will be transmitted even in the crossed position, although the amount will be quite small.

The crossed polarisers principle forms the basis of viewing projected images in directing the correct image to each eye. In the projector, two separate light beams are created, one for each image. After passing through the film image, each beam continues through a polarising filter to the projector lens and screen. However, the two polarising filters are orientated at right angles to each other so that the left light beam is polarised in the vertical plane, say, and the right beam horizontally. If the spectator wears polarising spectacles with the lenses orientated in the same way as the projector filters, the left eye will see only the left image; the right image, being cross-polarised with respect to the left lens of the spectacles, will be blocked out. In a similar way the right eye sees only the right screen image

In practice, the two polarisation directions used are not vertical and horizontal as described above but at 45° to form a "V" configuration. The left image is polarised in a direction from top left to bottom right (as imagined from behind the spectacles) and the right image in the direction running from top right to bottom left (**Fig 8.3**).

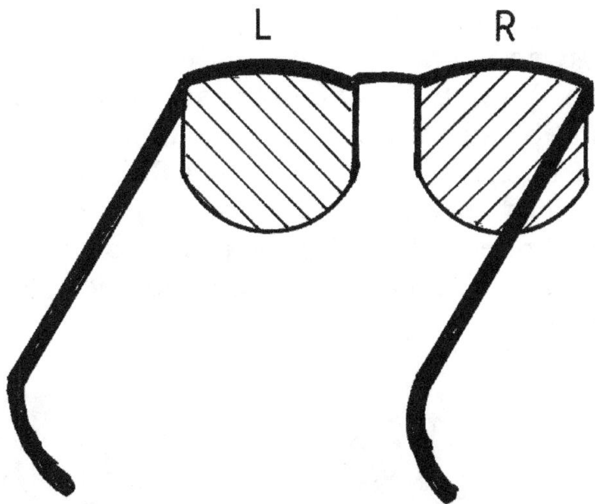

Fig 8.3
Standard polarising spectacles showing the "V" configuration of polarising directions.

In an ideal set-up the image separation would be perfect, but because it is virtually impossible to produce perfect filters and screens, the observer may see a faint ghost image of the right component in the left eye and vice versa. Usually, this is not too troublesome; ghosting is discussed further in Section 8.5.2.

In the early part of the twenty-first century, a number of 3D feature films have been made and shown in cinemas which have sparked a moderate response from the general public. Early showings, at least in the Imax cinemas, made use of shutter glasses in which the lenses blacked out rapidly and alternately in synchronisation with the alternate display of the left and right images. These were expensive so later screenings of 3D films used circular polarised light and passive spectacles with suitable filter lenses. Circular polarisation is produced by adding to a linear polarising filter an extra layer in the form of a plastic sheet with a thickness that retards the phase of one component of the light wave by either ¼ or ½ wavelength. This causes the polarising vector to rotate continuously to follow a spiral path as the light travels through. The plane polarisers are arranged as usual, with the polarising directions forming a V. One filter has just one extra layer (¼wavelength), which produces left-handed circular polarisation, while the other filter has two layers to produce right-handed polarisation. Left-circular polarised light will not pass through a right-handed polariser and vice versa. One of each type is used to project the images onto the screen and the glasses have corresponding filters. With linear polarisers a slight tilt of the viewer's head away from the vertical will cause a loss of the stereo effect. With circular polarisation the head can be tilted much further before the stereo effect disappears.

8.3 Stereo Projectors
8.3.1 General features extra

Even more so than stereo cameras, stereo projectors tend to be few and far between. A 1950's Hawk projector designed for the Realist 5P format using 101 x 41mm mounts is shown in **Fig 8.4**, together with a Russian FED projector, modified to work with quartz iodine lamps. The latter can also be used for the projection of European format stereograms, as well as mono 35mm full frame. It can even be modified to accept separated 50x50mm stereo pairs.

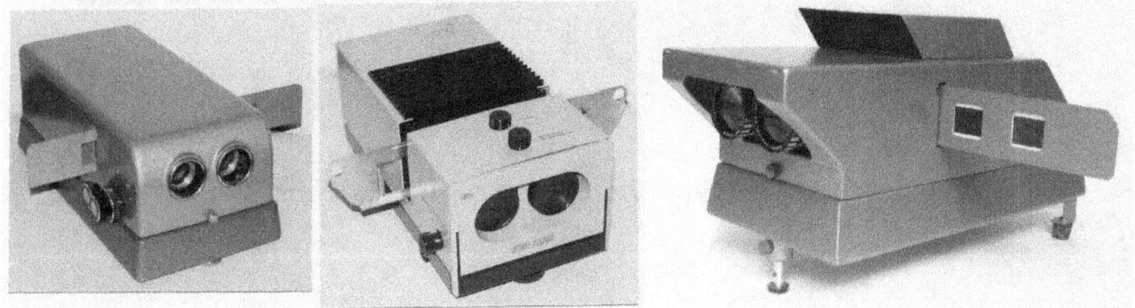

Fig 8.4
Examples of stereo projectors. Top left is an early Hawk Mark II (c. 1950's), which takes Realist format slides. Top right is a Russian FED projector, which can be used for both Realist and European formats. Bottom is a Hawk Mark VII probably the latest model in the series with zoom lenses and blacking out when changing slides

A few other projectors can also handle different formats. By changing the slide holder, condenser lenses and objective lenses, a universal projector is effectively created, which covers all needs. There are also in circulation, on the second-hand circuit, projectors for Viewmaster stereograms. As part of the Stereo Realist system in the 1950's a projector was also available.

The essential features of a good stereo projector can be listed as follows:

1. **a powerful light source or sources**. Most projectors have two bulbs. Nowadays, more powerful iodine quartz bulbs are used. With stereo projection, because of the need for polarising filters and spectacles, there is considerably more light loss than for projection of mono slides. Especially for larger auditoria, one needs to ensure an acceptable screen brightness for the images. Usually, the two lamps have separate switches so that either beam can be switched off, useful for setting up the projector. A single lamp, the light from which is split into two optical paths, is feasible, but overall image brightness will be halved compared with a twin lamp design. A mono projector is typically fitted with a 250W lamp, which gives a reasonably bright image in medium sized rooms. The more powerful the lamps used the better, especially if long viewing distances and larger images are desired.

2. **a slide holder** that locates accurately in the projector and holds mounts securely and precisely. Usually, in stereo projectors a "push-pull" type of holder is used; when one slide is being projected the previously shown slide is removed from the holder (jutting out from one side or the other of the projector) and replaced by the next to be shown. The slide holder is in essence a rectangular metal sheet with two pairs of apertures and has channels or the like attached to hold the stereograms in place (**Fig 8.5**). These should be designed to hold the mounts firmly and always in the same position. Small leaf springs may be included to press against the mount edge to hold it securely against a stop.

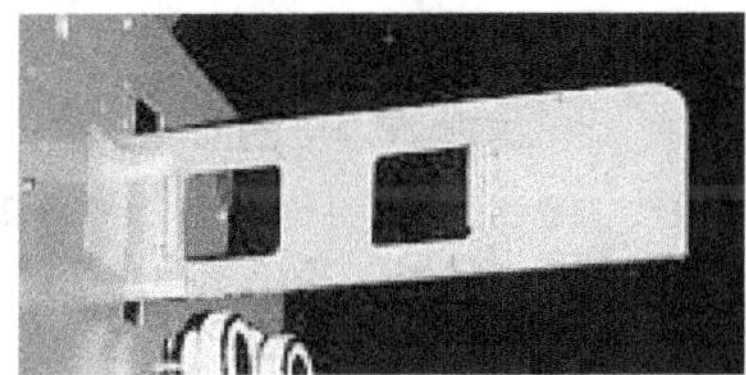

Fig 8.5
Slide carrier for the Hawk projector.

3. **a height adjustment control**. Usually a centrally located support can be turned to lift or lower the front of the projector in order to direct the light beams up or down. There may also be other adjustable legs to enable the projector to be levelled from left to right.

4. **objective lens separation control**. In projection one needs, in general, to set the infinity points at about 65mm separation on screen. Most projectors have a knob which, when rotated, moves one of the lenses towards or away from the other to shift one of the images sideways on screen. Thus the desired infinity point spacing can be achieved quite simply. The basic spacing of the projector lenses is about 65 to 70mm. In some projectors the control shifts both lenses equally closer together or further apart.

5. **vertical image adjustment control**. Another knob, when turned, raises or lowers within set limits one of the objective lenses. This enables the two projected images to be aligned height wise. (N.B. If mounting is carried out consistently and the mounts are accurately located in the slide holder, then once initial adjustments for lens separation and vertical alignment have been carried out, no further adjustments should strictly be necessary during projection. In practice, some occasional resetting is required because even very small differences between two stereograms will be magnified during projection.)

6. **focusing control**. The simplest form is a knob attached to the spindle of a simple rack and pinion arrangement. Rotation of the control moves a block, on which the objective lenses are mounted, forwards or backwards.

7. **good quality polarising filters**, correctly orientated. In addition to the above, versatility of a projector can be increased if it is fitted with zoom lenses. This allows greater scope in adjusting the projected image size in larger auditoria.

8.3.2 Basic optical geometry

As seen from behind a stereo projector, the left objective lens represents part of the optical path for the right image, and not the left, as might be assumed. Likewise, the right lens projects the left image. This is because the stereogram has to be inserted upside down, as is normal with any projector. More precisely it has to be in the configuration shown in **Fig 8.6**. The correct position can be achieved by holding the stereogram as if for normal viewing and rotating it about a horizontal axis at right angles to its plane. This turns the images upside down and transposes left and right while keeping the correct viewing side towards one's person.

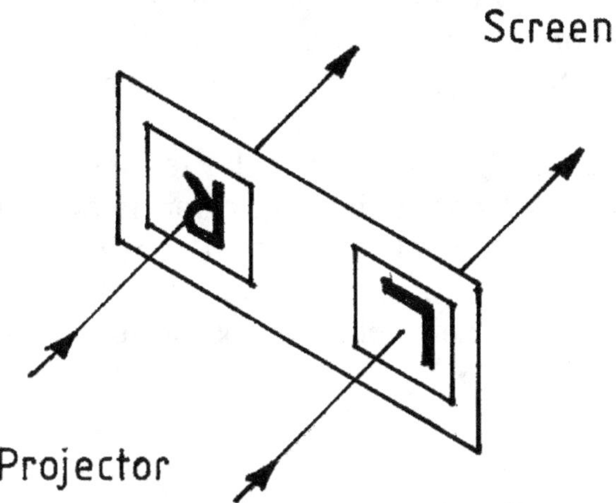

Fig 8.6
Correct orientation of a conventionally mounted stereogram for insertion into a projector.

All this is necessary to get the screen images upright and laterally correct (not mirror images). However, if the stereo projector were to be constructed in the form of two side-by-side mono projectors with parallel optical paths, the on-screen right image would lie further to the left than the left image, though there would be considerable overlap (**Fig 8.7**). This could result in the on-screen infinity homologues being too close together, or even transposed left and right. The projector is best designed so that the two beams cross before they strike the screen.

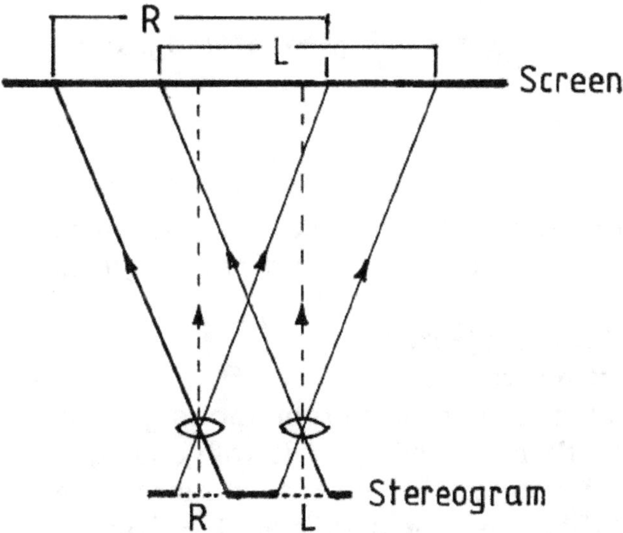

Fig 8.7
Incorrect screen image location in projection resulting from parallel light paths.

Clearly the optical paths could be arranged to converge; however, this would lead to slight convergence distortion of the form shown in Chapter 4, **Fig 4.5**, except that the images would be superimposed rather than lying side by side.

The more usual design is to have the lenses mounted slightly closer together (bearing in mind that their separation is adjustable) which causes the images to shift towards each other and cross over. The ability to shift the images laterally with the horizontal control on the projector takes into account the variations in their relative positions that occur with different projection distances (**Fig 8.8**).

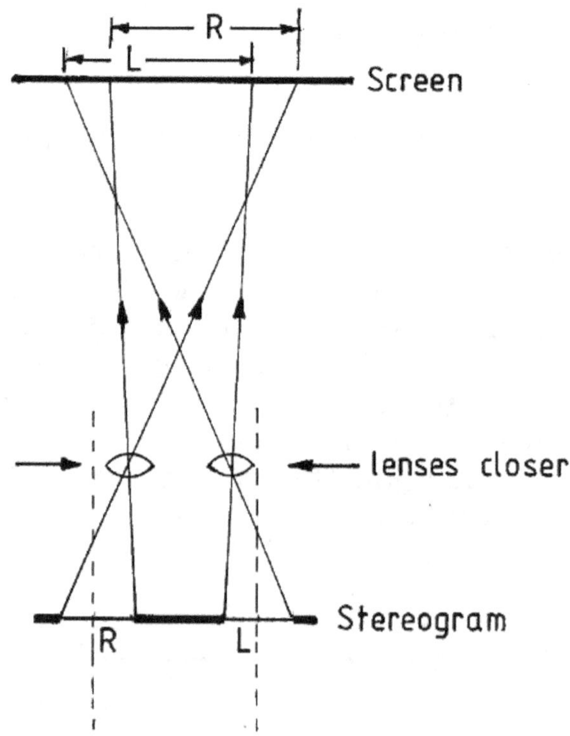

Fig 8.8
Moving the projecting lenses closer than the mount frame centre lines (shown dotted) shifts the screen images into a better configuration.

8.4 Using Twin Mono Projectors
8.4.1 General comments

If it is decided to use a pair of mono projectors for stereo slide presentations, then there is a wide choice of good equipment available. Not only can two such projectors be purchased more cheaply than a specialist stereo one but there is the additional advantage of having more sophisticated technology. With good optical performance and facilities such as autofocus, zoom lenses, remote control, the consumer can be somewhat spoiled for choice. A further advantage is the ability to use slide magazines, which avoids the chore of loading individual stereograms in semi-darkness with an ever-present possibility of dropping mounts on the floor or getting them out of sequence.

For best results, the two projectors should be identical models, with matched lenses. This means that their true focal lengths (as opposed to the nominal value stamped on the casing) should not differ by, say, more than 0.5%. Retail outlets specialising in 3D can often supply a matched pair. It is not practicable for the individual to do this himself, even if he possesses an optical bench.

Apart from using one of the newer multi-format stereo projectors, the stereo photographer who produces separate 50 x 50mm pairs with the aid of two mono cameras, or a Siamesed stereo camera, is more or less obliged to rely on twin mono projectors. The 5P or 7P format stereo buff will have to think in terms of separated pairs, too, using 50 x 50mm mounts but with readily available masks for the relevant image sizes. With separated pairs there is always a danger of a more permanent separation should one of them go missing, but, by using slide magazines, they can be kept more securely. It is worth drawing attention to the Agfa CS slide system, which uses plastic 50 x 50mm mounts that have fine grooves parallel to the four edges. These grooves "lock" the mounts into the magazine and prevent them from falling out even if the magazine is inverted. Added to that is the fact that the mounts are very thin; an Agfa CS magazine, roughly the same length as a normal magazine that takes 36 slides, will hold 100 Agfa CS mounts.

8.4.2 Setting up the projectors
Side-by-side.

This is, at first sight, a logical arrangement since it resembles the two parallel optical paths that exist in a stereo projector. Unlike the latter, however, there is no need to arrange for the optical paths to cross before they reach the screen because the stereogram is in the form of separate slides so that the left image can be placed, upside-down of course, in the left projector and the right image in the right projector.

The problem with this arrangement is that the optical paths will be separated by more than the width of one projector, to allow space for the operation of the slide changing mechanism. Used like this, the infinity homologues would be an identical distance apart on the screen, unless the projectors were "toed in". However, this would increase convergence distortion. If two projectors were set with their lenses 300mm apart, then for a projection distance of 3 metres each projector would have to be turned inwards by just over 2°, a total convergence angle of over 4°, to bring the infinity homologues to a spacing of 65mm. This angle will be smaller if the projection distance is increased.

Although this amount of convergence may not be excessive, it is never a wasted exercise to reduce it, if possible. Stacking the projectors one above the other affords a better solution, as discussed below.

Stacked configuration.

The ideal arrangement would be to place one projector above the other, not with their lenses in line, but offset about 65mm horizontally, so that the two projected images will be "square-on" to the screen and the infinity homologues separated by the correct amount. Usually, it is more convenient to mount them in line vertically, requiring some "toe-in"; this will be much less than that produced in the side-by-side arrangement, and the resulting distortion will be very small (**Fig 8.9**).

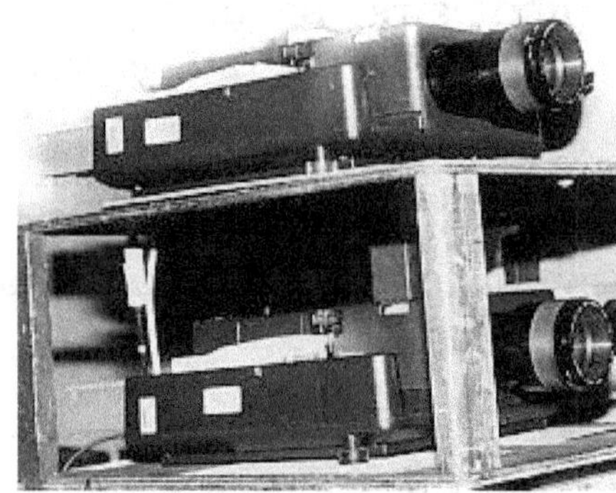

Fig 8.9

Two mono projectors stacked for stereo projection.

An additional distortion will occur because the two projectors have to be tilted vertically in relation to one another to ensure that the two screen images are at the same height. This gives a slight convergence distortion in one of the forms shown in **Fig 8.10** depending upon the exact geometry of the set-up. Again, this will be small because the two lenses will be much closer (this time in a vertical plane) than they would be in a side-by-side situation, more like about 100mm apart rather than 300mm.

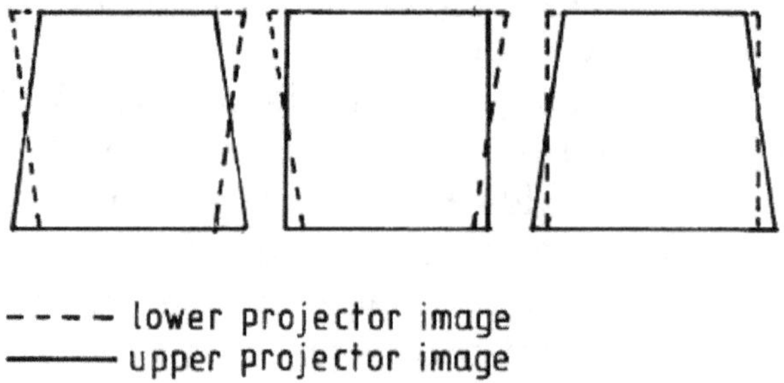

Fig 8.10

Possible "keystoning" configurations on screen that might arise from using two stacked mono projectors (exaggerated for clarity).

Whether the projectors are stacked or side-by-side, it is preferable to use some kind of jig to fix their relative positions quickly and accurately each time they are used. The design should enable at least one projector to be tilted and rotated relative to the other to facilitate image positioning on the screen, as outlined above. Lastly, the upper projector should not block the air circulation system of the lower one, or overheating could occur.

8.5 Screens
8.5.1 The silver screen

In Section 8.2 above it was stated that most surfaces receiving non-polarised light will cause some degree of polarisation in the reflected light. It is also true that most surfaces receiving polarised light will depolarise it to some degree, and these include plastic surfaces or coatings and white painted surfaces, the kinds of materials from which projection screens are commonly constructed. In stereo projection, any depolarisation that occurs will lead to ghost images, when each eye sees a faint version of the other eye's image in addition to its own. Although the stereo effect will still be observed, it will be spoiled by the spurious images, and these should be avoided, or reduced sufficiently to cause minimum interference.

Luckily, metallic surfaces do not depolarise incident polarised light to any great extent, and so screens made of fabric or plastic for stereo projection are "silvered" by coating with metallic aluminium paint. Silver screens can be purchased fairly readily, but the quality, as far as stereo projection ideals are concerned, varies considerably. A screen may be silver in colour but unless it has a high metallic particle content, it may be little better than a white one. There is no test that one can apply to determine how good a particular screen behaves in this respect, other than to try it out with a projector, stereograms and polarising spectacles. However, one can at least rely on the recommendations of photographic retailers who specialise in stereo equipment; they can usually supply satisfactory screens in various forms, or even the material itself, supplied off the roll.

Any projection screen, whether white or (inadequate) silver, can be made to work for 3D projection by the application of aluminium paint. There is a whole variety of aerosol paints available in silver, at auto accessory shops, craft and model shops and paint specialists. Even here, the effectiveness of such paints for 3D projection will vary, and it is still a matter of trial and error to find a suitable one. Roll-up collapsible and portable screens are usually made of plastic material (for the actual screen surface) and the solvents used in some paints may partially dissolve the plastic. This can cause some swelling and the paint may take a long time to dry out. There are, however, some acrylic based aluminium paints available that are safe to use; several silver paints can be found in the PLASTI-KOTE range, for example.

Spraying is probably the best way to apply the paint to achieve an even finish, and the best technique is to spray several coats, working from left to right and up and down alternately from a distance of about 2 feet, allowing each coat to dry thoroughly before applying the next. A final coat of clear varnish is recommended to help prevent sticking when the screen is rolled up.

One of the problems of roll-up collapsible screens is that, when erected, the surface may not be entirely flat, despite any built-in tensioning device. Indentation marks arising from contact with the roller may be visible; such screen defects can be distracting when 3D images are projected onto the screen. An alternative is to make a rigid, flat screen from hardboard, or a similar material, but the disadvantage is that very large screens will be cumbersome when it comes to transportation, and they may not fit easily into the back of a car.

Screens made from sheets of metal have been tried with varying success. As Ferwerda[20] has pointed out, the image brightness produced by such screens is far too uneven, although a sheet of polished aluminium has apparently performed satisfactorily, almost as well as some of the best fabric screens.

8.5.2 Optical characteristics of silver screens

As pointed out earlier, one of the drawbacks of projection is the appearance of ghost images that arise because polarising filters, spectacles and the screen are never perfect. Even with crossed polarisers the image extinction is never 100%. Extinction is defined as the difference in brightness between the left and right images as seen by either eye through the relevant polarising spectacle lens. It can be measured in stops and an acceptable difference is around 6 stops. This means that the brightness of the ghost left image would be 2^6 (= 64) times weaker than the bright (right) image. Obviously, it is advisable to use the best quality polarisers. Even so, the screen, too, should be chosen carefully (in terms of its optical characteristics) to keep ghost images to a minimum.

The degree to which ghosting interferes with the 3D image will vary with brightness of the image at different points on the screen and with the direction of viewing. It is particularly noticeable when bright regions in one image are partly or wholly superimposed on dark regions in the other image, so ghosting will vary from one stereogram to the next. According to Ferwerda[21] if the amount of extinction is subtracted from the overall brightness, the difference represents the brightness of the light that causes ghost images. Although the total brightness and extinction will differ greatly at different places on the screen, the brightness of the ghost image appears to be virtually constant.

Ferwerda[22] tested various screen materials, in different viewing directions, measuring in each case the reflected brightness of polarised light, direct from the screen and then through a crossed polariser, thus obtaining "total brightness" and extinction readings. A typical result is shown schematically in **Fig 8.11** for what would be regarded as a satisfactory material.

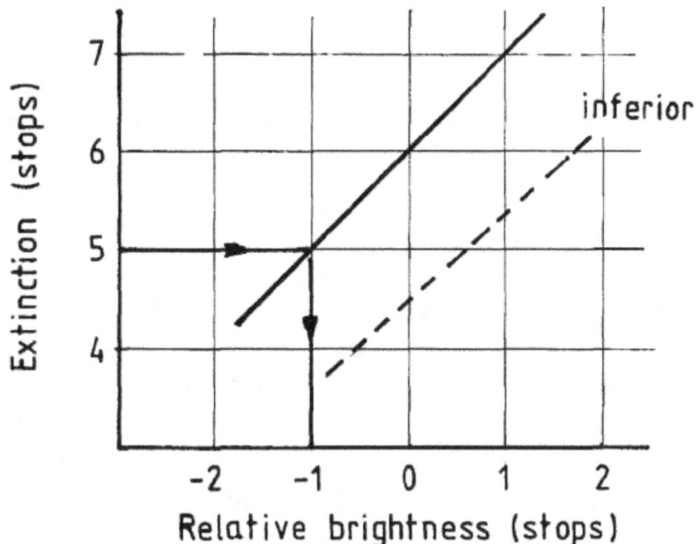

Fig 8.11

Characteristics of silver screen materials (schematic).Based upon results obtained by Ferwerda[22].

The vertical axis shows the amount of extinction in stops (1 stop is equivalent to a doubling or halving of the transmitted light) plotted against the relative screen brightness (shown on the horizontal axis), also measured in stops. The zero represents a reference brightness, so +1 signifies a brightness twice that value, -1 half that value, and so on.

Ferwerda's analysis of several such plots is rather brief so we shall consider the significance of this example in greater detail. The relationship in **Fig 8.11** is a straight line. If we now consider the reference brightness (marked 0, for convenience) then from this line we find that the extinction is 6 stops. In other words, the intensity of any transmitted light (i.e. ghost image brightness) is 2^6 (= 64) times weaker than the overall brightness. If, for illustration, we assume that the reference screen brightness (at zero) is 100 lux (1 lux = 1 lumen per square metre, a measure of the brightness of a surface), the ghost image will have a brightness of only 100/64 = 1.56 lux. If at another point on the screen the brightness is twice the reference value i.e. it is 200 lux (which is represented by +1 on the horizontal scale), the extinction here is 7 stops, so the ghost image is 2^7 times weaker than 200 lux, i.e. 200/128 = 1.56 lux. This is identical to the previous value and it will apply to any brightness values on the straight line. This shows that the brightness of the ghost image is uniform. Any image, whether genuine or ghost, has light and dark areas, so we take image brightness to mean average image brightness. The level of brightness depends upon the projection conditions, the strength of the lamps, the distance of the projector from the screen and so forth. If we project over a greater distance the brightness of the ghost image will be less, but then so will be the total brightness.

The constancy of ghost image brightness (for a given set of projection conditions) means that if we view the projected stereogram at an oblique angle to the screen, the ghosting effect will be more apparent, because the total brightness is less than it is at right angles to the screen.

A screen made from inferior material will have optical characteristics similar perhaps to those shown in **Fig 8.11**. The extinction values for all screen brightness levels are less than the corresponding values for the superior material, indicated by the dotted line.

In 1991, Colin Clay[59] carried out a comprehensive series of tests to assess the properties of various commercially available screens. For comparison, he also examined a spray painted surface and aluminium foil (matt side). He concluded that a metal surface had better characteristics than conventional screens as far as extinction of ghost images is concerned, but it was very directional. At a viewing angle of 22.5° from the centre line the brightness diminished by a factor of 45 to 1, which is totally unsatisfactory. The brightness variation with commercially produced screens was best if the screen surface was vertically ribbed, rather than flat. This gave a better spread of light. The best screen was a Reflecta Superstar, with a Harkness Miralyte running a close second. This gave more even brightness overall but somewhat less than the Reflecta near to the projector axis.

Ten years later, and the availability of good silver screens is much poorer. They are most likely to be obtained from dealers specialising in stereo equipment.

8.6 Projection and Viewing Conditions
8.6.1 Room layout for comfortable viewing

The ideal viewing position is the one at the correct distance away from the screen and on the centre line from screen to projector, and with the eyes level with the horizontal centre line of the image (**Fig 8.12**).

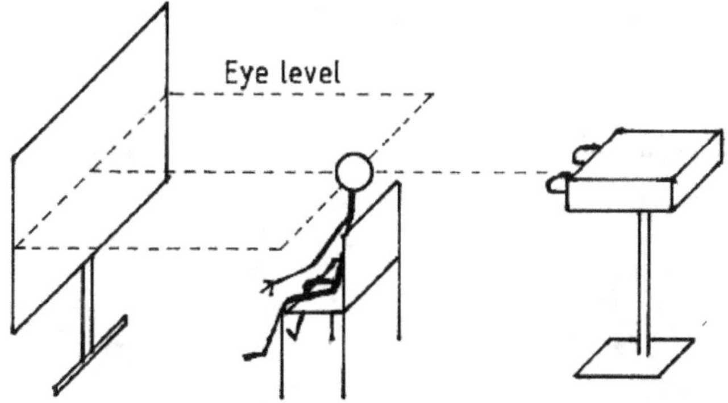

Fig 8.12

"Ideal" conditions for viewing projected images with the observer sitting centrally and with eyes level with the screen centre. The problem is that the observer's head will partially block the light beams.

This is impossible to set up, for one very good reason - the observer's head would block at least part of the beams of light. The usual arrangement, therefore, is to raise the screen and angle it downwards slightly, the projector being lilted upwards to keep the light paths normal to the screen surface. As long as the screen is not too close the sight lines from the eyes of the observers will be virtually perpendicular to the screen (**Fig 8.13**).

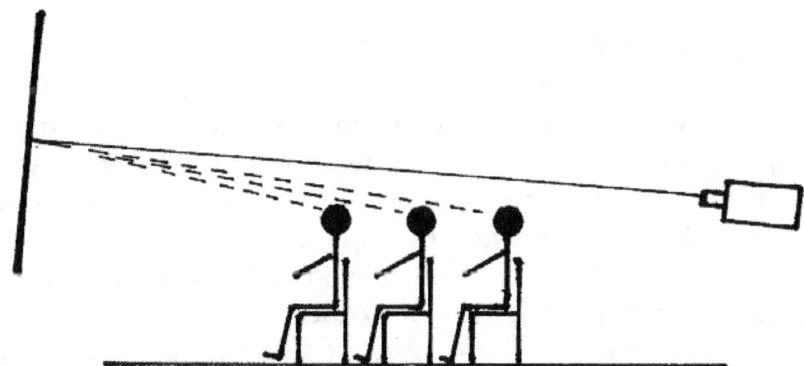

Fig 8.13

Common arrangement for projection with screen raised and tilted for better overall visibility.

The ideal, or orthostereoscopic seat (**OSS**) lies on the centre line. Only here will an observer's view match the perspective "seen" by the camera lenses. The orthostereoscopic distance depends upon the projected image size and is based upon the concepts discussed in Supplement S1. Further information is given in Supplement S10.

It is recommended that the seating arrangement is of the form shown in **Fig 8.14a**. The audience should, if possible, be confined to the triangular shaded area. Arranging the spectators as close as possible to the orthostereoscopic seat (**Fig 8.14b**) will help to reduce image distortions which are worse at the extremities of the auditorium.

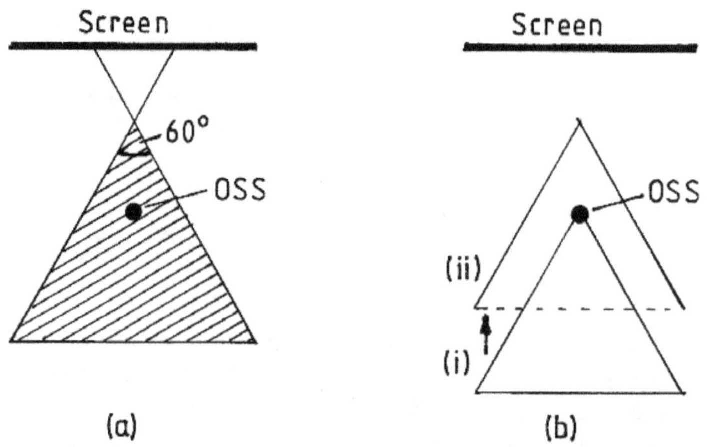

Fig 8.14
a *Recommended area to seat an audience, within a 60° angle.* **OSS** *is the orthostereoscopic seat.*
b *Arranging the audience behind the* **OSS** *means more extreme "stretching" of the image for those further back. It is best to group the audience to position* **ii** *rather than* **i**.

8.6.2 Infinity points on screen

For correct viewing (and to ensure that even the person seated in the orthostereoscopic position does indeed see an orthostereoscopic image!), the infinity homologues should be separated on screen by 65mm, or thereabouts, preferably slightly less. As always, we have to compromise to allow for those with below average eye spacings. However, an s_i spacing of 65mm in a stereogram viewed in a stereoscope by an observer with a 61mm eye spacing (at about 40mm distance) would produce more discomfort than the same 65mm spacing on a screen viewed from, say, 4 metres, since the eyes would be required to diverge much less in the latter case. In projection, then, the on-screen s_i value is less critical, as long as it is consistent throughout a presentation. Even so, it is advisable to keep s_i less than 65mm to be reasonably sure that nobody will suffer any viewing discomfort.

More important is accuracy in mounting, because any variations in the infinity homologue separation will be magnified some fifty or more times on screen. Mounting needs to be accurate to a fraction of a millimetre. Whilst any major variations in s_i on screen can be corrected by adjusting the projector lens spacing, this should be avoided if at all possible, because it spoils the professionalism of the presentation and can be hard on the spectators' eyes.

8.6.3 The stereo window in projection

The on-screen images of the edges of the mount apertures define the boundaries of the individual frames. In combination, as in a stereoscope, they will form a stereo window located in front of the audience. There are three possible locations for the stereo window relative to the screen surface, which depend upon the projector set-up and projection distance:

i.   on the screen surface itself
ii.   in front of the screen
iii.   behind the screen

In cases (ii) and (iii) the location of the window is not fixed in space. Its perceived position depends upon the observer's distance from the screen. The distance between window and screen will appear greater to those at the back of the audience in case (ii), for example, a consequence of "stretch" deformation. In case (i), the window location on screen will be observed by all spectators alike.

Of these three window locations, (i) is the most and (iii) the least satisfactory. To some extent, acceptability of (ii) and (iii) depends upon the lighting conditions, and how conscious one is of the physical presence of the screen. In a completely darkened room (as in a cinema) the only light is on the screen and one is not conscious of the screen's existence as a surface. The impression should be one of a window with dark surrounds through which the 3D image can be seen. In this case the position of the stereo window, in front of, behind or on the screen is not critical. Any blemishes on the screen surface may be distracting, however.

When the screen is clearly visible as an object, it can be slightly disorientating to the spectator if the stereo window is in front of or behind the screen surface. He sees a window in front of the screen, for example, but logic tells him that the picture "frame" ought to lie on the screen surface which he can locate in space because the screen and its supports are clearly visible.

The advantage of having the stereo window located on screen is that all spectators will see the window at the same position (**Fig 8.15**).

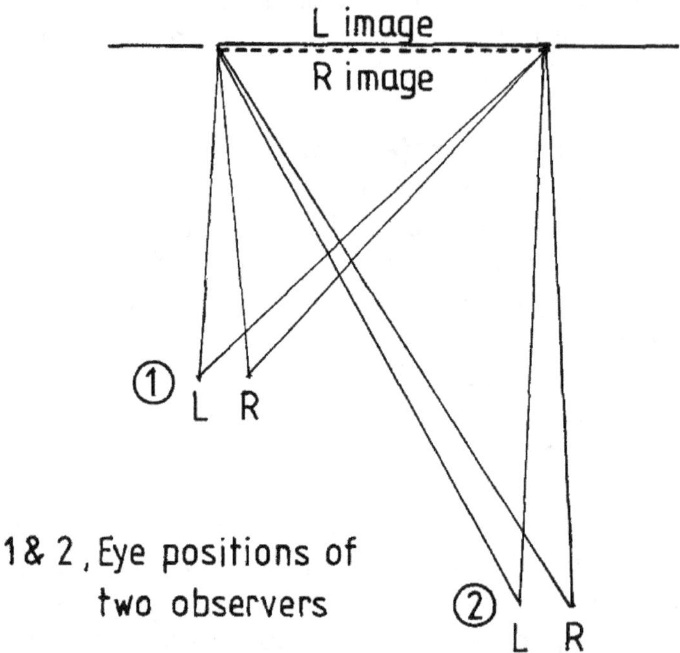

Fig 8.15
With the left and right images superimposed on the screen (coincident frame edges) all spectators will see the stereo window at the screen surface.

If the screen is now moved further away from the projector, the image size will be increased and the images will have to be refocused. At this point the image frames will overlap with the left image to the left and right image to the right (**Fig 8.16a**). However, the geometry of the situation, as explained in Supplement S10, is that after the infinity points have been brought back to 65mm the image frames will have "crossed over" as shown in **Fig 8.16b**.

Observers will now see the stereo window in front of the screen, its perceived position varying according to the spectator's distance from the screen as shown in **Fig 8.17**. This effect is analysed more fully in Supplement S10.

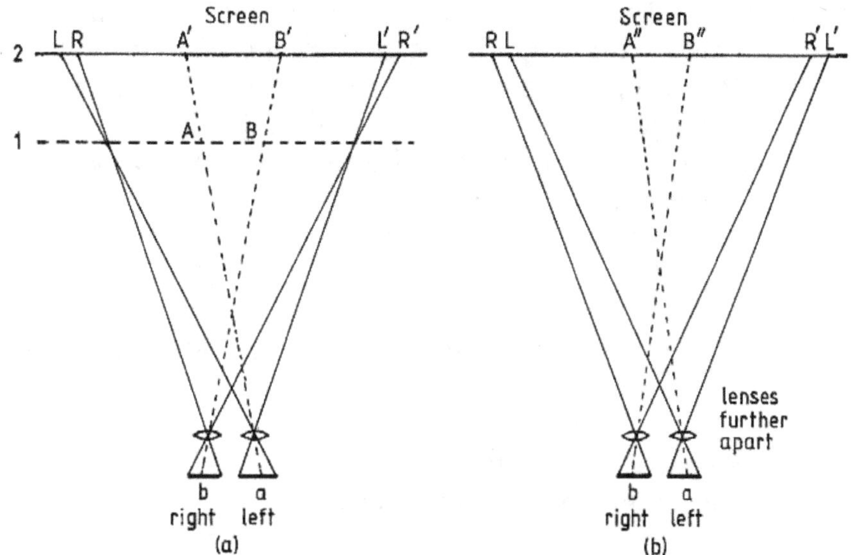

Fig 8.16
a *Screen position* **1** *is the ''window on screen '' setting. If the screen is moved back to position* **2**, *images* **A** *and* **B** *of infinity homologues* **a** *and* **b** *move apart to* **A'** *and* **B'**. **LL'** *and* **RR'** *are the left and right screen images respectively.*
b **A'** *and* **B'** *can be brought back to* **A"B"** (= **AB**, *the correct separation) by moving the projector lenses apart. Images* **LL'** *and* **RR'** *cross over as a result.*

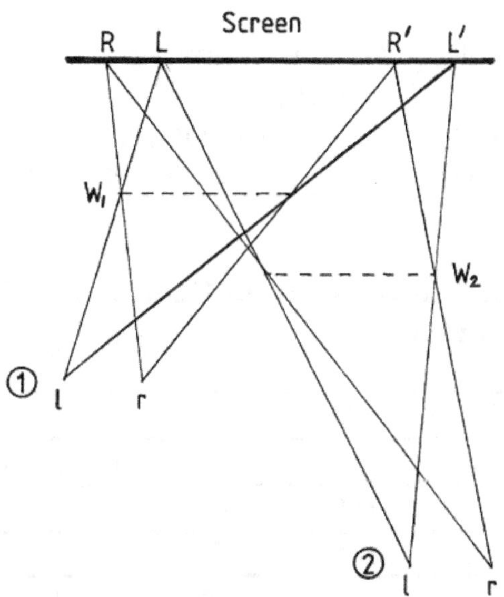

Fig 8.17
When the screen images **LL'** *and* **RR'** *overlap as shown, the stereo window will appear in front of the screen but its location varies with viewing position. The spectator at position* **1** *sees the window at* **W₁**, *whereas the spectator at* **2** *sees it at* **W₂**. *Eye positions are represented by* **l** *and* **r**.

If the screen is brought nearer to the projector from the reference position (stereo window on screen) the two image frames will immediately overlap with the left image slightly more to the left. To correct the infinity point spacing the projector lens spacing must be reduced, to move the images further apart. This will move the stereo window back behind the screen (Supplement S10).

The stereo window will coincide with the screen surface at a certain distance which depends upon the mounting parameters and projector lens focal length.

Taking s_i = on-screen infinity separation (assumed to be equal to that in the mount)

$$d = \text{parallax deviation}$$
$$f = \text{focal length of projector lens}$$

then, as demonstrated in Supplement S10, the projector/screen distance (**D**) is given by:

$D = s_i f/d$ (strictly, **f** should be replaced by **v**, the working focal length)

For the Realist format d = 1.2mm, s_i = 63.4mm and so, for 85mm lenses:
D = 4.49m

The following table gives the appropriate projection distances for various focal length projection lenses to give an on-screen stereo window. Note that, for a given format, the distance is proportional to the focal length. For all combinations of **D** and **f** the actual image sizes are identical.

TABLE 8.1
Projection Distance for an On-Screen Stereo Window
(Realist/European format)

f (mm)	25	45	60	70	80	85	90
D (m)	1.32	2.38	3.17	3.70	4.23	4.49	4.76
D (ft., in.)	4'4"	7'10"	10'5"	12'2"	13'10"	14'9"	15'7"

f (mm)	110	150	180	200	250	300
D (m)	5.81	7.93	9.51	10.57	13.21	15.85
D (ft., in.)	19'1"	26'	31'2"	34'8"	43'4"	52'

Some projectionists prefer to reduce the on-screen s_i separation to about 60mm. This is helpful for spectators with less than average eye spacing, especially if the screen is close when any divergence of the eye sight lines would be greater. At the same time, the image is not seriously distorted for other observers with greater eye spacing.

A smaller on-screen s_i value will affect values of **D** in the table above. For example the new **D** value for an 85mm projector lens and Realist format, if s_i is reduced to 60mm, will be:

$$\mathbf{D} = 4.49 \times 60/63.4 = 4.25m$$

This represents approximately 5% reduction in distance, which can be applied to all distances in the tables.

In practice, the **D** values in the table would be used merely as a guide to setting up the projection equipment quickly. The projector screen distance can be adjusted while viewing a correctly mounted stereogram to achieve an on-screen window without using a tape measure.

8.6.4 The orthostereoscopic seat

Following the principles of correct viewing perspective, discussed in Supplement S1, the ideal position for viewing a projected 3D image can be calculated from:

$$\mathbf{D_S} = 1.64\mathbf{W} \text{ (Realist/European Format)}$$
$$\text{or } \mathbf{D_S} = 1.39\mathbf{W} \text{ (Full frame 35mm, 50 mm camera lens)}$$

where **D_S** is the distance of the orthostereoscopic seat from the screen and **W** is the image width on screen. (See Supplement S10).

Seating is best arranged as close to this ideal distance as possible, some spectators closer and some further back, as illustrated in **Fig 8.14b**. The orthostereoscopic seat is, of course, located on the line from the image centre to the projector.

8.7 Back Projection

By using a screen made of translucent material it is possible to place the projector behind the screen, which has the advantage of producing a brighter image. To avoid a large projector/screen distance, which would add to the total room length requirement, short focal length projector lenses should be used. The projector beam should be directed slightly upwards, and not aimed directly towards the spectators, or they will be aware of a hot spot in the centre of the screen.

According to Waack[23] the screen material has to be selected carefully. Etched glass causes depolarisation; large glass screens will be heavy, transportation will be difficult and there will be a high risk of breakage. Special plastic plates, however, can be obtained, as well as materials in the form of rolls that can be cut to length. Any depolarisation tendencies would have to be checked out, of course.

For rear projection, the mounted stereograms have to be transposed laterally relative to their orientation in front projection. If the screen is thought of as a mirror, the projector and stereogram configuration in back projection will be mirror images of those used in normal projection. The stereogram should be orientated as in **Fig 8.18**, the emulsion side of the film chips facing away from the screen.

8.8 Accuracy in Projection
8.8.1 Mounting accuracy

Mounting to consistent standards is very important. For example, if a Realist format stereogram is set with s_i = 63.5mm instead of 63.4mm, the on-screen s_i separation will increase by about 5mm at a 4.49m projection distance with 85mm projection lenses. Using the principle illustrated in **Fig S10.2**, Supplement S10, the "extra" 0.1mm will be "magnified" to:

$$0.1 \times 4490/85 = 5.4mm$$

If we can mount to an accuracy of ± 0.1mm, then we can expect the on-screen value of s_i to vary from 55 to 65mm, assuming that the desired setting is 60mm.

There should be no need in these circumstances to adjust the projector for each slide, as the on-screen variation in s_i will be within acceptable limits. However, greater variations of the film chip positions than 0.1mm in the mount will cause greater problems.

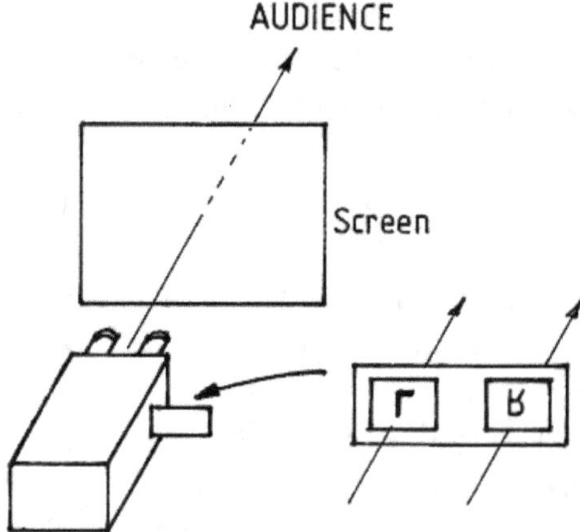

Fig 8.18
Set-up for back projection showing the correct orientation of the stereogram to produce a correct image for the audience on the far side of the screen.

8.8.2 Accurate location of mounts in the projector
Twin-lens stereo projector

A combined pair mount (e.g. the Realist type) should sit properly in the projector slide carrier, which ideally should support it along the whole of its length, or at least at both ends, with no possibility of forward or backward tilling.

Any lateral play in the position of the mount in the carrier is not too serious because this will simply cause the projected image to lie more to the left or right of centre on screen, as long as it is not so off-centre that part of the image moves off the edge of the screen. Fixing shims to the left or right edge of the carrier mount stops, or including a short piece of leaf spring to stop any movement are simple solutions.

The mount should be truly horizontal when in the slide carrier. If the carrier runs at a slight angle (**Fig 8.19a**) the images will appear slightly rotated on screen and at different heights. While the latter can be corrected by the lens height control on the projector, the rotation will persist. This fault can be corrected by fixing a suitable shim (**Fig 8.19b**) to the slide carrier.

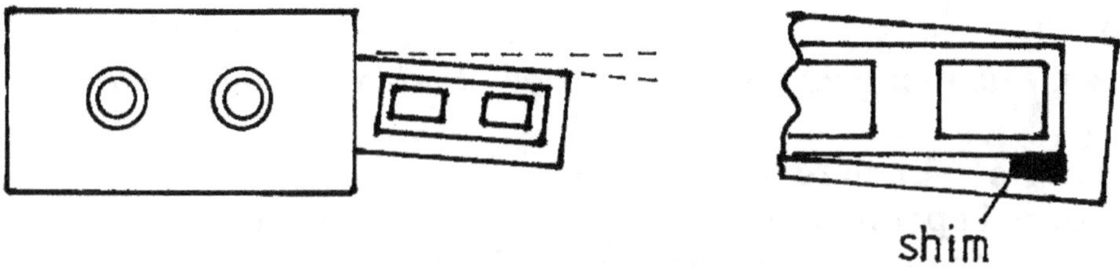

Fig 8.19
Correcting image tilt caused by a non-horizontal slide carrier by means of a shim.

Two mono projectors

Any lateral play in either or both of the projectors will cause significant variations in the on-screen s_i values from one slide to the next. Because the mounts are separated each must be located accurately in its carrier to give a consistent s_i on screen. This problem does not arise with combined pair mounts (e.g. Realist) as the two images are fixed in relation to each other.

Spring loaded mount holders will ensure that each slide is held firmly against either the left or right stops in the carriers.

If one projector shows the angled slide carrier fault as in the above it may be possible to tilt it laterally, using the height adjuster on the projector, or by fitting shims into the offending carrier.

To check for horizontal alignment of the two projectors, a 50x50mm slide with a horizontal line across it, is first placed in one projector and the light beam directed to a wall. The position of the line is marked on the wall by two crosses. The slide is then transferred to the second projector and its height adjusted until the new image of the line also passes through the crosses. This test will also show any relative tilting of the two projectors, revealed if the line does not pass through both crosses simultaneously.

A suitable slide can be made by sticking a piece of tape across a mount aperture (**Fig 8.20**). The edge of the tape, if accurately located, will project as a shadow.

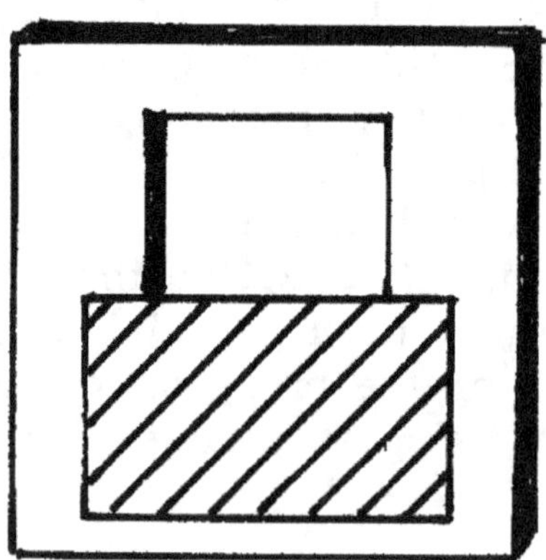

Fig 8.20
Test slide for twin projector set-up to check horizontal alignment.

8.9 Marking of Slides for Projection

Coloured spots are used to denote the correct viewing side and which way up it should be inserted into the projector.

Combined pairs (e.g. Realist format)

The convention is that with the mount the right way up and with the correct side facing the observer, a small self-adhesive spot is fixed to the bottom left hand corner. When the mount is inverted for projection this spot will lie at the top right corner, under the right thumb when normally handled (**Fig 8.21**); a spot drawn with a pen is also acceptable. The spot should be a red one to conform to the convention that red signifies the left image.

In a non-transposed pair of images, to suit a particular viewing device, the top right spot should be green to denote the right image. Such slides cannot be used in conventional stereo projectors and should not be mixed with normal stereograms.

Suitable coloured stickers, about 7mm in diameter, are available from most stationers.

For projection, the slide is turned so that the coloured spot faces the projectionist and lies at the top right hand corner. For back projection the mount is turned so that the red spot is at the top left but facing away from the operator.

Separated 50x50mm pairs

The left image is marked as for the combined pair mounts above, using a red spot. The right image is marked with a green spot (**Fig 8.21**)

8.10 Projection of Slides of Differing Formats

Stereograms produced from different camera formats will be mounted according to different criteria and a mixed selection should not generally be used in any single presentation. Realist and European formats could be mixed in a sequence if the slides are mounted with s_i = 63.4mm, say, and the screen set to allow the full width of the European format images to be fitted onto the screen. To include other formats in a presentation, it is better to set up another projector (or twin projectors) in advance, to avoid having to readjust the existing equipment during the show.

Much more of a problem is to include stereograms in which the window has been set closer than the "standard" 2m, which can be the case for close-up shots. If the projected stereo window keeps jumping from 2m to 1.3m, for example, it will be discomforting to the spectators. If close-ups are mounted to a 2m window, by using a different technique (see Chapter 20) there will be no difficulties.

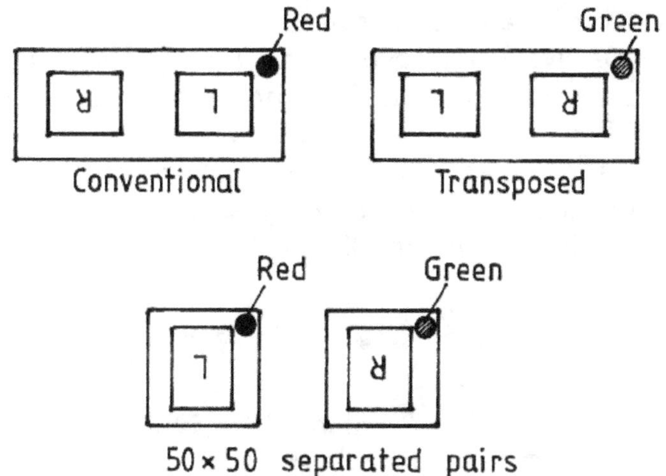

Fig 8.21
Conventional identification and marking of mounted stereograms. Facing the correct way for viewing but turned upside down, the slides are marked in the top right corner with a red or green spot. Red denotes the left image and green the right.

8.11 The "Puppet Theatre" Effect

This is also referred to as the **marionette theatre** effect and it arises when the projectors are set up in such a way that the on-screen infinity points coincide, or lie very close together (or even cross over so that their normal positions are transposed).

With objects supposed to be at infinity now lying close to the screen surface, the whole scene will be compressed into the space between this location and the spectator, resulting in a miniaturisation of the subject so that it resembles a model. Unlike the miniaturisation caused in hyperstereoscopy, the reduction in size is accompanied by frustum distortion, which is always present when infinity sight lines converge (or diverge). Frustum distortion is dealt with in Chapter 19, Section 19.3.4. The puppet theatre effect is avoided simply by increasing the infinity point separation to a value of around 65mm, by adjusting the projector lens spacing.

8.12 Mirror Attachments for Projectors

For projection of slides taken on a camera with a Pentax style mirror attachment, producing non-transposed images side-by-side in a single 35mm mount, similar attachments have been available that can be fitted to a mono projector. With the aid of polarising filters the images can be projected as well as viewed in the special viewer for this format. The attachments are essentially of the beam splitter type but with adjustable mirrors or prisms to allow correct on-screen placement of the images.

8.13 Customised Projection Systems

Two projection systems, developed by individuals, are worthy of note as they demonstrate both ingenuity and practicality, though requiring constructional skills that may be denied to many.

Neville Jackson[26] has based his system on the 5P format but, unusually, mounts the two images side-by-side on a 50 x 50mm sizes cover glass, masking the edges with tape (**Fig 8.22**).

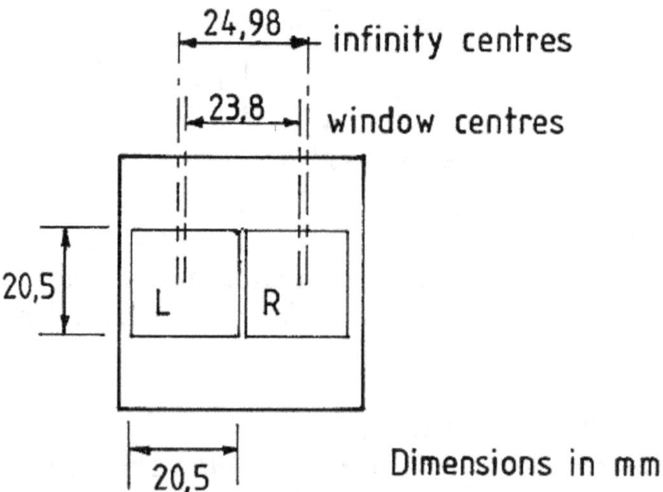

Fig 8.22
Method of mounting 5P format stereo pairs sandwiched between two 50 x 50mm cover glasses devised and used by Jackson[26].

His custom-made projector is based upon a standard mono projector fitted with a large condenser lens and two objectives (modified by slicing portions off each lens to allow the optical axes to be closer). Thus, each objective projects one of the images of the pair.

Mike Fisher[51] designed and built a special double projector to accept two continuous film strips (frames from each strip being projected alternately). The film strips were produced as full-frame 35mm pairs taken with a "Siamesed" camera and the whole system enabled the stereo images to be viewed on screen without any need to cut the film or to transpose and mount the images.

8.14 Projection vs Viewing by Stereoscope

It is probably fair to say that with a correctly mounted stereogram and a good stereoscope the image is generally superior to that of a projected one, certainly in terms of basic image quality. Also, each observer sees more or less an identical image to that seen by others, which is not the case with projected images, which vary in appearance with different seating positions.

The light intensity level in a stereoscope is likely to be higher than that encountered in projection. The eyes will be working at a wider aperture during a projected slide show. This will tend to reduce the depth of field of the image that can be viewed comfortably. A slide with a subject range from 2m to infinity may be more difficult to "take in" when projected, whereas in a stereoscope there is no problem. The spectator might experience diplopia in a projected image but have no such problem when viewing the same image in a stereoscope.

CHAPTER 9: AUTOSTEREOSCOPY

9.1 Introduction

The term **autostereoscopy** is usually taken to refer to a system that enables stereoscopic images to be viewed without the use of a stereoscope or similar device. In a sense it could include the method of free viewing as explained in Chapter 5, Section 5.2 but it is generally applied to systems which rely on special prints or special projection systems, either for slides or moving images (although the latter have been mainly experimental) that can be viewed as 3D images with the unaided eye.

In fact, all such systems do contain some kind of optical device that enables the 3D image to be reconstructed, but the essential difference between an autostereoscopic system and a conventional two-image one is that the optical aid is incorporated into the image or the screen, rather than being in the form of a separate item worn or handled by the observer. Free viewing is rather different because there is no certainty that a particular spectator will be able to see a 3D image, if he has not practised the techniques required.

9.2 The Raster Principle
9.2.1 Basic geometry

This is illustrated in **Fig 9.1** and forms the basis of the majority of autostereoscopic viewing systems. **Raster** is a term borrowed from the world of television where it is the term used to define the pattern of horizontal lines traced by an electron beam as it scans the screen. In stereoscopy, it refers to a vertical grid screen placed in front of a picture that is constructed from narrow vertical strips, arranged alternately from the left and right images. The raster consists of a series of separate parallel vertical slats, or is in the form of a transparent sheet ruled with opaque vertical lines (**Fig 9.1**) and it is placed at a precise distance, close to the strip picture. This arrangement allows the left eye of the spectator to see only the left image strips of the composite image and the right eye the alternating right image strips. Thus each eye sees a "complete" and correct image. However, the very presence of the grid degrades the images because neither is truly complete. Between the strips of either image there are a corresponding number of gaps (where the grid slats mask the strips of the other image). For better resolution, the number of strips needs to be as large as possible; this is akin to the improvement in the quality of TV images that occurred when the old 405 line standard in the UK was changed to 625 lines. With a properly designed raster, having a very small spacing to match up with a finely divided composite image, the individual lines will not be resolved and the image will appear continuous, as is the case with TV images and photographs in books and magazines. It also helps if the picture is relatively large to allow it to be viewed at a greater distance.

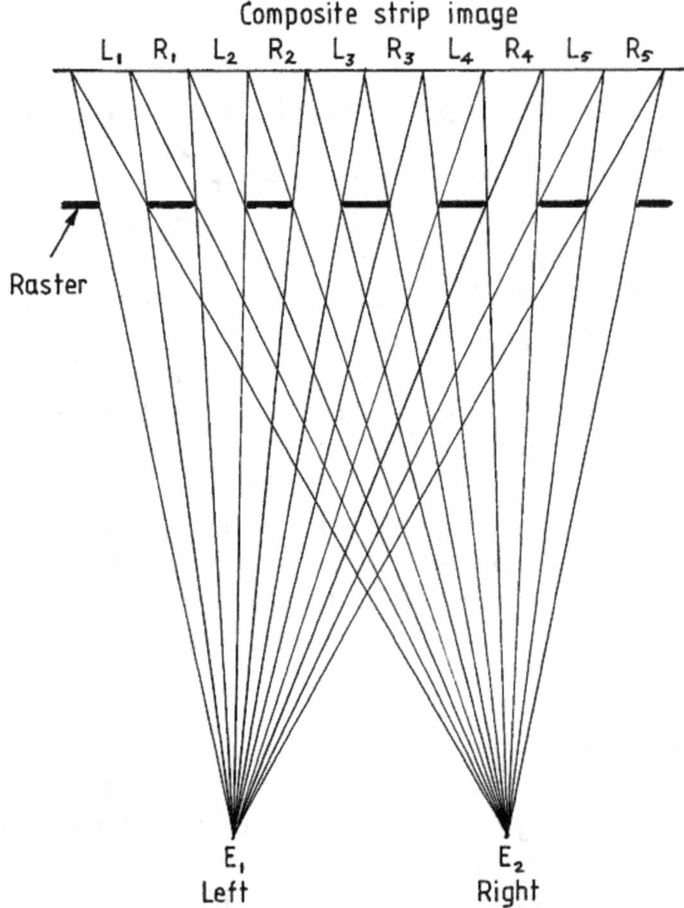

Fig 9.1
The raster principle. With correct positioning of the raster in front of a composite image of alternate left and right strips, each eye sees only the correct image.

The other disadvantage is that correct viewing of the stereoscopic image is often only possible from certain fixed viewing positions. Moving away from these positions could result in each eye seeing the incorrect image or parts of both images, which would destroy the effect, or give a pseudoscopic 3D image.

9.2.2 Additional viewing positions

The composite image constructed in the way described above is also known as a **parallax stereogram**. The method of viewing relies on essentially the same principle as the Elliot stereoscope (Chapter 5, Section 5.2.3).

So far it has been assumed, as depicted in **Fig 9.1**, that the raster is a regular one, in that the slats and gaps are of equal width. A modification to the design is to make the slat width larger than the gap width, as shown in **Fig 9.2**. In this way, extra picture element strips can be located directly behind each slat to provide additional viewing positions.

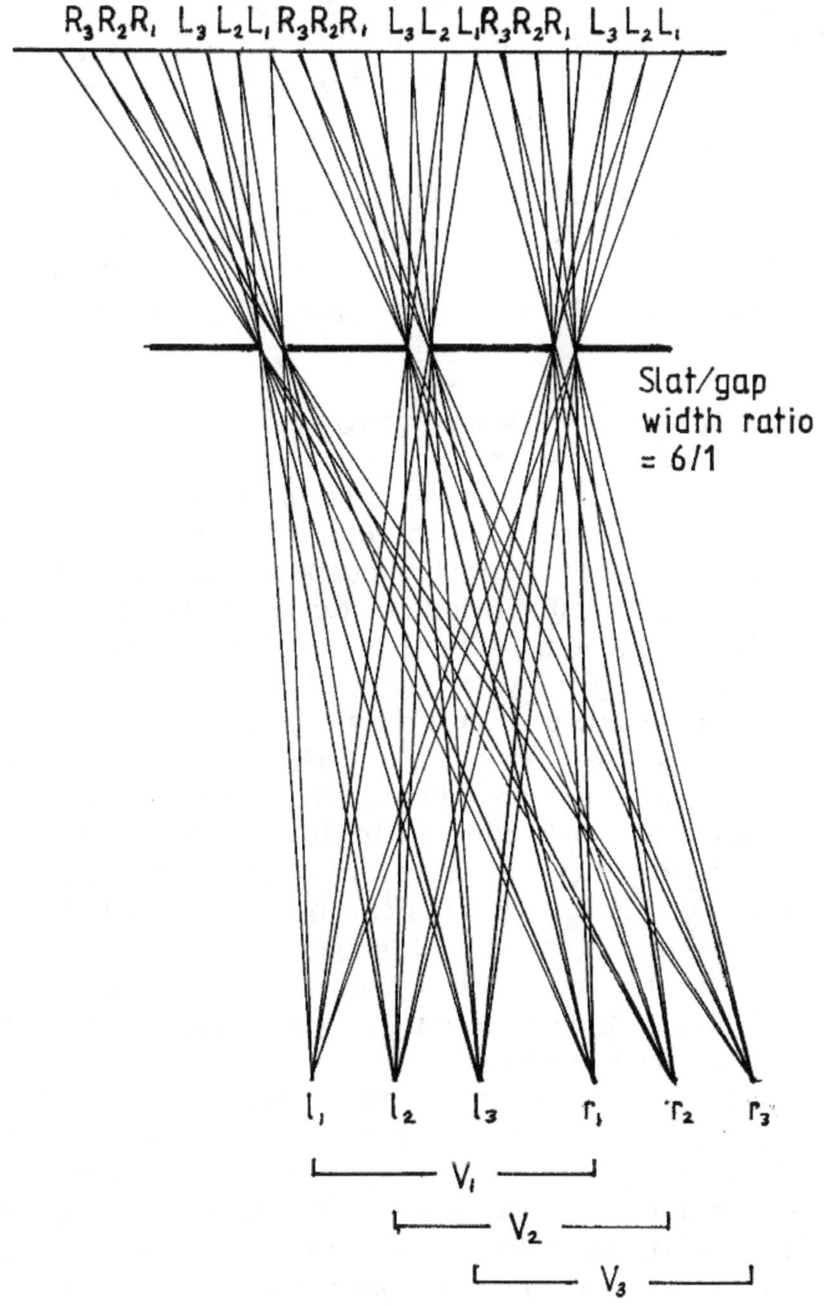

Fig 9.2
A raster with a slat/gap ratio greater than 1:1 gives more viewing positions,
V₁, V₂ *etc.*

The extra strips could simply be duplicates within a single group, but they might be made from images taken from slightly different viewpoints. As an observer moves his head from one viewing position to the next, there will be subtle changes to the images. This can enhance the perception of the total 3D image, replicating, somewhat crudely, the changes that occur as the head moves when looking at real objects.

The disadvantage of increasing the slat/gap width ratio is that less light is reflected from the image to the observer, and the picture appears darker. To preserve the original resolution of the picture, both slat and gap widths have to be reduced as does the picture element strip width. For example, suppose a parallax stereogram is constructed with a 6:1 ratio of slat/gap width, as in **Fig 9.2**. If the original 1:1 raster had been made from picture strips of 0.6mm width, say, then the new version would have to be made from 0.1mm width elements to maintain the gap spacing of 0.6mm. This represents a resolution of 1.67 lines per millimetre (just over 43 lines per inch).

9.2.3 Construction of a parallax stereogram

Making a parallax stereogram by physically cutting photographs into 0.6mm or, worse, 0.1mm strips and reassembling them is clearly out of the question; precision optical methods are required. The cutting method could, however, be used for special display purposes, using very large prints intended to be viewed at relatively long distances, but it is a tedious method and even in this case, some means of producing the alternate strips optically would be easier.

Fig 9.1 gives the clue to a possible method if we re-interpret the main features. Imagine two projectors at E_1 and E_2, the one at E_1 projecting the left image and that at E_2 the right image. By placing a raster as shown (a transparent sheet with black lines) in front of a film, which replaces the composite print, then we can capture the correct strip sequence directly onto the film with one exposure. This can be viewed with the same raster correctly in place, to give a correct 3D image.

With a 6:1 slat/gap ratio raster (or any other ratio) then several exposures have to be made, each from a different viewpoint. **Fig 9.2**, re-interpreted in like manner, illustrates this concept.

Developments of these principles have been used mostly for projection and direct 3D viewing in the cinema, mainly as experimental trials of autostereoscopy. None has succeeded in making a permanent impact in the public domain, though successful results have been reported[24]. Much work has been directed into the designs of the rasters to ensure that all the members of a fairly large audience can correctly observe the 3D images.

One such system, described by Symons[25], was the Cyclostereoscope devised by F. Savoye in France; it was first exhibited in 1949, in a smaller version for amateur use. It incorporated a raster in the form of a truncated cone (**Fig 9.3**) within which the screen was placed. Projection and viewing was made through the raster onto the screen. The raster revolved on a vertical axis, which had the effect of "smoothing out" the vertical stripe effects that result from low resolution. Viewing was possible over an angle of 40°.

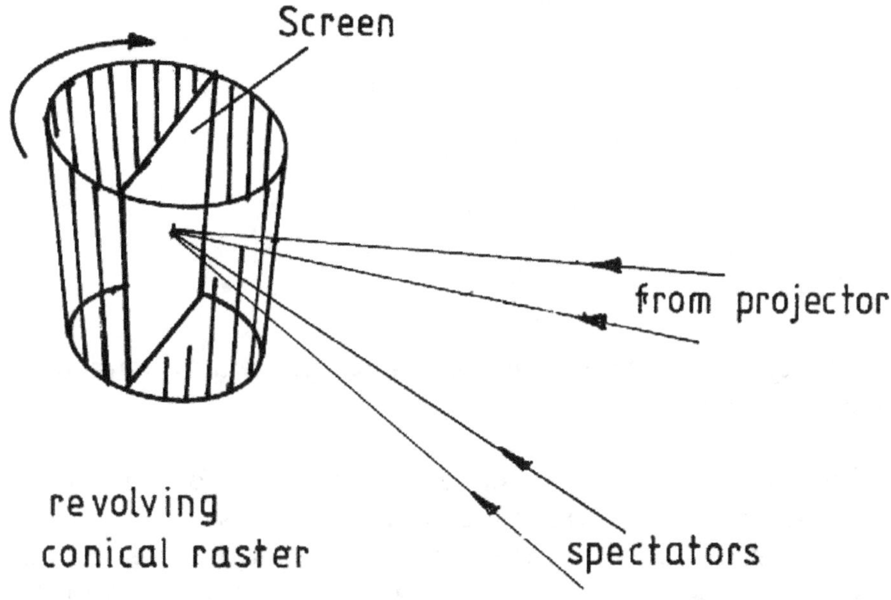

Fig 9.3
Principle of the Cyclostereoscope for moving images. The screen is surrounded by a raster in the form of an inverted truncated cone that revolves around the screen to improve image quality.

9.3 Lenticular Systems
9.3.1 Lenticular prints

Replacing what we might call physical rasters with optical ones offers much improvement in the quality of autostereoscopic images. The single viewpoint problem associated with the simple grid raster is eliminated, and acceptable resolution can be achieved. An autostereoscopic lenticular print consists of a composite strip photograph, often produced from four separate negatives (as with the Nimslo camera), the individual strips being produced by a precision optical printer onto photographic paper which has a thin transparent plastic coating in the form of many parallel semi-cylindrical lenses (**Fig 9.4**).

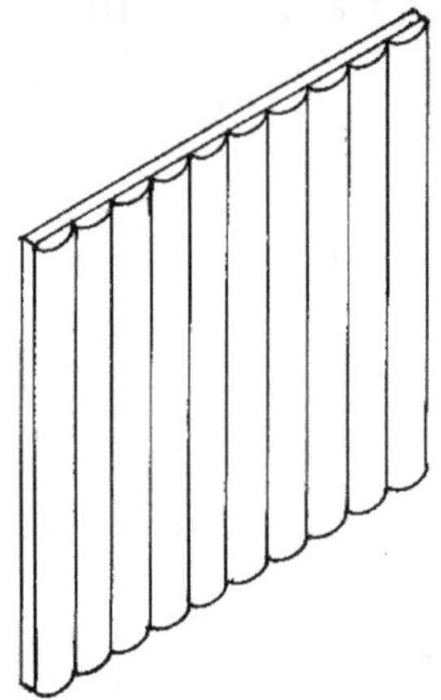

Fig 9.4
Enlarged view of part of the surface of a lenticular print showing the parallel semi-cylindrical lenses.

In the Nimslo system, designed specifically for the production of lenticular prints, there are just under 200 such lenses per inch. At normal viewing distances the ribbed surface can just about be discerned, so there is little apparent loss of quality compared with a standard (non-stereoscopic) photograph.

Each semi-cylindrical lens directs the sight lines of the two eyes of an observer to different image strips (left and right as appropriate) located behind the lenticular screen (**Fig 9.5**).

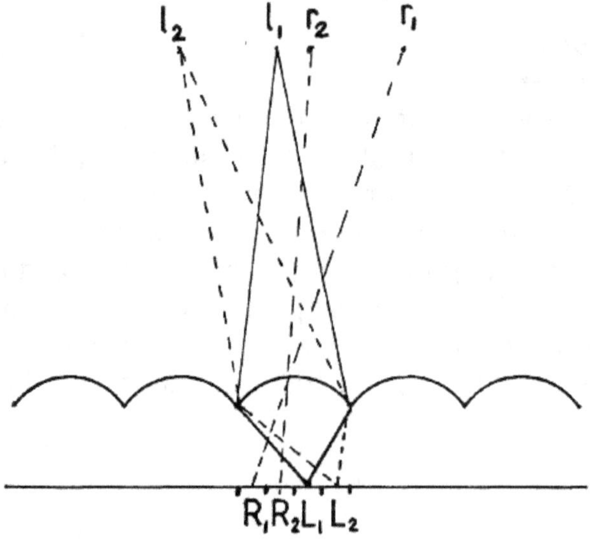

Fig 9.5
A lenticular print enables the observer to see the image correctly from many positions. With the eyes at l_1 and r_1, strips L_1 and R_1 are seen. From l_2 and r_2, the observed strips are L_2 and R_2.

Moving the head sideways when viewing the print causes different left and right image strips to be seen. There may be a slight jump in the continuity of viewing the picture as the viewpoint is changed from one position to another, several times as the head is moved, and parts of the image may appear pseudoscopic momentarily. However, the overriding effect is of an easy-to-view 3D image for which there is no critical viewing position. The slight changes in the image that are observed as different strips come into view give an impression of looking around the subject, as occurs when viewing real objects while moving the head slightly. With a continuous lateral head movement one will detect occasional relative movements between foreground and background that can enhance the perception of the total image.

9.3.2 Lenticular systems for the amateur photographer

Lenticular prints have been produced commercially for a number of years, usually in the form of picture postcards, birthday cards and the like, mostly as novelty items.

With the introduction of the Nimslo camera in 1983 (in the UK) the amateur photographer could now produce his own autostereoscopic prints. Admittedly, this was entirely due to the back-up processing facilities that were linked to the whole marketing package for the camera, which was really no more than a traditional stereo camera fitted with two additional lenses to provide four two-dimensional images from which the lenticular prints were produced. The Nimslo owner could not produce his own prints, of course, but had to rely on the special processing provided by designated laboratories.

In commercial terms the launch of the Nimslo was not a runaway success. The camera, although relatively sophisticated with its programmed exposure system, was rather expensive. Added to that was the cost of processing, some two to three times that for conventional prints, so the general public were not tempted to indulge in what it probably regarded as an expensive gimmick.

In the late 1990's there was a hint of a revival, because a number of simple compact cameras similar in form to the Nimslo, except that some had only three lenses rather than four, became available. Processing facilities were set up to support sales. These cameras are much cheaper and simpler than the Nimslo, and are perhaps more tempting to the casual photographer. However, these cameras are no longer available.

Examples of such cameras are:

1. **3D RITTAI**; A 4-lens compact with built-in flash and motorised drive. It takes 100, 200 or 400 ISO print film. 3 apertures available (f/11, f/5.6, f/4)
2. **IMAGE TECH 3D FX**; A 3-lens (30mm focal length fixed focus) compact with built-in flash. Shutter speed 1/100 sec only. The 3-lens design gave more stereo sets than 4-lens models, viz 24 stereo shots on a 36 (standard frame) length film.
3. **IMAGE TECH 3D WIZARD**; (3-lens fixed focus). A simpler camera with 3 aperture settings (manual) and shutter speed 1/100 sec.
4. **IMAGE TECH 3D WIZARD**; Self-contained recyclable cameras complete with film, one with integrated flash, the other without. Again, both are 3-lens types (fixed focus). The whole camera unit was sent off for processing and the hardware (lens, shutter mechanism etc.) is recycled by the manufacturers.

Clearly, the commercial provision of autostereoscopic facilities for the amateur is rather basic. Cameras are essentially of the point and shoot type, the greatest sophistication being programmed exposure, available in only some models. The wide exposure latitude of current print films compensates for the simple technology in most of these cameras to provide acceptable exposures in the majority of situations.

9.4 Limited Depth Range in Lenticular Prints

A distinctive characteristic of most lenticular prints is that the subject appears to have little depth. There are two main reasons. First, the three or four lens system results in a shorter stereo base than is customary in a stereo camera used for medium to long distance shots. For example, the Nirnslo camera effectively uses two adjacent standard 36mm wide frames for the four images, with the outer lenses spaced at around 55mm. In the three-lens cameras, using roughly 1.5 standard frame widths for the three images (to give 24 views on a 36 standard frame film), the outer lens spacing will be around 37mm. Thus, the images in both designs will be hyposstereoscopic. Second, and this is the main reason, the infinity separation on the prints is much less than that required for orthostereoscopic viewing.

Assume, for the purposes of analysis, that a lenticular print is made entirely of image strips from just the outer pair of images, using a 3 or 4 lens camera. In forming the print the overall left and right images are basically superimposed. Each image extends from the left to the right edge of the final print, ignoring the gaps. If two 35mm "separated pairs" slide images were superimposed in this way the infinity homologues would end up 1.6mm apart (= the deviation) if the lens focal length is 50mm. Now 152 x 101mm (6 x 4in) prints have an enlargement factor of about 4.2 in comparison so that the infinity homologues would be separated by 4.2 x 1.6 = 6.72mm. For shorter focal length lenses, the spacing on the final print will be even less than this. If near objects at 2m are superimposed (so they are located at the print surface) then the whole image will lie between the plane of the print and an infinity plane only a short distance behind it (**Fig 9.6**).

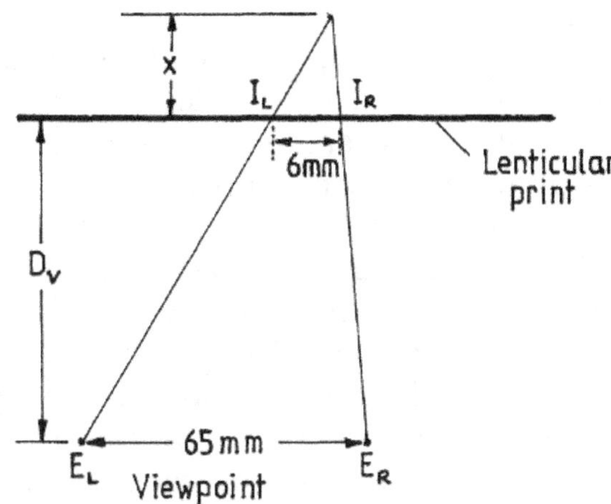

Fig 9.6
Limited depth range **x** *of lenticular prints. Infinity homologues* I_L *and* I_R, *typically 6mm apart, will give an image at a distance* **x** *, about 30mm at best.*

In this diagram, from similar triangles:

$$x/I_L I_R = (x + D_V)/E_L E_R$$

If $I_L I_R$ = 6mm (for simplicity)
       $E_L E_R$ = 65mm
and D_V = 300mm (viewing distance)
then $x/6 = (x + 300)/65$
i.e. $59x = 1800$
and $x = 30.5$mm.

The value of **x** will depend upon the value of $I_L I_R$, which is governed by the parallax deviation. The deviation for 35mm lenses is 1.2mm on the negatives, but this is obtained with a stereo base of 70mm. When the base is reduced the deviation, and hence **x**, will be smaller.

The image, therefore, is contained within a total depth of perhaps 15 to 30mm. It is frequently the case that the print is not set up exactly to superimpose the near (2m) objects. Consequently, the image may straddle the plane of the print, some objects appearing to float above the surface.

Lenticular prints are quite effective for low relief subjects but will have little appeal for those seriously interested in stereo photography. They are often used as the basis of novelty items, such as 3D birthday cards or postcards. Some very effective plastic bookmarks have been produced with an autostereoscopic geometric design that gives a distinct extra "thickness" to an object only 1mm thick. The unusual feature of these is that the 3D image is constantly present even if the bookmark is laid on a flat surface and rotated about a vertical axis while being viewed. A standard autostereoscopic print can be viewed as a 3D image only if it is correctly oriented, with the built-in lenses running from top to bottom in the field of vision of the observer.

A more notable application, reported in 1998, is a development by the electronics company, Philips, of a lenticular screen suitable for use with computers. This allows 3D-based software to be viewed without the aid of special glasses. In 2000 came information from Japan of a new stereo TV system in which the image changes as the viewer moves position, as with holograms, except that the TV system is based upon a matrix of lenses to produce multiple images in conjunction with a similar matrix on the screen.

A decade or so later and 3D TV has aroused interest amongst the general public for a while, although the novelty has perhaps worn off to some extent. Flat screen TVs are now common and some have been developed for autostereoscopic viewing of images. The problem of having only a few fixed viewing positions ("sweet spots") can be overcome by built-in tracking systems that can follow a viewer's position and maintain the correct perception of depth in the screen image as he moves. It is even possible to have multi-tracking so that several viewers can watch simultaneously and see images correctly in 3D. The technology is there but for it to be successfully marketed requires a greater interest and enthusiasm in stereoscopy from the general public. Unfortunately, although interest in 3D imaging emerges every few decades, it lasts for only a relatively short time before waning, and then lies dormant until some new technology appears and sparks a reawakening.

CHAPTER 10: EFFECTIVE PICTURE-MAKING IN 3D

10.1 Introduction

To a degree, all stereo photographs have a novelty factor, simply as a result of revealing the depth of the subject, which ordinary photographs cannot do. For many spectators, viewing 3D photographs is a relatively rare experience which usually elicits favourable comments, whether the actual picture is a good example of the art or merely run-of-the-mill. Some pictures have a particular visual impact that shows off the stereo effect to its best, with good composition and realism. Such stereograms frequently evoke comments to the effect that "it is just like being there!"

All stereo photographers attempt to produce results that justify such a response, but no matter what expertise and experience they bring, they can never be absolutely sure that a particular shot is going to be as effective as they imagined. However, with a sound knowledge of basic principles, they are likely to succeed more times than if they simply snap away thoughtlessly.

As far as the mechanics of stereo photography are concerned, the guidelines and procedures that have been described in previous chapters and in the supplements can be applied. In the main, these factors influence only the technical quality of the images, in that they help to create images that match the original scene as faithfully as possible without causing any viewing discomfort.

When it comes to aesthetic qualities, it is not so easy to give advice. In all the arts, whether they be graphic arts, literature or music, the teaching of composition is probably the most difficult task. The teacher can only help to develop the student's awareness of aesthetics; in the end the learner has to make his own judgments.

Past experience over many generations has at least given us many ideas and guidelines to use as a basis in our creative pursuits and some of these are discussed in this chapter.

10.2 Photographic Composition
10.2.1 General

There are several, now almost traditional, rules of thumb regarding photographic composition that have been used successfully in general photography, and many of them can be of great assistance in 3D work.

Composition is fundamentally about choosing a suitable camera viewpoint, to give a pleasing arrangement of the subject matter in the final photograph. In composing a picture, factors such as the following have to be considered:

1. what the main subject is within the whole scene
2. how far away to place the camera
3. how far to the left or right to place the camera
4. how high or low the viewpoint should be
5. how much to include within the frame
6. the lighting conditions
7. the overall geometric shape and balance of the subject
8. exposure – choosing aperture, shutter speed, plus any exposure compensation
9. light and shade – the tonal balance of the scene

10.2.2 Geometry of composition

Some of the traditional or conventional compositional arrangements that have become established as pleasing or sound are illustrated in **Fig 10.1**.

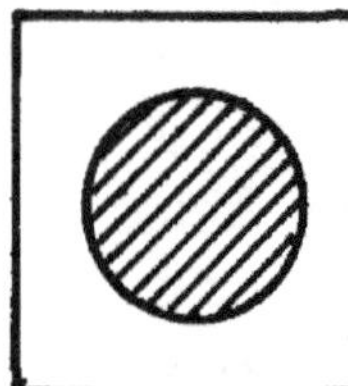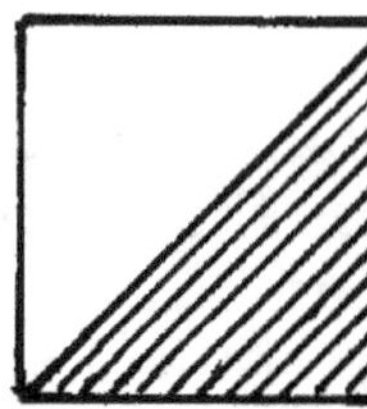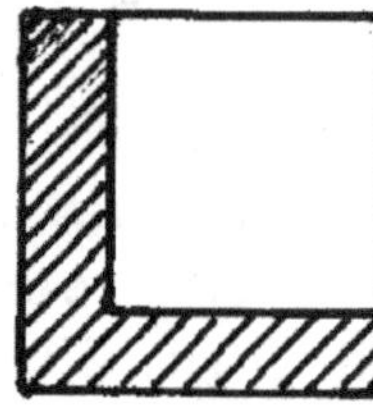

Fig 10.1
Geometry of picture composition – some basic forms.

According to the Focal Encyclopaedia of Photography[27], the qualities of these arrangements are:

triangular - a sense of symmetry
circle - an impression of unity or repetition
diagonal - departure from the static effect - stronger appeal
L-shape - used in foreground framing

Linked with these basic compositional forms is the idea of balance (**Fig 10.2**). Perfectly symmetrical arrangements may be visually somewhat uninteresting. Large single picture elements, not centralised, can make the picture look lop-sided, top-heavy, etc. Depending upon their location within the frame, but better balance can be achieved by including other elements (smaller, if they are of secondary importance) within the frame.

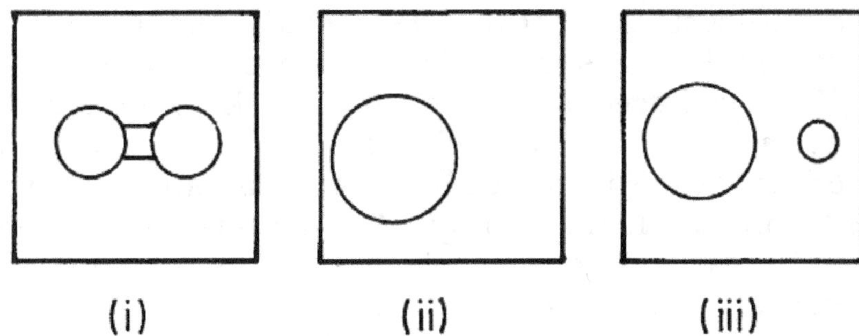

(i)   (ii)   (iii)

Fig 10.2
"Balance" in composition. Picture (i) shows perfect balance, (ii) shows an imbalance and (iii) shows a large area balanced by a small one.

10.2.3 Placement of main subject in the frame

Within a scene one can often identify a particular feature which is of principal interest and which may be regarded as the main subject. In deciding the viewpoint when composing the photograph, the photographer should take into account the position of this main subject both in relation to the picture frame as a whole and to other objects in the scene. The following points may help to identify some of the key decisions that have to be made:

1. the main subject can be close to the camera, virtually isolated from its surroundings, or viewed from further away so that it can be seen in the context of its environment. This is a matter of personal judgment.
2. objects of prime importance can be effectively emphasised by making use of the **rule of thirds (Fig 10.3)** by placing them close to the intersections of imaginary lines that divide the scene into thirds both vertically and horizontally.

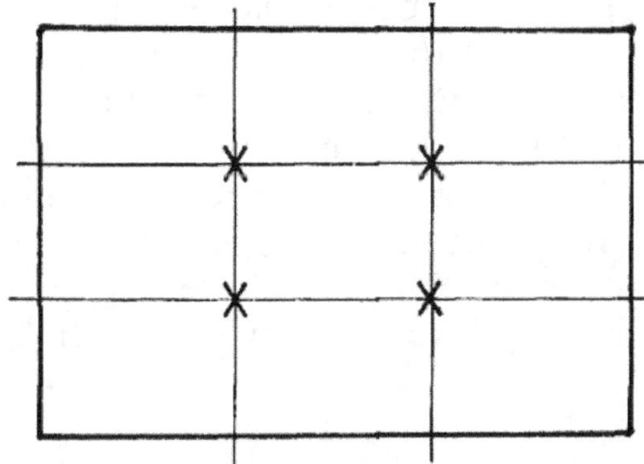

Fig 10.3
The rule of thirds in pictorial composition. Placing the main subject at any of the intersections tends to produce a strong composition.

3.   the main subject can be clearly delineated by finding a viewpoint that ensures that it is not surrounded by unnecessary secondary objects; it may be advantageous to have a light background for a dark object and vice versa, if this is possible. In stereo photography this may not be as critical as it is in mono photography because the depth element in the 3D picture helps to untangle what might otherwise appear to be a confused clutter of objects. Even so, one should not automatically abandon this principle in 3D work.

4.   moving objects should have space ahead of them in the frame. **Fig 10.4** illustrates this point. The principle also applies to people looking sideways in the picture. It is somewhat frustrating when looking at a photograph to see a figure at the right edge of the picture frame staring to the right at something that is out of sight as far as we are concerned, unless this is done for deliberate effect, to make some kind of "statement".

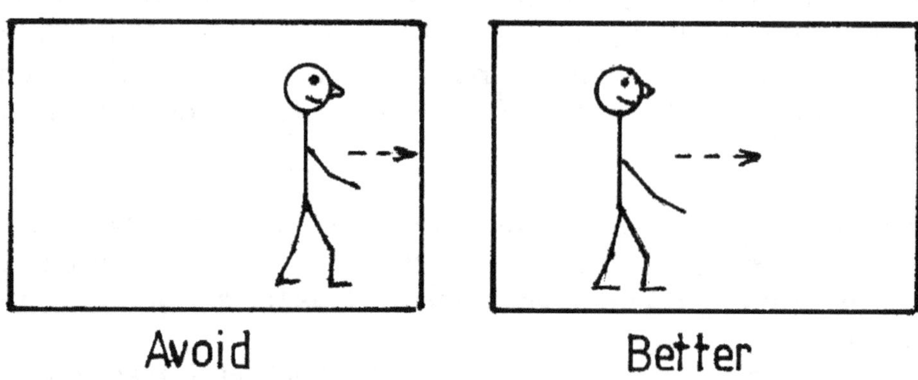

Fig 10.4
Objects or people moving or looking left or right in the frame need space ahead of them for better composition.

5.   the horizon is generally better placed either above or below the horizontal centre line of the picture frame (**Fig 10.5**). When central it tends to cut the scene into halves, creating "two" pictures. Whether the horizon should be low or high depends upon the relative importance of the sky in the scene. A dramatic sky with storm clouds, for instance, can be given greater prominence by choosing a low horizon, but for good stereo there should be something in the foreground to give depth to the scene as a whole.

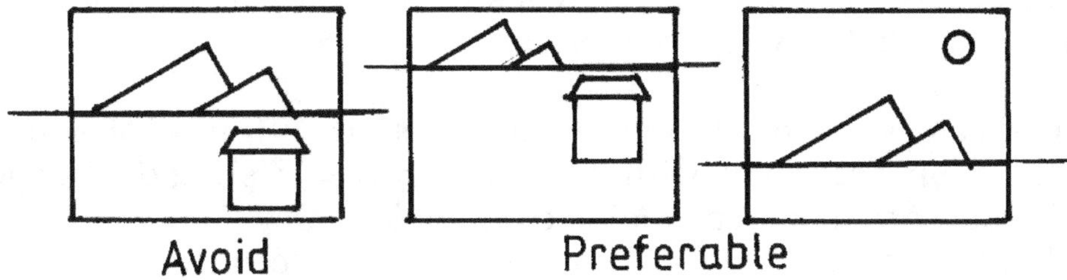

Fig 10.5
Generally it is better to avoid placing the horizon centrally as this tends to divide the frame into "two separate pictures".

10.2.4 Composition for stereo

The established "rules" of composition, several of which are discussed above, are not rules in the strictest sense, but guidelines based upon a consensus of opinions drawn from past experience. There is no suggestion here that they must be followed if successful artistic results are to be achieved. They can be broken, and frequently are, without necessarily producing poor pictures. Each photograph is an individual concept; whether the rules are followed or not, knowledge of them helps the artist to improve his value judgment.

Having said all this, some aspects of composition are unique to stereoscopic images. Certain scenes or subjects that produce disappointing results in two dimensions may work effectively in three.

Take the classic situation that is normally avoided in mono photography, a picture of a man with a lamp-post or tree directly behind him, apparently growing out of his head. To avoid this, the viewpoint is changed by moving the camera to the left or right of the original location. In stereo, however, the depth element in the image makes it quite clear that the figure and tree are quite separate. That is not to say we can freely disregard such configurations of subject matter in 3D work; it may still be better to shift position when taking the picture to improve the overall composition, but it is less of a problem.

A second type of picture that can be more acceptable as a stereo image is of the following type. Imagine a photograph of a thick cluster of foliage, plants, shrubs, or part of a hedgerow. In two dimensions a rather flat-looking picture would be produced, with no particularly distinctive features apart from a mass of branches and leaves, difficult to untangle visually. In 3D, the same picture could look lively, with the complex intertwining of the branches, leaves at different distances and so on, and turn out to be an effective study in depth.

There is a warning note, however; three-dimensional representations do not automatically convert poor two-dimensional ones into works of art. Those that do work effectively often have a kind of abstract quality about them. One must still choose such subjects with care.

With regard to what we might call "depth management" in taking stereo pictures, the following may prove helpful:

1. the greatest depth information is perceived with near objects. Stereo perception decreases with distance. Subjects should, therefore, be kept as close as is reasonable or feasible.
2. a landscape without foreground does not produce the most effective stereo, even though a sense of space may be perceived when the stereogram is viewed. One generally needs close objects and others at mid-distance to complete the picture. Even a close figure or overhanging branches can provide a necessary reference, but pictures that are "all front and back" with little in between can be somewhat crude.
3. the depth range from front to back of the subject should be kept within the limits suggested in Supplement S9. To avoid greater ranges than can be comfortably viewed, one can make use of "artificial" backgrounds such as walls of buildings, or hedges.
4. the inclusion of objects from 2m to infinity (or whatever is the recommended depth range for the particular subject) is not obligatory in every shot. Stereograms with a limited depth range, less than the maximum possible, can be just as effective.
5. the taking of several shots from different viewpoints (general views, closer shots showing particular details and so on) is well worthwhile, rather than relying on a single shot. With luck, one or two might produce the desired effects
6. leading lines such as footpaths or railings are helpful in guiding the observer from foreground to background. Some of the most effective stereo shots are those which include objects that recede and link the depth planes together, rather than just a number of isolated objects at different distances. Branches of trees, parapets, walls, bridges etc. fall into this category when photographed at appropriate angles.

10.2.5 Use of colour

In general photography, management of colour is an important aspect of composition and it is no less valuable in 3D. Some of the principles are outlined below:

1. creating a harmonious blend of colours in a scene using hues that go well together
2. emphasising the main subject as a bold colour against softer background colours
3. having the main subject as the only item with a particular colour to make it more prominent (e.g. the only red object)

4.   using only a limited range of colours in a scene (e.g. blues and greens) for special effects
5.   deliberately engineering a clash of vibrant colours for effect.

The reader should consult various photographic books on composition to develop these ideas further.

10.3 Lighting
10.3.1 General considerations

Brief mention was made in Chapter 1, Section 1.2, of the qualities of light that assist in providing depth clues in mono photography. They work equally well for 3D.

The solidity of real objects is more evident when the lighting is strong enough to cast shadows. With a suitable viewpoint, chosen to make shadows on the object itself visible, the roundness, squareness, surface roughness and so on are made evident. Dull, flat lighting, on the other hand, can render the object almost two-dimensional; one has to look harder to appreciate its depth. Flat lighting can be one of the factors that produce the effect known as **découpage**. This effect is characterised by a lack of detail, particularly in foreground and mid-distance areas, where objects appear to be flat "cardboard cut-outs" set at different distances, resembling a multi-layered scene cut from card in a child's peep-show.
Strong directional lighting can, in some circumstances, produce a similar effect. Taking pictures against the light (**contre-jour**), may cause the various objects to appear in silhouette, showing little or no shadow detail. Consequently, they will appear very flat. Contre-jour shots can be very effective, though, and more likely to be so if the stark blackness is reduced by increasing the exposure by a stop or so to reveal some shadow detail. **Fig 10.6** summarises some of the effects of lighting on stereo perception.

10.3.2 Artificial lighting and flash

Whatever the lighting conditions, natural or artificial, the points about "modelling" discussed in the section above are still relevant. With artificial lighting one should use the correct film stock, balanced for a lower colour temperature. Alternatively, one can use "daylight" film in conjunction with a blue filter (such as a Wratten 80B) to compensate for the yellowish colour cast that would otherwise be produced.

Techniques for studio lighting have been analysed in many photographic books. Principles of good lighting include the use of floodlights to give a base level of illumination, spotlights to highlight particular objects or to provide modelling and the use of reflectors to direct some of the ambient light towards shadow areas, to lighten them. The reader is advised to consult the many specialist books on photographic lighting for further details and information.

Flash lighting is an indoor substitute for natural daylight, in that no colour correction is required when using daylight balanced film. In 3D the subject must be relatively close or the level of illumination becomes too low for good exposure. Second, if sequential shots are taken, either by using a mono camera or by shifting a stereo camera (to reduce or enlarge the stereo base), the flashgun will move with the camera, and the lighting directions for the two images will be different. In these conditions, the flashgun must be separated from the camera and placed in a fixed position relative to the subject, for both exposures.

In close-up stereo photography, such as a still life, one technique is to take separate shots with a camera in a fixed position, and rotating the subject, on a turntable by a few degrees between shots. A fixed flash will again produce differing lighting angles for the two exposures. The answer here is to ensure that the lighting (i.e. the flashgun) rotates with the subject, so that these two items remain fixed in relation to each other.

LIGHTING THE SUBJECT

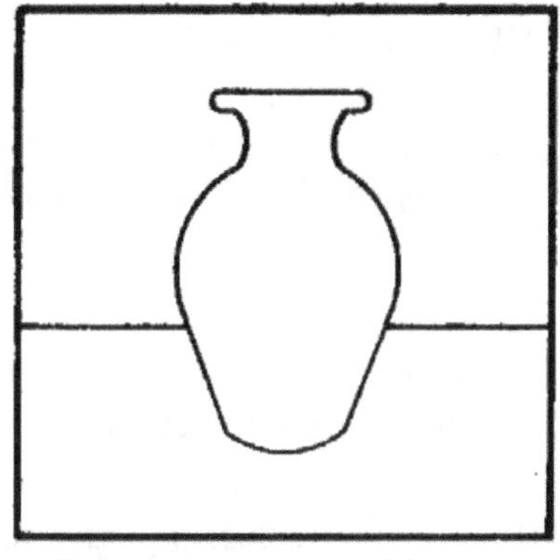 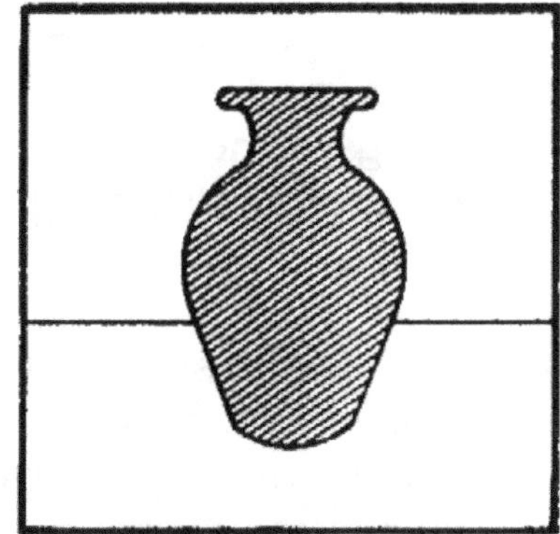

Flat lighting is seldom satisfactory: the subject merges with the background (*left*) unless it is different in tone, colour, or surface texture (*right*).

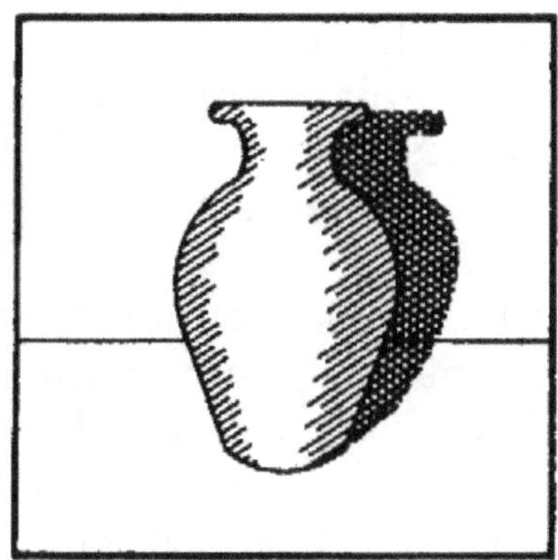 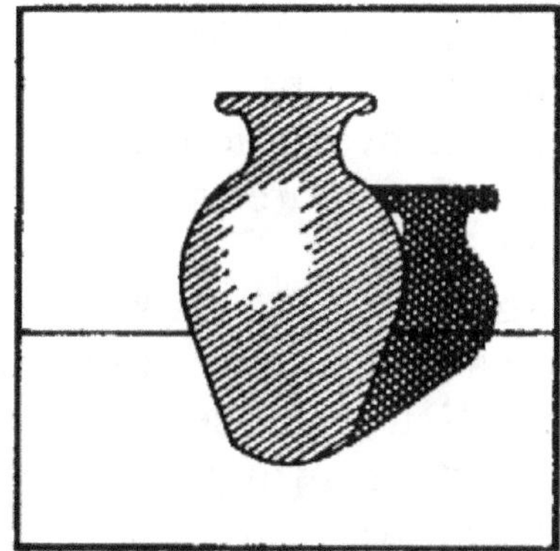

The roundness of a subject is revealed by side-lighting (*left*), and becomes accentuated when the light is also raised (*right*)

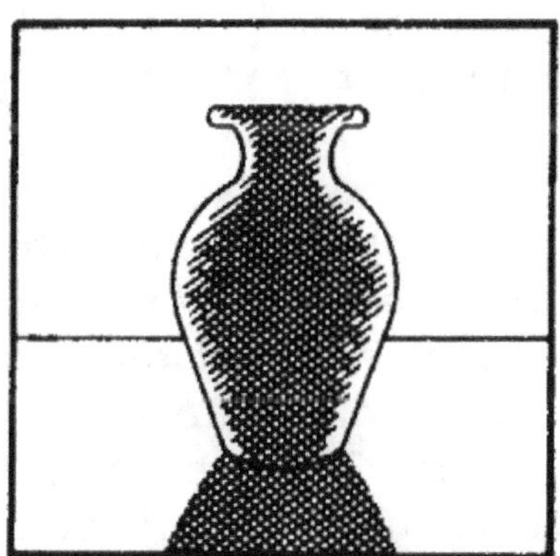 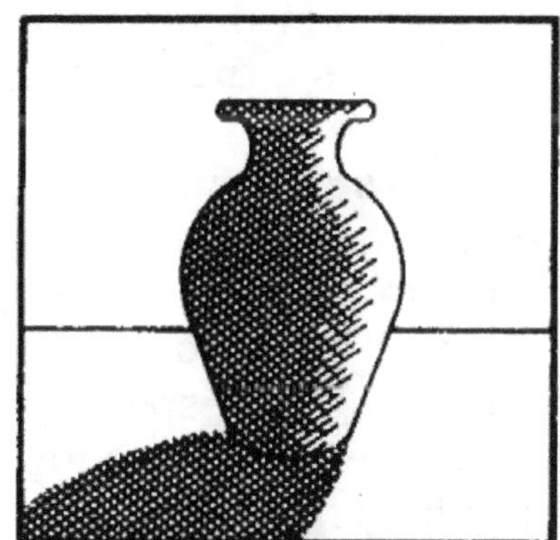

Backlighting also tends to diminish roundness (*left*). Side-backlighting is better, but some areas will lack detail unless illuminated by reflected light (*right*).

Fig 10.6
Importance of lighting in portraying the depth of a subject. From Symons[32].

10.4 Moving Subjects

As a general rule, it is wise to avoid taking stereo pictures of moving subjects, because they very often appear unnatural. What is acceptable in images of moving images in mono photography does not always "come off" in stereo. Once again the rule can be ignored, but one must be prepared for less than satisfactory results. To stand a better chance of success, the following points should be considered:

1. a sufficiently fast shutter speed must be used to avoid blurring of the moving object. A "solid" mass of blur looks most odd in 3D although one can sometimes get away with blur in some parts of a subject.

2. even when the movement of the object is frozen by a fast shutter speed, the resulting image can look static, not conveying any sense of movement. This can be so in mono photography too, where slight blurring is acceptable, to suggest movement. A sharply defined object may appear to be stationary; that itself may give it an artificial appearance, particularly if it is in mid-air. A picture of someone jumping over a fence, for example, looks most natural if it is taken when the figure is at its highest point rather than part way up or down.

3. images of people walking or running may look peculiar if legs or arms are caught at ungainly angles, one foot in the air, perhaps. If they are relatively close to the camera. The problem is much less if they are further away and only incidental to the scene as a whole.

4. running water (rivers, fountains) can appear very much as if frozen and can look more like ice if captured on film by a fast shutter speed. Still waters, lakes with no ripples, for example, are generally less troublesome in this respect. Very fast running water can look like a blurred mass if the shutter speed is too slow.

10.5 Focusing Techniques

Normally, one should take 3D photographs with the whole of the scene in focus, to give a sharp image from the nearest object to the furthest. To do this, careful choice of aperture is essential, so in deciding upon which of the available shutter speed/aperture combinations to use for a given exposure level, the aperture should take priority. The appropriate aperture can be determined from the depth of field scale on the camera, or from depth of field tables (see Chapter 17, Section 17.5 and Supplement S13). All of this assumes that, when the appropriate aperture is selected, the shutter speed is satisfactory for the particular subject or circumstances. In dull lighting conditions with a small aperture of f/11, for example, the correct shutter speed might well be too slow for a hand-held shot, or too slow to freeze any motion of objects within the scene. If so, the shot may have to be abandoned.

When focusing, it has to be remembered that zones giving acceptable image sharpness exist both in front of and behind the distance to which the lens is focused. As a rule of thumb, which applies to medium and long distances, about one-third of the total range lies in front of the focused distance and about two-thirds behind it. The technique known as **zone focusing** is recommended for general use. This is quite straightforward if the camera lens mount incorporates a depth of field scale (**Fig 10.7**).

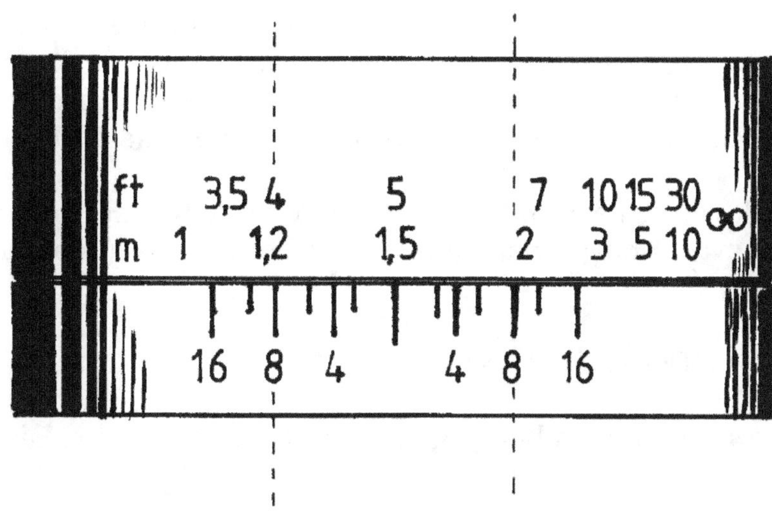

Fig 10.7
Typical depth of field scale on a camera lens. With the lens focused at 5ft., the depth of field for an aperture of f/8 extends from 4ft. to about 6½ft. as shown.

The lens mount is rotated until the near point and far point distances of the scene are aligned with one of the pairs of aperture markings, or fall between the two marks. If the camera is not equipped with a depth of field scale, then depth of field tables can be consulted, although this is a somewhat tedious exercise and not usable in situations where quick decisions have to be taken, or the moment will have passed. Simple cameras, without any focusing facilities, are usually designed to give a reasonably extensive depth of field, even at the wider apertures, so that the majority of photographs will be acceptably sharp. This situation can be imitated with a focusing camera by pre-setting the focus to a suitable distance and selecting an appropriate aperture. For example, with a camera lens of focal length 35mm set at f/8 and focused at 6m (20ft), subjects from about 2m (6ft) to infinity will be in focus. The only variable will be the shutter speed, which can be adjusted according to the lighting conditions and film speed.

Some modern SLR cameras have a depth of field preview facility. Normally, a scene is viewed through the viewfinder at maximum aperture. When the shutter release button is pressed, the iris diaphragm rapidly closes to the pre-set value for the actual exposure, then opens fully again. By pressing a depth of field preview button, the iris stops down to the pre-set value so that the photographer can check the range of focus prior to the exposure being made. The brightness diminishes in this mode, of course, and it can be difficult to assess the range in dull lighting conditions.

Certain cameras have a depth of field program setting, which can be advantageous, used along with autofocus facilities. The camera is first pointed to the nearest object that is to be rendered sharp and the shutter release button half-pressed to register the distance in the camera's electronic memory. Then, a similar reading is taken for the most distant object in the scene. The camera automatically sets the correct aperture to produce the desired depth range and focuses the lens to the appropriate distance.

A simple formula can be used to calculate the correct focusing distance D to give a sharp image for objects between D_N (near distance) and D_F (far distance):

$$D = 2D_N D_F / (D_N + D_F)$$

The aperture (n = stop number, e.g. 5.6) that must be set to give this range of sharpness is:

$$n = 1000f(D_F - D_N) / 2D_N D_F$$

where f is the focal length of the lens. (N.B. f must be in the same units as D_N and D_F)

Example

If the range of sharpness is to be from 3m (10ft.) to 10m (33ft.), then:
$$D = 2 \times 3 \times 10/(3 + 10) = 60/13 = 4.6\text{m (approx 15ft.)}$$

The aperture setting required for a 35mm (= 0.035m) focal length lens:

$$n = 1000 \times 0.035(10 - 3)/2 \times 3 \times 10 = 4.1$$
i.e. $n = f/4$

Thus, by setting the focus to 4.6m and the aperture to f/4, a 35mm lens will give acceptable sharpness for a subject range of 3 to 10m. Of course, smaller apertures than that calculated could also be used and would in fact give greater depth ranges. The aperture value calculated from the above formula is the largest that will produce the required depth of field.

For the maximum possible depth of field at a given aperture, the lens should be focused at the **hyperfocal distance** for that aperture (see Chapter

17, Section 17.5.2). By doing so, the scene will be in focus from half the hyperfocal distance to infinity. **Tables 10.1** and **10.2** give hyperfocal distances for various apertures and focal lengths.

TABLE 10.1
Hyperfocal Distance (metres) for given focal length and aperture

Focal length (mm)	Aperture							
	1.8	**2**	**2.8**	**4**	**5.6**	**8**	**11**	**16**
24	13	12	9	6	4.3	3	2.2	1.5
28	16	14	10	7	5	3.5	2.6	1.8
30	17	15	11	8	5.4	3.8	2.8	1.9
35	19	18	13	9	6.3	4.4	3.2	2.2
38	21	19	14	10	6.8	4.8	3.5	2.4
50	28	25	18	12	9	6.3	4.6	3.2
70	39	35	25	17	13	9	6.4	4.5

(Distances greater than 7m have been rounded to the nearest whole number).

TABLE 10.2
Hyperfocal Distances (feet, inches) for given focal length and aperture

Focal length (mm)	Aperture							
	1.8	**2**	**2.8**	**4**	**5.6**	**8**	**11**	**16**
24	44	39	28	19'9"	14'2"	9'11"	7'3"	5
28	51	46	33	23	16'6"	11'7"	8'5"	5'10"
30	55	49	35	25	17'8"	12'5"	9'1"	6'3"
35	64	58	41	29	21	14'6"	10'7"	7'3"
38	69	62	45	31	22	15'9"	11'5"	7'11"
50	91	82	59	41	29	21	15'1"	10'5"
70	128	115	82	58	41	29	21	14'7"

(Distances greater than 20ft have been rounded to the nearest whole number).

Accurate focusing is easy on modern SLR cameras with the advent of autofocusing, and often the depth of field scales are absent on autofocus lenses. On older stereo cameras there may be no aids to focusing accurately. The Stereo Realist has a built-in range finder, which is of great assistance, though much slower to operate compared with autofocusing. It is still possible to buy small range finders (**Fig 10.8**), mostly second-hand, and it is worthwhile investing in one for a relatively small sum. They can be fitted to the camera accessory shoe and are invaluable for checking the depth range and the distance of the main subject from the camera. Accuracy of focusing is most important for subjects at closer distances, say 6m (20ft) or less, and it is better not to place too much trust in one's ability to estimate them by eye.

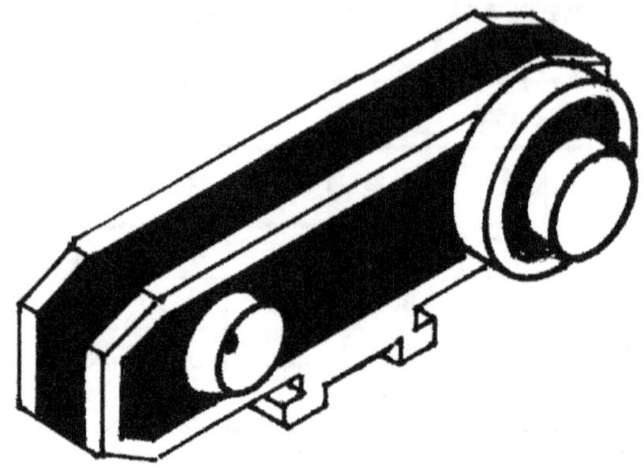

Fig 10.8
Typical rangefinder (not used much these days with the benefits of autofocus) that fits into the accessory shoe of a camera.

Although one should normally aim to produce a fully sharp image from front to back, there are occasions when the background in particular can be out of focus. For this to be acceptable, the background should be fairly inconspicuous and more or less uniform, with no distinctive features to catch the eye. In these circumstances, the less sharp it is the better.

10.6 Film

Amongst the many technological advances in photography that have been made over the past twenty years or so, the improvements to film emulsions must surely rank among the highest. Each year sees further progress as film manufacturers launch the latest versions of previously successful films, with better colour rendition, finer grain or whatever claims are made. The stereo photographer is provided with a wide choice of emulsions and can easily find one that he prefers.

Since the aim of stereo photography is to re-create the real world life size (for orthostereoscopic viewing at any rate), it is important to produce the highest quality images possible, because those images are going to be viewed at a relatively high magnification. The finer the detail that can be recorded by the camera, the better the result. With film images based upon 35mm film stock it is advisable to use film with only modest sensitivity, 100 ISO for example. For static subjects (e.g. close-ups in the studio), where fast shutter speeds are not required, one can use 25 ISO film stock; there are some excellent films of this speed available.

Even so, the faster emulsions should not be ignored for those occasions where lighting is less than desirable, e.g. flash pictures indoors at long range, or where a moving subject requires fast shutter speeds combined with a small aperture. Current 200 and 400 ISO film emulsions are remarkable in quality and so much better than their counterparts of a few years ago. The graininess of the image increases with film speed, and it is preferable to use slower film whenever possible for most work.

With transparency film, exposure accuracy is more critical and if older cameras having no built-in exposure facilities are being used, it is wise to purchase a hand-held exposure meter.

Film for colour prints has greater exposure latitude and is the obvious choice for the rather simple 3D cameras such as the Loreo and the various cameras intended for the production of lenticular prints.

10.7 Exposure

When taking stereo shots with modern cameras which have built-in metering, such as the better specified compact cameras, or SLR's with through-the-lens (TTL) metering (and that includes current models of the Siamesed type), the photographer can be fairly certain that 90% or more of his exposures will be perfect. Sophisticated metering systems are now common, and some cameras are equipped with more than one type, centre-weighted, integrated (from measurements in different parts of the image) and spot metering (from a small area), to give three examples. Just occasionally, tricky lighting conditions or very light (or dark) subjects may "confuse" the meter and give slightly inferior results.

With older cameras, one can use the basic guide to exposure that is printed usually inside the film carton, which will work for most straightforward situations, but sound judgment is required to assess the lighting conditions by eye. This is less of a problem with colour print film with its extra latitude, but slide film needs more precision. The use of a hand-held electronic exposure meter is recommended; even so, one has to learn how to use it properly.

It is recommended that if the photographer is unsure about a particular exposure he should err on the side of underexposure if using transparency film, and on the side of overexposure for print film. Better still, if the subject allows it, he should take two or three shots, each at a slightly different exposure, perhaps half to one stop either side of the measured one. Some SLR cameras will do this **bracketing** automatically when the appropriate function is selected. Usually, three shots are taken in quick succession, one at the exposure determined by the camera's meter, one at a stop above and one at a stop below. In some cameras the amount of under and over exposure for bracketing can be set from between half a stop to several stops.

With slides, erring on the side of underexposure should not be taken to mean gross underexposure. In the final stereogram, the shadow areas need to be exposed sufficiently to show some detail, or they will appear without much depth. At the same time one must avoid any burning-out of the bright (highlight) areas. Extremely contrasty lighting can be difficult to photograph successfully, if both of the above objectives are to be met.

Selecting the appropriate shutter speed/aperture combination is sometimes a matter of compromise. The aperture is often the prime consideration in stereo photography and must be small enough to give adequate sharpness over the depth range of the subject, as discussed in Section 10.5 above. This will determine the shutter speed for the prevailing light levels and one must then consider whether or not it is appropriate for the particular subject or the conditions under which the exposure is to be made. Too slow a shutter speed may rule out a hand-held shot or taking a picture of a moving object. The slowest usable shutter speed for hand-held shots is usually taken (in seconds) as the reciprocal of the lens focal length (in mm). With a 50mm lens, for example, the slowest hand-held shutter speed would be 1/50th sec on this basis. If a slow speed is unavoidable, then the camera will have to be supported on a tripod, or placed on a firm base for the exposure. If a cable release can be used to fire the shutter, this is desirable, for using finger pressure on a camera, even when it is fixed to a tripod, can cause some slight movement.

A cable release operated by a trigger mechanism (**Fig 10.9**) which screws into the tripod socket on the base of the camera can also be used when slow shutter speeds are necessary; this helps to avoid camera shake when hand holding, but it should not be regarded as a cure-all.

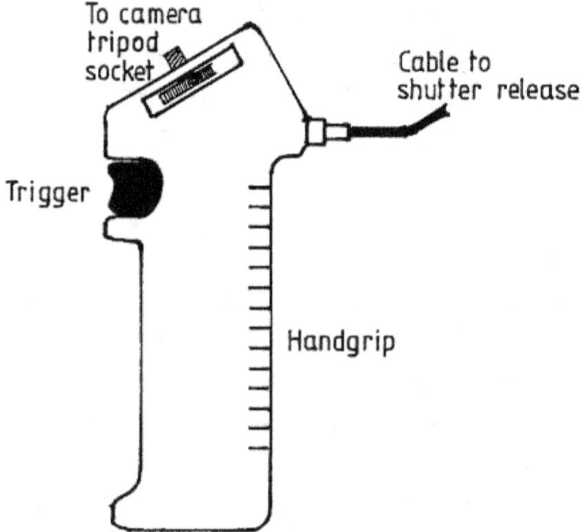

Fig 10.9
Trigger release for shutter that can be fixed to the camera base. It helps to minimise camera shake at slow shutter speeds.

CHAPTER 11: TRICK PHOTOGRAPHY AND SPECIAL EFFECTS

11.1 Unusual Images

Over the years many photographers, not content with merely recording natural scenes and events, even artistically, have employed a number of devices or techniques, either when taking the photographs or during the processing stages, to produce imaginative results. Unnatural effects, surrealist images or apparently impossible subjects count among the many pictures that have been created.

Trick shots could be defined as those in which a sense of illusion is produced, akin to the conjuror's art, whereas special effects might be considered as unusual or special treatments made to the image to produce changes that could not be achieved by straightforward exposure in camera, but the distinction is not particularly important.

Many "traditional" tricks and effects can be applied equally well to 3D photography. Some are inappropriate, while others have to be modified if they are to work in three-dimensional images. Even some of the more hackneyed tricks can gain a new lease of life in stereo and regain the impact that has perhaps been lost through familiarity.

Various ideas and techniques will be discussed in this chapter, but the list is by no means exhaustive.

11.2 Survey of Tricks and Effects
11.2.1 Scope

A number of tricks and effects that are fairly well established in conventional photography will be surveyed in the next section. How they can be adapted to work in stereo photography will be discussed in Section 11.3.

11.2.2. Optical tricks

These include the use of optical devices with the camera and special techniques when enlarging negatives to create prints in the darkroom.

1. **Use of mirrors**; a single mirror can produce symmetrical images. Two mirrors at 60° (or other angles) can be used to form multiple images as in a kaleidoscope. Concave and convex mirrors produce distorted images.
2. **Lenses**; the use of supplementary lenses is an established procedure for close-ups and does not really count as a trick. Using more unorthodox equipment such as binoculars or telescopes in front of the lens might be regarded as a special effect. Cheap simple lenses will tend to introduce distortion at wide apertures, or some softening of the image that can be used to produce changes.

3. **Effects filters**; special coloured and optical effect filters, such as those marketed by Cokin, are readily available. Almost any optical effect, soft images, soft surround to a clear central image, graduation of colour, multicolour, multi-imaging, diffraction effects and many more, enable the photographer to enhance (or ruin!) his picture.

4. **Use of an enlarger**: when enlarging negatives to produce prints, images can be changed in a number of ways. These include: deliberate soft focus (using a plain glass filter smeared with Vaseline); tilting the baseboard at an angle to correct or create converging verticals; arranging the print paper into curved surfaces to distort the image.

5. **Distortion of scale**; the classic trick is to produce a photograph of somebody with one hand outstretched, upon which stands what appears to be a tiny but real person. The figurine is actually a second person standing some distance behind the "full-sized" one to appear smaller. Careful selection of the camera position is the key to the success of this trick. The effect will not work directly in 3D because the images of the hand and small figure will be seen at their true relative distances.

11.2.3 Exposure tricks

1. **Long exposures**; one particular special effect can be produced with the camera on a tripod in a darkened room to allow a small torch to be moved around, thus producing a light-trail image. The torch can be attached to swinging objects to produce images against a black background. Very long exposures can be used to eliminate moving objects from a street, for example. Instead of using an instantaneous exposure of, say, 1/100 sec, which would record traffic, ten separate, spaced exposures of 1/1000 sec would be made. In any one of these, moving objects would be recorded at worst as only very faint images. Static objects, after the build-up of ten of these short exposures, will form a correctly exposed image. Obviously, with continuously flowing traffic, the method would fail. With long exposures and occasional moving objects, the aperture can be left open and the lens capped whenever vehicles move into and out of the scene.

2. **Double exposures**; a classic effect is to produce a "ghost". An empty room is photographed and a double exposure is made by superimposing a shot of a person standing against a black background. The final image shows a figure which is transparent. The picture of the person can be taken outdoors by flash in a dark open space, against the sky, if a black background is not available. The principle can be used to show the contents of, say, a wooden box, the latter appearing transparent to reveal what is inside. If any part of a normal scene is masked out with some black velvet, a

second exposure of an object against a black background (and positioned to coincide with the blacked out area in the first exposure), then a double image without ghosting can be produced. This method can be used to produce an object in a picture frame, for example. In normal photography this may seem to be rather circuitous but in 3D it is extremely effective and not easily created in any other way (**Fig 11.1**).

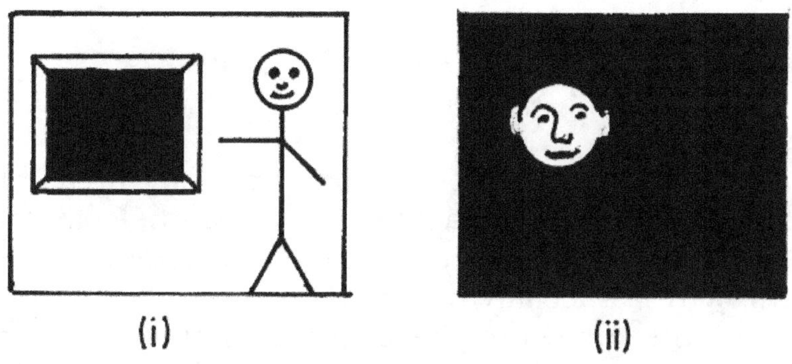

Fig 11.1
The "black art" principle using double exposures (i and ii) with various parts of the scene blacked out for each shot. When the above shots are superimposed, the effect will be of a 3D head in the picture frame.

Using an extended lens hood or a matte box (**Fig 11.2**), double (or multiple) exposures can be made side by side in one film frame, by masking half of the opening. The mask is shifted to the opposite side for the second shot. This device allows the same person to appear in both halves of the frame as twins or "doubles". The frame can be divided horizontally or diagonally at any angle by careful positioning of the mask. Three, four or more exposures of this type can be made on a frame by using masks that cover two-thirds, three-quarters etc. of the frame (**Fig 11.3**).

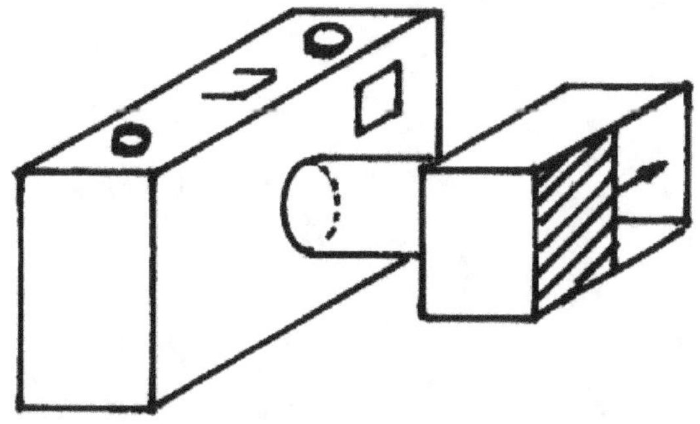

Fig 11.2
Mono camera with a matte box fitted to the lens. Various shaped masks can be fitted to the box front like the simple image divider shown, which can be moved across for double exposures.

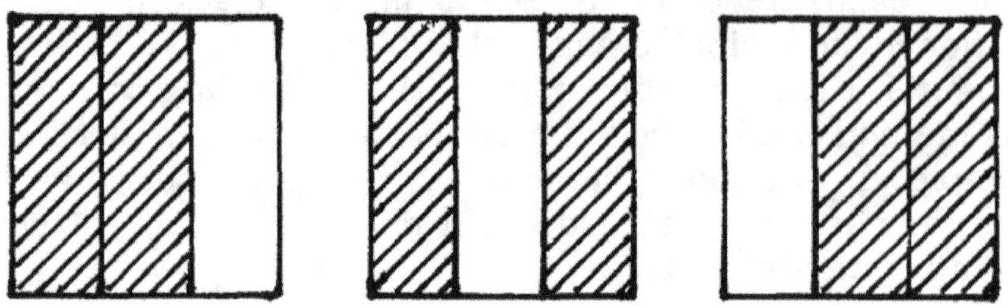

Fig 11.3
Successive masking for "3 image" multiple exposures.

11.2.4 Lighting effects

1. **Light sources**; concentrated lighting on small areas of the subject can be created by a large magnifying glass in the beam of an ordinary light, or by using a slide projector as a source, to create strong shadows. With a specially prepared slide in place, its pattern will be spread over the subject to give unusual textures or lighting effects.

2. **Projected images**; a slide projector can also be used to provide a background against which a person or object is photographed, an exotic location, for example. There are two problems with this: one is that the projected beam, if it is to avoid the figure, has to be directed obliquely to the screen (**Fig 11.4**) and this will give a distorted image. The second problem is to provide sufficient illumination to give a satisfactory exposure for the principal subject, without swamping the projected background. Back projection, with the slide laterally reversed, is one solution to the first problem. Another is to project the slide square-on to the screen and to take a photograph of the image at an oblique angle to produce a new slide (with a distorted image). If this second slide is projected at the same oblique angle behind the figure) its image will now appear correct when viewed perpendicular to the screen.

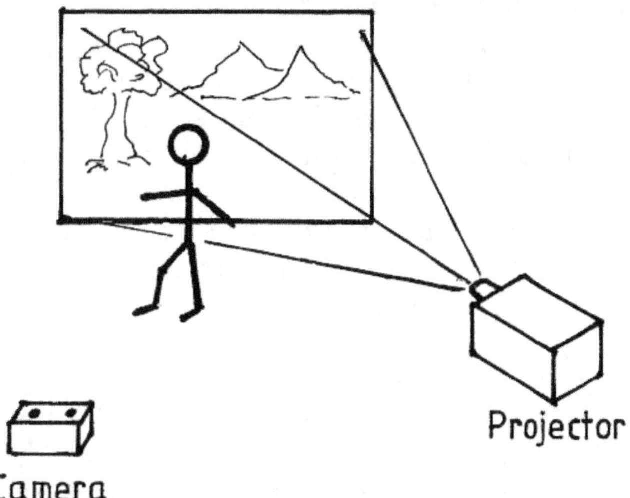

Fig 11.4
Use of a projected image to create a background. Because the beam must be angled to avoid the figure, the screen image will be distorted obliquely. In stereo work the screen image will be flat, destroying any illusion of the figure being in a real location.

11.2.5 Montage
Parts of a photograph can be cut out and pasted onto another to create either realistic or surrealistic images. The montage is usually re-photographed. This technique allows one to mix colour and black and white images, to create differences in scale and many more effects. For best results the cutting needs to be accurate and the cut edges blackened or coloured appropriately to blend properly with the background.

11.2.6 Computer imaging
In the computer world software is available that enables the operator to manipulate screen images. These may be captured on screen by scanning a photograph. The programs allow the images to be modified in many ways e.g.:

1. removing parts of the subject and filling in the gap electronically, to give a perfect match.
2. adding extra subject matter, the computer equivalent of montage.
3. altering colour, contrast, lighting effects and the like
4. altering image shapes.
5. reducing or enlarging parts of the image in relation to the background The final result can be printed out on high resolution colour printers to give images of excellent quality.

Further discussion of computer imaging is given in Chapter 14.

11.2.7 Chemically produced effects

Various effects, mainly in black and white photography but not exclusively so, can be produced by deliberately departing from normal processing procedures. Such techniques as switching on a light part way through development to form a combination of positive and negative images, raising the temperature of the fixing bath to produce reticulation (a network of fine lines where the emulsion is broken up) are examples of this category.

Unusual colour effects can be produced by processing slide film as if it were print film and vice versa.

11.3 Applicability to Stereo Images

Many of the tricks and effects described above can be applied successfully to stereo work. Those that require home darkroom facilities are not very evident these days, because few amateur photographers carry out their own processing.

The tricks and effects that are less easily adaptable to stereo imaging are:
Section 11.2.2 (4) Use of enlarger
Section 11.2.2 (5) Distortion of scale
Section 11.2.4 (2) Projected images
Section 11.2.5 Montage
Section 11.2.7 Chemically produced effects

To create stereo backgrounds from projected images, it would be possible to make two separate exposures using left and right images on screen in turn, but this is not so easy with a human figure present. The person involved would be required to stand or sit absolutely still while the background was changed.

Montage, too, would require two stereo pairs of prints and the pieces being added would have to be very accurately located, a fiddly process, though not impossible.

Reticulation, as described in Section 11.2.7 cannot be produced identically in both prints of a stereo pair and cannot be used for stereo work.

Optical effects such as those produced by double exposures are amongst the most widely practised tricks in 3D photography. To be successful they require a little more care, because the "extra" image has to be located not only in the correct position in the frame but at the correct depth plane in the scene.

11.4 Tricks Using the "Black Art" Principle
11.4.1 The basic technique

In its simplest form, this technique involves taking two images on one frame of the film, as illustrated in **Fig 11.1**. The "black art" principle involves blacking out parts of the scene by using matt black paint or covering with a black material such as velvet for the first exposure. The subject matter for the second exposure has to be accurately aligned in the frame so that it falls into these blacked areas. Correspondingly, those areas that form an image in the first exposure must be themselves blacked out for the second shot to avoid any overlap of the separate images, which would cause ghosting. This kind of effect can only be produced if the camera allows double exposures to be taken. Most cameras have a built-in double exposure lock to prevent accidental multiple images and for the trick effects this has to be over-ridden; with many cameras this is not possible.

To illustrate the trick, let us assume that the final picture is to consist of a person looking at a picture of himself (in 3D) hanging on a wall. The basic procedure will be as follows:

1. **Shot 1**. A picture of the person in a room looking at the picture frame, which contains nothing but a piece of black velvet. For illustration, we shall assume that the picture frame is on a wall and is 2.5metres (8ft.) away from the camera. The film is not advanced after this exposure.
2. **Shot 2**. This will be a picture of the person's head and shoulders only, with a completely black surround. This can be done by draping the person in black velvet apart from the head and shoulders, which are photographed against a black background. This could be in the form of a black velvet curtain, or a matte black wall; alternatively, the second picture can be taken outside by flash in a dark open space at night.

The head must be positioned in the frame so that it will coincide exactly with the position of the picture frame in the first shot; there is a device that can be used to facilitate this, described later. If, for example, the head and shoulders image is to be one-third of its normal size, this second exposure will have to be taken with the draped figure three times as far away i.e. at 7.5metres (24.5ft.).

However, there will be, a discrepancy because the "portrait", although one-third in size, will appear to be well behind the picture frame, at 7.5 metres. Therefore, in the second shot, the image must be brought forward to 2.5 metres. This is done by increasing the stereo base from 70mm to 3 x 70 = 210mm. This will mean taking sequential shots by covering each lens in turn and ensuring that the person remains stationary between shots.

In this example, there will actually be three separate exposures:
1. **Shot 1**. person plus "black" picture in frame at 2.5m
2. **Shot 2**. head and shoulders using left lens only, right lens covered, at 7.5m
3. **Shot 3**. head and shoulders using right lens only, left lens covered, at 7.5m but 210mm to the right of the position of the left lens in shot 2.

If the portrait is to be full size (on the same scale as the person in the first shot) then the second exposure will be a straightforward stereo shot taken at 2.5m, superimposed on the first. The technique can of course be extended, if required, to three or more superimposed shots.

11.4.2 Scale and image positioning

If both shots are taken with a normal stereo base (about 70mm), then images will appear in the final composite at distances roughly equal to their original positions in space. As we saw above, it is possible to manipulate both the scale of any image and its depth location.

In addition to reducing the size of an image, as in the example, it is possible to increase its size by photographing it at a closer distance.

These changes in scale and location can summarised by means of simple formulae:
1. **Scale**. If an object is to appear at a distance **D** in the final image, the desired size can be gauged by placing the object itself at this distance and estimating how much bigger or smaller the image needs to be. If **m** is the magnification factor, then the object has to be photographed at a distance D_P, where $D_P = D/m$. Note that if **m** is greater than unity, the image will be larger; if less than unity, the image will be smaller.

Example

To produce an image one-quarter size at 3m distance, **m** = 0.25 and the object should be photographed at 3/0.25 = 12m.

However, this image will also be located at 12m. To "bring it back" to 3m, the stereo base has to be modified as shown below.

2. **Location**. To relocate the final image (in its reduced size) back to distance **D** instead of D_P, the stereo base is simply increased by a factor D_P/D. Thus, the new stereo base **b'** is:

$$b' = bD_P/D$$

In our example D_P = 12m, **D** = 3m, and **b** = 70mm, say.
Hence   **b'** = (12 x 70)/3 = 280mm

This will relocate the image to **D** (3m) and it will be one-quarter size, compared with the actual object at 3m. In fact, the image can be relocated to any distance **D'** by using the formula for **b'** given above.

Example

Continuing with the previous example, the image to be photographed at 12m (to produce the correct scale) could be relocated to 6m by using a stereo base of:

$$\mathbf{b'} = 12\mathbf{b}/6 = (12 \times 70)/6 = 140\text{mm}$$

Summary

Using a reference distance **D** to estimate the scale required, and a magnification of **m**:

The distance at which to photograph the image to produce the correct scale is **D$_P$**, where:

$$\mathbf{D_P} = \mathbf{D}/\mathbf{m}$$

Stereo base required to relocate the image to a new distance **D'** is **b'**, where:

$$\mathbf{b'} = \mathbf{bD_P}/\mathbf{D'}$$

where **b** is the normal stereo base. (Note that **D'** can be smaller as well as larger than **D$_P$**)

Since **D$_P$** = **D**/**m**, the stereo base can be written in terms of the initial reference distance:

$$\mathbf{b'} = \mathbf{bD}/\mathbf{m}\ \mathbf{D'}$$

11.4.3 Image locating device

Without some form of assistance, it is difficult to ensure that the subject in the second exposure will fall exactly in the right places (black areas) of the first exposure. In the Stereo Realist Manual[28]; Tommy Thomas describes an "image locator" to help in this respect, designed specifically for the Stereo Realist camera. It is basically a rectangular Perspex sheet with two large holes cut into it to allow it to be clamped onto the lens hoods. It provides an area of clear Perspex in front of and slightly forward of the centrally placed viewfinder. By looking through the viewfinder when setting up the first "black art" exposure, the photographer can outline the masked area on the Perspex, using a chinagraph pencil. This outline helps to position the subject correctly for the second exposure.

A modification to this design by the present author. (**Fig 11.5**), allows the Perspex to be attached to the camera via the tripod socket in the base. This design does not, therefore, rely on fitting Realist lens hoods, which, fifty years after the camera's inception, are probably rather scarce. The new version gets round this problem. The vertical piece with the lens hoods is attached to the base off-centre to allow access to the shutter cocking lever on the Realist. The shape can be modified to fit other makes of camera, but it is more likely to suit those with a central viewfinder window, or there are likely to be parallax problems.

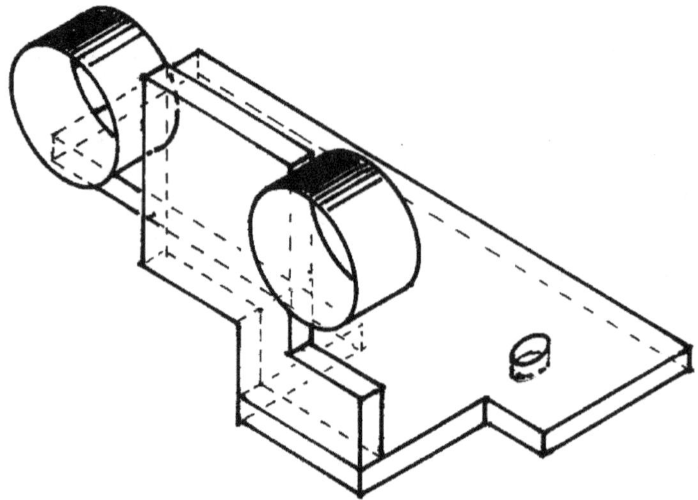

Fig 11.5

"Image locator" device designed by the author for the Stereo Realist camera, modified from the original idea by Thomas[28]. In this version, made in clear Perspex, the built-in hoods fit over the camera lenses when the device is attached to the tripod socket under the camera via the hole on the right. The central rectangle will locate in front of the viewfinder and can be marked with a grease pencil to denote the positions of key objects for alignment in multiple exposures.

11.5 Tricks Using Image Divider Caps

This, in stereo work, is the equivalent of using a matte box in mono photography (Section 11.2.3 2). Placing image divider caps over both lenses enables just part of each film frame (most commonly one half) to be exposed for the first shot. The caps are rotated by 180° to expose the remainder of each frame in the second shot. Usually referred to as D-caps (**Fig 11.6**) from their appearance, they resemble pillboxes with the end cut away across a diameter

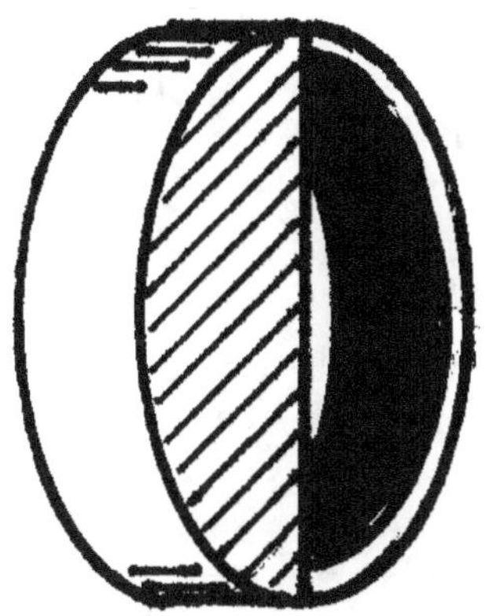

Fig 11.6
Divider cap (or D-cap) for multiple exposure work.

With the aid of these caps, a photograph showing the same person twice in the same frame, as if twins, can be produced, for example. With skill and practice the two figures can appear to be holding a single object, one at each side, or standing quite close to each other.

The D-caps can be set with the dividing edge vertical, horizontal or at any angle to suit the circumstances or the effect desired.

There is a minor problem arising from their use in that the first "half image" will extend slightly into the other, as yet unexposed, part of the frame. Similarly, the second "half image" will overlap into the first image. This central band (fusion zone) is a critical area within which nothing must change or move between the two exposures. Any part of the subject to be "doubled" that appears in this region will appear transparent, as a ghost effect.

In the final composite there will be no evidence of the transition zone, provided the necessary precautions are taken to avoid ghosting.

The width of the fusion zone depends upon the picture-taking geometry, both in the camera and in the D-caps. It is narrower for shorter focal length lenses, smaller apertures and longer D-caps (with the "D" further away from the lens).

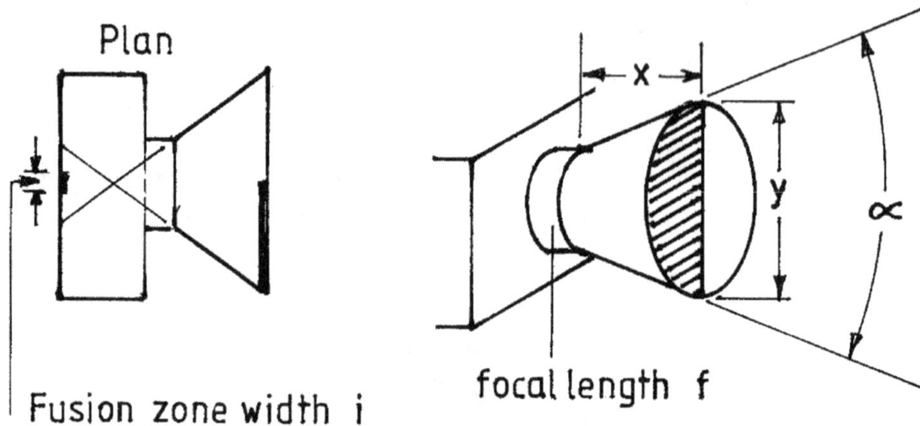

Fig 11.7
Key geometric features of D-caps.

Using the information given in **Fig 11.7** the width **i** of the fusion zone is given by:

$$i = f^2/nx \qquad \text{(see Supplement S11)}$$

where **f** = lens focal length
x = length of D-cap
n = aperture (stop number) (e.g. **n** = 11 for f/11)

The diameter **y** of the cap at its wide end (at the "D") is given by:
$$y = f/n_0 + 2x\tan(a/2)$$
where **n₀** = widest aperture available on lens
a = angle of view of lens based upon the frame diagonal

Example
For the Realist Format, 35mm focal length lenses and D-caps of length 40mm, the fusion zone width **i** calculated from the formula given will be, for an aperture of f/8:

$$i = 35^2/(8 \times 40) = 3.83\text{mm}$$

Expressed as a percentage of the frame width (23mm), the fusion zone (with D-caps dividing the frame vertically) will occupy:

$$(3.83 \times 100)/23 = 17\% \text{ of the total width.}$$

Example

For the same format and D-cap length (40mm), the diameter **y** can be calculated as follows:

Diagonal angle of view **a** = 50°48' (See Supplement S3)
a/2 = 25°24'
tan (**a**/2) = 0.4748

For an f/2.8 maximum aperture lens, and using the formula for **y**:

y = 35/2.8 + (2 x 40 x 0.4748)
= 12.5 + 38
= 50.5mm or 51mm rounded up.

Similar analyses have been made by H. Everett[29] in an article on the use of D-caps, in the Stereoscopic Society's Bulletin.

A summary of his results is given below in a slightly modified form, and with some additions, in **Tables 11.1, 11.2** and **11.3**.

TABLE 11.1
Fusion Zone Width (FZW) for D-Caps (Vertical Divider) REALIST FORMAT
(35mm lens, max aperture f/2.8)
%W = percentage of (23mm) frame width occupied by fusion zone

Cap Diameter y ▶	32mm		41mm		51mm	
Cap Length x ▶	20mm		30mm		40mm	
Aperture ▼	FZW (mm)	%W	FZW (mm)	%W	FZW mm)	%W
4	15.3	67	10.2	45	7.7	34
5.6	10.9	48	7.3	32	5.5	24
8	7.7	34	5.1	23	3.8	17
11	5.6	25	3.7	17	2.8	13
16	3.8	17	2.6	12	1.9	9
22	2.8	13	1.9	9	1.4	7
32	1.9	9	1.3	6	1.0	5

TABLE 11.2
Fusion Zone Width (FZW) for D-Caps (Vertical Divider) EUROPEAN FORMAT
(40mm camera lens, max aperture f/2.8)
%**W** = percentage of (30mm) frame width occupied by fusion zone)

| Cap Diameter y ▶ | 37mm | | 49mm | | 60mm | |
| Cap Length x ▶ | 20mm | | 30mm | | 40mm | |
Aperture ▼	FZW (mm)	%W	FZW (mm)	%W	FZW (mm)	%W
4	20.0	67	13.3	44	10.0	33
5.6	14.3	48	9.5	32	7.1	24
8	10.0	33	6.7	22	5.0	17
11	7.3	24	4.8	16	3.6	12
16	5.0	17	3.3	11	2.5	8
22	3.6	12	2.4	8	1.8	6
32	2.5	8	1.7	6	1.3	4

TABLE 11.3
Fusion Zone Width (FZW) for D-Caps (Vertical Divider) 35mm Full Frame
(50mm camera lens, max aperture f/2.8)
%**W** = percentage of (36mm) frame width occupied by fusion zone

| Cap Diameter y ▶ | 44mm | | 53mm | | 61mm | |
| Cap Length x ▶ | 30mm | | 40mm | | 50mm | |
Aperture ▼	FZW (mm)	%W	FZW (mm)	%W	FZW (mm)	%W
4	20.8	58	15.6	4.3	12.5	35
5.6	14.9	41	11.2	31	8.9	25
8	10.4	29	7.8	22	6.3	18
11	7.6	21	5.7	16	4.5	13
16	5.2	19	3.9	11	3.1	9
22	3.8	11	2.8	8	2.3	6
32	2.6	7	2.0	6	1.6	4

In these tables, the percentage width is calculated with the dividing line set vertically. The actual fusion zone width is constant for all settings of the D-Caps, vertical, horizontal or at any other angle.

While a narrow fusion zone is generally desirable, the ability to use wider apertures (and a wider fusion zone) gives more scope for faster shutter speeds. If the "doubles" are to be seated one at each end of a table the extra distance between the positions allows for the use of a wider aperture.

The technique can be extended so that three or more exposures are combined for the final image. It is simply a matter of using two-thirds or one-quarter D-caps etc., as depicted in **Fig 11.8**, and rotating the caps by the appropriate angles between each individual shot. Other shapes can also be devised.

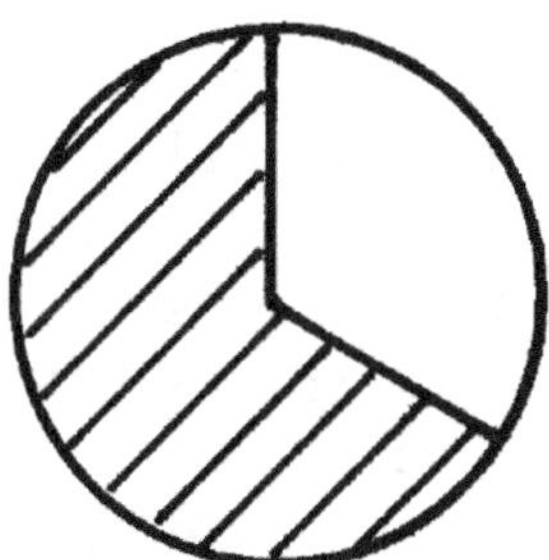 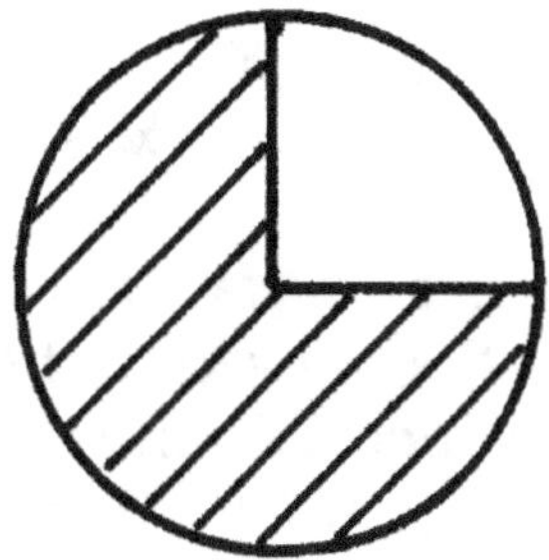

Fig 11.8
D-caps for 3 and 4 image multiple exposures.

As an alternative to D-Caps, a matte box similar to that shown in **Fig 11.2** can be made wide enough to cover both lenses of a stereo camera. Slides with pairs of apertures of different shapes and size can be fitted to the front of the matte box to produce the appropriate masking. Such a device was marketed in the 1950's for the Stereo Realist camera, by the Powers company of Cleveland USA, under the name "Powers Trick adapter".

11.6 "Floating Object" Tricks using Sequential Exposures
11.6.1 Basic principles

Individual objects, provided they can be moved, can be made to "float" if the stereo photograph is taken as two separate (sequential) exposures. Each object that is to be "floated" has to be moved laterally between the two shots.

The technique is as follows:
1. with the camera on a tripod or suitable support, the left shot is taken in the normal way. If a stereo camera is being used, the right lens has to be covered.
2. the object that is to be "floated" is moved a short distance to the left (as viewed from the camera position).
3. the second shot is taken using the right lens of the stereo camera, with the left lens covered, without advancing the film and using the double exposure prevention over-ride facility. If a mono camera is being used, it will have to be moved laterally by a distance equal to the stereo base between exposures, in the normal way.

The procedure can be reversed; if the right shot is taken first, then the object must be moved to the right prior to the second (left) exposure. An easy way to remember the principle is that the object is moved in the opposite direction to the exposure sequence. For example, with the two shots taken in the order left and right, the object must be moved from right to left. If one imagines the sequential exposures being taken with a mono camera, then the object and camera have to be moved in opposite directions.

The effect of this, if carried out correctly, is that the object will appear nearer to the camera than it actually is and will float in front of the background. It will also appear smaller than its normal size.

The distance by which the object has to be moved laterally depends upon:
1. its original distance from the camera
2. the distance from the observer at which the "floating" image is to be located in the final picture.

For a given object distance, the greater the amount of lateral shift, the nearer (and smaller) the object will appear in the image.

Fig 11.9 shows how the effect is achieved. In **Fig 11.9a** the on-film images of a point object photographed as a normal 3D pair are shown. The object **O** gives left and right images **M** and **N** respectively. **Fig 11.9b** again shows the right image of the stereo pair with **N** denoting the expected position of the image of **O** on film for a "straight" 3D shot. However, when the object is moved leftwards to **O'** before the film is exposed, its image will be formed at **N'** instead of **N**. After transposing and mounting of the film chips, points **M** and **N'** will be closer than **M** and **N** would have been in a normal 3D shot. Thus, the object will appear closer but, because the actual size of the image on film is unaltered, it will appear to be smaller (**Fig 11.10**), because the angle subtended by the object at the eye is unchanged.

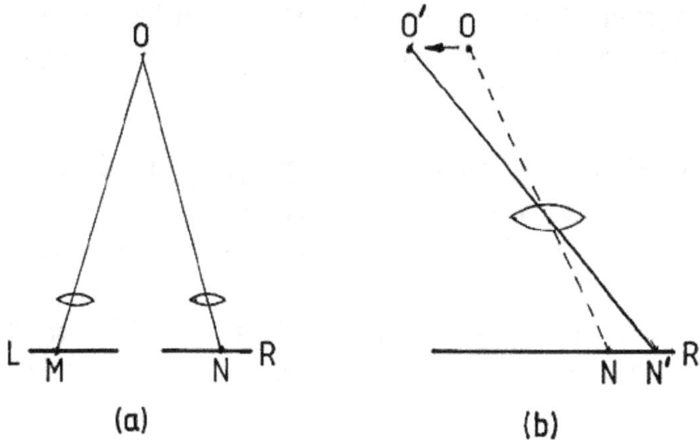

Fig 11.9
Principle of the "floating image" trick shots.
a. *homologues on film produced by normal stereo photography.*
b. *Effect of moving the object from **O** to **O'** between sequential exposures, left followed by right in this example. The homologue in the right film chip will appear at **N'** instead of **N**. The effect is to bring the image of **O** forward.*

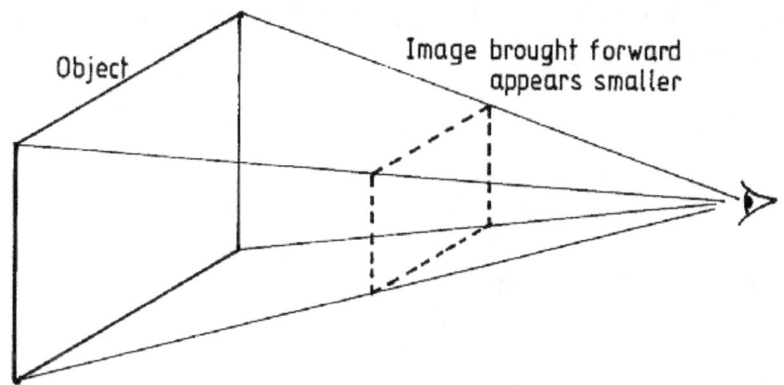

Fig 11.10.
The nearer image produced by the "floating" technique still subtends the same angle at the eyes, so it appears smaller.

For successful results, the following points are also important:
1. the object must be moved only laterally, as seen from the camera. There should be no movement towards or away from the camera
2. the object should look identical in both positions. With a car, for example, the wheel spokes should be set at the same angles for both shots or spurious images can arise.
3. if the object casts a strong shadow, this, too, will move with the object and will appear to float, giving an unsatisfactory effect.
4. no part of the object should be obscured by any nearer object, such as the branch of a tree. If the object is ultimately going to float nearer

to the observer than the branch there will be a discrepancy in the image. Of course this advice can be ignored if a surrealistic effect is desired.

11.6.2 Controlling the position of the floating image

This is a matter of controlling the location of the point N' on the right film chip; this location is determined by the distance through which the object is moved.

If an object is located at distance D_A and it is to be "floated" at some nearer distance D_B then the amount x by which the object has to be moved is given by:

$$x = b(D_A - D_B)/D_B$$

where b is the stereo base being used (see Supplement S12).

The easiest way to use this formula is to calculate x in the same units as b, the stereo base (in mm for example). Since $(D_A - D_B)/D_B$ is simply a ratio, any convenient units for D_A and D_B (the same for both, of course) can be used to calculate a "multiplying factor" for b.

Example

An object is located at a distance of 20ft from a camera and is to be "floated" at a distance of 8ft.

First, calculate the multiplying factor:

$$(D_A - D_B)/D_B = (20 - 8)/8 = 12/8 = 1.5$$

Then, for b = 70mm:
x = 1.5 x 70 = 105mm

Equally valid is to take b = 2.5in
i.e. x = 1.5 x 2.5 = 3.75in

Table 11.4 gives x values for various D_A and D_B combinations:

TABLE 11.4

Lateral movement x required for an object at distance D_A to "float" at distance D_B

(Stereo base **b** = 70mm)

D_A (actual object distance)	x values (mm) for required D_B value											
	D_B ("floating" distance required)											
	2	2.5	3	3.5	4	4.5	5	5.5	6	7	8	9
2.5	18	—	—	—	—	—	—	—	—	—	—	—
3	35	14	—	—	—	—	—	—	—	—	—	—
3.5	53	28	12	—	—	—	—	—	—	—	—	—
4	70	42	23	10	—	—	—	—	—	—	—	—
5	105	70	47	30	18	8	—	—	—	—	—	—
6	140	98	70	50	35	23	14	6	—	—	—	—
8	210	154	117	90	70	54	42	32	23	10	—	—
10	280	210	163	130	105	86	70	57	47	30	18	8

The value of **x** (in mm) is read directly as the value in the table at the intersection of the row and column for the relevant **D_A** and **D_B** values. Thus, for an object at 5 metres required to float at 3 metres, the **x** value is 47mm. The same **x** value would be used if **D_A** and **D_B** were 5" and 3" or 5' and 3', as long as the units are consistent for both distances.

The values of **x** in the table are rounded up or down to the nearest millimetre. The distances at which an object will be seen to float in the stereogram will be approximate but reasonably close to the nominal values, assuming that the images are accurately mounted. Adjustment of the film chip separation in the mount will change the perceived "floating" distance, but this will not affect the position of the object in space relative to other items in the scene.

In summary, the procedure for taking the two shots and moving the object is:

> take the LEFT shot
> move the object **x** mm to the LEFT
> take the RIGHT shot

Alternatively, the sequence can be:

> take the RIGHT shot
> move the object **x** mm to the RIGHT
> take the LEFT shot

These can be remembered by initialising the first two stages, as LL or RR, denoting the first exposure and the direction of movement of the object.

Inclusion of human figures in any of these floating shots presents problems, because anyone appearing in the scene must stay absolutely still during the whole exercise. If the figures are in the mid-distance, any slight movements will probably go unnoticed. It is easier for someone to keep still if they are comfortable, relaxed or supported in some way so that limbs do not wave about involuntarily when they are subjected to muscular tension.

A simpler version of the floating principle can be used in close-ups with a number of objects placed on a horizontal surface, such as a table top, and photographing them from above. Moving the objects laterally by various amounts will produce the illusion of objects floating at different levels. The formulae quoted earlier can be used in the same way but the distances through which objects have to be moved between exposures will be smaller. Care must be taken not to rotate objects about a vertical axis when shifting them. Most likely, a reduced stereo base will be used for close-ups and the correct value of **b** must be used in any calculations.

11.6.3 Enlarging objects

If the LL sequence described above is changed to LR (or RR to RL), that is moving the object in the same direction as the exposure sequence for a mono camera, the image will "sink" into the background instead of "floating" nearer. Although this will result in an unnatural 3D image, it can produce unusual or surrealistic photographs. If there is sufficient space behind the object, its image can simply be moved back without "colliding" with more distant objects. In this case, the object will appear to be larger than normal.

For example, if a model car is suspended relatively close to the camera, the LR sequence can be used to push it back so that it will appear as a much larger version (as big as a normal car, if desired) standing on the road further away in the scene.

A practical way of achieving this effect is shown in **Fig 11.11**. The model car can be fairly close to the camera; as long as it is to be pushed back beyond about 2m, it will end up behind the normal stereo window and there will be no viewing problems such as diplopia. To fix it in space, so that it is aligned correctly against the background with the wheels apparently on the road, it can be attached by hidden supports to a glass or Perspex sheet. The glass can be slid across in a supporting grooved frame to provide the necessary movement between exposures.

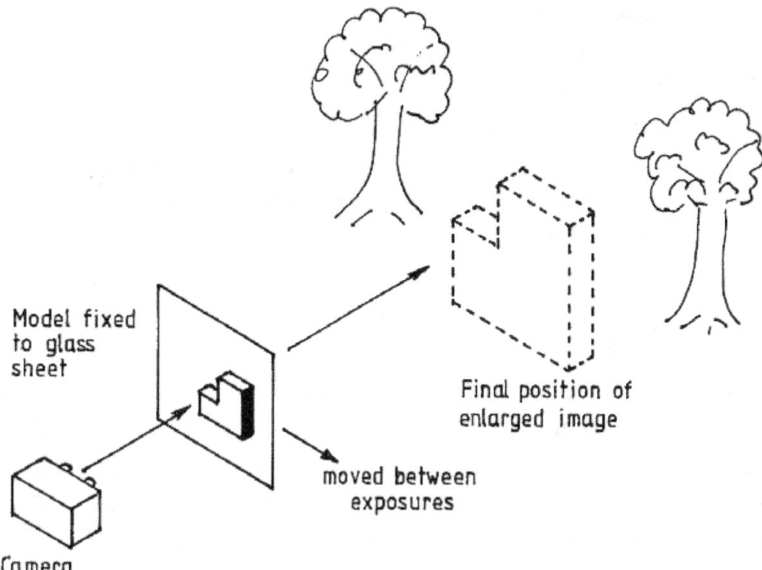

Fig 11.11 *The floating image principle used in reverse to produce an apparently larger object further away*

The formula for the lateral movement, **x**, is used in the same way as for the floating method. However, because in this case D_B is greater than D_A, the calculated **x** value will be negative. Mathematically, this simply signifies that the movement of the object must be made in the opposite direction to that required for floating. With the object fairly close (to give a larger apparent size in the stereogram, it is essential to use a small aperture (f/11, f/16 etc.) to give a suitable depth of field.

A 35mm lens focused at about 2m at f/16 will give a depth of field from about 1m to infinity. Distances closer than 1m can be used if the furthest object in the scene is closer than infinity. Depth of field tables should be consulted.

To move the image of a car from 1 metre to 6 metres, for example, will require the model car to be shifted by:

$$\mathbf{x} = \mathbf{b}(1 - 6)/6 = -5\mathbf{b}/6 = -58\text{mm (for } \mathbf{b} = 70\text{mm)}$$

The model is shifted in the same direction as the camera lens sequence used (LR or RL, as discussed earlier).

At a 1 metre distance for the car, the glass sheet will have to be about 700mm square, or slightly larger, to avoid the edges appearing in the picture.

11.7 Pseudoscopic Images

To produce a pseudoscopic stereogram, the left and right images are interchanged in the mount. The mounting procedure will be slightly modified because near point homologue separation, s_n, will be greater than that for infinity homologues, s_i. All depth information is reversed, so that near objects appear further away, and distant objects nearer. This will cause anomalies where one object partly obscures a more distant one in the normal stereogram. In pseudoscopic viewing the distant object, now seen nearer, will have a gap in it through which one sees what would normally be the near object further away.

With many stereograms, the effect is unnatural and often odd-looking; the exercise simply achieves nothing. However, with subjects that are perhaps somewhat abstract in nature, some interesting and surreal effects can be produced. An element of unreality or fantasy may be created.

D. McGraw[31] devotes part of a chapter in the Stereo Realist Manual to pseudoscopy. He notes the problems when one object is obscured by another, but points out that one can "get away with it" when outlines of objects are soft and the objects themselves are unfamiliar, meaning that their true nature is disguised. In fact, McGraw advocates that the film chips should be mounted upside-down (as well as being transposed) to make the final 3D picture more abstract and to help in disguising the objects. If a particular subject looks as if it might be suitable for pseudoscopic treatment, it is a good idea to take two identical stereo pairs, one of which can be used for a standard stereogram and the second for a pseudogram.

CHAPTER 12: ANAGLYPHS

12.1 The Nature of Anaglyphs

The term anaglyph derives from the Greek **anaglyphos**, which means "in low relief". The term is used to describe an ornament in low relief and a system for viewing stereoscopic pairs. The trade name "Anaglypta" used for heavily embossed wallpaper comes from the same etymological root.

In 3D, the anaglyph comprises a stereo pair, the left and right views being printed in complementary colours, usually cyan (blue/green) and red, though other combinations have been used. The pictures are viewed through spectacles incorporating red and cyan coloured filters, one for each eye.

The stereoscopic system based upon anaglyphs is attributed to Louis Ducos de Hauron, and it dates from 1881. It has been used widely as a means of popularising stereoscopy in books and magazines; it has also been used in the cinema as the basis for 3D films. In stereograms the left image is printed in the cyan colour and the right image in red. In the spectacles, the red filter is located in front of the left eye and the cyan one in front of the right. If one considers a piece of white paper with some lines drawn on it, some in red and others in cyan, the left eye looking through the red filter will see the white paper as red, and the red lines will blend into the background and not be visible. The cyan lines, being complementary in colour will appear near black. In a similar way, the right eye will see only the red lines. When a stereoscopic pair of images, correctly coloured, are printed one on top of the other, a 3D effect will be produced since each eye sees only its correct image (**Fig 12.1**).

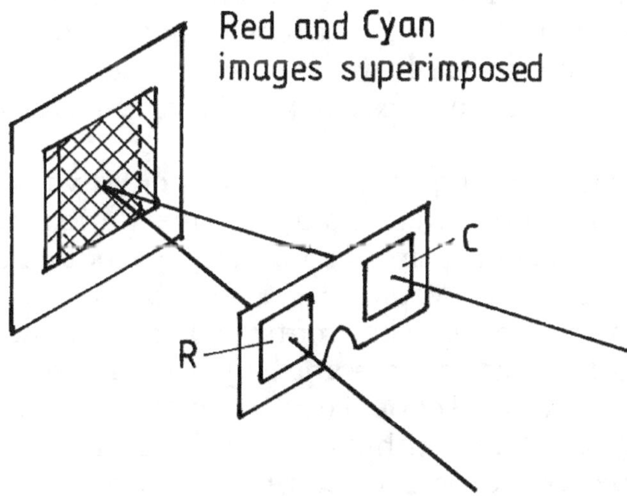

Fig 12.1
Viewing of anaglyphs.

In practice one can sometimes see a ghost of the incorrect image. This occurs mainly with the cyan image and the right eye. It is quite difficult to get a perfect match between the printed colour and the coloured cyan filter. If the cyan image is too densely coloured, the effect may be more pronounced. The left image should be printed in a fairly light hue for best results.

Sometimes the spectacles are fitted with a plain blue or green filter instead of the normal cyan colour but the stereo effect does not appear any the worse for these variations.

Occasionally one finds anaglyph stereograms printed with the colours reversed giving a pseudoscopic effect. This anomaly is overcome quite easily by reversing the spectacles when viewing. However, the accepted standard is - right image equals red.

12.2 Stereograms in Anaglyph Form

Since each eye ultimately sees a dark, nearly black, image, the anaglyph method as described above would seem to be restricted to the viewing of "black and white" images. The use of colour images would seem to be impossible. Anaglyphs have been used for monochrome images since their inception, but there now exists an interesting application of the technique, which combines coloured images and anaglyphic principles; it was developed in the 1980's (see Section 12.6.6).

Because there is no danger of either eye seeing the wrong image (assuming the spectacles are used correctly) there is no need to print the two images side-by-side, and it is usual for them to be superimposed to give a slightly fuzzy picture, which has a brownish colouration with areas of cyan or red fringing. Superimposed images have a great advantage over side-by-side pairs, as there is no limit to size; one is not restricted to a maximum print width of 65mm or so as is the case with normal stereograms.

The system lends itself well to the production of printed 3D photographs in books and magazines. Simple cardboard spectacles can be included at low cost.

Anaglyph production has not been a particularly favoured method for the amateur photographer. In the past, home darkroom workers could adopt the old Carbro colour print techniques to produce the cyan and red images on tissues that would be overlaid to produce the final stereogram/anaglyph. Those who continued into home colour printing could use the newer colour papers and superimpose two coloured images using red and cyan filters in sequence in the enlarger loaded with black and white negatives. Most stereo enthusiasts preferred full colour images, and viewing with stereoscopes or projectors, so the anaglyph method never really caught on as an amateur pursuit.

An interesting technique is to print colour negatives using filters to give the left image a cyan colour cast, and the right image a red cast, and then superimposing the two images. The composite, when viewed through standard anaglyph spectacles, appears almost normally coloured, the colour casts effectively cancelling out when combined. Although effective, it is a compromise and not ideal for producing 3D in colour.

12.3 Image Depth

Since the anaglyph method relies on exactly the same principles as normal stereo images, there is no reason why the image quality and depth information should be any different, apart from the lack of colour. However, because the images are superimposed in a particular way, most anaglyphs tend to have limited depth, which is attributable to the relatively small displacement of the images. It is common practice to superimpose the images with the edges aligned. Although this creates a neat image on the printed page, provided that the prints are trimmed correctly to avoid "floating edges", it means that infinity homologue separation is at the mercy of the enlargement factor. The frame edges will form a window located at the surface of the page (usually) and the scene should appear behind it. As an approximate guide, two 35mm negatives, if superimposed, would give an s_i value of 1.6mm, if the frames are aligned, and the camera lens has a focal length of 50mm. If these negatives are enlarged to make 152 x 102mm (6 x 4in) prints, the enlargement factor is about 4.2, which means that in the anaglyph the s_i value is just under 7mm. The same situation occurs in autostereoscopic prints (Chapter 9, Section 9.4) and in the standard View Magic mounting system for prints. However, in the latter case one print is located above the other (higher on the page), and not superimposed (see Chapter 6, Section 6.10.4). Infinity points in typical anaglyphs will be seen as located about 30mm below the page, at a viewing distance of 300mm.

Often in published anaglyphs the individual images are trimmed so that the picture frame is not the nearest part of the image, with the result that part of a scene may protrude through the stereo window. If the infinity points are arranged to coincide, then an object at infinity would appear to be level with the page surface in the stereogram, the rest of the scene standing proud.

Ideally, the images should be overlapped so that the infinity points are about 60 to 65mm apart. To some extent this depends upon the size of the anaglyph. An s_i value of 60 to 65mm is acceptable if the image is large enough to be viewed at about 300mm with the correct perspective (Supplement S1). For smaller sizes s_i should be reduced slightly. This will cause some miniaturisation but the final 3D image will still be acceptable to most people, even if it is technically distorted. With 60 to 65mm infinity separation and a fairly small picture, considerable stretching of the image would occur.

A normal infinity homologue separation means that the stereo window will lie behind the plane of the paper, because the frame edges of the two images will not be coincident. With the left image frame lying to the left of the right image frame, sight lines from the eyes will not meet at the print plane but further back. In the end, the way in which the two images are superimposed determines whether the anaglyph will be seen as an orthostereoscopic image or a (technically) distorted one that is more neatly arranged on the page, with the stereo window level with the page surface. Most commercially produced anaglyphs fall into the latter category.

12.4 Negative Anaglyphs

Consider the simple anaglyph depicted in **Fig 12.2a** consisting of a "V" shape with the left arm **Oa** red and the right arm **Ob** cyan. When viewed through coloured glasses the eye sight lines to points **a** and **b** cross at **X** and the image **OX** appears standing up from the page. This is a conventional anaglyph on a white background.

Fig 12.2b shows an identical V shape but on a black background. This is a negative anaglyph and it works in the opposite sense. The left eye sees **Ob** as before, as a black line, but this now becomes continuous with the background. Instead, the left eye will see **Oa** as a light area against the black. Similarly, the right eye will only be aware of the line **Ob**. The sight lines from the eyes will again cross, but behind the plane of the paper, at **Y**. Obviously, the length **ab** must be less than the eye spacing to produce a proper image. The image **OY** points away from the observer, but if the colours of **Oa** and **Ob** were reversed, the original image **OX** would be re-created. The advantage of negative anaglyphs is that ghosting is reduced considerably, to give a cleaner image. In some ways, however, the general darkness is less pleasing overall, but having a light image (virtually white) against a dark background can be effective with some subjects, such as line diagrams. If it is to work as a photograph then the images would have to be printed in the "wrong" colours and as negatives rather than positives.

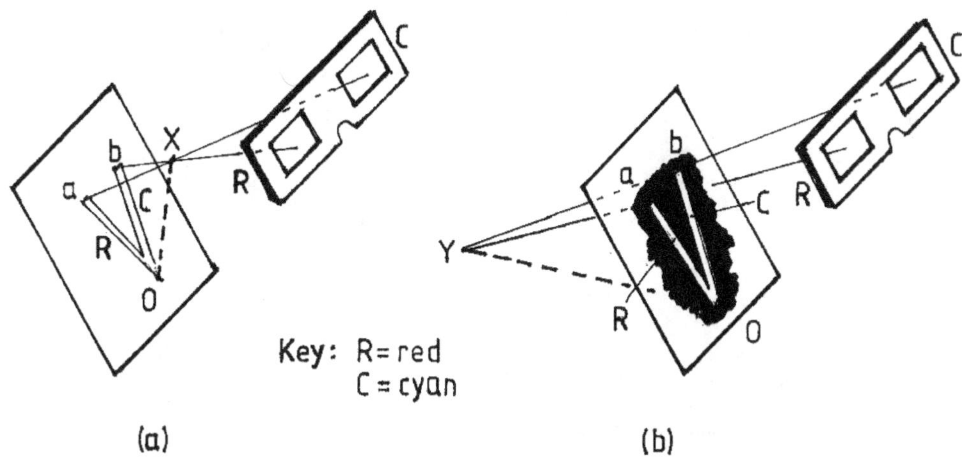

Fig 12.2
a *Positive anaglyph: the right eye sees the red line* **Oa** *and the left eye the cyan line* **Ob**. *The image appears as* **OX**.
b *Negative anaglyph: the same image as in* **a** *but on a black background. The right eye again "sees" only the red image but this time it blends with the background. Thus the right eye is aware only of the line* **Ob**, *which appears "white". Similarly, the left eye sees* **Oa** *as white. The final image appears as* **OY**.

12.5 Geometric Drawings

Anaglyphs can be used most effectively to display 3D line drawings, in engineering or mathematical contexts. Such drawings are usually designed to form three dimensional images that stand up from the page, which forms the base. The perspective is chosen so that the observer, wearing the customary spectacles and with the drawing flat on a table, views the page at 45°, which causes the image to stand up vertically. The observer can adjust his position so that the image is so produced (**Fig 12.3**).

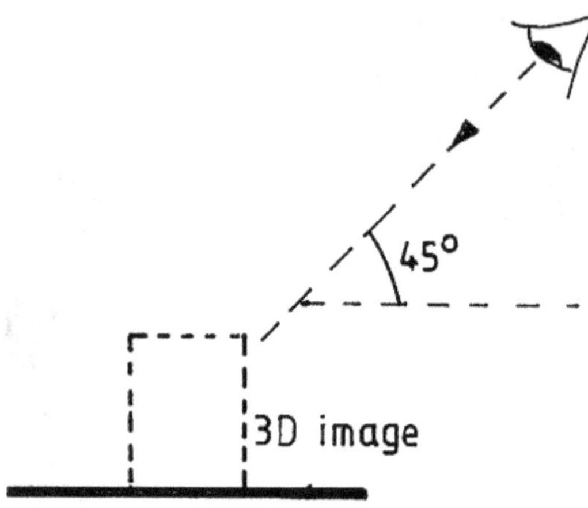

Fig 12.3
Anaglyphs of geometric shapes and engineering drawings are often designed to be viewed at 45° as shown to give a correctly proportioned image.

With any anaglyph, if the head is moved sideways when viewing, the image leans over in the same direction. Viewing from a greater distance increases the depth by "stretching". When the image is recreated in this way, its various features can be traced in real space with a finger or pointer and measurements made (approximately) with a ruler.

The author taught metallurgy for thirty years to degree level in a technical college and frequently made use of a book of anaglyphs[30] depicting ternary phase diagrams, which show the various changes that occur in ternary alloys (i.e. made up of three metals in various quantities) on cooling from the liquid state to room temperature. Whilst it is not easy to produce such diagrams, they are frequently superior to actual 3D models, constructed from cardboard or wire, because the drawings can be made to highlight certain features of the model, by using thicker lines for those regions, for example. Such drawings are an invaluable aid for the learning process, particularly for those who have difficulty in visualising objects in 3D from conventional diagrams in two dimensions, even if they are drawn in true perspective form.

One occasionally finds 3D material in children's comics. The traditional strip cartoon can have a greater impact and novelty value when presented in this way. It takes a good degree of skill to prepare the pairs of drawings superimposed as red and cyan images. Usually, the depth effect is not over-complex but it is nonetheless effective.

12.6 Projection of Anaglyphs
12.6.1 Introduction

Two methods can be used to produce anaglyph images on screen for viewing with the usual red and green spectacles. Curiously, what may seem to be the obvious way does not work in practice, as will be explained. The methods differ in the form of the transparencies used, whether they are coloured, (one red and the other cyan), or in the form of two black and white images.

12.6.2 Using coloured images

Separate positive transparencies for the left and right components have to be made with the left image converted to a cyan colour and the right image to red.

It would seem obvious to use two projectors, one for each slide of the pair, and to superimpose the images on screen. However, this is the method that does not work, as hinted above; it is illustrated in **Fig 12.4.**

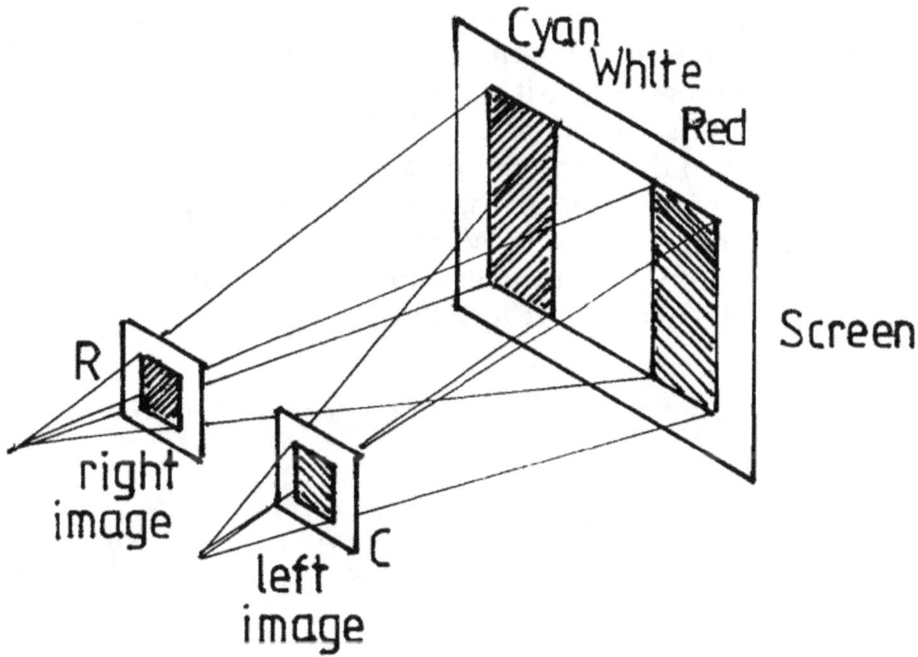

Fig 12.4

Incorrect way to project anaglyphs. Where the left (cyan) image overlaps the right (red) image on the screen the complementary colours are additive and produce (near) white light. For correct rendition of the image the white area needs to be black.

With reference to this diagram, suppose that the image is a simple square shape. Projected singly, the left image will appear as a cyan square and the right image as a red one. When projected so that they overlap as shown, the outer portions of each square will appear in the relevant colours, unchanged. However, the central portion is illuminated by both cyan light from the left image and red light from the right image. Mixing of coloured light is additive (not subtractive as in mixing pigments) and the cyan and red will combine to produce white light, or as near white as the particular dyes will allow. As pigments, they would produce near black.

When this white rectangle with green and red side areas is viewed through the spectacles the central region will stay white and the side areas will appear black and the illusion of a black square floating somewhere in space will be lost. Another method of projection of anaglyphs must be sought, therefore.

The solution is to sandwich the two slides and place them together in a single projector. This produces quite a different result. In this arrangement, light from the projector lamp first passes through the red image, say, and the blue/green component of the white light is absorbed. Only the red component of the light can continue, but where it strikes the green image of the second slide, it will be absorbed. The net result is that, ideally, no light can pass through any overlapping red and green parts in the slide sandwich, and the corresponding regions on the screen will appear black. Those parts of the image that are not overlapped will pass the appropriate coloured light to the screen unchanged. The clear regions surrounding the coloured square will allow white light to pass directly to the screen without modification (**Fig 12.5**).

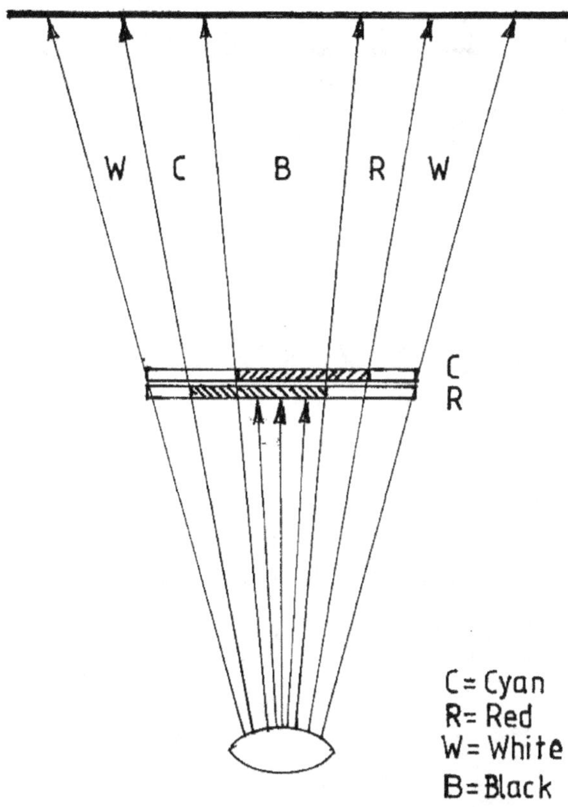

Fig 12.5
Correct method for the projection of cyan and red images by sandwiching the two slides.

12.6.3 Using black and white Images and filters

In this method, the separate images are left as normal black and white positive transparencies and placed in separate projectors. The light from the projector holding the left image is passed through a red filter, and that from the other projector, with the right image, through a cyan filter. At first sight this would appear to be the wrong way round. Analysis of **Fig 12.6** provides the explanation.

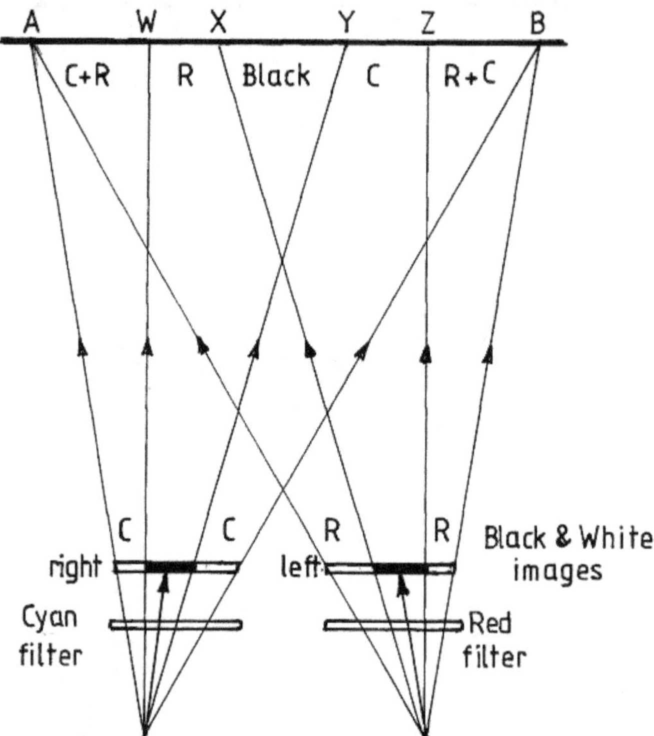

Fig 12.6
*Method of projecting black and white images using red and cyan filters. Superimposed red and cyan regions (**C+R** and **R+C**) will appear white.*

With a square image as before, the left projector alone will produce a screen image **WY** as a black square, since the black image blocks the light beam. The surrounding areas **AW** and **YB** will be cyan, owing to white light from the projector passing through the clear areas in the slide and then through the cyan filter (the emergent beams marked **C** in the diagram. Similarly, with the right projector alone, the right image will be a black square **XZ** with regions **AX** and **ZB** coloured red. When both projectors are used together, the region **WX** (black as far as the left projector is concerned) will be illuminated by red light from the right projector. Similarly, the section **YZ** will appear cyan.

The region **XY** receives no light from either projector, so appears black. Segments **AW** and **ZB**, illuminated by both red and cyan light appear white as a result of the additive effect of the two beams.

When all of this is viewed through the correct anaglyph spectacles, the left eye, looking through its red filter, sees **AW** as white, **WX** as white, **XY** as black, **YZ** as black and **ZB** as white. It sees **XZ**, therefore, as black, which is the correct image of the square for the left eye. A similar analysis shows that the right eye, looking through its cyan filter, sees its correct image of the square as **WY**.

12.6.4 Stereoscopic shadows illusion

This is a novelty live presentation suitable for display on a stage or in a large hall. The audience, equipped with standard anaglyph spectacles, watches a kind of shadow play in three dimensions on a large white screen.

The arrangement is shown in **Fig 12.7**. At the front of a stage, or at some point in a large hall, a large screen is set up. This is in the form of a sheet of white fabric, sufficiently translucent to allow shadows cast on one side to be seen from the opposite side.

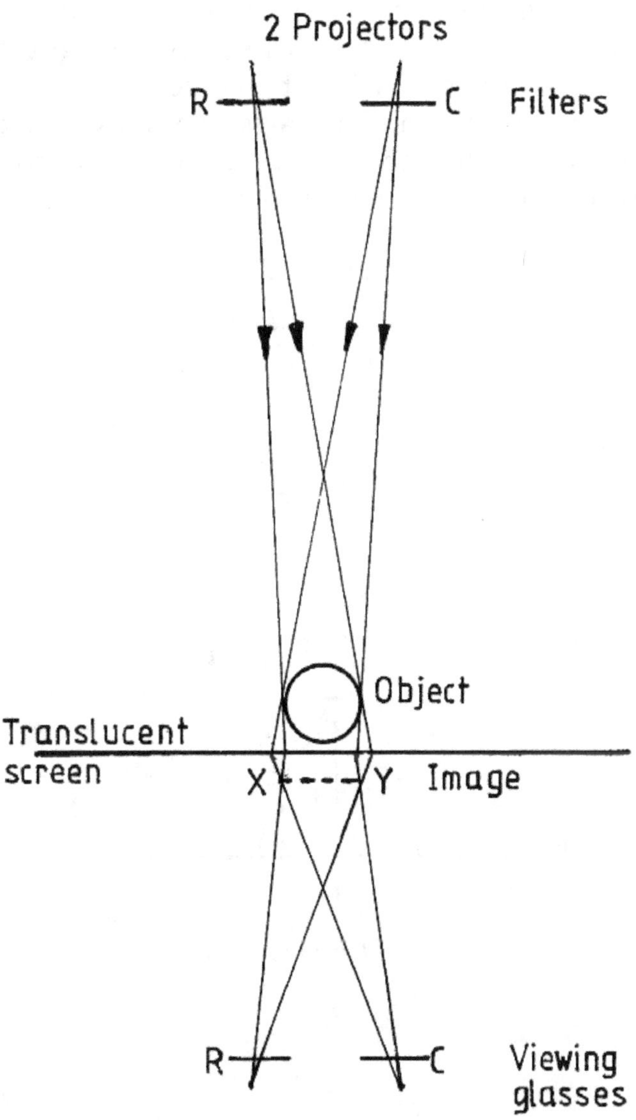

Fig 12.7

*''Stereoscopic shadows'' illusion. The red and cyan filters on the projectors cause colour fringing of the shadows of the object behind the screen to give an image at **XY** seen from the other side.*

The audience sits facing one side of the screen. On the stage side, two projectors are set up essentially parallel to each other to project shadows that are broadly superimposed on the screen. The projectors need to be set back as far as possible; a reasonable amount of "working area" is required.

The projector at stage left is fitted with a cyan filter and the other with a red filter (marked **C** and **R** in **Fig 12.7**).

The projectors will cast two shadows of any object standing between them and the screen, but they should be positioned so that the shadows are nearly coincident when the object is adjacent to the screen on the stage side, as shown. It will appear from the audience side as a single shadow with a red fringe to the left and a cyan fringe to the right, if viewed without the spectacles. The principles involved here are similar to those illustrated in **Fig 12.6**, in which non-overlapped parts of a dark image are coloured by the light from the "opposite" projector. Viewed with the spectacles, the shadow will be seen in front of the screen at **XY**.

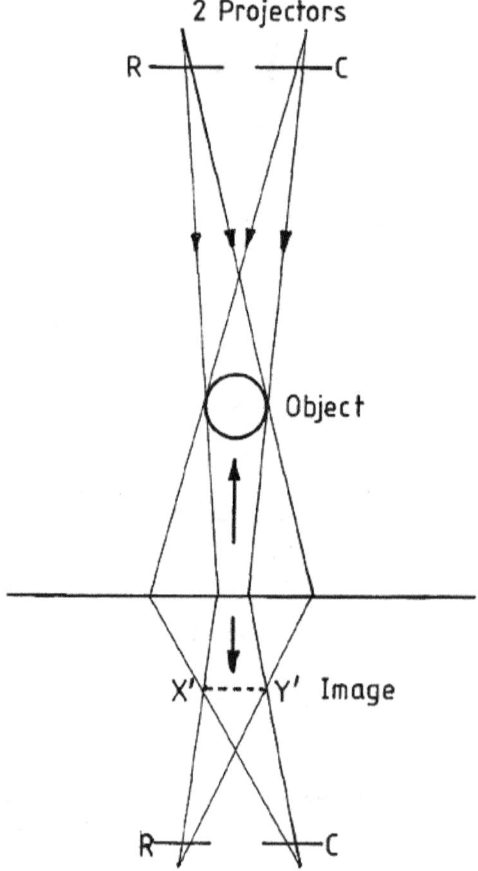

Fig 12.8
As for **Fig 12.7** *but here the object is moved away from the screen towards the projectors. The image moves to* **X'Y'***, closer to them.*

If the object, which could be a person, moves away from the audience towards the projectors, the two shadows will move further apart and will increase in size (**Fig 12.8**).

The effect of this on the audience is that the shadow is moving towards them. Small objects thrown towards the projectors will appear as shadows flying from the screen towards the spectators.

Apart from this somewhat gimmicky application, 3D shadowgraphs could be created with card shapes to produce interesting effects. The technique could also be set up in a miniature form with a much smaller screen for a limited number of spectators, but in this case, the shadows will have to be created by objects other than human beings.

12.6.5 Anaglyphs in the cinema

From time to time there is a burst of activity in the movie world and a few 3D films enter the cinema circuit for public showing. Many of the earlier productions in this genre were produced in anaglyph form. The red and cyan images were superimposed on each film frame so that only one projector would be required. One or two notable films, such as "The House of Wax" were made in both mono and stereo versions but in this case, it being a colour film, the polarisation principle was used for viewing. Anaglyph films were usually either short, consisting largely of spectacular demonstrations of 3D (roller coaster rides, objects thrown towards the audience - that kind of thing), or the 3D content of the film, if a full feature length drama, was limited to several short episodes, to limit possible visual fatigue. The bulk of the film would be in two dimensions only.

Nowadays, 3D films are generally in colour and are viewed with polarisers. With the development of the IMAX system, using two 70mm wide films for the separate images, projected onto a huge screen, spectators can now enjoy a realism that has not previously been available. Added to the impressive visual content is a surround sound system; together they create a memorable experience of stereoscopic cinema.

12-6.6 The Vivitar Q-DOS 3D lens system 70 – 210 zoom

This lens was first marketed by Vivitar, a subsidiary of Hanimex Ltd, in 1991. Based upon the principle of combining an anaglyph form of stereo with normal colour images, the lens was developed largely by David Burder, a professional photographer who has worked mainly in enterprises involving 3D imaging.

Q-DOS stands for Quantum Duplex Optical System. The lens incorporates a stereo optical encoder with red and cyan colour filters to separate the light path through the lens in order to produce the 3D effect. It includes a switch that enables the photographer to change from normal lens function to 3D capability.

The encoded stereo image appears on a single frame and looks very similar to a normal colour mono image, apart from areas of either red or cyan fringing, which do not detract too much from its appearance as a "mono" image. Viewing through normal anaglyph glasses reveals the full stereo effect.

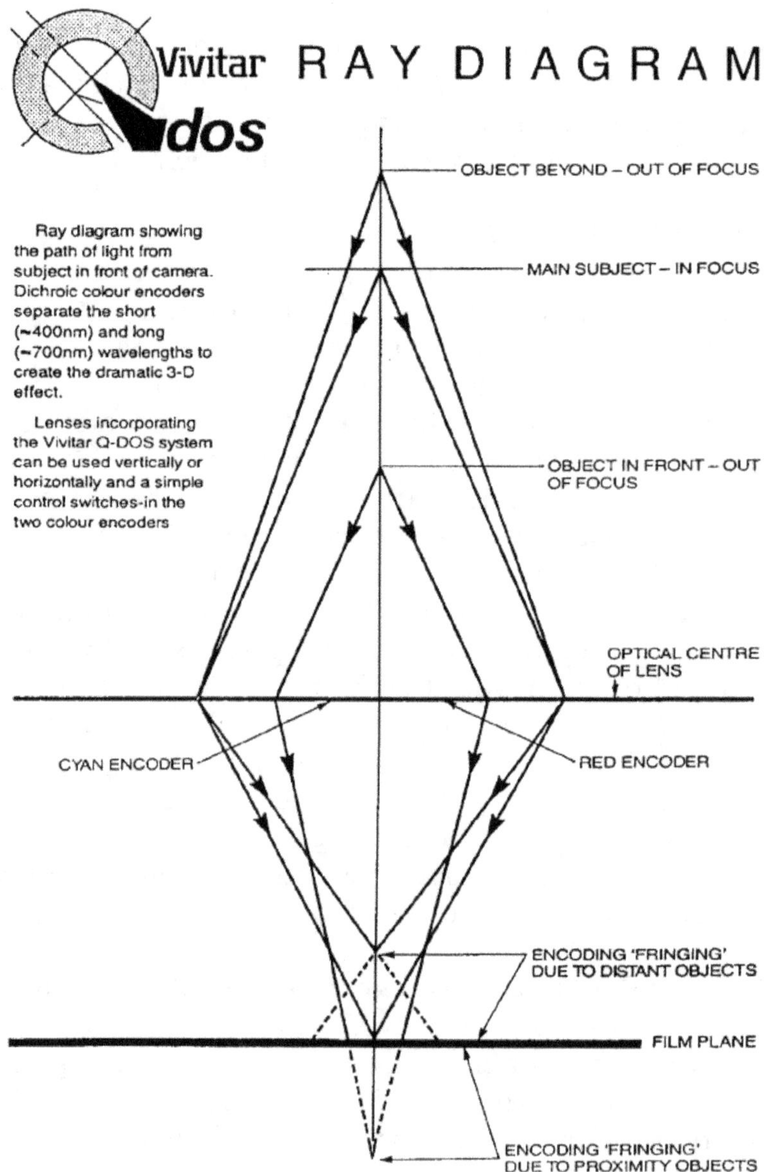

Fig 12.9
Ray diagram for the Vivitar Q-DOS lens which combines the anaglyph principle and normal colour photography. (Diagram taken from an advertising brochure).

The ray diagram (**Fig 12.9**) supplied by Vivitar gives a few clues to the principle behind the working of the lens, but it requires a little thought. When the encoder is switched in, rays from the subject passing through the left side of the lens encounter the cyan filter while those on the right half of the lens meet the red filter. If they come from the part of the subject that is in focus according to the lens setting they superimpose on the film surface and the red and cyan biased images produce a normal colour image by the additive principle. Rays that come from a nearer part of the subject (out of focus technically but within the sharpness range of the depth of field) will come to a focus behind the film emulsion, thus producing a fringing effect, with a red fringe to the left and cyan to the right. Rays from more distant parts of the subject will be focused in front of the film surface and produce fringing in the opposite sense. When viewed through the red/cyan glasses, the nearer parts of the subject appear in front of the final print, the truly "in focus" parts appear at the print surface, and the more distant areas below the surface.

Some of the colour rendition is lost, but the best results are seen if the filters in the spectacles are relatively pale.

The first publication of pictures taken by David Burder with this lens appeared in "Amateur Photographer" (UK weekly magazine) on August 25th 1984.

Since the Q-DOS relies on differential focus to produce the 3D image, it works best with longer focal length lenses, an aperture of f/5.6 being the most effective.

CHAPTER 13: STEREOSCOPIC DRAWING

13.1 Introduction

The principle of producing separate left and right views of a subject for viewing as a 3D image has been known for centuries, well before the discovery of photography. Several artists have been successful in creating such images, a considerable achievement in pictures produced by what amounts to a freehand technique. Control of line, colour and image location (in depth terms) requires detailed thought and concentration and makes demands that most of us could not meet, given our limited artistic abilities.

Line drawings, either in black and white or coloured in a simple way, are easier to create. With present-day technology, drawings can be produced large enough to ensure accuracy, then reduced on a photocopier to a size suitable for viewing.

An appreciation of the techniques that can be used for creating 3D drawings can be useful to the photographer, if only for the production of effective title slides to enhance any public showing of his work. The basic principles will be covered in this chapter, but for a greater understanding the reader is urged to consult specialist books on perspective drawing if more complex images are required.

13.2 Depth Layer Method
13.2.1 Basic technique

The principle involved here is to visualise the final image as being intersected by a number of parallel vertical planes at key distances from the observer, the planes being at right angles to the viewing direction (**Fig 13.1**). In simple drawings, perhaps only two or three such planes will be required to establish the basic skeleton of the drawing; their locations will be chosen with reference to easily identifiable features within the image. Starting, say, with the furthest depth plane, the left and right images for the objects that lie on that plane are drawn. It may be that only part of an object can be delineated, or a section through it to establish the edges. Then the exercise is repeated for the next nearest selected plane and so on, combining all the left images in one drawing and the right images in the other, to produce a stereo pair in outline form, with the key positions of various features identified. In placing the individual components into each drawing, the relative separations of homologous points at various distances should be borne in mind, as has been discussed in previous chapters.

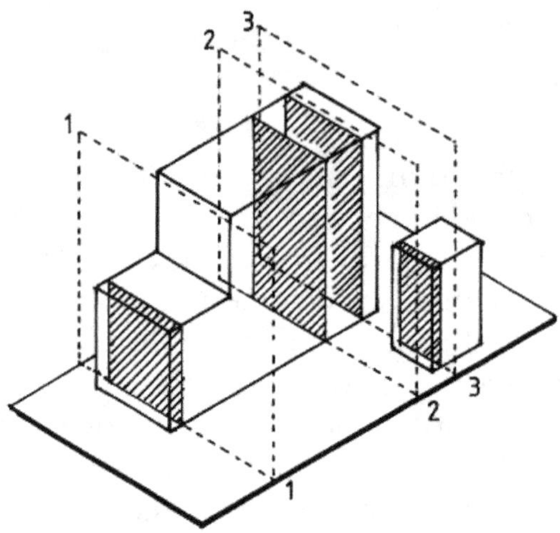

Fig 13.1
Visualisation of an object or scene as being intersected by a number of parallel planes (1, 2, 3) to assist in locating object positions when making 3D drawings.

A simple example will serve to illustrate the method, though it will produce a final 3D image that is no more than a set of two-dimensional objects located at different distances from the observer. In this instance the drawing will be made large enough for free viewing without the need for any further enlargement or reduction

The first step is to draw two frames, one for each image, as shown in **Fig 13.2**. The frames will form a stereo window at what will be the near point distance. Since we have chosen a 60mm separation for the frame edges, this value will also represent the separation of homologues for any objects located at the window distance. If desired, the frames can be erased from the final image, but it is better to start with clearly defined borders as an aid to correct placement of the various parts of the subject.

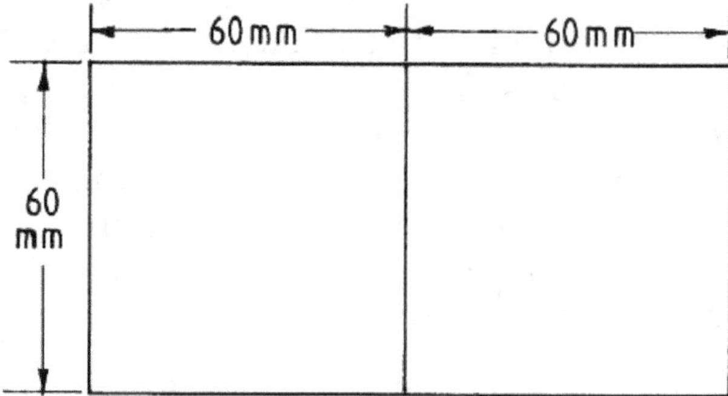

Fig 13.2
Suitable dimensions for left and right image frames for the construction of 3D drawings to be free viewed.

We shall use a value of 65mm for infinity point separation. For this image size the 5mm difference in the infinity and near point separation values is a reasonable one. **Fig 13.3** gives the necessary details for constructing a stereo pair comprising three circles, one located at infinity, another at the near point (picture frame) distance, with a third circle at an intermediate distance. For the most distant object, the two circles are separated by 65mm; they can be placed anywhere within the frame provided that their centres lie on a single horizontal line as shown. However, if the left circle of the pair is placed too close to the right, its counterpart in the right image will lie wholly or partly outside the frame. A similar problem will arise if the right circle of the pair is too far to the left.

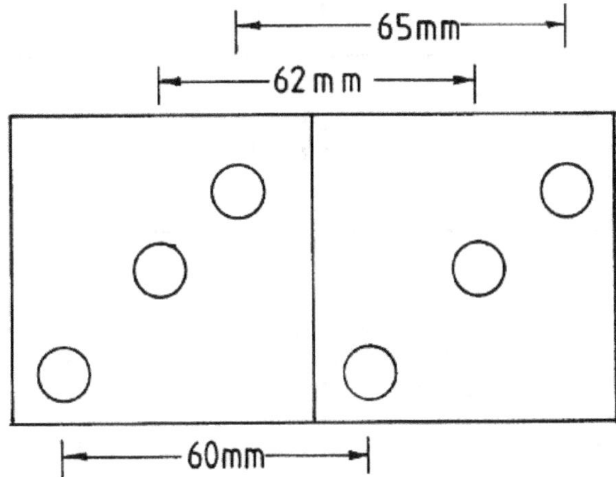

Fig 13.3
Typical values for homologue separations to place objects at different depths.

The nearest circle has its left and right images separated by 60mm, to place it in the same plane as the picture frame; again, the placement of the two images is arbitrary, subject to their being at the same height.

By selecting a separation of 62mm for the third circle image pair, the final image will lie somewhere between the other two in terms of distance from the observer in the final 3D picture. Any value between 60 and 65mm can be selected; the nearer the chosen value is to 65mm, the further away the final location of the relevant object will be.

If the circles are of different sizes as illustrated in **Fig 13.4b**, with the nearest being the largest, the final impression will be that the circles are similar in size but at different distances, following one of the principles of perspective, that objects further away appear smaller. On the other hand, making the circles identical in size will cause their apparent sizes to increase from front to back in the stereoscopic image. **Fig 13.4** shows the end result for both cases; the "apparent size" effect can be confirmed by viewing the diagrams as stereo pairs.

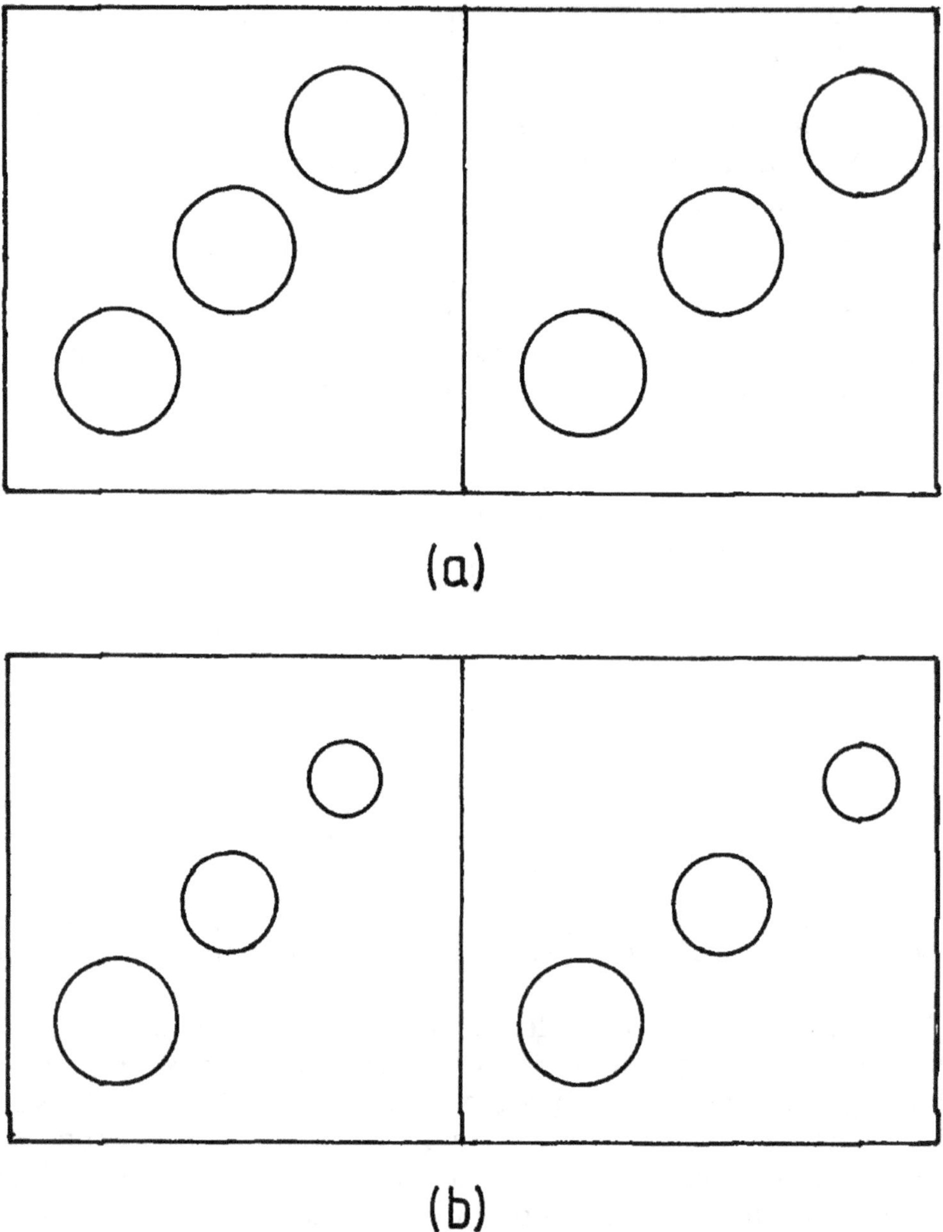

(a)

(b)

Fig 13.4
*In both diagrams the upper circle is furthest away and the lowest circle nearest when viewed as a stereo pair. In **a** the circles are identical in size but appear to increase in size from front to back in 3D. In **b** the effect of perspective on size is introduced to give the illusion that the circles are identical in size when viewed in stereo.*

A straightforward application of this basic technique is to produce titles in the manner of **Fig 13.5**. Individual letters can be arranged in echelon formation, whole words set at different distances, or various combinations of these effects can be employed. Sloping two corresponding letters from the two images in opposite directions will cause them to lean back or forward in the stereo image.

For a more pictorial effect, a number of two-dimensional picture elements, perhaps in the form of silhouettes, can be combined to produce a series of cut-outs at various depths, creating an image resembling a cardboard "peep-show" (**Fig 13.6**).

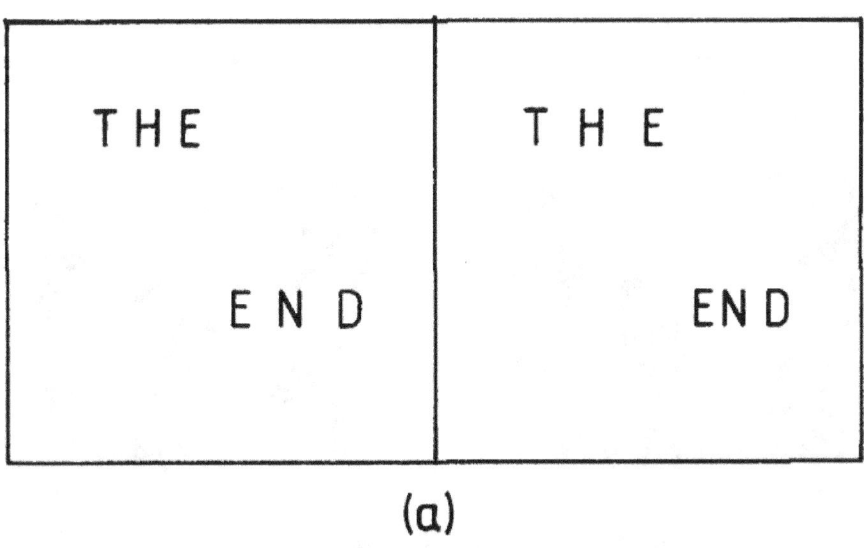

(a)

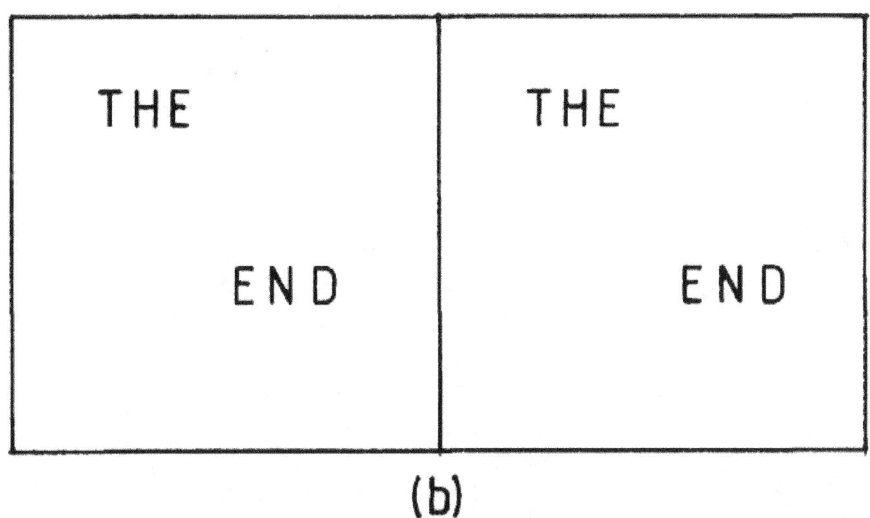

(b)

Fig 13.5
Two forms of 3D title.
a *individual letters at different depths*
b *whole words at different depths.*

13.2.2 Creating solidity

Fig 13.7a is derived from **Fig 13.4b** by drawing common tangents to the two nearest circles. When viewed in 3D, the two relevant depth planes are linked and the circles resemble the ends of a transparent solid or hollow cylinder. A little doctoring of the image can turn it into an opaque one (**Fig 13.7b**).

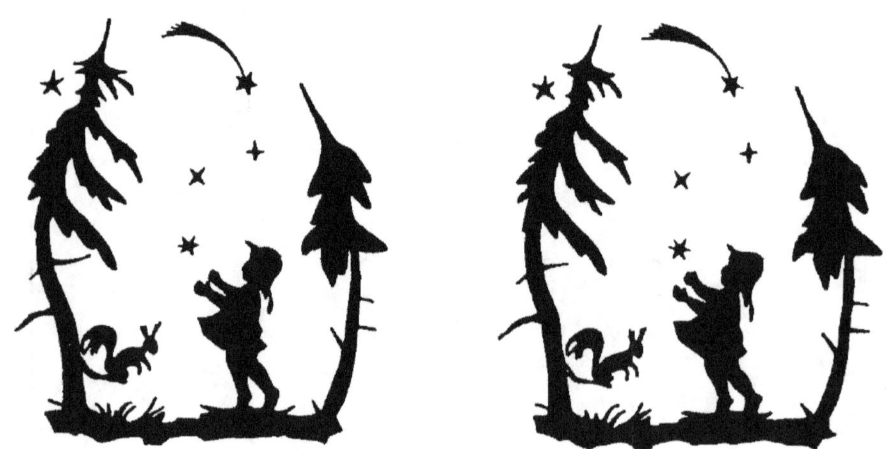

Fig 13.6
3D drawing in silhouette form. From Valyus[39].

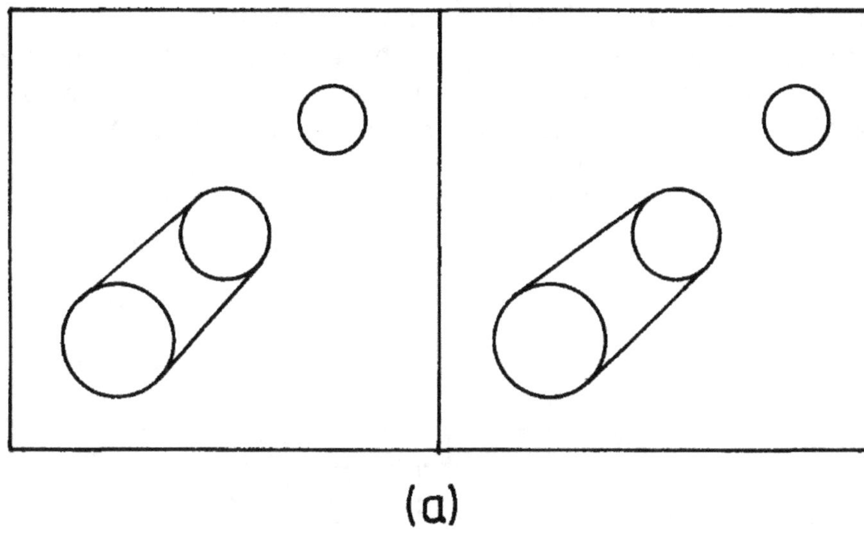

(a)

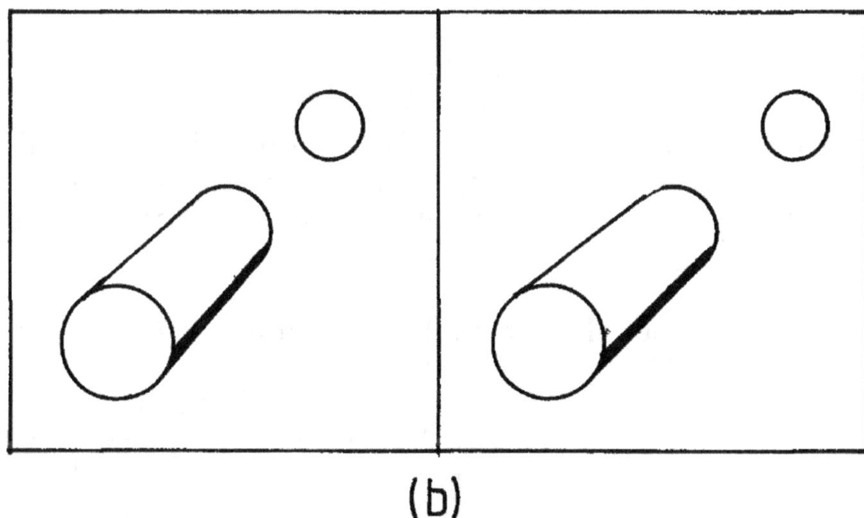

(b)

Fig13.7
*Lines connecting the circles of **Fig 13.4** produce solid objects. In **a** the object is a transparent rod or hollow tube. In **b** it is opaque.*

Since one of the effects of perspective is to make parallel lines appear to converge if they run in a direction away from the observer, the vanishing point principle, as used in two-dimensional perspective drawing, can be employed to produce a realistic effect.

Starting with a pair of frames identical to those in **Fig 13.2**, two squares **ABCD** and **A'B'C'D'** (as a simple example) can be drawn, spaced at 60mm to place them at the "frame near point" distance (**Fig 13.8**). Points **P** and **P'**, 65mm apart, are the vanishing points at infinity. By drawing the lines **AP, BP** etc. the picture begins to resemble a rectangular object of infinite length. These lines should be drawn faintly as they are merely for constructional purposes at this stage. Changing the object to one of finite length is simply a matter of drawing a horizontal line such as **HH'**. From the points of intersection of **HH'** and the lines **AP**, **BP**, **A'P'** and **B'P'** a box shape can be completed as shown.

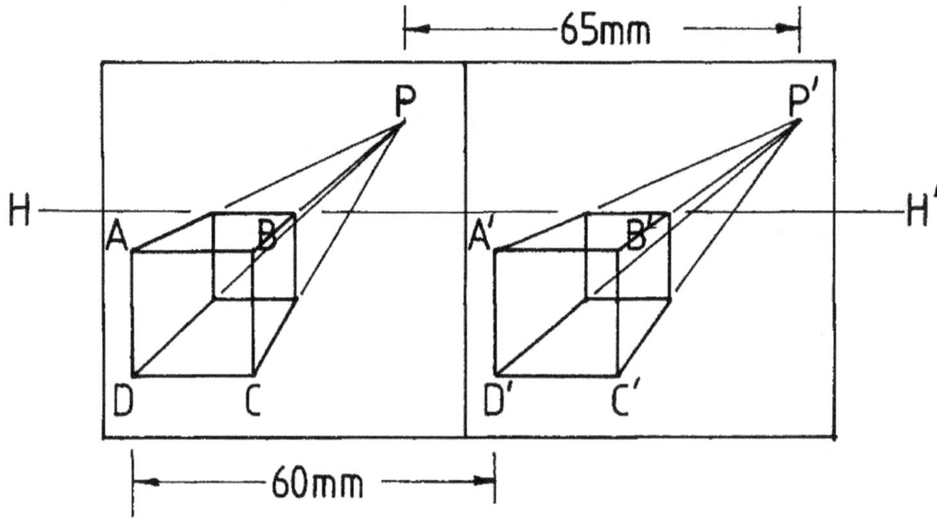

Fig 13.8
*Construction of a stereo drawing of a cube. Squares **ABCD** and **A'B'C'D'** are drawn as the front faces at 60mm separation (same as the picture frames). **P** and **P'** are vanishing points set at 65mm apart. HH' is used to locate the back face of the cube.*

By drawing additional horizontal lines, similar to **HH'**, a row of boxes can be drawn (**Fig 13.9**).

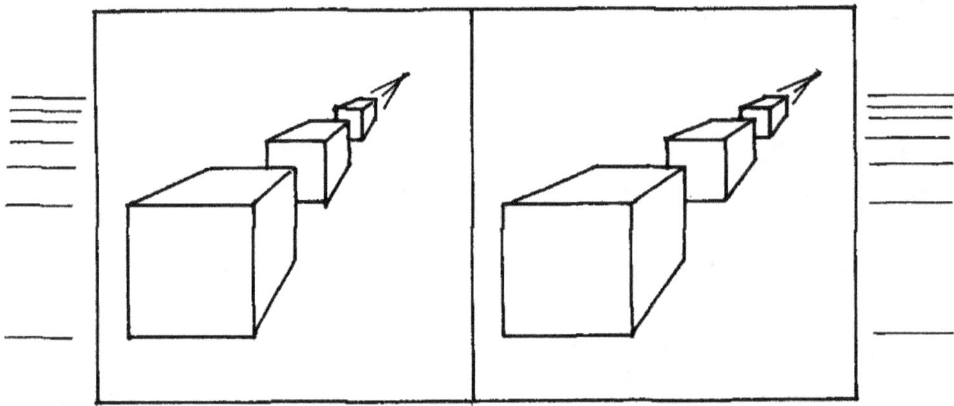

Fig 13.9
*Extension of the principle shown in **Fig 13.8**. By drawing several horizontal lines (shown at the sides of the frames a number of parallel cubes or blocks can be drawn.*

To draw parallel boxes, either in a single row or in two separate rows, as in **Fig 13.10a**, a common vanishing point is used, but if one box is rotated about a vertical axis so that it is no longer parallel to the first, it will be necessary to use a second vanishing point (**Fig 13.10b**).

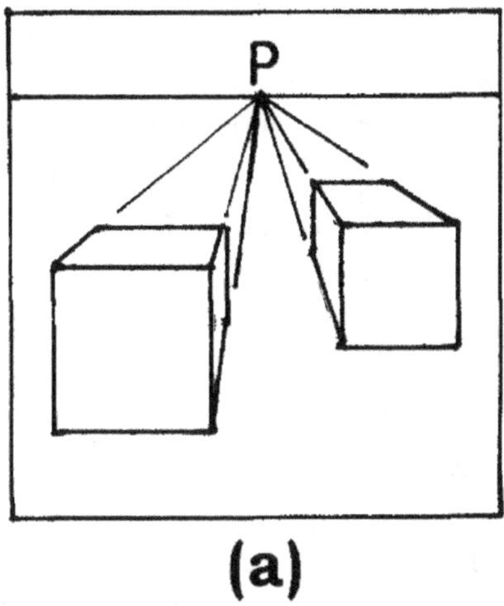

(a)

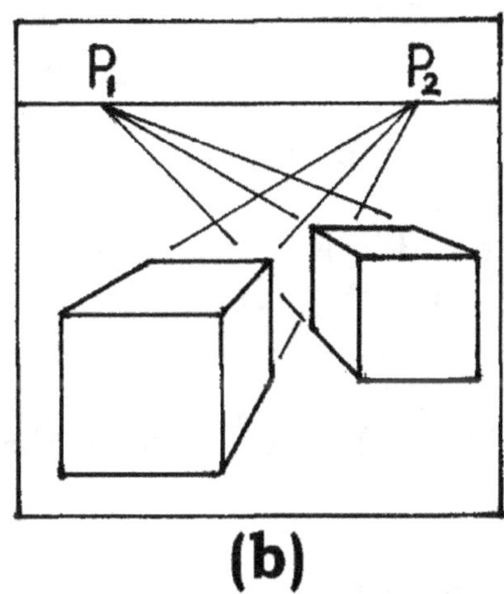

(b)

Fig 13.10
a. *Parallel blocks, even of different sizes and at different distances, have a common vanishing point* **P**.
b. *Non-parallel blocks have separate vanishing points.*

13.2.3 Special effects

1. **Protruding objects**. If the separation of the left and right images of a near object in a drawn stereo pair is deliberately made less than the frame spacing, then that object will appear in front of the stereo window; this can be very effective. A title, perhaps, can be made to

float in space part way between the observer and the screen in a projected slide show. Dramatic touches of this kind can add considerably to the entertainment value of the presentation.

It is wise, if one wishes to produce this effect, to follow the advice given in Supplement S9 and to ensure that the overall depth range of the stereogram is not excessive, or the full 3D image will not be taken in comfortably, and the audience is likely to experience the effects of diplopia.

Whilst in normal stereography the recommendation is to avoid image protrusion through the window, in the realm of drawings it can be more acceptable because one can more easily control the effect and the problem of protruding objects being "cut" by the frame borders (window violation) avoided.

2.   **Conflicting colours**. A curious effect can be produced by colouring two corresponding areas in the left and right images in different colours, or having one area black and the other white. When the images are fused in stereo viewing, each eye receives a different colour for that particular region and the brain attempts to resolve the conflicting information. The result depends upon the specific colour combination and perhaps upon the individual observer; the effect might be an alternate flickering of colours or a blending of the two colours, but not necessarily in the way one might expect from colour mixing theory. Using black in one image and a colour in the other can give a metallic lustre.

Because we all have a dominant eye, one of the two colours may be seen preferentially in images of this type.

This is not a technique that should be overindulged because a degree of eyestrain or discomfort may be experienced by the observer. Nevertheless, it could prove to be a useful novelty and the concept is worthy of experimentation.

13.2.4 Achieving greater accuracy

Stereo drawings made in frames 60mm apart, as in **Fig 13.2**, are probably the smallest that can be produced with reasonable accuracy. In preparing drawings, it is best to use a proper drawing pen to ensure a constant line thickness. Usually these pens have interchangeable nib units so that various line thicknesses are available. On this scale of diagram even small variations in the positioning of lines can cause discrepancies in the 3D image.

It is better to work on a larger scale and then either:

1. reduce the final image size by means of a photocopier with a reduction facility

or

2. take separate photographs of the drawings; the photographs are then mounted in the normal way

All dimensions will have to be scaled up from the values used for the 60mm size by the relevant magnification factor.

When using the second method, it is best to scale up from the film chip image size, and to construct the drawings so that they exhibit the correct parallax deviation when reduced in size.

Consider the Realist format, as an example of the method of working. The film chip images are approximately 23mm square, slightly wider than the mount apertures to allow for adjustments when mounting. The maximum parallax deviation is 1.2mm. For convenience the two drawings could be placed close together, as in **Fig 13.2**, but they will be photographed separately. The proximity of the two drawings affects only the separations of the various homologues but not the deviations (see Chapter 6, Section 6.4.3). Selecting, arbitrarily, a magnification of 8x will allow two squares to be placed side by side on an A3 sheet of paper in landscape orientation.

The squares will be 8 x 23 = 184mm in height and width. Using a value of 180mm for simplicity, and spacing the squares by 20mm, the frame separation will be 200mm. With a magnification of 8x, the maximum deviation is 8 x 1.2 = 9.6mm. This means that infinity homologues should be separated by 200 + 9.6 = 209.6mm. A value of 210mm will be accurate enough. Working with these values, the two images can be constructed as described above in Section 13.2.1 onwards.

Computer graphics are now very sophisticated and can be used to construct stereo pairs, following the various principles discussed so far in this chapter, which can make the task easier, or at least more accurate.

13.3 Use of Perspective Charts and Grids

Architects and technical illustrators have, for years, made use of special grids, over which tracing paper is placed, to prepare drawings, of an engineering component, an automobile, an artist's impression of a new building complex or whatever, in perspective. Such drawings often present the subject in dramatic or flattering form, but only as two-dimensional images.

Each chart or grid consists of sets of lines (representing parallel lines in real space) converging to one or more vanishing points, which, depending upon the viewpoint chosen for the particular grid, may or may not lie within the chart area.

Various types of grid design can be used. One version, shown in **Fig 13.11**, is based upon three axes mutually at right angles, together with sets of lines "parallel" to these at regular intervals. Although these lines represent parallel lines in the real world, they actually converge to vanishing points a long way off the chart, and the distances between them (equal in reality) will vary according to the laws of perspective.

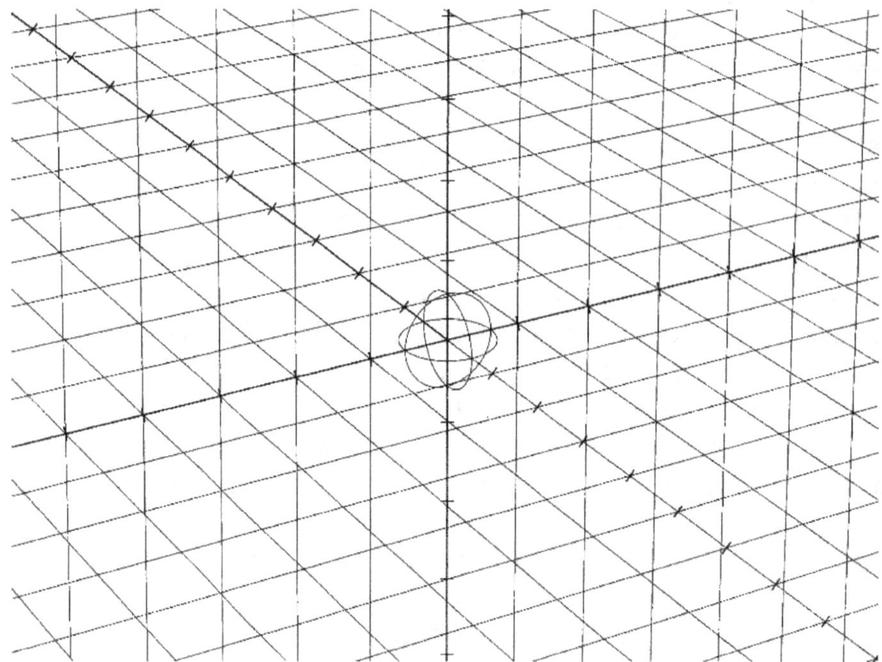

Fig 13.11
Typical perspective grid based upon three point perspective. Vertical and two sets of horizontal lines each converge to a separate vanishing point. (Chart kindly supplied by D Rainbow of Advanced Illustration, Congleton, Cheshire).

Another type of chart might be described as an "open box" design, the top and two nearest sides of the box omitted to give the shape shown in **Fig 13.12**. This diagram actually shows left and right perspective views of the box, the two drawings themselves constituting a stereo pair. Such charts are designed to give correct perspective (either for two- or three-dimensional use) when the final drawing is viewed from the correct distance and level; this information should be included in any published charts.

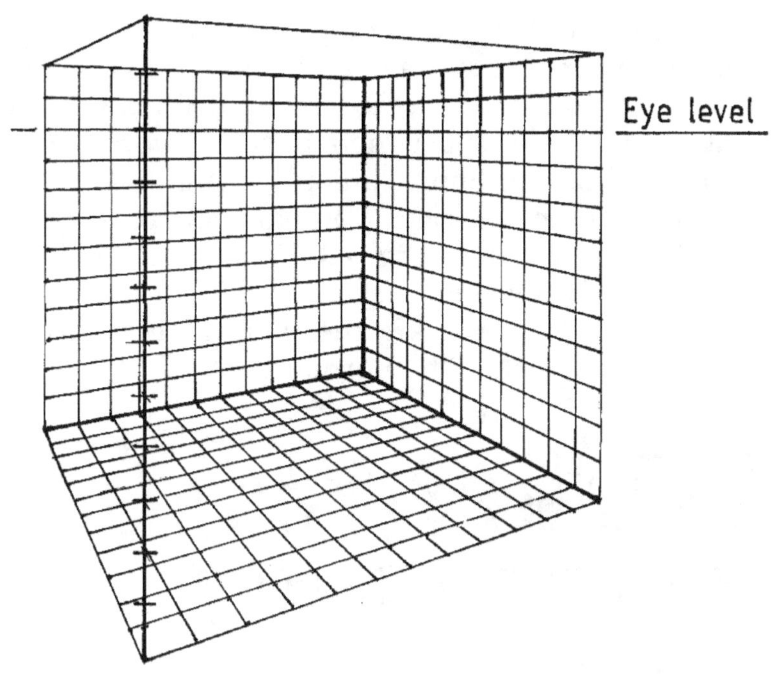

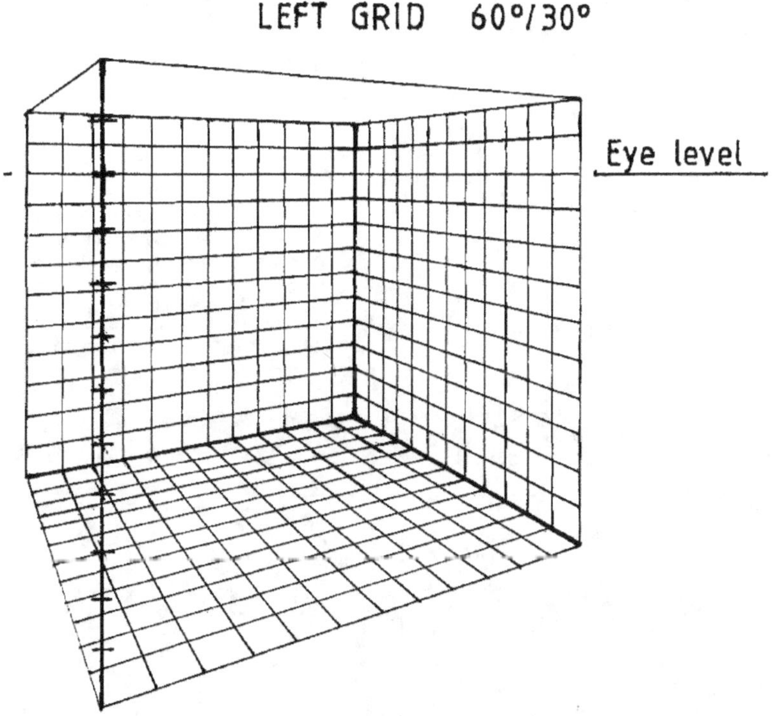

Fig 13.12
"Open box" type of perspective grid. The left and right grids shown form a stereo pair and can be used for constructing 3D drawings.

Perspective grids are of great help in preparing stereo drawings, though it has to be said that they have their limitations. They are ideal for geometric shapes based upon connected straight lines such as rectangles or triangles, but circular shapes, which have the form of ellipses when viewed other than head-on, are more difficult to handle.

Jerry Haines Sales, an American company, currently markets a set of "Phantogram" perspective charts (**Fig 13.13**) especially designed for the construction of anaglyph images; they are available in the UK[33]. Using coloured pencils provided with the kit, the right image is drawn in red and the left in cyan, superimposed in the normal way.

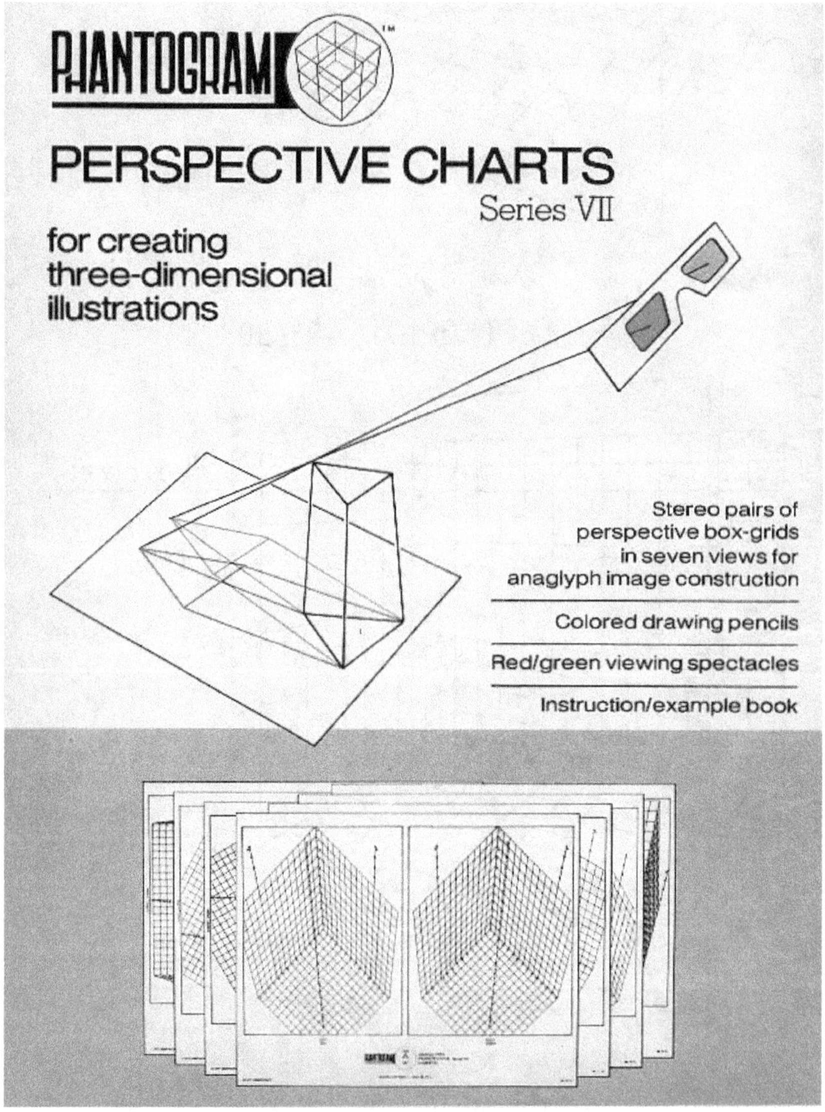

Fig 13.13
"Phantogram" perspective charts published by Jerry Haines Sales in the USA[33].

As shown in **Fig 13.14**, the images should be viewed at an angle of 45° and with the eyes at 450mm from the centre of the diagram. Under these conditions the 3D image will appear to stand up vertically on the page and be free of distortions. The charts are based upon one central vanishing point (one-point perspective) but dimensions in the "north-south" direction are elongated to allow for the foreshortening of the image at the 45° viewing angle.

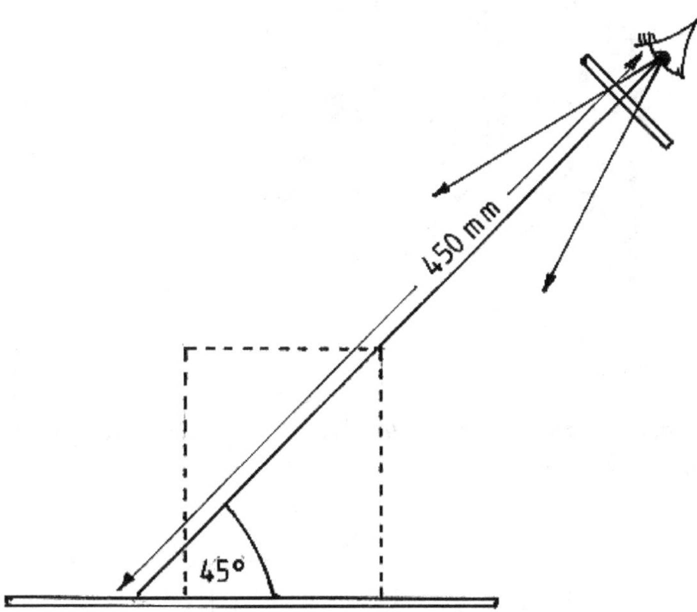

Fig 13.14
Correct angle and distance for viewing images produced with the aid of Phantogram perspective charts.

Whilst these charts can be used to produce two side-by-side images, in black lines instead of different colours, there will be some image distortion if the stereogram is viewed conventionally, at 90° to the page. Images would appear stretched vertically. This need not be a problem unless one is trying to draw natural objects or scenes realistically. With abstract subjects or titles the stretching is less important.

The solution is to use charts that are prepared without the built-in elongation factor, but they are not generally available. It is possible to construct one's own; this is not quite as formidable a task as it might seem.

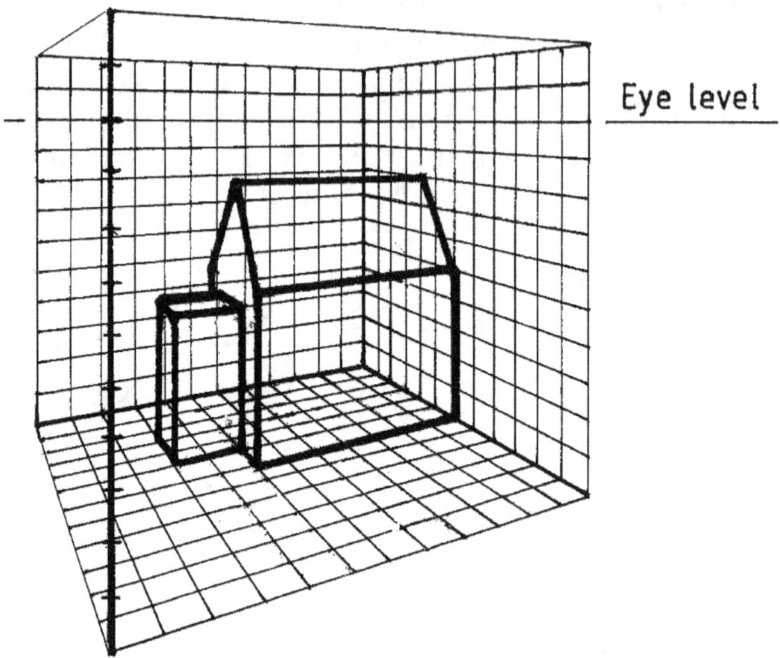

Fig 13.15
Drawing made on a perspective grid. Normally it would be made on tracing paper placed over the grid.

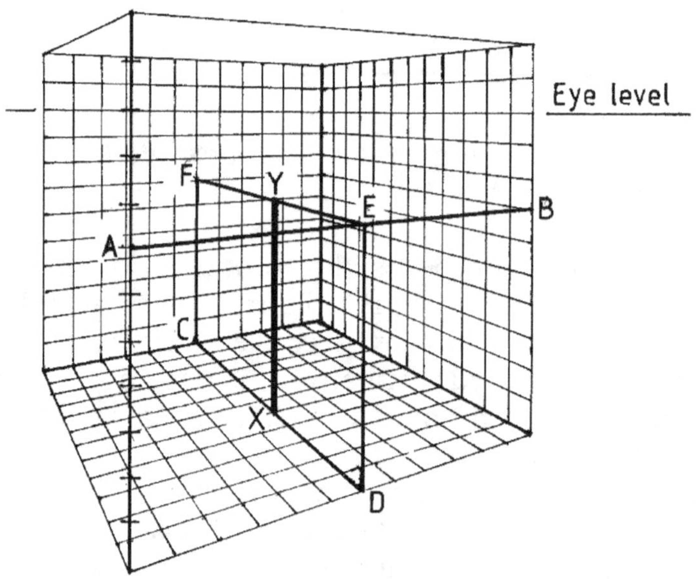

Fig 13.16
Method of constructing verticals of the correct height on a perspective grid. To draw a vertical line from **X** *height 7 units, points* **A** *and* **B** *(7 units from the base) are located and the line* **AB** *is drawn. From* **C** *and* **D** *on the base, verticals* **CF** *and* **DE**, *each equal to 7 units, are constructed. A line is drawn from* **X** *to intersect* **FE** *at* **Y. XY** *is the required vertical.*

The charts in **Fig 13.12** may be used as they are, or in enlarged form. **Fig 13.15** shows a drawing constructed on one of them, while **Fig 13.16** illustrates the correct method for establishing the heights of vertical lines and positions of horizontal planes.

All such charts and grids can be produced using computer programs that enable more accurate drawings to be made.

13.4 More Elaborate Pictorial Forms

The previous sections have covered some of the principles involved in the creation of relatively simple 3D drawings based primarily on simple geometric shapes that can be combined to produce a stylised version of a real scene. In theory, the techniques can be extended so that objects of greater complexity can be produced, by joining many of the basic elements together, but this approach does not lend itself readily to irregularly shaped objects, human figures, trees and so on.

To convert an "artistic" drawing into a stereo version requires much patience and painstaking work, but it can be done. One technique is to make a single line drawing to represent, say, the left view. The drawing should be constructed as simply as possible, using clear outlines, firm lines and simple shading, set inside a square or rectangular frame which will be used as a reference for making the right hand view, by application of the depth layering principle explained in Section 13.2, in a modified form.

The next step is to visualise the finished drawing as a 3D scene to establish in the mind the depth locations of key features. Having done so, it is advisable to make notes for consultation so that errors are less likely to be made at a later stage.

The second (right view) drawing is constructed by tracing the first picture in stages, starting with the most distant parts of the scene and working forwards for each successive (nearer) depth level. The tracing paper has to be shifted to the right by a small amount at each stage, calculated on the basis of a (magnified) deviation value appropriate to the relevant depth level. In this way, the locations of key points can be established. The drawing will have to be completed by some freehand copying, connecting the key points to match the original, bearing in mind the differences that will exist between the two aspects of any object seen from left and right viewpoints.

The procedure in greater detail, based on an approximately 8x magnification in the Realist format (see Section 13.2.4), is as follows:

1. draw a picture frame on the tracing paper to match that on the first drawing
2. place the tracing paper over the drawing with the frames exactly aligned
3. slide the tracing paper to the left by the maximum (magnified) parallax deviation of 8x1.2 =9.6mm (10mm will be accurate enough). Infinity homologues can now be marked.
4. slide the tracing paper to the right until the picture frame spacing is reduced by the relevant (magnified) deviation for that depth, in order to mark homologues on the next nearest depth plane, using the formula given below.
5. continue in this manner for each nearer depth layer until the picture frames are coincident. This setting is for the location of homologous points at the stereo window distance. Shifting the upper sheet further to the right will place the appropriate objects nearer than the window.

Parallax deviations for different depth planes can be calculated from the standard formula given in Supplement S7, modified by including the magnification factor **m**, which is simply the ratio of the width of the drawing to the width of the final image to be produced. Thus, if we make drawings of width 180mm to be photographed in Realist format (width 24mm before mounting), the magnification factor is 180/24 = 7.5. Using a value of 8 will be accurate enough; this follows the example in Section 13.2.4.

The modified formula is:

$$\mathbf{d'} = \mathbf{mfb}/\mathbf{D}$$

where

$\mathbf{f}$ = focal length
$\mathbf{b}$ = stereo base
$\mathbf{D}$ = distance of depth plane
$\mathbf{m}$ = magnification factor
$\mathbf{d'}$= magnified deviation value

So, for a plane at 15m, the magnified deviation using $\mathbf{f}$ = 35mm and $\mathbf{b}$ = 70mm is:
$\mathbf{d'}$ = 8 x 35x 70/15000 = 1.3mm

This means that the picture frames, initially set at 10mm apart for infinity point location must be set 1.3mm closer, i.e. at a separation of 8.7mm, to place objects at 15m.

If executed in pencil, the drawings can be converted to ink versions, with addition of colour if desired, or they can form the basis of full colour paintings, in which all colour gradations must be carefully matched in the two views.

The surrealist artist Salvador Dali has produced stereoscopic paintings for viewing by the crossed-eye method, on display in a museum at Figueras in Spain.

Several techniques for the production of stereoscopic drawings have been developed by the late Arthur Girling and these are explained with many examples in his book on the subject[43]. Girling is recognised as an authority on the subject and has used a number of techniques to achieve some excellent results with fine detail.

The Frenchman Sylvain Arnoux has designed and built mechanical devices which can be set to produce correct left and right views, essentially semi-automatic drawing machines, and he has developed the results into a number of impressive paintings on a wide variety of subjects.

CHAPTER 14: DIGITAL IMAGING

14.1 Introduction

The computer age has brought a wealth of gadgetry and techniques for the collection, organisation and distribution of all kinds of data and information. From number-crunching through word processing, data bases, spreadsheets and the like, computer science has been extended to explore and develop the graphic arts. Computer-based techniques are now widely used in advertising and the motion picture industry, notably in work involving animation which is, in the late 1990's, already astonishingly advanced and sophisticated. Computer graphics programs can generate images of many kinds, from simple line drawings to realistic art forms.

It was inevitable that sources other than computers would be developed to generate images. Consequently, in the world of photography, a new breed of camera, the digital camera, has come to the fore, capturing images on an electronic chip, a charge coupled device (CCD), instead of the traditional film. The captured image is immediately accessible for viewing in situ on a built-in screen and can be saved or deleted at will. Cameras have a built-in memory that can store a small number of images, but they can take a removable SD (Secure Digital) card that can accumulate hundreds of images depending on its capacity. Stored images can later be transferred to a computer and hard copies printed, all in full colour and with good definition. The first cameras were not able to match the image resolution of film, though great improvements in image quality have been made in the ensuing years.

Digital imaging carries with it a facility for modifying images in new ways, to produce effects that are either difficult or even impossible to achieve with film images. In stereo work, especially, there is scope to create amazing effects by building up pairs of images in stages and even converting mono photographs to stereo. In the sections that follow, the principles of digital processing will be explained with particular reference to 3D photography.

14.2 Digital Imaging

Traditional black and white photographic imaging is based upon chemical processes in which light-sensitive silver salts in a film emulsion are converted by development to metallic silver in those regions that are exposed to light, thus forming the black areas on the negative. The brightest parts of the original subject produce the densest (blackest) areas on the negative. When the negative is printed onto photographic paper the tones are reversed to give the familiar positive print. In colour films, the same principles apply but the film is more complex by having three layers in the emulsion that are sensitive to blue, green and red light respectively. During development, the silver images are converted to transparent coloured dyes in the primary colours, one for each layer. The various proportions of these dyes in different regions produce a range of hues identical (in theory) to that of the original subject.

In digital imaging technology the image is changed electronically to a very long string of "on" and "off" signals in binary code, in which all values of specific image characteristics such as light intensity or colour saturation are expressed by using only the digits 0 and 1; this is a number system with a base of 2 rather than the more familiar base of 10 with which normal arithmetical operations are performed. The numbers 0, 1, 2, 3, 4 and 5 become 0, 1, 10, 11, 100, and 101 in the binary system. To avoid confusion, binary numbers are pronounced as separate digits; thus binary 101 is "one zero one" or "one oh one" in speech and not "one hundred and one". If the binary digit 0 represents "off" and 1 "on", all quantities that binary numbers represent can be processed and stored as electrical pulses or charges.

In a digital camera the light rays from the subject are directed onto a CCD, an electronic chip consisting of a matrix of a large number of tiny picture elements (**pixels**). These pixels convert the light to electrical charge, the value of which is proportional to the brightness. Each of the individual charges is quantised into one of 256 steps, from black at level 0 to white at level 255, with mid grey lying at 128. The larger the number of pixels within a given area, the better is the detail that can be reproduced in the image. Pixels can be regarded roughly as the equivalent of grain in a conventional film. The problem with increasing the number of pixels to improve resolution is that more storage space will be required in the computer. For example, an image approximately 2" square converted to a digital one of 512 x 512 pixels gives a total of 262,144 pixels, which will require 768 kB (kilobytes) of storage. As a guide, Table 14.1 shows the number of pictures of size 10 Megapixels that can be stored on SD cards with different capacities [60]. For stereo pairs, with each image being 10 Megapixels in size, the numbers would be halved.

Table 14.1
Approximate number of images that can be stored on SD cards of different capacities

Megapixels	File size	1GB	2GB	4GB	8GB	16GB	32GB	64GB	128GB
10MP	3.0 MB	286	572	1144	2288	4577	9155	18310	36620

If the number of pixels in the 2" square image is reduced to 256 x 256 (65,536 pixels in total) the resolution is just about adequate to give a good image in which the individual elements cannot be distinguished in normal viewing. In comparing digital images, increasing the resolution to 512 x 512 pixels does not, at first sight, appear to produce a superior image, but the extra "hidden" resolution will allow for a degree of enlargement while maintaining image quality. It is important, therefore, to take the final image size into account when choosing a value for the resolution, to avoid coarsening the image.

It should be realised, however, that a digital image pixel is only a mathematical concept inside a computer and as such has no physical size until the program is set to reproduce it as a visual display or hard copy. On a computer screen one pixel is 1/72 of an inch in magnitude. If the whole image is enlarged by a linear factor of ten, each pixel will now occupy a square of a size originally occupied by 100 pixels, just larger than 1/8 of an inch square; this will obviously give a coarse image when it is viewed at the normal distance.

14.3 Digital Cameras

Digital cameras became commercially available early in the twenty-first century and proved to be increasingly popular amongst amateur photographers. Early cameras, although expensive, were relatively simple, with moderate resolution up to around 2 to 3 megapixels. As Henshall[34] has pointed out, these megapixel cameras were "in no man's land - producing better than necessary images for the Web, but still not good enough for a 10 x 8" photo quality print. Even at the low resolution of 200 pixels per inch, a 10 x 8" needs 3.2 megapixels". He also described digital cameras as below box cameras in quality terms, but up with single-lens reflexes in price. With the on-going improvements in modern chip technology, however, the achievable resolution increased at a pace and within a few years began to rival that of conventional film.

Digital photography has now largely taken over from film-based imaging, even among professionals. The debate as to which form is superior is ongoing; the two forms can produce very similar results. Some photographers use both, preferring film for some subjects or circumstances and digital for others. One of the distinct advantages of digital imaging is the reduced cost compared with the use of film.

Initially, the majority of digital cameras were of the compact "point and shoot" type but soon the more sophisticated digital single-lens-reflex (DSLR) cameras appeared. Since the inception of this new wave of technology, the specifications of both kinds have improved rapidly and costs have reduced greatly. Images of 12 megapixels or more taken on cameras of either type now seriously compete in quality with those produced from 35mm film cameras.

Digital stereoscopic cameras were not available until several years later, though one expert in stereoscopy managed to create a "siamesed" model from two compact cameras (Fig 14.1)

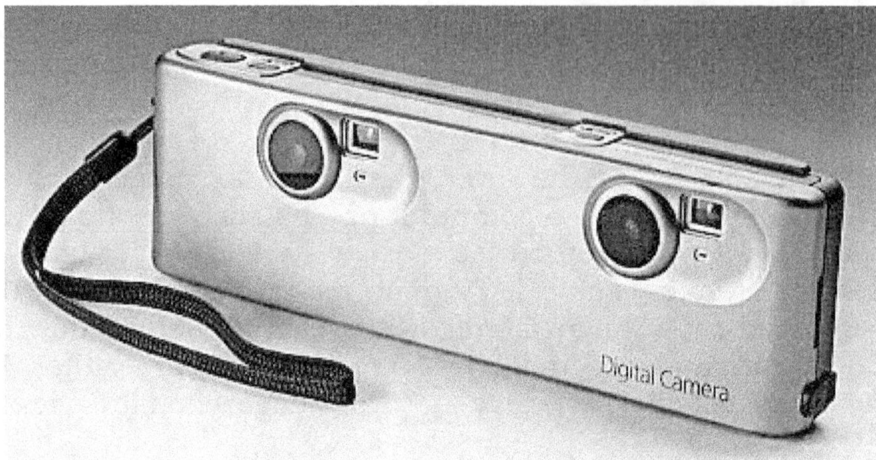

Fig 14.1
A "Siamesed" digital camera. (3D conversion is by David Burder of 3D Images Ltd, London, who kindly supplied the photograph).

The lack of stereo digital cameras meant that stereoscopic images had to be produced by other means, such as taking sequentials with a single camera (for static subjects only) or by using two identical digital mono cameras, a practice used by many stereographers with film cameras. The final stereograms produced can be downloaded into a computer and printed as side-by-side images, the format made popular in Victorian stereo cards. Alternatively, computer technology can be employed to retain images in digital form for them to be viewed with polarised glasses on suitable devices such as 3D computer monitors or 3D television, all of which is described in Section 14.7.3 and 14.7.4.

Whatever the final form of the stereo image, it is necessary to be able to process the left and right components to correct any discrepancies such as height errors and window violation, the equivalent of mounting as practised with film images. It may also be desirable to crop the final result to improve the composition. Fortunately there are at least two software programs, COSIMA and StereoPhoto Maker, which are designed especially for processing digital images and are readily available for amateurs and professionals alike. Digital image processing is discussed in Section 14.6.

Unfortunately with twin camera rigs there are inherent problems in obtaining satisfactory images suitable for viewing as stereo pairs. With film all parts of an image are captured simultaneously, whereas in digital technology the image arrives on the SD card as a flow of binary digits and this takes time to be completed. Even though this delay is a small fraction of a second the captured image may differ from the intended one because a person may turn away at the moment the shutter is pressed and the back of their head appears in the final picture instead of the face! Such signal delays are characteristic of all digital technology, and occur in digital radios and TVs. But more important is that the delay times vary from one camera to another. Worse is the fact that two apparently identical cameras can exhibit different delay times so there is no guarantee of perfect synchronisation if they are used in a twin rig. Significant differences in the left and right images caused by these variations are impossible to correct by using software.

The search for reliable ways to obtain good synchronisation was moderately successful. Simultaneously pressing the two shutter buttons (as can be used with film camera rigs - see Chapter 4, Fig 4.18) can give reasonable results, as long as the time delays for the two cameras are close in value. A better technique is to use a specially designed control device, such as the LANC Shepherd devised by Bob Crockett in the USA. This has built-in electronic circuitry and two leads, one for each camera. The unit monitors power-up, shutter, focus lock and zoom functions. Later models included extra features such as flash control. Other developers managed to make hardwire connections between the two cameras that worked satisfactorily, but all of these more sophisticated methods added to the cost of the equipment. One solution was provided in the form of a beam-splitter (the Tri-Delta Advantage) based upon the earlier Tri-Delta design (see Chapter 4, section 4.2.4). This was made to fit specific DSLR cameras, like the Canon Z 1200 which, with its 12 megapixel capacity, would give two half frame images at 6 megapixels each, of satisfactory quality. Unlike the original Tri-Delta this new version had adjustable mirrors to provide a variable stereo base. Synchronisation problems were non-existent, of course, but it was a fairly expensive solution.

Another method of obtaining two suitable images is to use a single digital camera with a fast shutter speed (lighting conditions permitting) and setting continuous shooting mode. The shot is taken by panning the camera left to right so that it records several images in rapid succession. This produces several possible stereo pair combinations with different stereo bases. One can choose a particular combination to give a satisfactory stereo image. With only very short time delays between the individual images any slight movement of the subject or parts of the scene may well be small enough not to cause disturbances or discrepancies in the final image when it is viewed. Of course, this technique is not likely to be successful for action shots with fast-moving subjects.

A breakthrough came in 2007 with a software programme devised by Suto and Sykes, creators of SPM. This was StereoData Maker (SDM) and, like SPM, was available on the internet as a free download. It derived from an earlier program published by a programmer named as "VitalyB" on a Russian website. His program, named Canon-Hack Development Kit (CHDK), was designed to replace the internal software (firmware) of several Canon compact cameras so that it could provide extra features not available on the standard product. Suto and Sykes developed and adapted this principle to solve the synchronisation problem for twin rigs; it was cleverly conceived and proved to be very successful.

For each of the various Canon cameras they compiled two software programs for downloading onto SD cards, one for the left camera and the other for the right (the two versions differ). Loaded with these SD cards the cameras work perfectly normally and independently. To achieve synchronisation the cameras have to be linked. For this a simple battery pack is required, consisting of battery power of about 4.5V, a "push to make" switch and two leads, one for each camera, plugged into its mini-USB socket. A typical twin rig with its battery pack is shown in Fig 14.2.

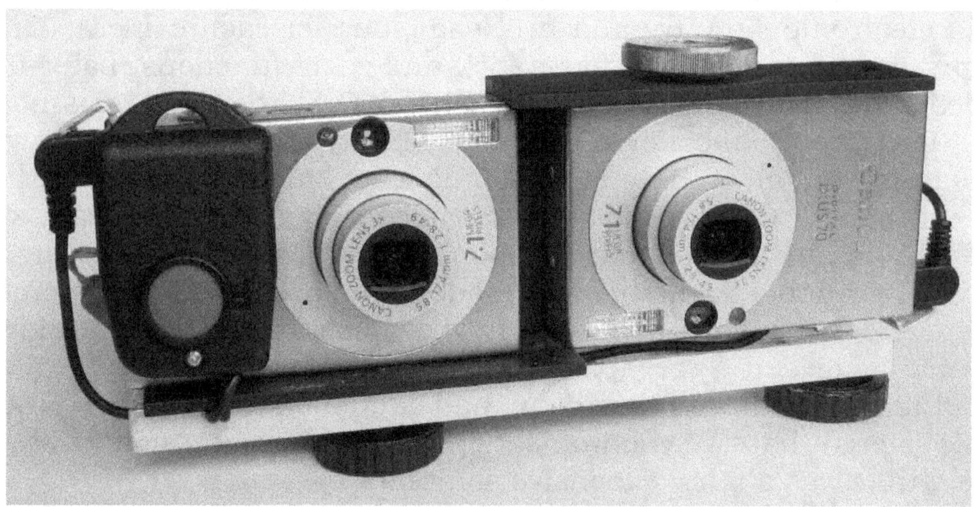

Fig 14.2
Twin rig of two Canon Ixus 70 cameras mounted on a "Z" bar and linked to operate with StereoData Maker software, to synchronise the shutters. The battery pack and its switch are seen on the left of the picture with two leads connected one to each camera's USB socket. The camera on the right in the picture is inverted to reduce the inter-lens spacing to 70mm from a minimum of 83mm if both cameras were mounted the same way up.

When the switch is pressed and held, each camera receives 4.5V and this activates the software downloaded onto the SD cards, overriding the cameras' firmware. At the same time the LCD screens black out. After ten seconds the shutters will be fired automatically in synchronisation, but the exposure can be made at any time during that ten seconds if the pressure on the switch is released. Although there is an occasional malfunction (generally when only one camera shutter fires) the system works extremely well, producing excellent synchronisation, Measured values of mis-synchronisation for a pair of Canon A460's are between 1/5000 and 1/10000 seconds [61].

The great advantage of SDM is that it costs very little to set up and the cameras are not modified in any way.

14.4 Digital Stereo Cameras
14.4.1 Background

Commercially-produced digital stereo cameras did not materialise until July 2009, when the Fuji company launched its FujiFilm W1. This had twin lenses capturing images at 10 megapixels each and an LCD screen displaying the 3D image autostereoscopically. It also incorporated a 3D video facility. Production ceased a year or so later when the improved version based upon the same technology, the FujiFilm W3, replaced it. Since then, a number of stereoscopic digital cameras (both still and video) have appeared from companies such Panasonic, Sony and others.

Panasonic produced a compact digital camera, the G1, designed to accept interchangeable lenses. One was a 3D lens, consisting of a normal-sized barrel that had two small lenses of focal length 12.5mm separated by 10mm as a stereo base. It resembled a Clemetson attachment (see Chapter 4, Fig 4.15), producing images cameras of good quality but, with its small stereo base, it was suitable only for close-up work.

14.4.2 FujiFilm Stereo Cameras

The FujiFilm W3 camera (Fig 14.3) and its predecessor the W1 have proved to be very successful and have been widely adopted by amateur stereo enthusiasts, though not perhaps by some professionals in this branch of photography who would presumably prefer a higher specification. Nevertheless, the Fuji cameras are capable of excellent results. Unfortunately, production ceased in 2014, so they are now available mostly on the second-hand market.

As far as the technology and facilities are concerned, the W1 and W3 have much in common. The lenses and CCDs are identical and their LCD screens are autostereoscopic though they use different technologies to display the images. The W1 displays the left and right images alternately at 120 frames per second with synchronised directional lighting that sends the images to the appropriate eyes. In the W3 the screen is a lenticular one with a very fine pitch to give a sharp image, but the viewing position is consequently more critical. The stereo base (inter-lens spacing) in the W1, at 77mm, is higher in value than in typical stereo film cameras, but Fuji reduced this slightly to 75mm in the W3.

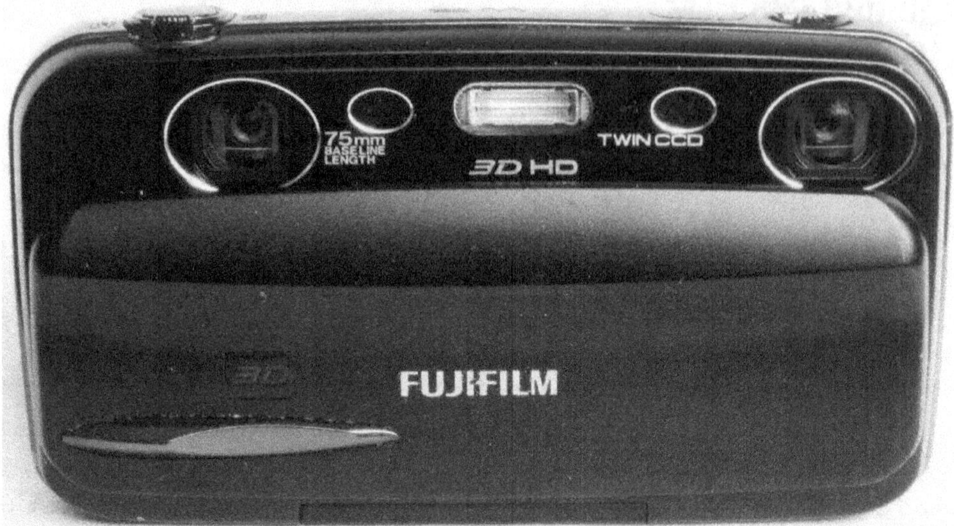

Fig 14.3
The FujFilm W3 digital stereo camera. The front panel (marked FUJIFILM) slides down to switch on the camera and to reveal the lenses. The central flash unit is located centrally between two microphones (for recording stereo sound when taking videos) and the two lenses.

A more detailed look at the specification of the W3 camera will essentially summarise the features for both cameras.

Specification: major features

Lenses:	Two Fujinon 3x optical zoom, f/3.7 (wide) to f/4.2 (telephoto) lenses, focal length 6.3 - 18.9mm (equivalent to 35 - 105mm on a 35mm camera).
Effective Pixels:	10.17 million
CCD:	Two 1/2.3 inch CCDs
Storage:	Internal memory 34 MB. Uses SD or SDHC memory cards
File Format:	Still pictures 3D: MPO + JPEG or MPO Still pictures 2D: Exif 2.3 JPEG (compressed) Movies 3D:Stero AV1 with two image channels Movies 2D:Motion JPEG with stereo audio recorded in AVI
Image Size:	Max 3648 x 2736 (10M) to in 1920 x 1080 (2M)
Zoom:	3D/Advanced 2D:combined optical and digital zoom up to approx. 3.8 times (35 mm format equivalent 39mm to 149mm) Advanced 3D: 3 x optical zoom 2D; 3 x optical zoom with up to approx. 5.7 x digital zoom (max combined zoom approx.17.1 x)
Stereo Base:	**75** mm (the W1 was slightly larger at 77mm)
Shutter Speeds:	3 seconds to 1/1000 second but the exact range varies according to the shooting mode
Apertures:	f/3.7, f/5, f/8 wide angle f/4.2, f/5.6, f/9 telephoto
Metering:	Through-the-lens Multi, Spot, Average
ISO:	Standard output equivalent to ISO 100 200 400 800 160 Auto(400) Auto (800) Auto (1600) These represent ranges 100 to 400, 400 to 800, and 800 to 1600 variable according to lighting conditions
Flash Modes:	Auto, fill flash, off, slow sync (*all these with red eye removal off*); auto with red eye removal, fill flash with red eye removal, off, slow sync with red eye removal (*all these with red eye removal on*).
Shooting Modes:	Auto, Manual, Aperture Priority AE, Program AE, Advanced 2D, Advanced 3D,plus SP1 and SP2 (*see next item*)
SP1 and SP2:	SP = Scene Position. SP1 and SP2 provide choices that match subject and situation to give suitable aperture/shutter speed combinations. There are 13 choices (the same for both modes) including anti-blur, portrait, landscape, sport, sunset, night, snow, beach, and underwater. Different scenes can be assigned to SP1 and SP2

MPO (Multi Picture Object) files are essentially two JPEG images joined side by side as a unit, but the camera can be set to record the images as MPO together with a JPEG file (single image, not a pair). When downloaded to a computer, MPO files appears as icons and not as photographs so images are not easily identifiable until opened in the StereoPhoto Maker (SPM) program as normal side-by-side JPEG images. The advantage of storing images as MPO plus JPEG is that the JPEG image is present as a 2D picture so that it is recognisable as a photograph on the computer screen. The disadvantage of this display format is that when SPM is set to bulk process the MPO files automatically, it also attempts to process the associated JPEG files as stereo pairs and this interrupts the proceedings.

The main control on the W3 is in the form of a dial on the camera back, a neater arrangement than the various buttons on the W1. The shooting modes are selected by rotating this dial. A useful setting is the advanced 3D mode in which two shots of the same subject can be taken from different positions sequentially. The camera automatically combines the two as a stereo image. This allows the photographer to use a reduced stereo base for close-ups or an increased base for hyperstereoscopic shots.

A Menu/OK button gives access to settings for both shooting and viewing modes, allowing one to change ISO values, white balance, image quality, aspect ratio and a host of other features. It is surrounded by a cursor ring which can be pressed at the top, bottom, left and right to choose macro, flash, self-timer, erase image and to increase the brightness of the LCD screen to increase its visibility in bright or dim light conditions.

On the top of the camera is a parallax control slider, whose function is to increase or decrease the lateral separation of the images prior to taking a shot, or when viewing a stored image. Operation of this control shifts the stereo image as a whole forward or backward relative to the stereo window, equivalent to the positioning of film chips in a card or plastic mount. Although in the menu there is an automatic setting for parallax control, this cannot guarantee avoidance of window violation in all shooting situation. It is wise, therefore to adjust the parallax control manually at the time of taking the picture. A useful feature is that window violation in a stored image can be adjusted by the parallax control and the corrected version stored on the SD card in addition to the original image. This could save one operation when processing the image in SPM.

The advanced 2D setting effectively converts the W3 into two separate cameras. The two lenses can be set to take two pictures simultaneously, one in black and white with the other in colour, or the two used at different zoom settings or with different sensitivities.

Of the three settings for video on the W3, the best resolution is classified as HD at 1280 x720 pixels at 24 frames per second, which is superior to that on the W1 camera.

There is a choice of three aspect ratios, **4:3**, **3:2** and **16:9** each with three size options **L**(arge), **M**(edium) and **S**(mall), based upon the largest sized quality image that can be printed. **L**arge pictures can obviously be printed to larger sizes with no loss of quality; **S**mall pictures require less memory, allowing more pictures to be recorded. Image quality based upon another factor can also be selected as Fine (**F** signifies low compression) for higher image quality or Normal (**N** signifies high compression) to increase the number of images that can be stored. An indication of the number of images that can be stored on 4GB and 8GB SD memory cards is given in Table 14.2 for two sizes and two aspect ratios.

Table 14.2
Number of images that can be stored on 4GB and 8GB SD memory cards for different image sizes (L and S), aspect ratio (4:3 and 16:9) and quality (Fine and Normal).

		4GB	4GB	8GB	8GB
Size	**Aspect Ratio**	**Fine**	**Normal**	**Fine**	**Normal**
L	4:3	260	530	530	1070
L	16:9	370	730	740	1470
S	4:3	830	1630	1680	3270
S	16:9	1250	1880	2510	3770

A minor problem with the W3 has its origin in the position of the flash, which lies midway between the two lenses. It arises when a flash photograph is taken of a person indoors, say, that produces a strong shadow on a surface such as a wall, close behind the subject. Because of the central location of the flash, the shadow in the left image appears to the right of the person, whereas in the right image it lies to the person's left. When the picture is viewed stereoscopically, the two shadows producc a retinal rivalry effect because each eye sees a different shadow. It also gives the shadow a strange halo-like appearance. If the background is far away or "busy" with several objects so that a clear shadow is not obvious then there is no problem. It is advisable, therefore, to avoid this effect, by covering the flash on the W3 with some exposed film or a small piece of card to block or greatly reduce the light reached by the subject. The piece of film or card should be attached in such a way that some light from the flash can escape sideways to trigger a remote slave unit attached to an external flashgun. This can be held freely in the left hand or attached to a flash bar together with the camera. It is best to have the camera on the right to make it easier to operate the shutter release.

In the USA, The Cyclopital range of adaptors and stereo equipment designed for various makes of cameras and camcorders (FujiFilm, Panasonic, JVC and Sony) provides extra facilities. For the FujiFilm W3 the list of products for use with the camera in shooting mode comprises a close-up/macro adaptor (which reduces the stereo base from 75 to 25mm), an auxiliary lens adaptor (to which can be attached wide-angle or fisheye lenses), a stereo base extender (which increases the base from 75 to 226mm for hyperstereoscopic images) and an optical viewfinder that can be attached to the base of the camera and used when the sunlight is even too bright for the screen brightness boost facility to be effective.

14.5 Other Digital Devices

Computers have reduced drastically in size and increased dramatically in what they can do since they first came into being. Now we have mobile telephones and tablets (the Apple company models are also known as iPads or iPods) all of which are basically miniature computers operated by touch-screen technology. Digital picture frames were amongst the earlier devices, partly replacing conventional photo frames. These were merely display units but capable of presenting slide shows of a number of images. A "smartphone" is not only a telephone; it has a screen, two built-in cameras (one pointing away and the other towards the person using it) and the software to achieve some of the functions that only larger computers could at one time achieve. A tablet is larger, in the form of a flat digital screen, typically from 7 to 10 inches (screen diagonal) in size, also with similar built-in cameras and a number of functions for communication. Thus one can send e-mails or messages using Wi-Fi technology, and see and speak live to friends and family via such applications (apps) using Facetime or Skype. .One can also connect to the airwaves and listen to radio or watch TV live or to catch upon previous programmes for a number of days after the original transmission.

For 2D photography digital photo frames began to gain popularity as more people turned to digital cameras for their snapshots. Stereo photographers often used them to display side-by-side stereo pairs, viewed with a lorgnette (Chapter 5, Section 5.3.7) or any simple viewer with wedge–shaped lenses suitable for viewing images too large to be free-viewed (Chapter 5, Fig 5.19).

Tablets and smartphones have taken over from digital photo frames because of the built-in cameras and the ability to display the image immediately on the screen. They, too, can be used for viewing side-by-side or anaglyph stereoscopic images. Sequential shots by moving the device laterally between exposures as with any mono camera (as described in Chapter 2) can produce a stereo pair. Two such images are normally displayed separately, but it may be possible to arrange them side-by-side if there is an "album" setting that shows a number of images simultaneously.

Stereo pairs taken with a digital stereo camera or twin rig can be downloaded to the tablet or phone, to be viewed as true 3D images with a simple two-lens stereoscope, or as an anaglyph by means of red/cyan glasses. There are a number of apps that can help to achieve this method of display. However, many so-called "3D apps" have no connection with stereoscopy. The term "3D" has in recent years been downgraded to describe drawings or images that look solid, with realistic shading and colouring. They can be rotated on the computer screen to be seen from different viewpoints, and they can give the illusion of depth. With continuously moving objects, as one might see in a cartoon film, the effect can be quite convincing but it is best described as "dynamic perspective". None of these types of image are truly stereoscopic.

Perhaps in the future an iPad that has twin cameras to take stereo pairs will be available, to rival the FujiFilm W3. The general public probably use iPads and iPhones more than compact digital cameras for photography. Perhaps this is because these devices do many other things that cameras do not. A "stereoscopic tablet" might be more effective in creating a greater interest in 3D imaging than a host of new 3D cameras.

14.6 Image Processing with StereoPhoto Maker

Digital images have to be aligned and adjusted by following the same principles used for film and print images as described in Chapter 6, though the procedures are carried out on a computer.

As mentioned briefly in Section 14.3, the first program, was COSIMA (**CO**rrect **S**tereo **IM**ages **A**utomatically) created in 2004 in Germany by Gerhard P Herbig. A later one, devised by Masuji Suto and David Sykes, is called StereoPhoto Maker (**SPM**). The Cosima program can be downloaded free, allowing users to produce images no larger than 640 x 480 pixels. Anything larger will cause a logo "mounted with cosima" to be superimposed on the images. If larger images are required, the user can pay for a licence to operate the program.

Both Cosima and SPM enable the user to adjust the stereo images on a computer with great accuracy and control, to correct alignment errors and to make changes to image quality (brightness, contrast, colour balance, for example) and to crop freely.

StereoPhoto Maker is available in its full capacity as a free download from the internet and like Cosima, has been continually refined and upgraded. It is possibly the most widely used of the two, so discussion of image processing will focus on this particular program.

The first step is to load the images from the camera(s) into the computer, into as many folders and files as desired, classifying them by date, subject or whatever. The main folder is best labelled "Source Images" or similar. These represent the original unprocessed images and should be retained for possible reprocessing in the future. Left and right images from a twin camera rig should initially be sent separately to "Left" and "Right" folders. SPM can then label all the images in bulk in a set with a title in the form, for example "Castle_l" and "Castle_r" with all pairs numbered in sequence. The left and right images can now then be moved or copied to a single folder so that the pairs are matched correctly and ready for processing.

Once the images are stored in the computer, SPM can be opened.

The essential steps required to process an image are very straightforward, as follows:

1. Open Stereo Image

Click on File on the menu bar and select "Open Stereo Image" on the drop-down menu for MPO or JPEG stereo pairs. MPO images are seen in folders as icons whereas JPEG images are pictorial.

Left and right images from a twin camera rig are entered by selecting "Open Left/Right Images". If they are identified by the "_l" and "_r" suffixes, a click on one will enter both into SPM as a side-by-side pair. The SPM screen display is now as illustrated in Fig 14.4.

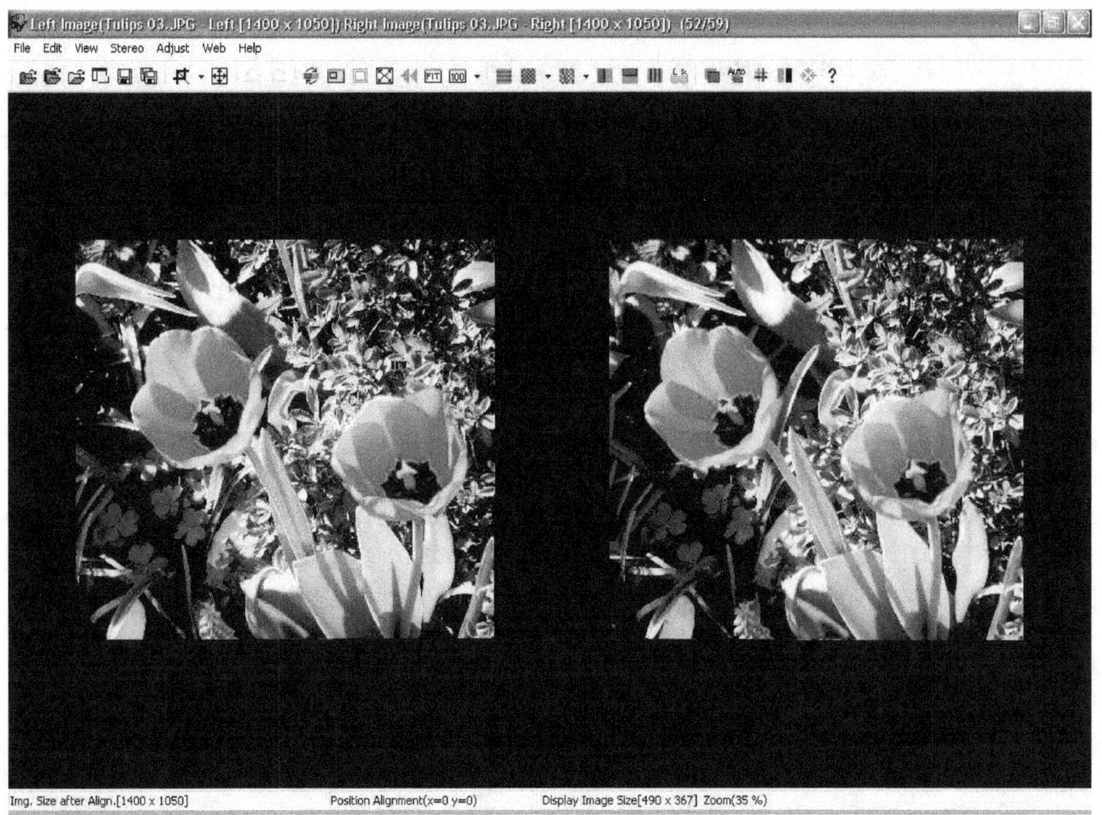

Fig 14.4
*This is the main display page of the StereoPhoto Maker (SPM) software program showing a stereo image pair in position for processing. Immediately above the images, the twelve principal function icons (the final twelve of the large central group) are, from left to right, **Interlaced; Grey anaglyph; Colour anaglyph; Side-by-side; Above/Below; Sharp 3D LCD; Page-flip for 3D shutter glasses; Easy adjustment, Auto alignment; Alignment mode; Auto colour adjustment; Alignment reset.** The icons seen on the left of the menu bar in Fig 14.4 are shortcuts to some of the options in the File and Edit menus. (This figure exhibits some window violation at this stage. The next step would be to correct it by using the Easy Adjustment control).*

2. Align the Left and Right Images

Selecting the "Easy Adjustment" icon (Fig 14.4), converts the images into a red/cyan anaglyph in a smaller screen with two sliders, one on the left and the other at the top. These can be adjusted to shift the images relative to each other both vertically and horizontally until they are correctly aligned. By wearing red/cyan spectacles it is easy to see when the horizontal adjustment places the image correctly in relation to the stereo window. To the left of this screen display there are various buttons for selecting other features. One of these enables a grid to be set over the anaglyph image. Choosing "30" produces a 30 x 30 grid and if infinity points are set at one column width apart (i.e. 1/30th of the image width), as a rule of thumb this is about right for most images.

One can also correct a rotational difference between the two images that could arise from a twin camera rig if one camera slopes slightly from left to right compared to the other. The right image, for example, can be rotated to bring its sloping horizon horizontal to match that in the left image.

Both images can be rotated by the same amount by selecting the "link both rotations together" button. This allows one to correct an image taken when the camera or twin rig was tilted about a horizontal axis (as shown in Chapter 2 Fig 2.1). However, there is a limit to how much rotation of this kind can be corrected before the stereo image becomes distorted too much for correct viewing (see Chapter 6 Section 6.3.1).

A control marked "barrel distortion" can be set to correct that particular fault. The correct value to be set can be determined by taking a test picture of a square grid or similar subject. This can be viewed in the Easy Adjustment mode, and the effects of different correction values for barrel can be assessed.

Using the Easy Adjustment mode is informative because one can see how different factors affect the image by correcting errors and placing it correctly in relation to the stereo window. However, the adjustment can be made simpler and speedier by first selecting the Auto alignment icon (Fig 14.4) instead of Easy Adjustment. This works automatically to correct vertical misalignment, differential rotational error between the left and right images, and barrel distortion (the optimum value has to be set in advance). In particular it adjusts the horizontal separation to a pre-selected option, one of which is locating the nearest object at the stereo window. Using this facility offers one great advantage because it can be used to process a whole file of images by selecting the Multi Conversion option from the drop-down File menu. In this mode one can include other options such as resizing, increasing sharpness, cropping, colour adjustment and contrast. Nevertheless, it may be better to apply most of these after auto alignment, because the images may not all require the same treatment to get the best results. Once auto alignment is completed the images should be sent to a new folder marked "Auto-aligned images" or something similar.

Auto alignment does not guarantee a perfectly adjusted stereo image. It is important to check the position of the image in relation to the stereo window and to alter the lateral separation of the images in the Easy Adjustment mode. Stereo windows are usually set at about 6 to 8 ft. distance and if the nearest object was 20ft. away, auto alignment may place it at the stereo window which is too close. In this example the lateral separation needs to be increased to move the image back, further behind the window. And any linked rotation should also be corrected in Easy Adjustment mode because only the photographer knows if there is an overall tilt to be corrected. There is no way Auto alignment would be able to recognise this kind of anomaly.

3. Other Adjustments

The next stage is to consider the aligned image and to decide what further changes might improve it. Various options might be necessary or desirable: colour adjustment to match the left and right images; increasing sharpness, changes in brightness or contrast; or cropping (which can be completely free or to any size with a fixed aspect ratio). All of this is in the realm of artistic judgement and not technical accuracy.

Resizing, not to be confused with cropping, is another option in which the dimensions of the final image are expressed as the numbers of pixels. This size may have to be restricted so that the image is compatible with the requirements of a digital projector, say 1400 pixels (width) x 1050 pixels (height), 2800 x 1050 for the pair. A cropped image of an arbitrary size can be resized to this aspect ratio by selecting "keep aspect ratio with borders" in the resizing menu. The original image is then reduced to a height of 1050 pixels and black borders are added to the top and bottom or sides as appropriate to make up the width or height of each image in this example to 1400 or 1050 pixels respectively.

4. Saving the Images

The final stage is to save the final images into suitably named files and folders. Clicking on "Save Stereo Image" in the File drop-down menu will automatically save MPO or JPEG images as JPEG images. Alternatively, either format can be saved as MPO images by clicking on "Save MPO File" in the same drop-down menu. They can also be saved as separate images by selecting "Save Left/Right Images".

Images can also be saved as anaglyphs (with choice of complementary colours), in "above and below" format for ViewMagic viewing (Chapter 5 Section 5.3.8), or "page-flipping" format (rapid alternation of left and right image) for use with suitable shutter glasses. Images saved in anaglyph or above/below form can be printed in those formats. One of the icons on the menu bar enables the left and right images to be interchanged, with the left image on the right and vice versa in a side-by-side pair or with the right image above the left in the above/below mode.

In this same menu is an option to print images as stereo cards in the same style as those used in a Holmes viewer. Stereo cards in other sizes can also be printed from this option. The menu also gives the choice of printing a title and brief description of the subject on the card.

14.7 Viewing Digital Images
14.7.1. Hand-held Viewers with Lenses

These are the digital equivalent of slide viewers of Brewster-type stereoscopes such as the Stereo Realist (Chapter 5, Section 5.3.5).

Two commercially produced digital hand-held viewers are shown in Fig 14.5.

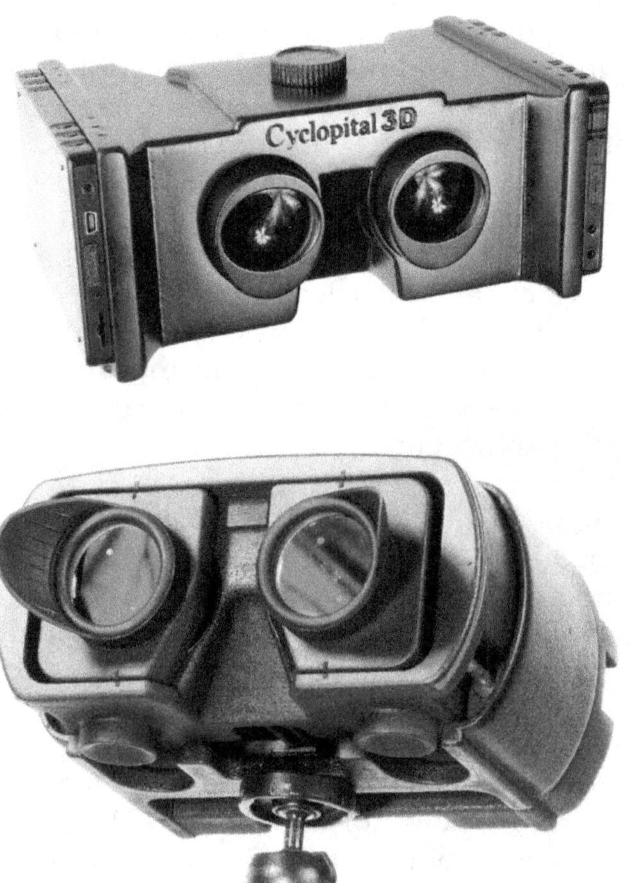

Fig 14.5
(a) *Cyclopital 3D digital hand viewer manufactured in the USA.*
(b) *HDD3 ViewVaster™ Cyclopital 3D viewer.*
(Photographs kindly supplied by Ken Burgess)

The screens in the Cyclopital viewer are located on the left and right sides of the viewer's body. This viewer has internal mirrors at 45° so it is similar in design to a Wheatstone stereoscope, which means that the images each have to be laterally reversed, to become mirror images of the originals. When this model first appeared, available screens were of low definition and, combined with the magnification from the lenses, images were rather coarse because individual pixels were discernible, but users did not find this distracting. It has now been replaced by the HDD3 ViewVaster which offers much higher definition. This is sold as a body designed to accept high definition cell phones (not supplied). It is claimed that the images are comparable to viewing a 65 inch HD3D TV from 6ft distance.

The quality of high definition digital images is now beginning to match that of film images, but not all viewers can display them to their full potential. Future improvements lie in producing a screen with a high enough resolution to match the high quality resolution of the best digital images.

Compared with film slide viewers the digital versions are much more expensive, but manufacturing costs are high because they are more complex in design and require high-priced ready-made components.

14.7.2 Freestanding Viewers

This category includes tablets and iPads which can be used as free-standing screens. While it is true that they can be hand-held, they have no in-built lenses so they are here regarded as in a different category from those in **i** above.

Along with their W1 and W3 cameras, FujiFilm marketed a small freestanding viewer, the FinePix Real 3D V3. The 7.2 inch lenticular screen provides autostereoscopic viewing of the 3D images. 2D images can also be viewed, so the viewer is a kind of updated version of a digital photo frame, but a more expensive one. The screen resolution is 800 x 600 pixels for each image of the stereo pair. Although this matches the resolutions of some of the better photo frames, it is only a moderate resolution figure. Nevertheless, it is an acceptable figure for viewing digital images when no extra magnification is involved. Individual pixels should not be discernible at normal viewing distances. The image quality is superior to that for a side-by-side pair on a digital photo frame with the same resolution viewed through lenses. On the photo frame each image would measure only 400 x 600 pixels maximum. The Cyclopital Company also manufactures the Cy-3D iPad lens-based viewer that fits over an iPad with a Retina (high resolution) display. It offers adjustable inter-ocular and focus and a 40° horizontal field of view.

The Gadmei Electronics Technology Co., Ltd in China has developed specialised tablets for autostereoscopic viewing of 3D images. Their first product of this kind was a "Glasses-Free 3D Media Player" (Fig 14.6) which displays still images (2D and 3D), 3D video (certain formats); it also functions as an e-book. The 8 inch (diagonal) HD lenticular screen has an aspect ratio close to 16:9, and it displays a good clear image with a resolution of 1280 x 768 pixels. The recommended viewing distance is 45 – 65 cm (about 18 – 26 inches). It has a rechargeable internal battery and comes with a remote control.

The device has stereo speakers and a choice of musical tracks that can be played while viewing. There is an automatic slideshow facility but individual images can be viewed and changed manually.

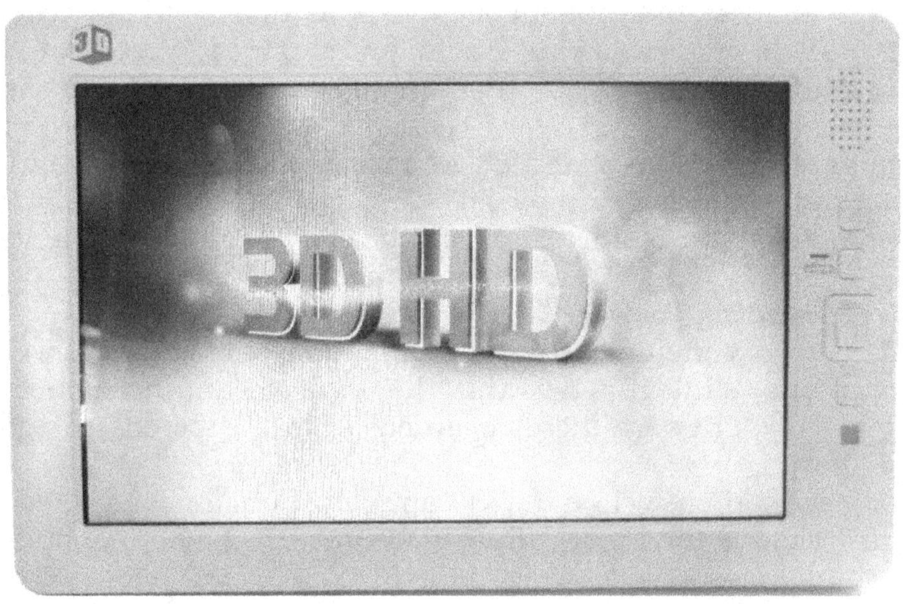

Fig 14.6
Gadmei "Glasses-Free 3D Media Player"

There are two inputs, a mini USB socket for connecting to computers or flash drives, and a card slot for SD and SDHC memory cards up to a capacity of 32 GB. Images. MPO stereos from the FujiFilm W3 camera are displayed automatically as 3D images;. Side-by-side JPEG images have to be first processed (in SPM or COSIMA) in half width format. They are compressed laterally, as shown in Fig 14.7.

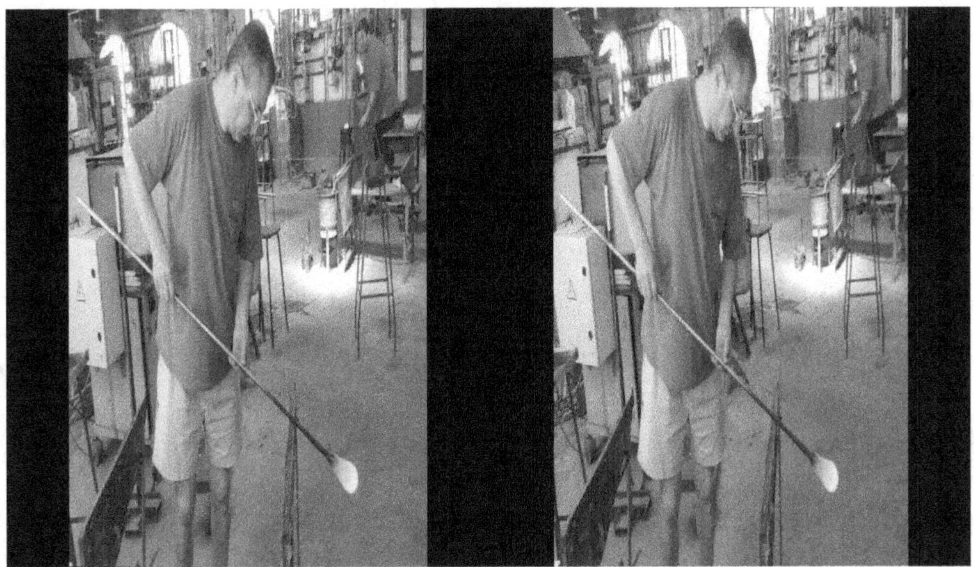

Fig 14.7
JPEG stereo pair compressed laterally to half width. The black borders were inserted when resizing the cropped image in SPM to 2800 x 1050 pixels for the pair. Then the width was reduced to 1400 total without maintaining the aspect ratio then reducing the total width to 1400 pixels.

In the Gadmei viewer these images first appear on the screen in compressed form as in Fig 14.7, but when the 2D/3D button is pressed the left and right images are interlaced vertically and the picture is now displayed at normal width to be viewed as an autostereoscopic 3D image. As with all such images, there are specific viewpoints ("sweet spots") for correct viewing, and the central position is the obvious one to choose. By moving the device or the head sideways left or right by 4 – 5 inches two more sweet so pots can be found but the image will be viewed at a slight angle. They are too close to allow more than one person to use the viewer comfortably at the same time. Each viewing position is quite critically defined. A slight sideways shift of the head and the image is seen as pseudoscopic. Holding the device for viewing requires a steady hand and it is better to stand the viewer on a flat surface at about head height, (there is a strut on the back that can be pulled out) and that makes it easier to maintain a fixed viewpoint and to look at the image from the recommended distance without having to stretch one's arms forward full length.

A later model from the Gadmei Company, similar in appearance to the original version, is marketed as the Gadmei E8-3D Tablet, with an 8.1 inch High Resolution 1280 x 800 touch screen (again for autostereoscopic viewing), and it includes Wi-Fi, front and rear cameras, microphone and USB socket. Like its predecessor it supports 2D and 3D video, MPO and JPEG still images.

14.7.3. Computer Monitors

Since about 2010, specialist 3D monitors for use with computers have been produced commercially. They function normally for general use but when the screen resolution is set to a suitable value, they can display 3D images, both still and video, using appropriate software. The monitor is fitted with circular polarising filters so viewing requires compatible glasses. Normally the left and right images of the stereo pair are interlaced on alternate horizontal rows of pixels.

The internet once again can offer free downloads of software such as Stereoscopic Player, which enables 3D videos to be shown, and there is a good choice of stereo stills and videos that can be watched and often downloaded from sites such as YouTube, in various formats, even as anaglyphs for viewing on standard computer monitors.

Laptop computers are becoming increasingly popular and there are now versions that have 3D monitors. Although portable, they have more in common with their desktop counterparts than with tablets, so they are included in this section.

14.7.4 3D Television

It was only from about 2010 that 3D TVs began to be sold to the general public, though the concept was not new. The first demonstration of 3D television was given by John Logie Baird in August 1928 and various companies developed the ideas that eventually led to commercial production. Television sets had by 2010 been transformed from moderately sized boxes to large flat screen panels, an ideal design for displaying large 3D images.

The stereo images are transmitted as a laterally compressed pair and appear on screen as in Fig 14.7 above. This will be transformed to a viewable form by pressing a 2D/3D button on the remote control, or perhaps by setting the TV to recognise any 3D image and convert it automatically in one of two ways, as explained below.

The two main types of 3D TV are passive and active, both requiring viewers to wear glasses. In the passive system the left and right images are oppositely polarised (circular polarisation) and interlaced on alternate horizontal rows of pixels and the picture is viewed with circular-polarised spectacles. The glasses are the same type as used in cinemas for viewing 3D films, and are relatively inexpensive. The system works well but there is a slight disadvantage in that the vertical resolution of the image as a whole is only one half of the corresponding screen resolution. As long as the distance between viewer and screen is great enough the discontinuities the alternate dark lines will not be visible.

The more expensive system (active) works differently. In this case the left and right images are displayed alternately full-screen, at a rate of at least 120 frames per second. The viewer has to wear special battery-operated shutter glasses. Each eye's glass has an LCD (liquid crystal display) layer which becomes opaque when a voltage is applied, being otherwise transparent. The glasses are controlled by a timing signal transmitted from the TV set by infrared or radio signals which cause the glasses to block each eye in turn, in synchronisation with the refresh rate of the screen. For the 120 frames per second rate each eye receives its images at 60 frames per second, sufficient to avoid flicker.

Because each image is displayed as full frame the full vertical resolution is employed so the picture is technically superior to that seen on a passive set. Both systems have advantages and disadvantages so in reality there is not a lot to choose between them.

Depending on the make and model, 3D TV sets will have various inputs to show stereoscopic image taken on digital cameras. An HDMI connection may be available and many sets will accept an SD or SDHC card via a slot. Through AV channels D TVs can screen 3D movies from 3D DVD or 3D Blu-Ray players.

For a while, some TV channels transmitted 3D programmes (both pre-recorded or live) and these could be viewed when transmitted and could also be recorded on 3D player/recorder DVD equipment. But as the public enthusiasm for 3D began to wane, as it seems to after every surge of interest, the number of stereo programmes has almost disappeared.

The stereo window will lie at the screen surface and there is usually a "3D Adjustment" or similar function that can be accessed to move the image relative to the window. Usually one needs to move the image back rather than forward. Some 3D movies come with built-in window violations that cannot be eliminated. In some circumstances this 3D adjustment feature may not be accessible. For example, it is not available when connecting a FujiFilm W3 camera directly to a Panasonic 3DTV via the HDMI lead. On the other hand, images displayed from SD or SDHC cards can be adjusted on screen. If they are first properly processed in SPM, they will appear correctly on screen without the need for any further tinkering.

Some 3D TVs have the facility to convert normal 2D images to 3D at the press of a button. This works to some extent but, in the author's experience, is not particularly impressive; in fact the conversion is hardly noticeable.

Quite a lot of research has gone into the development of autostereoscopic TV screens, so that viewers can view 3D images without special glasses. The usual problems of the number of sweet spots restricting the number of viewers that can watch the screen an any one time is an obvious disadvantage of this format. However, developments of head tracking systems have partially solved the problems, by producing regions in the viewing field, called exit pupils, where a particular image is seen across the complete area of the screen. As the viewer moves, the 3D image remains constant. A number of methods can be adopted to achieve this, but all of this technology is so far in the development stage and no TV sets of this kind are yet being marketed.

14.7.5 Digital Projectors

Digital projection has one advantage over film slide projection; it is much easier to prepare a programme and show many images as slideshows or as a pre-prepared AV presentation. In the past, Realist format mounts could be used only in projectors like the Hawk in the UK or the Realist and TDC Vivid in the USA. Slides had to be loaded individually and changed by hand. Projectors like the Kodak Carousels that used magazines loaded with a large number of slides made operation much easier. These projectors worked with 35mm slides in 50 x 50 mm mounts, left images in one projector and right images in the other. Hand-loading was no longer necessary; just a simple press of a button changed the projected image.

Automation was possible by using a tape recorder, on which recorded pulses on one track activated a device that triggered the projectors to change to the next slide at the pre—determined times. The other tracks would be recorded with a commentary and musical background. None of this was possible with the Realist format projectors.

Projecting a show is even easier with digital projection. The great advantage is that the images can be stored individually or in a given sequence as a pre-prepared show on memory sticks, CDs or DVDs which occupy little space, and is ready for projection at a moment's notice.

Although there are digital projectors designed especially for 3D image projection (as well as 2D), they operate in the same way as active 3D TVs, so shutter-type glasses have to be used. This is expensive for the amateur who wishes to present shows for large audiences, and indeed for showing 3D films in cinemas. In order to allow the use of circular or linear polarised spectacles, an additional piece of equipment is needed to polarise the images, such as the PolaRotator marketed by 3D Experience Ltd. The PolaRotator kit consists of an LCD screen that is an active shutter "window" in front of the projector, a driver box with controls for synchronisation rate and eye reversal, plus connecting cables. The device converts the images alternately to left and right circular-polarised ones in synchronisation with the alternating 3D frames so that they can be viewed with cheaper passive polarised glasses. But this alternative may be just as costly overall because the PolaRotator is an expensive piece of kit.

The most common method of projecting digital stereo images is to use two single (2D) projectors. A typical set-up is shown in Fig 14.8. The stand is an important component because it must incorporate some mechanism (adjusting screws, for example, as shown in Fig 14.8) to enable the two supporting platforms to be tilted forward, back, left and right, in order to align images correctly on screen.

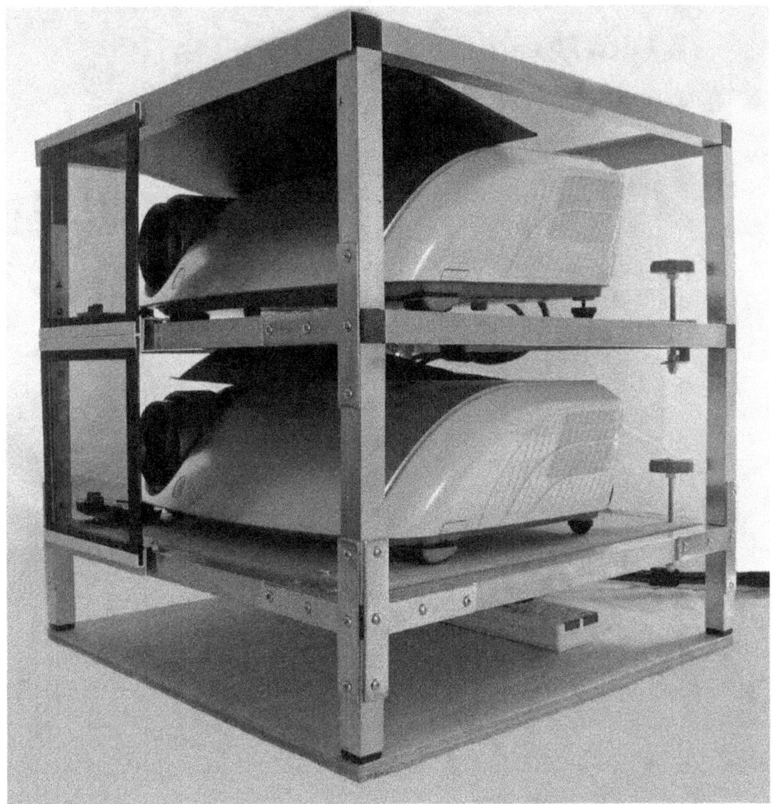

Fig 14.8
Two digital projectors in a rig with polarising filters (on the left front of the stand)

What is not shown in the above figure is the computer that acts as the control centre. Individual images, or pre-prepared AV programs, are downloaded into the computer, which must have two outlets that will send the left images to one projector and right images to the second projector. The problem with having to incorporate a computer in the system is the extra bulk to carry around. Laptops are more portable but any images nor already loaded into the computer prior to the showing have to be stored and then selected from the computer menus, all somewhat time-consuming.

A neater set-up is to use a media player plus some extra components (illustrated in Fig 14.9) to enable stored images to be "plugged in" as DVDs, or from memory sticks and the like, and then shown immediately, without the need to store them into the system in advance.

3D DIGITAL PROJECTION SCHEMATIC

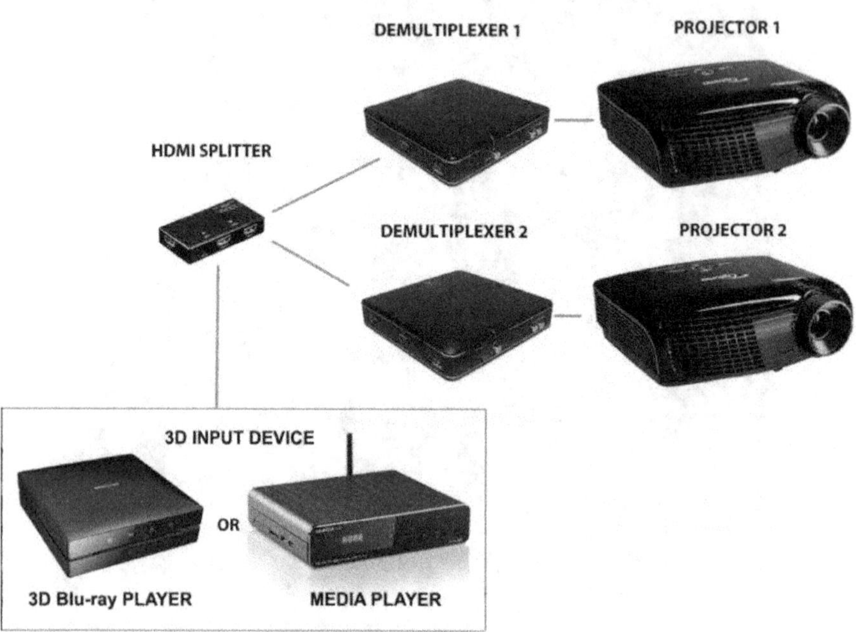

Fig 14.9
Schematic showing 3D digital projection using two projectors connected to a media player through an HDMI splitter and two multiplexers all that is needed to complete the set-up are polarising filters, a silver screen and loudspeakers for the audio content of the presentation. (Image kindly supplied by Barry Aldous: see www.aldous.net)

This set-up is ideal for AV presentations created by using computer software programs such as Magix or Cyberlink Powerdirector that provide sophisticated editing facilities for still and video images. The film maker can add commentary, musical background and can use many other options to produce shows of a high professional standard.

Digital projection as described so far has many advantages over slide projection. In general, viewing relies on polarised light. Circular polarisation is now common and is superior to linear polarisation because it allows a viewer's head to be tilted more freely without losing the stereo effect, However, both types are liable to suffer from ghosting. In passive systems the images are superimposed and that, logically, will contribute to that problem. However, in active systems the two images are always displayed separately and never superimposed, so in theory there should be no ghosting. However, the darkening of each lens is not perfect and so they are not completely opaque.

There is, however, a more recent development by Dolby and others of a projection system that uses interference filters in place of polarised ones.

The system is also known as **Spectral Comb Filtering** or **Wavelength Multiplex Visualisation**. The filters are designed to transmit specific wavelengths of blue, green and red light for the left eye, and three similar but different wavelengths for the right eye. For example the wavelengths could be:

Left eye: Blue 432 nm, Green 518 nm, Red 615 nm
Right eye: Blue 446 nm, Green 532 nm, Red 629 nm

The differences are shown in Fig 14. 10.

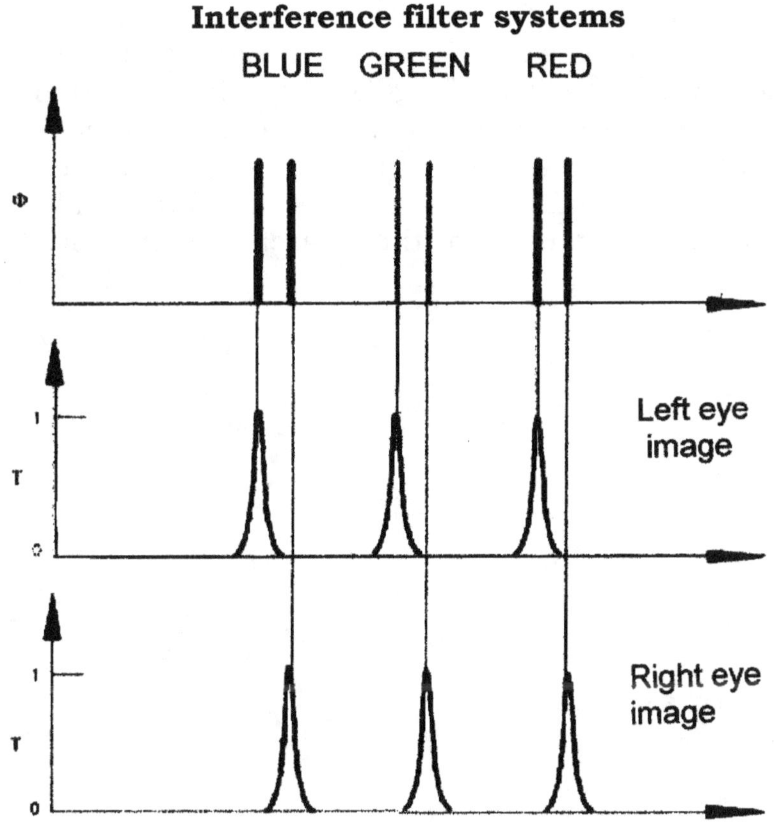

Fig 14.10
Interference filters for left and right images

These filters are used in the same way as polarising ones, in the projector and in the spectacles. Basically they divide the visible colour spectrum into six narrow bands, two in the blue region, two in the green and two in the red, denoted as B1, B2, G1, G2, R1, and R2. B1, G1, and R1 are used for one eye and B2, G2 and R2 for the other.

The Omega/Panavision system is based upon the same principle but uses a wider spectrum with more "teeth" to the "comb", five for each eye.

This eliminates the need to colour process the images and to give the viewer a more relaxed "feel".

The benefits of interference filter systems is that the glasses, while more expensive than simple circular polarised ones, are cheaper than shutter glasses. The unique construction of the filters gives excellent imaging with no ghosting. As well as what we might call "image leakage" from left to right images and vice versa, some ghosting is caused by the quality of the silver screen. If polarised light strikes a white screen it is depolarised. Silver screens maintain polarisation of reflected light but they are not perfect and some depolarisation does occur. The interference filter projection system does not rely on silver screens (though it will work perfectly well with them) so they can be used with ordinary white screens. The separation of the images is virtually perfect and ghosting eliminated.

The differences in the wavelengths in the left and right filters does result in slight differences in the colour rendition of the left and right images, but this is so small that the eye would not detect them. In conclusion, it is perhaps fair to say that this interference filter technology is a significant breakthrough in the search for improved 3D image projection.

CHAPTER 15: FURTHER STEREOSCOPIC TECHNIQUES

15.1 Introduction

In this chapter some additional methods of stereo imaging will be surveyed to provide a more complete picture of the state of the art. Only the basic principles will be covered, because to go into greater detail would require a separate book rather than a few pages. Indeed, there are already a number of books devoted to some of these topics and the reader is advised to consult them for further information.

15.2 Television and Video
15.2.1 The Pulfrich Effect

This is a curious phenomenon, which, though not in itself stereoscopic in nature, can lead to clearly observable stereo images. It has to be pointed out, however, that its applications are limited. Essentially, the Pulfrich effect gives a distinctly stereoscopic appearance to the image on a standard TV screen. The reader might like to experience the effect for himself by watching any TV programme while wearing sunglasses from which one lens has been removed, or by positioning one of the lenses of a normal pair of sunglasses over one eye. The sunglasses should not be too dark or it will be difficult for the covered eye to see the image with ease. When viewing normal TV in this way, for much of the time no special 3D effect will be seen, but when the circumstances are right, various objects or figures will appear to stand out from the background, or possibly recede into it to give a pseudoscopic effect. The stereoscopic effect will come and go according to the nature of the image being transmitted to the screen, as will become clear in the explanation that follows.

The Pulfrich effect relies on relative movement between, in the simplest case, a near object and its background, as shown in **Fig 15.1**. When a moving object on the TV screen is observed through the darkened lens of the sunglasses there is a delay factor such that it is perceived as being in a position other than its actual one. **Fig 15.1** is actually intended to depict a particular instant in time for a near object on screen moving to the right. In this example, the right eye is assumed to be the one covered by the darkened glass. The left eye sees the object at **A**, its true position on the screen, whereas the right eye experiences a delay and sees the object at **B**. This difference effectively creates a stereo pair and the near object will appear to float in front of the background (and the TV screen) at **C**. The same will apply at all successive positions of the on-screen object as it progresses.

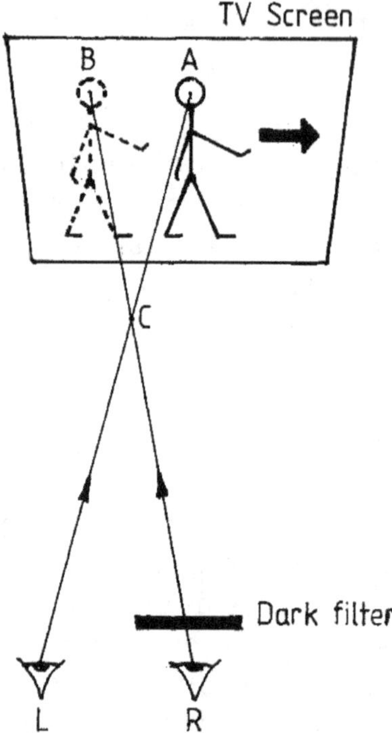

Fig 15.1
*The Pulfrich effect in TV images. An image moving to the right and seen by the left eye at **A** appears at **B** to the right eye, which is covered by a dark filter. The overall effect is that the image appears in front of the screen at **C**.*

A similar effect will occur if the near object maintains its position in the centre of the screen, say, but the background is moving from right to left, as would be the case when the TV camera follows the main subject by panning left to right to keep it centre screen. The difference here will be that the near object will be located at the screen surface, while the background will recede into the TV set.

An object moving from right to left will appear to recede into the background, thus producing a pseudoscopic image, but it can be made to stand proud of the background by transferring the dark glass to the left eye. If two or more objects are moving in different directions, then some will stand out and others will recede, depending upon their specific direction of movement and which eye is viewing through the dark filter.

The stereo image produced by the Pulfrich effect is somewhat crude, because depth differences will only exist between objects that are moving relative to each other. While a moving figure will stand out against the background, there will be no depth in the background itself, which will appear as a flat backcloth. All static objects at different distances will be located in the same single plane.

In 1994, BBC TV put on a 3D week in the UK in which various filmed sequences based upon the Pulfrich effect were shown at different times.

Audiences were provided with cardboard spectacles (with a dark filter for the right eye) supplied through newspapers and magazines. All the filmed items were shot with the camera moving continuously from right to left or circling round the main subject in a clockwise direction. Generally, the stereo effect was quite pronounced, but the constant movement of the camera or subject became irritating after a while. The technique can be used by the amateur video photographer but it requires extremely smooth camera movements to be effective. These can be achieved with the aid of a specially designed rig to which the camera is attached. Although the camera is still basically hand-held, any jerky movements are ironed out. Such a device of this kind was marketed under the name "Steadicam", as a simpler version of a professional one, but equipment of this kind is not cheap.

15.2.2 Stereo Video Camera

In the late 1980's the Japanese company Toshiba marketed a twin lens stereo video camera. This gave a full-sized image by recording left and right images from each lens in turn on alternate frames. To view the results in 3D required the use of special glasses of the "electronic shutter" type in which each lens was made of transparent material incorporating a liquid crystal that could be darkened momentarily by an electronic pulse. The glasses were connected to the playback system, the circuitry of which blackened each lens alternately in synchronisation with the alternating left and right images being displayed on the TV screen, so ensuring that each eye would see only the succession of images intended for it.

In the UK a TV image is reformed 25 times a second, which is more than enough to allow the persistence of vision effect to result in a continuous moving image. However, viewing stereo images in the Toshiba system revealed a shortcoming. Since each eye saw only alternate frames, the observed frame frequency was only 12.5 per second and this resulted in a distracting flicker. In the USA there was less of a problem as the normal frame frequency is 30 per second.

In the end, the Toshiba system, which at first sight seemed to provide a neat stereo package for the amateur video photographer, turned out to be rather disappointing.

More recently, companies like Panasonic and Sony have produced some excellent stereo video cameras. In addition, the Fuji W1 and W3 stereo (still) cameras are capable of producing good quality stereo video images.

15.2.3 Use of Beam Splitters

Before the video age, one or two mirror type beam splitters were commercially available for use with cine cameras, when amateur film making was a popular activity. The beam splitter was used not only on the cine camera but also on the projector lens for screening, in conjunction with polarising filters and glasses. For example, the Bolex stereo system was designed to produce the two images side by side in the frame in the same manner as the Pentax splitter for still photography (Chapter 4, Section 4.2.2) giving a vertical format. In contrast, the system used by the Japanese company Elmo developed a splitter that also divided the frame vertically but contra-rotated the two images by 90° (corrected on projection) to give a near normal aspect ratio to the stereo image.

Some stereo enthusiasts have developed systems along similar lines for use with video. For example, N. DuBrey of South Africa, has designed and built his own beam splitter to fit on an unmodified camcorder, to give left and right images side by side on the TV screen[35]. The TV images can be viewed in several ways:

1. with the aid of two lenses on a pocket-size TV
2. by using special glasses with built-in tiny mirrors
3. by attaching a mirror box to the front of the TV screen. This is designed both to superimpose and to polarise the images, which are viewed with polarising glasses.

A beam splitter for use with a camcorder recently made available for amateur use is the NuView adapter made by SD-Video of America. This consists of a plastic housing which contains a mirror and two liquid crystal panels or "light valves" with a semi-silvered mirror between them, as illustrated in **Fig 15.2**. In this device the left optical path is slightly longer than that for the right image but the resulting difference in image sizes will not be great enough to cause problems. The principle of its operation is based upon a format known as Field Sequential Video. In the PAL system the rapid succession of still pictures occurs at a rate of 50 per second. Each video frame consists of two fields; when displayed on screen; the first field is made up of the even numbered lines and the second field of the odd numbered lines. Each field is replaced by its successor 50 times per second, which gives a frame rate of 25 frames per second. The process is referred to as interlacing. In the NuView adapter one field is assigned to the left view (the light valve for the right view being blacked out), while the other field is assigned to the right view, for which the other light valve is blacked out. The screen is viewed through crystal shutter glasses, which are synchronised with the field changes.

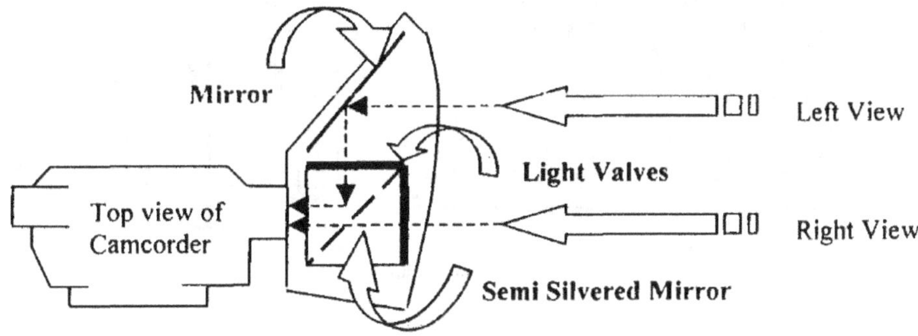

Fig 15.2
Principle of operation of the "NuView" mirror attachment for use with a camcorder. (Diagram by courtesy of Marcus Warrington).

To ensure that the subject appears behind the stereo window, the mirrors have a convergence adjustment. The nearest object can be used as the near reference and the convergence knob is rotated so that the two images of the near object merge into one.

15.2.4 Twin lens attachment

An alternative method, akin to the Elmo device for cine use referred to earlier, has been developed and patented under the name JC 3D™ by J. Christian[36] and marketed by his company, Stereoscopic Image Systems Ltd. In this system, the camera attachment rotates the images by 90° (both anti-clockwise) as shown in **Fig 15.3**. An attachment that fits to the TV returns the images to their correct orientation for viewing through polarisers. The two images can also be projected by means of an LCD video projector, fitted with polarising filters, onto a silvered screen. Christian claims that his system gives an improvement in perceived resolution and that it can also be used for photographic film and computer-generated images. In this TV stereo system, every line, field and frame contributes to both images so there is none of the flicker present in some other systems, as described earlier. Christian is currently developing the principle in projects such as a stereoscopic endoscope and robotic handling. Other applications are also being explored.

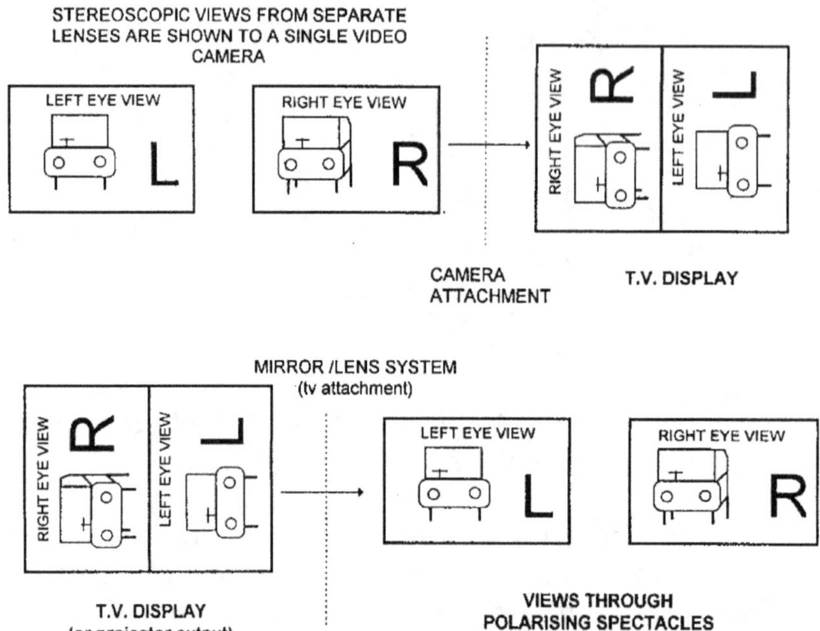

Fig 15.3
Principle of the JC 3D system for stereo video developed by Christian[36].(Diagram reproduced from The Stereoscopic Society Journal of 3D Imaging No 135, January 1997)

15.2.5 Autostereoscopic Screens

As reported by D. Ezra[37], Sharp Laboratories of Europe (SLE) has been developing autostereoscopic display systems since 1991, with particular emphasis on improving resolution, creating a wide viewing region and enabling the observer to see partly around the image, As implied in Chapter 9, Section 9.2.2, multiple viewing positions (or "windows") are needed if several observers wish to view an autostereoscopic image simultaneously, and SLE have concentrated their research on this aspect of the subject, as well as the creation of systems with "steerable windows" that can follow the movement of an observer's head.

A different approach is being made by researchers in Japan who are developing a stereo TV system which uses a bank of lenses on both the TV camera and screen to produce an autostereoscopic image that changes with head movements, as with holograms (see Chapter 9, Section 9.4.

15.3 Holography and Holograms

The word holography derives from the Greek **holos** (whole) and **graphis** (image) and a hologram is in essence a three-dimensional image produced, in its earliest form, by laser on a piece of glass coated with a special photographic emulsion. The theory of holography was developed in 1948, but it was only with the invention of the laser in 1961 that it could be realised in practice.

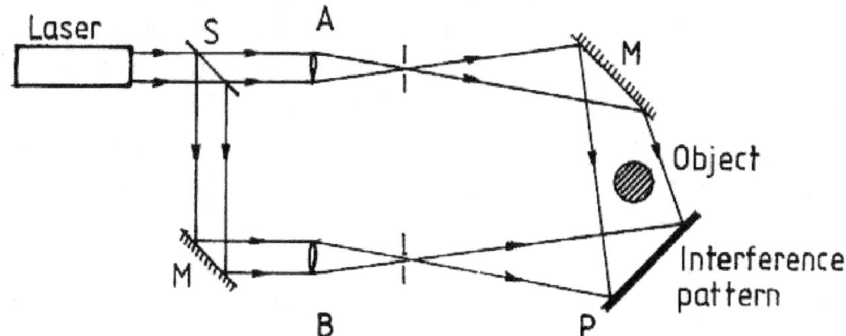

Fig 15.4
*Principle of holography. The beam from the laser strikes a semi-silvered mirror **S** and is split into two paths **A** and **B**. Mirrors **M**, lenses and pinholes direct beam **A** onto the subject and beyond where it meets the reference beam **B** to produce an interference pattern on the photographic plate at **P**.*

The principle of making holographic images is illustrated in **Fig 15.4**. A laser is used to provide a parallel beam of light, which is first passed through a semi-silvered mirror to give two beams. One of these is directed via a lens system to the film and acts as a reference beam. The other is passed through a similar lens system, and reflected by a mirror to illuminate the subject, a still life. Laser light reflected from the subject passes to the film where it combines with the reference beam to form an interference pattern. The film image is not a real image of the subject, like that produced by conventional photography, but a kind of random pattern of light and dark regions. When the film (glass plate) is illuminated from behind, an image of the original subject can be seen in stereoscopic form. The holographic image differs from a conventional 3D image in that the observer can actually see round the object by shifting his viewpoint, just as if he were examining the actual subject. This ability to see the object or scene from different angles is one of the intriguing features of holograms.

The need for a laser and a precision optical bench unaffected by the smallest vibrations means that the creation of holograms is not for the amateur. There is also a limitation in that the subject must be static to ensure that any slight movement does not spoil the image during the long exposures required.

If the glass plate containing the holographic image is cut into two, each piece, provided it is large enough to be viewed properly with both eyes, is capable of re-creating the complete image in 3D.

Since the early holograms of the type described above first appeared, the art has developed new forms and methods of production. The most common type of hologram is the embossed form on plastic that can be viewed with a strong directional light, or even daylight. Nowadays, a hologram in miniature form is an essential part of credit cards and the like, so that the manufacture of fakes is made more difficult.

Various companies are developing holographic TV systems that will project 3D images in the home, although the first displays are more likely to be public ones because of the high costs. Two such companies working independently, Philips and Samsung Electronics, have developed TV sets that use holography to give images that can be viewed without glasses. Both companies have based their systems on a flat screen, using a holographic optical element that acts as a kind of filter between the image and the viewer. Fully holographic TV sets, resembling a glass cube onto the surfaces of which four lasers project images, are likely to be the next step.

15.4 Photomicrography in Stereo

Photomicrography is a widely used procedure in much scientific work. From the relatively simple bench microscope to the sophisticated electron microscope, many substances, materials and biological specimens have been studied and images of great magnification have been produced to aid our understanding of the physical world. Occasionally, stereo images have been produced. Various simple microscopes are available to the amateur, and these will allow him to produce stereo images of reasonable magnifications. Most will allow a 35mm camera to be fitted in place of the eyepiece.

Basic types of microscope and techniques are outlined below:
1. **stereo microscopes** - these range from relatively low magnification types resembling binoculars mounted on stands and used for macro work to higher-powered stereo bench microscopes. To produce stereo images, the camera is fixed in turn to each of the eyepieces to produce the stereo pair. There are also some "binocular" microscopes, which have two eyepieces, but only a single active objective lens in use at any time. Both eyes see the same image, therefore, in two dimensions only. These should not be confused with true stereo microscopes.
2. **monocular microscopes** - there are two types, the biological, which uses transmitted light for transparent or semi-transparent specimens, and the metallurgical, in which the light is passed down through the objective lens and reflected back from the specimen surface to the eyepiece. In either case, it is necessary to arrange that the object is shifted in some way in order to produce the two views required for a stereo pair. There are two basic methods. The shift method entails placing the object on a mechanical slide (which may well be an integral part of the microscope) to allow it to be moved fractionally between exposures. The second technique is the tilt method, which involves tilting the slide like a seesaw between exposures.

A recent development in microscopy for scientific work is the 3D imaging R400 microscope manufactured by Edge Scientific of California, USA[38]. What is special about this instrument is that, while it has twin eyepieces, it is not constructed as a stereo microscope but essentially as a normal compound microscope. However, it has built-in to the illumination system a pyramidal mirror. Light is supplied via four fibre optic guides and the four beams are shifted towards or away from the central axis by moving the pyramid up or down. This increases or decreases the degree of oblique illumination produced. Polarisers are placed (mutually at right angles) in the left and right eye paths for direct viewing. The objective aperture is cut in half compared to that in a standard viewing system. This presents an oblique viewing angle and each eye receives information from its "own half" of the light collected by the objective.

The advantage of this microscope is that it provides high magnification real time 3D viewing, and is a valuable tool in the study of polymers, foams, microelectronics and particles, to quote a few examples.

15.5 3D Cinematography

In the amateur world, the video camera has replaced the cine camera to such an extent that the latter is virtually obsolete. As mentioned in Chapter 12, Section 12.6.6, the early commercial stereoscopic feature films relied upon the anaglyph system, though not very many were made. Some notable colour films, such as "The House of Wax", were made in two versions, one of which was in stereo for viewing with polarisers. 3D cinema, despite these significant attempts, never quite caught the public's imagination and such experiments were relatively rare.

The computer age has, however, resulted in a greater interest in technology-based entertainment and the UK at least is beginning to see some permanent 3D presentations in the form of wide screen films produced by the IMAX system. Even the mono films produced in this form are impressive and almost give a stereoscopic effect, but the true 3D films are particularly outstanding. Currently, three IMAX cinemas are operational in the UK.

15.6 Virtual Reality

This represents a step beyond the many ingenious and Interactive computer games, often set in a fantasy world involving exploration, encounters with hostile forces and problem solving.

With virtual reality, the player wears a special headset that allows him to see the computer-generated environment in 3D. Not only that, the player himself feels that he is located within it, instead of merely viewing it on a screen. Special hand controls allow the participant to interact with the imaginary environment and to "handle objects" and so on. The combination of a real person in an artificial world produces a most realistic effect for the participant.

15.7 Vectographs

The vectograph is a form of stereoscopic image not seen much these days. It consists of two transparent images (left and right) mounted in superimposition with a polarising filter and a metal reflector. The light from each image is polarised in opposite senses and a 3D image can be seen when the composite is viewed through polarising spectacles. In another form, the reflecting screen is omitted and the whole viewed by transmitted light. Vectographs can also be produced in full colour but they are not very common. Production of vectographs is not really a pursuit for the amateur because it requires specialist techniques and equipment.

15.8 Phantograms

Phantograms (variously known as phantaglyphs, Op-Ups, free standing anaglyphs, levitated images, or book anaglyphs) are special forms of anaglyph that produce the effect of a solid object or group of objects standing freely on a base, in some ways resembling a hologram but without the properties that enable an observer to move around the image and see its different perspectives. The phantogram represents a fixed view of the subject and has to be viewed with standard red/cyan filter glasses (or other complementary colour pairs to match the glasses used) from a specific position or it becomes distorted. The phantogram should be laid on a flat horizontal surface and viewed with the bottom edge nearest to the observer at a downward angle of 45°. The object appears to be solidly standing on the flat surface. A phantogram consists of a pair of images that are distorted in such a way that they re-create the perspective that would be observed for a three-dimensional object viewed from the phantogram's intended vantage point. The basic principle is illustrated in Fig 15.5.

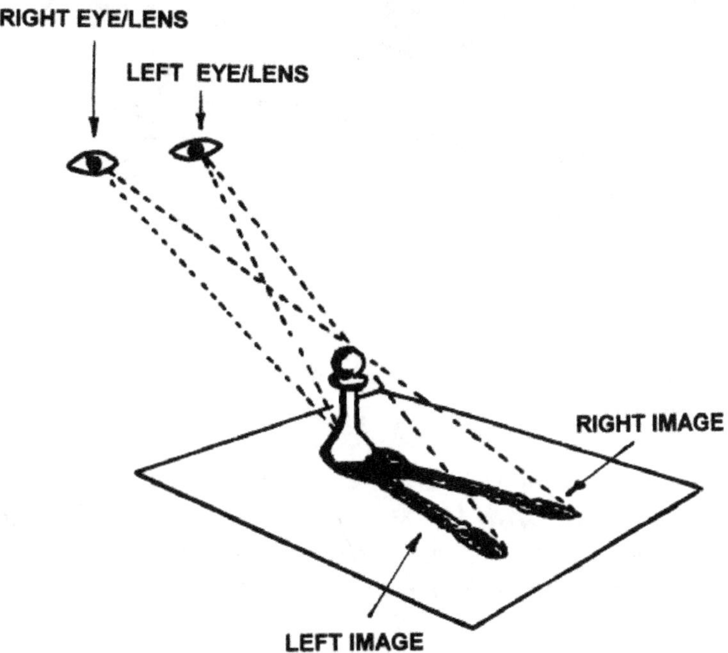

Fig 15.5
Basic geometry of a phantogram. The left and right images in complementary colours are in elongated "V" formation configuration. The eyes represent not only the camera lens positions for taking the initial stereo picture but also the eye positions for viewing r the final phantogram.

The left and right images in the diagram (usually photographs of a real object, drawings, or computer-generated images) are anamorphic projections onto a rectangular flat surface of a solid object which, viewed from the "eyes" position through anaglyph spectacles, produce the 3D image shown, standing up. Fig 15.5 can also represent the real object being photographed with a stereo camera pointing down at 45° from the same position (now regarded as "lens" position. Although the left and right images form a traditional stereo pair, they are not yet in the right form to be called a phantogram. They will not be exactly as shown in Figure 15.5; they will appear as in Fig 15.6.

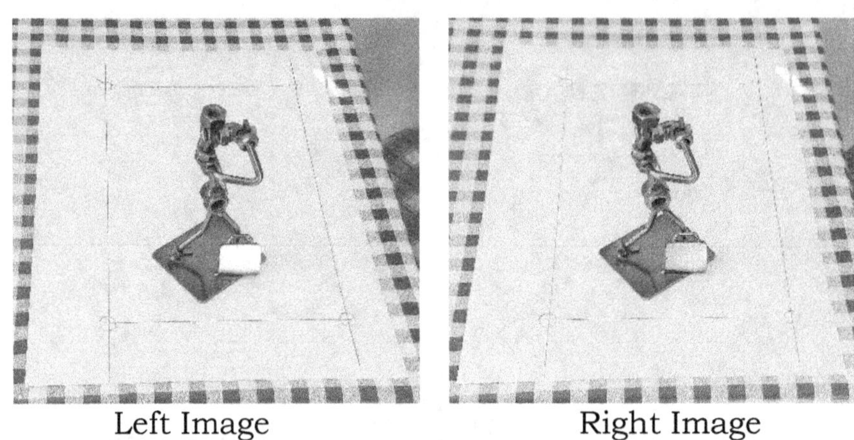

Left Image   Right Image

Fig 15.6

Stereo pair taken at an angle of 45°. The rectangular base on which the model stands is foreshortened and trapezium – shaped. (NB Each image will eventually be cropped to the pencilled areas (faintly visible) and these in turn will be stretched to correctly sized rectangles.

The background sheet and the pencilled area as real objects are truly rectangular, but, when photographed at 45° they are seen foreshortened and trapezium-shaped. To be viewed correctly as a phantogram according to Fig.15.5, the trapezium shapes have to be stretched back into rectangles of the correct aspect ratio. This is done on the computer in software programs such as Photoshop or SPM.

Each image is treated separately and, in Photoshop, consists of using the crop tool to place a rectangular marque large enough to enclose the trapezium-shaped image. Then, ensuring that the Photoshop's "perspective" box is checked, the corners of the marque are now dragged inwards by the cursor to coincide with the four corners (circled in Fig 15.6) of the trapezium image. Activating the cropping process causes the image to become perfectly rectangular (even close to a square). In SPM the same transformation is carried out by a slightly different method, At this point, however, the rectangle is not of the correct aspect ratio. By selecting the "image size" tool, it can now be resized to the correct proportions. The final form for the two images is shown in Fig 15.7. These can be converted to an anaglyph in SPM, which can be printed to any size, placed on a flat surface and viewed with full 3-D impact as depicted in Fig 15.5. A red/cyan anaglyph of these images can be seen at the back of this book in the Plates section.

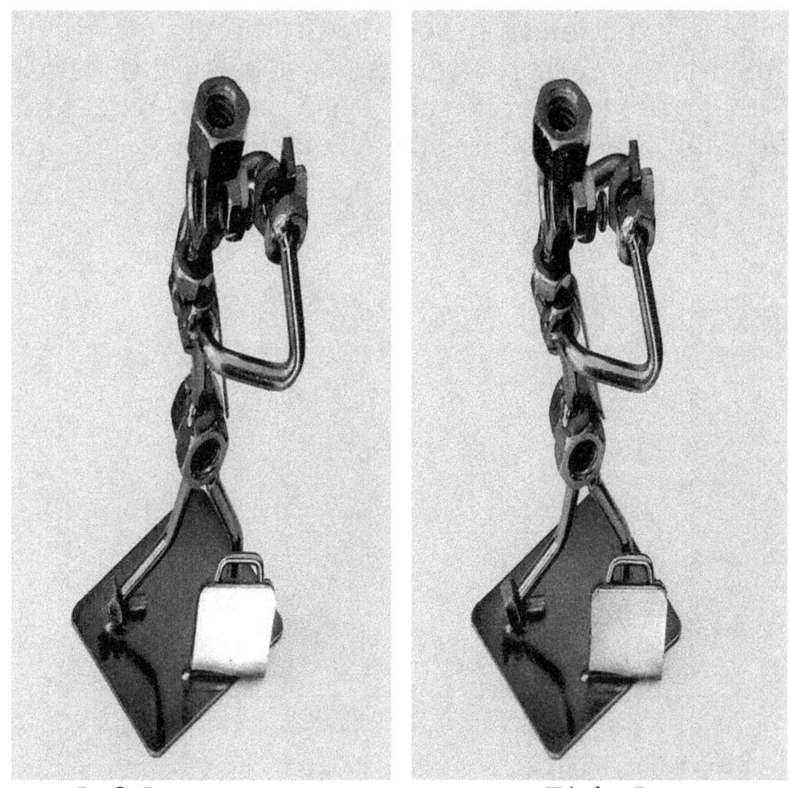

Fig 15.7
Left and right images after transformation and resizing to the correct aspect ratio.

The side-by-side images in Fig 15.7 can also be viewed as a phantogram in the same way as the anaglyph version by laying the book flat on a horizontal surface and viewing from above at 45°, either by free viewing or using a simple twin lens stereoscope. A full colour side-by-side version of this image is also included in the Plates section of this book.

All that remains is to display and print the images as an anaglyph to produce the finished phantogram. This can be printed to any size, placed on a flat surface and viewed with full 3-D impact as depicted in Fig 15.5. There can be a slight problem with printing an anaglyph because it is sometimes difficult to print the left (cyan) image pale enough for it to disappear when viewed by the right eye through its cyan filter in the anaglyph glasses. Yet the same anaglyph displayed on a computer monitor often shows no such ghosting, but it is not so easy to view at a 45° angle. A compromise solution is to darken the anaglyph so that the cyan image and background are closer in overall tone. A further possible improvement is to try viewing the red/cyan image with red/green glasses. This may reduce the ghosting even further.

If one does experience problems of this kind, there is another solution, as mentioned earlier. Instead of converting the final "stretched" images into anaglyph form, printing them side-by-side avoids ghosting altogether and allows them to be seen in full colour.

Part 2 - Analysis

CHAPTER 16: THE EYE AND BINOCULAR VISION

16.1 The Eye
16.1.1 Structure

The eye, the light-sensitive organ of vision, is a highly developed part of the human anatomy. Whilst the eye and the camera are often regarded as of similar construction, in that both have a lens, a shutter (eyelid), a variable aperture (iris) and a light-sensitive surface (retina), there are distinct differences in the way they function, so the resemblance is somewhat superficial.

Fig 16.1 shows a cross-section of the eye, which is roughly spherical in shape and approximately 25mm in diameter. The outer layer, the cornea partly focuses light rays that enter the eye and the lens completes the task of focusing them onto the retina. This is possible because the lens consists of a transparent elastic material and its shape, and hence its focal length, is varied by the action of a muscular ring surrounding it. The focal length of the lens varies between about 22mm for distant vision and 17mm for close vision.

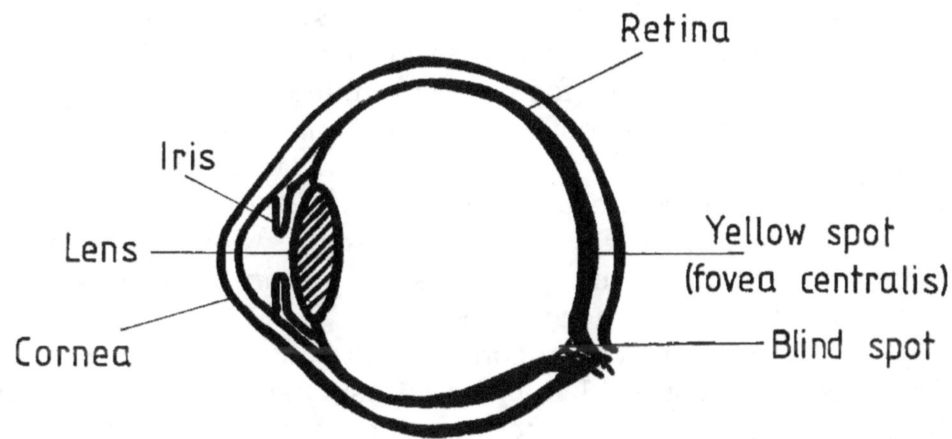

Fig 16.1
The human eye.

The interior of the eye is filled with fluid, the aqueous humour between the cornea and lens, and a jelly-like vitreous humour in the main chamber.

The iris is a variable aperture that adjusts itself automatically according to the light intensity. Normal working apertures range from about f/4 to f/8, but they can reach values of f/1.8 to f/12. The retina is the spherical inner surface at the back of the eye. Its curved shape helps to counteract most of the natural spherical aberration inherent in the lens performance. It is sensitive to light over a range of wavelengths from about

380nm (nm = nanometre. 1nm is 10^{-9}m) to 700nm. The retina consists of about 7 million cones (which are functional in daylight and are very sensitive to intensity and colour) and some 120 million rods, active in low light levels. They are much more sensitive than the cones but lack colour discrimination. The **yellow spot** or **fovea centralis** is situated more or less on the optical axis of the lens and has virtually no rods, so it is a particularly sensitive region with a high discrimination of detail and colour over a wide range of light levels. When light falls onto the retina, certain molecules within the rods and cones absorb energy and there is a change in electrical potential. This change is detected at the back of the cones and rods and a signal is sent to the brain via the numerous nerve fibres. Whilst each cone is connected to one nerve fibre, up to one hundred or so rods share a single nerve fibre; consequently the rods are less sensitive to fine detail in the image.

Just off-centre at the back of the eye is a small region where the main optic nerve, containing all the nerve fibres, joins the retina. This is known as the blind spot because it is insensitive to light.

16.1.2 Normal Vision

The image in a correctly focused camera is essentially sharp from edge to edge (ignoring the slight loss at the edges which is common). In the eye the situation is rather different; only that portion of the image that falls on the yellow spot is in proper focus. The remainder of the image, spread over the rest of the retina, is considerably poorer in quality and less distinct. The reason that we appear to see a whole scene in focus is that the eye continually darts about, scanning the subject, so that each part is focused on the yellow spot in turn. Even when we fix the view onto a particular detail, the muscles in the eye introduce a small continuous "wobble", which is in fact an essential part of normal vision.

A real image produced by a convex lens is always inverted, and the retinal image is no exception. The brain is responsible for interpreting the image as "the correct way up". Experiments have been performed in which a person has worn a special optical device to produce an inverted view. Initially this caused difficulty, but after about a week of continuous use, the subject's brain had corrected the image so that he saw everything as normal. Removal of the device caused only momentary confusion before correct vision was resumed.

16.1.3 Accommodation and Convergence

When viewing distant objects the lens in the eye is in a relaxed state. As the eye focuses on nearer objects, the muscles surrounding the lens move into action to change its shape and focus the image on the retina. This action is termed **accommodation**. At the same time, the eyes rotate in their sockets about a roughly vertical axis (assuming the head is upright) to allow the lines of sight of both eyes to move towards each other, this action being called **convergence** (**Fig 16.2**). Both of these, together with experience gained over many years, give us our sense of depth, the relative distance of objects in view at a particular moment. This sense of depth, it must be stressed, is a relative rather than an absolute one. All the same, one can develop a skill of estimating distances with some measure of accuracy.

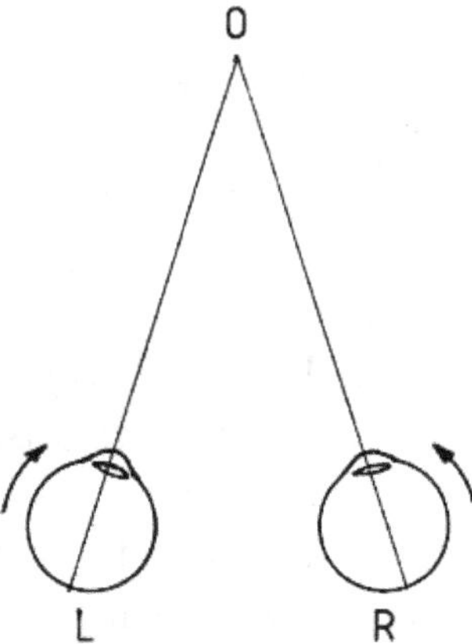

Fig 16.2
Convergence of the eyes.

Accommodation and convergence tend to work together, because viewing an object at a given distance will require so much of each effect, muscular action for focusing and eye-swing of the correct amount to cause the two lines of sight to intersect at the object being observed. However, the two are not permanently linked and they can function independently. This can be demonstrated by considering a stereogram being viewed in a conventional stereoscope, of the Brewster type, for example. The stereogram itself will be located approximately 40mm, say, from the stereoscope's lenses (of 40mm focal length) and light rays from all parts of the image will enter the eyes more or less parallel. This means that the eyes will be focused at infinity for every feature within the image. However, the eyes will converge as normal for objects at different distances, just as they would if viewing the actual scene. Thus the eyes converge while maintaining constant focus, a situation that is not encountered in normal vision.

16.1.4 Persistence of Vision

The eye responds mainly to the rate at which light is received rather than to its quantity. When the eye is functioning, it is subjected to a continuous image and not a static one. However, when it receives a short flash of less than about one-fifth of a second, it responds as if the quantity of light is spread uniformly over one-fifth of a second. Thus, a series of flashes arriving at a rate faster than five per second will appear to merge and appear as continuous illumination. This effect is known as the persistence of vision, and is the basis of the perception of continuous movement of an object produced by viewing a rapid succession of still images, as in cinematography. The frequency of the sequence of still images needs to be greater than about 16 per second to avoid flicker. The standard for cinematography in the commercial world of film-making is 24 frames per second.

16.1.5 Monocular vision

When an observer views a scene with one eye he sees it in much the same way as the single lens of a camera sees and records it on film. The image is two-dimensional and no sense of depth is apparent apart from the visual clues that were discussed in Chapter 1, Section 1.2. In reality, however, the sense of depth will tend to be better than might be inferred from the above because of the slight head movements that occur naturally in normal viewing. These will help to establish the relative distances of various objects in the scene more precisely as a result of the changes in parallax that accompany them. Although this depth information is limited and does not compare with true binocular vision, it does, for example, enable those people who have lost sight in one eye to cope with many everyday tasks, such as driving, in which some sense of distance is essential for success and safety.

16.1.6 Visual acuity and depth of field

Visual acuity is a measure of the eye's ability to see two closely spaced objects as two separate entities, and not as one. The two objects are usually taken as being side-by-side in the general case. When one is further away than the other and the distance between them is measured along the viewing direction then the depth difference is the important parameter, and this relates specifically to stereo acuity, as defined in Chapter 7, Section 7.2.1. Visual acuity is inversely proportional to the minimum angle subtended at the eye by the two objects. The smaller this angle, the smaller is the separation between the objects that the eye can resolve, which signifies a higher acuity. This minimum angle ($\mathbf{w_o}$) is itself a definition of the resolving power of the eye.

A typical value for visual acuity is 1 minute of arc, but this varies considerably, even in an individual, with the intensity of illumination and the contrast between two adjacent areas of the subject. It is also highest in the yellow spot region of the retina, falling to lower values outside that area where several rods and cones are connected to each nerve fibre. In these outer areas, two close images are more likely to be perceived as a single object.

According to Valyus[43] the depth of focus, **T**, (strictly this should be depth of field) expressed in dioptres (rad m $^{-1}$) is given by:

$$\mathbf{T} = \mathbf{w_o}/\mathbf{d} \ (\mathbf{d} = \text{pupil diameter})$$

This can be written as:

$$\text{Depth}\,\mathbf{D} = 1/\mathbf{T} = \mathbf{d}/\mathbf{w_o}$$

Taking **w$_o$** as 1minute (0.00029 radians) and **d** = 4mm:

$$\mathbf{D} = 0.004/0.00029 = 14 \text{ metres approximately.}$$

This means that with the eye focused at infinity, the depth of field ranges from 14 metres to infinity, in other words 14m represents the hyperfocal distance under these conditions. By focusing the eye at 14m, the depth of field will be even greater, from 7 metres to infinity.

The normal working aperture of the eye ranges from about f/4 to f/8, the corresponding pupil diameters being 3.8mm to 1.9mm [44]. If the eye is given time to adjust, the aperture range can extend from f/1.8 to f/12 (pupil diameters from 8.5mm to 1.25mm). Using the latter value in the above expression produces a new hyperfocal distance of 4.3m, giving a depth of field from 2.15m to infinity. This result forms the basis of the recommended 2 metres distance for the nearest allowable object in "normal" stereo photographs with a depth range to infinity. The eyes can view a scene or stereogram with this depth range comfortably, without experiencing diplopia.

16.2 Binocular Vision
16.2.1 Retinal Images and Depth Perception

The clue to stereoscopic vision lies in the way in which nerve fibres connect the retinae to cells within the brain. Each brain cell has two visual nerve fibres that run from two corresponding cones, one in each eye. Two such cones are referred to as **corresponding points**. When the gaze is fixed on a stationary object, the impression of a single object is generated. Strictly, this applies only to an individual point on the object; the whole object is perceived by a replication of this effect as the eye scans the scene. However, returning to the "fixed gaze" situation, then the part of the object on which the eyes are focused forms images on the corresponding points of the two retinae. Other objects, either in front of or behind the primary object will form retinal images in different locations in the two eyes, not on corresponding points[40]. Certain neurons in the brain, which are known as binocular disparity neurons, are activated only when this image difference occurs and the brain interprets the information as a difference in depth location of the various objects. Such interpretive skill is, as has been said before, gained through experience. The eyes determine distance by two main means, these differences in retinal images and the size of the image.

16.2.2 Extent of Binocular Vision

There are two parameters that are relevant in defining the ability of the individual to distinguish depth clues and establish object locations in space. **Stereo acuity** (see Chapter 7, Section 7.2.1) is the first of these and represents the smallest depth difference that can be resolved by the eye of the observer. It is also referred to as **stereopsis threshold** or **stereo definition**. The second factor is the maximum distance at which any depth differences can be identified, what might be regarded as a limit to stereoscopic vision, or **stereo infinity**. The two are linked, as will be made clear in the ensuing discussion.

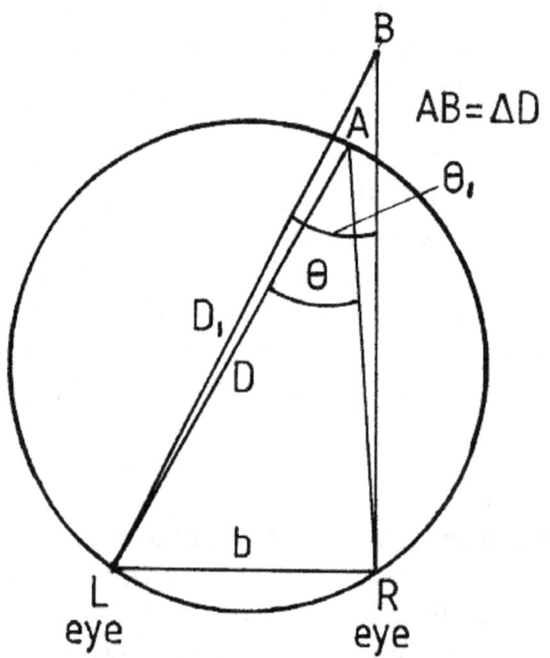

Fig 16.3
Horopter. Point **A**, *on which the eyes are focused, gives retinal images on corresponding points in the two eyes. The circle represents a section through the horopter, which is a spherical surface. This horopter defines the positions of points in space that give images on corresponding retinal points for the given focus setting. Point* **B**, *further away than* **A**, *can just be distinguished as lying at a different distance.*

In **Fig 16.3** the two eyes are shown fixated on a point **A** situated at a distance **D**. If **A** is "off-centre" then the lengths **LA** and **RA** will differ, but provided they are much larger than the eye spacing **LR** (=**b**), they can be taken as equal. The circle passing through **L**, **R** and **A** represents the section of the horopter in the plane of the diagram. This horopter is the locus of points in space that form images on corresponding points in the retinae, and is spherical. The geometric properties of the circle are such that the angle subtended by a chord (**LR**.) at the perimeter, angle **LAR** here, is constant for all points on the perimeter. If the eyes are focused on a more distant point then there will be a similar horopter of greater diameter, representing other object points that produce images on corresponding retinal points. Each horopter relates to a particular eye convergence, in other words.

Returning to **Fig 16.3**, with the eyes focused at **A**, now consider point **B**, lying just outside the horopter. The retinal images formed by **B** will not lie on corresponding points in the eye, and the image disparity will trigger the brain into registering the image of **B** as further away than point **A**, provided that **ΔD** is large enough. However, if **B** is too close to **A**, the two points will be seen as one. For the observer to be able to distinguish the depth difference between **A** and **B**, and to see two separate points, the difference between the two angles **LBR** and **LAR** has to be sufficiently large. If angles **LAR** and **LBR** are θ and θ_1 respectively, then the differential parallax angle is given by $\Delta\theta = \theta - \theta_1$.

Stereoscopic acuity is defined as the minimum discernible parallax $\Delta\theta_0$. Assigning a value to this is not straightforward because it varies from one individual to the next and in practice depends upon external factors such as subject brightness and observation time (duration). A value as low as 2" of arc has been reported[41] but, according to Valyus[42], 30" is a more representative value for use in calculations.

Assuming that **D** > **b** (**Fig 16.3**) then all parallax angles can be written in the form $\theta = b/D$ in radian measure. Accordingly, the expression can be used to determine the limit of stereoscopic vision. Rearranging and taking $\Delta\theta_0$ as 30" (0.000145 radians) with **b** = 65 mm:

D = **b**/$\Delta\theta_0$ = 65/0.000145 = 448 metres.

The value of 30" for stereo acuity can be regarded as taking into account the "unknown" factors that in many conditions effectively diminish a person's ability to distinguish small depth increments. The stereo acuity of most people is better than this, in the region of 5" to 10", which means that the limit of stereoscopic vision will be greater in magnitude. If 10" (= 0.000048 radians) is used in the calculation:

D = 65/0.000048 = 1354 metres.

From the above, it should be apparent that one cannot be pedantic about the extent of binocular vision as it depends upon so many factors.

1354 metres (just over 0.8 miles) is probably as good a value as any other quoted distance, though in many circumstances it is perhaps optimistic. However, figures as low as 200 metres, which are sometimes quoted, seem too pessimistic. Nevertheless, one must also remember that stereo acuity will be better in the actual location than when viewing the stereogram in a viewer. Under projection conditions it will be worse still.

16.2.3 Minimum Depth Discrimination

Stereo acuity, as relevant to a specific observer under given viewing conditions, is defined by the minimum parallax angle $\Delta\theta_0$ that just enables him to ascertain that two objects are at different distances away. As outlined in Chapter 7, Section 7.2.1, the constancy of this value for the conditions means that the minimum depth difference between the objects that can be detected increases as the observer-object distance increases, as shown in Table 7.1. The exact relationship between object distance and the size of the "depth step" can be determined from further analysis of **Fig 16.3**. The distance **AB**, normal to the horopter is given by:

$$\Delta D = D_1 - D$$

Since **D** and D_1 are much greater than **b**, then we can write $D_1 = b/\theta_1$ and $D = b/\theta$.
Hence:

$$\Delta D = b(1/\theta_1 - 1/\theta) = b(\theta - \theta_1)/\theta_1\theta$$
$$= b\,\Delta\theta/[(b/D_1)(b/D)] = \Delta\theta D_1 D/b$$
$$\text{i.e.} \quad \Delta D = \Delta\theta(D + \Delta D)D/b$$

which leads to
$$\Delta D = D^2\,\Delta\theta/(b - D\Delta\theta)$$

The minimum depth step, ΔD_0, is the value of **ΔD** when **Δθ** is equal to the stereo acuity $\Delta\theta_0$. Thus:

$$\Delta D_0 = D^2\Delta\theta_0/(b - D\Delta\theta_0)$$

This expression, which follows the analysis by Valyus[3], shows that the minimum discernible depth step is (approximately) proportional to the square of the object distance, measured from the observer. The significance is that our perception of depth falls off rapidly for distant objects and that the stereoscopic effect is more pronounced at relatively close range. As a general guide, the photographer should ensure that the important elements of a stereoscopic image lie within the 2 to 200 metres range, say, but this is not to suggest that more distant objects should be excluded.

To enlarge on this concept, it is worthwhile to calculate the number of discernible depth steps that occur in various distance ranges. For the purposes of this exercise the stereo acuity will be taken as 30" (0.000145 radians). This means that an observer will just be able to discern two objects as lying at different depths if the parallax of one is 30" greater than that of the other. With $\mathbf{b}$ = 65mm and $\mathbf{\Delta\theta_0}$ = 0.000145 then the minimum discernible depth step at distance $\mathbf{D}$ = 10m will be, from the equation above:

$$\mathbf{\Delta D_0} = (10^2 \times 0.000145)/[0.065 - (10 \times 0.000145)] \text{ metres}$$
$$= 0.228\text{m}$$
$$= 228\text{mm}$$

So, if an object is located at a distance of 10 metres, a second object will just be distinguished as lying further away than the first if it lies at 10.228 metres, but not if it lies closer, at 10.2 metres, say.

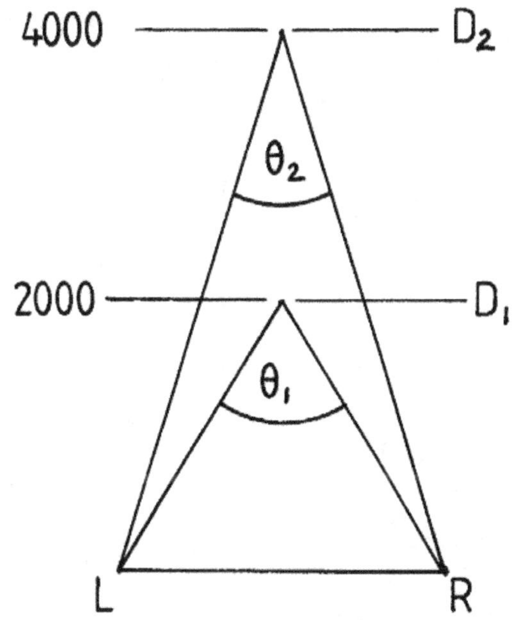

Fig 16.4
Variation of parallax angle with distance. The difference $(\theta_2 - \theta_1)$ enables the number of "depth steps" in the range $\mathbf{D_1}$ to $\mathbf{D_2}$ to be calculated.

To determine the number of such depth steps that lie between two points at different distances from an observer, the parallax angles must be considered, as illustrated in **Fig 16.4**. The calculation simply involves determining the parallax angles θ_1, θ_2 for the relevant distances $\mathbf{D_1}$, $\mathbf{D_2}$. The angular difference divided by the stereo acuity gives the number of depth steps. For example, the parallax angle for 1 metre distance, as seen by the eyes, is 224' of arc, and that for 2 metres is 112'. Since the stereo acuity value of 30" can be written as 0.5' of arc, the number of depth steps between 1 and 2 metres will be (224 − 112)/0.5 = 224 steps.

Table 16.1 gives the results of similar calculations for object distances from 0.3 metres (representing the nearest distance of distinct vision) to 400 metres, just short of the stereo infinity value of 448 metres for the chosen stereo acuity of 30". The table shows the number of depth steps in each distance range and the size of the step at each key distance.

TABLE 16.1
Variation of Number and Size of Depth Steps with Distance
(Based upon a stereo acuity of 30" of arc)

Object Distance (metres)	Parallax (minutes of arc)	Number of Depth Steps	Size of Depth Step (metres)
0.3	742		0.0002 (0.2mm)
		1036	
1	224		0.002 (2mm)
		224	
2	112		0.009 (9mm)
		112	
4	56		0.036 (36mm)
		56	
8	28		0.145 (145mm)
		28	
16	14		0.592 (592mm)
		19	
50	4.5		6.227
		4.6	
100	2.2		28.71
		3.28	
400#	0.56		3314

(# with a stereo acuity of 30", the limit of stereo perception is calculated to be 448m)

From these figures, it is clear that the eye can discern finer depth detail at close range, and successful stereo photography is likely to rely on the inclusion of objects in the foreground.

CHAPTER 17: LIGHT, LENSES AND OPTICS

17.1 Introduction

In this chapter, some of the basic principles of optics and the nature and behaviour of light will be outlined. The purpose is to provide a background to an understanding of the stereo image and the principles of operation of optical equipment. The material will also be relevant to certain topics covered in earlier chapters and in some of the supplements.

17.2 The Nature of Light
17.2.1 Electromagnetic radiation

Light is that part of the electromagnetic spectrum that has the correct wavelength range (400nm to 700nm approximately) to stimulate the nerve endings of the retina in the human eye. It can travel across empty space with a velocity of 300×10^6 metres per second (186,000 miles per second) as well as through several gaseous, liquid or solid media. It can be regarded as having a dual nature. In some respects it behaves as a stream of particles; in others it is wavelike in character.

The smallest basic unit of light is the photon, which represents an elementary packet (or quantum) of energy. When photons strike (rather like particles) a photographic emulsion, it is the energy associated with the photon that sets off the reaction whereby silver nitrate is reduced to metallic silver, thus forming the image.

17.2.2 Reflection, refraction and diffraction

Light travels in straight lines; when it strikes an object some will be absorbed and some reflected, the relative amounts being dependent upon the nature of the object and its material composition. Some materials allow light to pass through relatively freely and are called transparent materials, e.g. glass, various liquids and some plastics.

It is often convenient to regard a beam of light as consisting of a number of individual rays; a single ray is simply the path taken by photons of light energy travelling from a source to a receiver; these paths are straight lines. Now let us examine how these light paths are affected by interactions with objects:

1. **reflection**: when rays of light strike a polished surface such as a mirror or a pool of still water they are, for the most part, reflected. The rules of reflection are illustrated in **Fig 17.1** and summarised below:

    a)   the angle of incidence is equal to the angle of reflection.

    b)   the incident ray, reflected ray and normal to the reflecting surface at the point of reflection lie in the same plane.

    c)   the image formed in the mirror is laterally transposed and as far behind the mirror as the object is in front of it.

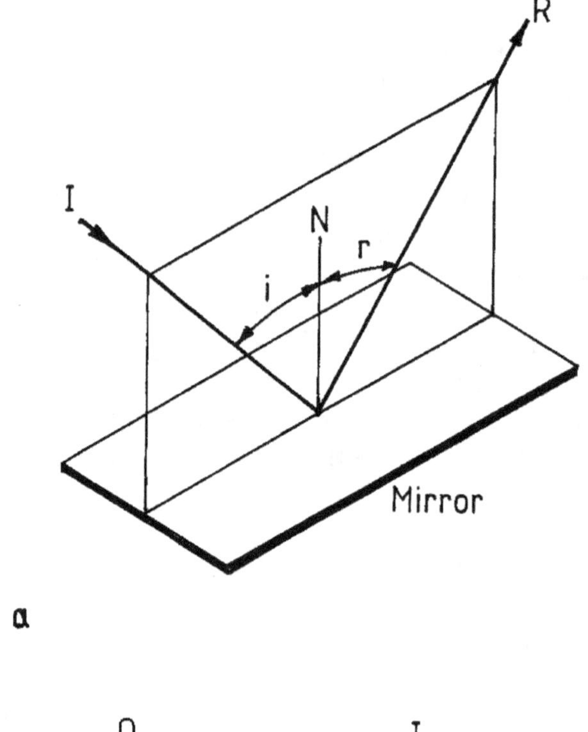

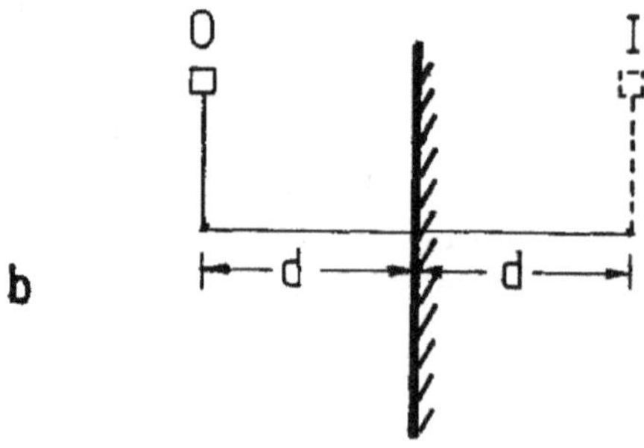

Fig 17.1
a *Reflection at a plane surface. Incident ray* **I** *is reflected as* **R**, *where angle* **i** *= angle* **r**. **I**, **R** *and the normal* **N** *are co-planar.*
b *Image* **I** *and object* **O** *are equidistant from the reflecting surface.*

Reflection can also occur at rough surfaces but, because of the varying angles of incidence at different points as "seen" by the beam of parallel rays, different rays are reflected at various angles to give a diffuse or scattered reflection, in contrast to the specular reflection from smooth surfaces.

Specular reflection is important in most optical devices, such as stereoscopes, cameras and projectors, and the laws of reflection allow us to analyse the light paths in these devices and to design them effectively.

2. **refraction**: when light rays pass from one transparent medium to another of a different density (from air to glass, for example) there is a change in direction, as shown in **Fig 17.2**. This change of direction is termed refraction. When the light travels from the lighter to the denser medium, the velocity is reduced and the rays are bent towards the normal as indicated. From a dense medium to a less dense one, they are bent away from the normal. This will be clear if the direction of the ray in **Fig 17.2** is reversed. All light paths are reversible.

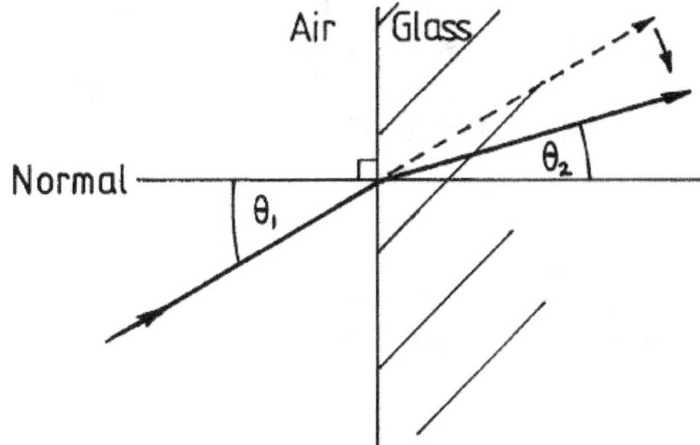

Fig 17.2
Refraction. An incident light ray travelling from a rarer to a denser medium (e.g. air to glass) is bent towards the normal. θ_1 and θ_2 are the angles of incidence and refraction respectively.

The rules of refraction are:
- the incident ray, refracted ray and normal at the point of refraction lie in a single plane
- for light of a given frequency and for a given pair of media:

$$\sin\theta_1/\sin\theta_2 = \text{a constant, } \mathbf{n} \text{ (Snell's Law)}$$

The constant **n** is known as the refractive index of the denser medium relative to the lighter medium. The absolute refractive index of a material is with respect to a vacuum. In practice, air is taken as the lighter medium but the difference in values is negligible.

Refractive indices of various glasses range in value from about 1.5 to 1.8. Larger values indicate a greater bending of the light rays.

The refractive index also depends upon the wavelength of the light; blue rays (shorter wavelengths) are bent more than red rays (longer wavelengths). Refraction can, therefore, cause white light to be split into a spectrum of colours; this is called dispersion. It is this effect that gives rise to colour fringing in an image, often found with simple lenses such as magnifying glasses.

3. **diffraction**: light not undergoing reflection or refraction can, nevertheless, experience some bending when it encounters the edges of opaque objects, especially if the edges are sharp. This is known as diffraction and it is relevant when taking pictures with a very small lens aperture, such as f/22. Diffraction at the edges of the iris diaphragm in a camera will cause the light to spread to some extent and this will lead to a loss of sharpness in the image. In fact, this effect occurs at all apertures, but with the smaller ones a greater proportion of the whole beam of light is affected and the reduction in image quality is more obvious.

17.2.3 Formation of images

If we trace several rays of light through an optical system we can determine the location of any images. In **Fig 17.3a** and **b**, **O** represents one point on an object[14]. A point image **I** will be formed if all the rays collected by the optical system either:

1. pass through a single point **I** after emerging from the system as shown in **Fig 17.3a**. This is called a **real image** and it can be captured on a screen placed at **I**.

or

2. appear to have come from a single point **I** (**Fig 17.3b**). This is a **virtual image** and it cannot be seen on a screen placed at **I**.

The whole image is formed in each case by similar sets of rays from all points on the object. Both types of image can be seen and photographed. A real image can be recorded by placing a photographic emulsion at **I**. A virtual image can only be photographed by using another optical system, which collects the divergent rays and brings them to a focus as a real image.

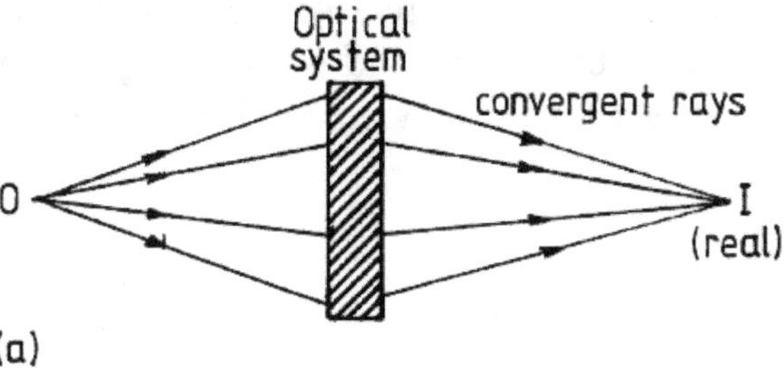

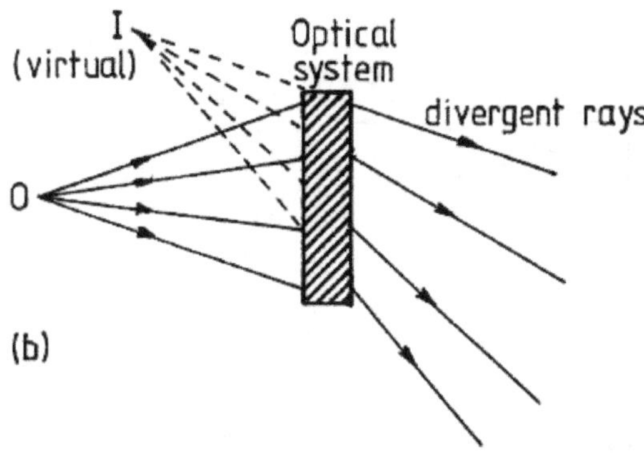

Fig 17.3
Image formation in optical systems (schematic).
a *If the rays emerging from the system converge to a point, a real image* **I** *is formed of the object* **O**.
b *Emergent rays that diverge appear to come from point* **I**, *which is a virtual image.*
(Only real images can be captured on a screen placed at image position **I**).

17.3 Refraction Through Prisms

A prism is a geometric shape that has a constant cross-section, both in terms of shape and area. In optics, it is a transparent glass or plastic block with several polished surfaces. There are usually two or three "working" surfaces. Those with two working surfaces are known as refracting prisms; knowledge of how they function is an aid to understanding how lenses work. Those with three working surfaces are designed to act as reflectors, to replace mirrors. In that capacity, they are more efficient, with less light loss and often feature in stereo attachments and viewers, as discussed in earlier chapters.

17.3.1 Prism with parallel sides

Fig 17.4 shows the path of a light ray incident at angle θ_1. At the first surface, refraction causes the ray to bend towards the normal. The angle of refraction, θ_2, becomes the angle of incidence at the second (glass to air) interface; this refraction is simply a reversal of the first, so the emergent ray is parallel to the original incident ray. Although it is not deviated from its original direction it is displaced sideways. By reducing the angle of incidence, the thickness of the prism, or both, the displacement will be smaller.

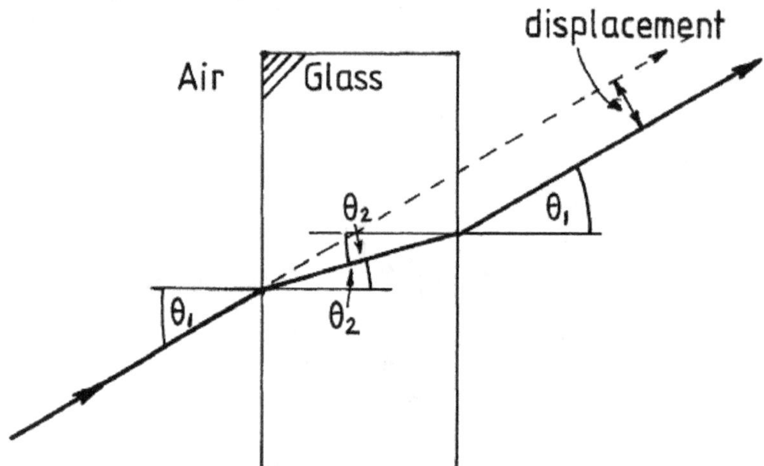

Fig 17.4
Double refraction in a parallel-sided prism. The emergent ray is undeviated but displaced relative to the incident ray.

17.3.2 Prism with non-parallel sides

A typical light ray path is shown in **Fig 17.5**. Here, the emergent ray is not parallel to the incident ray but is deviated by an angle **D**.

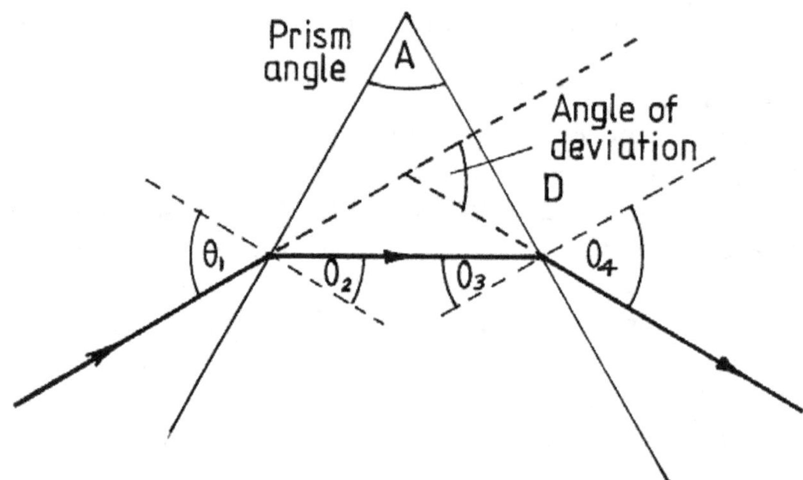

Fig 17.5
Double refraction in a prism with non-parallel sides. The light ray is deviated from its original direction.

From simple geometry it can be shown that:

$$\mathbf{D} = (\mathbf{\theta}_1 - \mathbf{\theta}_2) + (\mathbf{\theta}_4 - \mathbf{\theta}_3)$$

The value of **D** varies with the angle of incidence $\mathbf{\theta}_1$ but has a minimum value when the ray passes symmetrically through the prism, i.e. when:

$$\mathbf{\theta}_1 = \mathbf{\theta}_4 \text{ and } \mathbf{\theta}_2 = \mathbf{\theta}_3$$

As always in optics, the principle of reversibility applies; light energy can travel in either direction along the path shown.

If the prism angle **A** is small (less than about 6°), experiments have shown that all rays having small angles of incidence (i.e. nearly normal to the surface) will be deviated by the same amount, according to the relationship:

$$\mathbf{D} = (\mathbf{n} - 1)\mathbf{A}$$

(where **n** = refractive index of the prism material)

This is actually a slight approximation, but the errors are negligible for most practical situations. The relationship is important because it forms the basis of lens theory.

17.3.3 Total internal reflection

Consider the paths of rays travelling from inside the prism to the outside, as illustrated in **Fig 17.6**.

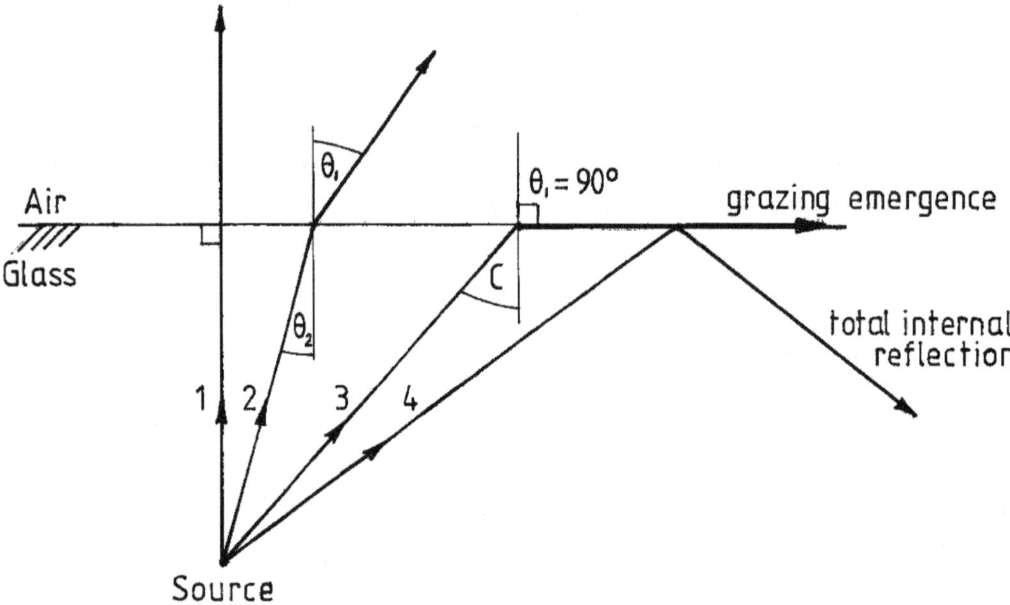

Fig 17.6
Total internal reflection.
Ray **1** *(incident angle = 0) passes straight through the interface.*
Ray **2** *is refracted in the normal way.*
Ray **3** *(at the critical angle of incidence* **C***) undergoes grazing emergence as* $\theta_1 = 90°$.
Ray **4** *(angle of incidence greater than* **C***) is totally internally reflected.*

Reading from left to right, the first ray, at 90° to the surface, passes through undeviated. At other angles the rays are bent away from the normal. As the angle of incidence (typified by θ_2) increases, there comes a point when the refracted ray is just parallel to the surface (grazing emergence). This occurs when $\theta_1 = 90°$ and the value of $\theta_2 = $ **C**, the so-called critical angle. If θ_2 is greater than **C** then no refraction occurs and the ray is subject to total internal reflection.

In glass the critical angle is about 41° to 42° depending upon the refractive index. This phenomenon is employed in various optical instruments, including stereoscopes, in which prisms are used in place of mirrors.

17.4 Lenses

A lens is a portion of transparent medium (e.g. glass or plastic), usually in the form of a circular disc, and bounded by either two curved surfaces, or one curved and one plane.

Lenses can be broadly classified into two groups, converging and diverging. Converging lenses produce a real image in the manner of **Fig 17.3a**, whereas diverging lenses create a virtual image (**Fig 17.3b**).

A simple lens consists of a single disc of material, and is termed an **element**. Compound lenses are constructed from a number of such elements, often from a number of different materials (with different refractive indices). The reason for this is that superior images can be produced, with fewer, or smaller distortions (**aberrations**) than are commonly present in simple lenses. Not even compound lenses produce perfect images, but technological developments in lens design and manufacture have led to the production of some excellent lenses for both professional and amateur markets. **Fig 17.7** shows some typical lens element shapes.

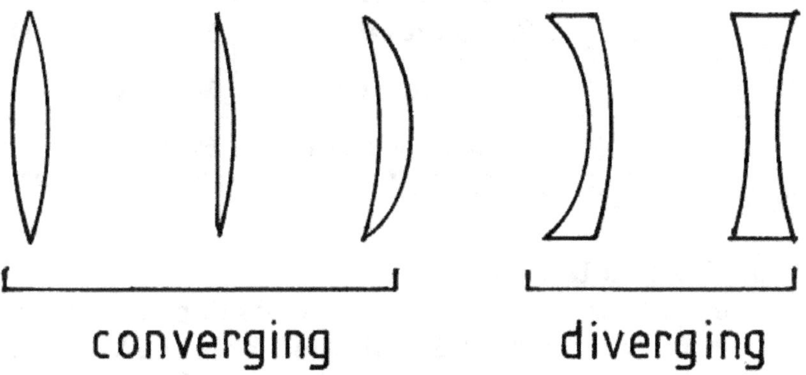

Fig 17.7
Basic lens element profiles.

Whether a lens behaves as a convergent or divergent optical system depends upon the nature of the curved surfaces. In optics, a curved surface when viewed from the rarer medium (air, in this case) is denoted as convex (+) or concave (–). A convex surface "bulges" towards the observer, for example. When both surfaces are convex (or one convex and the other flat) the lens will always be converging. If both surfaces are concave (or one concave and the other flat) it will always be diverging. When a lens has one face convex and the other concave, it will be either converging or diverging depending upon the relative curvatures of the two faces. If the two radii of curvature of the faces have a common centre then it will no longer be a lens, but simply a curved disc of uniform thickness. A summary of the various types is given in **Table 17.1**[15].

TABLE 17.1
Basic Types of Lens Element

Surfaces			Name	Thickest at:	Effect
Plane	Convex	Concave			
1	1		Plano-convex	Middle	Converging
1		1	Plano-concave	Edges	Diverging
	2		Bi-convex	Middle	Converging
		2	Bi-concave	Edges	Diverging
	1	1	Concavo-convex	Middle	Converging
	1	1	Concavo- convex	Edges	Diverging

(Source: Encyclopaedia of Photography[15].)

17.4.1 Basic optics of a lens

To understand how a lens functions, consider first the arrangement of three prisms depicted in **Fig 17.8** with just three individual rays of light Prisms **1** and **3** are identical, while prism **2** is parallel-sided. Rays **1** and **3** are bent equally (in opposite directions) while ray **2** passes through undeviated. All three emergent rays intersect at point **F** on the principal axis; that is, they are brought to a focus. This optical system represents a crude "lens". If we imagine that two extra prisms (with a slightly smaller prism angle) are inserted, one between **1**and **2** and the other between **2** and **3**, their emergent rays will be deviated less but will also pass through **F**, if the prism angle is chosen correctly.

Taking this concept to the limit produces a bi-convex lens, as shown in **Fig 17.9**, which can be regarded as an infinite number of such prisms. Parallel rays of light from an object at infinity will be brought to a focus at **F**, the focal point. The distance from the lens centre to **F** is termed the focal length of the lens. **Fig 17.10** shows some of the terminology used in lens optics.

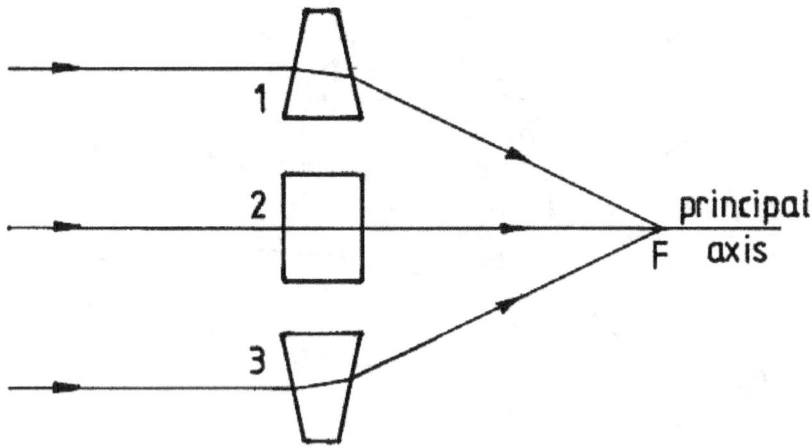

Fig 17.8
*Basic principle of the operation of a lens. Three prisms can be designed to bring three individual (parallel) rays of light to a common focus at **F**.*

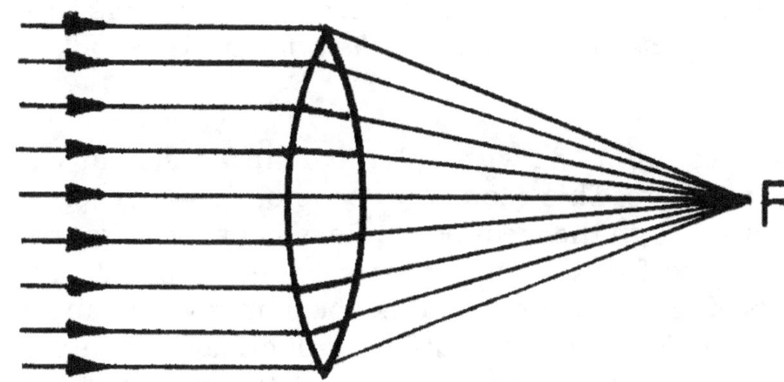

Fig 17.9
*A lens can be regarded as an infinite number of prisms with a range of prism angles joined together, an extension of the principle shown in **Fig 17.8**.*

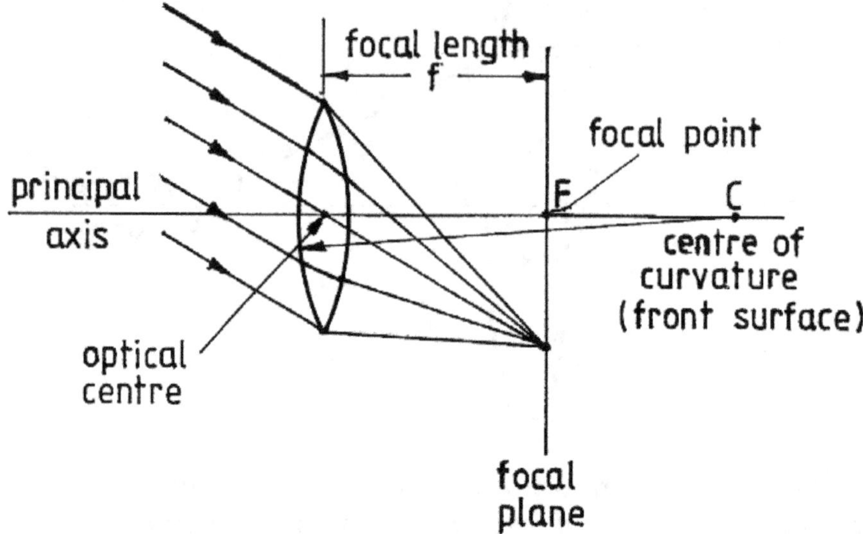

Fig 17.10
*Lens terminology. Parallel rays will be brought to a focus at a point on the
focal plane. Only if they are parallel to the principal axis will they be focused
at* **F***.*

Most lenses are made with spherical surfaces, that is, each surface
forms part of a sphere. This geometry does not, however, cause all the rays
to pass exactly through the focal point. Rays near the outer perimeter of the
lens are brought to focus slightly nearer to the lens than point **F**. This is
known as **spherical aberration**, and is one of many lens aberrations. It can
be corrected by making the lens surface aspherical, but this adds greatly to
the cost of manufacture. By stopping down the lens aperture, so that only
the central region of the lens is used, spherical aberration can be reduced.

17.4.2 Geometry of image formation

It is relatively easy to construct optical paths geometrically in order
to locate the image positions of objects at different distances from the lens.
The starting point is that an object at infinity produces an image at the focal
plane of the lens, as has already been demonstrated. Objects at finite
distances will give images further away from the optical centre of the lens,
beyond the focal point. As the object distance (measured from the optical
centre) decreases, so the image distance, also measured from the optical
centre, increases. **Fig 17.11** illustrates the principles of image construction,
which is based on the paths of three key rays of light, though generally any
two of them will enable the image position to be established.

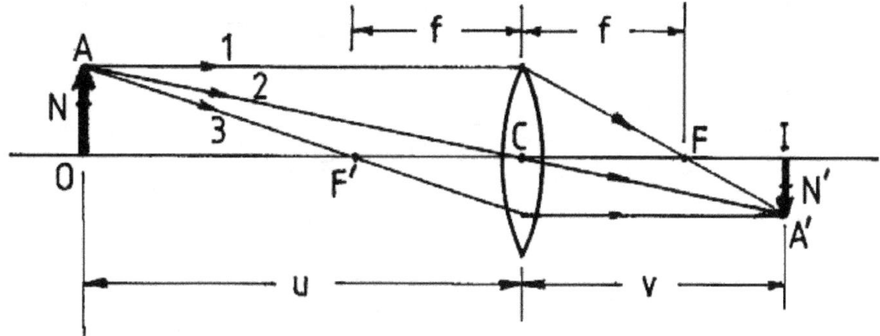

Fig 17.11
*Image formation with a converging lens. Object **OA** produces a real, inverted image at **IA'**. Rays **1**, **2** and **3** can be traced to establish the image position and size.*

In the figure, **OA** is the object at a distance **u** (greater than **f**) in the form of a vertical arrow. The paths of certain rays (marked **1**, **2** and **3**) are easily traced since:

1. a ray from the object parallel to the principal axis will be directed by the lens to pass through the far focal point **F** (ray **1**).
2. a ray that passes through the optical centre will not be deviated and if the lens is thin will not be displaced significantly.
3. a ray passing through the forward focal point **F'** will emerge parallel to the principal axis (converse of i).

The three rays all pass through point **A'**, beyond **F**. **IA'** represents the complete image, located at some distance **v** from the lens, on the far side. Similar constructions can be made for other points on the object to produce corresponding points on the image; point **N** will give **N'**, for example. However, it is not necessary to do any more than is shown in **Fig 17.11** in most examples of this type. The image can be located simply by considering point **A**.

It should be clear that the image is a real one and that it is inverted. As the object is moved nearer to the lens, the image moves further away from the lens and becomes larger (**Fig 17.12**).

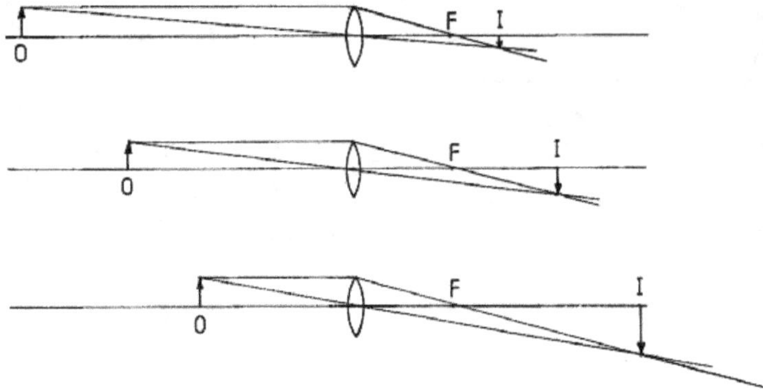

Fig 17.12
Sequence (from top to bottom): moving the object **O** *closer to the lens causes the real image* **I** *to move further from the lens (on the other side) and to increase in size.*

17.4.3 Lens formulae

A standard formula can be derived which relates the object distance, the image distance and the focal length of the lens. This formula is based upon the assumptions that the lens can be regarded as a system of small prisms and that the angles of incidence are small. In all calculations, a sign convention has to be adopted to ensure correct interpretation. Following Whelan and Hodgson[14], the convention is summarised as follows:

1. all distances are measured to the optical centre. (In compound lenses there are two nodal points instead of a single optical centre. Object distances are measured to the forward nodal point and image distances to the rear point. This, however, need not concern us in our analyses).
2. distances are taken as positive if actually traversed by the light rays, i.e. distances to real objects and images.
3. distances are taken as negative if they are only apparently traversed by light rays i.e. distances to virtual objects and images.
4. radius of curvature is positive for surfaces which are convex when viewed from the rarer medium (air). (**See Fig 17.13**). A positive radius of curvature causes a deviation towards the principal axis.

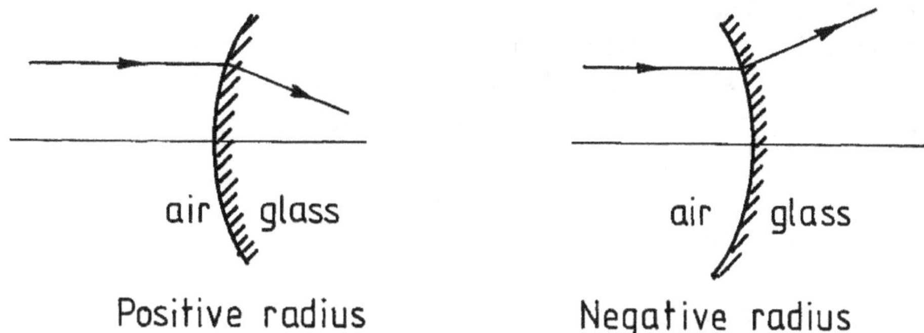

Fig 17.13
*Distinction between positive and negative radii of curvature of a lens surface.
(See Section 17.4.3 iv).*

The usual symbols are as follows:
  u = object distance
  v = image distance
  f = focal length
  R = radius of curvature (of lens surface)

The standard lens formula is:
  $1/\mathbf{u} + 1/\mathbf{v} = 1/\mathbf{f}$

In this equation **f** will be positive for a converging lens and negative for a diverging one. The term $1/\mathbf{f}$ is also referred to as the **power** of the lens, measured in dioptres (now rad m⁻¹) when **f** is measured in metres. Thus a 50mm focal length lens has a power **P** = 1/0.05 = 20 rad m⁻¹.

Another version of the lens formula is known as the "lens-maker's formula" since it includes the radii of curvature of the lens surfaces. The focal length of a lens is dependent upon the refractive index of the material, **n**, and the radii of the two surfaces. The focal length is smaller for greater curvature and higher **n** values.

It can be shown geometrically that:

$$1/\mathbf{f} = (\mathbf{n} - 1/(1/\mathbf{R_1} + 1/\mathbf{R_2})$$

where **R₁** and **R₂** are the radii of curvature of the front and back surfaces.

Hence:

$$1/\mathbf{u} + 1/\mathbf{v} = (\mathbf{n} - 1)(1/\mathbf{R_1} + 1/\mathbf{R_2}) = 1/\mathbf{f}$$

Although we shall not be making use of this relationship, it is worth being aware of its existence.

17.4.4 Lens calculations

A few representative calculations using the lens formula will give some insight into how lenses function. Taking three object distances in turn the corresponding image distances will be calculated. For this exercise the focal length of the lens will be taken as 50mm.

Example 1: Object distance 200m

$$\mathbf{u} = 200\text{m}, \ \mathbf{f} = 0.05\text{m}$$

Rearranging the lens formula;

$$1/\mathbf{v} \ = 1/\mathbf{f} - 1/\mathbf{u}$$

i.e. $1/\mathbf{v} \ = 1/0.05 - 1/200 = (200 - 0\ 05)/(200 \times 0.05)$

$$= 199.5/10 = 19.995$$

Therefore

$$\mathbf{v} \quad = 1/19.995\text{m} = 0.0500125\text{m}$$
$$= 50.01\text{mm}$$

This shows that an object 200m away produces an image only fractionally beyond the focal point of a 50mm lens. It will probably appear as much in focus as an object at infinity, if we were to place a film 50mm behind the lens.

Example 2: Object distance 2m

Here $1/\mathbf{v} \ = 1/0.05 - 1/2 = 1.95/0.01 = 19.5$
And $\mathbf{v} \quad = 1/19.5 \text{ m}$
$$= 51.28\text{mm}$$

In this case the object would not be in focus on a film placed at 50mm from the lens. Either the film must be moved back, or the lens forward, by 1.28mm to produce a sharp image. In fact, moving the lens forward will reduce the object distance from 2m to 1.99872m but if this value were to be used for a revised calculation there would be only an insignificant change in the value of $\mathbf{v}$ as calculated above.

Example 3: Object distance 300mm

$$1/\mathbf{v} = 1/0.05 - 1/0.3 = 0.2/0.015 = 13.33$$

And
$$\mathbf{v} = 1/13.33 \text{ m}$$
$$= 75\text{mm}$$

Here the lens has to be screwed out by 25mm from its infinity focusing position. The significance of this is that for close-up work, when the subject is nearer than about 2 metres, the lens cannot be assumed to be at a distance from the film equal to its focal length. In these circumstances, the actual film-image distance **v** must be used in any calculations; this distance is often referred to as the "working focal length".

For general stereo work (subject distances between 2m and infinity), the difference between the actual focal length **f** and the working focal length **v** is very small, as shown by examples **1** and **2** above. In many calculations the value of **f** can be used without introducing significant errors, thus avoiding an additional calculation to determine **v**.

When an object is placed close to a lens at a distance less than the focal length, the lens acts as a magnifying glass, producing a virtual, upright image larger than the object itself (**Fig 17.14**). The lenses in a stereoscope are essentially used in this way. When the object is close to the forward focal point (but still located within the forward focal distance) then the image will approach infinity.

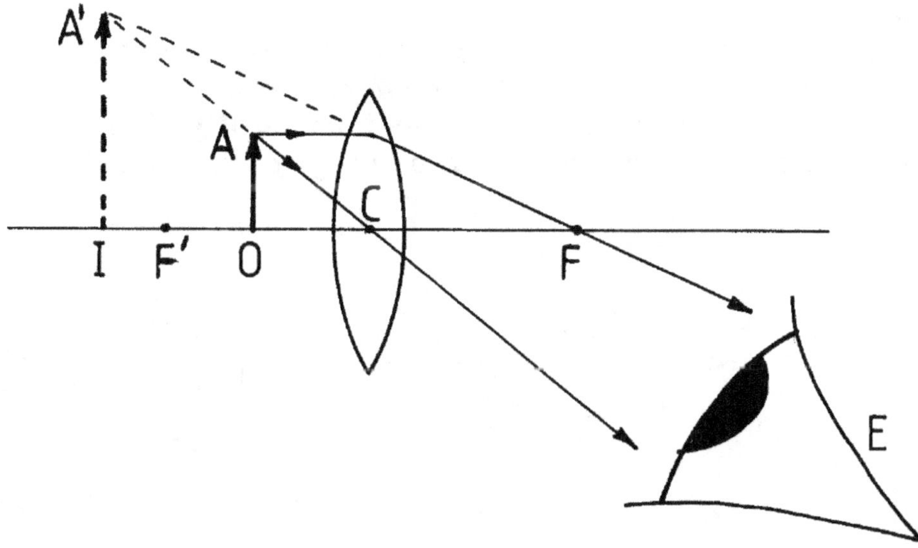

Fig 17.14
*The lens as a magnifying glass. When the object lies within the forward focal length (between **F'** and **C** in the diagram) the image is magnified, upright and virtual, on the same side of the lens as the object.*

17.5 Depth of Field
17.5.1 Basic concept

According to the lens geometry analysed so far, confirmed by the calculations, a lens can be focused on only one object distance at a time. If focused at 200m then an object at 2m is technically out of focus. However, examination of many photographs would seem to indicate that objects at several distances can be in focus at the same time. The reason for this is that the eye will tolerate a certain degree of unsharpness in part of an image and cannot distinguish between this and a properly focused section elsewhere.

Depth of field is the term used to denote the range of object distances, from the closest to the most distant, that will be seen as "sharp" to the eye in an image.

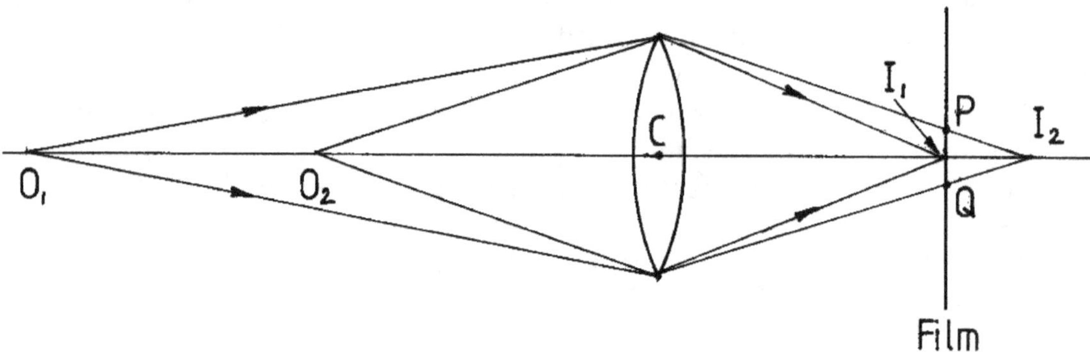

Fig 17.15
Depth of field principle (i): Point object O_1 produces a point image I_1 at the film plane. A nearer object O_2 would produce a sharp image at I_2, behind the film plane. The image on film is a blurred circle diameter PQ. If this circle is no greater than a critical size, it will appear to the eye as sharp as I_1.

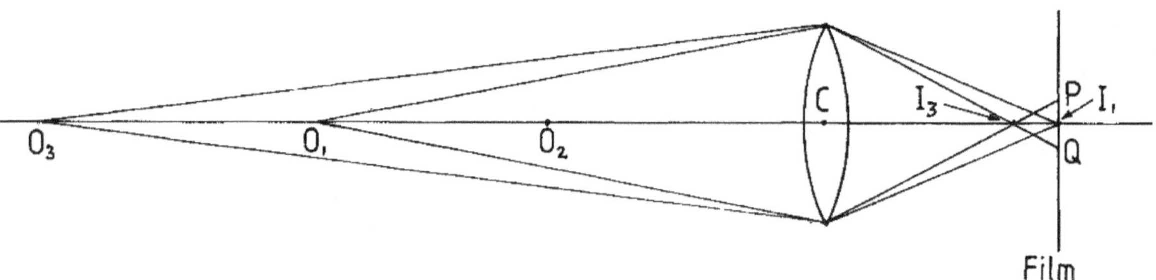

Fig 17.16
*Depth of field principle (ii). Similar to **Fig 17.15**, but showing a more distant object O_3 that gives an identical circle of confusion. In this case the true focus point is at I_3, in front of the film plane.*

Figs 17.15 and **17.16** demonstrate the basic principle. In **Fig 17.15**, a point object O_1 produces a point image I_1 exactly in focus on the film at some distance **v**. Now a nearer point object O_2 would give, for this setting, an image at I_2, slightly further away from the lens. However, the film plane cuts the cone of rays from O_2 just ahead of their point of focus, and this results in a small circular image, diameter **PQ**, on the film, instead of a single sharp point. This is known as a **circle of confusion**. If this circle is small enough, the eye will see it as a single point and it will appear as sharp as I_1. An object placed even nearer to the lens than O_2 will produce a larger circle of confusion. For a certain object distance the circle of confusion will be large enough for the eye to discern that the image is no longer in focus. If we assume that O_2 produces the largest "tolerable" circle **PQ** that the eye will accept as sharp, then all objects between O_1 and O_2 will appear to be in focus within the total image.

A similar argument applies to objects further away from the lens than O_1, as shown in **Fig 17.15**. In this case, the light rays in the cone intersect in front of the film and cross over before forming the circular image. This means that there is an additional range of object distances, from O_1 to O_3, that will appear sharp, giving a total range from O_3 to O_2, assuming that O_3 is the object distance for the maximum allowable circle of confusion. The identical principle applies to all other points on an object in a scene to produce the overall Image with its varying degrees of sharpness in different regions.

In calculations, the circle of confusion is usually taken as $1/1000$ of the focal length value.

Depth of field (i.e. the distance range from O_3 to O_2) depends upon the distance of the focused object and the lens aperture that is being used. In general terms, it varies as follows:

1. the total range is reduced as the focused object distance O_1C is decreased.
2. the distance from O_3 to O_1 is much greater than that from O_1 to O_2 except in extreme close-up conditions. There is usually more of the scene "in focus" behind the focused object than in front of it. A very rough guide is to assume that the distance O_3O_1 is about twice the distance O_1O_2 but it can be greater than this.
3. for any given focused distance the total depth of field is greater with smaller apertures.
4. if the degree of blur that is acceptable as still being sharp is greater, ie the tolerable circle of confusion is larger, the depth of field will be greater. The more critical the standard of sharpness, the smaller will be the depth of field.

17.5.2 Hyperfocal distance

If a lens is focused at infinity it can be shown that the depth of field will extend from a certain distance **H**, known as the hyperfocal distance, to infinity. The value of **H** depends upon the same factors as depth of field, standard of sharpness, aperture and focal length of the lens. For a 50mm focal length lens, for example, **H** varies from about 25m to about 1.5m as the aperture is reduced from f/2 to f/32. Focusing the lens at infinity, therefore, will give a large depth of field, from **H** to infinity.. However, by focusing the lens at the **H** value appropriate to the aperture in use, the range is even larger, extending from **H**/2 to infinity. This represents the maximum possible depth of field for a given aperture and standard of sharpness. (See also Chapter 10, Section 10.5).

Focusing on the hyperfocal distance is most useful practically to ensure that all (or most) of a scene is acceptably sharp, so important in stereo photography, assuming that the subject extends to infinity. If lighting conditions are poorer so that a wider aperture has to be used, with a reduction in the depth of field, the lens can always be focused closer than **H** so that the new depth of field range includes the nearest object. The more distant objects may now lie outside the range but some unsharpness in this region is less important.

When the overall scene does not extend as far as infinity one can adjust the aperture and focused distance so that the subject range and depth of field more or less coincide. If the lens barrel incorporates a depth of field scale, the lens can be set so that the relevant pair of aperture markings lie opposite the distance markings corresponding to the nearest and furthest objects. This method, called **zone focusing**, is widely used in stereo photography and often produces better results (in terms of overall sharpness of the image) than simply focusing on the principal subject of interest.

Hyperfocal distances and the depth of field can be found in published tables but can also be calculated from the formulae that follow:

Hyperfocal distance

$$H = f^2/cn$$

But if $\quad c = f/1000$

then $\quad H = 1000f/n$

Depth of field limits

$$D_N = D/(1 + ncD/f^2)$$

and $\quad D_F = D/(1 - ncD/f^2)$

But if $\quad c = f/1000$

then $\quad D_N = D/(1 + nD/1000f)$

and $\quad D_F = D/(1 - nD/1000f)$

Simplified depth of field

$$D_N = HD/(H + D)$$

and $\quad D_F = HD/(H - D)$

Key to symbols:

D = focused distance

D_N = near limit of depth of field

D_F = far limit of depth of field

n = lens aperture stop number

f = focal length of lens

c = limiting circle of confusion

Supplement S13 gives depth of field information for some commonly used lens focal lengths.

CHAPTER 18: THE ORTHOSTEREOSCOPIC STEREO IMAGE

18.1 The Perfect Image

In an ideal world a stereo image when viewed would exactly match the original subject, both in its size and location in space. Although such perfection is rarely achieved in practice, the 3D photographer should always aim to approach it as closely as possible. There are a few situations where special techniques are used which will rule this out, but the final result should be made to look as natural as possible. Sometimes, special effects are desired that deliberately make use of a distorted image, but this is the exception rather than the rule. Replicating reality as closely as possible is all a matter of having a sound grasp of the underlying principles and applying them competently.

The concept of orthostereoscopy, even if it is difficult to realise in practice, nevertheless provides a valuable benchmark against which a stereo image can be judged; it should not be dismissed as a mere abstraction, of interest only to theorists and academics.

18.2 The In-camera Stereo Image

To understand orthostereoscopy, it is necessary to start by examining the two images as formed in the camera. If the stereogram is ultimately to be seen orthostereoscopically, it must be produced according to certain basic conditions, as outlined in Chapter 2, Section 2.3. Of first importance is that the two lens axes are parallel (as will be the case in a stereo camera) or, if the sequential exposure technique is used, the camera is moved from one position to the next without "toe-in" (Chapter 2, **Fig 2.3**). For simplicity, we shall assume from here on that a "conventional" stereo camera is being used.

We know from earlier discussions that the left and right film chips will differ from each other by virtue of the following:

1. differing separations between various homologues
2. monocular areas to the right in the left image and to the left in the right image (Chapter 6, **Fig 6.11**).

As should be clear from **Fig 6.11**, the extent of the monocular regions increases with distance behind the stereo window. At the window itself there is no monocular region in either image. In the mounted stereogram, objects at the window distance will be located identically in both film chips. This leads us directly to the subject of the "built-in" window in many stereo cameras. **Fig 18.1** shows the formation of images in a camera without this feature; the optical axis of each lens intersects its image frame centrally.

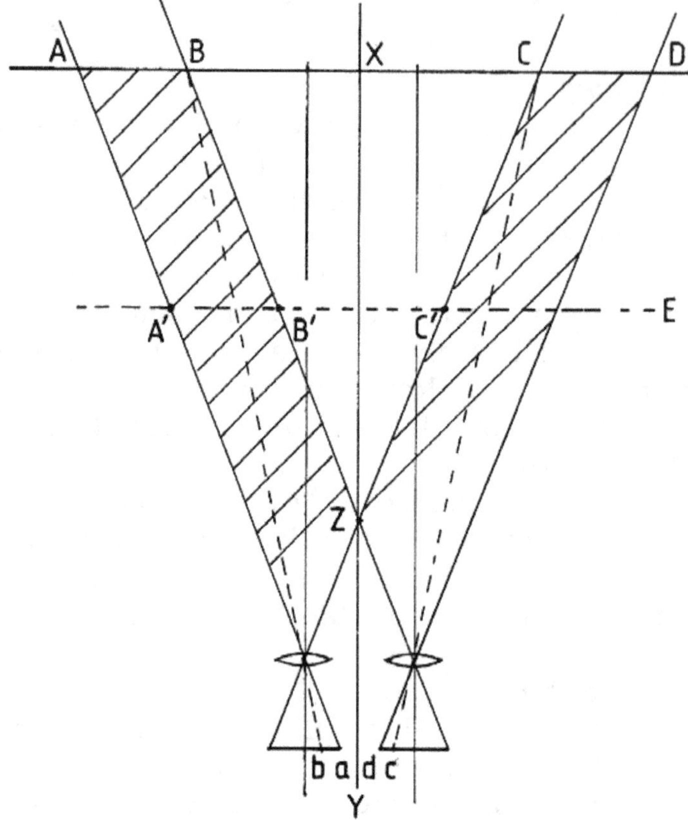

Fig 18.1
*Images produced in a stereo camera without a built-in stereo window. Lens axes are in line with the frame centres giving rise to areas **AB** and **CD**, each of which appears in only one image (**ab** and **cd** respectively).*

The shaded areas in the diagram indicate monocular regions, each of which appears on only one film chip. At 2 metres from the lenses, which is the distance at which the stereo window will appear for normal subjects, objects lying along the line **AB** will appear only in the left chip along the segment **ab**. Similarly, objects on **CD** will give images along **cd**, only in the right chip. These parts of the film images will be lost when mounting because only those objects lying along **BC** can appear in both images at the window location in the stereogram. This is not a problem; it simply means that the full width of each frame cannot be used, and there is some wastage.

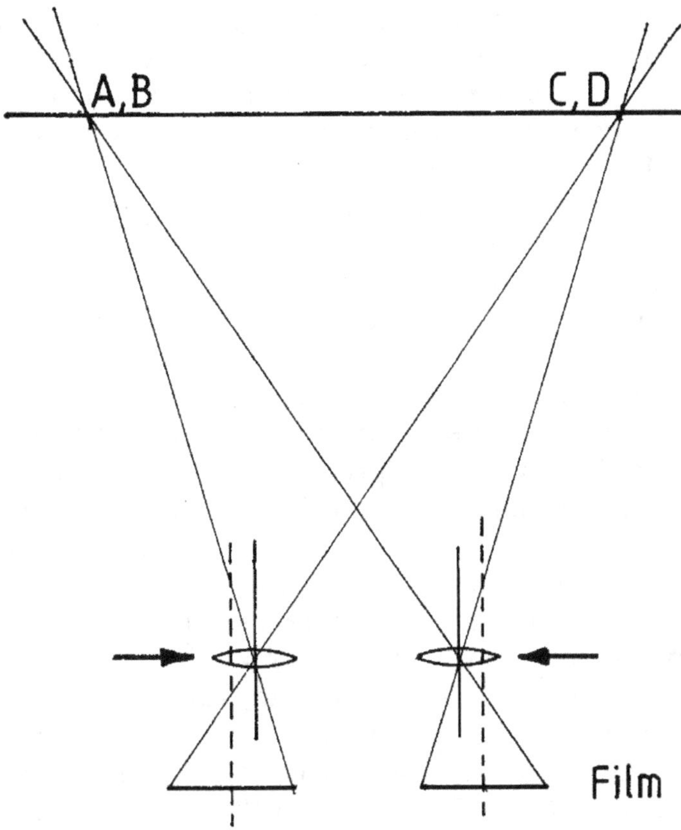

Fig 18.2
Images formed in a camera with a built-in stereo window. The lenses are set closer than the frame centres (dotted lines). The window is at **A,B** *–* **C,D** *and is common to both film images.*

A camera with a built-in window (**Fig 18.2**) has its lenses shifted towards each other by about 1.2 mm (for the 5P format); they are closer than the frame centres by this amount. This has the effect of eliminating the monocular regions (**AB** and **CD** in **Fig 18.1**) at the window distance itself. In short, points **A** and **B** now coincide, as do **C** and **D**. Now the whole of each film frame is usable. The difference between **Fig 18.1** and **Fig 18.2** may perhaps more easily be visualised by imagining that the film frames in the first diagram are moved apart until the inner frame edges (marked **a** and **d**) end up at **b** and **c** respectively. This would have the same effect, but shifting the lenses closer is the more practical option as the frame geometry, which is based upon the film perforation spacing, is not so easily changed.

This geometry is frequently referred to as converging. Terms such as "built-in convergence" are bandied about, and it is true that the light ray paths from the frame centres converge to the central point of the built-in window. However, the optical axes of the lenses are still parallel; there is no toe-in and hence no convergence distortion of the type shown in Chapter 5, **Fig 5.9b** (although this diagram relates to a different cause of this type of distortion). Consequently, reference to convergence in the context of the built-in stereo window is rather misleading. The differential separation of the camera lenses and frame centres simply avoids image loss, allowing the whole of each frame to be used (apart from the masking effect of the mount apertures that is necessary to allow for fine adjustments of the film chips during mounting).

As a subject approaches the camera, its images in the two film frames move towards the outer edges. At a certain distance at least one of the images will disappear from its frame. An object moving along **XY** in **Fig 18.1**, for example, disappears from view at point **Z**, in both frames simultaneously.

This does not imply that a standard stereo camera with a 70mm stereo base, say, cannot be used for subjects closer than 2m. If it is used for nearer subjects, however, two "problems" can arise. If the subject is too close there may be some violation of the 1 in 30 rule, although this is usually not serious at distances greater than about 500mm (see Supplement S8). Since most stereo cameras cannot be focused closer than about 1m, this problem will not occur very often. Of more significance is that as the subject distance is reduced the amount of "lost image" or frame width wastage is increased. For example, in **Fig 18.1**, the subject width at the window distance captured by the left frame is **AC**, of which the portion **AB** has to be disregarded. For the right film frame the corresponding segments are **BD** and **CD** (**AC** = **BD** and **AB** = **CD** = 70mm). If the lens angle of view is 36°, and **XY** = 2m, then **AC** = 2 x 2000 tan18 = 1300mm (= 1.3m) and 70mm is "lost", which represents about 1/20 of the width. This translates to 1.2mm on each film frame in the Realist format. At 650mm distance (about 2ft, plane **E**) the subject width is reduced to **A'C'**. The discarded portion **A'B'** is equal to **AB** (70mm) which, in this case, represents a greater proportion of the whole. A similar calculation to the above gives the proportion wasted as just over 1/6, equal to about 4mm of the film frame width.

If the camera has a built-in window (**Fig 18.2**) the effect is less severe in comparison, but it is not entirely eliminated for subjects in this closer range. In a stereo camera the left and right image configuration on the film, as seen from the back of the camera, is as depicted in **Fig 18.3**, top diagram.

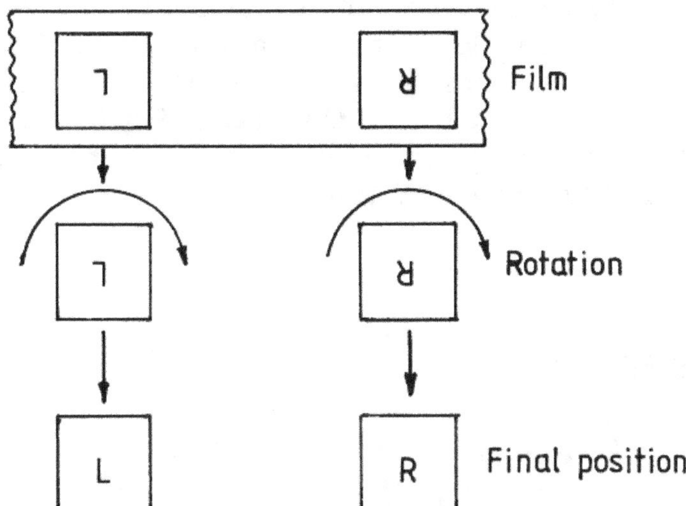

Fig 18.3
One method of transposing film images for mounting.

The film chips have to be transposed before viewing as has been explained in previous chapters. There is another way of achieving this transposition, which may help in keeping track of the image configurations in-camera and after mounting. Instead of starting with upright images, and then exchanging them left for right, the method shown in **Fig 18.3** can be used. Here the images are cut from the film while in the inverted position, as they were in the camera. Keeping the left image on the left and rotating both chips by 180° brings them into the correct configuration for viewing. The explanation of image reconstruction given in the next section will be more easily followed if this method of transposition is kept in mind.

18.3 Orthostereoscopic Viewing of a Stereogram
18.3.1 Images In a stereoscope

Fig 18.4a illustrates the creation of a pair of images in a typical stereo camera of an object PQR, which is in the form of an equilateral triangle in plan view. The apexes **P**, **Q** and **R** give image points **p,q** and **r** respectively on the left film chip, and **p',q'** and **r'** on the right. Points **i** and **i'** are infinity homologues generated along the lens axes. The lenses are separated by the stereo base **b**, and are assumed to be at a distance equal to the focal length **f** from the film plane. The separation of points **i** and **i'** in the camera will be equal to the stereo base **b**.

Now if we carry out the 180° rotation described in Section 18.2, and mount the film chips with **i** and **i'** separated by a distance **b**, then the stereogram shown in **Fig 18.4b** will be produced. When this is placed in a stereoscope as shown with lenses focal length **f** (the same value as that of the camera lenses) spaced by **b**, then the image **P'Q'R'** produced is identical to the original object **PQR** in respect of its size, shape and location in space. This can be verified by considering the situation at plane **E** in **Fig 18.4a**, at a distance **f** in front of the camera lenses. The various triangles between **O** and **gk** are identical to those between **O** and **ri** in **Fig 18.4b**. The upper part of **Fig 18.4a** (from **O** to the object) is identical to the upper part of **Fig 18.4b**, which confirms that the image is orthostereoscopic.

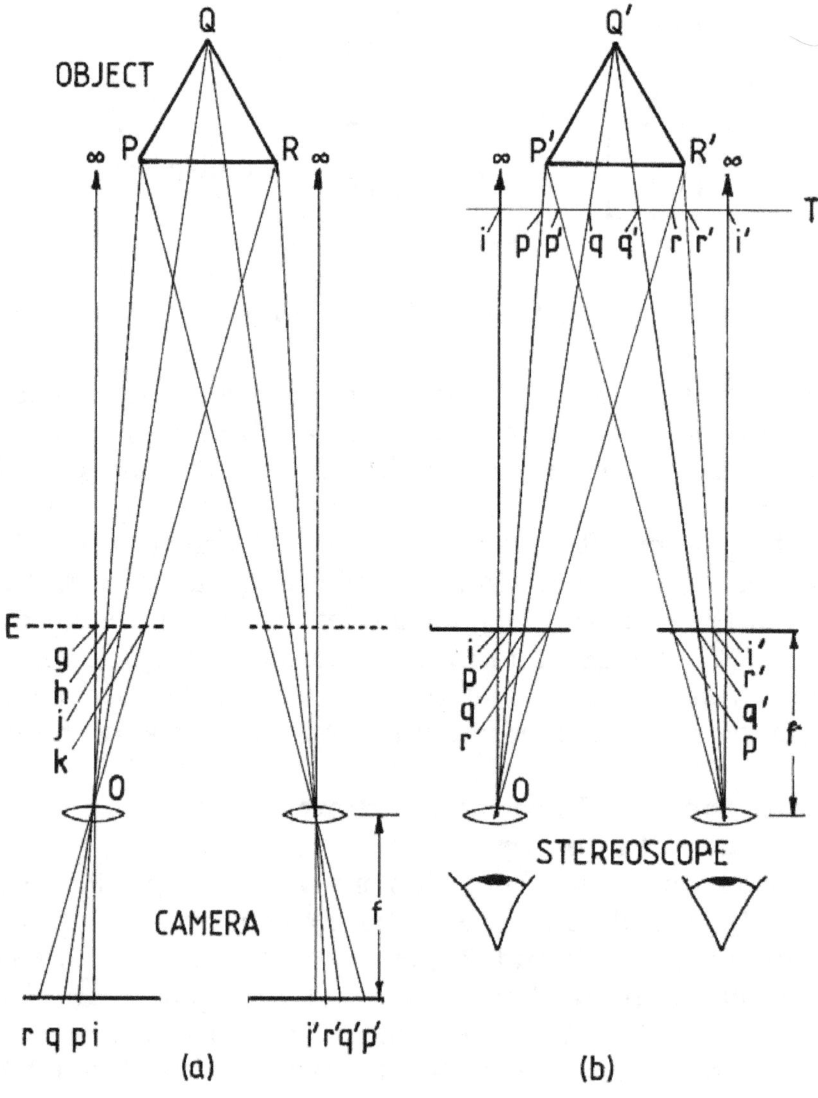

Fig 18.4
Orthostereoscopic viewing of an image.
a *Original formation of the image in the camera.*
b *Viewing of the transposed images in a stereoscope with lenses of focal length equal to that of the camera lenses.*

It should be apparent that the identities between the two diagrams, and hence the conditions for orthostereoscopy, rely on three factors:

1. the focal lengths of camera and stereoscope lenses must be identical
2. the stereoscope lens spacing must match that of the camera lenses
3. the film chips should be mounted so that infinity homologues are separated by a distance equal to the stereo base used.

In practice these pose some problems. Commonly, the focal lengths of camera and stereoscope are different (e.g. Stereo Realist camera 35mm, Stereolist viewer 44mm). In addition, the camera lenses would not necessarily be set at the actual focal length f for correct focus, but at some greater value, depending upon the subject distance. Furthermore, many cameras operate with a stereo base of 70mm and if the film chips were to be mounted with a 70mm infinity homologue separation there would be difficulties in viewing the stereogram if the observer's eye separation is significantly below this. Usually, the infinity separation adopted in mounting is around 63 to 64mm. The effects of these variables on the image will be discussed in detail later, but even at this stage it seems that true orthostereoscopic viewing may be rather an elusive pursuit.

Fig 18.4 is drawn as a general representation that is correct in principle for any stereo camera, whether or not it has a built-in stereo window. The only difference the latter will make is in the location of the film frame edges in the image.

It should be pointed out that the diagram is not in true proportion; the object distance is compressed in relation to the focal length to exaggerate the homologue separations on the film chips to give greater clarity. This does not, however, invalidate any of the arguments.

18.3.2 Projected images

For simplicity, we shall assume that projection conditions have been set up to produce the stereo window at the screen surface, although this is not a prerequisite for orthostereoscopic viewing of projected images. As demonstrated in Chapter 8, Section 8.6.3, and Supplement S10, the screen images will adopt the following configuration:

1. infinity homologues at the correct spacing (which in the context of this particular discussion must be equal to the stereo base e.g. 70mm)
2. left and right image frames coincident.

(These are both illustrated in **Fig S10.3**, screen position **1**, in Supplement S10).

Perhaps surprisingly, the focal length of the projector lens is not critical in establishing orthostereoscopic viewing conditions; it merely sets the projection distance at which the correct image configuration occurs.

The superimposed images on screen, with precisely registered frame edges, are no more than an enlarged version of the result that would be produced by sandwiching the two halves of a mounted stereogram, aligning the frame edges as shown in **Fig 18.5**.

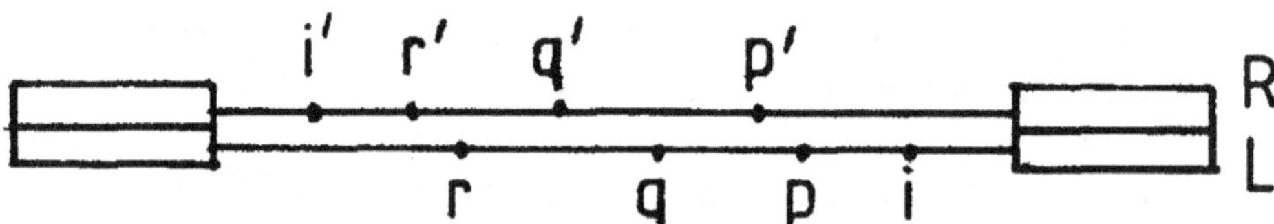

Fig 18.5
Hypothetical "sandwich" of superimposed left and right images (pictured edge-on from the top), showing the relative positions of homologues.

If this "double" slide were to be projected from a mono projector of the same focal length as the original stereo projector, an identical screen image would be produced, except that the differential polarisation of the two images would not be retained. (This use of a "sandwich slide" is, of course, only a concept for analysis of image configurations, and not a practical method of projecting stereo images). Thus, the pairs of homologues **pp'**, **qq'** etc. will appear on screen as an enlarged version of their configuration in the double slide (**Fig 18.6**). Points **L** and **R** represent the observer's eye positions (assuming the interpupillary distance is equal to the on-screen infinity separation **ii'**), the spectator being located at a distance D_s from the screen. D_s is the orthostereoscopic distance, equal to $1.59W_s$, where W_s is the width of the screen image, for the Realist format (Supplement S10). Placing the observer at distance D_s simply means that the viewing geometry obeys the principles covered in Supplement S1 (on perspective) and that the triangle **Lpr** in **Fig 18.6** is geometrically similar to triangle **Opr** in **Fig 18.4b**.

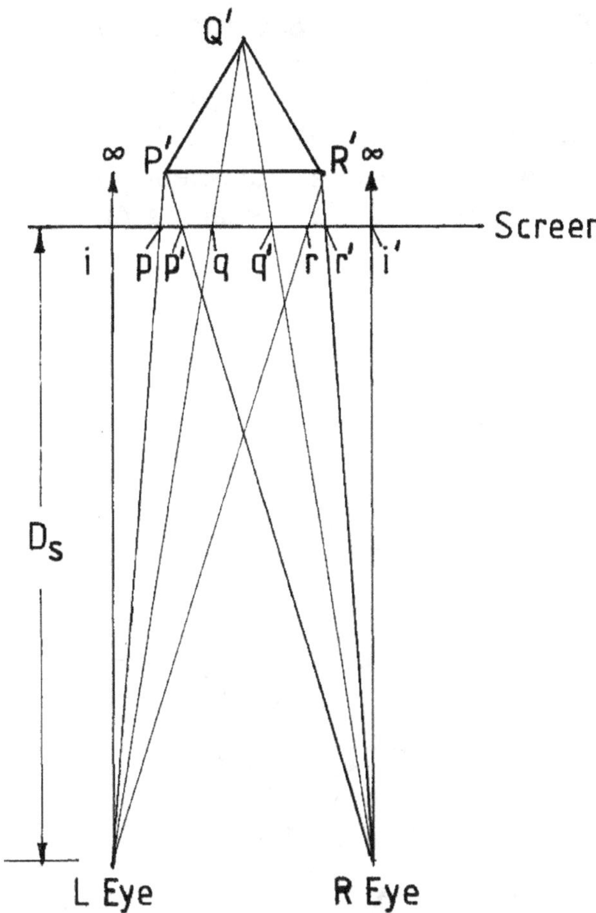

Fig 18.6
*Orthostereoscopic viewing of a projected image for a spectator sitting in the orthostereoscopic seat at a distance **Ds** from the screen.*

Now consider plane **T** in **Fig 18.4**, especially in relation to the paths of the light rays as they pass through it. The points of intersection of these rays with the plane correspond with the homologues **p**, **p'**, **q**, **q'** etc. and this plane becomes a "duplicate" of the screen of **Fig 18.6**. If plane **T** is chosen to coincide with the stereo window plane, then **Figs 18.4** and **18.6** become exact replicas. This analysis confirms that the image observed on screen as depicted in **Fig 18.6** is orthostereoscopic, provided that the projected images are properly spaced.

As long as the infinity homologues are set at the correct separation, it does not matter if the stereo window lies in front of or even behind the screen surface. The orthostereoscopic seat (**OSS**) distance is always measured from the stereo window position and not from the screen. This is discussed in Supplement S10.

To summarise, orthostereoscopic conditions for projected images require that the on-screen s_i value is set correctly and that the observer sits at the correct distance, in the orthostereoscopic seat.

18.3.3 Natural deviations from orthostereoscopy

Even though viewing conditions are set up to achieve orthostereoscopic images, most observers will experience some distortion. This is clearly the case with projected images because not everybody can occupy the orthostereoscopic seat simultaneously. But a more general factor is the variation in interpupillary spacing of human eyes from one person to the next.

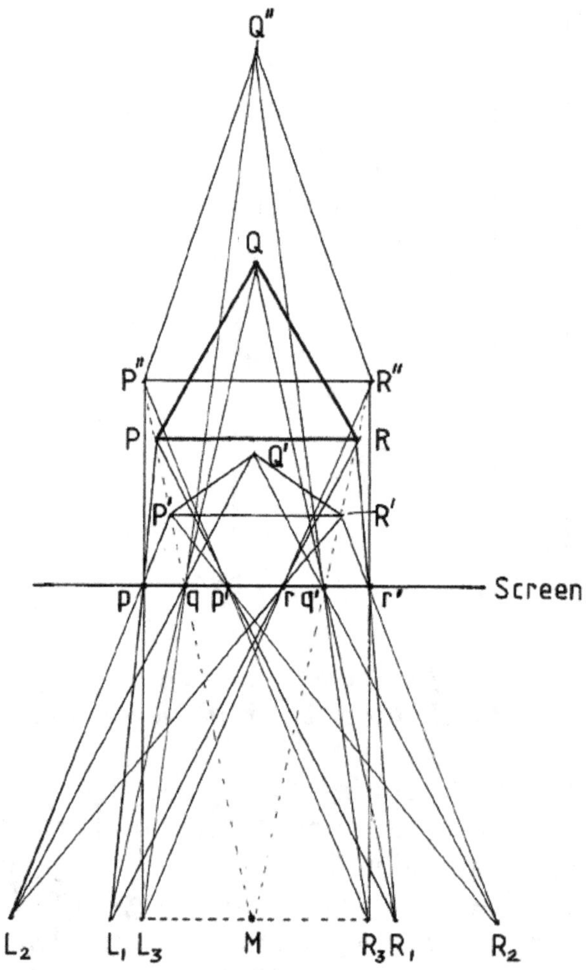

Fig 18.7

Effect of eye spacing on the perception of a projected image. Homologues **pp'**, **qq'**, *and* **rr'** *produce an orthostereoscopic image* **PQR** *for eye spacing* **L₁R₁**. *Spectators with larger* **(L₂R₂)** *or smaller* **(L₃R₃)** *eye spacings will see a squeezed* **(P'Q'R')** *or stretched* **(P"Q"R")** *image respectively. (The effect is exaggerated in the diagram for clarity).*

The effect of different eye spacings on the perception of the image is illustrated in **Fig 18.7**. Triangle **PQR** represents the orthostereoscopic image as seen by an observer's eyes at **L₁** and **R₁** as a result of homologues **p**, **p'**, **q**, **q'**, **r** and **r'**. The projected image, rather than one seen in a stereoscope, is easier to analyse. Following the previous example, the eye spacing is assumed to be 70mm to match the camera lens spacing, for consistency. The observer is also assumed to be located on the centre line **QM** at the orthostereoscopic distance. From exactly the same position, a different observer with a larger eye spacing L_2R_2 (which has been exaggerated for clarity) will see the image as **P'Q'R'**, the position of which is found by drawing the rays from L_2 and R_2 through the homologues **p, p'** etc. Note that this image, compared with **PQR**, is closer, narrower and compressed from front to back; it exhibits distortion. The effect is, of course, magnified in this diagram because of the foreshortening of the distance scale. With an actual image no closer than about 2m or more, the amount of distortion will be less obvious but will still exist. The translation of **P** to **P'**, **Q** to **Q'** (all points on the image, in fact) is along lines **PM, QM, RM** and so on. The distance by which a point on the image is shifted, measured at 90° to the screen, ignoring any lateral shift, increases rapidly with its distance from the observer. This can be seen by comparing the distance **QQ"** with the distance between the positions of the lines **PR** and **P'R'**. This difference gives rise to the compression, or **squeeze**, which is the term usually applied to this type of distortion.

A closer eye spacing, represented by L_3 and R_3 produces the image **P"Q"R"**, which is further away, wider and elongated. **P** moves to **P"** along the line **MP** produced, and **R** moves along the line **MR** produced. This type of distortion is known as **stretch**.

The depth change of any point in an image caused by differing eye separations can be determined from the geometries given in **Fig 18.8**. Homologues **p** and **p'** produce a point **P** when viewed with eye spacing L_1R_1. It lies at distance **D**, and has been located on the left eye's axis for convenience. **Fig 18.8a** shows the apparent shift of **P** to **P'** as a result of viewing the stereogram with a larger eye spacing L_1R_2 and **Fig 18.8b** shows the effect of a smaller spacing.

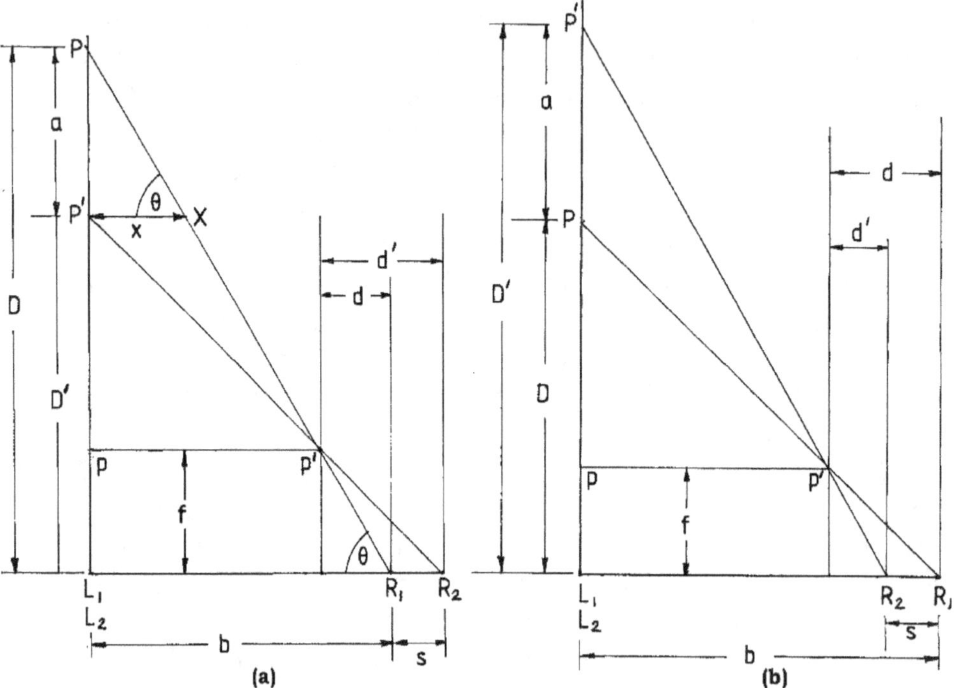

Fig 18.8
a *Homologues* **p** *and* **p**'*produce an image* **P** *when viewed with an eye spacing of* **L₁R₁**. *A person with a larger eye spacing* **L₂R₂** *will see the image at* **P'**. *The image shift* **PP'** *(=* **a***) can be calculated (see Section 18.8.3).*
b *Similar to* **a**, *but for a reduction in the eye spacing. The image appears further away (at* **P'***) in this case.*

From **Fig 18.8a**, the familiar relationship **D** = **fb/d** can be applied to the two eye spacings in turn:

$$\mathbf{D = fb/d}$$
$$\text{and} \quad \mathbf{D' = f(b + s)/d'}$$
$$\text{i.e.} \quad \mathbf{D' = f(b + s)/(d + s)}$$

Again, using the notation in **Fig 18.8a**, the distance **a** is found as follows:

$$\mathbf{a = x\,\tan\theta = xf/d}$$

Now, from similar triangles **P'Xp'** and **R₂R₁p'**:

$$\mathbf{x/(D' - f) = s/f} \text{ (using triangle heights } \mathbf{D'} \text{ and } \mathbf{f})$$
$$\text{i.e.} \quad \mathbf{x = s(D' - f)/f}$$

Substituting in the equation for **a**;

$$\mathbf{a = s(D' - f)f/df}$$

Cancelling **f**, substituting (**D − a**) for **D**', and simplifying, this reduces to:

$$\mathbf{a = s(D - f)/(d + s)}$$

As **s** increases, the numerator increases faster than the denominator leading to an overall increase in the value of **a**, but the change in depth is greater in the early stages as **s** increases from zero.

A similar analysis for **Fig 18.8b** gives related expressions:

$$\mathbf{D' = f(B - s)/(D - s)}$$
$$\text{and} \quad \mathbf{a = s(D - f)/(d - s)}$$

(These are valid for values of **s** from 0 to **d**).

Both formulae for the depth change, **a**, show that as **D** increases, the shift of the image caused by a change in eye spacing also increases. As with changes in **s** the effect is not linear. As **D** increases, the numerator of each expression increases; at the same time an increase in **D** means a reduction in the deviation **d** so there is a simultaneous decrease in the denominator of each equation.

Moving the film chips laterally, but keeping the eye spacing constant, can produce similar changes in the appearance of stereo images. Moving the chips closer together is roughly the same as viewing the original pair with a larger eye spacing and vice versa. Similar equations to those above can be derived. In terms of the effect on an object at a given distance, the values of **s'** and **s** that produce the same image shift are related to each other geometrically with **s'** less than **s**, but the ratio is not constant over the whole depth range. The effect of film chip displacements is discussed in Chapter 19, Section 19.3.4.

18.3.4 Interocular adjustments in a stereoscope

Superior stereoscopes of the Brewster type are fitted with adjustable lens spacing, activated by rotating a knob or swinging a small lever. This allows the lenses to be positioned so that their optical centres are aligned with the principal lines of sight from the observer's eyes to give comfortable viewing. Strictly, the optical centres of the lenses should be set at the same separation as infinity points in the stereogram. Ideally, this separation would also match the eye spacing.

It is a useful exercise to view a stereogram by starting with the lenses at maximum separation and slowly moving them to their closest setting. It is not recommended that this is done too often as the resulting eyestrain is somewhat uncomfortable. The image changes continuously during this adjustment, but it may take a few attempts before one appreciates exactly what is going on. As the lenses move closer, the stereo image, which initially appears slightly restricted in depth, becomes more natural and less compressed; it will appear to increase in size, becoming less like a scale model and more like a full-sized version of the subject. These changes are actually quite subtle but should be recognised more easily with experience.

At first one might expect that moving the lenses closer would have a similar effect on the image as increasing the eye separation, namely that the image would appear to reduce in depth rather than increase. However, the circumstances are rather different from those discussed in the previous section. The presence of viewing lenses provides an extra factor in the perception of the image.

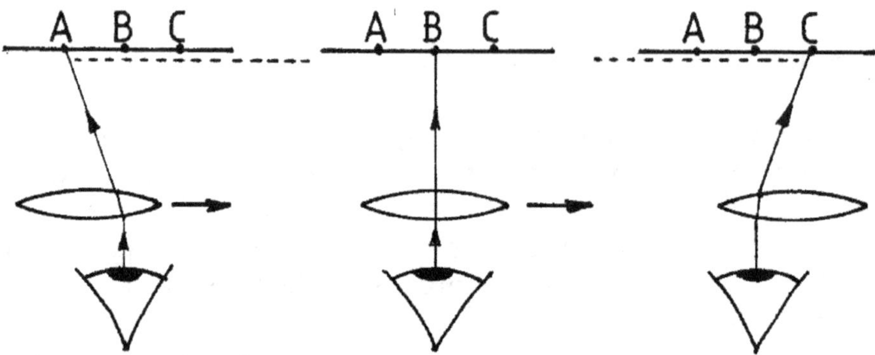

Fig 18.9
Varying the interocular spacing in a stereoscope. The sequence from left to right shows the apparent movement of the image for the left eye as the lens moves from left to right. The dotted lines give the apparent positions of the image at the start and end of the operation.

What happens here is that the principal line of sight for each eye is deviated according to the position of the stereoscope lens in front of it. As the lens moves past the left eye, for instance, from left to right, the sight line is made to scan the film chip in the same direction, as the sequence of drawings in **Fig 18.9** should make clear. The effect for the right eye is similar but the opposite way round. Reading from left to right in **Fig 18.9**, the left lens of the stereoscope moves to the right past the left eye. The line of sight initially passes through the lens at a point near to its right edge and the ray is refracted to point **A** on the image. With the lens in the central position, the sight line passes through the optical centre to point **B** on the image (the normal viewing position) without being deviated. When the lens is fully to the right, the sight line is deviated rightwards to point **C**. As the lens moves, points **A**, **B** and **C** in turn appear to lie straight ahead. In fact it appears that the image is moving from right to left. This apparent shift in image position may not be obvious when viewing with both eyes at the same time, but is very apparent if one eye is closed during the exercise.

In summary, as the lenses of the stereoscope are moved closer to each other, the two images appear to move further apart; this accounts for the increase in depth and shift of the overall subject to greater distances that are observed.

CHAPTER 19: THE DISTORTED STEREO IMAGE

19.1 The Imperfect Image

The main conclusion to be drawn from Chapter 18 is that it is very difficult to achieve orthostereoscopic viewing conditions in the majority of situations. Nevertheless, getting as close as possible to the perfect image should always be a priority.

One might well challenge this aim as being a waste of effort, because the brain will tend to accept significant degeneration of images without the observer apparently even noticing that anything is "wrong". There is always a psychological factor in the interpretation of stereo images. Although the eyes may be fed with information indicating that an object is half its normal size, the brain appears to "correct" this impression and the observer subconsciously doubles all dimensions and sees the object as being full size, at least if the object is a familiar one. All the same, a near-perfect image is more likely to produce comments such as "it's just like being there" than an image that is severely distorted.

In this chapter, the factors that cause various image distortions will be analysed, quantitatively as far as possible, so that the magnitudes of any changes can be appreciated. This will provide the necessary information on how distortion can be controlled and minimised.

19.2 Deformations and Disturbances

The term "distortion" is really a general term that covers two types of image defect, namely, **deformations** and disturbances, to use the terminology of Ferwerda[45], who discusses the various examples of these two forms of distortion but does not provide a general definition of either. The problem with formulating definitions is to ensure that they are all-inclusive. Too many exceptions challenge the validity of the definition. For that reason, the following definitions are offered with some reservations:

Deformation - a change in shape, dimensions or location (or any combination of these) of an image that has the potential to be viewed as an orthostereoscopic one. Such changes are in theory correctable.

Examples are stretch and squeeze, as outlined in Chapter 18, Section 18.3.3.

Despite the reference to orthostereoscopic viewing and the ability to correct a deformation, in practice neither may be possible. An example should resolve this apparent paradox. To human eyes, a landscape photographed as a hyperstereoscopic pair, using a stereo base of 10m, will appear as a scale model when viewed. No amount of adjusting the film chip positions will ever remove this deformation, but to a giant with a 10m eye spacing the stereo image would appear as an orthostereoscopic one if the infinity separation were to be set at 10m. From our standpoint the deformation (one of scale) cannot be corrected, because we cannot increase our eye separation, but the stereo pair is hypothetically viewable as an undistorted image.

Disturbance - this is a distortion that is a result of differences between the two images that are not caused by parallax. A disturbance is not correctable, unlike a deformation, because it is a permanent feature.

Examples will serve to clarify this definition:

1. an object (or part of one) "floating" or receding nearer or further than its true position in space because of movement between sequential exposures
2. a difference in scale between the two images, either in the whole area of view or part of it
3. a height error resulting from the stereo camera not being horizontal at the time of exposure.
4. images rotated during mounting to "correct" a height error. There are still likely to be residual non-homologous areas in the images.
5. left and right images that do not belong to each other, e.g. a stereo "pair" consisting of a circle (L) and a square (R). The brain will be unable to fuse these and the images will come and go alternately, a case of "retinal rivalry". This is an extreme example of a disturbance.

All these represent image differences that are in a quite separate category from the proper and acceptable ones, namely parallax deviations.

There are a few distortions that are best described as disturbances, even though they do not fit our definition precisely, because they are reversible and not permanent. They are best regarded as special cases.

19.3 Origins and Analysis of Deformations
19.3.1 Introduction

The easiest way to tackle the subject of distortions and their control is to consider the variables that give rise to them rather than to examine each distortion in turn. This is because the individual distortions are not easy to recognise without some experience in viewing stereograms. Studying the causes will lead more directly to the solutions.

The starting point for the analyses in the sections that follow is the orthostereoscopic image reconstruction shown in **Fig 18.4** in the previous chapter. As far as possible, the stereogram depicted in **Fig 18.4** will be used as a "standard".

19.3.2 Differing focal lengths of camera and stereoscope

The image in **Fig 18.4b** is reconstructed for viewing lenses of focal length identical to that of the camera lenses (**f**). **Figs 19. 1a** and **19.1b** show the effect on the image of reducing or increasing the focal length of the stereoscope lenses. When the viewing focal length is less than **f**, the image is squeezed and brought closer to the observer; when it is greater, the image is stretched and moved further away from its orthostereoscopic location. Usually, the focal length of the stereoscope lens is the larger, which means that the observer is more likely to encounter stretch deformation in practice.

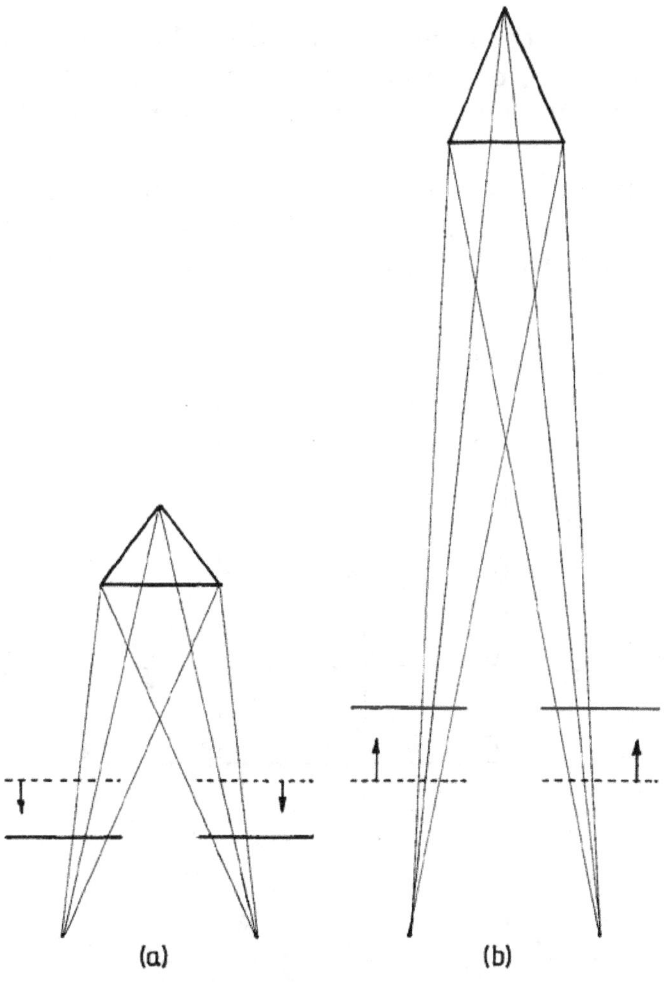

Fig 19.1

Effect of **a**. *shorter and* **b**. *longer focal length lenses in a stereoscope (relative to the camera lens focal length). In* **a**, *the image is closer and squeezed, whereas in* **b** *it is more distant and stretched. The dotted lines indicate the stereogram position for orthostereoscopic viewing. Image width remains constant.*

The quantitative effect of focal length differences can be derived from **Fig 19.2**. The two positions of the stereogram, **1** and **2**, relate to the focal lengths **f** and **f'** respectively. Homologous points **h** and **h'** produce a point image at **X** located at distance **D** for orthostereoscopic viewing, and at **X'**, distance **D'** when the focal length of the lenses is increased from **f** to **f'**. The parallax deviation for **h** and **h'** is **d**.

From similar triangles, the familiar relationships:

$$\mathbf{d = fb/D} \text{ and } \mathbf{d = f'b/D'} \text{ apply.}$$
Hence $$\mathbf{D' = Df'/f}$$

Thus any point in the image will be shifted to a new location **f'/f** times its original distance. The distance increases when **f'** is greater than **f** and decreases when **f'** is smaller than **f**. This also applies to the position of the stereo window.

Although the factor **f'/f** is constant for a given pair of focal lengths, the amount of image shift increases as **D** increases. The more distant parts of an image shift more than the nearer parts.

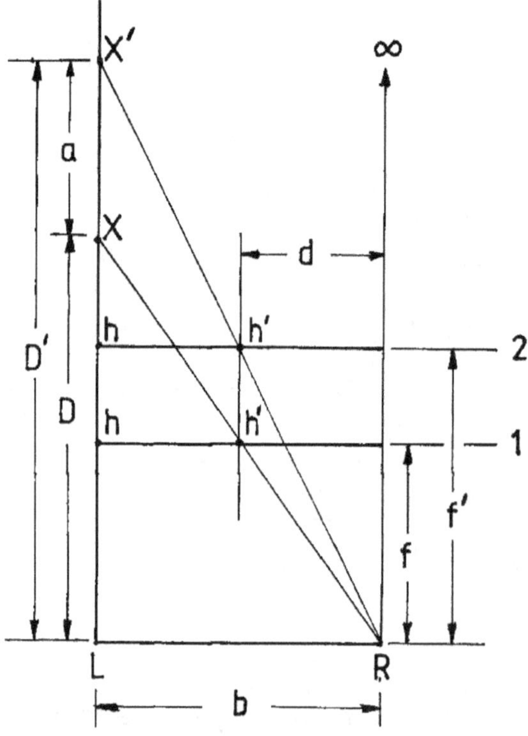

Fig 19.2
*Effect of stereoscope focal length on the image. With the stereogram in position 1 (orthostereoscopic viewing) homologues **h** and **h'** give a point image at **X**. With a longer focal length **f'**, the image is at **X'**.*

However, the width remains constant (as does the height) and the combination of constant width and variable depth is responsible for the stretch or squeeze observed.

If the amount of apparent movement is denoted by **a**, for a point at distance **D** for orthostereoscopic conditions, then a direct expression for **a** can be derived as follows:

$$\mathbf{a} = \mathbf{D'} - \mathbf{D} = (\mathbf{Df'}/\mathbf{f}) - \mathbf{D}$$
$$= \mathbf{D(f' - f)/f}$$

The constancy of width can be derived from **Fig 19.3**.

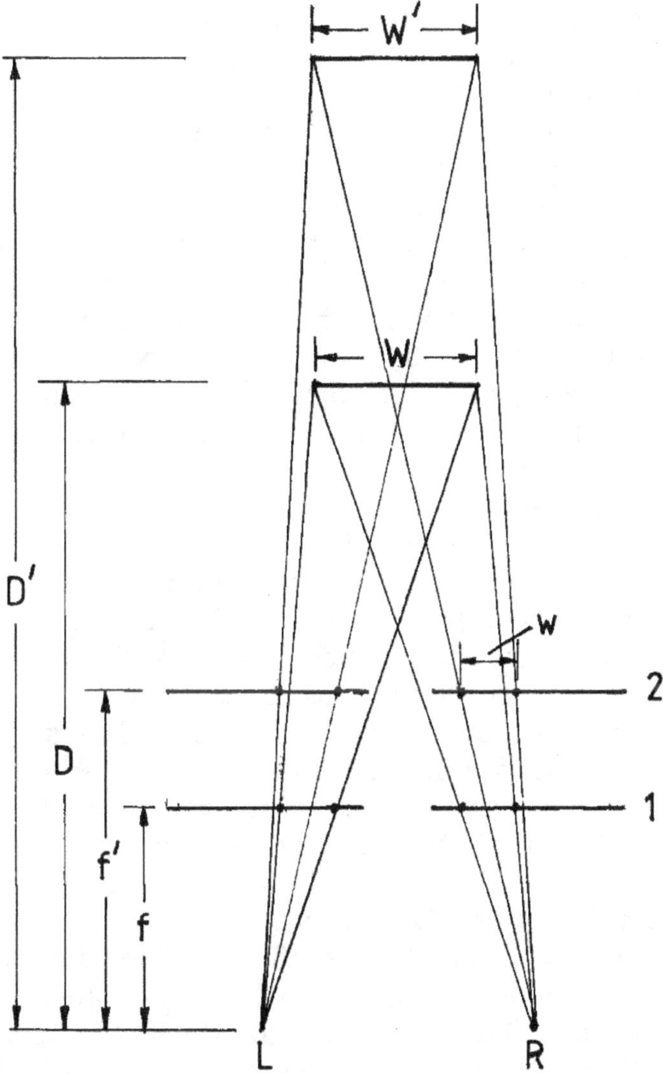

Fig 19.3
*Viewing a stereogram orthostereoscopically (position **1**) gives an image width* **W** *at distance* **D**. *Increasing the focal length to* **f** *moves the image to distance* **D'**. *Its width* **W'** *can be shown to be equal to* **W**.

An image on film of width **w** on each of the two film chips of a stereogram is seen as a stereo image of width **W** under orthostereoscopic viewing conditions (position **1**) and as an image of width **W'** when the lens focal length is increased from **f** to **f'**.

From similar triangles:

$$\mathbf{w} = \mathbf{Wf/D} \text{ and } \mathbf{w} = \mathbf{W'f'/D'}$$

Hence $$\mathbf{W'} = \mathbf{WfD'/f'D}$$

But $\mathbf{D'/D} = \mathbf{f'/f}$ (as shown earlier)

Therefore $\mathbf{W'} = \mathbf{W}$

This means that as the image moves towards or away from the observer as a result of focal length changes its size (in terms of its width and/or height as opposed to depth) remains constant, just like that of a real object placed at different distances. It appears smaller or larger only as a result of the "rules" of perspective.

As an example, consider the image of a cube of 1m side located at 5m distance from the observer when viewed orthostereoscopically. This replicates the original object location. If the stereogram is photographed with 35mm lenses and viewed with 45mm lenses then the front face (with the cube viewed square on) will appear to lie at(5 x 45)/35 = 6.43m.

The back face will lie at (6 x 45)/35 = 7.71m. Thus the depth of the image has increased from 1m to 1.28m while its width remains at 1m. The stretch effect is now clear.

When projected images are being viewed, stretch or squeeze will be experienced in seating positions on the centre screen axis other than in the orthostereo seat. Observers closer to the screen than the **OSS** will see a squeezed image while those further away will see a stretched one. Sitting closer to or further away from the screen is equivalent to viewing in a stereoscope with shorter or longer (than the ideal) focal length lenses respectively. The further away from the **OSS**, the greater will be the deformation. Other observers in the audience will also experience oblique deformation, alone or in combination with one of the other deformations, depending on their location. This will be discussed in Section 19.3.5.

19.3.3 Different stereo base for viewing

Fig 19.4a and **b** illustrate the effect of viewing, with normal eye separation, a stereo pair photographed with a larger stereo base. The stereo image appears nearer than the subject of the actual scene and will be perceived as a scale model, this effect being termed **lilliputism**. Apart from this, no other deformations (such as stretch or squeeze) will be present.

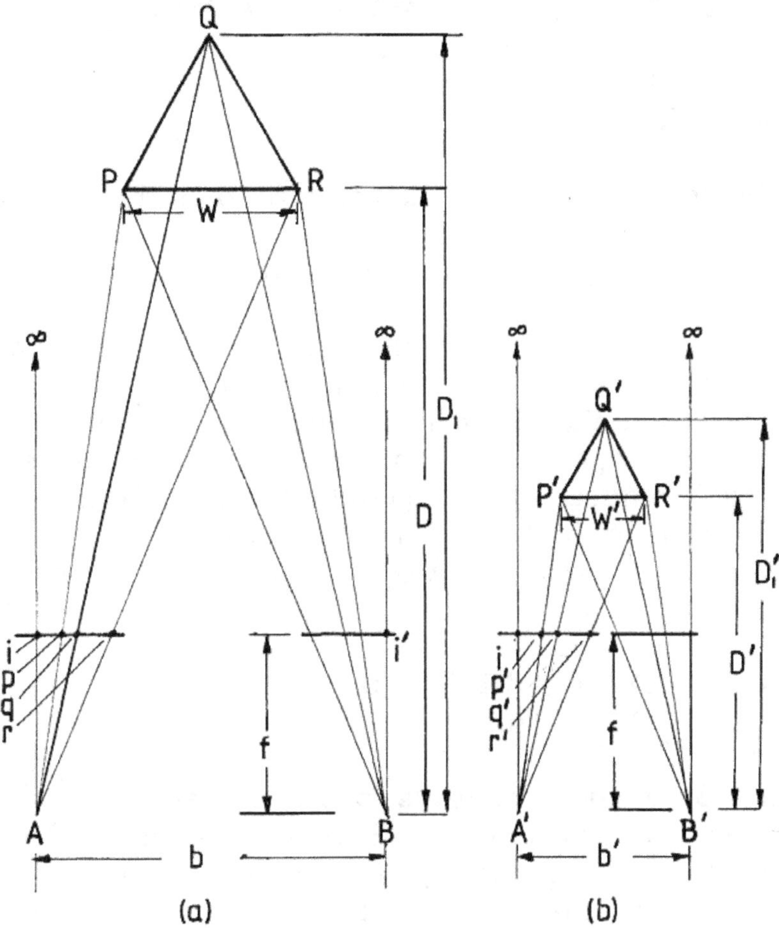

Fig 19.4
a *Hyperstereoscopic image taken with base* **b**. *Reconstruction of the image as it would be seen if viewed with an identical, large (hypothetical) eye spacing.* **b** *The same image viewed with a smaller base* **b**' *(in this case* **b**' = **b**/2*). The image is scaled down and closer.*

Whatever the technique actually employed, the stereo pair can be regarded as being produced in a super-large stereo camera with an inter-lens spacing of **b**. To view these as a 3D image the film chips have to be moved closer so that the original separation of infinity points **i**, **i**' is reduced from **b** to **b**'. The focal lengths of the camera and stereoscope lenses are the same, so triangles **ipqrA** and **i'p'q'r'A'** are identical, in fact, all angular relationships are maintained. Hence, triangles **APB** and **A'P'B'** are similar, which means that:

$$\mathbf{D/b} = \mathbf{D'/b'}$$

i.e. $\mathbf{D' = Db'/b}$

Also from similar triangles **AQB** and **A'Q'B'**, $\mathbf{D_1' = D_1 b'/b}$, and likewise for all points of the image.

From the similar trapeziums **APRB** and **A'P'R'B'**:

$$W/b = W'/b'$$
So $\quad W' = Wb'/b$

Thus the width changes in the same ratio as the other dimensions, unlike the case discussed in Section 19.3.2. The significance of this is that the image retains its proportions, in other words it becomes a reduced scale model.

In hypostereoscopy, the viewing stereo base is larger than the taking base and so the image is magnified, again in proportion. This can be visualised by regarding **Fig 19.4b** as the situation in camera and **Fig 19.4a** as that in the stereoscope. This magnification is referred to as **giantism**.

The image is reduced (or enlarged) by the factor **b'/b**, that is the ratio of the stereo bases ("viewing" base/ "taking" base).

Again, a direct expression for the actual shift, **a**, of any point, can be derived:

$$a \quad = D' - D = (Db'/b) - D$$
$$= D(b' - b)/b$$

19.3.4 Separation of the film chips in the mount

As pointed out in Section 18.3.3, there is a correlation between the effect on the stereo image of varying the film chip spacing and the differences in the form of the image as seen by observers with different eye separations. An increase in eye spacing of **s** will have a similar effect as shifting the chips by a smaller amount **s'** (geometrically related to **s**) closer together, but the link between **s** and **s'** is more complex than it might appear.

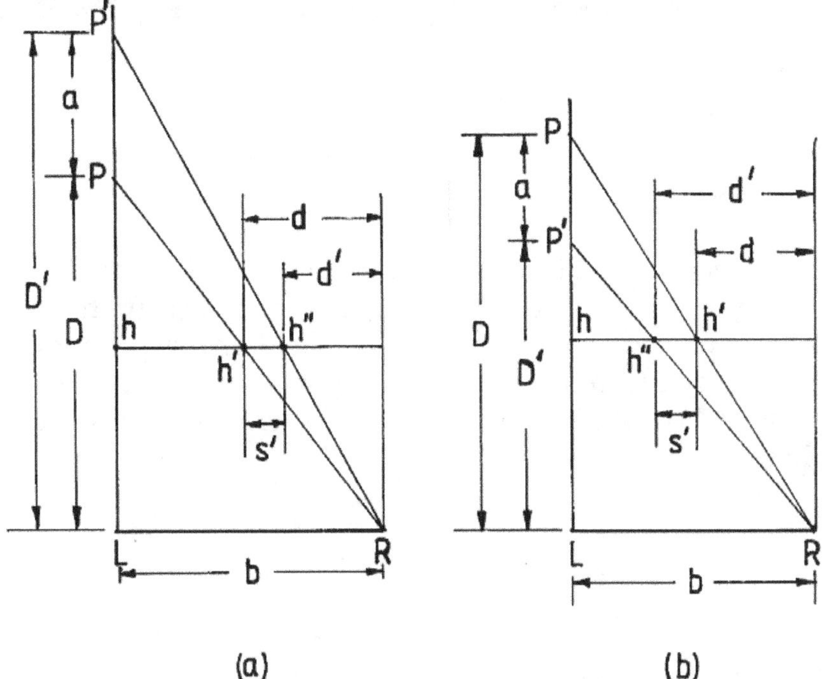

(a)   (b)

Fig 19.5
*Effect on the image of moving the film chips relative to the mount apertures by an amount **s'** outwards (**a**) or inwards (**b**). Homologues **h** and **h'** are on the left and right chips respectively. Image point **P** moves to **P'** in each case and the parallax deviation is changed from **d** to **d'**.*

In **Fig 19.5a**, **h** and **h'** are two homologues giving a point image at **P**, at a distance **D**. If the right film chip is moved to the right by an amount **s'** as shown, **h'** moves to **h"** and **P** goes to **P'**. The parallax deviations of **h'** and **h"** are **d** and **d'** respectively, where:

$$\mathbf{d' = d - s'}$$

From the familiar relationships **d** = **Db/f** and **d'** = **D'b/f**:

$$\mathbf{D' = Dd/(d - s')}$$

The image shift **a** is found as follows:

$$\mathbf{a = D' - D = D(d/(d - s') - 1)}$$

which simplifies to

$$\mathbf{a = Ds'/(d - s')}$$

When the film chips are moved closer together, as in **Fig 19.5b**, a similar analysis gives:

$$D' = Dd/(d + s')$$

And $\quad a = Ds'/(d + s')$

As was pointed out in Chapter 18. Section 18.3.3, there is a similarity between the image deformations as seen by observers with different eye separations and those caused by shifts in the film chip separation. The image shift caused by an increase in eye separation **s** can be equated to a film chip shift inwards of **s'** which produces an identical change for an object at a specific distance.

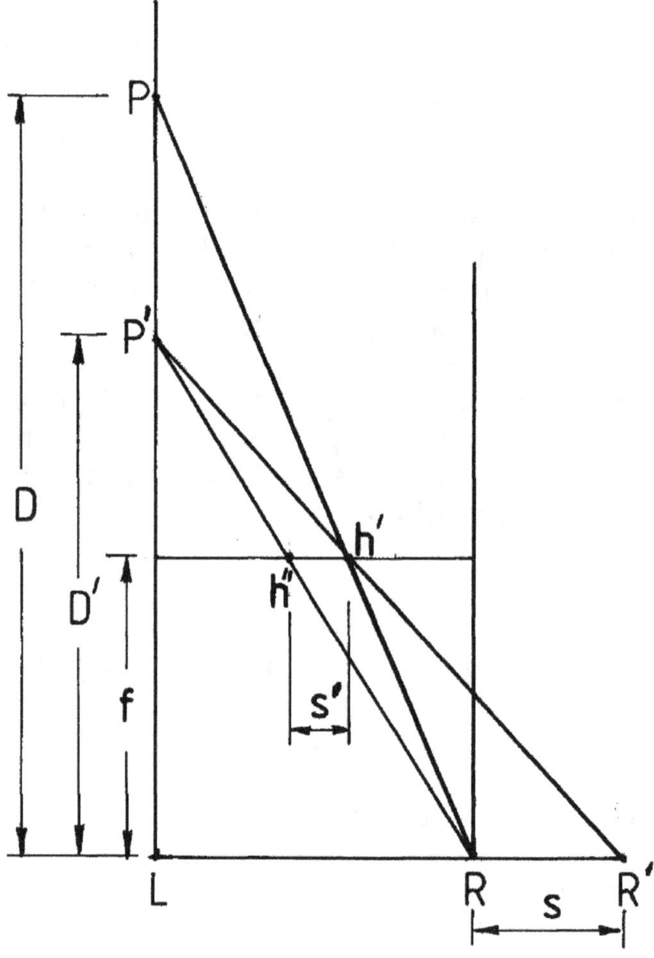

Fig 19.6
*Relationship between a film chip shift **s'** and increase in eye separation **s** for a given image change.*

Fig 19.6, which combines the key features of **Figs 18.8** and **19.5**, shows the geometric relationship between the two factors. Image point **P** shifts to **P'** either by moving the right film chip leftwards (homologue **h'** moves to **h"**) by an amount **s'** or by viewing the chips with an increased eye separation **LR'** (with the film chips in their original locations). The increase in eye separation is **s**. The diagram shows clearly that **s** is greater than **s'**.

From similar triangles **P'h'h"** and **P'RR'**:

$$\mathbf{s}/\mathbf{D}' = \mathbf{s}'/(\mathbf{D}' - \mathbf{f})$$

i.e. $\quad \mathbf{s}/\mathbf{s}' = \mathbf{D}'/(\mathbf{D}' - \mathbf{f})$

The value of this ratio varies with the value of **D'** so there will be no single correspondence of **s** and **s'** over the entire subject depth range. The two expressions above for image shift **a** (one for chip separation and the other for variation in eye separation) can be used to calculate the differences in image perception. For example, moving the film chips further apart by 0.2mm from the correct setting in the Realist format will shift an object originally at 2m to a new distance of 2.4m. At the same time, an object at 10m will move to 50m. Now, someone whose eye separation is smaller by an amount 0.203mm will also see the 2m object shift to 2.4m, but in this case the 10m object will move further, to just over 53m. The stretch effect is thus different in the two situations.

Shifting the film chips laterally, in either direction, causes not only a relocation of the image in space but a distortion called **frustum deformation**. This is displayed in **Fig 19.7** in which the image **ABCD** represents a cylinder in plan, **AD** and **BC** being the circular ends. If it is regarded as a hollow tube then both circular ends will be visible. The image **ABCD** with the film chips properly separated, as shown by the homologues **a**, **a₁**, **b**, **b₁** etc., is orthostereoscopic. When the film chips are moved closer, as indicated by the new positions of the homologues **a'**, **a₁'** etc., the image is also shifted nearer, to a position **A'B'C'D'**. Clearly, the new image shows compression and its plan view is no longer rectangular but trapezoidal. This means that the overall shape resembles a frustum, part of a cone, with, in this case, the wider end nearer to the observer.

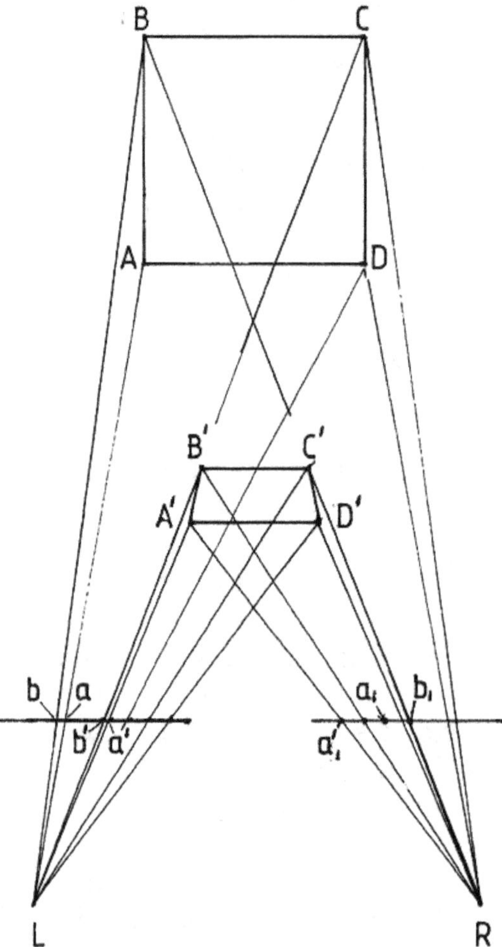

Fig 19.7
*Frustum distortion caused by moving the film chips closer together than the separation required for orthostereoscopic viewing. Homologues **a**, **b** etc. move to **a**', **b**' etc. and the image transforms from **ABCD** to **A'B'C'D'**.*

    This deformation can be attributed to the fact that the width of any part of the image is reduced by an amount which depends on the original depth location of that part. The "face" **AD** is reduced in width to **A'D'**. The width of face **BC**, further away, is reduced more, to **B'C'**, which is smaller than **A'D'**. The original depth of the object (the distance between **AD** and **BC**) is reduced to the distance between **A'D'** and **B'C'**.

    Moving the chips further apart from the original position will cause the image to move back, stretch and again exhibit frustum deformation, but in the reverse sense, with the back face being larger. This is illustrated in **Fig 19.8** in simpler form.

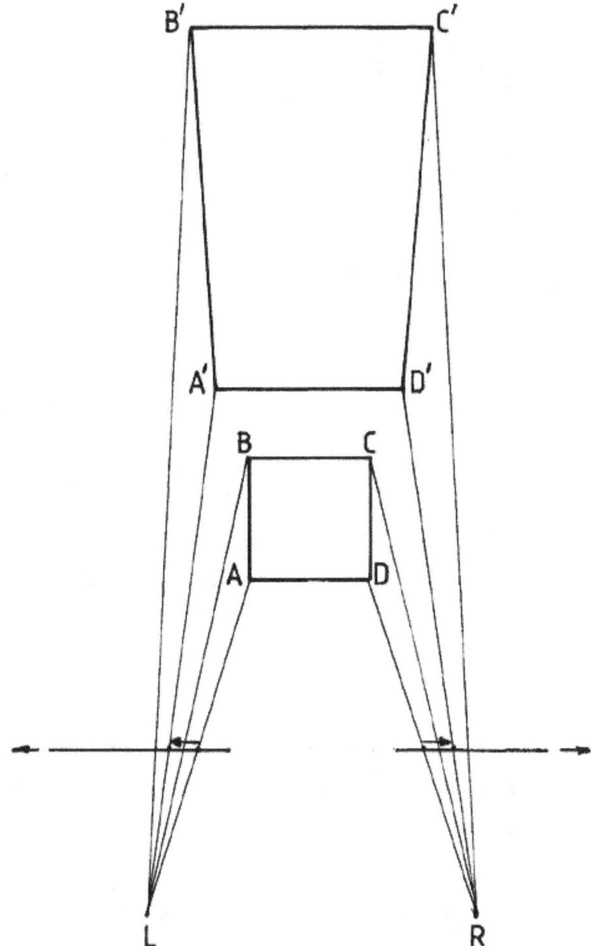

Fig 19.8
Alternative form of frustum distortion caused by moving the film chips too far apart.

The effect can be visualised from **Fig 19.7** by regarding **A'B'C'D'** as the original image which transforms to **ABCD**. The greater increase in width of the rear face should be clear (though here the starting image is not cylindrical as in **Fig 19.8**.

The deformation can easily be visualised by considering the infinity sight lines. If they diverge away from the observer then any parallel-sided object seen end-on will appear to get wider towards the far end, the sides diverging in the same way as the sight lines. Objects further away will thus appear bigger than when seen orthostereoscopically. Conversely, when the sight lines converge away from the observer, the more distant objects will seem smaller than they should.

It should be pointed out that the effect is quite a subtle one and may only become obvious in a real situation if the image is a simple geometric shape and the change in separation of the film chips is large.

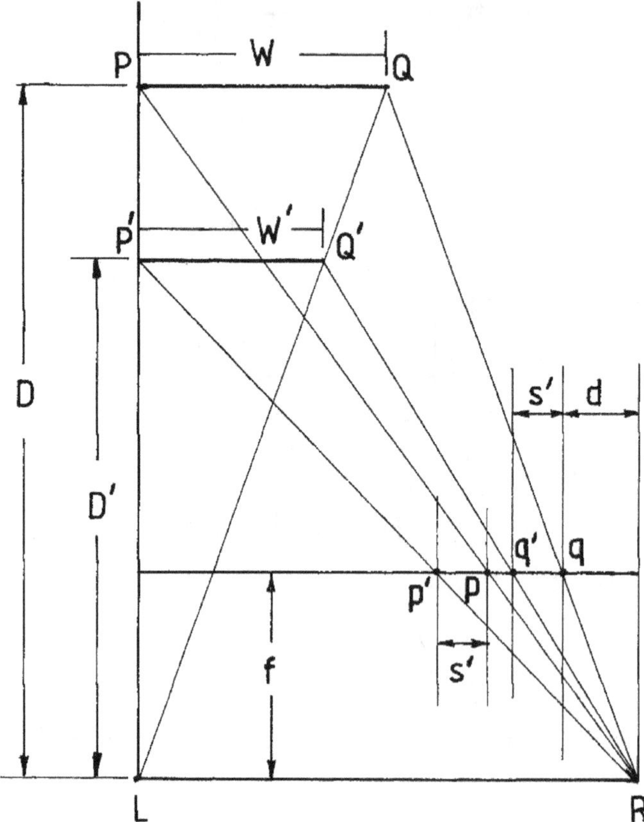

Fig 19.9
Change in width of an image due to changes in film chip separation. In this diagram the right chip is moved closer to the left chip by an amount **s'**.*Homologues* **p** *and* **q** *on the right chip move to* **p'** *and* **q'** *respectively. The image at* **PQ** *shifts to* **P'Q'** *and its width decreases from* **W** *to* **W'**.

The variation in image width with film chip separation can be deduced from **Fig 19.9**. In this diagram, **PQ** represents a linear image of width **W**, with point **P** on the left eye axis for convenience. A lateral inward shift of the right film chip of **s'** causes the image to move to **P'Q'**, from a distance **D** to **D'** and the width to decrease to a new value, **W'**. From similar triangles:

$$\mathbf{W'/W = D'/D}$$
$$\text{i.e.} \quad \mathbf{W' = WD'/D}$$

Since, as shown earlier $\quad \mathbf{D' = Dd/(d + s')}$:

Therefore $\quad \mathbf{W' = Wd/(d + s')}$

In this case, **W'** is smaller than **W**. When the chips are moved outward the relationship between film movement and width is:

$$\mathbf{W'} = \mathbf{Wd}/(\mathbf{d} - \mathbf{s'})$$

where **W'** will be greater than **W**.

An example will give some idea of the scale of the deformation. If an image of a cube of 1m side is seen orthostereoscopically at a distance of 5m (front face location), the effect of moving the film chips closer by 0.3mm can be calculated as follows:

Taking **f** = 35mm focal length, **b** = 65mm stereo base, we have **W** = 1000mm and **D** = 5000mm (near face) and 6000mm (far face). The values of deviation **d** for front and rear faces of the cube are calculated from **d** = **fb**/**D**. The film chip shift is 0.3mm.

Deviation **d** for the front face is (35 x 65)/5000 = 0.455mm.

For the rear face **d** is (35 x 65)/6000 = 0.379mm.

Front face; D' = **Dd**/(**d** + **s'**) = (5000 x 0.455)/(0.455 + 0.3) = 3013mm.
        W' = **Wd**/(**d** + **s'**) = (1000 x 0.455)/(0.455 + 0.3) = 603mm.

Rear face; **D'** = (6000 x 0.379)/(0.379 + 0.3) = 3349mm.
        W' = (1000 x 0.379)/(0.379 + 0.3) = 558mm.

This calculation shows that the cube is nearer (front face at about 3m instead of 5m), its depth (front to back) is 3349 – 3013 = 336mm, considerably less than its new width of 603mm at the front. Also, the width at the rear is less than that at the front, at 558mm, clearly demonstrating the frustum distortion. The depth to width ratio of roughly 1:2 shows the compression effect

The equivalent situation in viewing images projected onto a screen occurs when the infinity points are set closer or further apart than the norm. The extreme example is when the infinity points are actually superimposed on the screen. In this case, the infinity sight lines from the eyes converge and meet at the screen to define infinity. The entire image will now lie in front of the screen as a miniature version of the original scene and this configuration is termed the **puppet theatre** or **marionette theatre** effect. With incorrectly separated infinity points, frustum distortion will also be present. This is not the same as **lilliputism** (see Section 19.3.3), in which the image is an exact scale model of the original, with no other form of distortion present.

The puppet theatre effect will still be present when the infinity homologues, even though not coincident, are closer than the correct spacing. In this case the image will lie partly behind and partly in front of the screen. A similar effect occurs with "crossed-eye" free viewing of prints because the infinity sight lines from the two eyes will cross in front of the print surfaces, placing infinity at that distance. There will also be some convergence distortion (Section 19.4.7) as each of the two component images is being viewed obliquely.

19.3.5 Oblique deformation

This form of distortion is a result of the observer viewing a stereogram at an oblique angle, in other words not from a viewpoint on the central axis. This can occur in projection, free viewing and when viewing with lorgnettes. Any optical device in which the location of the stereogram is not fixed in relation to the eye position would be prone to the effect. In Brewster, Holmes and many other stereoscopes, this distortion will not arise.

Viewing of a projected image is depicted in **Fig 19.10**, in which L_1 and R_1 represent the eye positions for orthostereoscopic viewing.

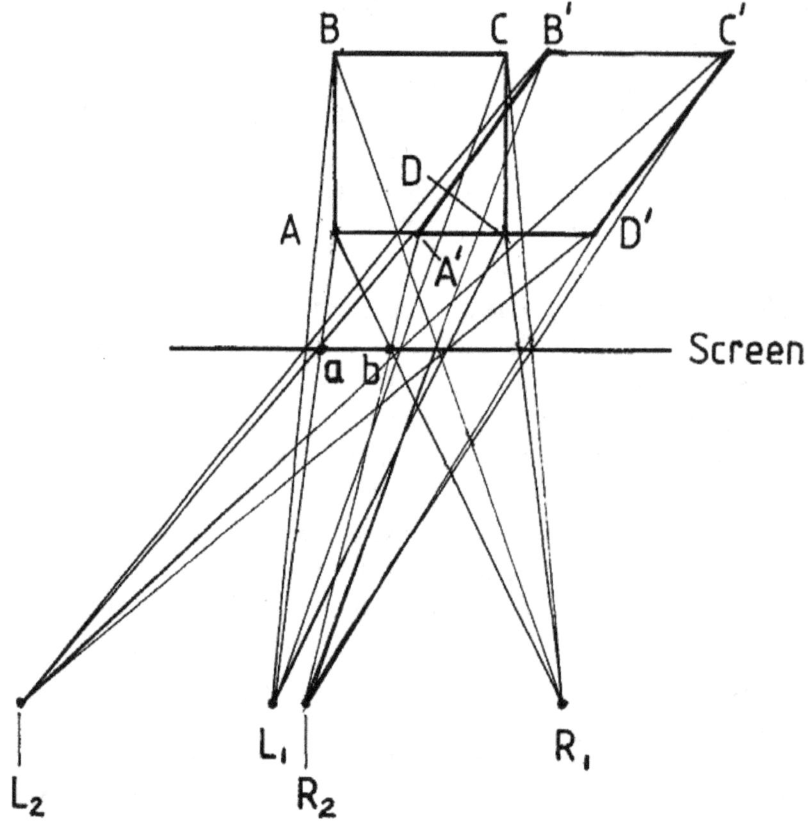

Fig 19.10

Oblique deformation as experienced by an observer viewing from a position (L₂R₂) to one side of the orthostereoscopic seat (eye positions L₁R₁)

The image **ABCD**, in the form of an open-fronted box shape, is orthostereoscopic as seen from eye positions L_1R_1. It is generated from the homologous points **a**, **b** etc. on the screen. If the observer moves to a new viewing position L_2R_2, the image becomes distorted obliquely into the shape **A'B'C'D'**. The observer-screen distance (measured at right angles to the screen) is unchanged from that at L_1R_1. The greater the distance from the centre line, the greater will be the distortion. The effect has been exaggerated in the diagram by placing the eye positions much closer to the screen than would be the case in an actual viewing. In reality the effect will be subtler, and perhaps not even noticed by most observers.

If the observer moves from L_2R_2 closer to the screen, then squeeze deformation will be superimposed onto the oblique deformation. If further away from the screen, the observer will experience a superimposed stretching of the image.

Consideration of triangles L_1AR_1 and $L_2A'R_2$ shows that **ab** is common to both and they have equal bases, since $L_1R_1 = L_2R_2$. Therefore, from standard geometry, their heights will be identical. This means that **A'** is at exactly the same distance behind the screen as **A**. This applies to all points on the image, so the image does not move forward or back with the change in eye positions as long as the observer-screen distance is unaltered.

Apart from the obliqueness of the image, there may be a psychological factor in how it is perceived. In the **OSS** the observer will see the image shown in **Fig 19.10** as an open-fronted box. Whatever his position in the room, he will see the sides **AB** and **CD** from the inside. If **ABCD** were an actual box and not an image, the spectator, by moving from L_1R_1 to L_2R_2 would expect to see the outside of the box along **AB**, as shown in **Fig 19.11a**. Instead, the image appears essentially the same as it was when viewed centrally (as in **Fig 19.11b**), except that it now suffers oblique deformation, of course.

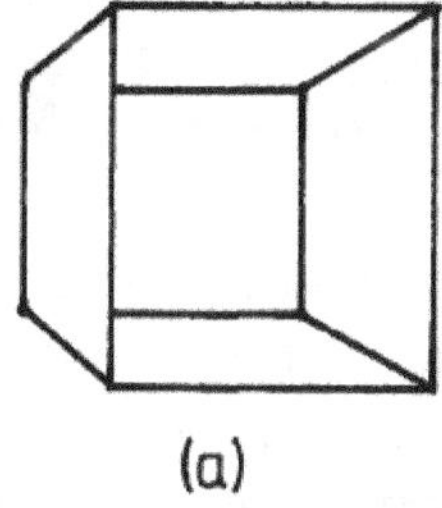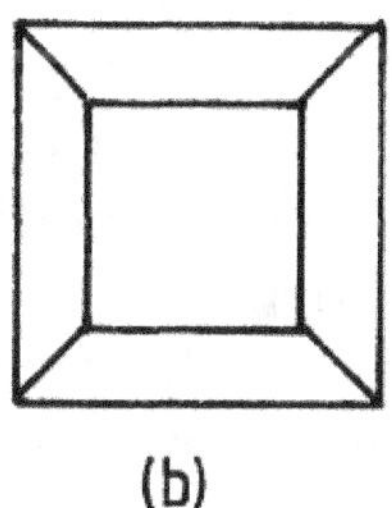

(a)   (b)

Fig 19.11
a *Oblique view of an open-fronted box*
b *Screen image of an open box which will appear the same from all spectator positions. Psychologically, one would expect to see the image as in **a** from left-of-centre positions.*

19.3.6 Pseudoscopy

This is not a serious problem, for it occurs only when the two images of the stereo pair are placed in the "wrong" positions for normal viewing. In most stereoscopes and viewing systems, the left image is usually located on the left and the right image on the right. Transposing the film chips or prints from their correct positions causes all the depth information to be reversed. Near parts of the image become distant and vice versa. The results can often look rather odd because objects that are partly obscured by nearer ones in the normal image appear to have gaps in the pseudoscopic configuration. Concavities in the original image become convexities, so everything is turned inside out. In some cases, with very familiar subjects such as human faces and figures, the brain finds great difficulty in accepting the transformations, and the observer might see that part of the image in normal relief; the brain can sometimes override the information received by the eyes, by some mechanism that is not well understood.

The effect can arise by accident during mounting if the film chips are simply confused, and the problem is soon put right by remounting them in their correct configuration. However, some photographs lend themselves to deliberate pseudoscopic treatment to produce an abstract effect. Some workers recommend mounting the chips upside-down to enhance the abstract nature of the image.

19.3.7 Summary

Having completed the analysis of deformations from the standpoint of their causes, it may be helpful to summarise the information on the basis of the individual deformations:

1. **stretch**: this is caused by the focal length of the stereoscope being greater than that of the camera, or by the observer being too far away from the mounted or projected image in relation to its size. The remedy is to match the camera and stereoscope lenses or to view the image from a closer position.
2. **squeeze**: opposite to the above. The stereoscope lenses have too short a focal length or the observer is too close. The remedy is to match the lenses or for the observer to sit further away.
3. **lilliputism**: the image is smaller than life-size The stereo base for viewing is smaller than that used in taking the picture. This is an unavoidable situation in hyperstereoscopy.
4. **giantism**: the image is larger than life-size. The stereo base for viewing is greater than that used for taking the picture. This is an unavoidable situation in hypostereoscopy.
5. **frustum deformation**: the two images are set at an incorrect separation in the mount or on the screen, converting a cylindrical shape into a frustum caused by the infinity point sight lines not

being set parallel to each other. If the infinity points are too far apart, the wider end of the frustum is furthest away; if too close, the wider end is nearer. The remedy is to reset the image separation.

6. **oblique deformation**: rectangular shapes are distorted into parallelograms with adjacent sides no longer at right angles. This is a consequence of viewing the stereogram from a position off the centre line. The remedy is to ensure that the viewing position is centralised. With projected images such distortion is inevitable from most parts of the room.

7. **pseudoscopy**: left and right images are transposed in relation to their proper positions in the mount. Corrected by exchanging their positions.

19.4 Origins and Analysis of Disturbances
19.4.1 Introduction

Most disturbances arise from differences, other than parallax deviations, between the two images of the stereogram. Once present, they cannot generally be neutralised either by altering the viewing conditions or the mounting procedure, apart from a few exceptions. Some can be avoided by using proper techniques when the photograph is taken. Others may be unavoidable but can be minimised, again by careful choice of procedure at appropriate stages in the production of the stereogram.

Broadly, the effect of all disturbances is to create some eyestrain or cause some difficulty in fusing the images, so it is not appropriate to analyse them in the same way as deformations; it is simpler to study each in turn. Some are very straightforward and will not require a lengthy explanation.

19.4.2 False stereo effect

This occurs when part of a subject changes its position during the time period between the two separate exposures when using the sequential method. Typical examples are leaves blowing in the wind, or distant figures or vehicles in continuous motion. All one can do is to be aware of the problem when taking the photographs and attempt to avoid it. If the moving objects are far away, as, for example, traffic viewed from the top of a skyscraper, the effect will hardly be noticed. As discussed in Chapter 11, Section 11.6, the principle can be employed deliberately to produce trick shots or special effects.

19.4.3 Differences in scale

Although there may be some cases where only part of the total image is affected, usually this problem will involve the whole of it. The principal causes of scale differences are:

i.   differences in the enlargement factor of two prints or drawings

ii.   differences in the focal lengths of the two lenses of a stereo camera, or the lenses of two mono cameras

iii.   use of two mono cameras in a fixture where one camera is set partly behind the other (see Chapter 4, Fig 4.17c).

The chances of (i) occurring are rather remote, but one should at least recognise it as a possible source of error. Regarding (ii), the manufacturers of stereo cameras will normally ensure that the two lenses are carefully matched, so again the problem will rarely come from this source. When two separate cameras are used in tandem, however, it is a matter of chance as to whether there is a significant difference in focal lengths or not, even with identical models of a particular brand. Without knowing the tolerances to which a manufacturer works, the maximum possible difference cannot be estimated. What can be said is that many photographers using twin cameras bought "as seen", as it were, seem to find few problems with scale difference. Perfectionists will take the trouble to measure the focal lengths of their camera lenses and will probably demand something like no more than 1% difference in values. Certainly, those who build their own stereo cameras, often for particular techniques such as close-up work, will do so, often creating two matching lenses by grinding both from a single, larger lens.

One has to realise that a 1% difference, say, between the scale of two images will be more noticeable for those parts of the subject that occupy a large proportion of the frame. An object whose image is 20mm in height in one film chip would be 0.2mm taller (or shorter) in the other, and 0.2mm is a significant difference on this scale, in a projected image, this will be magnified perhaps 50 times or more. The difference is far less on an object occupying only 2mm height in the film chip.

19.4.4 Height errors (1)

If the two images of a stereo pair are taken at different levels, there will be permanent differences in the heights of various objects within the scene relative to others at different distances. The tops of the two posts shown in **Fig 19.12a** lie on the same horizontal line when viewed at a certain eye-level. From a higher viewpoint, as in **Fig 19.12b**, the top of the far post will now be located higher up in the image than the top of the near post. Such a height error could easily be produced when taking sequential images, or with two cameras side-by-side with the lens of one higher than that of the other. Taking the two shots in this way introduces parallax deviations in the vertical direction, which is at odds with normal stereo practice. It will be impossible to mount the two images successfully unless the height differential is very small. Even so, there will be parts of the image that, to a greater or lesser extent, do not "gel". Because of the variation in levels of various homologous points, only one pair can be aligned horizontally at a time. The rest will be "out".

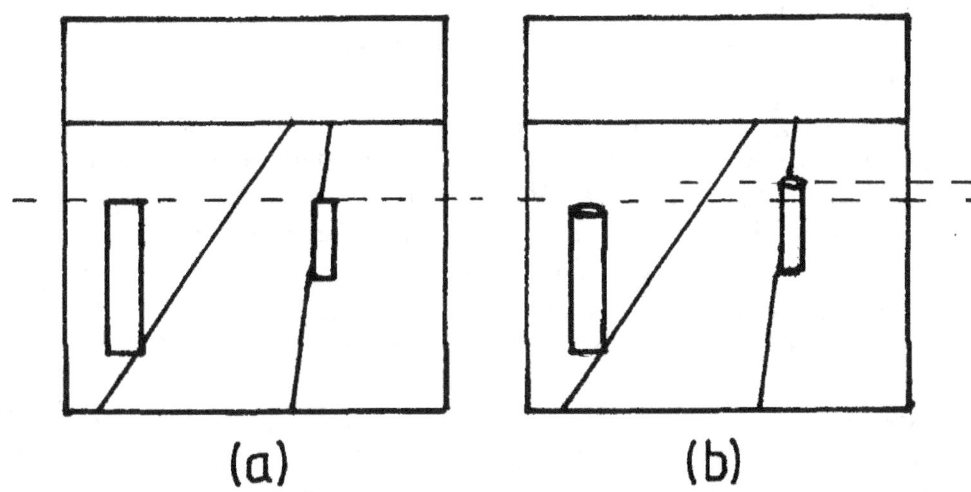

Fig 19.12
Illustrating height differences that can arise from sequential exposures.
a *Here the tops of the posts are in line in the left image.*
b *A height difference is present in the right image, taken from a slightly higher viewpoint. Also, the tops of the posts are now visible, and this will lead to a disturbance on viewing.*

19.4.5 Height errors (2)

When a stereo camera is tilted so that one lens is higher than the other, then height errors similar to those discussed in the previous section will result. However, the problem is compounded by the rotation and the situation is worsened. In this case the resulting stereogram can be mounted successfully, using normal procedures, but, of course, the final image will be tilted. The obvious way to remove the tilt is to rotate each of the film chips separately, in the manner of **Fig 6.7b**, Chapter 6, but this will not eliminate the discrepancies. Due to the tilt, homologous points close to the left and right frame edges will be at different levels in the separate images. Rotation of the chips changes the levels but does not eliminate the differences. Those parts of the image at the centre are less prone to height errors than those close to the frame edges; the discrepancies get worse moving outwards from the centre.

Other differences will appear when height errors are produced. The different vertical viewpoints imply that monocular areas in the vertical direction will appear as one lens "sees" part of the background not visible to the other. Referring again to the two posts in **Fig 19.12**, it could happen, for example, that the right image shows the top surfaces of the posts, whereas the left image, taken from a lower viewpoint, records them as straight edges. To summarise, the conditions that lead to height errors, as discussed in this and the previous section, will produce additional disturbances.

19.4.6 Disparities

This term is used for disturbances caused by significant differences in shape or colour between parts (or even the whole) of the subject in the left and right images. It also covers the case when a feature is present in one image but absent in the other. However, this does not include the monocular areas that are normally present in images because these are natural and proper ingredients of a correctly produced stereogram.

The definition implies image differences in the main stereoscopic area of the image, such as occur in the image of the top of the post discussed in Section 19.4.5 above. Examples of disparities are:

i.   any object that appears in only one image because it was absent for one of the shots in a sequentially taken stereo pair

ii.   a variation of the above - subjects like flowing water which, although present in both shots, are constantly changing

iii.   reflections that differ considerably in the two shots even when taken simultaneously because of the different angles of view. With highlights on rippling water and the like, it is often the case that the sparkle is captured on only one image

iv.   different colours in corresponding parts of the image. The iridescent surface of an oil film on water could lead to colour mismatching

v.   two unrelated images put together as a "stereo" pair

vi.   blemishes such as scratches, processing marks or dirt particles.

In most cases the specific differences produce retinal rivalry in the visual perception of the image. The relevant part of the image will "flicker" between the left and right versions; one or the other may dominate. With reflections, as in (iii) above, the effect can seem unnatural because in real life the pattern is constantly changing and we are much less aware of the disparities which are very short-lived. In the stereogram, they are "frozen" in time and we are stuck with the anomaly.

Incorrect mounting can produce "floating edges". They amount to monocular regions at the frame edges, but they are "on the wrong sides". As has been discussed in Chapter 6, one expects such regions on the right side of the left image and vice versa. If the film chips are too far apart, this situation can be the opposite way round and disturbances are observed in these regions on viewing. Floating edges can also occur at the top and bottom if the two images are not set at the same height in the mount. Unlike most of the disturbances described in this section, this one can be corrected by repositioning the film chips, or, with prints, by correctly trimming the sides.

19.4.7 Convergence distortion

Convergence distortion has been referred to a number of times in previous chapters; it is characterised by a change in appearance of an image that is most easily depicted as the distortion of rectangles into trapeziums, (also described as **keystoning**) as illustrated in Chapter 4, Fig 4.5.

The distortion will occur when the optical axes of the camera lenses are not kept parallel, as when using "toe-in", using either sequential exposures or two mono cameras simultaneously. In these cases the distortion will be captured on film, but the effect can also arise if two images that are free from this defect are tilted when being viewed (with the inner vertical edges further away than the outer edges, for example) instead of being placed at right angles to the two lines of sight from the eyes. In viewing there will be some degree of either discomfort or difficulty in fusion of the images, because the brain is essentially being asked to fuse pairs of verticals of unequal heights.

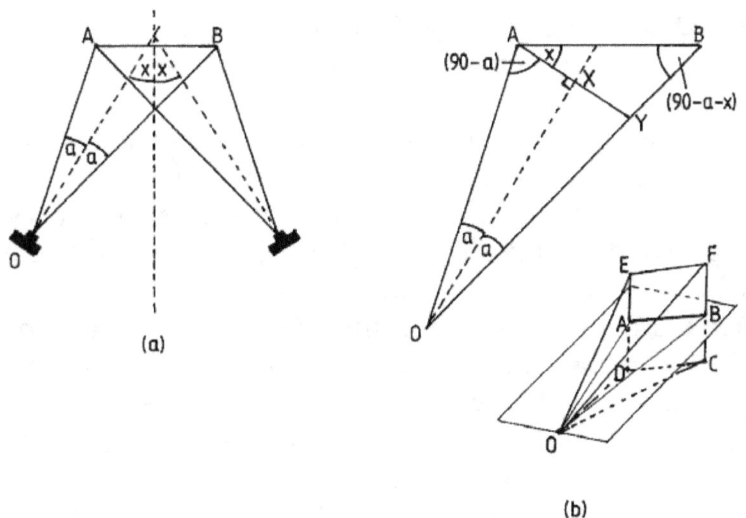

Fig 19.13
a *Toe-in of camera leading to convergence distortion.*
b *Detailed geometry of left camera position in* **a**. *The smaller picture is a pictorial view of the set-up.*

Fig 19.13a shows a typical arrangement of the two camera positions using a toe-in technique. **AB** is the plan view of a rectangle, which just fills the field of view of the camera lens. The convergence angle is 2**x** and the angle of view of the lens 2**a**. **Fig 19.13b** shows an enlarged plan view of the geometry for the left hand camera position, which will be mirrored on the right hand side. For reference, the small drawing gives a pictorial view of this half of the set-up.

Now the vertical edge **FBC**, being further away, will produce a smaller image on the film than the edge **EAD**. The ratio of the greater height **EAD** to the smaller one **FBC** (as recorded on the film) will be in inverse proportion to their distances from the camera lens. If **AXY** is drawn at right angles to the lens axis **OX**, **OA** = **OY** and the various angles can be derived from basic geometric relationships, as shown on the diagram. The ratio of the two images of the vertical edges will be equal to **OB/OA**, where **OB/OA** = **OB/OY**

Applying the sine rule to triangle **ABY**:

$$\mathbf{BY}/\sin\mathbf{x} = \mathbf{AY}/\sin(90 - (\mathbf{a} + \mathbf{x})) = \mathbf{AY}/\cos(\mathbf{a} + \mathbf{x})$$

Now $\quad\mathbf{AY} = 2\mathbf{AX} = 2\mathbf{AO}\sin\mathbf{a}$

Therefore $\quad\mathbf{BY}/\sin\mathbf{x} = 2\mathbf{AO}\sin\mathbf{a}/\cos(\mathbf{a} + \mathbf{x})$

i.e. $\quad\mathbf{BY} = 2\mathbf{AO}\sin\mathbf{a}\ \sin\mathbf{x}/\cos(\mathbf{a} + \mathbf{x})$

Now $\quad\mathbf{BO} = \mathbf{YO} + \mathbf{BY} = \mathbf{AO} + \mathbf{BY}$

Therefore $\quad\mathbf{BO} = \mathbf{AO} + 2\mathbf{AO}\sin\mathbf{a}\ \sin\mathbf{x}/\cos(\mathbf{a} + \mathbf{x})$

So $\quad\mathbf{BO}/\mathbf{OY} = \mathbf{BO}/\mathbf{AO} = 1 + 2\sin\mathbf{a}\ \sin\mathbf{x}/\cos(\mathbf{a} + \mathbf{x})$

$$= [\cos(\mathbf{a} + \mathbf{x}) + 2\sin\mathbf{a}\ \sin\mathbf{x}]/\cos(\mathbf{a} + \mathbf{x})$$

Replacing **BO/AO** by the symbol **y**, this reduces to:

$$\mathbf{y} = \cos(\mathbf{a} - \mathbf{x})/\cos(\mathbf{a} + \mathbf{x})$$

This expression allows us to calculate the ratio of verticals for any format, defined by angle **a**, that correspond to various convergence angles, as determined by angle **x**. All such calculations give the "worst case" as the analysis given above compares the heights of verticals at the extreme edges of the frame where the differences are greatest.

Table 19.1 shows results obtained for the Realist format (horizontal angle of view 35°, angle **a** = 17.5°) and for 35mm full frame landscape format with a 50mm lens, angle of view 39.6°, in which angle **a** = 19.8°. The angles of convergence are equal to twice the value of angle **x** used in the calculations.

TABLE 19.1
Convergence distortion
(Realist Format – 35mm lens)

Convergence angle (deg)	Height ratio y	Height difference %
2	1.0111	1.1
4	1.0222	2.2
6	1.0335	3.4
8	1.0451	4.5
10	1.0567	5.7

(35mm landscape Format – 50mm lens)

Convergence angle (deg)	Height ratio y	Height difference %
2	1.0126	1.3
4	1.0254	2.5
6	1.0384	3.8
8	1.0516	5.2
10	1.0650	6.5

Convergence distortion is inherent in some optical devices, such as the beam splitter attachment used with a mono camera (see Chapter 4); its presence is unavoidable but at least it is constant and, with proper design, acceptable. It is also present when the toe-in technique is used; here the amount can be excessive if care is not taken when the method is employed. With close-up work, one of the main problems is the image loss at the frame edges when adopting a standard stereo base (Chapter 18, Section 18.2) and it is tempting to swing the camera lens inwards for each exposure so that the frame coverage is roughly the same for both images. Too much swing and the convergence distortion will be too great. Reducing the stereo base will solve the problem of image loss and produce a better image, accepting that the resultant image will appear larger, as discussed earlier.

To assess the acceptable level of this type of distortion, consider the use of a toe-in technique for an object at 2m, using a 70mm stereo base, as shown in **Fig 19.14**. Of course, at this distance toe-in is unnecessary but the analysis will provide a basis for judgment. From the geometry the half angle of convergence is found from:

$$\tan\mathbf{x} = 35/2000 = 0.0175$$
$$\text{giving} \quad \mathbf{x} = 1.003°$$

This is just over 1° (total convergence angle just over 2°) and, according to **Table 19.1**, will produce slightly more than 1.3% maximum height difference for a 35mm format camera with a 50mm lens. A similar analysis by Charles Smith[46] using 2.5in as stereo base and 7ft distance, gives just over 1% height difference for this format. As he points out, in a projected image on a 6ft wide screen the vertical error is about one-quarter of an inch. This is only at the extreme corners of the picture. There is no vertical error at the centre or along the vertical or horizontal centre lines. The maximum vertical error at the corners of the film chip is only one-eighth of a millimetre. Mounting errors of this magnitude would be quite acceptable, so Smith concludes that convergence distortion on this scale is "not worth bothering with".

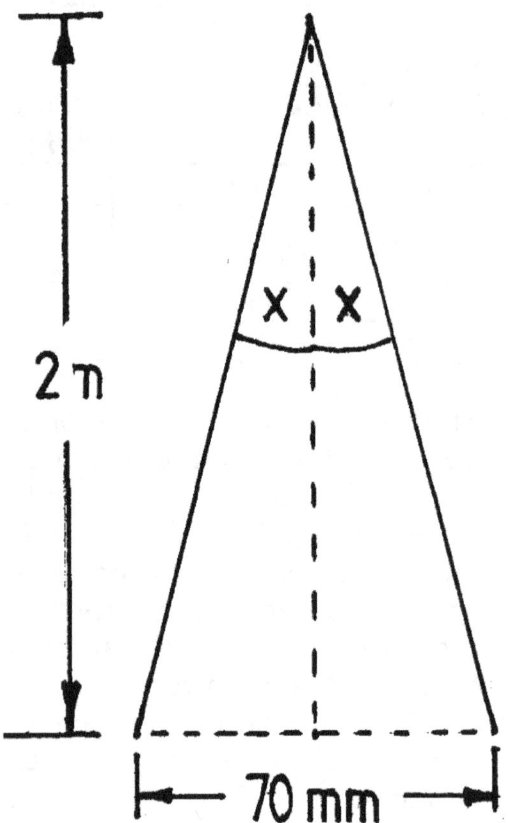

Fig 19.14
Geometry of convergence for a subject at 2m using a standard stereo base.

We may perhaps conclude that if the convergence angle is less than about 2° there is no serious problem. The geometry of **Fig 19.14** can be duplicated at closer distances by application of the 1 in 30 rule to establish the correct stereo base to be used in each case.

A significant effect of convergence distortion arises from the use of two mono projectors side by side when projecting separated pairs[50]. Of necessity, the lenses will be separated by around 300mm, so the two projectors have to be toed-in to superimpose the frames on screen, thus introducing convergence distortion, even though the actual images on film show no such effect. This is illustrated in **Fig 19.15**.

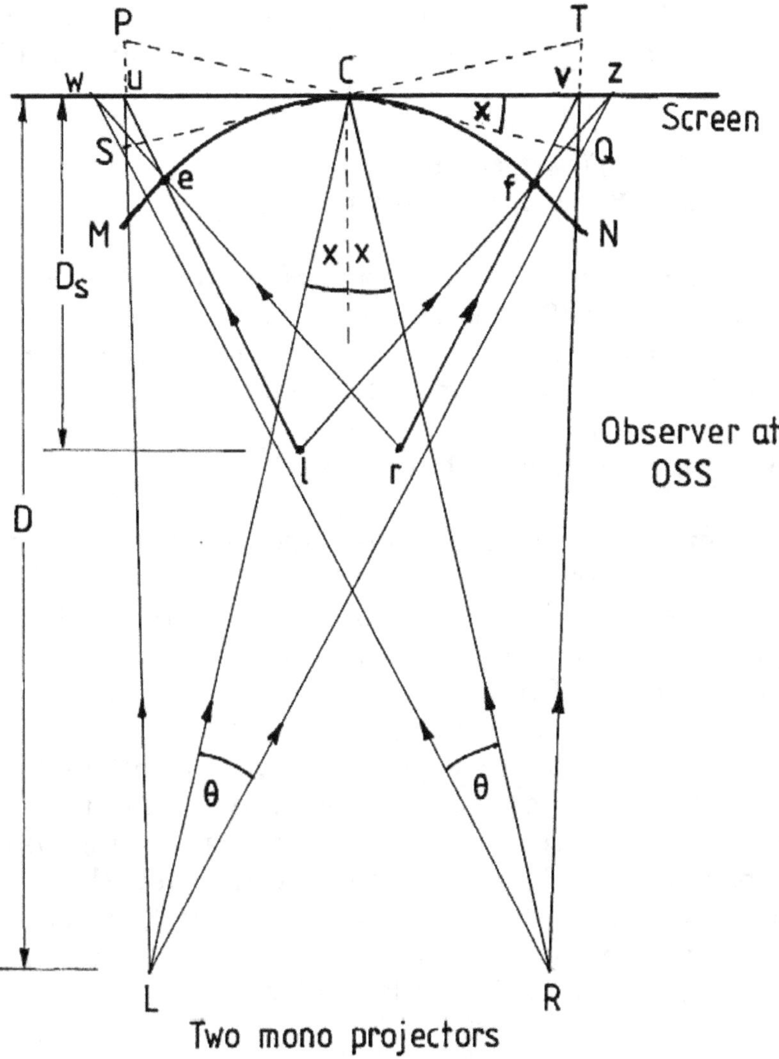

Fig 19.15
*Convergent mono projectors introduce convergence distortion, which causes the image plane to become elliptical (**MeCfN**).*

Each projector is angled inwards at an angle **x** (convergence angle = **2x**) so that the centres of the two images are superimposed at **C** on the screen. The image from the left projector is actually in true focus along **PCQ** and that from the right projector along **SCT**. Because of the toe-in, the left screen image extends from **u** to **z** where **uC** is shorter than **Cz**. Similarly,

Cv is shorter than **Cw**. If we consider the near points in the two images, as exemplified by the mount aperture edges that create the stereo window, the diagram shows that they coincide at the centre **C** but get further "out of step" towards the left and right boundaries of the screen image (**w**, **u** and **v**, **z**). An observer at the orthostereoscopic viewing position will see the stereo window on the screen at point C but in front of the screen at **e** and **f**. Between these extremes the near points will lie closer to the screen the nearer they are to **C**. These near points actually lie on the ellipse **MeCfN**.

With reference to the symbols and angles marked on **Fig 19.15**, it can be shown that:

$$\mathbf{Cz} = \mathbf{D}\sin\theta/(\cos\mathbf{x}\,\cos(\theta + \mathbf{x}))$$
$$\text{And} \quad \mathbf{Cv} = \mathbf{D}\sin\theta/(\cos\mathbf{x}\,\cos(\theta - \mathbf{x}))$$

Assuming the projector lenses are of 85mm focal length and the projection distance **D** is 4.491m to give an on-screen stereo window (ideally), with projector lenses 300mm apart, then the value of **vz** (= **Cz** – **Cv**) can be calculated from the above equations. The result is:

$$\mathbf{vz} = 5\text{mm approximately}$$

An observer seated in the orthostereoscopic seat, in this case at 1.39**W**, where **W** is the screen image width (see Chapter 8, Section 8.6.4) will see the frame edge at **f**. A calculation similar to that based upon Fig S10.5 in Supplement S10 shows that **f** is approximately 110mm in front of the screen, so the result of projector toe-in is significant. It will be less at greater projection distances, of course.

A similar curvature can be experienced with prints mounted side-by-side and viewed by the crossed-eye free-viewing technique, or if the two prints are angled inwards relative to each other (as if lying on facing pages in a partly opened book) and free-viewed with parallel sight lines. The magnitude of the effect will be greater as the angle between the eye sight lines and the image normals increases. With only small convergence angles the curvature will most probably not be noticed.

CHAPTER 20: FURTHER MOUNTING TECHNIQUES

20.1 Introduction

The basic principles of mounting of film images have been covered in some detail in Chapter 6 but entirely in relation to "standard" stereo images in which the subject matter lies within the range 2 metres to infinity. Most stereo photography will fall into this category, but there will be occasions when part of the subject will be closer than 2 metres, either by accident or because its nature or size requires a closer approach to do it justice. One can use a traditional stereo camera, with a stereo base of around 70mm, for subjects as close as about 0.75m and still produce acceptable results, but for closer subjects a smaller stereo base should be used.

The images produced by the above methods will require specialised mounting techniques to create satisfactory stereograms, as discussed in the sections that follow. It will be assumed that all such images have been produced with reference to the permissible depth ranges of subjects as outlined in Chapter 7, Section 7.3.4. While stereograms that include subject matter extending well beyond the recommended depth ranges can be mounted, viewing is likely to be uncomfortable. Such examples are always unsatisfactory, and should generally be ignored for public exhibition.

20.2 Close-ups with a Normal Stereo Base

This category covers subjects in which the nearest object is closer than the recommended 2 metres. As suggested in the Introduction above, the nearest possible distance is likely to be no closer than about 0.75 metres (2½ft.) because of the disparities between the camera images at close range, using a normal stereo base of around 70mm (see Chapter 18, Section 18.2).

Examination of the permissible depth ranges of subjects (Supplement S9, Table S9.1) will reveal a dramatic difference in the allowable far point distance (D_F) as the near point (D_N) moves closer. With a D_N value of 2m the depth range extends to infinity. Changing D_N to 1m means that the "safe" depth range now extends only as far as 2m. All such ranges are based upon a maximum "eye swing" of 1° 52' for comfortable viewing; this provides the key to one method of mounting, even though, technically, it causes image distortion.

20.2.1 Repositioning the stereo window

First, let us consider what must seem to be the obvious way of dealing with close subjects in mounting, and that is to use a mount in which the stereo window is set closer than the usual 2m. Commercial mounts nearly all have a 2m window so this will mean creating one's own. The simplest way is to adapt a standard mount. As shown in **Fig 20.1** this entails masking the existing aperture frames at the outer edges only. By doing this, the vertical centre lines are shifted towards the centre of the mount, thus reducing the separation of the two apertures, and bringing the stereo window forward. In order to bring the apertures closer by **x** mm, each must be masked off by **x** mm as shown, to shift its vertical centre line by **x**/2 mm.

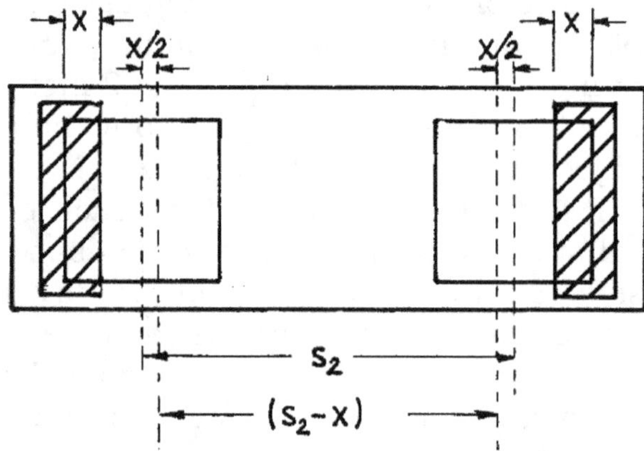

Fig 20.1
The stereo window can be brought closer than the standard 2m by masking the outer edges of the mount apertures as shown. Masking each aperture by **x** *mm brings the aperture centres (and hence their separation) closer by* **x** *mm. In doing so, the aperture width is reduced.*

The amount of masking required can be calculated from the parallax deviation formula **d** = **fb**/**D**. Assuming that the Realist format is being used, consider objects at infinity, at 2m (window location of standard mount) and at 1m, which is to be the desired window position in the example that follows.

For a 70mm stereo base and camera lens focal length of 35mm:

$$\text{For} \quad \mathbf{D} = \text{infinity} \quad \mathbf{d} = 0$$
$$\mathbf{D} = 2m \qquad \mathbf{d} = (35 \times 70)/2000 = 1.2mm$$
$$\mathbf{D} = 1m \qquad \mathbf{d} = (35 \times 70)/1000 = 2.4mm$$

Using $\mathbf{s_n} = \mathbf{s_i} - \mathbf{d}$ and taking $\mathbf{s_i}$ = 63.4mm, the separations of nearest objects (and hence mount apertures, to create the desired stereo window) will be:

$\mathbf{s_n}$ = 63.4 – 1 2 = 62.2mm for a 2m window (as in the standard mount)
$\mathbf{s_n}$ = 63.4 – 2.4 = 61mm for a 1m stereo window.

To create a stereo window at 1m then the outer edges of the mount apertures of a standard mount should each be masked by 1.2mm to reduce the separation from 62.2 to 61mm. Obviously, any desired window position can be calculated in the same way to suit the particular image. The separation of the film chips will be the same as it would be in a normal mount. This means that the various parts of the stereo image will appear at their correct locations in space, as in the original scene. The only difference is that the window will be nearer. With a standard stereogram the infinity homologues are set at 63.4mm and the near point homologues will fall correctly into position at 62.2mm to coincide with the stereo window location at 2m. With the close-up stereogram there are no infinity homologues (provided that the permissible depth range has not been exceeded) but the most distant points (at 2m) can be set 62.2 mm apart, just as they would be set in a standard mount. This automatically places the 1m near points at 61mm to coincide with the new window position.

By masking the mount apertures in this way, the width of each image is reduced by as much as 1.2mm, from about 21.3 to 20.1mm but this is no serious loss. It is, of course, possible to have a mount with apertures of 21.3mm width separated by 61mm, as shown in **Fig 20.2**. This could in theory be made from a standard mount by masking the outer aperture edges by 0.6mm (instead of 1.2mm as in **Fig 20.1**) and slicing a 0.6mm strip from each inner edge. Bringing these inner edges of the apertures closer might lead to a problem because the frame margins on the film chips could be exposed, the right hand side of the left chip and vice versa. To mask these edges, the chips would have to be moved towards each other. This in turn would move the film chips away from their original (correct) setting. On the whole, it is better and easier to stick to the method given in **Fig 20.1**.

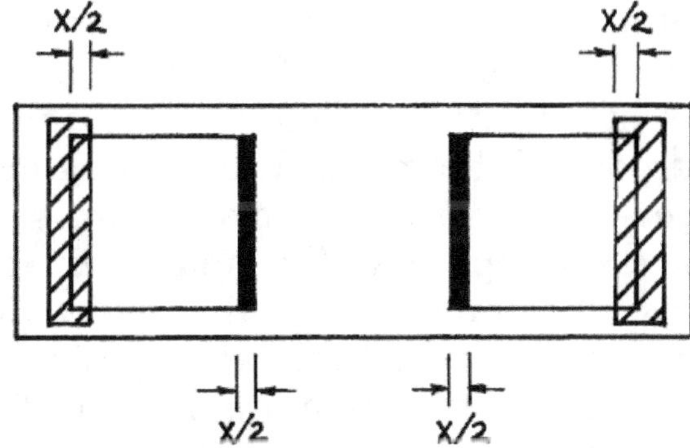

Fig 20.2
*If the outer edges of the mount apertures are masked by **x**/2 mm and the inner edges trimmed by the same amount (solid black strips removed), the aperture centres will move closer by **x** mm but the aperture width is maintained, unlike the example in **Fig 20.1***

Because the deviation **d** at a distance of 1m is double the value at 2m, this method has been described as "double depth"[52]. While it is true that there will be twice as many depth steps in the range 1 to 2m (see Chapter 16, Section 16.2.3), the terminology suggests that some kind of "improvement" has been made to the image. Actually, the image is simply mounted so that it appears at its correct distance. The description "double depth" is not particularly enlightening or, in the author's view, necessary.

The simple concept of adjusting the window position as described is perfectly acceptable and it will allow the stereogram to be viewed orthostereoscopically. However, the results are not particularly suited to viewing by projection, especially when stereograms of this type are mixed with normal ones having a standard 2m window. The audience will be subjected to drastic changes in the position of the stereo window from one slide to the next, which can be visually jarring. This will happen in a stereoscope too, but the effect is much less distracting, for reasons that are not entirely obvious.

For projection purposes a different mounting technique is adopted to preserve the normal stereo window position at 2m, as explained in the next section.

20.2.2 Repositioning the stereo image

The earlier calculations of parallax deviations showed that the value of **d** for the 2m to infinity range is identical to that for the range 1m to 2m, at a value of 1.2mm (for the Realist format). This is true for each of the depth ranges given in Supplement S9, **Table S9.1**, and is simply a manifestation of the constancy of the eye swing (1° 52') from the nearest to furthest distance in each range. Provided that the whole subject lies within one of these depth ranges, one can adjust the apparent location of the stereo image by decreasing or increasing the film chip separation within the mount. A subject that in reality lies in the range 1 to 2m can be "reset" to any other "safe" range, such as those in Table S9.1 in Supplement S9. The image can be made to "fit" any of them, stretching from 2m to infinity in the extreme case. The purpose of the modified mounting method is to relocate the image so that it lies entirely behind the standard stereo window.

In doing so, one has to accept that the image will be stretched in the process. On the positive side, it means that the stereo window remains fixed for all types of subject, which is preferable when projected images are being viewed. Krause[53] refers to this type of adjustment of film chips as "push-pull". In this specific case of close-ups it is of the "push" type because the image is being moved away from the observer. This means that the far points in the scene are being converted to "pseudo infinity" points in the new stereogram, with a separation of 64mm or thereabouts.

As the separation of the film chips is increased, there is the danger that gaps will appear adjacent to the inner vertical edges of the mount apertures, or that the film frame margins become visible. To avoid this, the mount apertures are made narrower.

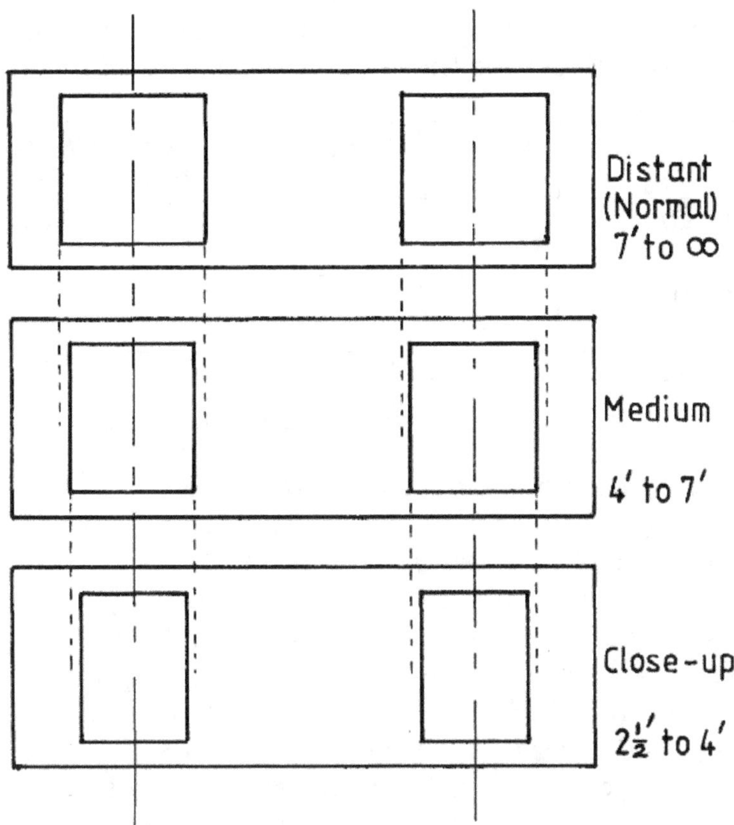

Fig 20.3
The three types of Stereo Realist mount. The mount apertures are concentric but narrower reading from top to bottom of the diagram. The stereo window is constant at about 2m in each mount and the film chips are mounted so that the image lies behind the window in each case, rather than at its "natural" distance.

Fig 20.3 shows the three types of mount introduced as part of the Stereo Realist mounting system during the 1950's. The width of the apertures decreases by about 1.5mm from the distant to medium and medium to close-up mounts. However, these apertures have common vertical centre lines, which means that the separation of corresponding vertical edges is constant at 62.2mm. Thus the stereo window position is fixed at 2m.

The original designs were actually based upon imperial units, and so the depth ranges of subject for the three mounts are:

Mount	Subject Range	Mount Aperture Width (mm) #
Distant (or normal)	7' to ∞ (2.13m to ∞)	21.3
Medium	4' to 7' (1.22m to 2.13m)	20.4
Close-up	2½' to 4' (0.76m to 1.22m)	19.1

#These figures are taken from British Standards BS 1487:Part 3:1979[54].

20.3 Close-ups with a Reduced Stereo Base

This is the realm of true close-up photography, and the techniques have been discussed in Chapter 7, Section 7.3 and Supplement S8. Mounting of stereograms taken as hypostereoscopic pairs presents no real problems, because they should be set in standard mounts, when they will be seen as magnified images (giantism). In the close-up range, the subject depth has to be somewhat restricted because of the need to keep everything sharp when the depth of field is limited, and so it is unlikely that the subject depth ranges of Supplement S9 will be exceeded. The only distortion that should appear is one of scale, as long as the 1 in 30 rule (with any correction for very close subjects) has been followed at the picture-taking stage.

Stereograms of this type will be accepted as normal enlargements of reality just as they are in conventional photographic images. The opposite effect, a reduction in apparent size (lilliputism), is experienced with hyperstereoscopic images. Both forms of distortion are unavoidable in these circumstances and should be accepted as just another part of the overall stereo experience.

20.4 Mounting for Projection
20.4.1 Projection mounts

The terms "projection mounts" and "mounting for projection" are frequently met in the stereo literature but it is not always clear to the newcomer exactly what the distinction is between mounts for hand viewing and those for projection. To some extent they are interchangeable; projection mounts can always be used in a stereoscope but not all mounts for hand viewing are suitable for projection. The differences are explained as follows:

1.   some earlier mounts were designed with slip-in compartments into which the film chips were inserted. There was little or no facility to adjust the film chip separation and they were suitable only for hand viewing in which discrepancies in mounting are more readily tolerated.

2.   mounts as described in Section 20.2.2 above are the preferred choice to give a stereo window at about 2m for all projected images

3.   in a hand-held stereoscope the luminance (or brightness) is usually greater than that found with projected images. One consequence of this is that the eyes will be functioning at a smaller aperture when viewing with a stereoscope. The enhanced depth of field of the eye makes it easier to view images with an increased depth range, from, say, four feet to infinity instead of the more usual six feet to infinity, for example. This arises from the increased angle of swing of the eyes that can be tolerated in these conditions.

In addition to the three mounts shown in **Fig 20.3**, British Standards BS 1487:Part 3:1979, referred to earlier, includes a design for a mount suitable for hand viewing. This has apertures separated by 61.9mm instead of 62.2mm as used for the projection mounts. This produces a stereo window at 1.6m (5ft). In terms of the allowable deviation this translates to a **d** value of just over 1.5mm instead of the normal 1.2mm (Realist format).

20.4.2 Mounting jigs

Accuracy and consistency in mounting are of prime importance and the stereo worker should try to uphold the highest standards in producing the finished stereograms, whatever the method of viewing that is planned. However, accuracy is particularly important for stereograms that are to be viewed by projection, as minor inaccuracies are magnified on screen to an extent that is more disturbing than appears to be the case in a stereoscope. Both accuracy and consistency are perhaps best achieved by using a mounting jig. Relatively few such devices are or have been made available commercially; most have been designed and built by individuals to suit their own circumstances. It is not too difficult to make a suitable jig. The key features and requirements are as follows:

1.   **background illumination**: the easiest way to provide this is to base the design on a simple light box used for viewing slides.

2.   **mount holder**: some simple clip is required to hold the mount steady as the film chips are placed in position. The mount position needs to be adjustable sideways so that relevant parts of the images can be aligned with any reference grid.

3. **film chip holders**: the film chips need to be held in place temporarily in some way that allows them to be adjusted into the correct alignment.
4. **mounting gauge** or reference grid: though not absolutely essential, reference marks of some kind are extremely valuable in achieving accuracy.
5. **viewing lenses**: ideally these should have the same focal length as the camera lenses but this is not critical. It is helpful if they can be moved sideways as a pair to remain in line with the mount as it is shifted over the mounting grid. If they can also be tilted back or removed it will improve access when fixing the film chips in place.

A simple design of mounting jig is described in Supplement S14.

20.4.3 Mounting technique

As an addition to the basic principles explained in Chapter 6, Section 6.3.2, the procedure is as follows, assuming that mounting is performed with the chips emulsion side up, as shown in **Fig 6.8**:

1. place the right chip over the left mount aperture and affix it temporarily in place, aligned with the image frame edges parallel to the aperture edges.
2. slide the mount sideways to align an infinity point or near point with the appropriate reference line or mark on the mounting gauge.
3. while viewing through the lenses, roughly position the left film chip over the right mount aperture with the aid of tweezers.
4. still viewing through the lenses, adjust this chip in order to align the infinity or near point homologue with the correct right hand reference line on the mounting gauge. The chip can be moved left or right as required to place the image behind the stereo window. The relative positions of image and window will be seen clearly in stereo.
5. make fine adjustments up, down, left, right, or even make a slight rotation until the horizontal grid lines pass through pairs of identical points in all regions of the image. If this is difficult to achieve, then the right image film chip (over the left mount aperture) may need to be repositioned and the whole exercise repeated. Eventually the correct position for the left image chip (i.e. the one being adjusted on the right side of the mount) will be found when the image "clicks" into place and is seen against the grid with no disturbances. Particular attention should be paid to the similarity (or otherwise) of the images near to the bottom and top edges of the frames because this will reveal whether the mount is correctly aligned with the grid, for example.

6. fix the chips in position and check the accuracy in a stereoscope. Remount if necessary.

The above description is based upon the use of mounts similar to that depicted in Chapter 6, **Fig 6.10**. In this type of mount there are no restrictions, registration pins or the like, and the film chips can be moved freely over the mount apertures. Some specialist mounts do include such aids to positioning the film images and this can greatly assist in locating them correctly and more rapidly. For example, mounts supplied by the German company RBT for use with stereo shots taken on their various "Siamesed" cameras (see Chapter 4, Section 4.4) allow the film chips to be placed accurately by means of registration pins that can be moved horizontally and vertically in four steps each of 0.1mm. However, the type of mount does not change the basic principles of good mounting technique to achieve accuracy as outlined above.

Mounts made by Spicer in Australia are available in a number of formats (4P, 5P, 7P and 8P) and the range also includes reduced height and reduced width versions, useful for masking out excessive sky areas or unwanted objects to the left or right of the main subject. These mounts are of the fold over card variety, The rear apertures are slightly larger than the front ones so that, when the mount is folded, the front apertures give a clear sharp edge to the frame.

20.5 View Magic Mounting

This system uses standard principles for trimming prints to produce a stereo window (see Chapter 6, Section 6.10.4), but differs from the norm by having the right image above the left instead of side-by-side. The View Magic handbook gives advice on picture taking to avoid excessive parallax deviations but the result of aligning the vertical print edges is that infinity points will be separated horizontally by only 6mm or so, which is equivalent to the 1.6mm parallax deviation for a 50mm lens multiplied by the enlargement factor of just over 4 for 152 x 102mm (6 x 4in) prints.

The problem with this method of mounting is similar to that found with autostereoscopic prints (Chapter 9, Section 9.4) in that the depth of the image is very restricted, at around 30 mm. The whole purpose of "over and under" mounting is to allow wide prints, too large to be placed side-by-side, to be viewed conveniently. Reducing the infinity point separation by aligning the vertical edges of the two prints is illogical.

It can be argued, therefore, that the two images, still in the over and under positions, should be staggered to give an infinity separation of around 60 to 65mm, as illustrated in **Fig 20.4**. This will produce a stereo image closer to orthostereoscopic. To improve things even further, lenses could be placed over the View Magic viewer eye apertures, of focal length about

200mm (5 rad m^{-1} or dioptres) to overcome the fact that the normal viewing distance is too long relative to the print size (see Supplement S1).

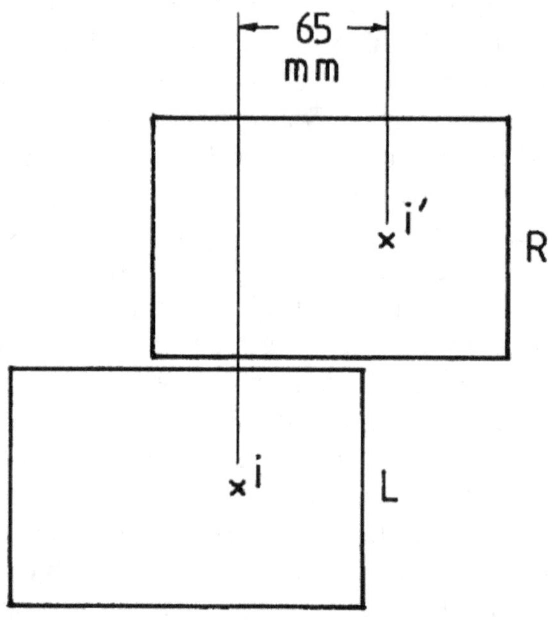

Fig 20.4
*Suggested improvement in mounting prints for the View Magic system. Infinity points **i** and **i'** are separated by about 65mm instead of the 6mm or so normally used in the standard method. (Compare this diagram with* **Fig 5.29** *in Chapter 5).*

The modified mounting technique described above will also apply to pictures trimmed to give "pop out" images for special effect. Trimming the prints according to the View Magic method, so that far points are aligned vertically, will now offset the near points by about 6mm. This is just as unsatisfactory as having infinity points 6mm apart. The depth range will again be no more than about 30mm. Instead, the far points should be offset by a distance appropriate to their location in orthostereoscopic space, which can be calculated from parallax deviations in conjunction with the enlargement factor.

CHAPTER 21: IMAGE CONTROL IN STEREO SPACE

21.1 Basic Concepts

One of the major objectives in stereo photography is to produce an orthostereoscopic image, or at least one that appears as natural as the circumstances allow (as in hypo- and hyperstereoscopy). There are, of course, exceptions to this, For example, in some trick photography part of the image is deliberately changed in scale, relocated in space, or changed in form to achieve special and unusual effects. Such image manipulation is referred to as space control, but the term can be applied equally to the minor adjustments made in mounting to "tweak" the image to a position behind the stereo window.

As explained in Chapter 11 on trick photography, part of a subject can be duplicated in miniature or magnified form, and relocated closer to or further away from the observer. Controlling the image size on the film is achieved very straightforwardly, by varying the subject distance. In order to make it appear smaller, the particular object is simply photographed at a greater distance and vice versa. However, this method alone gives no control over the position of the image. Assuming standard mounting procedure, the image will end up at a distance equivalent to that of the original object. To relocate it further away or nearer requires a change of stereo base as described in Chapter 11, Section 11.4.

The floating effect, produced by deliberately moving objects between sequential exposures, is another example of space control. This is covered fully in Supplement S12.

The other important area in which space control is invaluable lies in the field of stereo photography with long focus lenses. In this case, space control can help to produce images that are more natural in appearance than those produced by taking stereo pairs with these lenses and a normal stereo base, followed by conventional mounting. However, no manipulation of the image in this way will produce an orthostereoscopic one. This particular topic forms the basis of this chapter.

Space control relies on principles that have already been discussed in Chapters 11, 18 and 19, and the key factors that control image size, shape and location can be summarised as follows:

1. If **b** is the "taking" stereo base and **b'** the "viewing" base, then all image dimensions are changed by a factor **b'/b**. If this ratio is less than unity there is a reduction in size; if greater than unity, there is enlargement. This ratio also affects the distance at which the image is perceived by the observer. The image retains its correct proportions in all cases.

2. If **f** and **f** are the focal lengths of camera and stereoscope respectively, then the image distance and its depth (front to back dimension) are changed by a factor **f**/**f**. However, height and width remain the same. Thus the resultant image is either compressed or stretched, depending on whether the ratio is smaller or greater than unity.

3. If, in the mount, the film chips are moved closer together or further apart than the "correct" separation (i.e. the separation which gives parallel sight lines to infinity points) then the image moves closer to or further away from the observer, and undergoes squeeze or stretch. In addition, the image will be subject to frustum distortion.

These factors can be altered individually or in combination to produce the required image changes; this is space control.

21.2 Using Long Focus Lenses for Stereo Imaging
21.2.1 Squeezed images

Telephoto and zoom lenses are widely used in mono photography to give magnified images of distant objects that cannot easily be approached closely, wildlife being a typical example. Using such lenses for stereo images does not generally produce satisfactory results, however. The fundamental problem lies in the image distortion caused by the change of focal length from camera to viewer. The image, though magnified several times, is severely compressed and so lacks depth. This rather extreme form of squeeze also tends to promote the effect known as **cardboarding** or **découpage**. The compression associated with long focus lenses is evident in mono images too, so it is not simply a stereoscopic problem. Of course, if the images were to be viewed in a stereoscope fitted with long focus lenses (of focal length equal to that of the camera lenses), the stereo image would look "natural", in the sense that it would appear the same as the original subject did when it was viewed in the camera. The image, even under these conditions, is still compressed. The same effect is experienced when viewing a scene through binoculars. (The converse effect, stretching of the image, is to be found when viewing a subject through a wide-angle lens).

The basic compression effect produced by long focus lenses is associated with the magnification of the image and can be explained with reference to **Fig 21.1**. Dimensions in this diagram are marked in arbitrary "distance units" to help in the explanations that follow.

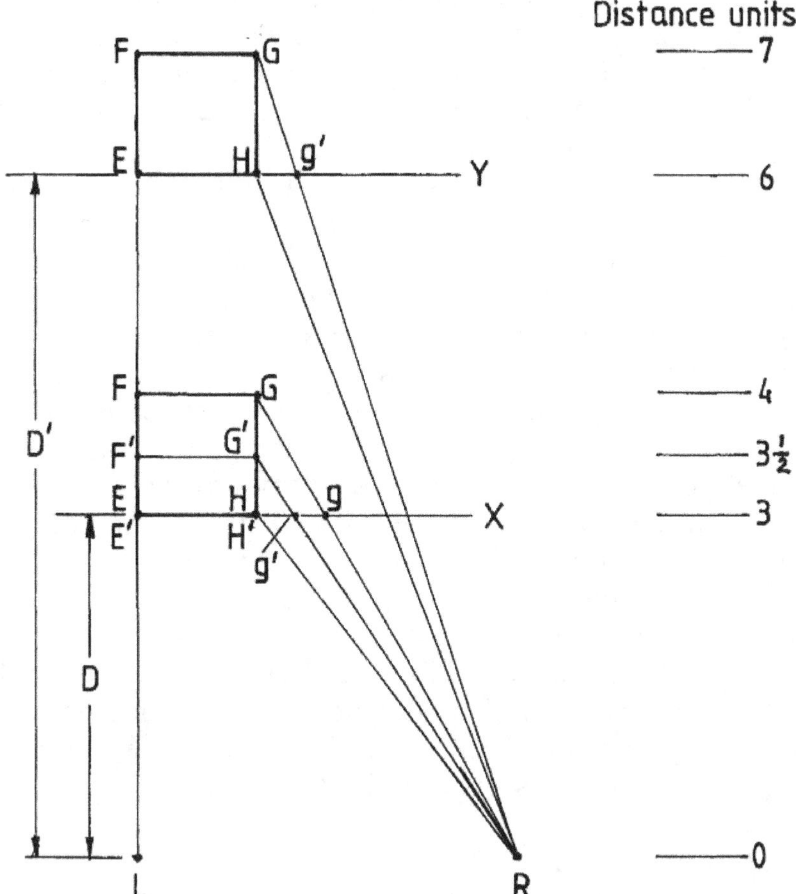

Fig 21.1

*"Compression" of an image caused by the use of long focal length lenses. Doubling the focal length of the camera lenses brings the front face of the cube image **EFGH** forward from plane **Y** to plane **X**. Because it is only magnified, its perspective is the same as it is when at **Y**. As a result the image is compressed to **E'F'G'H'**.*

In **Fig 21.1**, **EFGH** is a unit cube shown in two positions, one with the front face **EH** in plane **X** located at 3 distance units, and the other with the same face in plane **Y**, 6 distance units from the observer. The eye positions are **L** and **R** and the left face of the cube, **EF**, lies on the left eye axis for simplicity. The retinal images of the cube placed at **Y** will be half the size of those produced when the cube is at **X**, but they will also differ in their appearance. The right eye will see more of the face **GH** when the cube is at **X**, as indicated by the distance **Hg** on the projection plane at **X**, which is greater than the corresponding distance **Hg'** on the projection plane **Y**.

If the cube at **Y** is viewed through lenses of twice the focal length used for viewing the cube at **X** the image will be magnified by a factor of two and will appear twice as close, at **X** in fact. The front face **E'H'** will coincide with

EH for the cube itself placed at **X**. However, the view of the right face, represented by the length **Hg**', will be the same as that seen when the cube is located at **Y**, because the actual perspective is determined by the distance **D**' and not **D**. Thus the rear face will be seen at **F'G'** instead of **FG**, and the image will appear to be compressed.

Although the front face **E'H'** is identical to **EH**, the new image will be seen as an enlarged version of the original subject. This is a psychological phenomenon, similar (though in the opposite sense) to the experience of perceiving a hyperstereoscopic image as a small-scale model. This is only a rough analogy because the two distortions, squeeze and lilliputism, are quite distinct and have different origins.

Another way of analysing the focal length effect is to consider the object distances. Using the long focus lenses (twice the original focal length in this example) brings the front face **EH** forward from 6 distance units (plane **Y**) to 3 distance units from the observer and the rear face from 7 distance units to 3½ units. If the original cube were truly located at **X**, its rear face would be located at a distance of 4 units.

It should be emphasised that this compression will also be observed with mono images; it is not specifically a stereoscopic distortion. But if "long focus" stereo images are viewed in normal stereoscopes the compression will be even more pronounced as a result of what we might call classic stereoscopic squeeze effects as previously discussed.

21.2.2 Lack of depth in the image

Compression distortion, from whatever cause, produces an image that has less depth in proportion to its height and width, as compared with the original object. The quality of the image will be degraded by this effect, as will be understood by reference to the number of discernible depth steps in a given range. If an orthostereoscopic image of a subject is produced which extends from 4m to 8m, for example, then the number of depth steps that can be distinguished is 56, according to **Table 16.1** in Chapter 16, for a stereo acuity of 30". If, however, the image produced suffers squeeze, so that it extends from 4m to 6m, then the number of depth steps is reduced to 38, based upon the formula given in Chapter 16, Section 16.2.3.

Apart from the reduction in depth of the image caused by compression, depth information is restricted for a magnified image that has been produced by long focus lenses and apparently brought closer. Since the image is bigger and closer than in reality, the number of depth steps should be greater than would be the case if the image were located at its "correct" position in space. However, whatever benefit might have been gained in this way will more or less be cancelled out by the reduction of the depth of the object, which is a result of the compression that accompanies the magnification and relocation of the image.

21.2.3 The PePax concept

The term **PePax** was coined by McKay[55] for a principle that has been recognised virtually since stereo photography began. PePax is a contraction of the words "**Pe**rspective" and "**Pa**rallax" and is based upon a combination of the techniques outlined in Section 21.1, (1) and (2), using different stereo bases and focal lengths for recording and viewing. The principle is to "match" the differences between the corresponding parameters. As Themelis[56] expresses it, "if you increase the focal length of the recording lens then you should also increase the stereo base proportionally, in order to get closer to orthostereo". So, if the camera lens focal length is three times that of the stereoscope lens, one should use a stereo base of three times the normal value. With 135mm camera lenses and 45mm stereoscope lenses, therefore, the base ought to be about 3 x 65 = 195mm (7½in).

The larger stereo base has a hyperstereoscopic effect and causes the image to be miniaturised (lilliputism). Referring again to **Fig 21.1**, a larger stereo base would allow the right lens to see more of the right face of the cube located at **Y** and, as with all hyperstereoscopic images, this will increase the depth perception as measured by the number of discernible depth steps within a given distance range.

Unfortunately, the reality turns out to be less than ideal, because the focal length difference produces compression as discussed, and changes in the stereo base have no effect on the proportions of an image, as was shown in Chapter 19, Section 19.3.3. For example, if a subject is photographed with 135mm lenses, in place of the standard 45mm lenses, the image depth will be reduced to one third of what it will be when the image is seen as an orthostereoscopic one. Increasing the stereo base from 65mm to 135mm to "compensate", following the PePax principle, just reduces the size of the whole image by a factor of three (but maintaining its proportions).

Fig 21.2 shows the effect of the application of the PePax principle to an image of a cube **PQRS** at distance **D**. L_1 and R_1 represent the camera lenses (focal length **f** with a stereo base **b**) which would produce images on the film plane (not shown) at a distance **f** below the line L_1R_1. With the stereogram correctly transposed and placed at distance **f** as given in the diagram (plane **Y**), then L_1 and R_1 represent hypothetical eye positions to give the reconstructed image, which will be orthostereoscopic, at **PQRS**.

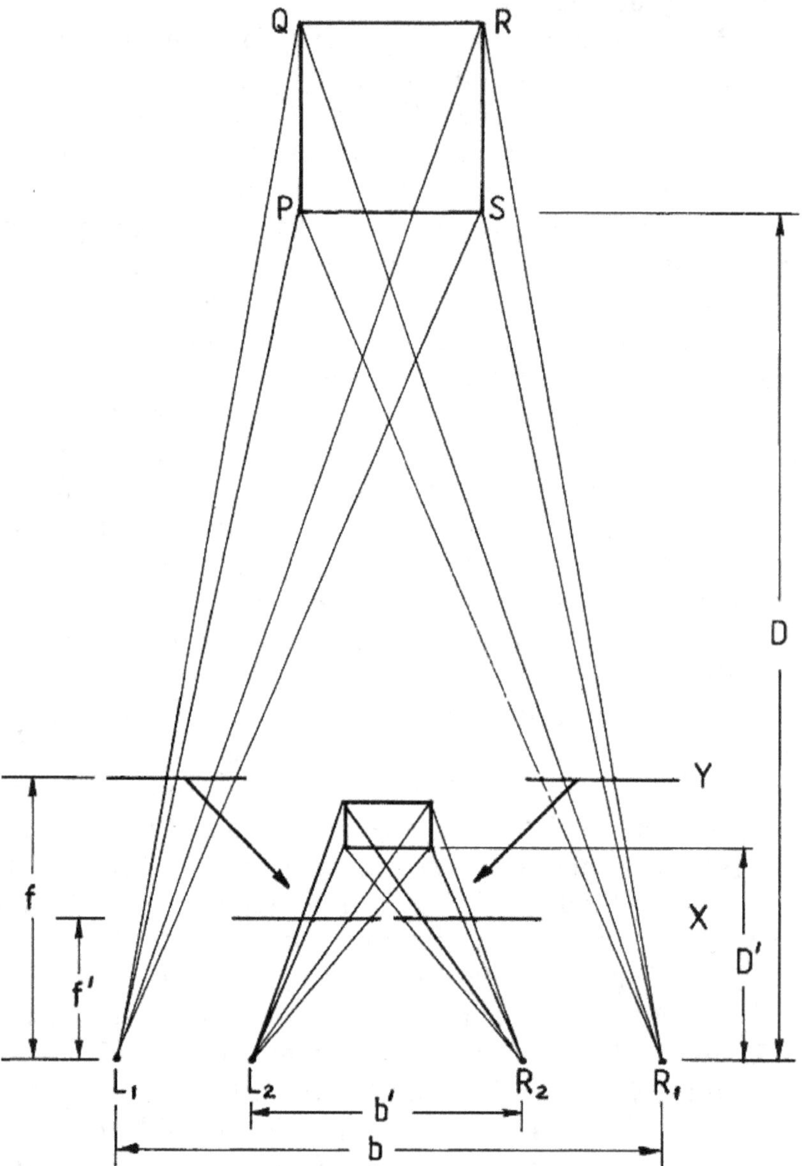

Fig 21.2
Effect on the location, size and shape of an image **PQRS** *when viewed with reduced focal length lenses and smaller stereo base (***f′** = **f**/2 *and* **b′** = **b**/2 *in this example).*

When this stereogram is viewed with a reduced base **b′** (= **b**/2 in this example) from eye positions **L₂** and **R₂** and in a stereoscope with lenses of focal length **f′** (= **f**/2) then the film chips have to be moved towards each other and closer to the observer, to the positions shown in plane **X**. The new image is half the original width, one quarter of the original depth and at a distance **D′** which is equal to **D**/4.

This kind of transformation of the image can be determined from the simple relationships quoted in Section 21.1 (1) and (2). Each factor modifies the image size or proportions and its distance from the observer. Using **b**, **b'**, **f**, **f'**, **D** and **D'** as defined in **Fig 21.2**, **W** for the width and **T** for the "thickness" (i.e. depth of the object from front to back), the factors **b'/b** and **f'/f** can be applied in turn to give the final distance, depth and width as follows:

$$\mathbf{D' = Db'f'/bf}$$
$$\mathbf{T' = Tb'f'/bf}$$
$$\mathbf{W' = Wb'/b}$$

(NB the width is unaffected by focal length differences)

By substituting **b'/b** = **f'/f** = 1/2 as in the earlier example, the results obtained for the image proportions and location as depicted in **Fig 21.2** can be verified.

The relative proportions of the object and image can be expressed as an aspect ratio of depth to width. From the last two expressions:

$$\mathbf{T'/W' = (Tb'f'/bf)/(Wb'/b)}$$
$$\mathbf{= Tf'/fW = (f'/f)/T/W)}$$

In simple terms, the depth to width ratio of the image is **f'/f** times that of the original object.

Clearly, the PePax principle goes only so far in recreating an orthostereoscopic image, though McKay[55] claimed that using 2x standard focal length camera lenses with a twice than normal stereo base would give a normal size image at half the distance, and that it would appear undistorted. As we have shown, the image produced in this way would be only half the width of the original object and would be located at one-quarter of the original distance. It would also suffer from squeeze. It was Dalgoutte[57] who pointed out that McKay had, without reference to the fact, incorporated in his explanatory diagram an additional factor. This was an outward shift of the film chips, just sufficient to push the image back to half the original distance and to increase its perceived width back to its original value. Although the image suffered frustum distortion as a result, the deformation was not obvious in the triangular shape chosen by Mckay to represent the object.

21.2.4 PePax and parallax deviations

Increasing the focal length of the "taking" lenses and using a larger stereo base will lead to greater parallax deviations for homologues within the subject range; this might lead to "too much depth" in the scene and uncomfortable viewing. For example, consider an object at 20m distance photographed with 35mm lenses and a 70mm stereo base in the Realist format. The deviation will be given by $\mathbf{d} = \mathbf{fb}/\mathbf{D}$. Thus:

$$\mathbf{d} = (35 \times 70)/20000 = 0.12\text{mm}$$

Using 105mm lenses and a 210mm stereo base (both parameters increased by a factor of three) the deviation for this distance will be nine times larger at 1.08mm. If the object at 20m is to become the near point at 2m in the stereogram and the whole scene extends to infinity then this deviation is acceptable, since it is less than the 1.2mm maximum for the Realist format. On the other hand, using 210mm lenses and a 420mm stereo base will increase $\mathbf{d}$ to 4.41mm. With a subject range including infinity, the eye swing needed to survey the image from nearest to furthest objects will be too great and the stereogram will be uncomfortable to view. However, if the subject depth range is restricted such that the furthest object has a deviation of 4.41 – 2.2 = 3.21mm, diplopia can be avoided.

This value of $\mathbf{d}$ corresponds to a distance of $(210 \times 420)/3.21 = 27.5\text{m}$ approximately. Restricting the subject to this depth range (20 to 27.5m) in these conditions is based upon the same principle as that used for close-ups (see Supplement S9).

With such a large deviation, the near object will appear in front of a 2m stereo window if mounted "traditionally" but the film chips can be moved apart to push this image back. The far point homologues (representing an object at 27.5m in the actual scene) can be separated to the conventional infinity point value of around 64mm, so that they form a pseudo-infinity. A slight mounting problem can arise because, when the film chips are separated by a distance of this magnitude, gaps may well appear at the inner edges of the mount apertures. This can be corrected by careful masking or by using mounts with reduced width apertures.

21.2.5 The "PeShPax" analysis

So far, the discussion has shown that the PePax principle alone does not lead to natural-looking images in stereo photography using long focus camera lenses. In addition to perspective and parallax changes, a third contribution in the form of an outward shift of the film chips in the mount is required.

Dalgoutte[57], in his analysis of the PePax principle, summarised in typically elegant fashion the basic geometry of what he called "Big Bertha stereo", the term used for longer-than-normal focal length stereo and named after the German long-range cannon which shelled Paris in 1917. It is quite clear from Dalgoutte's explanation that the key factors are the focal length change from camera to viewer and the shift of the film chips. The role of the larger stereo base, though important, is somewhat secondary in nature as far as image distortion is concerned.

What is needed is a rethink of the PePax principle to include this "third factor" of film shift. With a degree of reticence, the present author suggests designating this component by the abbreviation **Sh** (from **Sh**ift) so that, more realistically, the PePax principle becomes the **PeShPax** principle, of which the **PeSh** components represent the important factors in producing an image with the least distortion. The **Pax** influence is one only of size.

We shall now present Dalgoutte's explanation and extend it to provide a fully quantitative analysis. **Fig 21.3** illustrates the combination of focal length and film shift (the **PeSh** part of **PeShPax**). It should be pointed out that in this diagram the object and image distances have been shortened to exaggerate the effects. The object is much closer than the 1 in 30 rule would recommend but the geometric construction is nevertheless accurate and will illustrate the basic principles correctly. The actual distances (in mm) measured from the original scale diagram, or calculated from formulae, will be used in the explanation. They should simply be regarded as numbers for illustration and not realistic values of the various dimensions and distances.

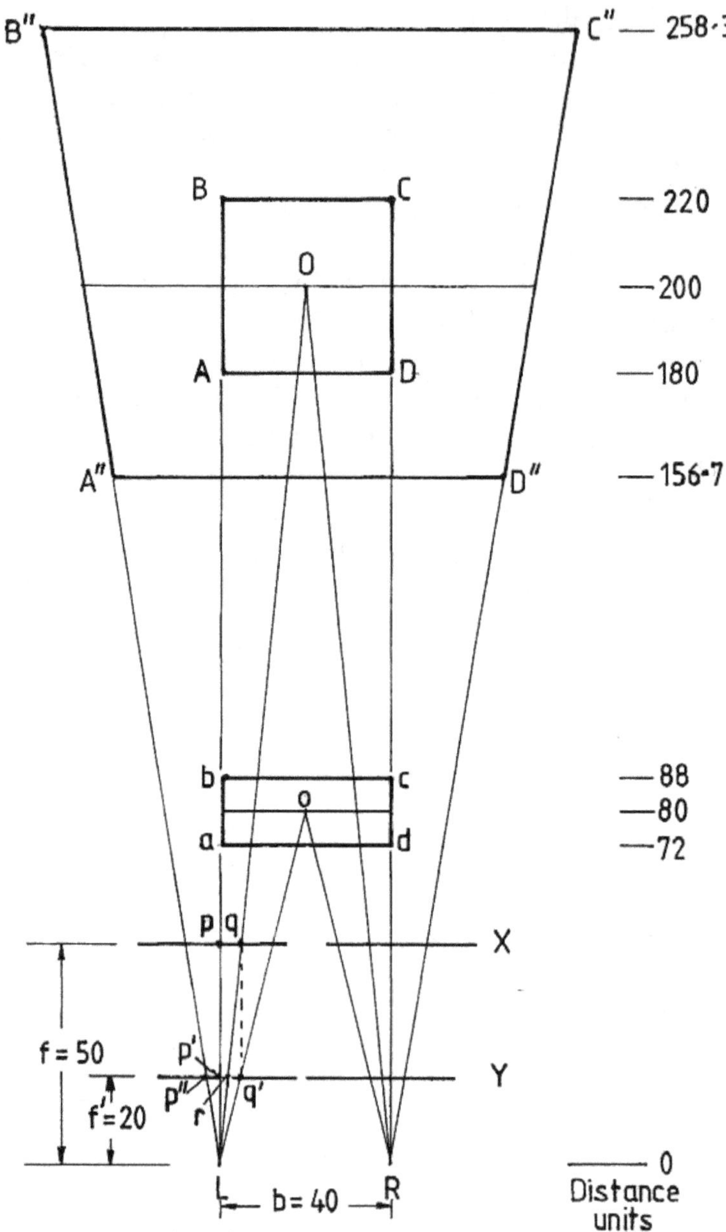

Fig 21.3
*The **PeShPax** Principle. Cube **ABCD**, when viewed with shorter focal length lenses (**f** = 20 units) appears compressed (**abcd**). By shifting the film chips outwards by a suitable amount, the image moves back to its original position, using the centre point **O** as a reference, but in an enlarged form (**A"B"C"D"**) which exhibits frustum distortion.*

In this diagram, **ABCD** represents a cube 40 units square, photographed with its centre (**O**) 200 units from the camera lenses focal length **f** (= 50 units) at **L** and **R**. Although at this stage we are ignoring the "Pax" component, it has to be remembered that the stereo base **LR** (40 units) will be larger than that to be used for viewing. In fact, the original PePax principle would be used to select the stereo base according to the focal length difference between camera and stereoscope. The size of the cube has been chosen so that the side faces **AB** and **CD** lie along the lens axes for simplicity.

The stereogram produced in this way, when placed at position **X**, will produce an orthostereoscopic image at **ABCD**, if we imagine it to be viewed with an eye spacing of 40 units, with the eyes at **L** and **R**. Points **p** and **q** on the left image are the homologues of the left face **AB** and the centre **O** of the object, respectively.

When the stereogram is viewed with a smaller focal length f'(= 20 units) it will lie at **Y**. The resulting image will be produced at **abcd**, changing its form to the rectangle as discussed earlier. The width remains at 40 units but the depth is reduced because all distances in the "depth direction" are reduced by a factor f'/f = 20/50 i.e. 0.4. Thus the locations of **AD**, **O** and **BC** are changed from 180, 200 and 220 units to 72, 80 and 88 units respectively. (All distances are measured from the base line passing through **LR**). The depth of the cube is reduced to 16 units.

If the left film chip (in plane **Y**) is now moved outwards so that **q**' shifts to **r** then the line **Lq'o** swings to position **LqO**. At the same time the right film chip is moved to the right so that **Ro** swings to **RO**, thus causing the image centre to move back from **o** to **O**, the original location of the object centre. Point **p**' also moves leftwards to **p**" by the same amount (= **q'r**) so that the left face of the cube image now shifts so that it lies along **LB**". In fact, the corners **a** and **b** move to **A**" and **B**", the positions of which can be determined by calculating the increase in distance that the cube faces **ad** and **bc** will move as a result of the film chip shift and noting where they intersect the line **Lp**" produced (see below). The other corner positions **C**" and **D**" can be located in similar fashion. Alternatively, the new corner positions can be determined geometrically by incorporating homologues for **C** and **D** on the film chips. It can be seen that the final image is reasonably "cube-like", its depth and average width being roughly equal, but it does exhibit the expected frustum distortion caused by (in this case) diverging infinity sight lines. Overall, the image size is roughly 2½ (= f/f') times that of the original object.

The exact location of the front and back faces **A**"**D**" and **B**"**C**" can be calculated from parallax deviations (using **d** = **fb**/**D**) and the formula for film chip shift derived in Chapter 19 (**D'** = **Dd**/(**d** - **s'**)).

The parallax deviations for **O**, points along **AD** and points along **BC** are calculated as follows:

For **O**: $\qquad$ **d** =(50 x 40)/200 = 10 units
(the distance **pq** (= **p'q'**) on the stereogram is equal to **d**/2)

For points on **AD**: **d** = (50 x 40)/180 = 11.1 units
For points on **BC**: **d** = (50 x 40)/220 = 9.1 units

Now **o** is at 80 units distance (= **D**). When the film chips are shifted it moves to **O**. The segment **q'r** in plane **Y** is equal to **s'**/2 where **s'** is the total shift for both chips. Since **p'q'** = **d**/2 (= **pq**) then:

p'r = (**d** − **s'**)/2.

From similar triangles **Lp'r** and **Lpq**:

p'r/**pq** = **f'**/**f**
i.e. (**d** − **s'**) = **df'** /**f**

For the move **o** to **O**:

$\qquad$ (**d** − **s'**) = (10 x 2)/5 = 4 units. Therefore **s'** = 10 − 4 = 6 units.
$\qquad$ **D'** = **Dd**/(**d** − **s'**) = (80 x 10)/4 = 200 units

For the move **ad** to **A"D"**:
$\qquad$ **D'** = (72 x 11.1)/(11.1 − 6) = 156.7 units

For the move **bc** to **B"C"**:
$\qquad$ **D'** = (88 x 9.1)/(9.1 − 6) = 258.3 units

The distances calculated together with the divergent lines from **L** and **R** enable the corners of the image to be located as shown in the diagram.
The expression derived above for (**d** − **s'**) can be rearranged to give:

s' = **d**(**f** − **f'**)/**f**

This shows that the amount of shift required to restore the shape of the image to its "correct" proportions (ignoring the frustum distortion) is a fraction (**f** − **f'**)/**f** of the parallax deviation for the centre point of the image, which is the most convenient reference point to use.

The above analysis represents the "PeSh" component of the "PeShPax" concept. It will be remembered that the stereo base **b** used for this will be greater than the viewing base, chosen to complement the focal length difference, eg both parameters increased by a factor of three (105mm lenses and 210mm base instead of the normal 35mm and 70mm values). The "Pax" element comes into being with normal viewing with the reduced base **b'**. The image will be reduced in scale from **A"B"C"D"** and brought closer by a factor **b'/b** as discussed previously. The frustum distortion will not be affected and so will remain in the final image.

It should be remembered that the importance of the "Pax" input is that the large stereo base used for recording improves the depth information within the image.

21.2.6 "PeShPax" in practice

Whilst the theory developed in the previous sections provides the necessary information to produce reasonably natural images, there will be many variables in practice that will make it difficult to adhere to the recommendations. Take the original PePax concept in which the stereo base is increased in proportion to the increase in focal length; if 300mm camera lenses are to be used, for example, then the recommended base would be:

(70 x 300)/35 = 600mm

This is quite acceptable if the sequential exposure method is being used, but for wildlife one needs to take simultaneous exposures, and such a large lens separation is unlikely to be used in any two-camera rig. The lens separation would really have to be adjustable because another subject might require only a 200mm focal length, and hence a different stereo base. These variations also cause changes to the values of parallax deviation and will therefore affect the permissible depth range of the subject.

Even without these complications, there is a serious limitation in attempting to apply the PeShPax principle in a real situation. The analysis of the simple cube object based upon **Fig 21.3** shows that the magnified image produced by longer-than-normal focal length lenses can be adjusted to look reasonably normal. As stated earlier, the image **A"B"C"D"**, apart from showing frustum distortion, more or less retains the shape of the original object **ABCD**. Its depth and average width are virtually the same so the final image appears "square". This result was achieved by basing all the calculations upon the reference point **O** and the line **EOF** at a distance of 200 units. However, images of objects at other distances in the same scene will not be properly corrected. The amount of film chip shift for full "correction" will vary with the image distance. This is shown in **Fig 21.4**.

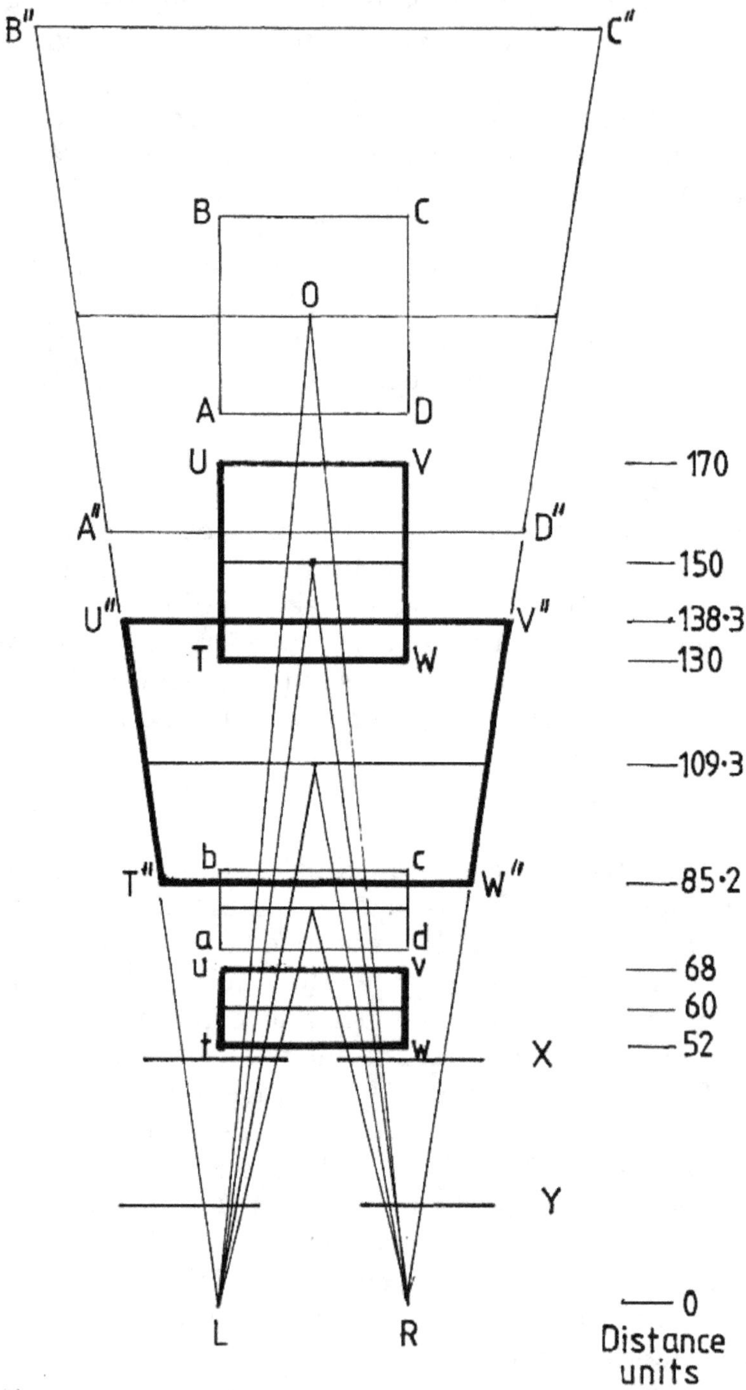

Fig 21.4
*Cube **ABCD** and its final image **A″B″C″D″** are shown as before (in **Fig 21.3**).*
***TUVW** is a nearer cube that transforms to **tuvw** with the change in focal length. However, the shift in the film chips that "corrects" **abcd** to **A″B″C″D″** only partly "corrects" **utvw** by shifting it only to **T″U″V″W″**, which still shows some compression.*

Here, the image **A"B"C"D"** is included to the same scale as in **Fig 21.3** but another cube object/image **TUVW**, with its centre line at 150 distance units, has been added. The change in focal length from **f** to **f** transforms this image to **tuvw**. However, the film chip shift **s'** used to "correct" the image **abcd** moves **tuvw** only as far as the position **T"U"V"W"**. The centre of this image is at 109.3 distance units (by calculation) and so it falls short of the original 150 units. It still exhibits some compression, as well as frustum distortion.

In a similar way, more distant objects will, with the same film chip shift, be relocated further away than desired and the image will suffer stretch. Any single calculation to correct an image will only apply to a specific distance. It is impossible to correct all images simultaneously if they lie at different distances. In any case, even a correction for a single image is a compromise.

Mike Fisher[58] has taken many exposures of wildlife with a two-camera rig, using the PePax principle as a starting point, with the addition of film chip shifts. His analysis was aimed at producing acceptable projected images. Using lenses of up to 300mm focal length and with a 75mm or 150mm stereo base, he set a maximum parallax deviation at 2mm (rather than 1.6mm) to represent the differential between the nearest and furthest objects. A computer program was developed to calculate the mounting offset (film chip shift) required to restore the apparent image size after increasing the focal length and stereo base. Fisher found that if the target subject distance was maintained in proportion to the focal length, the required shift was constant. For example, using a 150mm base, the focal length/target distance combinations of 50mm/10m, 100mm/20m or 300mm/60m all required an off-set of 18mm on screen, corresponding to about 0.38mm on film.

Since these film shifts are going to be fractions of a millimetre, it is not easy to measure them accurately when mounting. The idea of working to a focal length/target subject distance combination to standardise the location of the image in relation to the stereo window in all (or most) of the exposures is a sound one, as long as the PeShPax principle has been worked out in advance to ensure that the final image is going to look reasonably natural at its intended location in stereo space.

In the world of stereo cinematography, when sequences involving the use of zoom lenses are shot, control of stereo space is vital to maintain acceptable images, which would otherwise change from a natural to a highly squeezed appearance as the camera zooms in. This requires sophisticated equipment so that the stereo base can be changed continuously while zooming, and the framing adjusted in-camera, equivalent to the film shift in still photography.

Part 3 - Supplements

SUPPLEMENT S1 - PERSPECTIVE

Perspective, from the Latin **perspicere** (= to see through), relates to the representation of an image by projection from a central point (usually referred to as the vanishing point) onto a plane. This principle is illustrated in **Fig S1.1**, which shows the construction of an image of a cube. If, for the purposes of this analysis, we regard the cube as a simple wire frame, the wires forming the cube edges, we are able to see more features in the image than if the cube were solid.

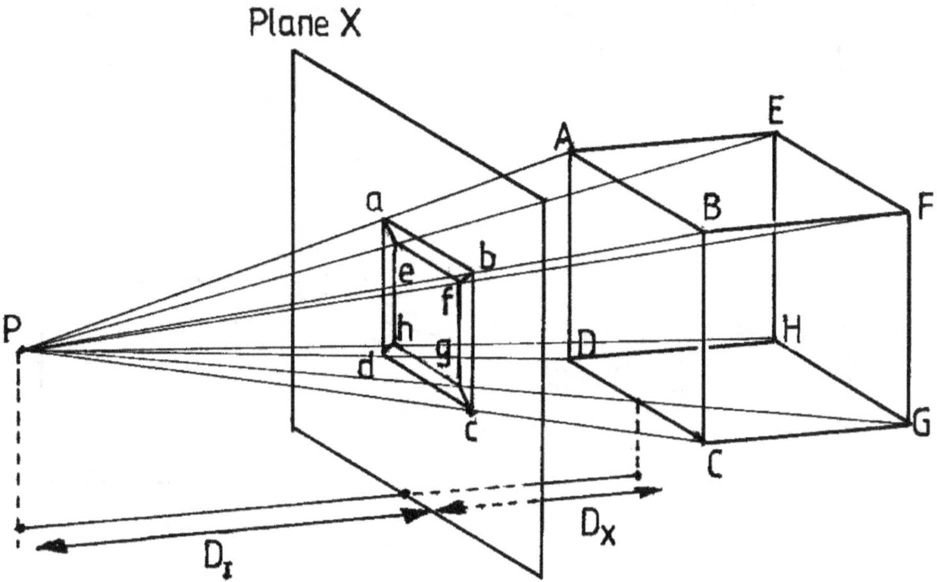

Fig S1.1
The image **abcdefgh** *of a "wire frame" cube* **ABCDEFGH** *is formed by central projection from point* **P** *(perspective projection).*

The method of construction is to draw straight lines from the central point **P** to every point on the cube in turn and to mark the points of intersection of these lines with the plane **X** to define the image. Since, in this form of projection, straight lines in the object appear as straight lines in the image, we need only project the eight corners of the cube **A, B, C** etc. to produce the corresponding points **a, b, c** etc. in the image, and then join corresponding points **ab, af** etc. to produce the final image. In this way we have represented the object as a perspective drawing.

This construction is quite different from that used in engineering drawing, because the latter is based upon orthographic projection, in which all projection lines such as those from the cube corners **A, B, C** etc. do not converge towards point **P** but run at right angles to plane **X**. In orthographic projection, therefore, points **a** and **e** would coincide, as would the other pairs **bf**, **cg** and **dh**. The orthographic image would consist of just the square **abcd**, points **e**, **f**, **g** and **h** being "hidden". Also, for a given D_x value, this square **abcd** would be larger than its counterpart in the perspective image.

The position of the plane **X** in perspective projection is immaterial. If we move it nearer to the central projection point **P** the image becomes smaller but does not change in general appearance, and it remains geometrically similar. Plane **X** can even be located behind the cube to produce an enlarged image; it may even be placed further away from the object (but on the same side as shown) to the left of point **P**, in which case the image will be inverted both vertically and horizontally (**Fig S1.2**). This arrangement now resembles the object and image configuration found in photography where point **P** would represent the position of the camera lens, plane **X** denoting the film plane.

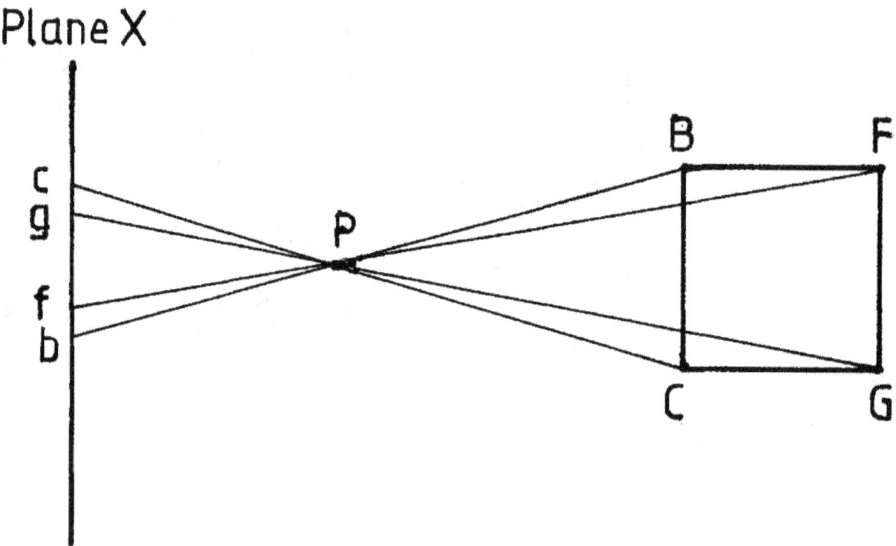

Fig S1.2
Side view of **Fig S1.1** *with plane* **X** *behind the vanishing point* **P**, *giving an inverted image.*

The image **abcdefgh** of the cube **ABCDEFGH** produced by central projection also illustrates the change in an image produced by changing the viewpoint when looking at an object. The cube is essentially made up of 6 identical wire squares **ABCD**, **AEHD**, **CDHG** etc. but each is orientated differently to the viewer situated at **P**. Each of these squares could be regarded as an object in itself. The image of square **ABCD** is the square **abcd** because we are looking at this face "head on". In contrast, square **AEHD** is at a different angle to the observer and its image **aehd** appears as a trapezium. If we were to rotate the cube about a vertical axis passing through the centres of the top and bottom faces (**ABFE** and **DCGH**) then we would see the images **abcd** and **aehd** change correspondingly. **Fig S1.3** shows the kind of change in the image produced by rotating the cube anti-clockwise through an angle less than 45 degrees. Here all six faces of the cube are at different angles to the observer and we see in the image a variety of trapezium and other shapes.

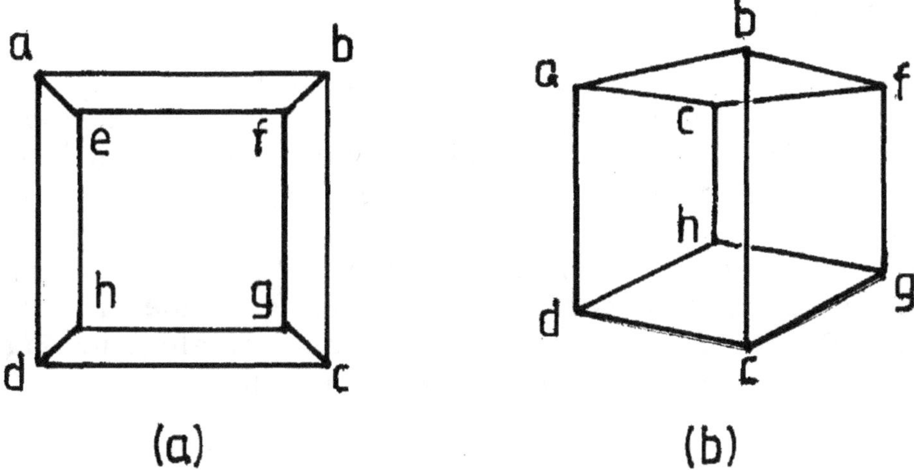

Fig S1.3
a *Perspective image of a cube as set up in* **Fig S1.1**
b *Image after rotation of the cube about a vertical axis (anti-clockwise rotation of less than 45°).*

If, in **Fig S1.1** plane **X** represents a piece of tracing paper with the image drawn on it and we place our eye at point **P**, then our perception of the image **abcdefgh** is identical to our perception of the actual object **ABCDEFGH** which we see directly when the tracing paper is removed. In other words, by placing the traced image in exactly the position shown, the lines **ab**, **ae** etc. appear to coincide exactly, with the lines **AB**, **AE** etc. seen on the object itself.

If we were to draw a new image of the cube, by reducing the distance D_I, but not altering the distance D_X, so that **P** is moved nearer to plane **X** then we would discover that this new image **a'b'c'd'e'f'g'h'** differed from the first in two ways:

1. the whole image will be smaller, as indicated by the reduced size of the square **abcd** (transformed to **a'b'c'd'**)
2. the proportions of the various parts of the image will change. The new image is not simply a smaller version of the original. For example, the trapezium **aehd** will change its proportions (from **aehd** to **a'e'h'd'**)

These changes are illustrated schematically in **Fig S1.4**.

Since the exact form of the image depends upon the position of the projection point **P**, it follows that this is the only viewing position that will allow the observer to replicate the experience of viewing the object from the same point.

If, for example, the observer moves from point **P** towards the object (**Fig S1.1**) the original image **abcdefgh** will no longer coincide with the direct view of the object itself. The observer will see the original tracing **Fig S1.4a** and the new image of the object **Fig S1.4b** superimposed.

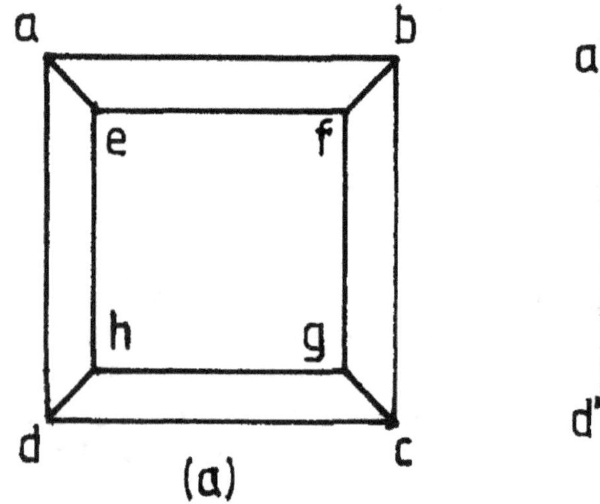
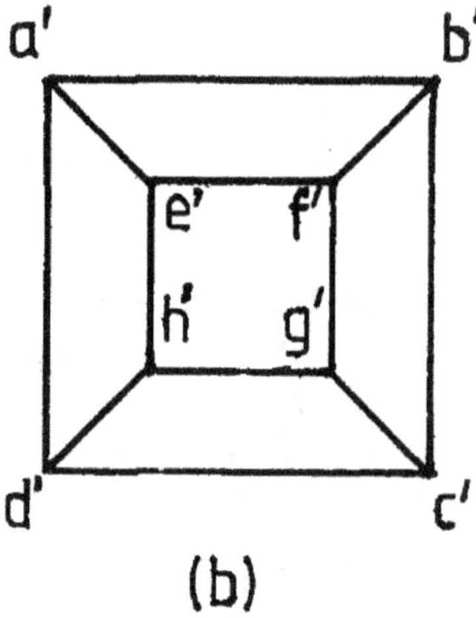

Fig S1.4
a *Perspective image of a cube as in* **Fig S1.1**
b *New image produced by moving the projection point* **P** *nearer to the cube, reducing the distance* D_I *(**Fig S1.1**) but keeping* D_X *constant.*

In everyday situations, we are unlikely to find ourselves viewing a perspective image and the actual object simultaneously in this way, but it is important to realise that there is only one correct viewing position, corresponding to the distance D_I from the image, that "re-creates" the visual experience of viewing the object itself from the distance $(D_I + D_X)$. In the correct viewing position, the "projection lines" **PaA**, **PbB** etc. will lie at the same angles in space as they did in the original construction of the image.

Consider a picture taken in a 35mm camera fitted with a standard 50mm focal length lens. In producing the image, the lens-film distance will be approximately 50mm (depending upon the subject-camera distance). Since the lens effectively acts as the central projection point, we should view a contact print (i.e. the same size as the negative) at a distance equal to the focal length of the lens, in this case, 50mm. In practice this would be difficult, since the human eye can focus only as closely as about 250mm. However, a larger print can be made, and a currently popular size is 152 x 102mm approximately (6 x 4in). This represents a linear enlargement of about 4.2 times the negative size of 36 x 24mm, ignoring the slight image loss at the edges that occurs during commercial printing. So that the projection lines from the eye to the various parts of the image retain their correct orientation in space, and hence the correct perspective, the photograph will have to be viewed at 4.2 times the distance used for viewing the contact print. As illustrated in **Fig S1.5**, the print should be viewed at 4.2 x 50 = 210mm. This is still too near for some people to focus comfortably, but by viewing the print as closely as possible, the difference will only be slight. This principle can be applied to any size of print and any lens focal length. The formula is:

$$\mathbf{D_V} = \mathbf{fV}$$

where $\mathbf{D_V}$ = ideal (correct) viewing distance

$\mathbf{f}$ = focal length of lens
$\mathbf{V}$ = enlargement factor
= (image size on print)/(image size on negative)

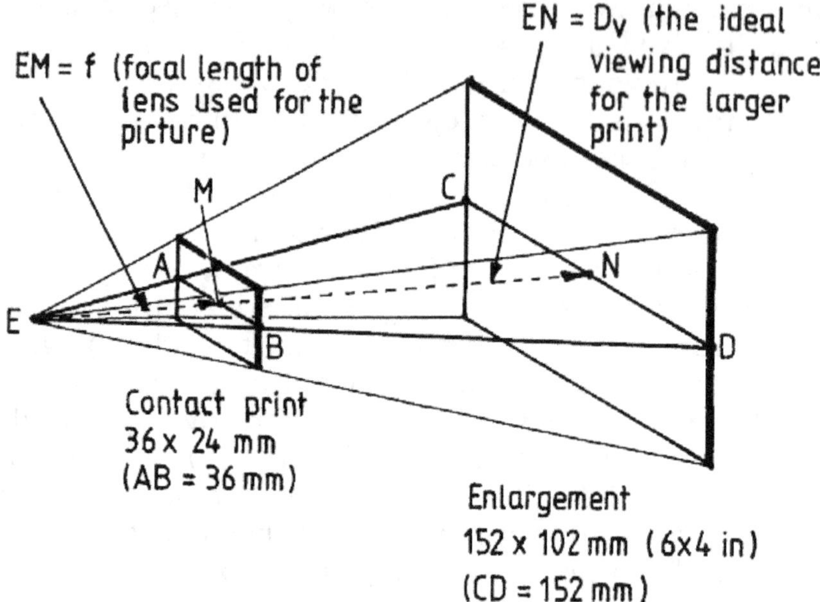

Fig S1.5
Ideal viewing distance **Dᵥ** *for viewing a photographic image. An enlargement should be viewed with the same perspective as that for a contact print to match the in-camera perspective.*

When perusing our family snapshots or even looking at the exhibits in a photographic display, we do not have to worry unduly about correct viewing distances. In most cases we would not even have the information required to work out what they should be. However, if three-dimensional space is to be re-created accurately by means of stereoscopic photography, correct viewing conditions are rather more important.

Even though in practice we may rarely achieve the ideal, the 3D photographer aims to reproduce images as close to reality as possible. The final result depends ultimately upon the means by which the images are produced, the way in which they are mounted and the conditions under which they are viewed. These factors are examined in the main text of this book.

SUPPLEMENT S2 - THE PANTOGRAPH

Construction of a working model

We can take the dimensions given in **Fig 2.11** in Chapter 2, use wood for the platform and base, each of 12mm thickness, and incorporate a bridge of, say, 20mm (about 0.8in). These dimensions are not critical; neither are they too small to make construction fiddly, nor too large to make the device too heavy. The tricky part is to make the linkage arms the right size and to fix them correctly so that the pantograph produces the required stereo base. This can be achieved practically by adopting the following method:

1. make the two platforms 150 x 75 x 12mm as shown in **Fig 2.11**, Chapter 2.
2. mark the positions of the pivot points (**P, P'** etc.) and make central reference marks on the front and back edges of the two platforms as shown in **Fig S2.1**. **P** and **P'** can be placed about 25mm (1in) from the ends, as a rough guide. Holes should now be drilled at the pivot points to take screws. Using screws with an unthreaded portion near the head is recommended so that when the linkage arms are in place they can swivel freely.
3. with the 20mm high bridge in position, assemble the pantograph as shown in **Fig S2.2** with the central reference marks offset horizontally by half the required stereo base (i.e. **b**/2). For a base of 65mm the offset will be 32.5mm.
4. measure the distance **PP'** (**Fig S2.2**). This represents the distance between the pivot points on each linkage arm. The four linkage arms can now be cut and drilled with holes this distance (**PP'**) apart.

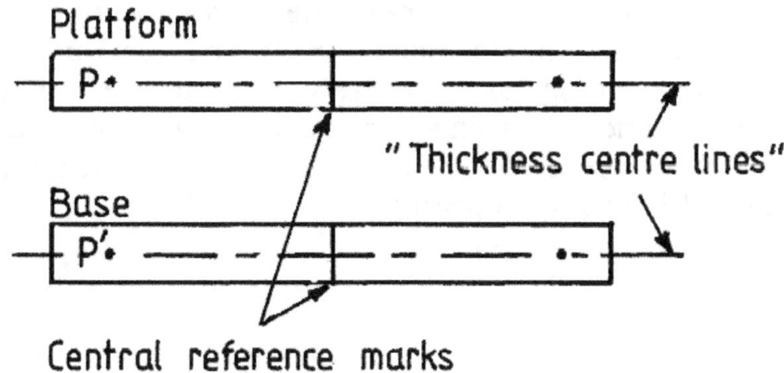

Fig S2.1
Locations of the pivot points **P** *and* **P'** *and the central reference marks on a pantograph prior to assembly.*

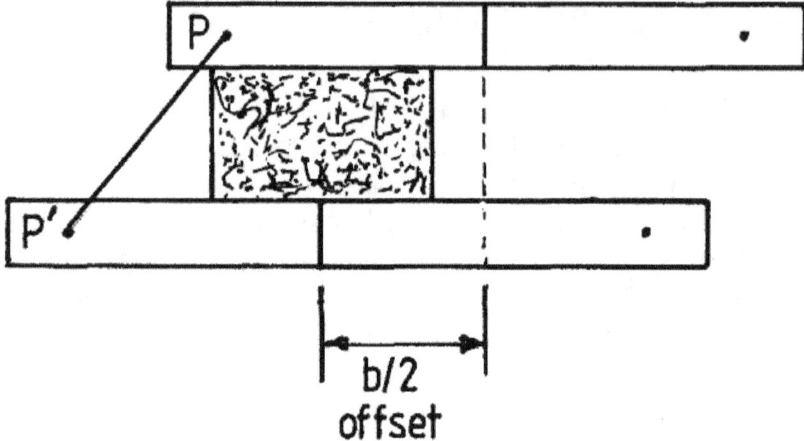

Fig S2.2
*Assembling the pantograph. Platform and base are offset by **b**/2 (**b** = stereo base required) to establish the distance **PP'** between pivot points.*

The pantograph can now be assembled. The holes in the linkage arms should be just large enough for the arms to rotate freely without too much slack. For those who like to work out their design in advance, the geometry of the pantograph is explained below so that the various dimensions can be calculated.

Calculating Dimensions
The key to the effective working of this device lies in the movement of the linkage arms. One of these arms is shown in **Fig S2.3**; it has to swing from position **OA** to **OA'**, the two end positions of its travel. The distance **AA'** is the desired stereo base **b**, normally around 65mm.
The value of this lateral displacement is determined by the length **AO** of the linkage arms (measured between the pivot points) and the angle **AOA'** through which the arms swing when the pantograph is operated. To produce a specific lateral displacement **b** (= stereo base) one can design the pantograph with long linkage arms; these will require only a small angle of swing. Alternatively, shorter linkage arms swinging through a larger angle will achieve the same result. Since using long arms will make the device rather top-heavy, it is best to compromise.

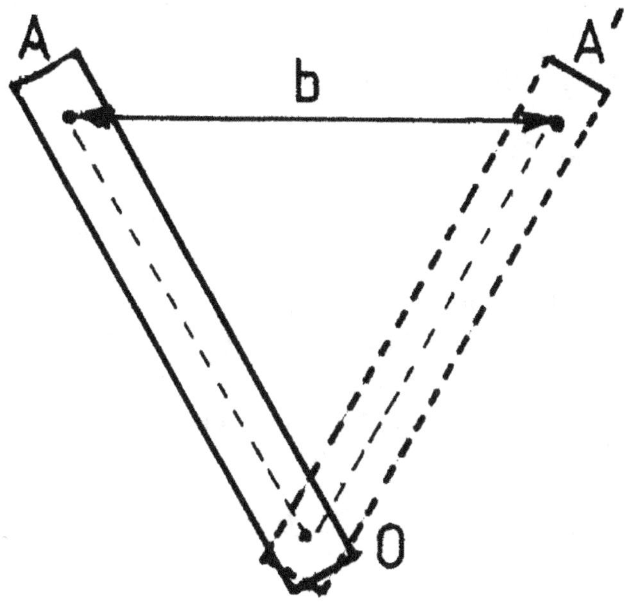

Fig S2.3
Movement of the linkage arm from **OA** *to* **OA'** *during the operation of the pantograph.*

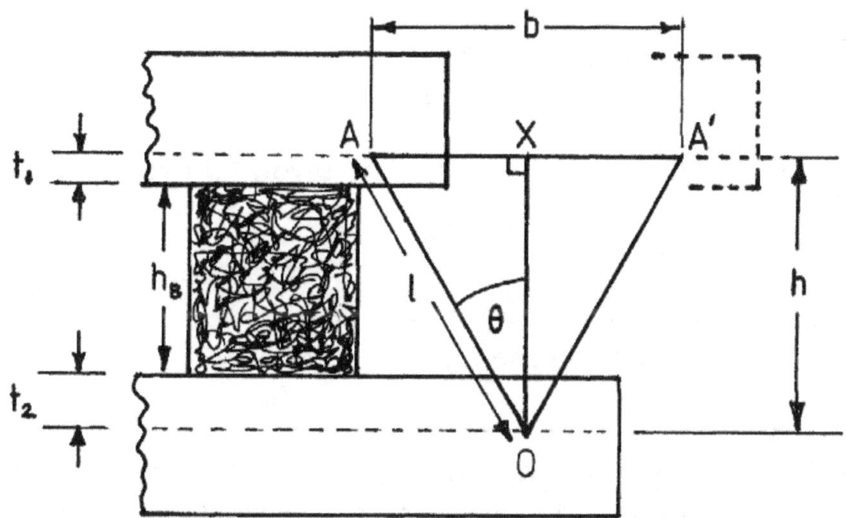

Fig S2.4
Basic geometry of the pantograph. **X** *is the mid-point of* **AA'**. **O, A** *and* **A'** *are pivot points. (The linkage arms are omitted for clarity).*

Fig S2.4 shows the configuration of a pantograph, incorporating a bridge, in one of its rest positions. To make this design a general one, we shall assume that the linkage arm pivot points are located at distances t_1 and t_2 from the "inner" surfaces of the two platforms as shown. If the two platforms are made the same thickness **t** and the pivot points are located on the "thickness centre lines" then $t_1 = t_2$ and $t_1 + t_2 = t$, which simplifies the calculation.

Applying simple trigonometry to triangle **AXO** gives:

$$\mathbf{AO} = \mathbf{I} = \mathbf{b}/(2\sin\theta)$$

This formula enables us to calculate the linkage arm length for any stereo base, provided we first choose a suitable angle of swing. For example, selecting a swing angle of 90° (i.e. $\theta = 45°$) which is not excessively small or large, the arm length for $\mathbf{b} = 65$mm will be: $\mathbf{I} = 65/(2\sin 45) = 65/(2 \times 0.7071) = 45.46$mm $= 46$mm to the nearest mm.

To complete the design we need to calculate the height of the bridge, $\mathbf{h_B}$. From **Fig S2.4** it can be seen that:

$$\mathbf{h_B} = \mathbf{h} - (t_1 + t_2)$$

From triangle **AXO**:

$$\mathbf{h} = \mathbf{b}/(2\tan\theta)$$

Continuing with our example:

$$\mathbf{h} \quad = 65/(2\tan45) = 65/(2 \times 1) = 32.\,5\text{mm}$$
$$= 33\text{mm to the nearest mm}$$

With 12mn thick platforms and centre line pivots, then:

$$t_1 + t_2 = \mathbf{t} \quad = 12\text{mm}$$

$$\text{and} \quad \mathbf{h_B} = \mathbf{h} - \mathbf{t} \quad = 32.5 - 12 = 20.5\text{mm}$$
$$= 21\text{mm to the nearest mm}$$

Alternative method

Instead of choosing a swing angle as a starting point, one can begin the design by selecting a value for $\mathbf{h}$, the vertical spacing of upper and lower pivot points.

In triangle **AXO** we can make use of Pythagoras' theorem:

$$\mathbf{l}^2 = (\mathbf{b}/2)^2 + \mathbf{h}^2$$

Choosing suitable values for **b** and **h** enables the linkage arm length **l** to be calculated from:

$$\mathbf{l} = \sqrt{(\mathbf{b}^2/4) + \mathbf{h}^2}$$

The bridge height is determined, as before, from:

$$\mathbf{h_B} = \mathbf{h} - (\,(\mathbf{t_1} + \mathbf{t_2})\ \text{or}\ \mathbf{h_B} = \mathbf{h} - \mathbf{t}\ \text{as appropriate}$$

Example

For **b** = 65mm, **h** = 40mm and **t** = 12mm, the linkage arm length **l** (between pivots) will be:

$$\mathbf{l} = \sqrt{(65^2/4) + 40^2}$$
$$= \sqrt{1056.25 + 1600}$$
$$= \sqrt{2526.25}$$
$$= 51.54\text{mm}$$

The bridge height will be 51.54 − 12 = 39.54mm
= 40mm to the nearest mm.

Varying the stereo base

The pantograph lends itself readily to close-up work, requiring smaller stereo bases. To restrict the lateral movement of the upper platform, it is an easy matter to design the pantograph with a removable bridge that can be replaced by others of appropriate heights. A taller bridge will reduce the stereo base. The relation between bridge height and stereo base is derived as follows:
applying Pythagoras' theorem to triangle **AXO** (**Fig S2.4**):

$$\mathbf{l}^2 = (\mathbf{b}/2)^2 + \mathbf{h}^2$$

Rearranging:

$$\mathbf{h}^2 = (\mathbf{l}^2 - \mathbf{b}^2/4)$$

and $\mathbf{h_B} = \sqrt{\mathbf{l}^2 - (\mathbf{b}^2/4)} - (\mathbf{t_1} + \mathbf{t_2})$

or $\mathbf{h_B} = \sqrt{\mathbf{l}^2 - (\mathbf{b}^2/4)} - \mathbf{t}$ (for centre line pivots and equal thickness **t** for platform and base).

Using this expression, the bridge height h_B for any stereo base within the capabilities of the particular design can be determined.

Example

For a pantograph in which I = 50mm and base thickness t = 12mm (centre line pivoting) calculate the bridge heights for stereo bases of 65mm and 10mm.

65mm base

$$h_B = \frac{\sqrt{I^2 - (b^2/4)}}{} - t$$

$$= \sqrt{50^2 - 65^2/4} - 12$$

$$= \sqrt{2500 - 1056.25} - 12 = \sqrt{1443.75} - 12$$

$$= 37.99 - 12$$

$$= 25.99\text{mm or } 26\text{mm (to the nearest millimetre)}$$

(This will be the "standard" bridge height for a normal stereo base using this pantograph.)

10mm base

As above, using b = 10mm:

$$h_B = \sqrt{50^2 - 10^2/4} - 12$$

$$= \sqrt{2500 - 25} - 12$$

$$= 49.75 - 12$$

$$= 37.75\text{mm (38mm rounded)}$$

Thus the 10mm stereo base can be achieved by inserting an extra thickness of 12mm (38 – 26) above the original bridge.

Finally, the maximum possible stereo base for a given pantograph will be realised when there is no bridge in place, i.e. when h_B = 0.

Putting h_B = 0 into the expression and rearranging:

$$T = \sqrt{I^2 - (b^2/4)}$$

i.e. $\quad t^2 = I^2 - (b^2/4)$

thus $\quad b = \sqrt{4(I^2 - t^2)}$

or $\quad b = 2\sqrt{I^2 - t^2}$

In our example, with $\mathbf{I}$ = 50mm and $\mathbf{t.}$ = 12mm, the maximum stereo base will be:

$$\mathbf{b} \quad = 2\sqrt{50^2 - 12^2} = 2\sqrt{2356}$$
$$= 97\text{mm to the nearest mm.}$$

This is more of academic than of practical interest because there is no great advantage in using a stereo base greater than about 65mm unless it is about 2 metres or more in magnitude (see Chapter 7, Section 7.2.3).

SUPPLEMENT S3 - ANGLE OF VIEW

Maximum Angle of View

The total image produced by any camera lens is actually circular and, for sharpness, lies on part of a spherical surface. Even so, the image quality deteriorates from the centre to the periphery of the "circle of illumination". Within this total image we can define a "circle of good definition" in which the image quality is of a predetermined standard of acceptance in terms of sharpness and relative freedom from aberrations. This circle of good definition represents the "covering power" of the lens and it is within this particular boundary that the image frame is located (**Fig S3.1**)

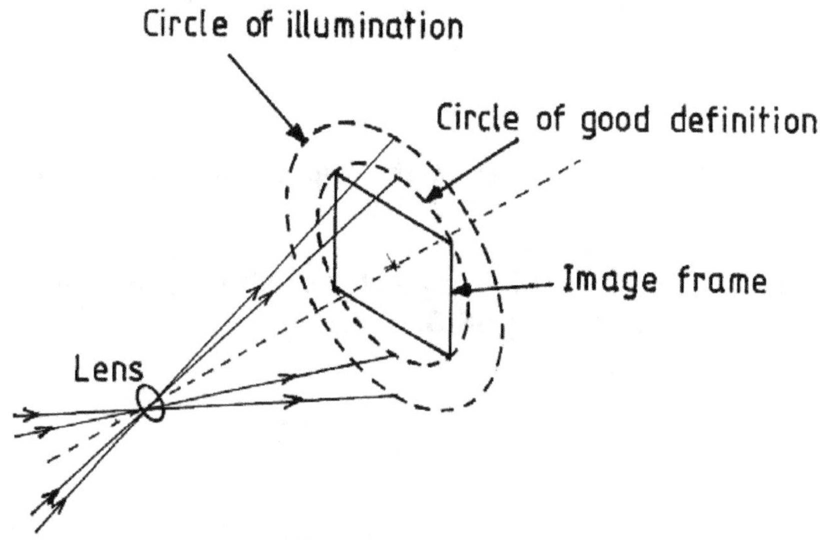

Fig S3.1
Covering power of a lens.

The covering power of the lens can be meaningfully expressed by the angle of view, which simply indicates the angle between two boundary rays of light on opposite sides of the cone of rays that enters the lens to form part of the framed image. Because the image frame is square or rectangular, depending upon the camera design, the widest angle involved will relate to the frame diagonal (**Fig S3.2**).

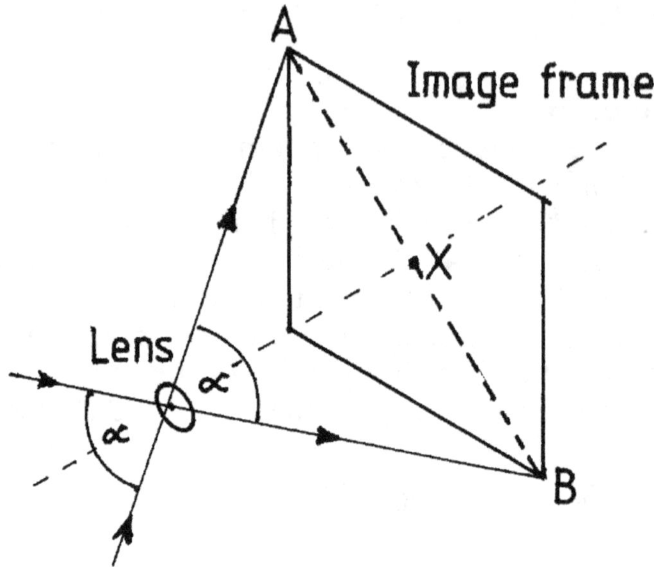

Fig S3.2
Angle of view of a lens subtended by the image frame diagonal at the lens centre.

In order to calculate this angle we need to consider the camera geometry, which is shown in Fig **S3.3**.

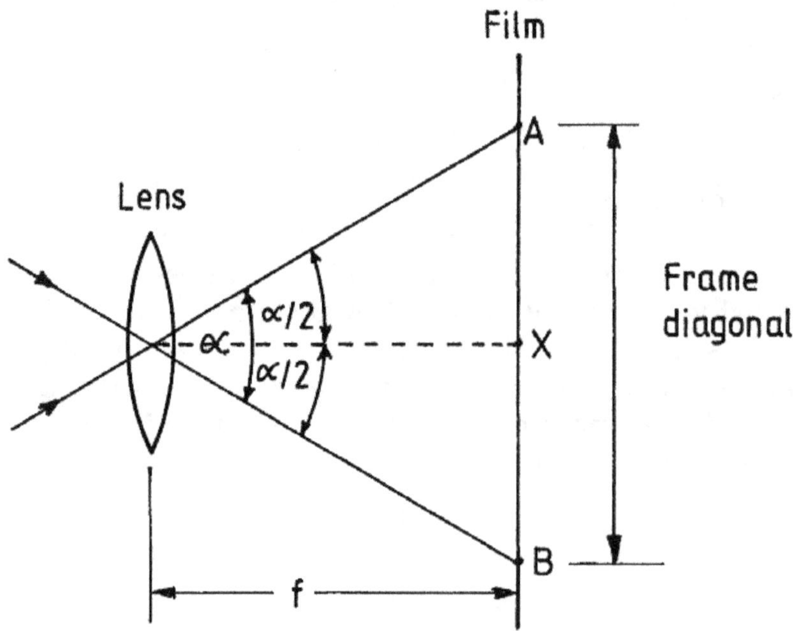

Fig S3.3
Camera geometry for calculation of the angle of view of a lens.

When focused at infinity, the lens will be situated at a distance equal to its focal length, **f**, from the film. If the frame diagonal is **AB**, **X** the mid-point of **AB** then by considering the half angle $a/2$ we have from simple trigonometry:

tan $(a/2)$ = **AX**/**f** = ½(frame diagonal)/(focal length)

From this equation, $a/2$ and hence a can be calculated.

When the length of the frame diagonal is equal to the focal length of the lens, the geometry is close to that in the human eye, and the perspective is therefore essentially the same in both the eye and the camera, giving a "natural" appearance to the image. In this case we refer to the lens as "standard" as opposed to "wide-angle" which gives a greater angle of view, or "telephoto" which has a smaller angle of view. Both wide-angle and telephoto images give a less natural perspective unless the images are viewed under strictly correct viewing conditions (see Supplement S1).

A normal 35mm image (24 x 36mm) has a diagonal of 43.27mm, so a 45mm focal length lens would be regarded as "standard". Nowadays, most standard lenses for 35mm cameras have a focal length of 50mm but this is not a major deviation from the basic principle. Many cameras are supplied with "standard zoom" lenses, typically 28 to 70mm focal length, rather than a fixed focal length. For a medium format camera with an image size of 60 x 60mm the image diagonal is 84.85mm, and in this case an 80mm focal length lens becomes the "standard" lens. The angles of view in these two examples will be virtually the same.

Using the formula quoted above and substituting **f** = 50mm and frame diagonal = 43.27mm:

$$\tan(a/2) = 43.27/(2 \times 50) = 0.4327$$

i.e. $a/2 = 23°24'$

and $a = 46°48'$

Calculations such as the above are based upon the configuration shown in **Fig S3.3**, in which the lens is focused at infinity, which means that the lens-film distance will be equal to the focal length **f**. If, however, the lens is focused on a nearer object, the geometry changes, because the lens-film distance will now be greater than **f**, the exact value depending upon the focused distance.

For example, if the lens is focused on an object 500mm away then the image distance **v** (lens-film distance) can be determined from the lens equation: $1/\mathbf{u} + 1/\mathbf{v} = 1/\mathbf{f}$.

Rearranging the equation:

$$1/v = 1/f - 1/u$$

Substituting **f** = 50mm and **u** = 500mm:

$$1/v = 1/50 - 1/500$$
$$= (10 - 1)/500$$
$$\text{so } v = 500/9 = 55.56\text{mm}$$

Therefore the angle of view will be given by:

$$\tan (a/2) = 43.27/(2 \times 55.56) = 0.3894$$

i.e. $a/2 = 21°17'$

giving $a = 42°34'$

This is slightly less than the angle of view for infinity focusing of the lens.

Despite this variation in angle of view with the lens focus setting, the value normally quoted is that for the infinity setting.

Horizontal angle of view

Of rather more practical use is the horizontal angle of view, which determines the width of the image, in other words how much of the subject from left to right is included within the film frame.

For any given lens focal length and film format the horizontal angle of view, based as it is upon the frame width, will clearly be less than that based upon the frame diagonal.

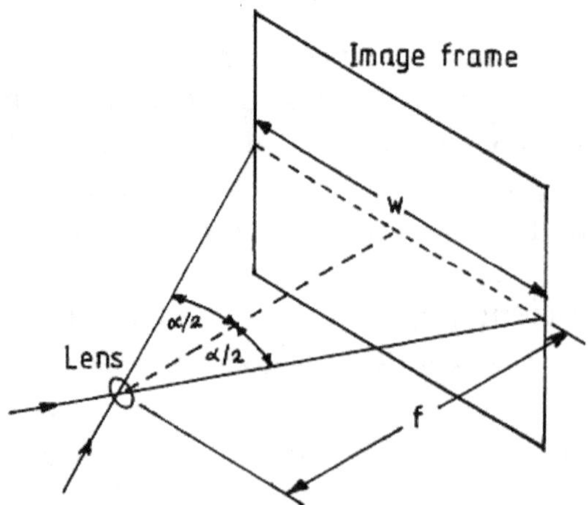

Fig S3.4
Horizontal angle of view of a lens.

Referring to **Fig S3.4**:

$$\tan(a/2) = (w/2)/f = w/2f$$
i.e. $\quad a = \tan^{-1}(w/2f)$

The horizontal field of view of the eye is quite large. With both eyes in action together it is approximately 180°. At the extreme edges of the field of view only peripheral vision is experienced, in which one is more conscious of movement rather than image detail. "Normal" vision lies within about a 50° angle.

One might assume that the most natural photographic images would be those in which the horizontal angle of view matched that of the eyes. Apart from panoramic cameras, no cameras, mono or stereo have view angles that are anywhere near 180°. However, if they approach 50°, the field of vision will not be too dissimilar to that of normal vision, excluding peripheral vision. Many stereo photographers prefer wider images although the reasons may only be subconscious ones. After all, everyday vision has no frame edges and we do not view the world through a stereo window, as we do when looking at a stereogram. Adopting a wider format, therefore, should give a more natural result.

In Chapter 3, the values for horizontal angle of view that are present in different cameras are included in the individual reviews. With the addition of angles of view for the standard 35mm mono image in both portrait and landscape formats, the figures are summarised in the table below:

Camera	Horizontal Angle of View
35mm - portrait format	27°
35mm - landscape format (8P)	39°36'
Wray Stereographic (5P)	36°22'
Stereo Realist (5P)	35°
FED Stereo (European format 7P)	43°05'
Nimslo (4P)	33°24'
View-Master (20mm focal length)	33°24'
View-Master (25mm focal length)	27°

When images from any of these formats are mounted, a small portion of each will be masked by the mount. This is necessary to allow for horizontal adjustments but it means that the angle of view for viewing is slightly less than that in the camera. However, the figures in the table are useful in making comparisons.

The table shows that none of the cameras gives an angle of view that matches that of the human eye (quoted as 50° earlier) but experience has shown that in the majority of cases the stereoscopic images are perfectly acceptable. The major formats (5P and 7P), of which there are many more examples than are included here, produce images with horizontal angles of view between about 35° and 45°. The exceptions are 35mm mono portrait format, the Nimslo and the View-Master. Some stereo workers might find the 27° angle rather too narrow for general use, but the Nimslo (at 33°24') is more acceptable, though borderline. The 20mm focal length View-Master format, with the same angle of view as the Nimslo, perhaps looks more natural because the image is virtually square. The Nimslo format is taller in comparison.

SUPPLEMENT S4 - TWO-MIRROR BEAM SPLITTER

The two-mirror device (see Chapter 4, Section 4.2.1) is set by placing the mirrors vertically and at a small angle θ relative to each other. The combination is then aligned at 45° to the camera lens axis. Thus the mirrors will actually lie at angles of $\theta/2$ relative to a 45° reference line, as illustrated in **Fig S4.1**, which is a plan view of the arrangement.

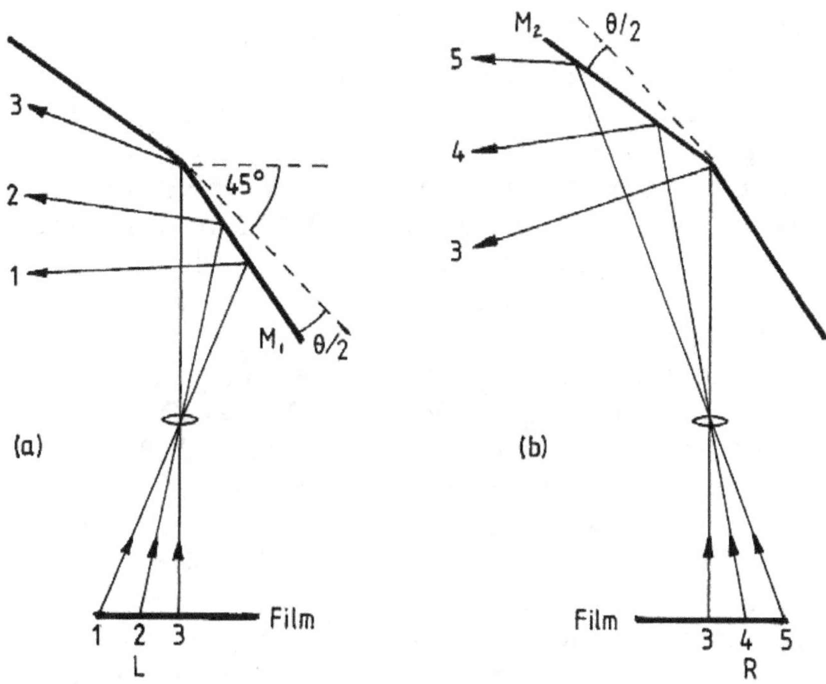

Fig S4.1
Two-mirror beam splitter showing the formation of the left image in mirror **M₁** *(a) and the right image in mirror* **M₂** *(b).*

Fig S4.1a shows how the left image is produced on the left half of the film frame as a result of the scene being reflected by mirror **M₁**. Light rays **1** and **3** are the outermost rays of the cone covering the field of view on the left image half frame. Ray **2** is the central light ray which represents the overall line of sight and which bisects the angle of view. Because this ray is not perpendicular to the film it means that the cone of rays as a whole strikes the film obliquely and there will be some slight convergence distortion of the image. This is a direct consequence of the fact that both principal optical axes have to pass through the one lens as they cross over to form the images on the film. This is unavoidable, but it does not cause a major problem.

Fig S4.1b shows, in like manner, the formation of the right image via mirror **M**$_2$.

In both diagrams the light rays are shown to be travelling from the film towards the subject via the mirrors. In reality they travel from the subject to the film, but assuming the opposite makes the optical analysis easier to follow. In optics, all such light ray paths are reversible; object and image are interchangeable, so the assumption will not lead to false conclusions.

In addition to the convergence distortion referred to above, additional distortions will be introduced unless the device is set up correctly. This is achieved by setting the angle between the mirrors to a value appropriate to the film format, and placing the mirrors at a suitable distance from the camera lens to produce the required stereo base.

Fig S4.1 represents an arbitrary setting of the device; in fact it is an unsatisfactory one because the sight lines (rays **2** and **4**) converge as they approach the subject, equivalent to "toeing-in" as illustrated in Chapter 2, **Fig 2.3**. In this case, the mirrors are set at too great an angle relative to each other, but if each mirror is rotated slightly, towards the 45° reference line, thus reducing both angles by the same amount, the sight lines will swing away from each other as indicated in **Fig S4.2**. At a certain angle, which can be denoted as **θ**$_C$/2 for each mirror, the sight lines will be parallel (**Fig S4.3**). The angle between the mirrors will be **θ**$_C$, which can be regarded as the critical angle. This critical angle is not unique; the actual value depends upon the film format and camera lens focal length, in other words, the in-camera geometry.

With parallel sight lines, the subject is "seen" in the same way that it is "seen" by a stereo camera, except for the slight convergence distortion referred to earlier.

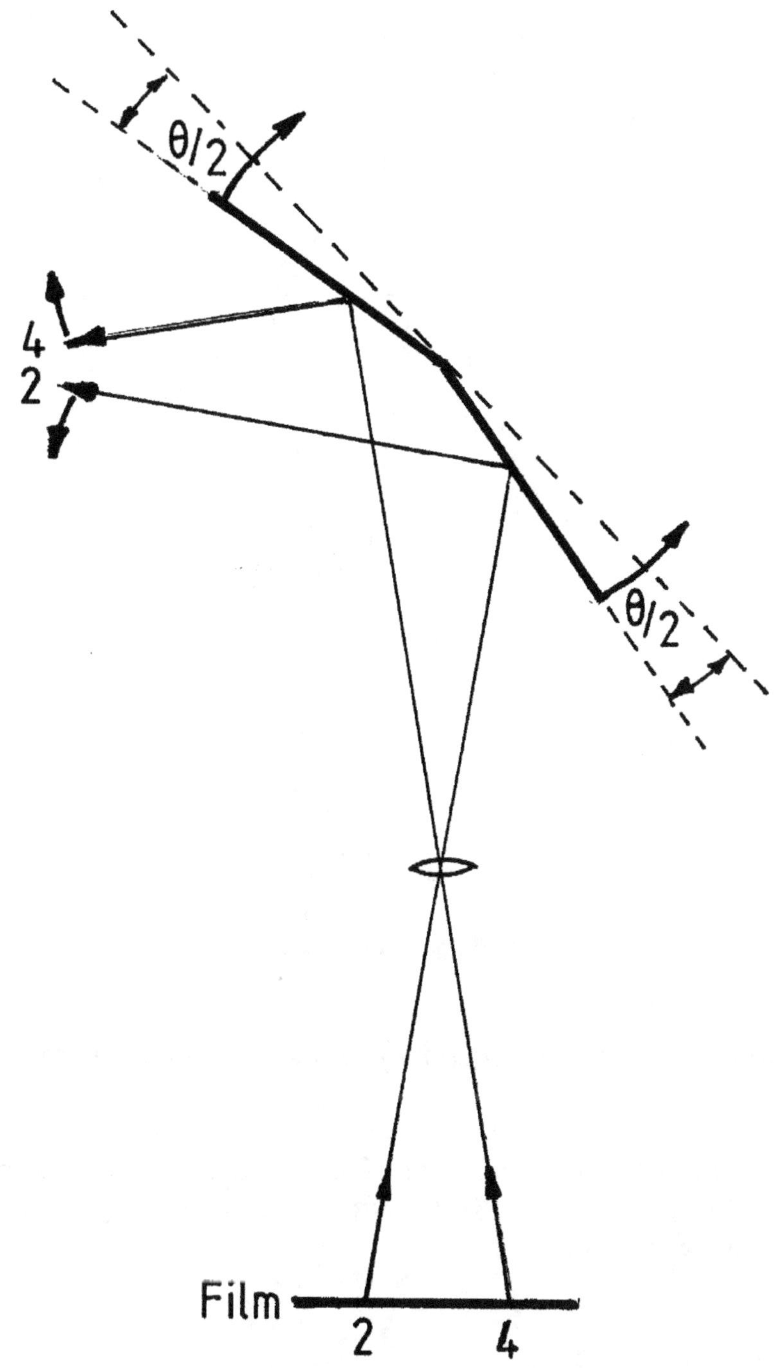

Fig S4.2
Rays **2** *and* **4** *(as in* **Fig S4.1***) converge after reflection in the mirrors, which are set at an arbitrary angle* **θ***. Reducing the mirror angle will reduce the convergence of the two rays.*

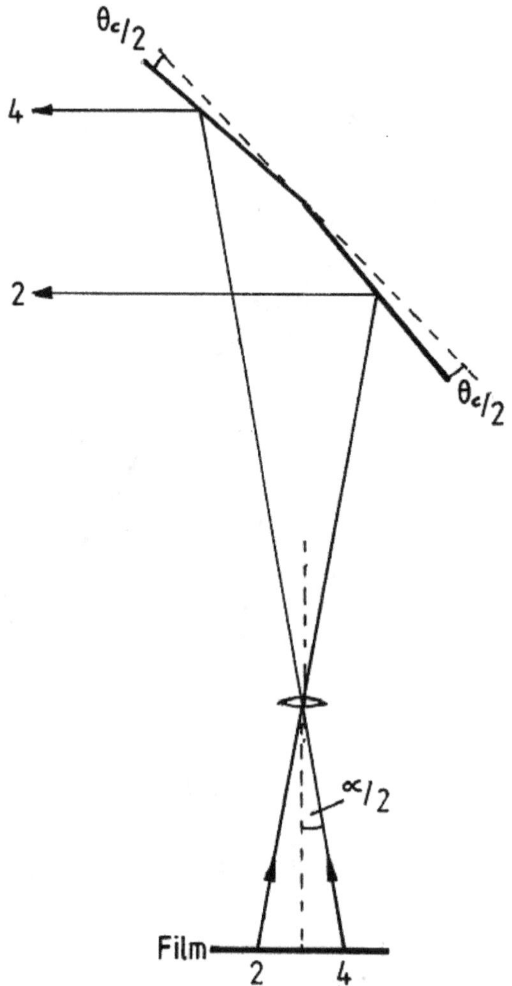

FigS4.3
*The sight lines (rays **2** and **4**) become parallel when the mirrors are set at the critical angle **θc**.*

    To determine the critical angle **θc**, for correct use, suppose that the mirrors are set at an angle **θ** = 0, which means that they effectively become one long mirror (**Fig S4.4**)

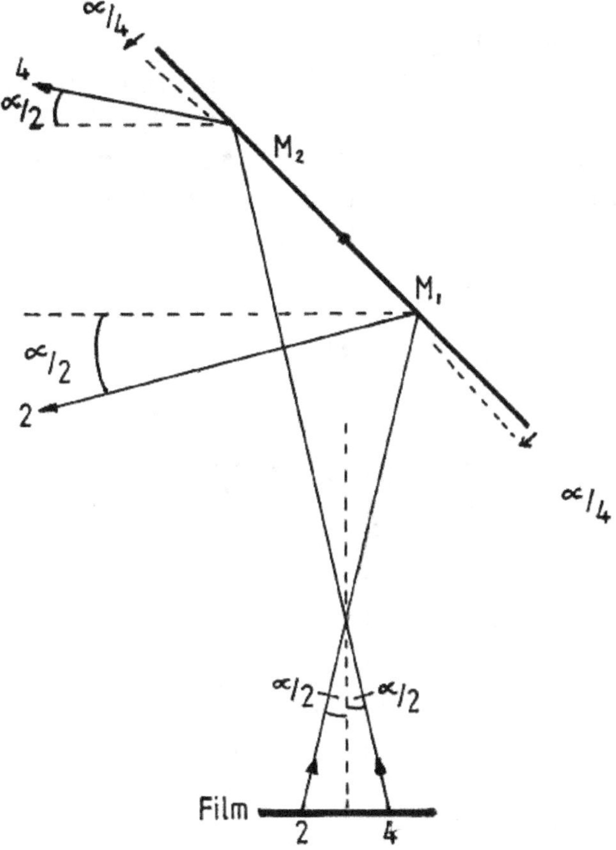

Fig S4.4
With mirrors **M₁** *and* **M₂** *set in line (zero angle), rays* **2** *and* **4** *diverge towards the subject, each by* **a**/2 *from parallel. Rotating each mirror by* **a**/4 *as shown will bring the rays parallel.*

Sight lines **2** and **4** will be found to diverge as they approach the subject. Simple geometry shows that both rays diverge by an angle **a**/2 from the paths they would follow in the correct setting (shown in **Fig S4.3**). These rays can be brought parallel by rotating mirror **M₁** clockwise and **M₂** anticlockwise by equal amounts. Now optical theory shows that if a mirror is rotated by any angle **Z**, a reflected ray will rotate in the same sense by an angle 2**Z**. It should be clear from **Fig S4.4** that the two mirrors should each be rotated by an angle of **a**/4 towards each other to bring the sight lines parallel. The angle between the mirrors after this adjustment will be **θc**, the critical value, which is equal to half the angle of view for the image, based here on one half-frame image, i.e. **θc** = **a**/2.

Example

To calculate the critical angle for a two-mirror device to be used with a 35mm SLR camera with a 50mm lens, the relevant half frame angle of view can be determined by reference to **Fig S4.5**. This is a slight approximation of the true geometry because the central ray is assumed to strike the film frame centrally. In fact, the point where it strikes the film will lie slightly to the right of the position shown. However, the error introduced will be negligible.

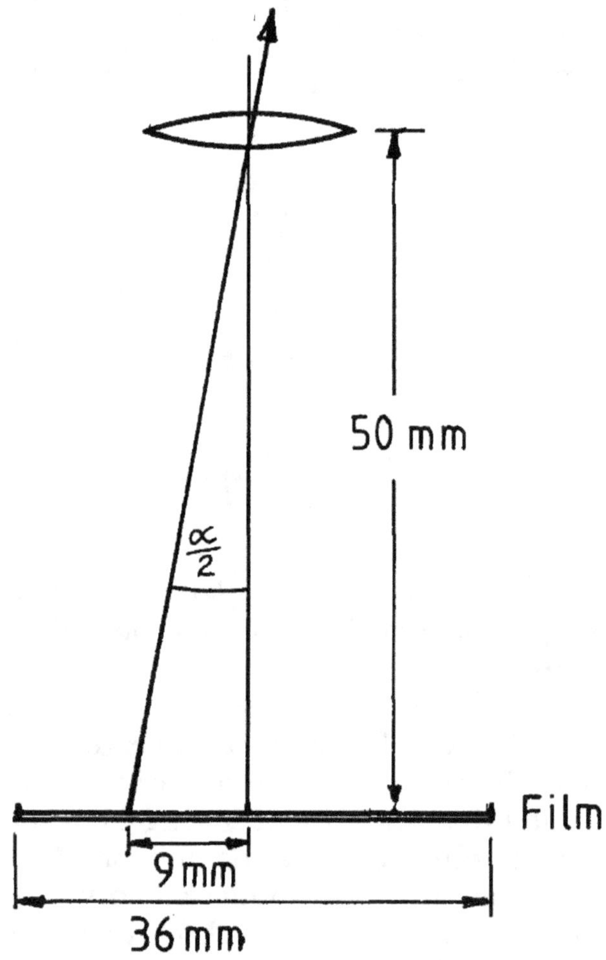

Fig S4.5
Camera geometry for 35mm landscape format.

From **Fig S4.5**:

$$\tan(\mathbf{a}/2) = 9/50 = 0.18$$

Therefore $\mathbf{a}/2 = 10.2 = 10°12'$

This is the angle to which the mirrors should be set; in practice a value of 10° will be accurate enough.

Since this value is approximately 1/4 of the horizontal angle of view of the camera lens (based upon the full frame width), the critical mirror angle can be taken as equal to this, for simplicity.

Setting the stereo base

In Fig **S4.6**, the paths of rays **2** and **3** are traced as they are reflected by mirror **M$_1$**, which is angled correctly at **a**/4. It is an optical fact that the angle between any two rays is unaltered by reflection in a plane mirror, so rays **2** and **3** remain at an angle **a**/2 to each other. They appear to originate from the point **S$_L$** behind the mirror; this point is simply the image of **S** in mirror **M$_1$**. Geometrically, the position of **S$_L$** is such that **SS$_L$** is at 90° to **M$_1$** and **SX** = **XS$_L$**. Now triangles **SOP** and **S$_L$OP** are similar, which means that **OS$_L$** = **SO** = **D** and angle **OS$_L$P** = **a**/2.

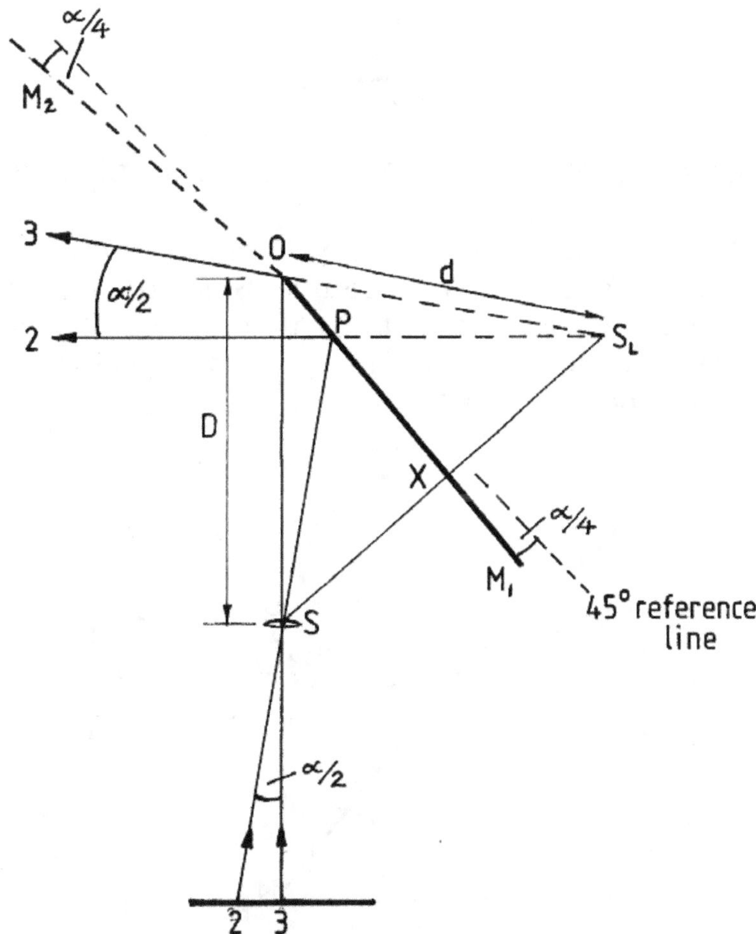

Fig S4.6

*With the mirrors set at the critical angle, rays **2** and **3** appear to originate from **S$_L$**. This is the effective viewpoint for the left image.*

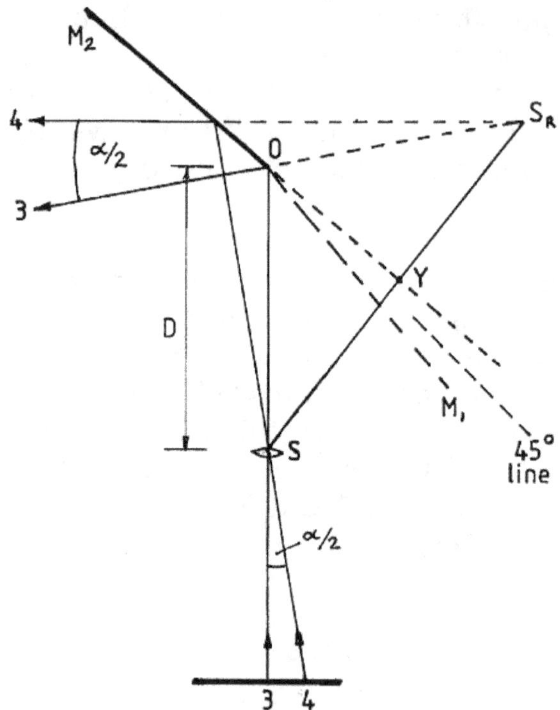

Fig S4.7
Similar to **Fig S4.6** *but showing the effective viewpoint* **S_R** *for the right image.*

Fig S4.7 shows the geometry for rays **3** and **4** and the right image. In this case **S_R** represents the apparent source. Since the lines **S_L O** and **S_R O** in these two diagrams are equal in length and equally inclined to the horizontal line running left to right through **O**, the positions of **S_L** and **S_R** are symmetrical as shown in **Fig S4.8**.

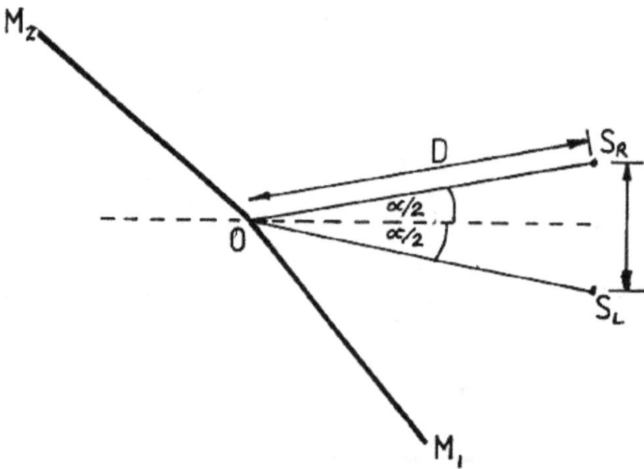

Fig S4.8
Positions of **S_L** *and* **S_R** *in relation to the mirror junction* **O**.

$\mathbf{S_L}$ and $\mathbf{S_R}$ are the effective viewpoints, or "lens positions" for the stereo images and the distance $\mathbf{S_L S_R}$ is the stereo base $\mathbf{b}$.

From trigonometry:

$$\sin(\mathbf{a}/2) = \mathbf{b}/2\mathbf{D}$$

so $\quad \mathbf{b} = 2\mathbf{D}\sin(\mathbf{a}/2)$

or $\quad \mathbf{b} = 2\mathbf{D}\sin\mathbf{\theta_C}$ since $\mathbf{a}/2 = \mathbf{\theta_C}$

Alternatively, the equation can be rearranged as:

$$\mathbf{D} \quad = \mathbf{b}/(2\ \sin\mathbf{\theta_C})$$

Example

Using the same parameters as in the previous example, the distance $\mathbf{D}$ at which the assembly should be placed in order to produce a stereo base of 65mm will be:

$$\mathbf{D} \quad = 65/(2\sin 10)$$
$$= 65/(2 \times 0.1736) = 65/0.3472$$
$$= 187\text{mm to the nearest mm.}$$

So, for normal base stereo photography, using the 35mm full frame format, the mirrors should be angled at 10°, placed with the vertical "join" 187mm (7.4in) from the lens. The mirrors will have to be about 150mm (6in) in width, to cover the whole horizontal angle of view.

SUPPLEMENT S5 - THE ELLIOTT STEREOSCOPE

As explained in Chapter 5 Section 5.2.3, this simple stereoscope (**Fig 5.5**), which uses no mirrors or lenses, is designed to assist in the free viewing of images by the convergent sight lines (crossing the eyes) technique. Its dimensions are calculated so that each eye can see only a single image, the correct one for that eye. This makes fusion of the two images considerably easier, but the stereo pair have to be mounted unconventionally, with the left image to the right and vice versa. This type of stereoscope is normally used to view large prints, though it could be used equally well with suitably illuminated large transparencies.

Any particular Elliott stereoscope will have been designed to work for a particular size of image, but it will function effectively with smaller or larger images provided that they are reasonably close in size to the "ideal".

Fig S5.1 shows the basic geometry of an Elliott stereoscope; this is depicted in its most general form, for viewing a stereo pair in which the infinity homologue separation s_i differs from the eye separation **b**. For convenience, we shall assume that **b** is also the value of stereo base used to photograph the stereo pair. In addition, the individual image width is assumed to be equal to the infinity separation s_i. In practice it will be slightly smaller (to produce a stereo window) but equating it to s_i will simplify the analysis without introducing any significant error.

In the diagram, triangle **XCE** represents the cone of rays entering the left eye as it views the left image **CE**; triangle **YAC** is the equivalent for the right eye. Each eye views its image through the "window" **QR** at the far end of the stereoscope; the surrounds of the window, **PQ** and **RS** prevent either eye from seeing any part of the wrong image, provided that the width of the window **QR** (= **L**), the stereoscope length **y** and the overall viewing distance **D$_V$** are correctly proportioned. In designing such a device, we select appropriate values for **D$_V$**, s_i and **b**, and calculate **y** and **L**.

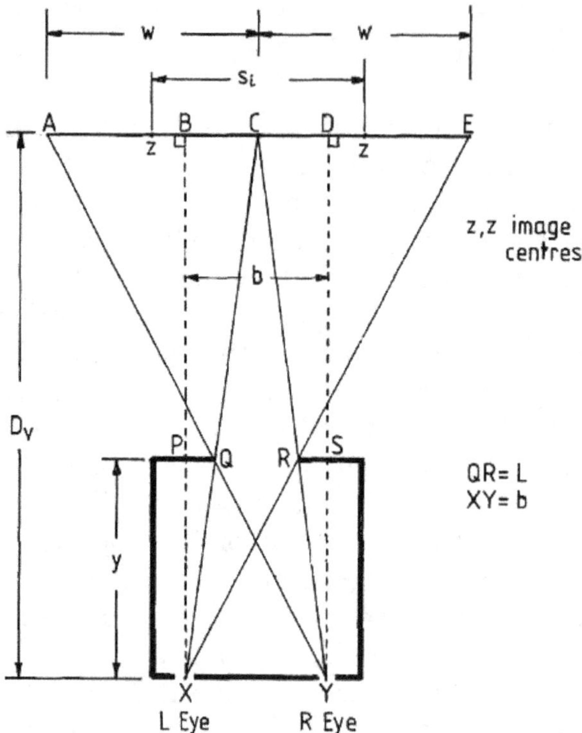

Fig S5.1
Basic geometry of the Elliott stereoscope.

Using the dimensions in **Fig S5.1**, where **QR = L**, **AC = s_i** and **XY = b**, we can, from simple geometry, establish formulae for **L** and **y**, as follows:
From similar triangles ACY and **QRY** of heights **D_v** and **y** respectively:

$$L/y = s_i/D_v$$

Now consider similar triangles **CQR** and **CXY**:

$$L/b = (D_v - y)/D_v$$

Rearranging:

$$L/y = b/y - b/D_v$$

Substitute for **L/y** to give:

$$s_i/D_v = b/y - b/D_v$$
i.e. $$y = bD_v/(s_i + b)$$

Since **$L/y = s_i/D_v$** then **$L = ys_i/D_v$**
i.e. $$L = bs_i/(s_i + b)$$

Example

Calculate **L** and **y** for an Elliott stereoscope suitable for viewing 80mm prints at a distance of 300mm.

Taking s_i = 80mm, **b** = 65mm and D_V = 300mm and substituting these values in the equations gives:

$$\mathbf{y} = (65 \times 300)/(65 + 80) = 134.48\text{mm}$$
$$= 134\text{mm to the nearest mm.}$$

$$\mathbf{L} = (65 \times 80)/(65 + 80) = 35.86\text{mm}$$
$$= 36\text{mm to the nearest mm.}$$

Standard print size: When an Elliott stereoscope is to be designed for viewing standard size prints with infinity homologues set at the normal spacing, the above formulae are simplified. By putting s_i = **b** they become:

$$\mathbf{Y} = D_V/2$$
$$\text{and } \mathbf{L} = b/2$$

Thus with D_V = 300 mm and **b** = 65mm

$$\mathbf{y} = 150\text{mm}$$
$$\text{and } \mathbf{L} = 32.5\text{mm}$$

Image height: The height of the end window in the stereoscope is not as critical as its width, but it is necessary to make it large enough so that the tops and bottoms of the images are not cut off when viewed.

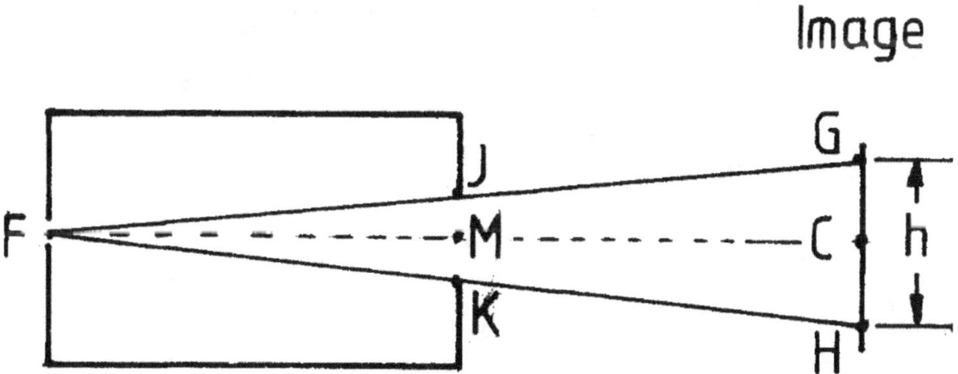

Fig S5.2
Side view of the Elliott stereoscope. **JK** *is the aperture height that can be calculated from the geometry shown.*

Fig S5.2 shows a side view of the stereoscope, in which **JK** is the (minimum) window height required to see the whole height **h** of the image. From similar triangles **FJK** and **FGH**:

$$JK/GH = FM/FC$$

Or $$JK = FM \times GH/FC$$

Now $$FM = y, \ GH = h \text{ and } FC = D_V$$

So the window height $$JK = yh/D_V$$

In other words, the window height is y/D_V times the image height. This is, of course, a minimum value; the window can be made larger in height because there is nothing above or below the images to cause any viewing problems.

Design variations: In the above analysis we have assumed that the two images of the stereo pair are butted together at the centre. For D_V = 300mm we find that the length of the stereoscope is of the order of 150mm. This may be felt to be rather long to be a convenient viewing aid, but the viewing distance cannot be reduced or the eye will be unable to focus the images, 300mm is about the closest distance for normal viewing. Anything closer than this would normally require lenses and the whole purpose of the Elliott stereoscope would be defeated.

The length of the stereoscope is determined by the distance from the eyes at which the sight lines cross (points **Q** and **R** in **Fig S5.1**). If, however, the two images are placed further apart and the "squinting" increased, these points can be brought closer together and the length of the stereoscope decreased. The end window will also need to be made smaller, as illustrated in **Fig S5.3**.

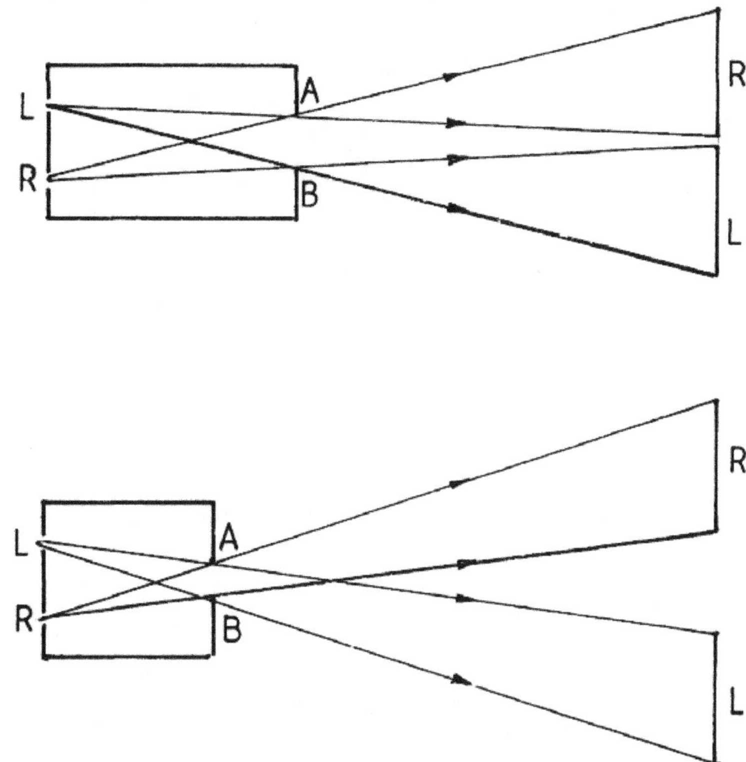

Fig S5.3
Variation in design of the Elliott stereoscope. By separating the images (lower picture) the amount of "squinting" is greater but the stereoscope can be shorter. The end aperture **AB** *will also be smaller.*

Greater convergence of the eyes will occur with this modification to the design; convergence should not be excessive or it will lead to eyestrain. To reduce this, each image could be tilted inwards as illustrated in **Fig 5.10** in Chapter 5. On balance, it is probably best to reduce eyestrain by keeping to the original design and accepting that the stereoscope will be somewhat bulky.

SUPPLEMENT S6 - DESIGN OF A CAZES STEREOSCOPE

Basic Geometry: The Cazes stereoscope is a simple viewer based upon two pairs of parallel mirrors set at 45° to the overall line of sight. Its principal use is to enable large prints to be viewed comfortably when they are mounted side-by-side, which will cause the infinity point separation to be substantially greater than the normal 65mm or so. If the two images of the stereo pair are large enough, they can be butted together. This not only simplifies mounting but also allows the stereoscope to be smaller in width. In the analysis that follows it will be assumed that the images are mounted in this way, at least as a starting point. If this arrangement does not work in any specific case, the prints can always be separated and the stereoscope made wider. Ideally, the instrument should be designed to allow viewing with the correct perspective (Supplement S1). With most applications this will probably not be achieved and viewing distances are likely to be longer than ideal. Consequently, when designing a model, the viewing distance should be kept as small as is feasible. Any increase in the spacing of the outer mirrors increases D_V, the viewing distance; if it is possible to butt the images side by side, then D_V will be kept to a minimum.

Whilst construction of a Cazes stereoscope is not complicated, the mirrors have to be fixed in place with precision, perhaps using spring-loaded supports and adjusting screws so that the mirrors can be tweaked into exact alignment.

The optical geometry is shown in **Fig S6.1**, which depicts only the left half of the stereoscope; the images are butted together for this model. The right half is similar but, appropriately, a mirror image.

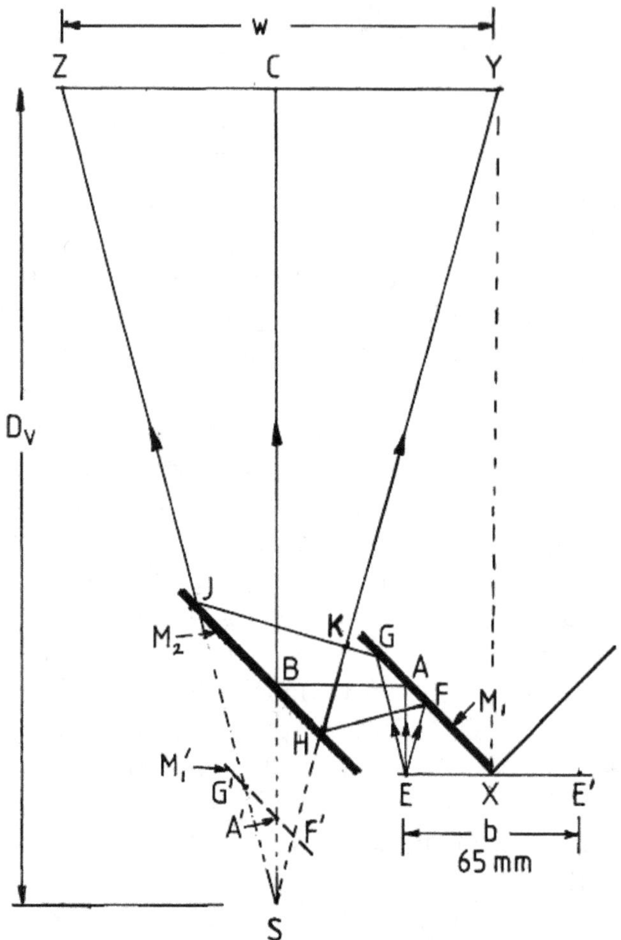

Fig S6.1
*Geometry of the Cazes stereoscope showing the left eye (**E**) view of the left image **ZY**. The effective viewpoint is at **S**. A similar construction can be made for the right eye.*

Lines **EFHY** and **EGJZ** are the outer rays of the cone of light that enters the left eye from the left image **ZY** and undergo a double reflection. For simplicity, the two inner mirrors are assumed to meet at **X**, the midpoint of the two eye positions **E** and **E'**, although in practice these mirrors need not extend as far as **X**. For **M₁**, the section marked **GAF** is all that is required to "collect" the whole cone of light rays, though in practice the mirror would be made slightly wider, extending slightly beyond **G** and **F**.

Mirror **M₂** (and its right hand equivalent) has to be larger than **M₁** in order to cover the greater width of the cone of light in this region. The distance between the mirrors, marked as the line **AB** on the diagram, has to be large enough to allow ray **YH** to avoid the edge of mirror **M₁**. The closest possible spacing of the mirrors will occur when point **G** lies at the very edge of **M₁** and coincides with point **K**.

We shall assume that the left and right images are butted together at the centre, represented by point $\mathbf{Y}$, which is in direct line with $\mathbf{X}$, the mid-point of the line joining the eye positions. Point $\mathbf{C}$ is an infinity point in the centre of the left image; there will be a corresponding point $\mathbf{C}'$ in the right image. These infinity homologues will be separated by s_i. With the image configuration shown, s_i will be approximately equal to $\mathbf{w}$, the individual image width. We shall also assume that $s_i = \mathbf{w}$ for simplicity; this will not introduce any significant errors.

The stereoscope has to be designed so that the principal sight line $\mathbf{EABC}$ has components $\mathbf{EA}$ and $\mathbf{BC}$ parallel to $\mathbf{XY}$, with $\mathbf{AB}$ at 90° to these.

Extending lines $\mathbf{ZJ}$, $\mathbf{CB}$ and $\mathbf{YH}$ shows that the light rays appear to originate at point $\mathbf{S}$ (**Fig S6.1**). This is the effective viewpoint for the left eye. The line $\mathbf{G'A'F'}$ is actually the image of $\mathbf{GAF}$ (i.e. mirror $\mathbf{M_1}$ itself) in mirror $\mathbf{M_2}$, and triangles $\mathbf{G'F'S'}$ and $\mathbf{GFE}$ are identical. This construction will help to establish design details, as discussed below. The image of $\mathbf{M_1}$ is denoted as $\mathbf{M_1}'$.

Determining the dimensions

The simplest way to determine suitable dimensions is to make a scale drawing from which the important parameters can be measured. Before describing the procedure, there are two important dimensions that result from the geometry of **Fig S6.1**.

First, since $\mathbf{M_1}$ is set at 45°:

$$\mathbf{AE} = \mathbf{EX} = \mathbf{b}/2.$$

Second:

$$\mathbf{AB} + \mathbf{EX} = \mathbf{CY}$$
i.e. $\quad \mathbf{AB} = \mathbf{CY} - \mathbf{EX}.$

Thus $\mathbf{AB} = s_i/2 - \mathbf{b}/2$
Or $\quad \mathbf{AB} = (s_i - \mathbf{b})/2$

It follows that

$$\mathbf{SB} = \mathbf{BA} + \mathbf{AE}$$
$$= \mathbf{BA} + \mathbf{EX}$$
$$= s_i/2$$

For accuracy, the drawing should be fairly large, but there is no need to make it larger than actual size. **Figs S6.2** and **S6.3** illustrate the first steps in the procedure and **Fig S6.1** should be used as a general reference. The instructions given below lead to the scale drawing of the left half, which can be duplicated as a mirror image to produce the right half.

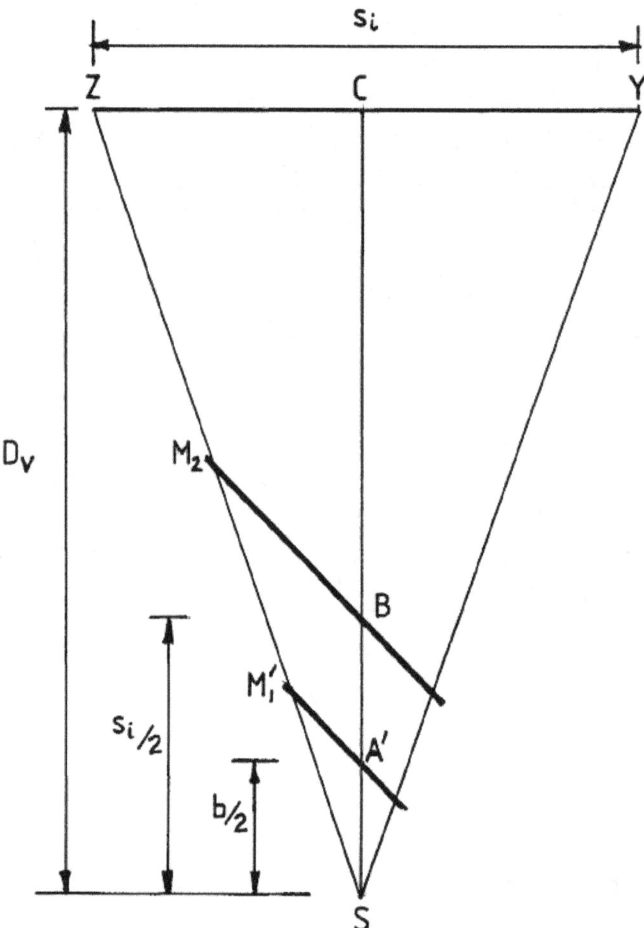

Fig S6.2
First stage in the design of a Cazes stereoscope, to locate mirror positions.

Start by drawing the triangle **ZYS** with **ZY** = s_i, **C** as the mid-point of **ZY** and **CS** = D_V, the viewing distance, at least 300mm (**Fig S6.2**). Then proceed as follows:

1. On the line **CS** mark points **A'** and **B** such that **SA'** = $b/2$ and **SB** = $s_i/2$ (**Fig S6.2**).
2. Draw lines through **A'** and **B** at 45° to **CS** to represent the mirror positions, bearing in mind that the line through **A'** is actually an image of the true position of mirror **M₁** (**Fig S6.2**).

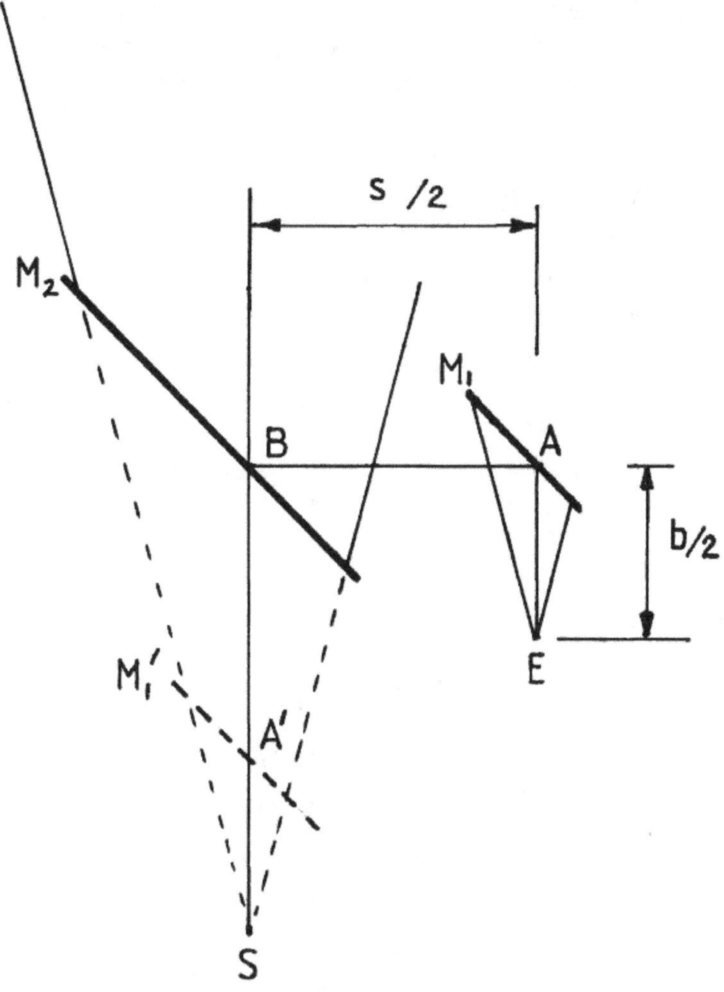

Fig S6.3
Locating the exact position of mirror **M₁** *from its "image" at* **M₁'**.

3. Now draw the line **BA** at 90° to **CS** such that its length is equal to **BA'** (**Fig S6.3**). This establishes the actual point for the location of **M₁**.
4. Draw **AE** at 90° to **BA**, of length **b**/2, to locate the left eye position.
5. Draw the line **EG** parallel to **SZ** (**Fig S6.1**). If point **G** lies to the right of the line **SY** then the design is satisfactory. However, if it lies to the left of **SY** the design must be modified, as explained in the next section. It may be helpful to draw the line **GJ** and to mark point **K**. Point **G** should lie to its right, although it will not lie exactly on a horizontal line drawn through **K**.
6. Draw line **EF** parallel to **SY** (**Fig S6.1**)
7. Draw **EX**, length **b**/2, at 90° to **AE** (**Fig S6.1**).

The key features of the design are now in place. If drawn correctly, **YX**, which marks the centre line of the stereoscope, should be parallel to

CS. Points **A** and **B** enable the mirrors to be positioned correctly (at 45° to **YX** and **CS**) and the lengths **JH** and **GF** can be measured to determine the mirror widths, allowing a little extra to ensure that there will be no image cut-off.

Correcting a "faulty" design

If the initial plan results in point **G** lying to the left of **K**, the solution is, as illustrated in **Fig S6.4**, to shift mirror **M₂** to the left. At the same time, the left image must be moved by the same distance to keep the sight line **BC** parallel to its original direction.

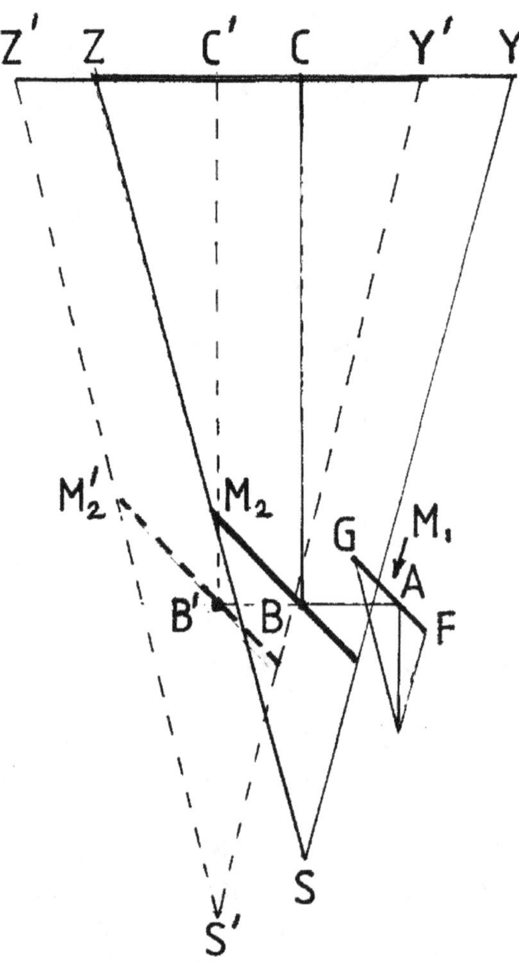

Fig S6.4

*Correcting a design problem. With the image at **ZCY** and mirror **M₂** at **B**, the ray **SY** will be impeded between **G** and **A**. Shifting **M₂** leftwards to **M₂'** and the image to **Z'C'Y'** provides the solution, In doing so, the viewing distance is increased from **CS** to **C'S'**.*

The right image will have to be shifted to the right (along with the equivalent outer mirror) by the same amount. The infinity separation is thereby increased. The amount of the shift needs to be sufficient to allow point **K** to lie to the left of **G**, with a little extra to accommodate the section of mirror **M₁** to the left of **G**.

Moving **M₂** in this way increases the viewing distance **Dᵥ**. **C'S'** will be longer than **CS** and the cone angle **Z'S'Y'** smaller than **ZSY**. If, therefore, the initial design is faulty, it may be easier to start again, using a larger value for **Dᵥ**.

The further apart mirrors **M₁** and **M₂** are set, the larger mirror **M₂** must be if it is to "capture" the whole cone of rays, so it is advisable to place the mirrors as close as is feasible. This will keep the overall size of the stereoscope to a minimum.

Mirror heights

Mirror **M₂** must be tall enough to accept the complete cone of light rays from the image at the point of reflection. So too must **M₁**, but here the cone diameter is smaller than it is at **M₂**, which means that **M₁** can be made shorter. If so, it will be necessary to mount the mirrors with their horizontal centre lines at the same height, as indicated in **Fig S6.5**; the line **CBA'S** is horizontal (for convenience the image **M₁'** of mirror **M₁** is shown in the diagram) and points **C**, **B**, **A'** and **S** correspond to those in **Fig S6.1**.

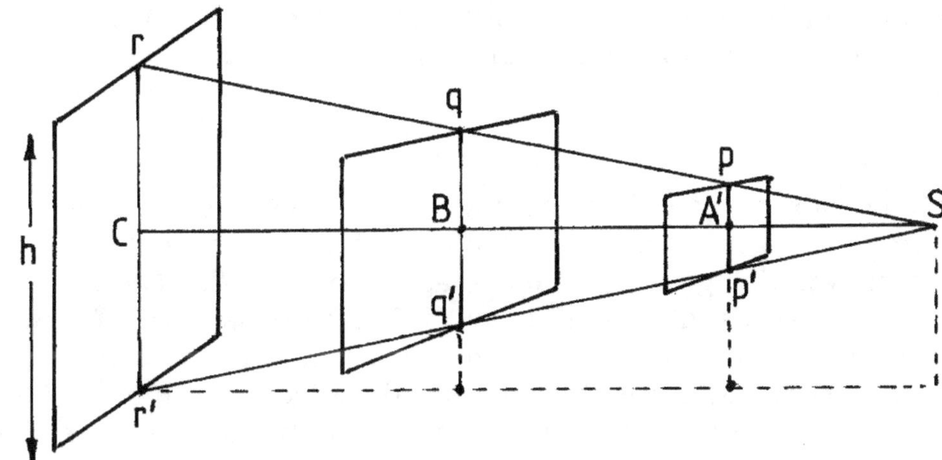

Fig S6.5
*Geometry of mirrors to enable heights **pp'** and **qq'** to be calculated.*

The heights **pp**' and **qq**' can be determined by proportion, using the image height **h** and similar triangles **Spp**', **Sqq**' etc. and from the known distances **SA**' = **b**/2, **SB** = s_i/2 and **SC** = D_v.
Thus:

$$\mathbf{pp}'/\mathbf{h} = \mathbf{SA}'/\mathbf{SC}$$

i.e.   **pp**' = **bh**/2$\mathbf{D_v}$
Similarly   **qq**'/**h** = **SB**/**SC**
i.e.   **qq**' = s_i**h**/2$\mathbf{D_v}$

These formulae give the absolute minimum heights; in practice the dimensions should be increased slightly. Alternatively, having established the required height of $\mathbf{M_2}$, mirror $\mathbf{M_1}$ can be made to the same height. It does not matter if it is taller than necessary, and construction of the stereoscope is simplified because all the mirrors can be mounted on a common baseboard without having to adjust the vertical position of $\mathbf{M_1}$ to align its centre with that of $\mathbf{M_2}$.

Casing

Once the mirrors have been set correctly and the stereoscope checked in its operation, the whole thing could be enclosed in a wood, metal or plastic case with appropriately placed apertures, or it can be left as an open structure.

Calculations

It is possible to calculate the key dimensions of a Cazes stereoscope directly from the geometry instead of constructing a scale drawing as described above. Using the "butted images" format, **Fig S6.6** shows the critical design that just allows light ray **YKS** to by-pass mirror $\mathbf{M_1}$, which is assumed to be of exactly the minimum width to accept the cone of rays. In this case, points **K** and **G** are coincident at the edge of the mirror. Although this configuration is idealistic, it enables us to establish the nearest possible viewing distance for a given pair of butted images. This can then be compared with the "correct" distance for orthostereoscopic viewing and any necessary adjustments made to the design. In this model, an image of width **w** (= s_i) can be correctly and completely viewed. From the geometry we can calculate the minimum possible $\mathbf{D_v}$ value. This should be increased slightly in practice to give a "margin of safety". An increase in $\mathbf{D_v}$, however, will automatically reduce angle **a**, and require the outer mirrors and the two images to be moved further apart.

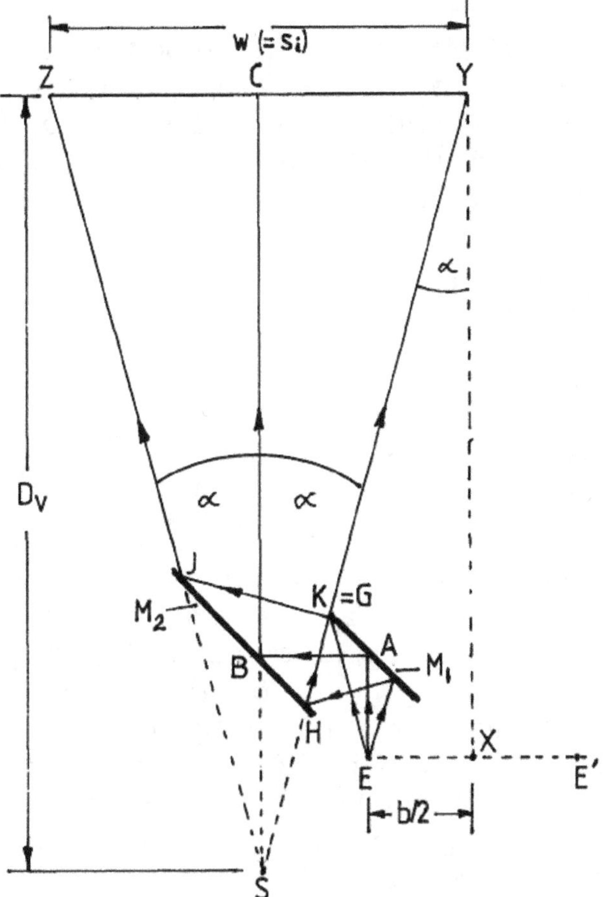

Fig S6.6
*"Critical" geometry of the Cazes stereoscope for abutted images. The left image **ZY** and mirror positions at **A** and **B** give the closest mirror distance **AB** that will allow boundary light ray **SY** to pass mirror **M₁** at **K**, which is coincident with **G** (see **Fig S6.1**).*

From **Fig S6.6**:

$$\tan\alpha = w/2D_v \ (= s_i/2D_v \text{ in this model})$$

i.e. $\quad D_v = s_i/2\tan\alpha$

It can also be shown from **Fig S6.6** that:

$$\tan\alpha = \frac{\left[s_i - \sqrt{\left(2s_ib - b^2\right)}\right]}{\left[s_i - b\right]}$$

The value of $\tan\alpha$ can be determined from this last expression and then used in the earlier expression to give **D_v**.

Example

The starting point is the image size to be viewed by the stereoscope. Suppose the individual image width is 216mm (= s_i); this represents a six-fold enlargement from a standard 35mm film frame. The left and right images are to be butted together. The eye spacing **b** will be taken as 65mm. Using the above formula for tan **a**:

$$\tan \mathbf{a} = \frac{\left[216 - \sqrt{28080 - 65^2}\right]}{[216 - 65]}$$
$$= 0.4076$$

Hence $\quad$ **Dv** $\quad$ $216/(2 \times 0.4076)$
$$= 265\text{mm}$$

Since this is slightly too close for most people to view comfortably, the distance should be increased to, say, 300mm. This increase in **Dv** of 35mm will be made by increasing the separation of each of the two images by the same amount, i.e. making s_i equal to 216 + 70 = 286mm, instead of 216mm as originally planned. This means that, in this case, the prints are going to be separated rather than abutted. The outer mirrors will also have to be moved apart by an extra 35mm each (i.e. a total increase in separation of 70mm from 216 to 286mm) to ensure that the sight lines are parallel. The new design will now look like **Fig S6.4**.
Key dimensions will be as follows:

SB = s_i/2 = 286/2 = 143mm
BA = (s_i − **b**)/2 = (286 − 65)/2 = 110.5mm

Increasing **Dv** from the original (minimum) calculated value of 265mm to 300mm in this example results in correct perspective when viewing. The individual image magnification by a factor of 6 requires a viewing distance of 6 times the focal length of the camera lens; for a 50mm lens this distance is 300mm. With other image sizes it will not always be possible to achieve this ideal, but the stereoscope should be designed as far as possible to approach it.

Mirror sizes

The mirror widths **GF** and **JH** can be calculated from relatively simple formulae; the mathematics is simplified by the fact that the mirrors **M₁** and **M₂** are related geometrically. The width of **M₂** is larger than that of **M₁** by a factor of **w/b**, that is **JH** = **(w/b)GF**.

The length **GF** is calculated as the sum of lengths **GA** and **AF** from the following formulae:

$$\mathbf{GA} = \mathbf{b}\sin\mathbf{a}/(2\sin(45 - \mathbf{a}))$$
$$\text{and} \quad \mathbf{AF} = \mathbf{b}\sin\mathbf{a}/(2\sin(45 + \mathbf{a}))$$

Having determined the width **GF**, it is then multiplied by the factor **w/b** to determine **JH**. The angle **a** is the half angle of view, as before. Since $\tan\mathbf{a} = \mathbf{w}/2\mathbf{D_V}$ the value of **a** in degrees can be found from trigonometric tables.

Example

Using the dimensions calculated in the previous example we have **b** = 65mm, **D$_V$** = 300mm and **w** = 216mm. It is important to remember that the value of $\tan\mathbf{a}$ for the "critical" design was determined as 0.4076, leading to a minimum **D$_V$** of 265mm. However, **D$_V$** was increased to 300mm and so the value of angle **a** will now be smaller than it was in the original plan and so has to be recalculated to determine the mirror sizes.

So $\quad \tan\mathbf{a} = 216/(2 \times 300) = 0.36$

i.e. $\quad \mathbf{a} = 19.8°$ or $19°48'$

Hence $\qquad\qquad$ **GA** $\quad = 65\sin 19.8/2\sin(45 - 19.8)$
$\qquad\qquad\qquad\qquad\quad = (65 \times 0.3387)/(2 \times 0.4258)$
$\qquad\qquad\qquad\qquad\quad = 25.9\text{mm}$

Similarly $\quad$ **AF** $\quad = 65\sin 19.8/2\sin(45 + 19.8)$
$\qquad\qquad\qquad\qquad\quad = (65 \times 0.3387)/(2 \times 0.9048)$
$\qquad\qquad\qquad\qquad\quad = 12.2\text{mm}$

Therefore $\quad$ **GF** $\quad = 25.9 + 12.2 = 38.1\text{mm}$
and $\qquad\quad$ **JH** $\quad = (216/65) \times 38.1 = 126.6\text{mm}$

As mentioned earlier, these are the theoretically smallest possible values; in practice the mirrors should be made slightly wider.

Some Cazes type viewers, such as the "Mirrorscope", were marketed in the early part of the 21st century. The outer mirrors were about 6 inches apart and could be rotated by turning a central knob to allow different sized images to be viewed.

SUPPLEMENT S7 - DEVIATIONS (PARALLACTIC DIFFERENCES) IN STEREO IMAGES

Homologue separations

Various references have been made in this book to the basic differences between the left and right images of a given stereo pair. Commonly, these differences are expressed in terms of the variation in separation between homologues of distant objects and those of near objects. Of particular importance are the separations s_i (for objects at infinity) and s_2 (for objects at 2 metres), this being a specific value for s_n (s_n being a general symbol for the separation of near object homologues).

The values of s_i and s_2 (and any other s value for objects between 2 metres and infinity) are usually taken as being measured on the mounted stereogram (Chapter 1, **Fig 1.6**, for example). As individual values, s_i and s_2 are purely arbitrary, because they depend simply upon how far apart the two images have been placed. If the separation of two images in a mount is increased by 1mm, for example, the values of each of these two separations would be greater by this amount. However, the difference (s_i - s_2) is unaffected by the image spacing and thus remains constant. It is a measure of the small differences between the two images, which is constant however far apart or close together the images are placed.

If s_x is the (mounted) separation of two homologues for an object located **x** metres from the observer, then:

$$(s_i - s_x) = d_x$$

where d_x is called the parallactic difference (pd) or deviation for that object (or strictly, the particular homologues representing a particular point on the object).

It will be clear from the formula that d_x will increase as the object distance from the observer decreases. Deviation for objects at infinity will be zero. These deviations all arise from the geometry of the subject and camera as will be explained shortly.

Acceptable range of depth

Let us consider the choice of s_2 as a reference or limiting value of s_x in addition to s_i. One of the strong recommendations for general stereoscopic photography, constantly urged in this book, is not to include objects closer than about 2 metres, at least if the most distant object is at infinity. The reason is straightforward and a simple demonstration will identify an important fact of normal vision. Try the following experiment: hold the forefinger of one hand vertically at about arm's length from the face and in front of, say, a window a metre away or more (the distance is not critical). Focus the eyes on the window and you will be conscious of two images of the forefinger (out of focus); focus on the finger and you will be aware of two window images. This double image effect is known as **diplopia**. If you repeat the experiment with the forefinger in front of a wall (and close to it) this double imaging is absent. In this case, the eyes can take in both objects more comfortably. If the distance between two objects is excessive, one object is seen as double when the eyes focus upon the other, and this is irritating when reproduced in a stereo image (although, somewhat strangely, less so in real life).

When the most distant of the two objects is at infinity, then the closest object that can be tolerated, without causing diplopia, is about 2 metres away (which seems surprisingly close). This distance is by no means exact; the effect will vary from person to person, but general opinion has settled upon 2 metres as an acceptable value.

In focusing separately on an object 2 metres away and then on one at infinity, the eyes also have to converge (rotate in their sockets). In **Fig S7.1** the two objects are located for convenience on the left eye's principal axis. It can be seen that the rotation of the right eye (in this example) is the angle **θ** as it swings from the near object to infinity, or vice versa.

Geometrically the angle **LNR** is also equal to **θ**. If we take $\mathbf{D_N}$ = 2m and **LR** = 65mm then:

$$\tan \mathbf{\theta} = 65/2000 = 0.0325$$
$$\text{i.e.} \quad \mathbf{\theta} = 1.86° = 1°52'$$

This represents (approximately) the maximum "swing" that the eyes can make without experiencing the double image effect. The angle **θ** at point **N** formed by the lines **NL** and **NR** is also termed the parallax of **N**.

If point **N** moves closer to the eyes, say at a distance 1 metre away, it will still be possible to see other objects behind it without diplopia, but only if the more distant objects are no further back than the distance determined by a 1°52' eye rotation from the near point. For a 1 metre near point, the furthest tolerable distance is 2 metres (**Fig S7.2**). Supplement S9 gives further details.

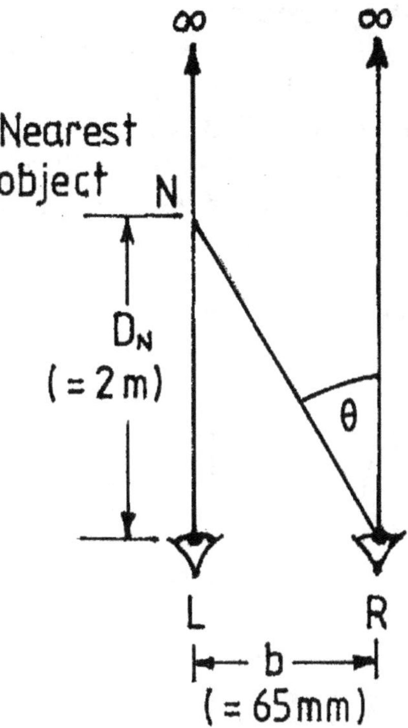

Fig S7.1
Maximum depth range (2m to infinity) for comfortable viewing. This defines a "maximum permissible eye swing" angle θ.

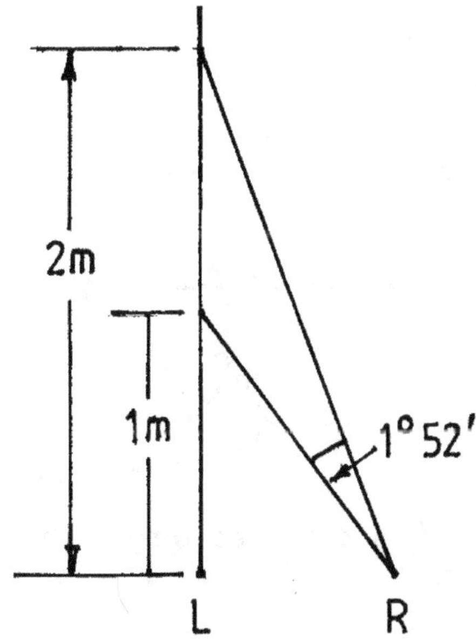

Fig S7.2
The "comfortable" depth range is reduced markedly if the nearest object is brought closer, to 1m. The depth range, for an "eye swing" of 1°52' now extends only from 1m to 2m.

Deviations (parallactic displacements)

The different displacements produced in the two images of a stereo pair arise from the two viewpoints of the camera lenses, and the basic geometry is summarised in **Fig S7.3**. From optical theory we can easily locate the image positions of point objects on film by considering light rays that pass through the optical centre of each lens, for they will do so without deviation from a straight line path (see also Chapter 17, Section 17.4.2).

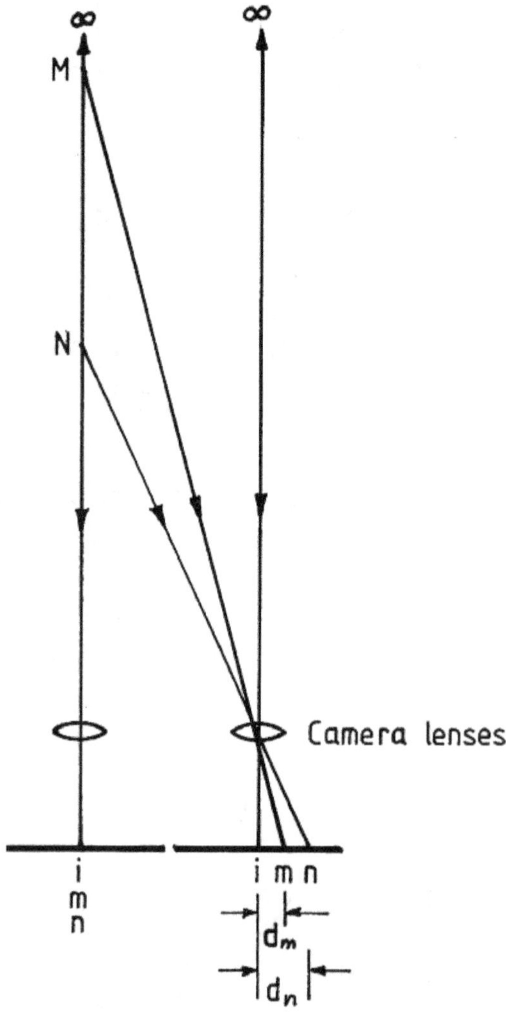

Fig S7.3
Parallax deviations d_m *and* d_n *produced on film by point objects* **M** *and* **N** *respectively.*

The objects at infinity, mid distance (**M**) and near distance (**N**) produce images **i**, **m** and **n** as shown on each film frame. (For convenience the objects are all located on the left lens axis). The distances **im** and **in** on the right image are the parallactic displacements or deviations for objects **M** and **N** respectively (d_m and d_n). The magnitude of **d** is greater for a nearer object. The separation between near point homologues (distance **nn**) from one film frame to the other is greater than that for infinity homologues (**ii**) when the film is in the camera but this will be reversed when the images are transposed for viewing. When mounting is complete, therefore, the homologue separations will conform to the familiar concept that s_i is greater than s_n.

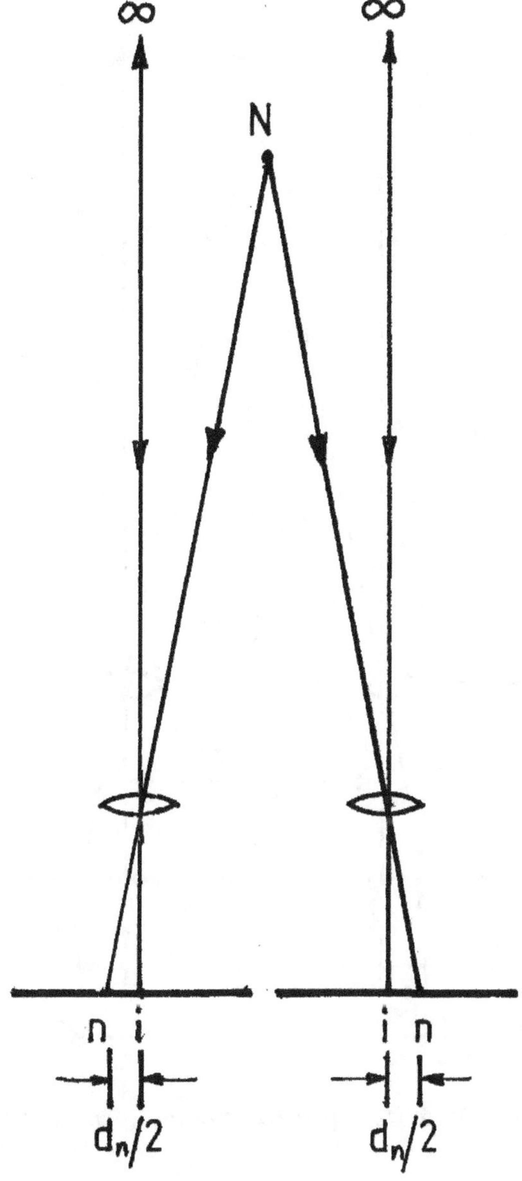

Fig S7.4
*For a centrally located object the deviation **d_n** is equally divided between the two images.*

If the objects lie on a line midway between the two lens axes then the deviation is divided equally between the two images (**Fig S7.4**). The total deviation is unchanged in value, however. Taking this further, if the object **N** in **Fig S7.4** is further to the left or right of the position shown (but still at the same distance from the camera) the "partial" deviations **ni** and **in** in the two film images will be unequal, but their sum will still be the same as the total deviation as measured in **Figs S7.3** and **S7.4**.

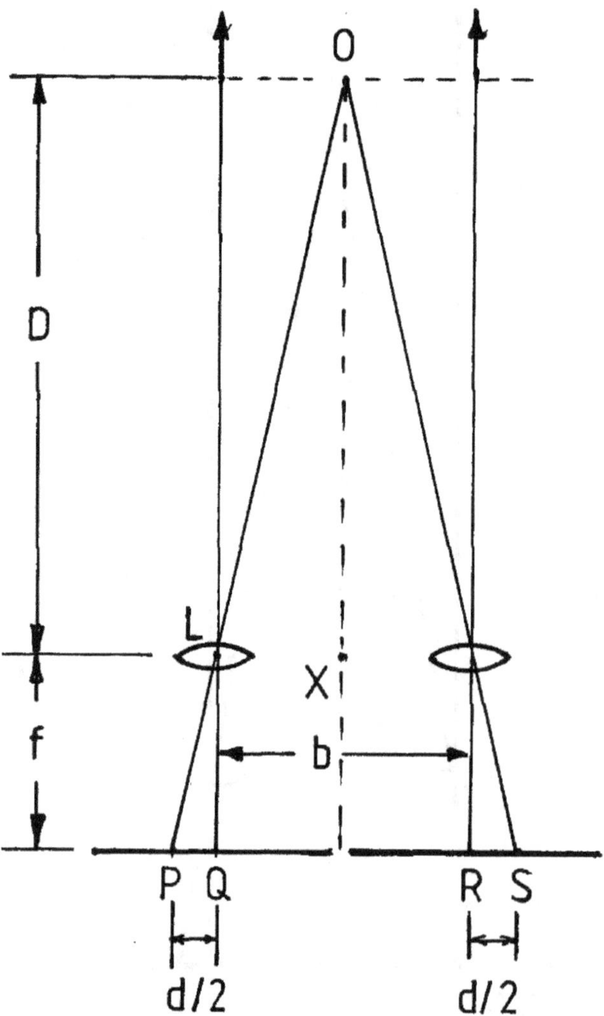

Fig S7.5
Determination of deviation **d** *in camera images for an object at distance* **D**. *Lens focal length is* **f**.

The relationship between deviation **d** for a given pair of homologues and the distance at which their stereo image appears in space (measured from the lens) can be calculated quite simply. From **Fig S7.5**, which is a generalised form of **Fig S7.4**:

> **b** = lens spacing (= stereo base)
> **f** = focal length of lens
> **D** = object distance
> **d** = deviation

Assuming that the lens is at a distance equal to its focal length from the film plane, consider the two triangles **OLX** and **LPQ**. Since they are similar triangles:

$$\mathbf{PQ/QL = LX/XO}$$

So $\quad \mathbf{PQ = (QL \times LX)/XO = f(b/2)/D)}$

i.e. $\quad \mathbf{d/2 = fb/2D}$

or $\quad \mathbf{d = fb/D}$

This simple formula tells us that the deviation is directly proportional to the focal length and stereo base and is inversely proportional to object distance. For example, if we double **f** (or **b**) we will double **d**; if we double **D** we will halve **d**, and so on.

We can now use this formula to calculate the maximum deviation **d**, which occurs for the closest permissible object, at 2 metres, for different formats.

35mm lens
(**5P**): **f** = 35mm, **b** = 70mm and **D** = 2000mm.
So $\quad$ **d** = (35 x 70)/2000 = 1.225mm

(**7P**): **f** = 35mm, **b** = 63.4mm and **D** = 2000mm.
So $\quad$ **d** = (35 x 63.4)/2000 = 1.11mm

50mm lens
$\quad$ **f** = 50mm, **b** = 70mm and **D** = 2000mm
So $\quad$ **d** = (50 x 70)/2000 = 1.75mm

For the 5P and 7P formats the deviation is standardised at 1.2mm (the original standards were based on the imperial measure of 7ft, which is 2134mm rather than 2000mm. Using 2134mm in the calculation gives slightly lower values for **d**.

With the 50mm focal length lens full frame format the deviation is usually standardised at 1.6mm, although 1.5mm is sometimes quoted.

The formula can be applied to any format and focal length so that the appropriate **d** value can be determined. As should be apparent from Chapter 6, these deviations are important in mounting the images "correctly"

Strictly, the value of focal length, **f**, which appears in the formula should be replaced by the actual lens-film distance that was present in the camera when the image was focused. As the lens barrel is rotated to focus on nearer objects it screws outwards, increasing the lens-film distance from the value **f**, which only applies when the lens is focused at infinity. As an aside, it must be remembered that in practice the focused distance is usually greater than the nearest object distance to give a suitable depth of field with an appropriate aperture setting. In calculations involving near object distances, the image distance **v** (from the lens formula; see Chapter 17, Section 17.4.3) should be used in the formula rather than the focal length **f**. However, in most cases the error is only slight. For example, using a 35mm lens at f/8 will give a sharp picture extending from about 2.3m (7' 7") to infinity if we focus the lens at 4.6m. The lens/film distance **v** for this focused distance is determined as follows:

using the lens formula $1/\mathbf{u} + 1/\mathbf{v} = 1/\mathbf{f}$ and working in mm:
$$1/4600 + 1/\mathbf{v} = 1/35$$
i.e. $\quad 1/\mathbf{v} = 1/35 - 1/4600$

giving $\quad \mathbf{v} = 35.27\text{mm}$

Replacing **f** by this value of **v** in the deviation formula (with **b** = 70mm, **D** = 2000mm):

$$\mathbf{d} = (35.27 \times 70)/2000$$
$$= 1.234\text{mm}$$

This is slightly higher than the value calculated previously (1.225mm) but the difference is negligible.

The lens-film distance, or image distance, is usually referred to as the **working focal length** for convenience.

The working focal length increases markedly as the focused distance becomes less than a metre or so and this can cause problems. The calculation above shows only a small difference in the **d** values obtained by using **v** or **f** but in extreme close-up photography, the working focal length will be significantly greater than the focal length and will lead to a larger deviation **d** on film. The danger is that it may exceed the maximum permitted value of 1.2mm (or the appropriate value) for the format, which, as discussed earlier, is related to the maximum angle of eye swing for comfortable viewing in the 2m to infinity, 1 metre to 2 metre, or any equivalent range of depth. If the maximum deviation is exceeded on the film image, there will be "too much depth" and viewing will be uncomfortable.

To correct any possible misconceptions, it should be pointed out that not all stereograms will necessarily exhibit this maximum deviation. A scene containing objects from 5 metres to infinity will show a deviation of less than 1.2mm. The exact value can be calculated from the deviation formula:

using $\mathbf{d} = \mathbf{fb}/\mathbf{D}$
and taking $\mathbf{f}$ = 35mm, $\mathbf{b}$ = 70mm and $\mathbf{D}$ = 5000mm

$$\mathbf{d} = (35 \times 70)/5000$$
$$= 0.49\text{mm}$$

Such calculations can be of assistance in the positioning of the film chips during mounting, even if the information leads to only approximate solutions. Accurate positioning requires precision of the order of fractions of a millimetre, and relies on the photographer knowing exactly how far away the nearest object (or any other notable feature) was from the camera at the time the picture was taken.

Nevertheless, in case this kind of information is to hand when mounting, the following table gives the deviations that correspond to various object distances. Values for other formats or focal lengths can be calculated from the deviation formula, as in the example above.

TABLE S 7.1
Values for parallax deviation d at various distances D

Focal Length 35mm										
D (m)	2	2.5	3	3.5	4	5	6	8	10	20
d (mm)	1.2`	0.98	0.82	0.7	0.61	0.49	0.41	0.31	0.25	0.12

Focal Length 50mm										
D (m)	2	2.5	3	3.5	4	5	6	8	10	20
d (mm)	1.6	1.31	1.09	0.93	0.81	0.65	0.55	0.41	0.33	0.16

From this table, the mount separation of homologues for an object at a particular distance **D** can be determined, starting with the s_i value recommended for the particular format. An example will make this clear.

Taking s_i = 63.4mm for the Realist format (35mm lens), the actual mount separation for an object at 10 metres, say, (this can be any object whose distance in the original scene is known, not necessarily the nearest one) is calculated as follows.

The table above gives a **d** value of 0.25mm for this distance (D = 10m). Therefore, the mount separation of homologues at this distance will be (63.4 – 0 25) = 63.15mm. If these are set correctly all other homologues will be correctly spaced. The principle is the same as that for setting infinity points at 63.4mm or 2m distant near points at 62.2mm and can be used when there are no 2m or infinity objects in the images. If the exact distance of the reference object is not known, an approximate value can often be recalled and used instead, so that the film chip locations in the mount are at least somewhere close to the ideal.

SUPPLEMENT S8 - CALCULATION OF THE STEREO BASE IN CLOSE-UP PHOTOGRAPHY

The 1 in 30 rule

The basis for this rule has been given in Chapter 7, Section 7.2.4. As illustrated in **Fig 7.3**, the normally accepted closest distance for objects that can be included in a scene that extends to infinity, namely 2m, is almost exactly thirty times the normal stereo base of 65mm. Even using a base of 70mm or 63.4mm as commonly found in stereo cameras does not significantly alter the ratio.

For example:

$$65/2000 \quad = 0.0325 \quad = 1/30.8$$
$$70/2000 \quad = 0.035 \qquad\quad = 1/28.6$$
$$63.4/2000 \quad = 0.0317 \quad = 1/31.5$$

When the distance of the nearest object is greater than 2m, there is generally no need to alter the stereo base unless that nearest object is several hundred metres away. This is a situation that calls for hyperstereoscopic treatment, using a larger stereo base in accordance with the information given in Chapter 7, Section 7.2. The one in thirty rule can be used as a guide, though it is not obligatory, as long as the base is not excessive in relation to the nearest object distance.

With close-up stereo photography, the one in thirty rule comes into its own. This rule states that the correct stereo base **b** can be determined from the distance $\mathbf{D_N}$ of the nearest object by taking $\mathbf{b} = \mathbf{D_N}/30$. This ensures that the geometry of the camera/object configuration is identical (but on a reduced scale) to that in normal stereo photography with a base of 65mm (**Fig S8.1**). The scaling down means that the maximum deviation (e.g. 1.2mm) is not exceeded.

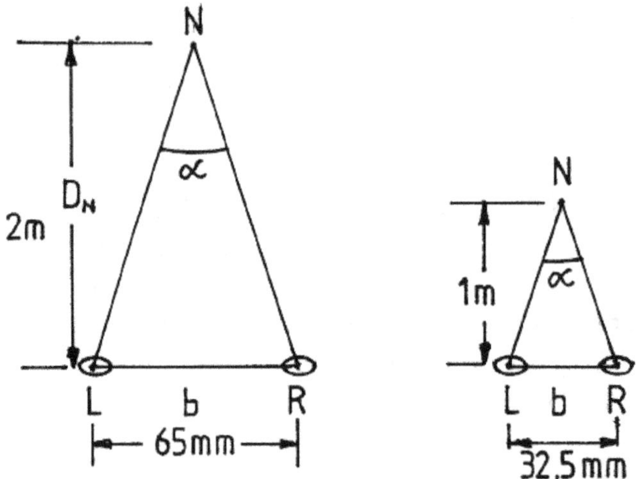

Fig S8.1
Reducing the stereo base in proportion to the distance of the nearest object **N**
*retains the essential geometry of the "normal" subject range (2m to infinity,
for "comfortable" viewing). The ratio* **b**/**D_N** *is constant at around 1/30.*

Breakdown of the rule

Although the 1 in 30 rule is a slight approximation, the errors become
significant only when it is applied in extreme close-up situations, at 500mm
or less, depending upon the focal length of the camera lens. For these
conditions the ratio **b**/$\mathbf{D_N}$ has to be reduced from 1/30 to smaller values
such as 1/40, 1/50 etc., depending upon the nearest object distance.

To understand the breakdown of the rule, first consider the formation
of an image in the camera of a subject that extends from 2m to infinity, a
typical "normal" subject. If the lens focal length is 35mm, then to achieve
sharpness over the whole depth range the aperture could be set to f/8 and
the lens focused at 4m, utilising the available depth of field.

The basic geometry is shown in **Fig S8.2**. In this diagram the points
M and **N** are on the centre line so the deviation **d** is "split" into two parts,
d/2 in each image. The lens-film distance is marked as **f**, the focal length;
strictly this should be the "working focal length" (i.e. the image distance **v**,
as determined from the standard lens formula), which will be greater than
f. Problems with the 1 in 30 rule arise only when **v** is significantly larger
than **f**, as will be shown in the analysis that follows. To avoid any confusion,
it should be remembered that the distance $\mathbf{D_N}$ is used for the rule itself but
the focused distance **D** is used to determine the value of **v**.

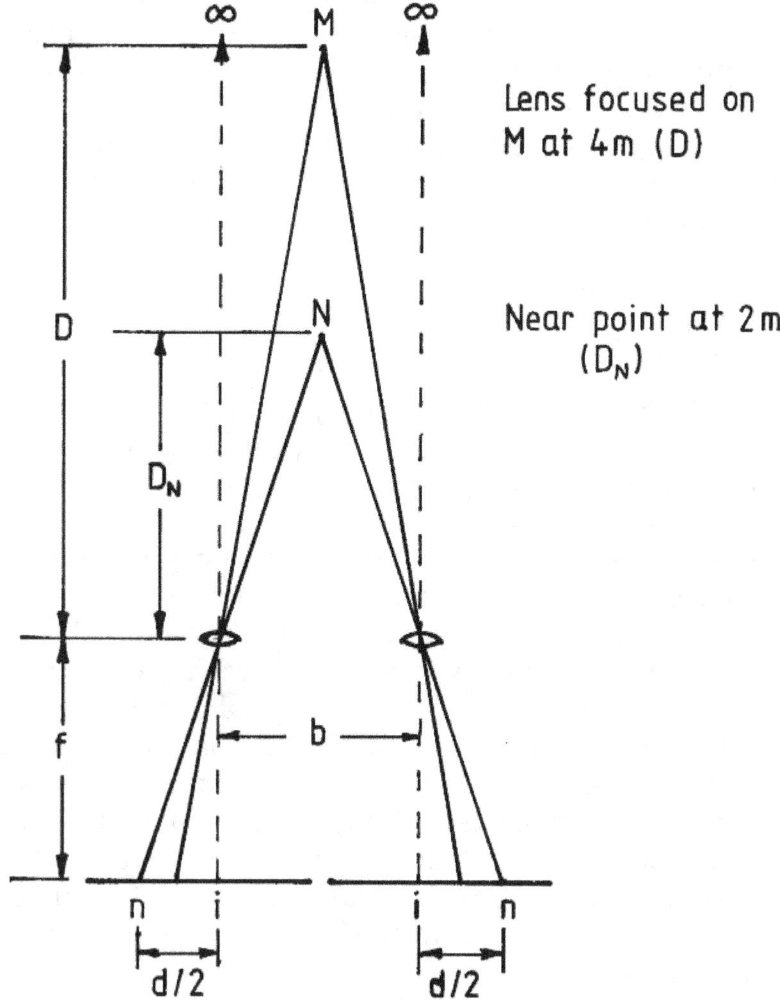

Fig S8.2
*The maximum deviation **d** depends upon the near object distance **D_N** and the lens–film distance ("working focal length" **v**). When the lens is focused at a point **M** to give a sharp image from **D_N** to infinity, **v** will be greater than the lens focal length **f**. Using **f** in calculations is accurate enough in all but extreme close-up situations.*

The validity of the rule can be demonstrated with reference to the deviation formula derived in Supplement S7:

$$\mathbf{d} = \mathbf{bf/D_N} \quad \text{(more strictly, } \mathbf{d} = \mathbf{bv/D_N} \text{ as discussed above)}$$

Rearranging:

$$\mathbf{b/D_N} = \mathbf{d/f} \quad \text{(strictly } \mathbf{d/v}\text{)}$$

The left hand side of this equation represents the 1/30 ratio, approximately, on which the rule is based and this ratio is used to determine the appropriate stereo base for a subject with a nearest object distance D_N. Taking $b/D_N = 1/30$, then $b = D_N/30$.

If this ratio is used to determine the stereo base for all possible values of D_N (in the range 0 to 2m say) then the right hand side of the equation is being kept at a constant value of 1/30. This means that:

$$d/f = 1/30$$
i.e. $$d = f/30$$

Since d and f are fixed values, only dependent on the choice of format, this would seem to be correct. However, the right hand side of this equation should be $v/30$ rather than $f/30$. As D_N decreases, v increases, so the deviation d will also increase.

If we assume that the subject being photographed extends over the complete depth range (e.g. 1 to 2m, 400 to 500mm as given in Supplement S9) then the images will show the maximum parallax deviation values (1.2mm for the Realist format). The problem with the extreme close-up situation is that as v increases significantly above the value of f, the deviation d will become greater than the "safe" maximum for comfortable viewing. The circumstances must be changed, therefore, to keep d at or below this maximum. This means looking at the expression for b/D_N from the point of view of the right hand side, d/v. As v increases, d/v decreases (keeping d constant) so that b/D_N must also be reduced. Since D_N is fixed by the particular subject, then b must be made smaller than the value calculated on the basis of 1/30.

The situation in **Fig S8.2** can be used to demonstrate the principle. In this case, with $D_N = 2000$mm and $b = 70$mm the ratio is actually 1/28.6 rather than 1/30, but this does not alter the argument.

First, the value of v is calculated from the lens formula in the form:

$$1/v = 1/f - 1/u$$

(u is the focused distance, in this case 4000mm)

So: $1/v = 1/35 - 1/4000$
Giving $v = 35.31$mm

Using this value in place of **f** to calculate **d** gives:

$$\mathbf{d} = 35.31/28.6 = 1.235\text{mm}$$

Putting **f** (= 35mm) into the equation instead of **v** gives **d** = 1.224.

This shows that the true **d** value is already greater than that based upon the standard formula using **f** instead of **v**. Here, though, the difference is not large and the rule may be regarded as valid. The stereo base **b** can safely be calculated as $\mathbf{D_N}/28.6$.

Now suppose that the set-up in **Fig S8.2** is changed so that the lens is focused at 150mm. With an aperture of f/8 as before, depth of field calculations show that the closest distance in focus will be about 145mm (= $\mathbf{D_N}$). If we apply the 1 in 30 rule, the stereo base should be:

$$145/28.6 = 5.1\text{mm}.$$

For a 200mm focused distance, the value of **v** is, by calculation, 42.4mm. Using the recommended stereo base of 5.1mm means that the ratio **d**/**v** = 1/28.6, i.e. **d** = 42.4/28.6 = 1.48mm which now exceeds the permissible maximum. To reduce the deviation to 1.2mm, the **d**/**v** ratio has to be reduced to 1.2/42.4 = 1/35.3. This means reducing the ratio $\mathbf{b}/\mathbf{D_N}$ to the same value, making the required stereo base 145/35.3 = 4.1mm instead of the 5.1mm value predicted by the 1 in 30 rule.

The same principle applies to even closer distances, when the discrepancy between the stereo base values will be even greater.

Despite its shortcomings, the 1 in 30 rule can be applied down to fairly close distances, as far as about 200mm with a 35mm lens. Any closer and the stereo base will have to be calculated by following the method given above. A more complete analysis is given in the next section.

Stereo base calculations

A slightly different approach leads to a more general formula for calculating the stereo base for all $\mathbf{D_N}$ values while maintaining the correct deviation **d** for the relevant format.

The deviation formula can be rearranged as:

$$\mathbf{b} = \mathbf{dD_N}/\mathbf{v} = \mathbf{dD_N}(1/\mathbf{v})$$

From the lens formula we know that $1/v = 1/f - 1/u$ so we can substitute for $1/v$ in the above equation. The focused distance u in the lens formula will be the focused distance D, as in **Fig S8.2**. Thus we have:

$$\mathbf{b} = \mathbf{dD_N}(1/\mathbf{f} - 1/\mathbf{D})$$

Now $\mathbf{d}$ = 1.2mm when $\mathbf{f}$ = 35mm
and $\mathbf{d}$ = 1.6mm when $\mathbf{f}$ = 50mm.

This means that we can calculate $\mathbf{b}$ values for any $\mathbf{D_N}$ value for either format, indeed, for any format for which we know the $\mathbf{d}$ value and $\mathbf{f}$.

We need to know $\mathbf{D}$ values (focused distance) for each $\mathbf{D_N}$ value. The information about permitted depth range in Supplement S9 can be used to determine corresponding values for $\mathbf{D}$ and $\mathbf{D_N}$ using the standard formula:

$$\mathbf{D} = 2\mathbf{D_N}\mathbf{D_F}/(\mathbf{D_N} + \mathbf{D_F})$$

in which $\mathbf{D}$ is the focusing distance to give a depth of field from $\mathbf{D_N}$ (nearest distance) to $\mathbf{D_F}$ (furthest distance) There is another formula that gives the necessary aperture to achieve this, but this need not concern us here.

The formula for $\mathbf{b}$ can be written:

$$\mathbf{b} = \mathbf{d}(\mathbf{D_N}/\mathbf{f} - \mathbf{D_N}/\mathbf{D})$$
i.e. $\mathbf{b} = 1.2(\mathbf{D_N}/35 - \mathbf{D_N}/\mathbf{D})$ for 5P and 7P formats
or $\mathbf{b} = 1.6(\mathbf{D_N}/50 - \mathbf{D_N}/\mathbf{D})$ for 35mm full frame

From a table of $\mathbf{D_N}$, $\mathbf{D_F}$ and $\mathbf{D}$ values we can select corresponding $\mathbf{D}$ and $\mathbf{D_N}$ values to use in the equation for stereo base, e.g.: (all dimensions in mm)

Nearest Object	$\mathbf{D_N}$	200	400	etc.
Furthest Object	$\mathbf{D_F}$	222	500	etc.
Focused Distance $\mathbf{D}$		210	444	etc.

The following tables give examples of stereo base values calculated from the above equations:

TABLE S8.1
Stereo Base Values in Hypostereoscopy

(For 35mm lens and **d** = 1.2 mm)
(all dimensions in mm)

Nearest Object Distance D_N	Focused Distance D	Stereo Base b	Ratio b/D_N
50	51	0.5	1/100
100	103	2	1/50
150	156	4	1/38
200	210	6	1/33
400	444	13	1/31
1000	1333	33	1/30
2000	4000	68	1/29

An aperture of f/11should be used in each case to ensure that there is an adequate depth of field. As the table makes clear, the 1 in 30 rule is invalid at D_N values of about 200mm or less.

TABLE S8.2
Stereo Base values in Hypostereoscopy
(For a 50mm lens and **d** = 1.6mm)
(All dimensions in mm)

Nearest Object Distance D_N	Focused Distance D	Stereo Base b	Ratio b/D_N
100	103	1.5	1/57
150	156	3	1/50
200	210	5	1/40
400	444	11	1/36
600	706	18	1/33
1000	1333	31	1/32
2000	4000	63	1/32

Again an aperture of f/11 will ensure sharpness from front to back. (Calculated value is f/9). Here the 1 in 30 rule begins to break down at D_N values below about 400mm.

Conclusions

The analysis is based upon that of Waack[5] who goes to great pains to produce graphs of **b** values for various focal lengths. He uses magnification factor (**v/u**) as one of the parameters for determining those **b** values. However, as has been made clear in this supplement, special calculations for stereo base are only required at very close distances, either around 400mm or 200mm, depending upon the format. On the rare occasions that ultra close-ups are used, it is easier, in the author's opinion, to calculate base values by following the method described in this supplement, than to use the over-complex and confusing nomogram in Waack's book.

With a 50mm lens focused at D_N = 100mm, the stereo base is only 1.5mm as shown in **Table S8.2**. In practical terms this will be very difficult to work with. Any closer than 100mm and the stereo base becomes too small to measure accurately unless some form of precision slide bar is used, with a screw device to shift the platform accurately. This is really the domain of the specialist.

For moderate close-ups, the one in thirty rule has been shown to be both logical and valid.

SUPPLEMENT S9 - MAXIMUM DEPTH RANGE OF SUBJECT

General analysis

In Chapter 7, Section 7.3.4 the need to restrict the depth range in a subject is explained. The distance between the nearest and furthest points has to be kept under control so that, in viewing the stereogram, the eyes are not required to rotate more than 1°52' as they swing from nearest to furthest object, or vice versa. As the near object distance decreases below about 2m the furthest tolerable object distance decreases rapidly from infinity.

To determine the link between near object distance and the permissible depth range beyond it, the general case is illustrated in **Fig S9.1**, which shows a near point **N** and a far point **F** defined by the largest allowable eye swing **θ** (equal to 1°52').

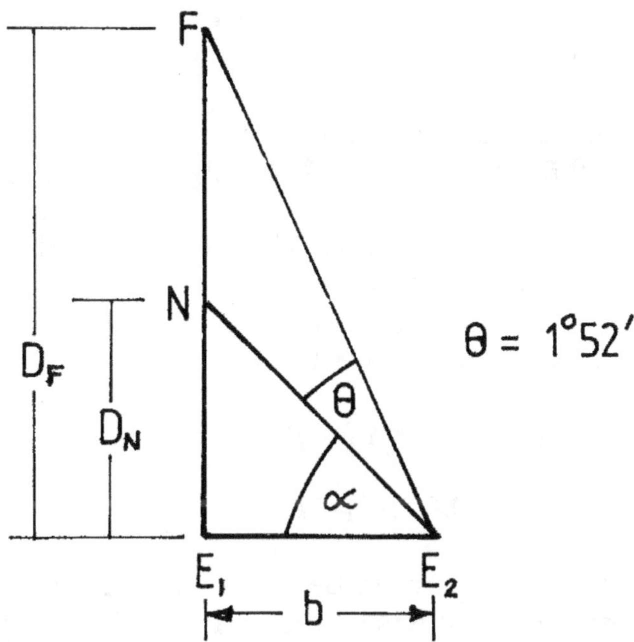

Fig S9.1
*General case for the location of the furthest (**F**) and nearest (**N**) points that can be included within the "maximum eye swing angle of 1°52' to avoid double imaging (diplopia).*

From the figure:

$$\tan(\alpha + \theta) = \mathbf{D_F}/\mathbf{b}$$

From standard trigonometrical relationships:

$$\tan(\alpha + \theta) = (\tan\alpha + \tan\theta)/(1 - \tan\alpha\,\tan\theta)$$

i.e. $$\mathbf{D_F}/\mathbf{b} = (\tan\alpha + \tan\theta)/(1 - \tan\alpha\,\tan\theta)$$

From the diagram:

$$\tan\alpha = \mathbf{D_N}/\mathbf{b}$$

Substitute in the equation;

$$\mathbf{D_F}/\mathbf{b} = ((\mathbf{D_N}/\mathbf{b}) + \tan\theta)/(1 - (\mathbf{D_N}/\mathbf{b})\tan\theta)$$
$$= (\mathbf{D_N} + \mathbf{b}\tan\theta)/(\mathbf{b} - \mathbf{D_N}\tan\theta)$$

Or $$\mathbf{D_F} = (\mathbf{b}\mathbf{D_N} + \mathbf{b}^2\tan\theta)/(\mathbf{b} - \mathbf{D_N}\tan\theta)$$

Divide right hand side by $\tan\theta$ top and bottom:
$$\mathbf{D_F} = (\mathbf{b}\mathbf{D_N}/\tan\theta + \mathbf{b}^2)/(\mathbf{b}/\tan\theta - \mathbf{D_N})$$

Now consider the case shown in **Fig S9.2** where the near distance is 2m and the furthest distance is infinity:

$$\tan\theta = \mathbf{b}/\mathbf{D_M} \text{ (where } \mathbf{D_M} = 2 \text{ metres).}$$

Substitute for $\tan\theta$ in the equation for $\mathbf{D_F}$:

$$\mathbf{D_F} = (\mathbf{D_M}\mathbf{D_N} + \mathbf{b}^2)/(\mathbf{D_M} - \mathbf{D_N})$$

Now as $\mathbf{D_N}$ decreases, $\mathbf{b}$ must be reduced to keep deviation constant (see Supplement S8) and since $\mathbf{b}$ is small in comparison to $\mathbf{D_N}$ we can ignore the term $\mathbf{b}^2$ in the numerator so that the equation becomes:

$$\mathbf{D_F} \approx \mathbf{D_M}\mathbf{D_N}/(\mathbf{D_M} - \mathbf{D_N})$$

where $\mathbf{D_N}$ = Distance of nearest object
$\mathbf{D_F}$ = Distance of furthest allowable object
$\mathbf{D_M}$ = Value of $\mathbf{D_N}$ when $\mathbf{D_F}$ = infinity (ie $\mathbf{D_M}$ = 2m, usually)

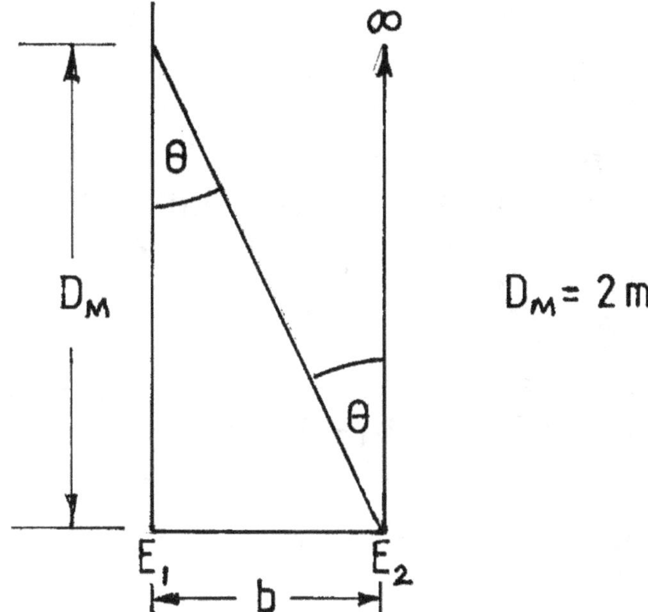

Fig S9.2
When the far point is at infinity the nearest point is at a distance D_M (=2m).

From this equation we can calculate the D_F value corresponding to any D_N value. The table below gives examples.

TABLE S9.1
Permissible Far Point D_F for a given Near Point D_N
(All dimensions in mm)

Near distance D_N	200	400	600	800	1000	1200	1400	1600	1800	2000
Far distance D_F	222	500	857	1333	2000	3000	4667	8000	18000	∞

Depth range ΔD

In some situations it may be more convenient to know the total permissible depth range ΔD beyond the given D_N value, rather than the value of the allowable far point D_F. With a close-up subject, it may be easier to know that at 400mm (nearest object) the depth range is 100mm (i.e. it extends to 500mm). Of course, ΔD can be found by subtracting D_N from D_F but this difference can be determined directly.

Since $D_F = D_N + \Delta D$, substitute this in the equation for D_F:

$$D_N + \Delta D = D_M D_N / (D_M - D_N)$$

Therefore

$$\Delta D = D_M D_N / (D_M - D_N) - D_N$$
$$= D_M D_N / (D_M - D_N) - D_N (D_M - D_N) / (D_M - D_N)$$
$$= (D_M D_N - (D_M - D_N) D_N) / (D_M - D_N)$$
$$= (D_M D_N - D_M D_N + D_N{}^2) / (D_M - D_N)$$

i.e $\quad \Delta D = D_N{}^2 / (D_M - D_N)$

Application of this formula gives us the following values for ΔD, which will be seen to correspond to the $(D_F - D_N)$ values of the previous table.

TABLE S9.2
Permissible Depth Range ΔD for a given Near Point D_N
(All dimensions in mm)

D_N	200	400	600	800	1000	1200	1400	1600	1800	2000
ΔD	22	100	257	533	1000	1800	3267	6400	16200	∞

Summary

i.   Knowing the D_N value we can calculate D_F values from:

$$D_F = D_M D_N / (D_M - D_N)$$

and ΔD values from:

$$\Delta D = (D_F - D_N)$$

ii.   Knowing only the D_N value and D_M (= 2m) we can calculate ΔD directly from:

$$\Delta D = D_N{}^2 / (D_M - D_N)$$

SUPPLEMENT S10 - CRITERIA FOR PROJECTION OF STEREO IMAGES

Introduction

As discussed in Chapter 8, most of the audience viewing 3D images will see, to a greater or lesser extent, a distorted image. There is only one position in the auditorium where the spectator sees an orthostereoscopic image. It is important, therefore, to analyse the geometry of projection so that equipment can be set up quickly and in a way that results in acceptable viewing conditions for the majority of observers.

It is generally agreed that the stereo window should lie as close as possible to the screen, preferably at the screen surface itself. At the same time, infinity homologues should be spaced at an agreed distance, at about 65mm or preferably slightly less, if the projection distance is not very long.

First, the conditions that satisfy these two criteria simultaneously will be analysed. Since it is not always possible to realise this ideal in practice (when larger audiences are present, for example), the effects of placing the screen nearer or further away than the "correct" distance will also be examined.

Locating the stereo window at the screen surface

For this analysis, two assumptions will be made for simplicity; first, that a twin-beamed projector is being used, and second, that sideways adjustments of the two screen images is produced by moving both projector lenses equally towards or away from each other; in some projectors only one lens is adjustable, but this assumption makes no difference to the general arguments

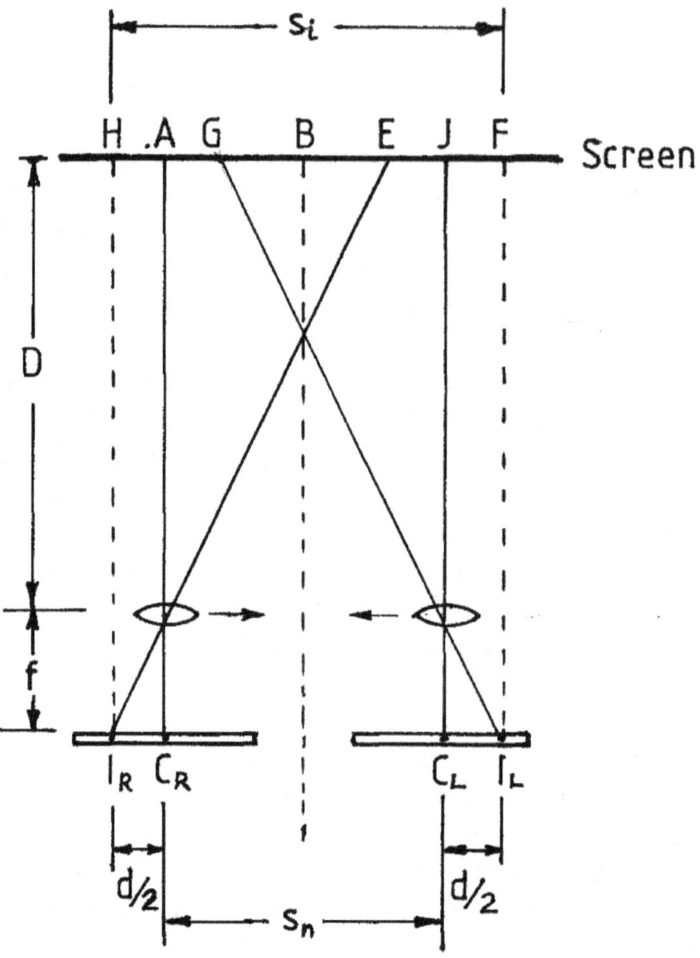

Fig S10.1

Geometry of projection. To place the stereo window on the screen, images **E** *and* **G** *of the infinity points* I_L *and* I_R *must be shifted to* **F** *and* **H** *respectively, while the frame centre images* **A** *and* **J** *must coincide at* **B**. *The frame edges will also be superimposed on each other. Distance* **D** *to achieve both of these simultaneously can be calculated from the geometry shown.*

As a starting point, consider **Fig S10.1**, which shows the optical axes of the two lenses aligned with the film frame centres, C_L and C_R separated by s_n in the stereogram. Infinity homologues for a centrally placed object at infinity are I_L and I_R for left and right images respectively. C_L and C_R produce screen images **J** and **A**, also separated by s_n while I_L and I_R produce images at **E** and **G**. For simplicity, the projector lens-film distance is taken as **f** (the focal length) and the lens-screen distance as **D**. In practice the lenses will be racked out for focusing, thus increasing **f** to **v** (working focal length) and reducing **D** accordingly. However, the errors in using **f** and **D** as marked in the diagram will be negligible.

Clearly, in this arrangement, the frame centre images **A** and **J** will be separated by s_n on the screen, as will corresponding frame edges. To produce a stereo window at the screen surface, the frame edge images must be made to coincide. This means that the frame centres **A** and **J** will also superimpose. This is done by reducing the inter-lens spacing on the projector, thus shifting **A** rightwards and **J** leftwards to the same point **B**, each moving by a distance $s_n/2$. Obviously, all corresponding points in the two screen images will move towards each other by the same amount, including the infinity homologues **E** and **G**. These, however, will not end up superimposed because their original separation was greater than s_n. They will move to two new positions **F** and **H**. For comfortable viewing, the final separation **HF** must be the required infinity homologue spacing s_i. This condition will be met only at one specific projection distance (for the particular value of focal length of the lenses being used).

Let us assume that **Fig S10.1** represents the correct projector-screen distance to produce the stereo window exactly at the screen surface, once the projector lenses have been adjusted. This means that, after **E** and **G** have moved to **F** and **H** respectively, **FH** = s_i and we can analyse the geometry to establish the value of **D** in terms of the other parameters.

In **Fig S10.1**:

$$\mathbf{EF} = \mathbf{HF} - \mathbf{HE}$$
$$= \mathbf{HF} - \mathbf{HA} - \mathbf{AE}$$

Now **HF** = s_i and **HA** = $\mathbf{I_R C_R}$ (= $\mathbf{C_L I_L}$) = $d/2$ where **d** is the parallax deviation.

From similar triangles **ALE** and $\mathbf{C_R L I_R}$:

$$\mathbf{AE}/\mathbf{D} = (d/2)/f$$

i.e. $\quad \mathbf{AE} = \mathbf{D}d/2f$

Therefore **EF** = $s_i - d/2 - \mathbf{D}d/2f$ and this must be equal to $s_n/2$ for frame coincidence, with s_i as the separation of infinity points.

Therefore $\quad s_n/2 = s_i - d/2 - \mathbf{D}d/2f$

i.e. $\qquad \mathbf{D}d/f = 2s_i - s_n - d$
$$= 2s_i - (s_n + d)$$
$$= 2s_i - s_i = s_i$$

i.e. $\qquad \mathbf{D} = s_i f/d$

This formula is confirmed if one envisages the left and right film chips being superimposed (with the mount apertures aligned) and projected in a single lens projector as illustrated in **Fig S10.2**

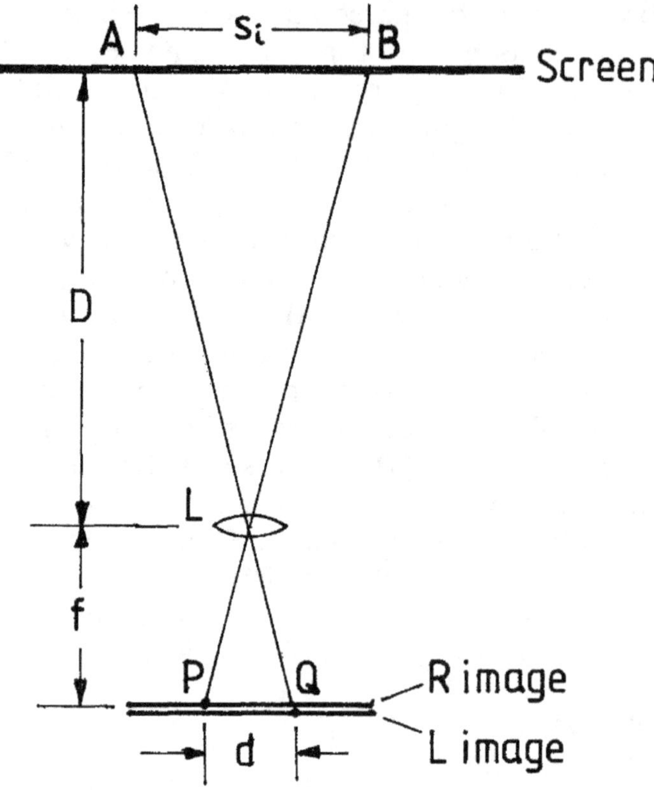

Fig S10.2
*Hypothetical "sandwich" of left and right images that can be used to calculate the "window-on-screen" distance. Infinity homologues **P**(on the right image) and **Q** (on the left image) will be **d** apart (e.g. 1.2mm).*

The frame edges will thus be coincident on screen at all projection distances, but the infinity point separation (equal to the deviation **d** in the film plane) will increase as the projection distance increases. It is a simple matter to find the distance **D** at which the deviation **d** is magnified to s_j on screen.

From **Fig S10.2**, triangles **ABL** and **PQL** are similar:

Therefore $D/s_i = f/d$

So $D = s_i f/d$ as before

Example

With the Realist or European format (d = 1.2mm), and using projector lenses of focal length f = 85mm, the correct projection distance for an on-screen stereo window will be:

$$D = (63.4 \times 85)/1.2 = 4490\text{mm}$$
$$= 4.49\text{m}$$
$$= 14'\,9''\text{ approx.}$$

For simplicity, s_i is taken as 63.4mm for both formats.
With 35mm full frame format (d = 1.6mm):

$$D = (63.4 \times 85)/1.6 = 3370\text{mm}$$
$$= 3.37\text{m}$$
$$= 11'\text{approx.}$$

Knowing these values enables the projectionist to set the screen quickly at roughly the right distance. Moving the projector backwards and forwards from this point, while projecting a stereogram, allows the window to be located more precisely.

The expression $D = s_i f/d$ shows that D is directly proportional to the focal length of the projector lens for a given value of s_i. A projector with 180mm lenses would have to be placed at 180/85 times the distance for an 85mm lens (at about 30ft) for the Realist format.

Rearranging the formula:

$$D/f = s_i/d$$

It can be seen that D/f is constant because s_i and d are both fixed for a given format. Now D/f is also equal to the ratio of the screen and film image widths W_S/W_F, in other words the screen magnification. Thus, for "window on screen" conditions, the screen image size is constant for all focal lengths.

So, for example, with 85mm lenses the correct distance D is 4.49m for the Realist format and the screen image width is 4490/85 times the film image width. In this format W_F = 22mm (approx.) so W_S= 1162mm = 1.162m or approximately 3'10". With 180mm lenses the projection distance will be greater, at about 30' as stated above, but the screen image size will still be 3'10", for an on-screen stereo window.

For 35mm full frame format, D is 3.37m and W_F is 36mm. These give a screen image width W_S = 1.427m (4' 8").

The formula for D has been used to calculate various projection distances for different focal length lenses. These appear in Chapter 8, Section 8.6.3.

Variations in screen position

It is not always possible to place a screen at the correct distance for an on-screen stereo window. Projecting images for large audiences may necessitate moving the screen further away from the projector. One advantage of this is that the projected image is larger, but the stereo window will be brought forward from the screen surface, so that it "floats" in front of it. However, the location of the window is not fixed in space; it will depend upon the spectator's distance from the screen. The distance between the screen and the window in front of it will appear greater to an observer at the back of the auditorium than it will to one sitting at the front. In other words, this distance is "stretched" for spectators sitting further back, as is the 3D image as a whole.

If a spectator is aware of the screen as an object in its own right, he may sub-consciously expect the stereo window to lie on the screen surface, and if the window appears nearer to him he may feel that the image or its location in space is "not quite right". In well-darkened rooms the problem is less likely, especially if the screen appears as a simple rectangle with uncluttered surrounds, as in a cinema. In these circumstances the screen itself effectively becomes invisible.

To examine the effect of placing the screen further away from the projector, it is convenient to start from the window on screen position, indicated by screen position **1** in **Fig S10.3**. The screen lies at distance **D** from the projector; infinity points lie at **A** and **B** on screen, s_i apart.

Now consider moving the screen further back to position **2** (at distance **D'**) and refocusing the lenses, but not as yet altering the inter-lens spacing. For simplicity, the lens-film distance will be assumed to be constant at **f**, as previously discussed. The infinity homologues will now lie further apart, at **P** and **Q**, while the frame edges will no longer be coincident. The left edges of the two frames will be located separately at **G** and **H**.

To restore the infinity point separation to the required s_i value, the inter-lens spacing must be increased so that **P** moves to **P'** and **Q** to **Q'**. This will also shift the frame edge **G** to the right and **H** to the left. Now it can be shown that the length **PP'** is greater than the length **GH**, which means that points **G** and **H** will cross as a result of the lens adjustment to finish at points **G'** and **H'**, such that **GG'** = **HH'** = **PP'**. Similar movements will occur on the right side of the screen for the other frame edges, but these are omitted for clarity.

By calculating the distance **H'G'** (which we shall denote as **a**), the stereo window position as seen from any location in the auditorium can be determined, so that the overall acceptability of the set-up can be assessed.

If the geometry of **Fig S10.3** is analysed, the distance **H'G'** (= **a**) can be expressed, using the parameters given in the diagram, as:

$$a = (s_i + d)(D' - D)/(D + f)$$

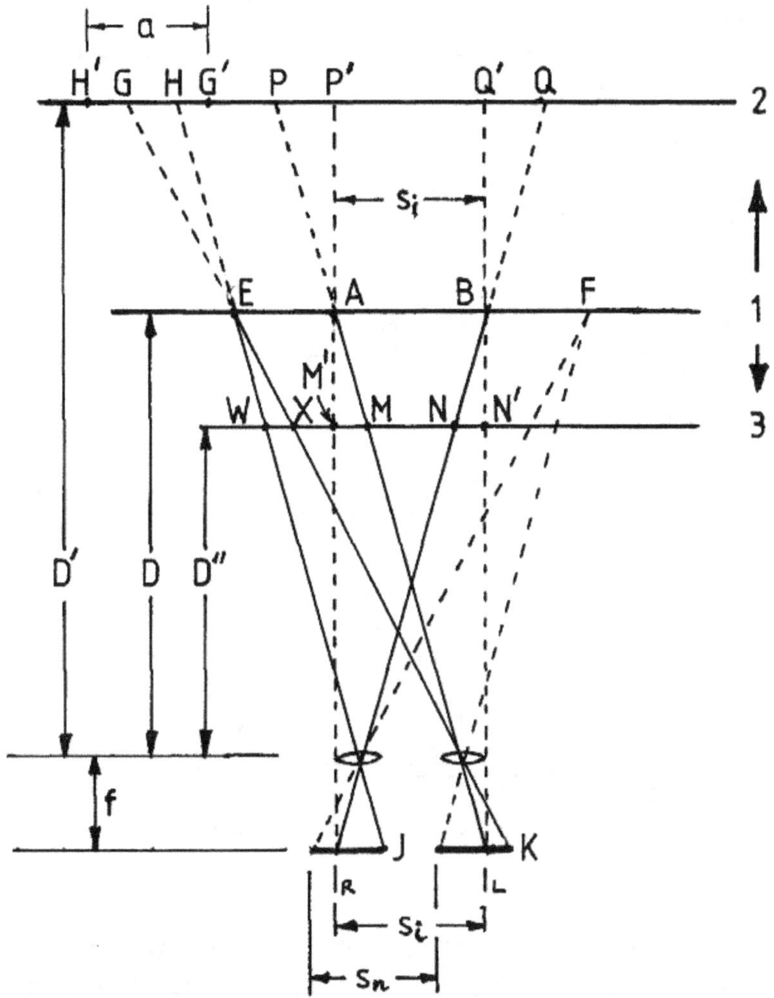

Fig S10.3
*Varying the screen position. Position **1** is the window-on-screen position, image frames superimposed at **E** and **F**, with infinity points at **A** and **B**. In position **2**, infinity points are wider apart at **P** and **Q** and must be adjusted to **P'** and **Q'** by increasing the projector lens spacing. With position **3**, infinity points **M** and **N** must be adjusted to **M'** and **N'** by decreasing the lens spacing. In positions **2** and **3** the stereo window will lie in front of and behind the screen surface respectively.*

The geometric analysis of this rather complex diagram is not given here, because it is somewhat tedious. However, there is a much simpler approach based upon **Fig S10.4**. Like **Fig S10.2,** this is a hypothetical set-up in which the left and right images are superimposed and projected in a mono projector, to allow us to visualise the relative positions of key points on screen. In **Fig S10.4**, the infinity homologues **P** and **Q** are aligned (rather than the frame edges as in **Fig S10.2**). Hence, it will be these frame edges (e.g. points **j** and **k**) that will be separated by the deviation **d**.

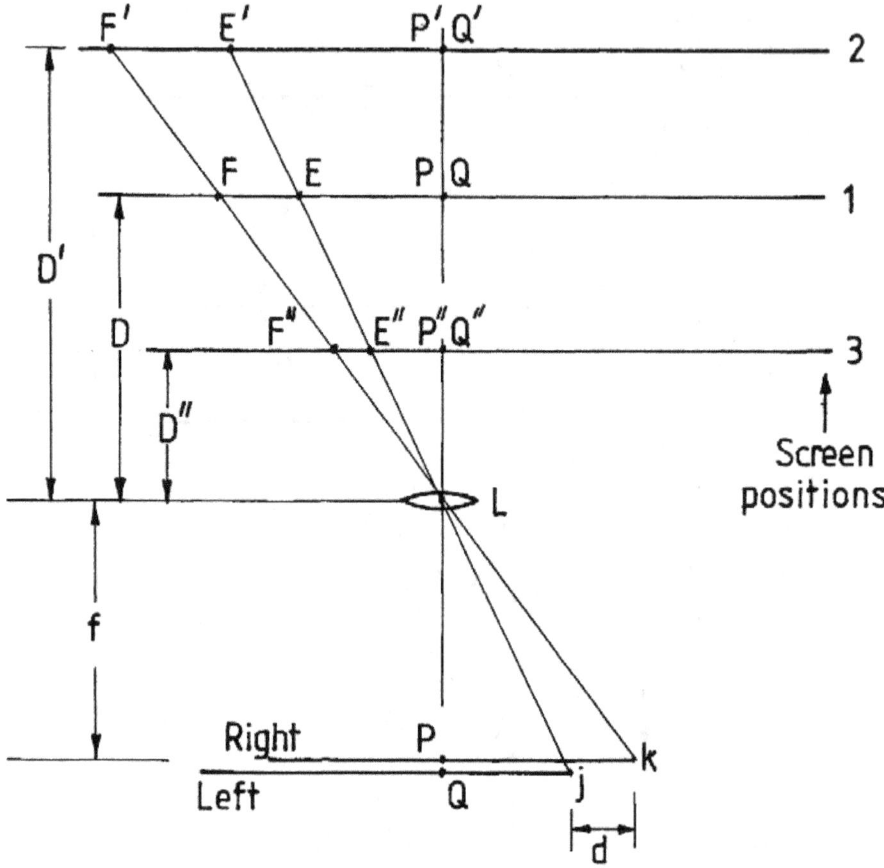

Fig S10.4
*Projection of a hypothetical slide "sandwich" with infinity points **P** and **Q** aligned. The frame edges **j** and **k** give images **E**, **F**, **E'**, **F'** etc. and the stereo window position depends upon the lengths **EF**, **E'F'** etc. for the different screen positions.*

Now imagine that the two parts of the sandwich in **Fig S10.2** (which represents the window on screen setting) are slid sideways while in the projector so that **P** and **Q** coincide; this transforms the diagram into **Fig S10.4**, screen position **1**. In doing so the screen images of **P** and **Q** will move by a distance s_i (= 63.4mm, say) and so will the frame edge images. In other words, the distance **EF** on screen will be 63.4mm too.

If we now move the screen away from the projector to position **2**, **E** and **F** move to **E'** and **F'** respectively. Infinity points are still coincident (**P"** and **Q"**). The lens will have to be refocused, thus slightly increasing the lens-film distance marked **f**, but this can be ignored in comparison with the lens-screen distances **D**, **D'** etc. The distance **E'F'** is found from similar triangles **LF'E'** and **LBA** as follows:

$$\mathbf{E'F'}/\mathbf{D'} = \mathbf{d}/\mathbf{f}$$

i.e. $$\mathbf{E'F'} = \mathbf{dD'}/\mathbf{f}$$

To obtain a proper image configuration on screen, infinity points **P"** and **Q"** must be separated by s_i (63.4mm) by adjusting the relative positions of the two parts of the sandwich, (equivalent to altering the lens separation in a stereo projector). Thus points **P"** and **F'** move to the right and **Q"** and **E'** to the left. **P"** and **Q"** will end up 63.4mm apart and **E'** and **F'** 63.4mm nearer than they were prior to this adjustment. They will now lie at the positions corresponding to points **G'** and **H'** in **Fig S10.3**. Hence this distance **H'G'** (= **a**) is given by:

$$a = (dD'/f) - s_i$$

Example

Data - 85mm lenses, Realist format, window on screen distance 4.49m as calculated earlier. Suppose the screen is now moved from 4.49m to double that distance (i.e. to 8.98m from the projector) to obtain a projected image twice as large in height and width (four times the area), the projector being adjusted to bring the infinity points back to a separation of 63.4mm.

Substituting values in the equation:

$$\mathbf{a} = [(1.2 \times 8980)/85] - 63.4$$
$$= 126.8 - 63.4$$
$$i.e. \quad \mathbf{a} = 63.4\text{mm}$$

This figure of 63.4mm, equal to the original on-screen infinity separation is no coincidence. Clearly, doubling the screen distance will double the original separation and subtracting 63.4mm for the readjustment will bring the 126.8mm figure back to 63.4mm.

The earlier equation, $[a = (s_i + d)(D' - D)/(D + f)]$ gives the same answer).

Stereo window position

Fig S10.5 shows how an observer at a distance D_V from the screen sees the stereo window at a distance D_W in front of the screen, that is a distance $(D_V - D_W)$ away from him.

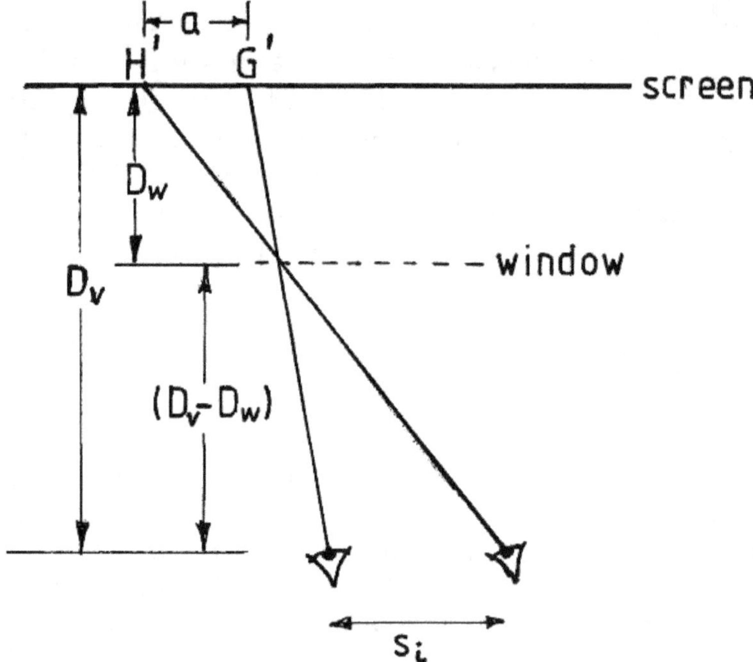

Fig S10.5
*With the screen in position **2** (**Fig S10.3**) a spectator at distance **Dv** from the screen sees the stereo window as shown. **H'** and **G'** are the frame edge images. The window position **Dw** depends upon the spectator's distance from the screen.*

From similar triangles, heights **Dw**, and (**Dv − Dw**):

$$D_W / (D_V - D_W) = a/s_i$$

i.e. $D_W s_i = D_V a - D_W a$

so $D_W, = aD_V(s_i + a)$

Here, s_i is the spectator's eye spacing, assumed to be identical to s_i on the screen, e.g. 63.4mm.

For a spectator sitting 5m from the screen:

D_W = (63.4 x 5000)/(63.4 + 63.4)

       = 2500mm or 2.5m (8' 2"approx)

For a spectator who is seated 10m from the screen, the window will appear to be even further in front of the screen, at 5m. In the first case the spectator sees the window (5 − 2.5) = 2.5m away from him, half-way between him and the screen, and in the second case 5m away, still half the screen distance away from him.

These variations are unavoidable. The obvious way to project over longer distances is to use a longer focal length lens in the projector, but, as shown earlier, the image size for the window on screen condition is the same for all lenses. For example, this condition will be met by using 150mm projector lenses at 7.925m (from Chapter 8, Table 8.1). The image width will be 1.162m (based upon the Realist image width of 22mm). To obtain a doubly dimensioned screen image (four times the original area), the screen will have to be moved back to 2 x 7.925 = 15.85m.

The on-screen frame edge separation will be, from the formula:

$$\mathbf{a} = [(1.2 \times 15850)/150] - 63.4$$
$$= 63.4\text{mm}$$

This is not surprising because we are merely doubling the 63.4mm infinity point separation on screen, by doubling the projection distance as in the last example. This means that the perceived window position for all spectators is halfway between their location and the screen, as before, so nothing is changed. A spectator seated 5m from the screen in this example will see the window 2.5m away from him and 2.5m in front of the screen.

The stereo window can be "pushed back" closer to the screen surface only by reducing the final separation of points $\mathbf{G}'$ and $\mathbf{H}'$ (**Fig S10.3**), that is by moving infinity points $\mathbf{P}''$ and $\mathbf{Q}''$ further apart, exceeding the "standard" 63.4mm. According to Krause[48], the average young or middle-aged person will have no trouble diverging each eye half a degree (one degree total). This translates to 330mm (13in) separation of on-screen infinity points viewed at a distance of 15.24m (50ft), or about 65mm (24in) at 3.66m (12ft). (Other values can be determined by simple proportion, using these figures as a basis).

In our second example (150mm lens and 15.85m projection distance) the infinity point separation could, reasonably safely, be increased from 63.4mm to twice that value, 126.8mm, which would bring the frame edges into coincidence, with the result that the stereo window would move back to the screen. The resulting eye divergence would be the maximum tolerable at 3.66m (12ft) and became less at greater viewing distances.

Often the best way to deal with large screen image projection is to adjust the projector to give frame superimposition and hence window on screen conditions. The infinity homologue separation must be checked, however, to ensure that it is not excessive as far as the front row of the audience is concerned. This is another reason for the recommendations regarding seating plans, as illustrated in Chapter 8, Fig 8.14, in not having spectators too close to the screen.

Of course, one can compromise by having the frame edge images separated by a small amount, say by 10mm or so. This means adjusting infinity points to 116.8mm, which will place the stereo window at about 680mm, i.e. two-thirds of a metre, in front of the screen for an observer at 5m. This is much less drastic than 2.5m with $\mathbf{s_i}$ set at the standard 63.4mm.

The orthstereoscopic seat (OSS)

In a correctly adjusted stereoscope with a conventionally mounted stereogram in place, the stereo window will be located about 2m from the observer (ignoring close-up mounts with closer windows). With projected slides, the window position in not fixed, since it depends upon the projection conditions and the spectator's location, as discussed above.

There is only one correct viewing position, the orthostereo seat (**OSS**), which can be determined by applying the principles explained in Supplement S1. The **OSS** will be in a direct line with the screen centre and lie at a distance that gives the spectator the same perspective view as that of the camera lens.

If the screen image width is W_S, camera lens focal length f and film image width W_F, then the distance D_S of the **OSS** from the screen will simply be W_S/W_F times the focal length, i.e.:

$$D_S = fW_S/W_F$$

More conveniently, D_S can be regarded as a factor f/W_F times the screen width W_S.

For the Realist format, f = 35mm typically, and W_F = 22mm, giving:

$$D_S = 35W_S/22 = 1.59W_S$$

Similarly, for the 35mm full frame format:

$$D_S = 50W_S/36 = 1.39W_S$$

For window-on-screen projection conditions the screen image width is 1.162m for Realist format and 1.427m for 35mm full frame (see earlier in this supplement) which means that:

$$D_S = 1.59 \times 1.162 = 1.848\text{m (Realist)}$$

Similarly, $\quad D_S = 1.39 \times 1.427 = 1.984\text{m (35mm full frame)}$

These values also represent the distances between the spectator and the stereo window for the two formats, because the window is on the screen.

Suppose the screen is now moved further back, so that a larger image is produced. The stereo window will now appear to float in front of the screen, as discussed earlier. The new **OSS** position is calculated in the same way as before, from the screen image size. With 85mm lenses, the window on screen distance is 4.49m (see earlier). Moving the screen further away to 8.98m gives a new image width W_S' of 8.98/4.49 times the width at 4.49m:

$$\text{i.e.} \quad W_S' = 8.98W_S/4.49 = 2W_S = 2 \times 1.162$$
$$= 2.324\text{m}.$$
$$\text{So} \quad D_S = 1.59 \times 2.324 = 3.695\text{m}$$

The position of the stereo window as seen by a spectator at this distance is determined from the formula derived earlier i.e. $D_W = aD_V/(s_i + a)$. Taking values used and calculated in the previous example for a and s_i;

$$D_W = (63.4 \times 3.695)/126.8$$
$$= 1.848\text{m}$$

Thus the window is 3.695 – 1.848 = 1.847m in front of the spectator, exactly as it was for the **OSS** in the window-on-screen arrangement. The significance of this result is that, whatever the screen/projector settings, the **OSS** always gives the same viewing conditions for the observer who sits there, as long as the on-screen s_i value is constant for all such settings.

Stereo window located behind the screen

Projection conditions for which the stereo window is located on the screen, or slightly in front of it, as analysed so far should be regarded as the norm. In setting up the projector and screen in a particular room, it may happen that the stereo window falls behind the screen; this is usually an undesirable configuration.

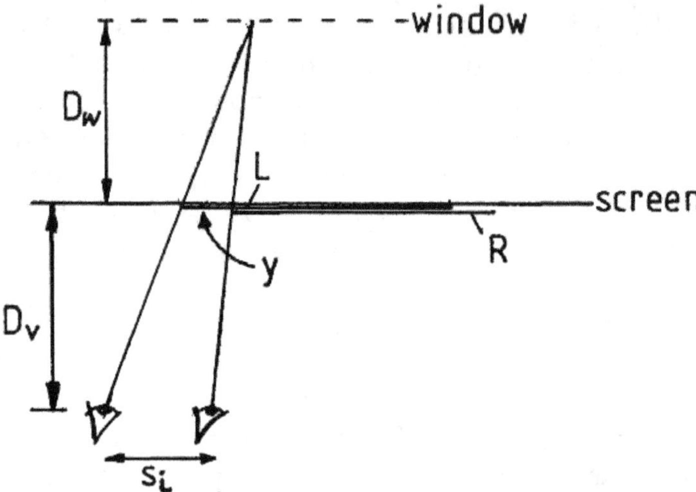

Fig S10.6
Stereo window located behind the screen. This occurs when the screen images overlap in the way shown. As the overlap is increased, the window will recede, eventually to infinity. Further overlap will require divergent viewing, which will be uncomfortable or even impossible.

When the stereo window appears behind the screen, the viewing conditions are more likely to be unsatisfactory. This situation can arise only when the two screen images overlap as in **Fig S10.6**, with the left image further to the left than the right image. This image configuration is the opposite of that which occurs when the window lies in front of the screen. With the frame edges displaced as in **Fig S10.6**, an observer will see them as a single edge at some distance behind the screen. If the two images are moved apart, the stereo window will be displaced away from the observer to an even greater distance behind the screen.

If the frame edge separation is less than s_i then the window will appear as in the diagram. However, if the edge separation is equal to s_i, the window will appear to lie at infinity. Worse, if it is greater than s_i, the eyes will be forced to diverge. Additionally, in either of these situations s_i will differ considerably from the normal 65mm.

There are three ways in which the "window behind screen" configuration can arise, and it is convenient to describe them with reference to the window on screen set-up because this is relevant to the means by which the problem can be corrected

i.   Moving the screen further away from the window on screen position (and refocusing, but not increasing the projector lens spacing, or not increasing it sufficiently).

Here, the configuration is the same as that shown in **Fig S10.3** (position **2**). The left hand side frame edges are at **G** and **H**. The distance **GH** (= **y**), can be determined from the geometry of the similar triangles **GHE** and **KJE** in **Fig S10.3**, to give:

$$\mathbf{y} = \mathbf{s_n}(\mathbf{D'} - \mathbf{D})/(\mathbf{D} + \mathbf{f})$$

The value of **y** increases from zero at the window on screen position as the screen is moved further back. When **y** is less than $\mathbf{s_i}$ then eye sight lines will converge to give a window behind the screen. When **y** = $\mathbf{s_i}$ the window will appear at infinity. If **y** is greater than $\mathbf{s_i}$ then the eyes have to diverge, but it will still be possible to fuse the frame edge images as long as the divergence required does not exceed about half a degree for each eye, as discussed earlier in relation to infinity point separation on large screens.

Whenever the screen is moved back from the window on screen position, the infinity points, typically at **P** and **Q** in **Fig S10.3**, will be further apart than the norm and difficulty in fusing these points will occur before the same problem affects the frame edges. The solution is simply to increase the inter-lens spacing to return to a "window in front of screen" configuration as described previously.

ii.   Moving the screen forward from the window on screen position and reducing the inter-lens spacing (and refocusing).

"Forward" here means towards the projector. The situation after moving the screen and refocusing (but before the lens spacing has been altered) is illustrated by screen position **3** in **Fig S10.3**. It is clear from this diagram that the infinity point spacing has been reduced from a distance **AB** to **MN**. The left frame edges of the two images are shown at **W** and **X**. The configuration is akin to that for position **2** but with some features interchanged and smaller spacings between key points. To restore $\mathbf{s_i}$ to its correct value (equivalent to the length **AB**) the inter-lens spacing must be reduced so that **M** moves to **M'** and **N** to **N'**. This action will also move **X** leftwards to **X'** and **W** rightwards to **W'** by the same amounts. (For clarity, points **X'** and **W'** are not shown in the diagram).

From similar triangles it can be shown that:

$$\mathbf{MM'} = s_i(D - D'')/(D + f)$$
$$\text{and} \quad \mathbf{WX} = s_n(D - D'')/(D + f).$$

Thus MM' is greater than **WX** because s_i is greater than s_n. This signifies that points **W** and **X** cross over to **X'** and **W'** (not shown in **Fig S10.3**) as **M** and **N** are shifted to **M'** and **N'** respectively. The final result is that the image frames overlap as in **Fig S10.5**, the actual separation increasing as the distance **D''** is reduced. The action is essentially the reverse of what happens when the inter-lens spacing is increased in position **2** as described earlier, and similar mathematical relationships can be derived.

From **Fig S10.3**, geometric analysis gives the final frame edge separation **X'W'** (= **a**) as:

$$a = (s_i + d)(D - D'')/(D + f)$$

Analysis of position **2** in **Fig S10.4** gives a simpler relationship for the length **F''E''** (the equivalent of **X'W'** in **Fig S10.3**):

$$\mathbf{F''E''} = y = dD''/f$$

If **X'W'** (or **F''E''**) is calculated for a specific distance **D''**, the value can be used to find the location of the stereo window for any seating position, from the geometry of **Fig S 10.5**. From similar triangles:

$$D_W/y = (D_W + D_V)/s_i$$
$$\text{i.e.} \quad D_W = aD_V/(s_i - a)$$

This is similar to the expression for D_W- relating to position **2** in **Fig S10.3** but with a minus sign in the denominator.

iii.   Wrongly set inter-lens spacing in the window-on-screen position.

This is a more trivial example of the problem that might occur while the window-on- screen conditions are being set up. Although the projector/screen distance is correct, the window appears behind the screen. This simply means that the projector lens spacing is too small and the solution is to increase it until the images of the frames coincide. This will automatically shift the window to the screen and establish the correct s_i value.

General comments

In all the projection conditions discussed in this supplement, derivations of formulae and calculations are based on exactitudes that will not be met in practice, when projection distances will be set only approximately and final adjustments made while viewing a correctly mounted test stereogram. However, the theory and principles outlined in this supplement are included to enable the important variables in the projection process to be better understood so that the screening of stereo images is not all left to chance.

SUPPLEMENT S11 - USE OF D-CAPS FOR TRICK SHOTS

Introduction

The double exposure technique using D-caps for trick shots is described in Chapter 11, Section 11.5. For successful results the D-caps must be properly designed for the camera being used, and the camera settings chosen with care.

In this supplement, we shall consider simple D-caps designed for two-exposure use, of the form shown in Chapter 11, **Fig 11.6**. The principles apply equally well to quarter D-caps and similar designs.

The fusion zone

Fig S11.1 shows the plan view of a camera fitted with D-caps (only one lens is shown), the partition at **Q** being vertical.

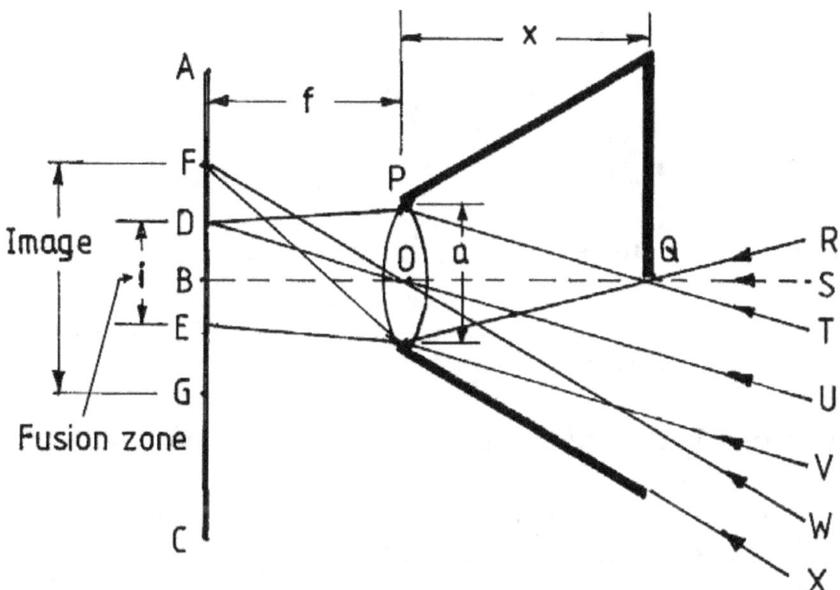

Fig S11.1
Fusion zone formation when using a D-cap.

AC represents the film. Light rays from the right half of the subject as seen from the camera position (rays **S, T, U, V, W, X**) all produce images on the left half of the film. Ray **S** is focused at **B** (image centre). Ray **X** (the outermost ray that can enter the cone) is focused at **F**, as is **W**, which is parallel to **X**. **F** is the left frame boundary of the image. Thus, rays **S** to **X** produce images between **B** and **F** on the film.

However, some rays above **S** in the diagram will also register an image on the left half of the film. Ray **R** represents the limiting ray in this group. This is a mirror image of ray **T**, which is focused at **D** (as is the parallel ray

U), which passes through the optical centre of the lens without being deviated. From symmetry, ray **R** will be focused at **E**, where **BE** = **BD**.

This means that, in addition to the right half of the subject registering as an image along **BF**, part of the left half of the subject produces an image along **BE**.

When the cap is rotated with the masked portion obscuring the right side of the lens for the second shot, ray **T** from the right half of the subject will still "get through" to give its image at **D**. **DE** becomes a fusion zone of width **i** as marked in **Fig S11.1**.

Let   **f** = focal length of the lens
       i = width of fusion zone
       x = length of D-cap hood
       a = lens aperture diameter

Since rays **U** and **T** are parallel, angle **DOB** = angle **PQO** and triangles **DOB** and **PQO** are similar.

Hence   **OQ/PO** = **BO/DB**
i.e. $\mathbf{x}/(\mathbf{a}/2) = \mathbf{f}/(\mathbf{i}/2)$
so $\mathbf{i} = \mathbf{fa}/\mathbf{x}$

But the aperture diameter **a** can be expressed as:

$$\mathbf{a} = \mathbf{f}/\mathbf{n} \text{ (where } \mathbf{n} = \text{ the stop number e.g. 5.6)}$$

Therefore $\mathbf{i} = \mathbf{f}^2/\mathbf{xn}$

From this expression it is clear that the fusion zone can be decreased by:

    i.   decreasing the focal length **f** of the lens
   ii.   increasing the hood length **x**
  iii.   increasing the aperture number (i.e. using a smaller stop)

either singly or in combination. One cannot generally change the focal length of the lens (unless the camera is fitted with a zoom lens) so to reduce the fusion zone width the lens hood should be made as long as possible without obstructing the viewfinder, and a small aperture should be used. The formula for **i**, the fusion zone width, has been used to compile the tables in Chapter 11 Section 11.5.

The width values are also expressed as percentages of the relevant image widths to give a better idea of the extent of the overlap.

D-Cap diameter

Assuming that the lens hood, of which the D-cap mask forms the outer boundary, is conical, the diameter of the circular shape can easily be calculated. This has to be large enough so that the hood does not block any of the light rays that form the edges of the image. The minimum usable cone angle will be equal to the angle of view for the camera lens, based on the frame diagonal which is the widest span (See Supplement S3).

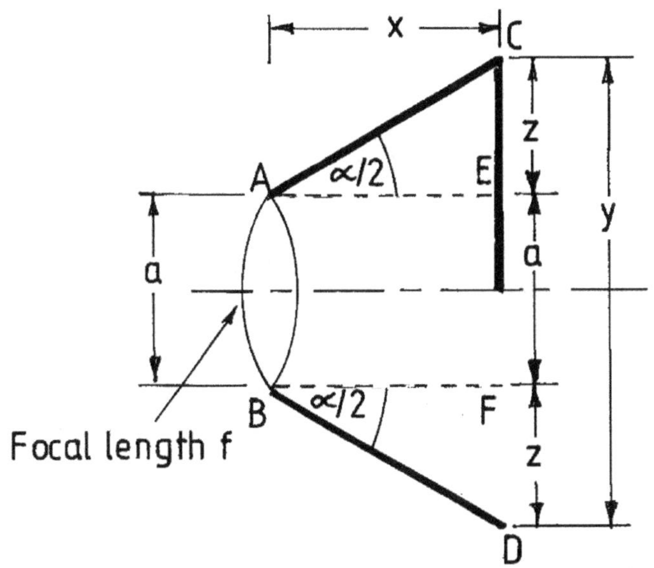

Fig S11.2
Geometry of D-cap.

Fig S11.2 shows a side view of the lens hood, with the lens **AB** set at its widest aperture, diameter **a**.

AE and **BF** are at right angles to **CD**, so **EF** = **a**. The cone angle **a** will be set to the angle of view of the lens, as already mentioned. In practice it should be slightly greater to give a margin of safety. Angles **CAE** and **FED** will both equal **a**/2.

From the diagram, the diameter of the D-mask (**y**) is given by:

y = **a** + 2**z**

From triangle **CAE**, **AE** = **x**, the cone length, so:

$$\mathbf{z} = \mathbf{AE}\,\tan(\mathbf{a}/2)$$
$$= \mathbf{x}\,\tan(\mathbf{a}/2)$$

But the aperture diameter **a** = **f**/**n₀**
Where **n₀** = widest aperture available (e.g. f/2.8) and **f** is the focal length of the lens.

Therefore $\quad \mathbf{y} = \mathbf{f}/\mathbf{n_o} + 2\mathbf{x}\tan(\mathbf{a}/2)$

This formula has been used to calculate the cap diameter values shown in the Tables in Section 11.5 based upon cap length values of 20, 30, 40 and 50mm.

SUPPLEMENT S12 - MOVEMENT OF OBJECTS TO PRODUCE "FLOATING" TRICK SHOTS

In Chapter 11, Section 11.6, the sequential exposure technique during which an object is moved laterally between shots to produce an illusion of "floating" is described. In addition to the floating effect, the object appears closer and smaller. The amount by which the object is moved sideways controls the floating position; the relationship between the two can be predicted and is determined as explained below.

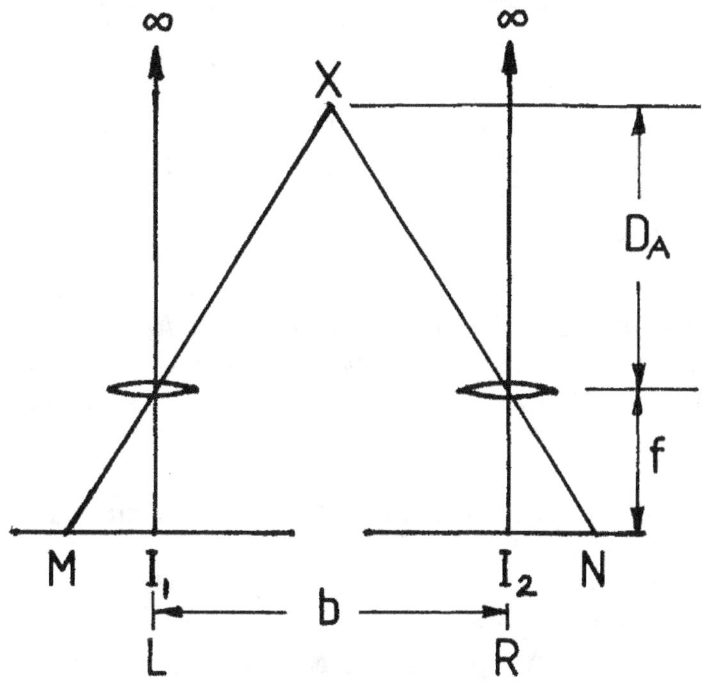

Fig S12.1
Sequential or simultaneous exposures of object **X** *produce homologues* **M** *and* **N** *in the normal way.*

Fig S12.1 shows infinity homologues I_1 and I_2 for an object at infinity and homologues **M** and **N** for object **X** situated at a distance D_A in a conventional stereo shot. If the two exposures are taken sequentially in the order left and right and the object **X** is moved to **X'** between exposures (**Fig S12.2**) the homologues **M**, I_1 and I_2 will be identical to those in **Fig S12.1** but **N** will move to **N'**. Homologues **M** and **N** relate to point **Y** situated at a closer distance D_B; this is effectively where **X** will appear to be located when the stereogram is viewed.

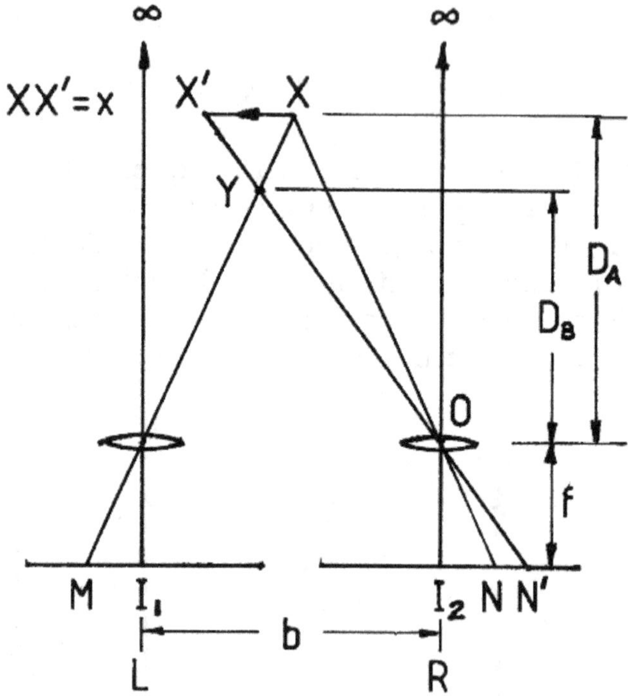

Fig S12.2
Sequential exposures. The left image is taken with the object at **X** *to give homologue* **M** *as in* **Fig S12.1**. *The right exposure is taken after the object is moved to* **X''** *laterally, to give a homologue at* **N'** *instead of* **N**. *The object will appear at* **Y** *when viewed.*

From similar triangles **X'OX** and **NON'**, and using the triangle heights **D$_A$** and **f**:

$$X'X/D_A = NN'/f$$

Putting $X'X = x$ and $NN' = d$:

$$x = D_A d/f$$

Now $(MI_1 + I_2N) = d_x$ the parallax deviation for **X**

And $(MI_1 + I_2N') = d_y$ the parallax deviation for **Y**

Therefore $(MI_1 + I_2N') - (MI_1 + I_2N) = NN' = d_y - d_x$

As given in Supplement S7, the familiar deviation equation is:

$$d = fb/D$$

so $d_y = fb/D_B$

and $d_x = fb/D_A$

therefore $d = fb(1/D_B - 1/D_A)$

           $= fb(D_A - D_B)/D_B D_A$

Substituting this in the equation for **x** above:

$$x = D_A fb(D_A - D_B)/fD_B D_A$$

i.e. $$x = b(D_A - D_B)D_B$$

So, if an object is located at a distance D_A and it is required to float it at a nearer distance D_B, the above expression enables us to determine the lateral displacement required. Chapter 11, Section 11.6 gives examples of such that can be used. This includes the correct sequence of exposures related to the direction of lateral movement to produce either "floating" or "receding".

SUPPLEMENT S13 - DEPTH OF FIELD

Depth of Field Tables

Depth of field tables can be calculated from the various equations given in Chapter 17, Section 17.5.2. The information can be presented in different ways, however, and a few words of explanation will be useful at this point.

As should be clear from the expressions for D_N and D_F in the form: $D_N = D/(1 + nD/1000f)$ etc., the nearest and furthest limits (and hence the total depth of field) are dependent upon the focused distance D, the lens focal length f and the aperture f/number n. From these specific equations, depth of field tables can be compiled for different lens focal lengths. This is probably the form of the information that is simplest to use, but it does involve a lot of calculation to produce the many tables required to cover a wide range of focal lengths.

Some depth of field information is given in **Tables S13.1 to S13.6**, for three focal length values (30, 35 and 50mm), at the end of this supplement. **Tables S13.1** to **S13.3** are in metric units while the others are in imperial units. In each table, the near and far limits of depth of field are shown in the "box" at the intersection of the relevant row and column for the aperture and focused distance respectively. The near and far distance values are rounded up or down to the nearest 100mm or 6" as appropriate.

Simplified Depth of Field

Examination of **Tables S13.5** and **13.6** will show that the depth of field range for a 35mm lens at f/2.8 is identical to that for a 50mm lens at f/4 for all focused distances; the hyperfocal distance H is the same for both, at 20½ft. This is also true for the metric tables, but there are a few slight differences in some of the "corresponding" entries as a result of the rounding up or down of values. This correspondence of hyperfocal distances will occur with many other focal length/aperture combinations. Since $H = 1000f/n$ we can substitute this in the equations for D_N and D_F quoted above and in Chapter 17, Section 17.5.2, to give simpler expressions $D_N = HD/(H + D)$ and $D_F = HD/(H - D)$. These expressions show that, for a given value of H, fixed by the aperture and focal length, the depth of field values are always the same. Some depth of field information is set out in this way so that a single table can show near and far distances as a function of H for any lens. In calculating H, it must be remembered that the value will be in the same units as those used for f (e.g. millimetres) and will have to be converted to metres for the depth of field tables.

If focused distances other than those given in the tables are used, it is not too difficult to interpolate between any two columns; the same applies to intermediate apertures.

Choice of Suitable Aperture

In Chapter 10, Section 10.5, the principle of choosing a suitable focusing distance and aperture in order to give a predetermined depth of field range, from a specified near distance to a specified far distance, was outlined. This can be a useful technique in, for example, low light conditions because it enables the photographer to use the largest aperture for the specified depth range and hence a faster shutter speed to allow for a hand-held shot. Although the method of calculation is given in Section 10.5, this is not something that the average photographer would wish to do in the field. However, this information can be gained from the depth of field tables by finding a suitable depth range from within a table and noting the aperture value at the end of the row in which that range appears.

Close-up depth of Field

Tables S13.7 and **S13.8** give depth of field ranges for subjects placed in the range 50 to 600mm from the lens. At close distances and with wide apertures the depth of field range is roughly symmetrical about the focused distance. Only at the greater distances and small apertures is the range behind the point of focus greater than that in front of it. All values in these tables are in millimetres, which are more convenient for measuring smaller distances.

DEPTH OF FIELD TABLES – METRES

NB. ALL TABLES (metric and imperial): in each "box" the upper figure is the near distance D_N and the lower figure the far distance D_F. H is the hyperfocal distance.]

TABLE S13.1
(FOCAL LENGTH 30mm)

30mm lens	DEPTH RANGE WHEN FOCUSED AT D(m)					
	D(m)					
APERTURE	H	2	3	6	15	30	∞
2	15	1.8	2.5	4.3	7.5	10	15
		2.3	3.8	8.2	∞	∞	∞
2.8	10.7	1.7	2.3	3.8	6.2	7.9	10.7
		2.5	4.2	13.7	∞	∞	∞
4	7.5	1.6	2.1	3.3	5	6	7.5
		2.7	5	30	∞	∞	∞
5.6	5.4	1.5	1.9	2.8	4	4.6	5.4
		3.2	6.8	∞	∞	∞	∞
8	3.8	1.3	1.7	2.3	3	3.4	3.8
		4.2	14.5	∞	∞	∞	∞
11	2.7	0.9	1.4	1.9	2.3	2.5	2.7
		7.7	∞	∞	∞	∞	∞
16	1.9	0.9	1.2	1.4	1.7	1.8	1.9
		∞	∞	∞	∞	∞	∞
22	1.4	0.8	1	1.1	1.3	1.3	1.4
		∞	∞	∞	∞	∞	∞

TABLE S13.2
(FOCAL LENGTH 35mm)

35mm lens		DEPTH RANGE WHEN FOCUSED AT D(m)					
		D(m)					
APERTURE	H	2	3	6	15	30	∞
2	17.5	1.8	2.6	4.5	8.1	11.1	17.5
		2.3	3.6	8.1	105	∞	∞
2.8	12.5	1.7	2.4	4.1	6.8	8.8	12.5
		2.4	3.9	11.5	∞	∞	∞
4	8.8	1.6	2.2	3.6	5.5	6.8	8.8
		2.6	4.6	18.9	∞	∞	∞
5.6	6.3	1.5	2	3.1	4.4	5.2	6.3
		2.9	5.7	126	∞	∞	∞
8	4.4	1.4	1.8	2.5	3.4	3.8	4.4
		3.7	9.4	∞	∞	∞	∞
11	3.2	1.2	1.5	2.1	2.6	2.9	3.2
		5.3	48	∞	∞	∞	∞
16	2.2	1	1.3	1.6	1.9	2	2.2
		∞	∞	∞	∞	∞	∞
22	1.6	0.9	1	1.3	1.4	1.5	1.6
		∞	∞	∞	∞	∞	∞

TABLE S13.3
(FOCAL LENGTH 50mm)

50mm lens		DEPTH RANGE WHEN FOCUSED AT D(m)					
		D(m)					
APERTURE	H	2	3	6	15	30	∞
2	25	1.9	2.7	4.8	9.4	13.6	25
		2.2	3.4	7.9	37.5	∞	∞
2.8	17.9	1.8	2.6	4.5	8.2	11.2	17.9
		2.3	3.6	9	92.6	∞	∞
4	12.5	1.7	2.4	4.1	6.8	8.8	12.5
		2.4	3.9	11.5	∞	∞	∞
5.6	8.9	1.6	2.2	3.6	5.6	6.9	8.9
		2.6	4.5	18.4	∞	∞	∞
8	6.3	1.5	2	3.1	4.4	5.2	6.3
		2.9	5.7	126	∞	∞	∞
11	4.5	1.4	1.8	2.6	3.5	3.9	4.5
		3.6	9	∞	∞	∞	∞
16	3.1	1.2	1.5	2	2.6	2.8	3.1
		5.6	93	∞	∞	∞	∞
22	2.3	1.1	1.3	1.7	2	2.1	2.3
		15.3	∞	∞	∞	∞	∞

DEPTH OF FIELD TABLES - FEET

TABLE S13.4
(FOCAL LENGTH 30mm)

30mm lens		DEPTH RANGE WHEN FOCUSED AT D(ft.)					
		D(ft.)					
APERTURE	H	6	10	20	50	100	∞
2	49	5.5	8.5	14	25	33	49
		7	12.5	33.5	∞	∞	∞
2.8	35	5	8	13	20.5	26	35
		7	14	46.5	∞	∞	∞
4	24.5	5	7	11	16.5	19.5	24.5
		8	17	107	∞	∞	∞
5.6	17.5	4.5	6.5	9.5	13	15	17.5
		9	23	∞	∞	∞	∞
8	12	4	5.5	7.5	10	11	12
		11.5	53.5	∞	∞	∞	∞
11	9	3.5	4.5	6	7.5	8	9
		18	∞	∞	∞	∞	∞
16	6	3	4	4.5	5.5	6	6
		246	∞	∞	∞	∞	∞
22	4.5	2.5	3	3.5	4	4.5	4.5
		∞	∞	∞	∞	∞	∞

TABLE S13.5
(FOCAL LENGTH 35mm)

35mm lens		DEPTH RANGE WHEN FOCUSED AT D(ft.)					
		D(ft.)					
APERTURE	H	6	10	20	50	100	∞
2	57.5	5.5	8.5	15	26.5	36.5	57.5
		6.5	12	30.5	388	∞	∞
2.8	41	5	8	13.5	22.5	29	41
		7	13	39	∞	∞	∞
4	28.5	5	7.5	12	18	22.5	28.5
		7.5	15.5	66	∞	∞	∞
5.6	20.5	4.5	6.5	10	14.5	17	20.5
		8.5	19.5	820	∞	∞	∞
8	14.5	4	6	8.5	11	12.5	14.5
		10.5	33	∞	∞	∞	∞
11	10.5	4	5.5	7	9	10	10.5
		15	249	∞	∞	∞	∞
16	7	3.5	4	5.5	6.5	6.5	7
		36.5	∞	∞	∞	∞	∞
22	5	3	3.5	4	4.5	5	5
		∞	∞	∞	∞	∞	∞

TABLE S13.6
(FOCAL LENGTH 50mm)

50mm lens		DEPTH RANGE WHEN FOCUSED AT D(ft.)					
		D(ft.)					
APERTURE	H	6	10	20	50	100	∞
2	82	5.5	9	16	31	45	82
		6.5	11.5	26.5	128	∞	∞
2.8	58.5	5.5	8.5	15	27	37	58.5
		6.5	12	30.5	76	∞	∞
4	41	5	8	13.5	22.5	29	41
		7	13	39	∞	∞	∞
5.6	29.5	5	7.5	12	18.5	22.5	29,5
		7.5	15	63	∞	∞	∞
8	20.5	4.5	6.5	10	14.5	17	20.5
		8.5	19.5	820	∞	∞	∞
11	15	4.5	6	8.5	11.5	13	15
		10	20.5	∞	∞	∞	∞
16	10	4	5	7	8.5	9.5	10
		14.5	410	∞	∞	∞	∞
22	7.5	3.5	4.5	5.5	6.5	7	7.5
		31	∞	∞	∞	∞	∞

CLOSE-UP DEPTH OF FIELD TABLES – METRIC

(All dimensions in mm)
Because of the very small depth ranges in certain conditions, all distances
have been calculated to an accuracy of 0.1mm with no rounding up or
down.

TABLE S13.7
(FOCAL LENGTH 35mm)

35mm lens	DEPTH RANGE WHEN FOCUSED AT D(mm)						
	D(mm)						
APERTURE	50	100	200	300	400	500	600
2	49.9	99.4	197.7	294.9	391.1	486.1	580.1
	50.1	100.6	202.3	305.2	409.4	514.7	621.3
2.8	49.8	99.2	196.9	293	387.6	480.8	572.5
	50.2	100.8	203.3	307.4	423.2	520.8	630.3
4	49.7	198.9	195.5	290.1	382.5	473	561.5
	50.3	101.2	204.7	310.7	419.2	530.3	644.2
5.6	49.6	98.4	193.8	286.3	375.9	463	547.4
	50.4	101.6	206.6	315.1	427.4	543.5	663.7
8	49.4	97.8	191.3	280.7	366.5	448.7	527.6
	50.6	102.3	209.6	322.1	440.3	564.5	695.4
11	49.2	97	188.2	274.2	355.3	432.1	504.8
	50.8	103.2	213.4	331.2	457.5	593.2	739.4
16	48.9	95.6	183.2	263.8	338.2	407	470.9
	51.2	104.8	220.1	347.7	489.5	648.1	826.7
22	48.5	94.1	177.7	252.4	319.6	380.4	435.7
	51.6	106.7	228.8	369.7	534.3	729.1	963.3

TABLE S13.8
(FOCAL LENGTH 50mm)

50mm lens	DEPTH RANGE WHEN FOCUSED AT D(mm)						
	D(mm)						
APERTURE	50	100	200	300	400	500	600
2	49.9	99.6	198.4	296.4	393.7	490.2	585.9
	50.1	100.4	201.6	303.6	406.5	510.2	614.8
2.8	49.9	99.4	197.8	295	391.2	486.4	580.5
	50.1	100.6	202.3	305.1	409.2	514.4	620.9
4	49.8	99.2	196.9	293	387.6	480.8	572.5
	50.2	100.8	203.3	307.4	413.2	520.8	630.3
5.6	49.7	98.9	195.6	290.2	382.8	473.5	562.2
	50.3	101.1	204.6	310.4	418.8	529.7	643.2
8	49.6	98.4	193.8	286.3	375.9	463	547.4
	50.4	101.6	206.6	315.1	427.4	543.5	663.7
11	49.5	97.8	191.6	281.4	367.6	450.4	530
	50.6	102.2	209.2	321.2	438.6	561.8	691.3
16	49.2	96.9	188	273.7	354.6	431	503.4
	50.8	103.3	213.7	331.9	458.7	595.2	742.6
22	48.9	95.8	183.8	265	340.1	409.8	474.7
	51.1	104.6	219.3	345.6	485.4	641	815.2

SUPPLEMENT S14 - SIMPLE MOUNTING JIG

Introduction

This was designed and constructed by the author for the mounting of both 5P and 7P formats but it can be used for any format based upon 35mm transparency film and is illustrated in **Fig S14.1**.

The basis of the jig is a photographic light box, made for the viewing of transparencies. The particular model in this case is the HAMA LP550, with a top surface measuring 160 x 110mm overall. The viewing screen itself has dimensions of 125 x 90mm, the greater dimension in each case running from left to right. Six AA size batteries located in the base act as the power source. Alternatively, there is an input socket on the left hand side for use with a mains adapter supplying 6V/500mA. On the right hand side (not visible in the diagram) is an on/off switch.

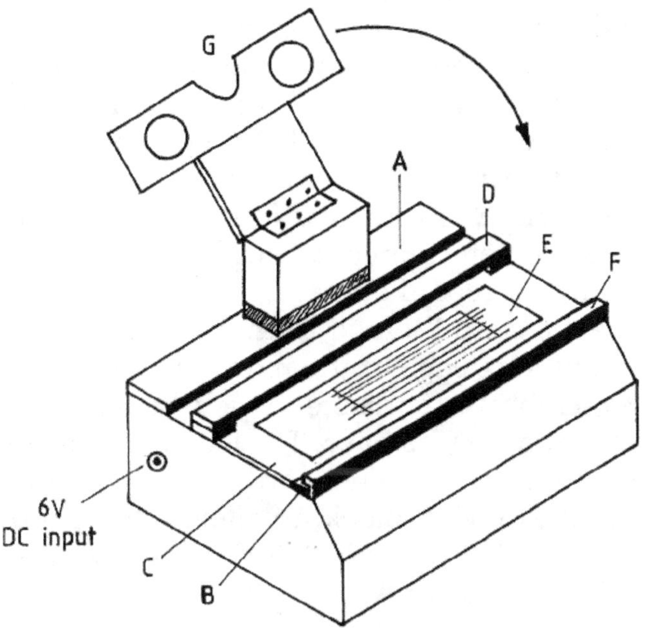

Fig S14.1
Mounting jig based upon a slide-viewing light box.

Construction

The jig is designed for use mainly with "double" card mounts that have four apertures and which are folded in half to enclose the film chips. The positions of some of the components are determined by the size of the opened out mount but nothing is critical as long as there is some room for adjustment.

The "additions" to the light box (see **Fig S14.1**) are as follows:

1. a thin steel strip **A**, about 20mm wide, running across the back edge from left to right. This is attached to the top surface by double-sided transparent tape and acts as a track for the lens mount, which incorporates a magnet in its base. The track can be covered with a layer of green baize (self-adhesive, made by Fablon).

2. a thin steel strip **B**, about 5mm wide, running adjacent to the front edge. The sloping front of the light box projects upwards past the top surface to form a natural "stop". This metal strip will allow magnets to be used for holding the film chips temporarily in position over the mount apertures. This strip is attached to the surface of the box with double-sided tape.

3. a clear acetate (or "Plasticard") sheet **C**, to cover the rest of the top surface. It abuts the metal strip **B** and should be of the same thickness to avoid a step where they meet. This is fixed to the top surface by double-sided tape at the left and right edges.

4. a rigid metal or plastic strip **D**, fixed at either end and raised slightly to leave a gap underneath. One long edge of the opened mount can be wedged under this strip so that it is held in position. A couple of layers of baize wrapped around the strip before it is attached will provide a slight "grip".

5. the mounting grid **E** is attached to the clear acetate sheet. Its exact position must be determined by aligning it with an empty mount in place to ensure correct alignment.

6. a narrow plastic strip **F** glued to the raised ridge to form a flange to retain the front long edge of the mount when it is in place.

7. the lens assembly **G** consists of a wooden block with a strong rectangular magnet as its base. The lenses (focal length about 40mm) are attached to a piece of Plasticard sheet, which is hinged to the top back edge of the wooden block, to allow it to be tilted back out of the way when required. The lens assembly as a whole can be positioned anywhere along the strip **A**.

Fig S14.2 shows a plan view of the jig with a mount in place. The far long edge is held under the metal strip **D** and the front edge by the flange **F**. The metal strip **B** lies just under the mount bottom edge, clear of the apertures. When the film chips are placed over the mount apertures they can be held in place temporarily with the aid of small but strong magnets over the bottom edges in line with strip **B**.

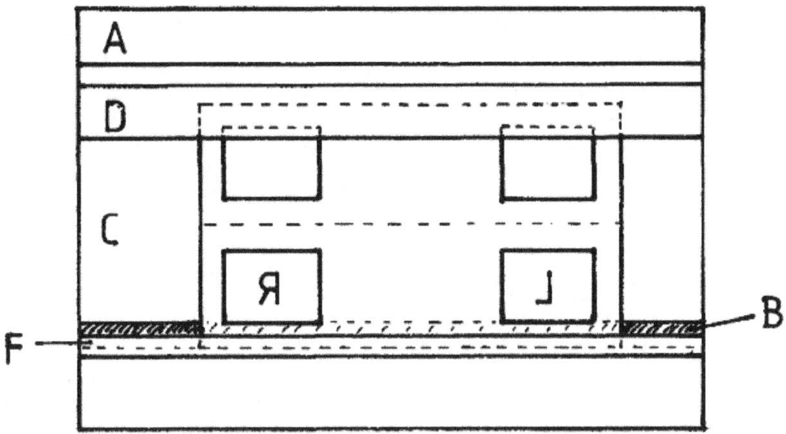

Fig S14.2
*Plan view of the mounting jig showing a fold-over card mount held in place by the strip **D** and the flange **F**. Film chips can be held in position over the mount apertures by magnets over the metal strip **B**. The mount can be slid sideways over the mounting gauge underneath it (omitted for clarity).*

REFERENCES

1. **Chibisov, K.B.** in "Stereoscopy" by N.A.Valyus, Focal Press, London 1966, p 9.
2. **Valyus, N.A**. Ibid, p 20.
3. **Valyus, N.A**. Ibid, p 44
4. **Ferwerda, J.G.** "The World of 3D – a practical guide to stereo photography", 3D Book Productions, Borger, The Netherlands, 2nd Edition, Third Printing, 1990, Chapter 1, Section 1.3, p 20.
5. **Waack, F.G.** "Stereo photography", Self-Edition 1985, Chapter 8, pp 53–56.
6. **Hofstetter, H.W.** "Interpupillary Distances in Adult Populations", Journ. Amer. Optom. Ass.,. Vol 43. 1972.
7. **Morgan, W.D.** and **Lester, H.M.** "Stereo Realist Manual", Morgan and Lester, New York, 1st Edition, October 1954.
8. Bulletin Mensuel du Stéréo-club Français, October 1995, quoted by Barton-Jones, B in The Stereoscopic Society Journal of 3-D Imaging No 134, October 1996, p 14.
9. **Starkman, D.** and **Pinsky, S.** "The Nimslo 3D Book", Reel 3-D Enterprises, California, USA, 1986.
10. **Symons, K.C.M.** "Stereo Photography", The Focal Press, 1st Edition, 1957, pp 70–72.
11. **Symons, K.C.M.** Ibid, pp 72–74.
12. **Butt, E.** "Beam splitter with a difference", The Stereoscopic Society Journal of 3-D Imaging No 134, October 1996, pp 2-5.
13. **Speel, S.** "A Modern Auto-exposure Stereo Camera", Stereoscopic Society Bulletin No 106, October 1989.
14. **Whelan, P.M.** and **Hodgson, M.J.** "Essential Principles of Physics", 2nd Edition, 1989, John Murray, p 256.
15. Encyclopaedia of Photography, Focal Press, London and New York, Desk Edition Reprint, April 1975, p 831.
16. **Ferwerda, J.G.** "The World of 3D" (See Ref 4), Section 10.12, p 116.
17. **Ferwerda, J.G.** Ibid, Section 10.8, p 107.
18. **Ferwerda, J.G.** Ibid, Section 10.9 pp109-112.
19. **Valyus, N.A.** "Stereoscopy" (See Ref 1), p 101.
20. **Ferwerda, J.G.** "The World of 3D", (See Ref 4), Section 19.4, p 197.
21. **Ferwerda, J.G.** Ibid, p 195.
22. **Ferwerda, J.G.** "A Comparative Examination of Silver Screens", Technical letter ISU, Nos 11,12, 1981-82. Abstract in Stereoscopy (ISU) No 9, 1979 and PSA Journal, 1978.
23. **Waack, F.G.** "Stereo Photography" (See Ref 5), pp 37-38.
24. **Valyus, N.A.** "Stereoscopy" (See Ref 1), Chapter III
25. **Symons, K.C.M.** "Stereo Photography" (See Ref 10), pp 203-205.

26. **Jackson, N.** "The Development of a System", The Stereoscopic Society Bulletin, No 53, 1976.
27. Encyclopaedia of Photography, (See Ref 15), p 330.
28. **Thomas, T.** "Stereolusions", Stereo Realist Manual (See Ref 7), Chapter 10, p 231ff.
29. **Everett, H.B.** "Double Exposure with D-Caps", The Stereoscopic Society Bulletin, July 1986.
30. **Tamás, F.** and **Pál, I.** "Phase Equilibria Spatial Diagrams, First published in 1970 by Iliffe Books, an imprint of the Butterworth Group, Joint Edition with Akadémiai Kiadó (Budapest, V., Alkotmány u. 21)
31. **McGraw, D.** "Stereo Realist Manual" (See Ref 7), Chapter 5, p 169ff.
32. **Symons, K.C.M.** "Stereo photography" (See Ref 10), p 89.
33. "Phantogram Perspective Charts". A kit including instructions, coloured pencils and anaglyph spectacles, published by Jerry Haines Sales, USA, 1994.
34. **Henshall, J.** "Expert Opinion", Digital Photo FX Magazine, August/September 1998, p 55.
35. "DuBrey 3D Video System on Offer". Article in The Stereoscopic Society Journal of 3-D Imaging, No 139, January 1998, p 5.
36. "3D Video – Two Different Approaches". Article in The Stereoscopic society Journal of 3-D Imaging, No 136,January 1997, p 2.
37. **Ezra, D.** "Look, no glasses", The Stereoscopic Society journal of 3-D Imaging, No 136, April 1997, p 25 (Reprinted from IEE REVIEW September Issue).
38. **Foster, B.** " A leap into the third dimension", Materials World, Journal of The Institute of Materials, Vol 6, No 7, July 1998, p 402.
39. **Valyus, N.A.** "Stereoscopy", (See Ref 1). Part of Plate XXXV opposite p 344.
40. **Ackermann, U.** "Essentials of Human Physiology", Mosby–Year Book Inc., St Louis, Mo, 1992.
41. **Klooswijk, A.I.J.** "Natural and Photographic Stereo Acuity", Stereoscopy (ISU) No 5, 1978.
42. **Valyus, N.A.** "Stereoscopy", (See Ref 1), p 42.
43. **Valyus, N.A.** Ibid, p 32.
44. Encyclopaedia of Photography (See Ref 15), p 569.
45. **Ferwerda, J.G.** "The World of 3D", (See Ref 4), Sections 24.6– 24.8, pp 239–248.
46. **Smith, C.** "Plain Words about Convergence", The Stereoscopic Society Journal of 3-D Imaging, No 133, July 1996, p 2.
47. **Girling, A.** "Stereoscopic Drawing", Author's Publication, 1990.
48. **Krause, E.E.** "Three-Dimensional Projection", Greenberg, New York, Second Printing, April 1955, p 93.

49. **Themelis, G.A.** "How to use and maintain your STEREO REALIST", Author's Publication, Cleveland, Ohio, USA, 1st Edition July 1999, 2nd Printing November 1999.
50. **Everett, H.** "The Projected Image", The Stereoscopic Society Bulletin, No 114, October 1991.
51. **Fisher, M.** "A Novel Method of Stereo Projection", British Journal of Photography, Part 1, April 1st 1977, p 276: Part 2, 8th April 1977, p 305.
52. **Ferwerda, J.G.** "The World of 3D", (See Ref 4), Section 25.3, p 251.
53. **Krause, E.E.** "Three-Dimensional Projection", (See Ref 48), p 79.
54. BS 1487:Part 3:1979 "Specification for picture sizes on photographic film" Part 3. Stereo systems using 35mm objectives on 35mm film, 5-perforation format (Fig 3).
55. **McKay, H.C.** "Three-Dimensional Photography", American Photography Publishing Company, New York, 1953.
56. **Themelis, G.A.** "(See Ref 49) p 118.
57. **Dalgoutte, W.C.** "Big Bertha Stereo Geometry", The Stereoscopic Society Bulletin, No 45, 1974.
58. **Fisher, M.** "3D Space: Measured, not Ruled!" (Part 2). The Stereoscopic Society Journal of 3-D Imaging, No 146, October 1999, pp 6-13.
59. **Clay, C.A.E.** "Clay's Clinic Part 7 – Screen Tests", The Stereoscopic Society Bulletin, No 111, January 1991, pp 21-28.
60. http://kb.sandisk.com/app/answers/detail/a_id/69/~/number-of-pictures-that-can-be-stored-on-a-memory-device
61. **Aldridge, R and Sykes, D**, "StereoData Maker", The Stereoscopic Society Journal of 3D Imaging, No 180, Spring 2008, pp 21, 24 and 25.

Plates

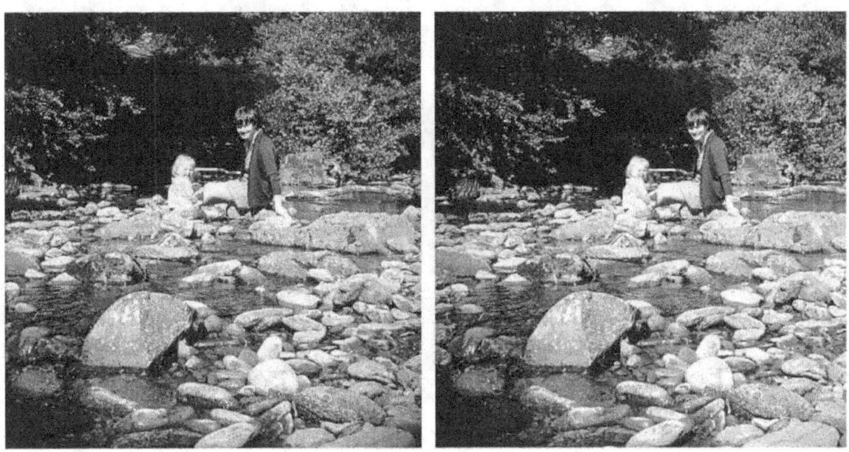

"STRANDED"
Taken with a Wray Stereo Graphic camera around 1969

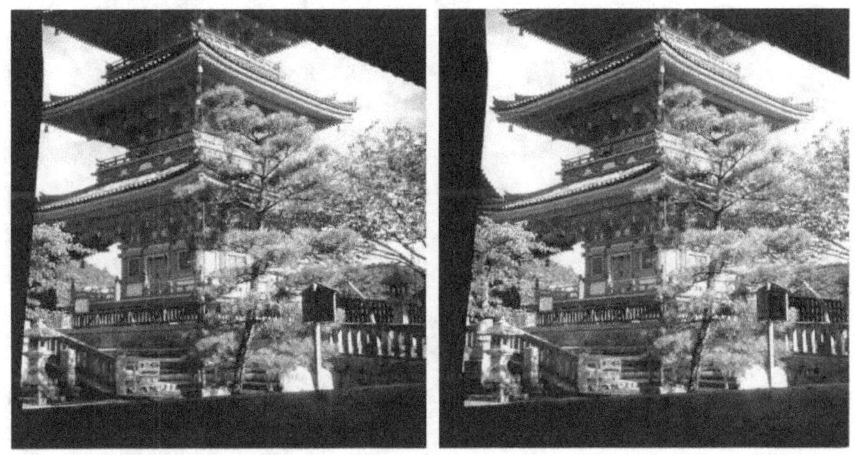

"PAGODA AT KIYOMIZU TEMPLE"
Taken with a Wray Stereo Graphic camera in 1988 in Kyoto, Japan

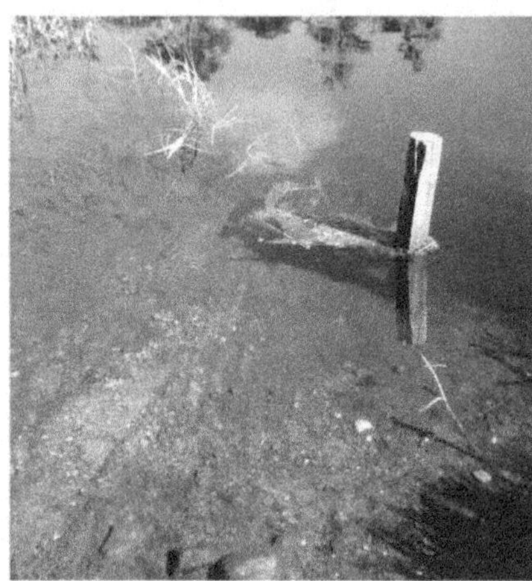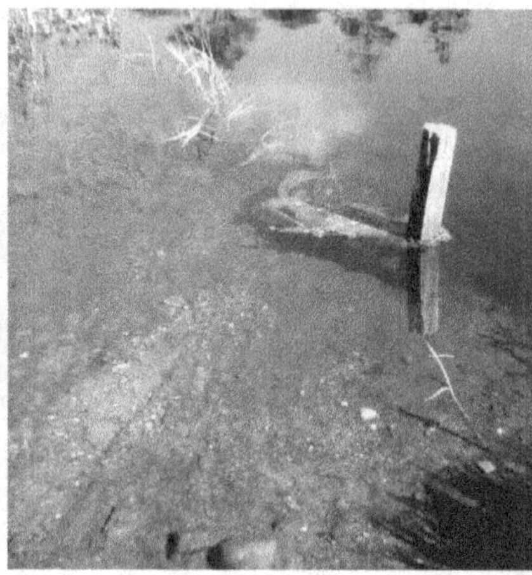

"SHALLOW WATER"
Taken with a Stereo Realist at Kylemore Abbey, near Clifden, Eire, in June 2000

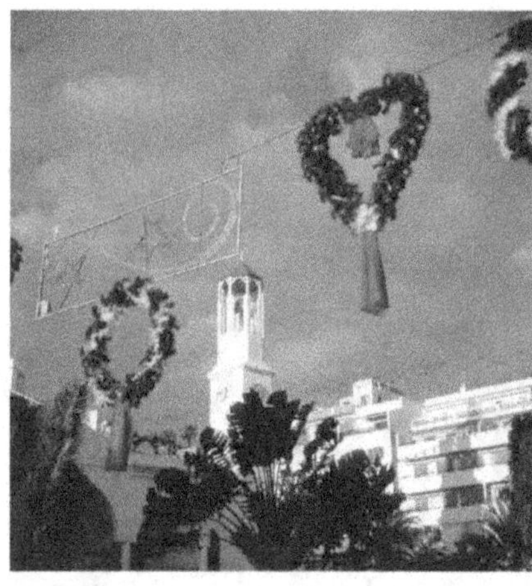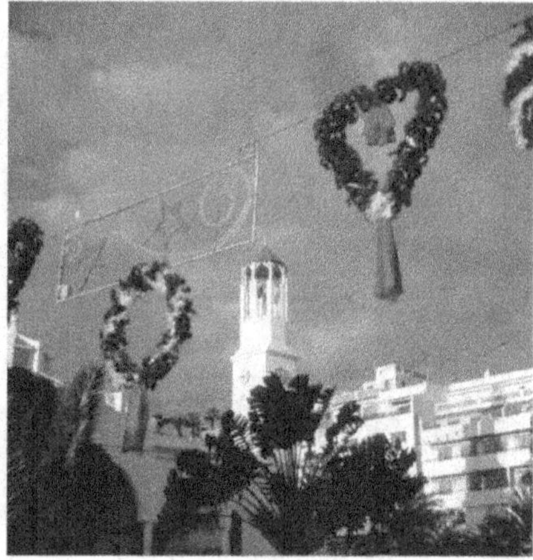

"EPIPHANY"
Street decorations in Los Cristianos, Tenerife, which enhance the celebrations on 6th January each year. Taken with a Stereo Realist, January 2000

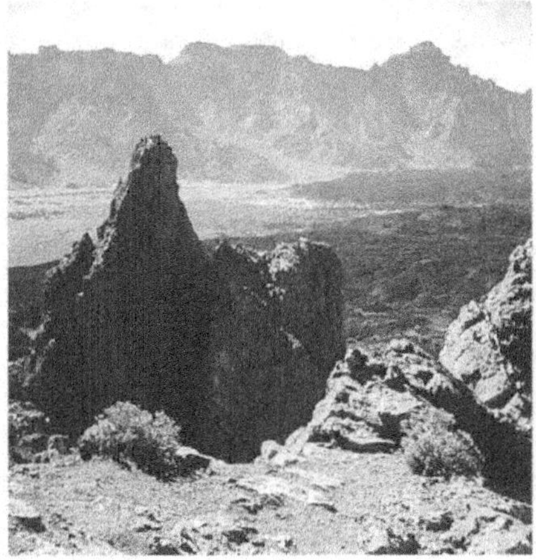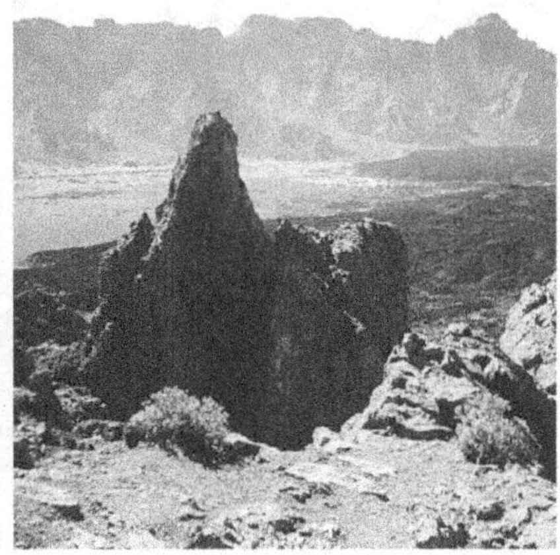

"ANOTHER PLANET?"

Volcanic landscape at Mount Teide in Tenerife, Taken with a Stereo Realist camera in January 2000

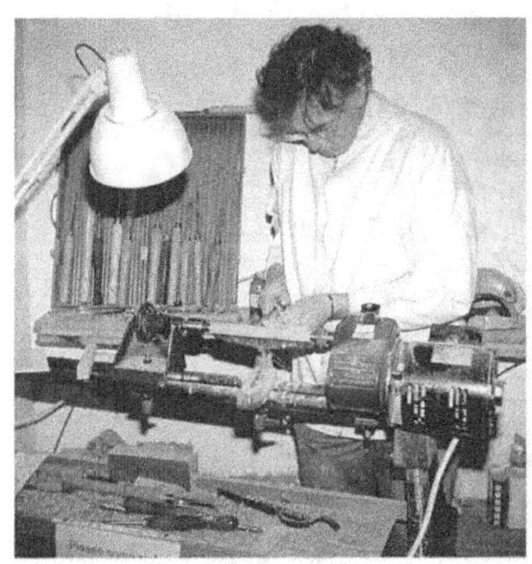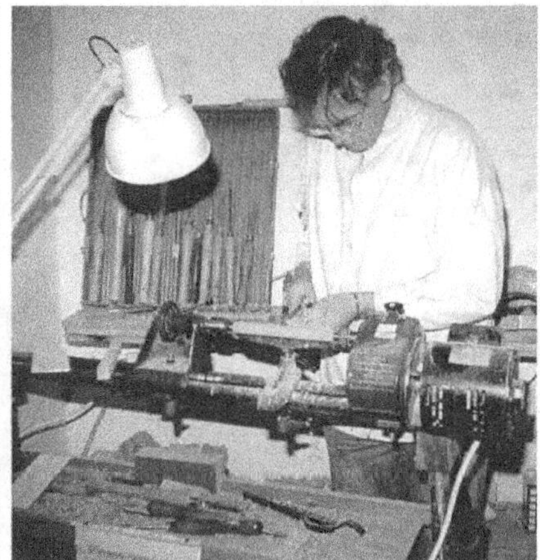

"CHIPS OFF THE OLD BLOCK"

Wood turning at a craft centre. Taken with a Stereo Realist camera in May 1999 and using flash

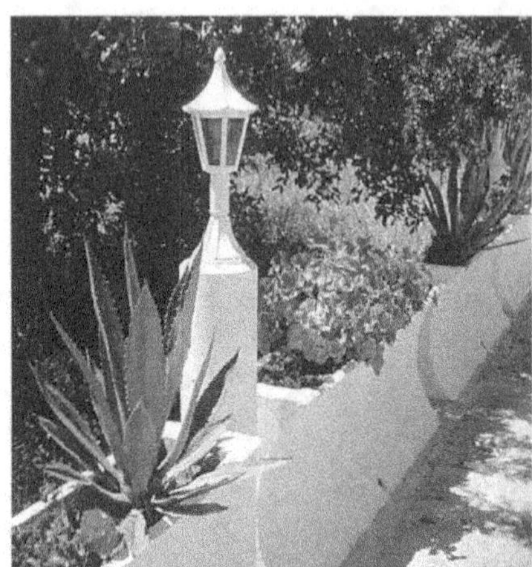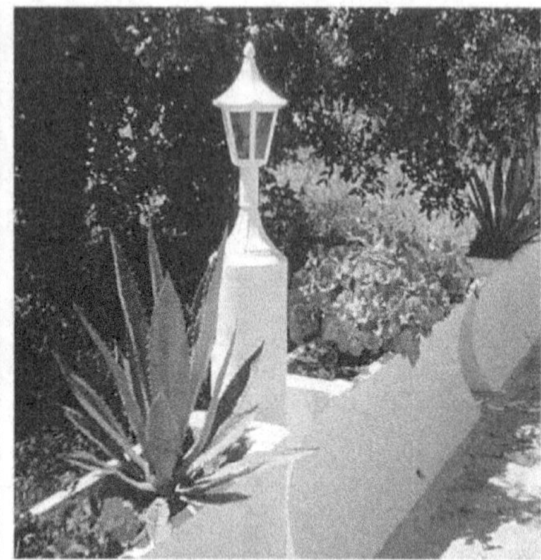

"LONE LAMP"
Taken with a Stereo Realist camera in The Algarve, Portugal, in May 2000

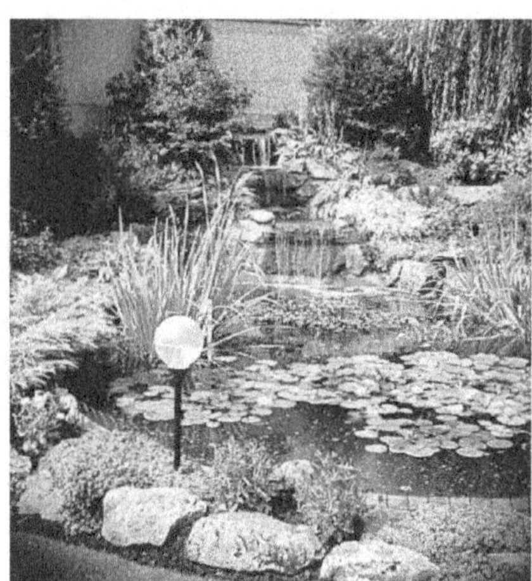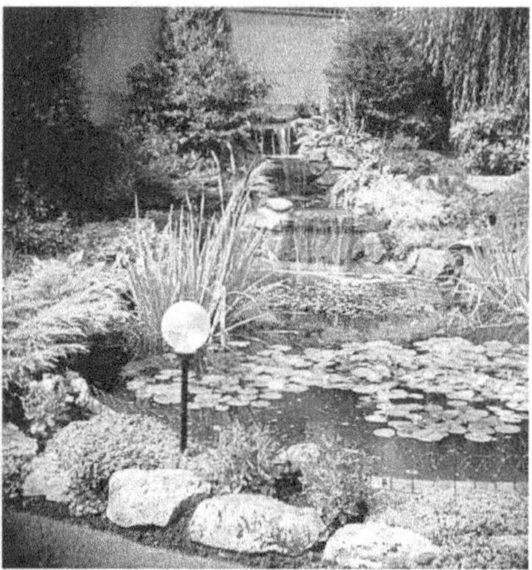

"WATER GARDEN"
Taken with a Wray Stereo Graphic camera in 1995

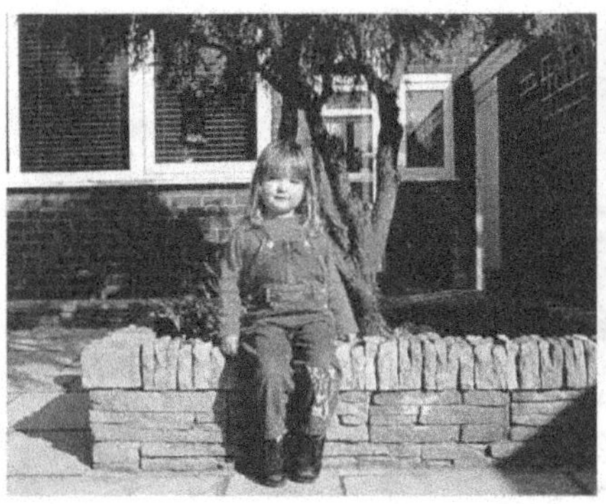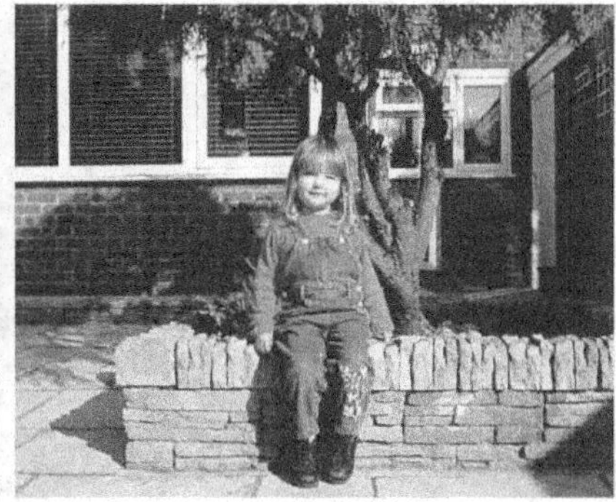

"VICTORIA"
Taken with an RBT XRX3P "Siamesed" camera at Stafford in March 2000

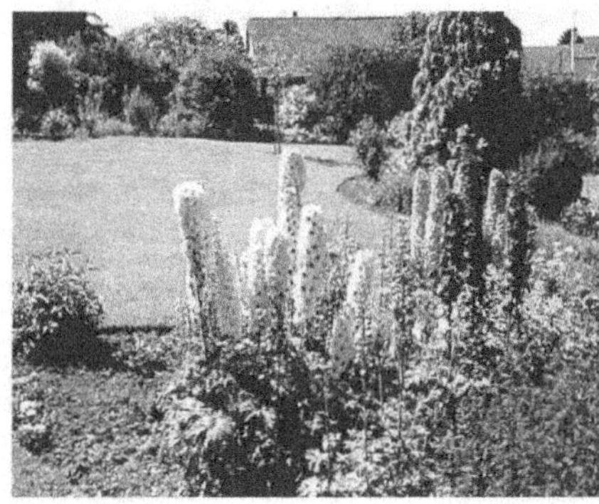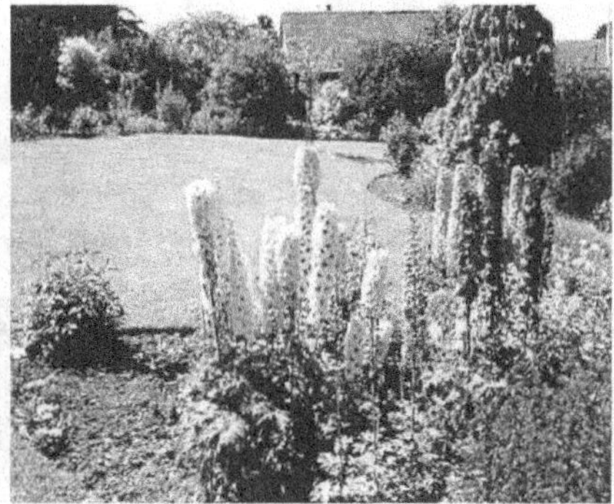

"COUNTRY GARDEN"
Taken with an RBT XRX3P camera near Pershore in June 2000

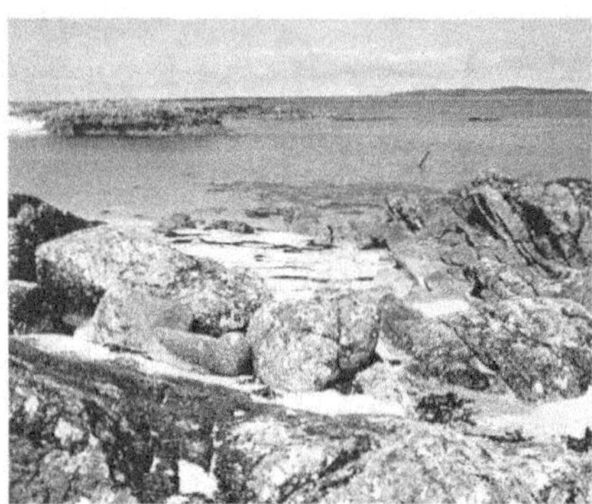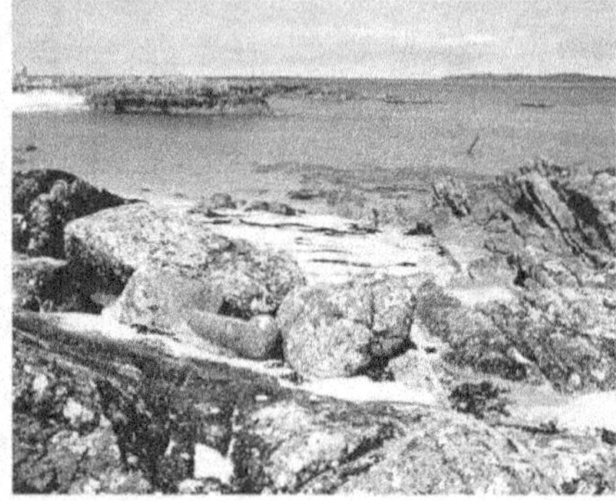

"CONNEMARA BEACH"
Taken with an RBT XRX3P camera in June 2000

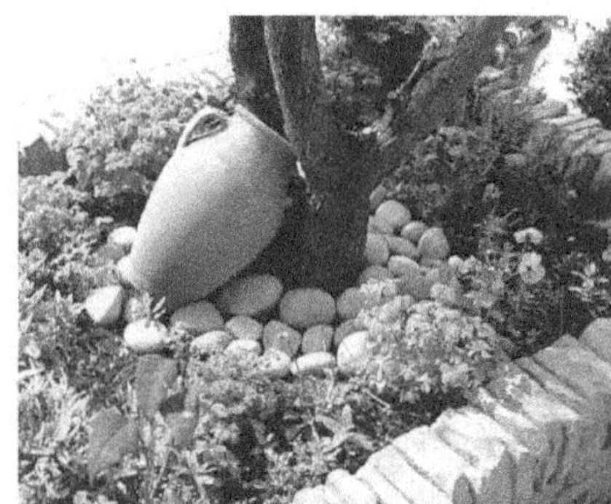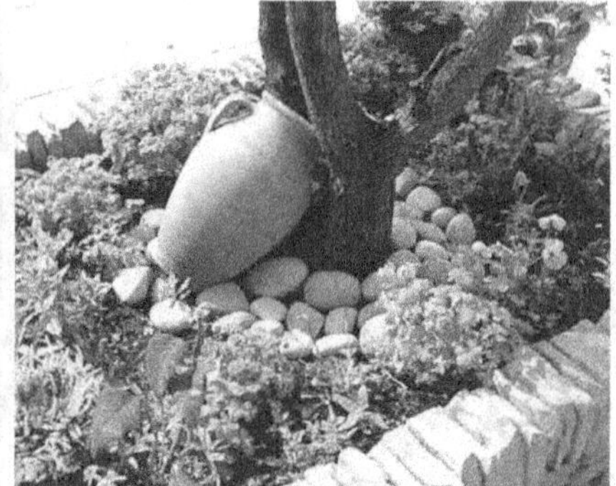

"ECHOES OF THE MED"
Taken with an RBT XRX3P camera at Stafford in May 2000

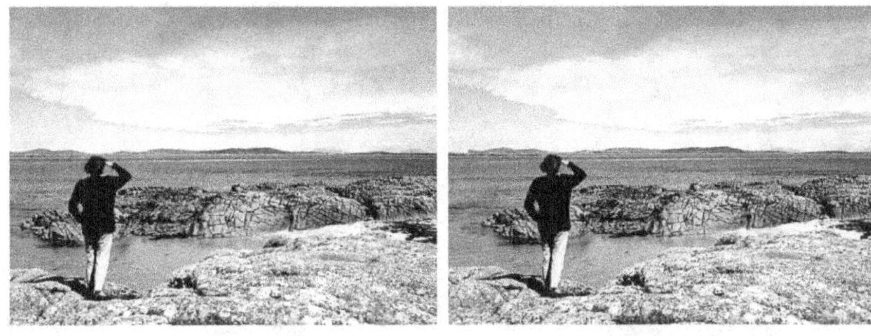

"THE LONELY SEA AND THE SKY"
Taken with an RBT XRX3P near Clifden, Eire, in June 2000

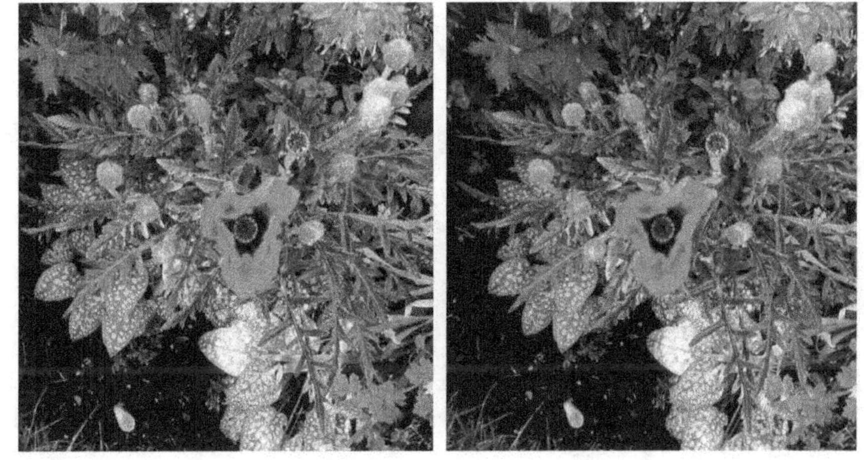

"POPPING POPPY"
Taken with a Stereo Realist in August 2000

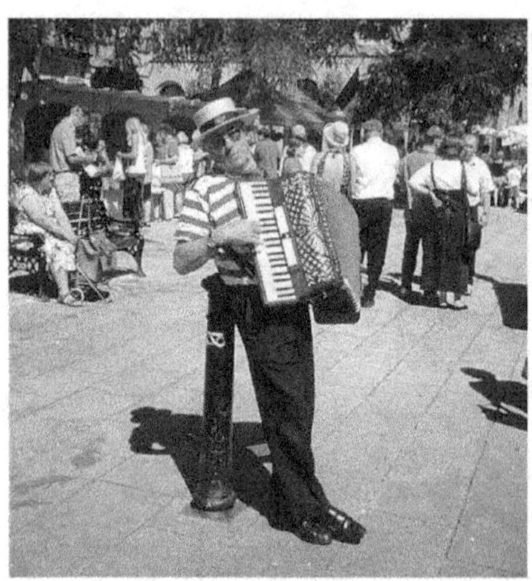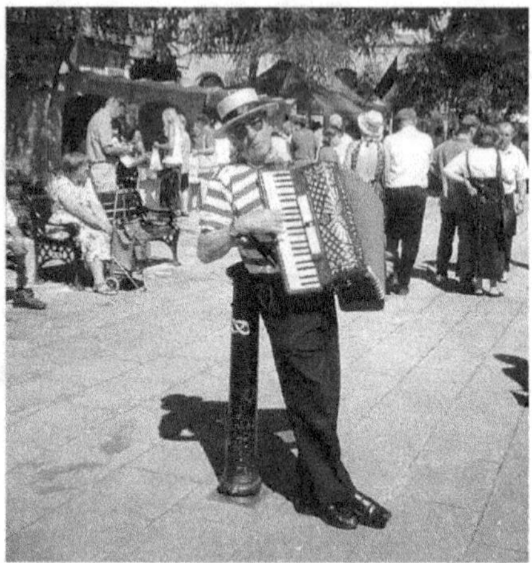

"LISTEN VERY CAREFULLY – I SHALL PLAY THIS ONLY WERNCE!"
Taken with a Stereo Realist camera at Stafford in July 1999

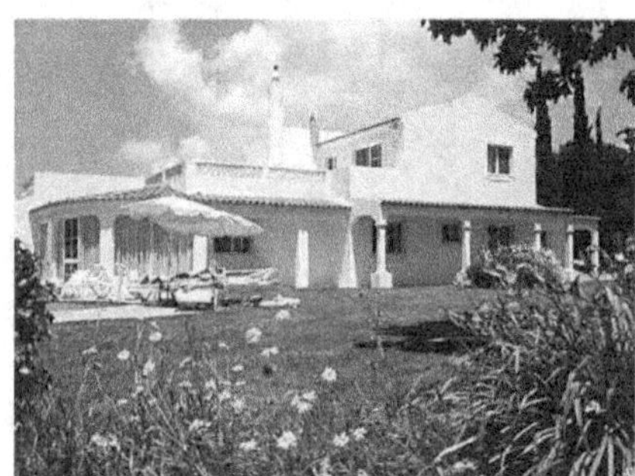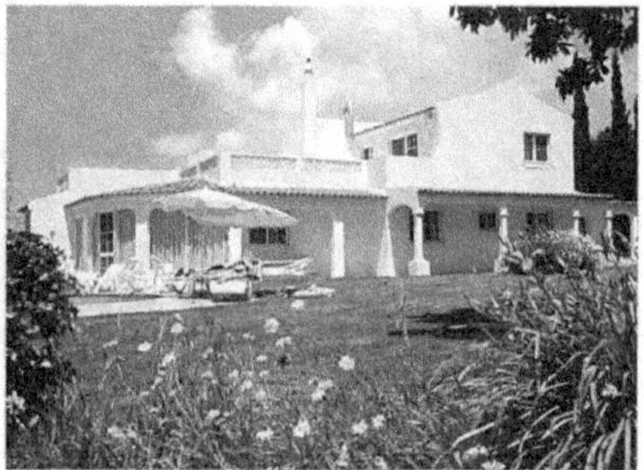

"HOLIDAY VILLA"
Taken with an RBT XRX3P in the Algarve, Portugal, May 2000

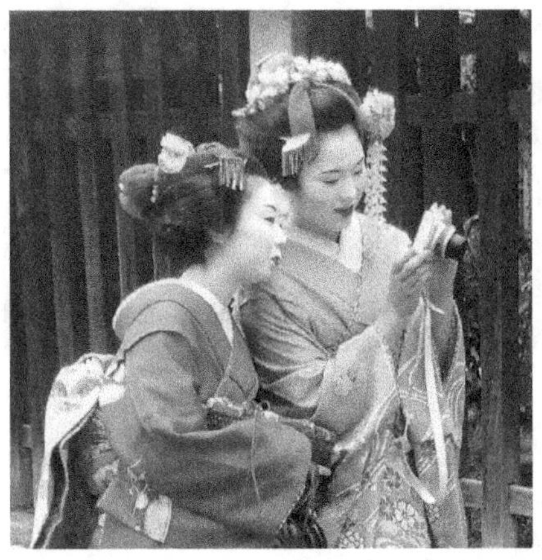 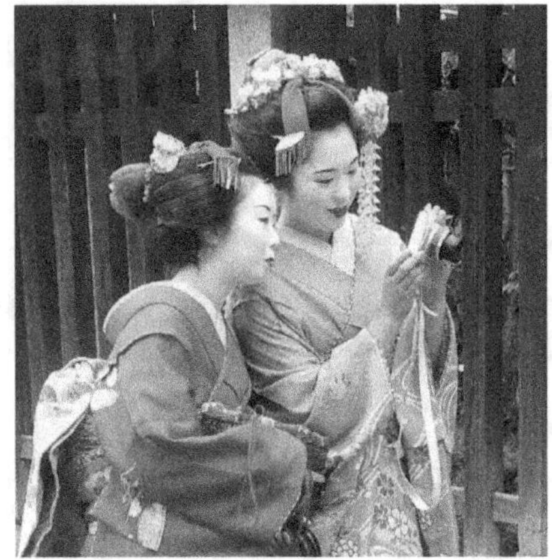

"ANCIENT CULTURE MEETS NEW TECHNOLOGY"
Taken with a FujiFilm W3 digital camera in Kyoto, Japan in October 2012

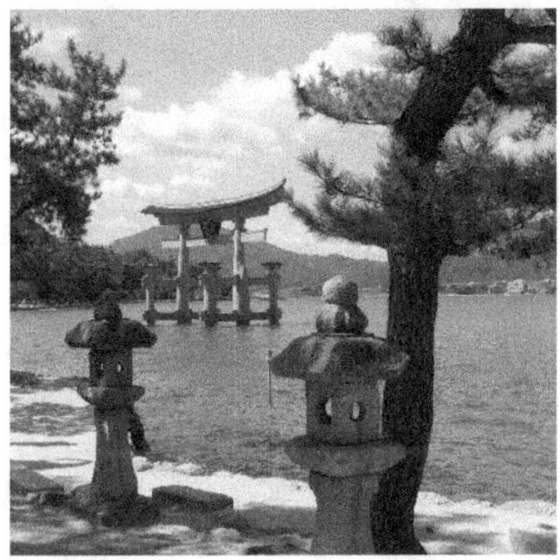 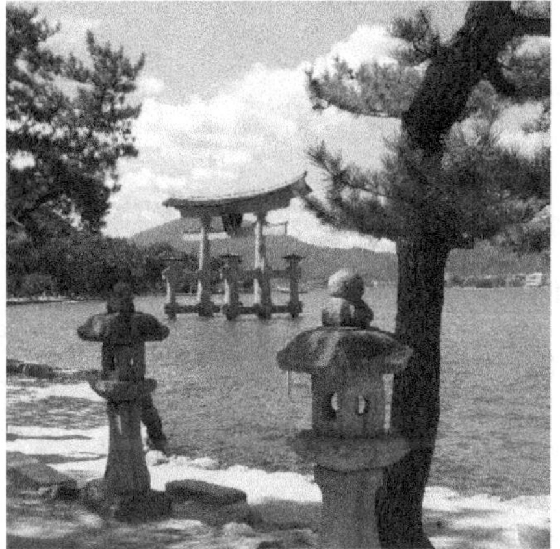

"RED TORII GATE"
Taken with a FujiFilm W3 digital camera in Miyajima, Japan in October 2012

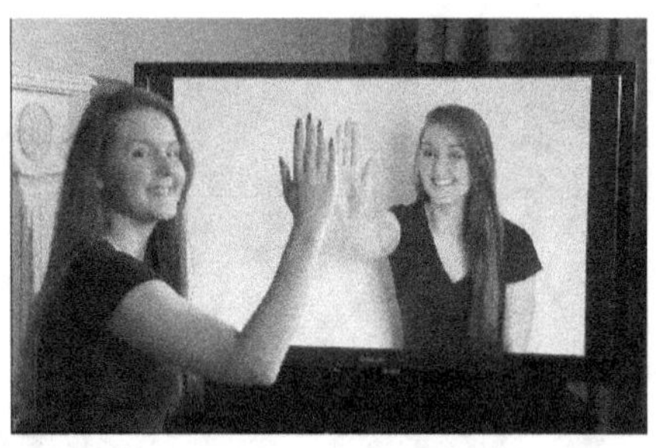 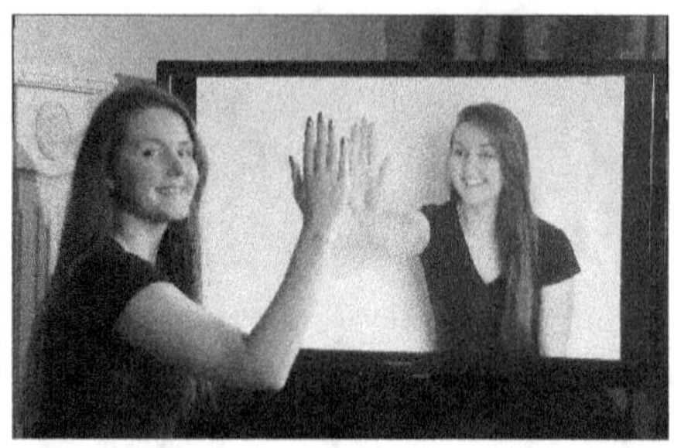

"HI SOPHIE!"
Taken with a FujiFilm W3 digital camera in Stafford, UK in January 2015

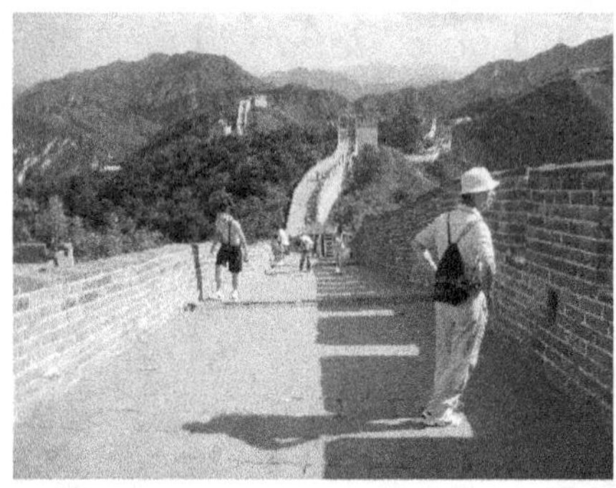 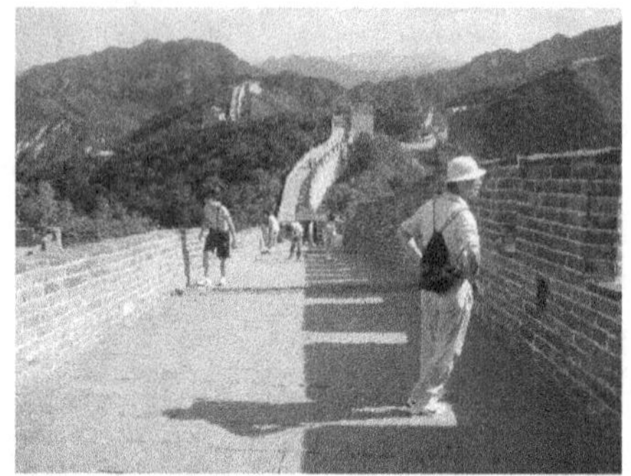

"SEEMINGLY ENDLESS"
Taken with a twin rig of Canon Ixus 70 digital cameras (linked by StereoData Maker software) on the Great Wall of China in July 2010.

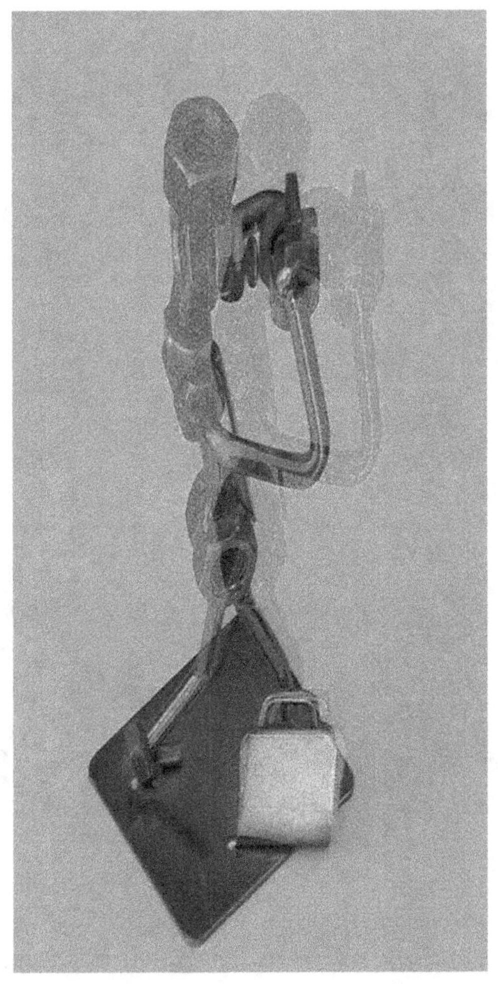

"PHOTOGRAPHER"

Phantogram taken with a FujiFilm digital camera
This should be viewed with the page lying flat on a horizontal surface and viewed from above at a 45°angle (as in Chapter 15 Fig 15.5). Although the image is a red/cyan anaglyph, it may be better to view through red/green glasses to reduce ghosting. The picture is printed darker than is ideal to reduce ghosting.

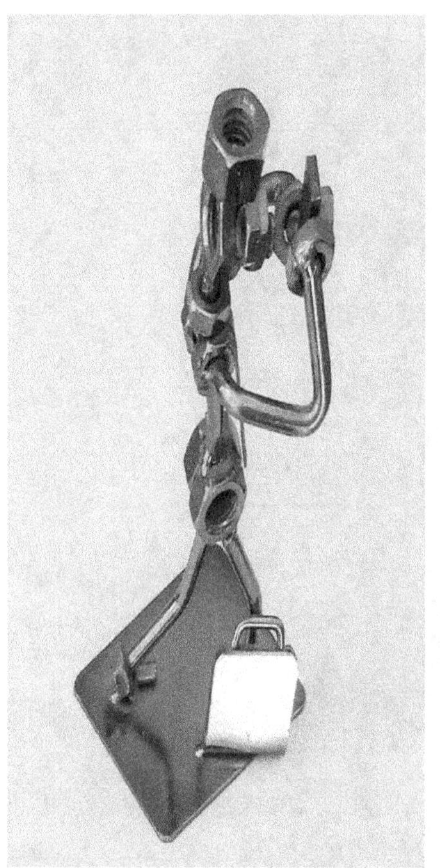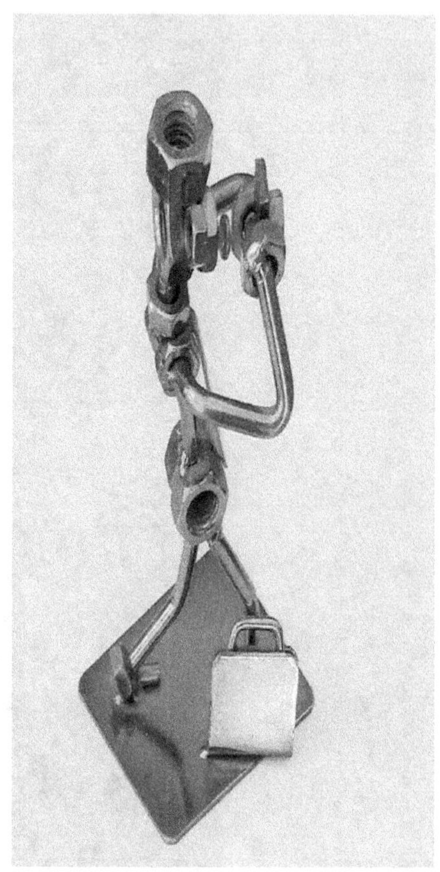

The same image as the anaglyph above but printed in colour side-by-side. It should be viewed in the same way at 45° but with a simple stereoscope with two lenses instead of anaglyph glasses, or by free viewing.